Empire of
the Columbia

EMPIRE OF THE COLUMBIA

A History of the Pacific Northwest

by Dorothy O. Johansen

Reed College

and the late Charles M. Gates

University of Washington

SECOND EDITION

BY DOROTHY O. JOHANSEN

Harper & Row, Publishers

NEW YORK, EVANSTON, AND LONDON

CONTENTS

MAPS

TABLES AND GRAPHS

WHILE it is often helpful to illustrate history with these devices, statistical information so presented may prove misleading when it covers only a short span of time. Short-term trends may lose significance if shown out of the context of longer periods. In order to set short-term information in proper perspective, much of the statistical information in this book is gathered in appendixes and references to it are made where appropriate in the text.

TABLES

Tables and Graphs

GRAPHS

PREFACE

THE HAPPY collaboration in which Charles Gates and I had produced *Empire of the Columbia* in 1957 prompted us to look forward, as he said, to "further joint ventures in regional writing." We also anticipated a revision of *Empire*, but then it seemed so far in the future that we delayed firm decisions and mutual commitments. We knew that we wanted to retain the organization in which each chapter remained, as much as possible, a separate essay, and we talked in general terms about putting more emphasis on the flow of events and on the interaction of political and economic factors in the twentieth century.

In undertaking this task alone, I have had to make a difficult decision and one which I could not have made without the generous and understanding help of Mildred Gates. To keep the book from growing to impracticable length and yet at the same time to enlarge our treatment of the twentieth century required cutting, combining, and rewriting as well as the incorporation of new materials and new chapters. In the process, much to my regret, Charles Gates' independent, tightly constructed, and highly useful chapters have lost their identities. It is my consolation, however, that his complete essays are available to students in the first edition.

I am grateful to those who have generously helped me in this task: Herman Deutsch and Keith Murray whose analytical critiques of the first edition were of great assistance, and Murray for compiling the Supplementary Readings; Stephan Michelson for his expert advice with regard to statistical data; John Sherman for the beautiful and useful new maps; the researchers who performed so nobly: Larry Kuehn, Tara O'Toole, Barbara Courts, and Roy Ekland; Helen Hoover whose disciplined mind and critical eye excised some, if not all, my excessive verbiage; Mirth Kaplan and Irene Hora who performed magic in turning my scrawl into a typed manuscript; Priscilla Knuth of the Oregon

Historical Society for whose many years of friendship and assistance I am doubly grateful. My colleagues, Arthur Leigh, Carl Stevens, Mason Drukman, Maure Goldschmidt, and Charles McKinley gave advice which I have deeply appreciated, while I regret that my performance does not match the excellence of their counsel.

To students of history I would say that much, much work needs to be done in this field. If what is written in these pages in some measure compels others to explore the region's past in order to clarify what here has been dimly or faultily seen, then, indeed, this revision of *Empire of the Columbia* has served the purpose for which it was intended.

DOROTHY O. JOHANSEN

BIBLIOGRAPHIC NOTE

IN ORDER to simplify footnote citations, the references to supporting documents and source materials are usually given only by author and title. In the case of diaries and journals the references are to the more accessible published editions rather than to the originals. Thus there are a number of citations to the *Oregon Historical Quarterly*, the *Pacific Northwest Quarterly*, and other periodicals which can be found in most libraries and schools.

Following is a list of abbreviations used:

AHR	*American Historical Review*
BCHQ	*British Columbia Historical Quarterly*
MVHR	*Mississippi Valley Historical Review*
OHQ	*Oregon Historical Quarterly*
PHR	*Pacific Historical Review*
PNQ	*Pacific Northwest Quarterly*
WHQ	*Washington Historical Quarterly*

Land and Water

The golden sandstone cliffs of Cape Kiwanda, Oregon coast. During the mid-eighteenth century, Russian, Spanish, English and American ships nosed along these turbulent waters.

BELOW. Cape Disappointment painted by James Henry Warre about 1850. Ships ventured into bays and inlets all along the coast seeking safe anchorage from which to explore and exploit the unknown west of the new continent. Many searched for a great fresh-water stream vaguely known as the "River of the West."

BELOW. In May 1792, the American Captain Robert Gray, in his ship Columbia, found haven in the mouth of a vast river which he named for his ship. On the river he discovered, Gray traded with Chinooks "well stocked with land furs and capital salmon."

The calm of the "nobel river" at the western
end of the Columbia Gorge. BELOW. Eastward,
the river twists and boils through the Cascade
Mountains.

LEFT. Wild Scenery *painted by Alfred Jacob Miller about 1840. As adventurers inched into the northwest wilderness from the sea, others determined to reach it overland. After the hazards of plain and river, these Rocky Mountains had still to be crossed. Courtesy Walters Art Gallery, Baltimore. © 1951 Oklahoma University Press.*

BELOW. The Source of the Columbia River *painted by James Henry Warre, high in the mountains which later became part of British Columbia. Not far from here, David Thompson built Kootenai House (1807) and planned his Voyage of a Summer Moon.*

BELOW. *Castle Peak in Idaho's White Cloud Mountains. At Lemhi Pass, Captain Meriwether Lewis (1805) saw the forbidding wall of "immense ranges of high mountains still to the West of us."*

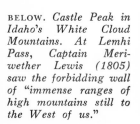

Two aspects of the Snake River, mighty tributary of the Columbia. ABOVE. Shoshone Falls, southern Idaho. The overland Astorians abandoned canoes where the Snake River dropped 200 feet to form a "whirling and tumultous vortex." RIGHT. Hells Canyon which forms part of the common Oregon-Idaho state boundary.

BELOW. Grand Coulee Dam, the largest concrete structure ever made by man, was completed across the Columbia near Spokane in 1941. Columbia's erratic, often wasteful waters have been disciplined in recent decades by numerous water control projects throughout the northwest.

BELOW. The Willamette River, western Oregon, is another Columbia tributary. The river's sweeping valley is one of the most bountiful of the Northwest.

PART I

The Nations in the Pacific Northwest

OVERVIEW

THE EARLIEST CHAPTERS *in the history of the Pacific Northwest belong to the story of Europe's expansion in the sixteenth and seventeenth centuries. Discovery of the Western Hemisphere inspired men to adventure, both in the realms of imagination and things-as-they-are. By the eighteenth century exploration limited imagination with outlines of reality, and poets surrendered to scientists the task of describing the physical New World.*

Sixteenth-century maps exaggerated the extent of the known world. In the next two centuries, as explorers charted the seas and roughly defined the major continents, the tight little world neatly represented in symmetry of land mass and sea scope, was vastly expanded. So were the ambitions of nations challenged to add to science great new discoveries, and to their economies riches in land and commerce.

After the Spanish conquests, dreams of finding another treasure of Montezuma and a new Peru led men to search North America for the fabulous Seven Cities of Cibola and the legendary Kingdom of Quivira.

1

The hope that Europe's merchant ships could reach the Orient from the west by shorter routes, polar or continental, led to the quest for a Northwest Passage. Visions of wealth in land, treasure, and commerce, as well as hunger for knowledge, drew men to the shores of the Pacific Ocean and the land we know today as the Pacific Northwest.

The first treasure found on Pacific shores was neither gold nor pearls nor a strategically valuable passage to India; it was the pelt of the sea otter. Russia's and England's state-sponsored voyages of discovery captained by Vitus Bering and James Cook led to the opening of the sea otter trade. Traders who followed Cook learned the principal features of the coastline, such as the Strait of Juan de Fuca and the entrance to the Columbia River.

In the last decade of the eighteenth century, France, Spain, Britain, and Russia carried out official explorations of the Northwest Coast, and England and Spain came close to war over Spain's claims to sovereignty on the Pacific shores. Spain claimed and lost the most. In principle and practice, she was defeated by England who claimed rights to trade in lands where title was not backed by occupancy. As a result of the Nootka Convention (1790) the coast between Russian settlements in Alaska and Spanish colonies in California was free and open to all nations.

On the continent, the Indian trade, with beaver fur a principal commodity, followed interior waterways to the West. The Canadian trader Alexander Mackenzie reached the Pacific in 1793. Ten years later the Louisiana Purchase pushed the boundary of the United States to the Rocky Mountains, and the Lewis and Clark expedition set the course for further American expansion.

Between 1807 and 1846, British and American diplomats argued their national claims to dominion beyond the Rockies, while Canadian merchants of the North West Company and later the Hudson's Bay Company, effectively exploited the fur trade of the region.

The advance of American traders to the Rockies, on the heels of the Lewis and Clark expedition, all but ceased for ten years after the War of 1812. But when in 1824 American trappers moved through South Pass to the Pacific Slope they asserted American rights over what they called the Oregon Country.

Fundamental differences between British and American trading practices ultimately affected the solution of the "Oregon Question." As a commercial corporation endowed with special privileges and powers, the Hudson's Bay Company adopted long-range policies for the development and control of the region's trade and resources; but its monopoly position eliminated free colonization by British subjects. On the other hand, the American trade, competitive, exploitive, without any policy, helped to open the way for agricultural and commercial adventurers and the establishment of an American colony and American sovereignty in the Northwest.

The Nations in the Pacific Northwest

Here, as elsewhere on the continent, the Indians were prime movers in the white man's occupation of the land. They produced furs and consumed a limited range of manufactured goods. In the exchange process, the white men made enormous profits while the Indians were all but destroyed. The British trade system encouraged—if it did not achieve—protection of the Indians and their ways of life. But to the Americans the Indian trade was a brief and violent phase of economic exploitation; Indians did not fit into the American pattern of expansion.

The aboriginal cultures of the Pacific Northwest were background to the history of the region. They were also unique and of sufficient interest to deserve some attention as prelude to our story.

CHAPTER
ONE

The Indians of the Northwest

THE BASIC FEATURES of the land occupied by the first people were formed through millions of years of violent geologic action. Liquid granite oozed from the sea; a great up-thrust and folding of the earth's crust formed the Rocky Mountains. At one time the Blue Mountains of eastern Oregon were part of the shoreline. Volcanoes spewed out lava flows that pushed back the sea and formed the Cascade Mountains; the Coast Range emerged. Glaciers, advancing and retreating, scarred the face of the land, scooping out great inland seas that were fed by torrential rains and melting ice waters.

Eons of tropical climate engendered giant fern forests. Fossils found in the uptilted strata of central Oregon's river walls tell of palm forests and great monsters overwhelmed by lava flows thousands of feet deep. After each ice age, new vegetation and animal life appeared, to be submerged in turn by fresh flows of molten rock. The last significant volcanic action occurred about 8000 years ago, when Mount Mazama, in whose dead crater lies spectacular Crater Lake, blew up and spread the ashes of its destruction over hundreds of miles. Human beings witnessed this cataclysm.

A land-form map, like the one used in this book, illustrates the varied character of Northwest physical geography. The extensive complex of north-south ranges composing the Rocky Mountain chain forms the eastern boundary of the region. The Cascades, dominated by lofty, skeletal frames of once active volcanoes (Mt. Rainier, for example, 14,410 feet high; or Mt. Hood, 11,245 feet), divide the region into two major climatic zones: the high dry lands of the immense interior plateau, and the wet valleys and low mountainous terrain of the coast.

Through this land of contrasts the Columbia River flows 1210 miles from its source in Canada to the Pacific. With its principal tributaries, the Kootenai, Pend Oreille, Snake, John Day, Deschutes, Yakima, Willamette, and Cowlitz, the Columbia is one of the great river systems of North America, draining 250,000 square miles, of which approximately 37,500 lie in British Columbia.

THE ABORIGINES

It is believed that even while the last great glaciers covered northern parts of the continent an open, ice-free passage extended from Asia into North America, over which came the first people and later waves of migration. They traveled to the central plains of the continent and to the southwest. Recent scholarship suggests that the original inhabitants of the Pacific Northwest moved from the Great Basin of Utah and Nevada into southern Oregon, then a great inland sea. Here were conditions to sustain life: a steady supply of water and food, and shelter in caves around the water's edge. Using the radiocarbon method of dating, scientists have demonstrated that men lived in these caves 10,000 years ago.[1]

Archeological research reveals that these cave dwellers were skilled in weaving sagebrush bark, tule, and cattail leaves into foot coverings, baskets, and mats, and that they used stone awls, flakers, punchers, smoothers, and polishers. Chipped obsidian arrowheads found with the small bones of birds and the larger bones of bison and deer reveal that the cavemen were hunters. They first propelled weapons by means of a throwing-stick, the *atlatl*, and later became skilled in the use of bows and arrows. They decorated their bodies with strips of fur, feathers, and bone beads. They gathered nuts, berries, and roots, but did not develop techniques for cultivation.

It is probable that these people originally differed little from one another, whether they lived in Oregon, Washington, Idaho, or northern Nevada. But with the passage of time, differences began to

[1] Luther S. Cressman, Howel Williams, and Alex D. Krieger, *Early Man in Oregon: Archaeological Studies in the Northern Great Basin* (1940).

emerge. Some people remained relatively isolated and retained their old customs longer. New migrations destroyed or displaced others or, mingling with them, stimulated the development of new living patterns. Changes in climate, recession of lake waters, disappearance of a food supply, and contact with peoples of different customs were factors of change.

The Coastal Peoples

On the lower Fraser River in British Columbia evidences have been found of a culture that flourished about 2000 years ago. When it began is not known. It was extinct and forgotten long before the white man came. Stone carvings of animal and human figures indicate that the culture developed exceptional artistry and craftsmanship and a body of complex ritualistic and symbolic lore. This culture may have influenced the whole Northwest Coast.[2] Stone sculptures similar in design have been found at village sites on the Columbia River and Sauvie Island at the mouth of the Willamette River. The refinements of the northern coastal peoples' canoes, fishing tackle, and utensils suggest a strong tradition of arts that may have come from the Fraser River culture.

Dominant characteristics of the coastal cultures are notable among the Tsimshians, Tlingits, Nootkas, Bellacoolas, Kwakiutls, and Haidas, who occupied the islands and mainland inlets from southern Alaska to the Strait of Juan de Fuca. Although there were differences among these peoples, the Kwakiutls may serve to illustrate characteristics common to most.

The social unit was the extended family in which descent was traced both patrilineally and matrilineally, and was represented in heraldic crests or *totems*, carved on poles or painted on boards. Status in the group was determined by heredity and wealth, and the chieftain was custodian of the family's possessions and prestige.

It was an individualistic society, materialistic and competitive. Values were determined by family or individual power in goods—canoes, blankets, fish oil, copper, and slaves. The *potlatch*, celebrating the naming of a child, his puberty, or his assumption of a place in the group, was a feast which demonstrated the status of the host. It was also a force for holding the group together and an economic weapon against a rival family or contenders for position within the group. In the *potlatch*, the host in effect challenged a guest chieftain to exceed him in his "power" to give away or to destroy goods. If the guest did

[2] Marian W. Smith, "The Cultural Development of the Northwest Coast," *Southwestern Journal of Anthropology*, vol. 12, no. 3 (1956).

not return 100 percent on the gifts received and destroy even more wealth in a bigger and better bonfire, he and his people lost face and so his "power" was diminished. Societies engaging in this form of competition were kept busy building a treasure of goods that were expendable for ego satisfaction. The *potlatch*, the *totem*, status competition, secret societies, elaborate masks and ritual dance dramas, were expressions of what Ruth Benedict has called a megalomaniac society.

Most of these Kwakiutl customs were shared by natives elsewhere on the Northwest Coast, notably by those of northwestern Washington and the Puget Sound country, and less strikingly by peoples to the south. Their influence appears to have decreased in direct proportion to the distance from the source. People south of the Columbia River had less in common with their northern neighbors, while natives of southern Oregon shared cultural patterns of northern California and the Great Basin.

The Northwest contained many mutually unintelligible language groupings. In western Washington, the predominant tongue was Coast Salish. In Oregon from the mouth of the Columbia to Tillamook Bay and east to the Cascades, Chinookan languages were spoken. The Tillamooks belonged to the Coast Salish. The Klatskanie on the Columbia, a band on the Willapa River, and another on the Rogue River, were enclaves of Athabascan-speaking peoples. Within the major language groups so many different dialects were spoken that neighbors could not easily communicate verbally with one another.

The coast peoples were politically atomistic. They had no conception of the tribe, though one village might be known to another as "of our people." The governmental unit was the village, which was sometimes simply an extended family. Leadership was inherited, but was affected by possession or lack of wealth. Through personal prestige the chief man of one village might exert influence over other villages. Nevertheless, each village was independent. It had its own fishing and hunting sites and lands for berry-gathering, and within a given area a village moved from summer to winter habitations as the seasonal economy required. There seems to have been no intervillage competition for possession of these locations.

Neither were there widespread alliances or combinations of villages for purposes of war. Wars were local, of short duration, and the exception rather than the rule. The usual provocation seems to have been the demand for slaves. British Columbia coast Indians raided villages of the interior and along the shores of Washington. The Chinooks were less aggressive and got their slaves in trade from southern Oregon and northern California.

8

Intervillage quarrels and slave raids produced warlike posturing—war dances and the massing of war canoes. Lower Columbia River warriors encased themselves in *clamons*, armor of thick elkskin that could turn an arrow, and carried small round shields of skins hardened in fire. Their weapons were bows and arrows and stout clubs. But the purpose of battle was to save face rather than to slaughter or reduce the enemy; after a casualty or two, peace was restored.

Coast Indians enjoyed an unusually rich environment. Famine and poverty were practically unknown except as a passion for gambling might drive individuals to throw away their freedom and, with it, the right to acquire goods for themselves. Ruth Underhill has called these the richest Indians of North America because a wealth of consumable goods was available with a minimum of labor. Wood and water were the sources of their livelihood and both were abundant.

The forests of the Northwest stretched solidly from Alaska to northern California and inland to the rain shadow of the Cascade Mountains. While the pine grew almost exclusively east of the mountains, the coast forests contained stands of spruce, fir, hemlock, and cedar. And wherever the straight-grained, easily split cedar was found, housing, utensils, and clothing were made from it.

Houses were built of split planks set over shallow pits, their gabled roofs supported by posts and covered by overlapping boards. A "long house," or feast house, could hold several hundred persons. A building 100 feet in length might shelter ten to twelve families. Low doorways gave access to a single windowless room warmed by one or more open fires whose smoke escaped through holes in the roof. A continuous platform lining the interior walls was divided into family units separated from one another by hanging mats or wooden chests for food supplies and personal properties.

The soft fiber between the bark and wood of cedar was woven into large conical umbrella-like hats, rain capes, and skirts. According to a sharp-eyed observer, the women wore

> . . . a kind of fringed petticoat suspended from the waist down to the knees, made of the inner rind of the cedar bark, and twisted into threads which hang loose like a weaver's thrums and keep flapping and twisting about with every motion of the body, giving them a waddle or duck gait. This garment might deserve praise for its simplicity, or rather for its oddity, but it does not screen nature. . . . In a calm the sails lie close to the mast, metaphorically speaking, but when the wind blows the bare poles are seen.[3]

[3] Alexander Ross, *Adventures of the First Settlers on the Oregon or Columbia River* (1923), 99.

For much of the year the women wore only such lightweight skirts and the men went naked. But in the cold wet days of winter, the more prosperous donned otter or beaver robes. Washington Indians wove blankets from the hair of a special breed of dogs or of mountain goats obtained in trade with mountain Indians.

Cedar, a fine straight-grained wood, was skillfully fashioned into household articles and utensils. Thin boards, wetted and steamed, were bent along partial cuts to form tight, square-cornered boxes, with joining ends and bottoms sewed together with thongs, and the lids decorated with painted designs or inlaid shells and stones. When used for cooking, these boxes were filled with water which was heated with hot stones; by replacing the rocks from time to time the cook could maintain a steady boiling. Oregon and Washington Indians made greater use of sea grasses and plant fibers than did their northern neighbors. Baskets served for carrying, gathering, and storing, and tightly woven ones were used for cooking just as the northern Indians used boxes.

Large cedar logs were skillfully fashioned into canoes which were so important to these coastal people that they have often been called Canoe Indians. The Makahs and Quinaults of Washington were artisans of the seagoing Nootka or Chinook craft, which were flat-bottom dugouts, sometimes forty to fifty feet long, capable of carrying thirty or more warriors or a crew of five and a ton and a half of dead weight.

The canoemaker split a log down its length, leaving something more than half of its thickness to be shaped by chipping and burning until a rough form was achieved. Final shaping required small chipping strokes, expert use of hot coals, and extreme patience. After the thin walls were made pliable with water heated by hot rocks they were stretched out with thwarts. The canoe was then painted inside and out and sometimes adorned with high end-pieces carved in animal or human figures.[4]

"If perfect symmetry, smoothness, and proportion constitute beauty," one observer remarked of the product, "they surpass anything I ever beheld." William Clark, in less elegant language and more elementary spelling, spoke of them as "butifull," "neeter made than any I have ever Seen and calculated to ride the waves, and carry emence burthens."

The Makahs hunted whales by canoe. The Chinooks traveled to Vancouver Island and California in these low, fragile craft propelled

---

[4] George Durkham, "Canoes from Cedar Logs," *PNQ*, April 1955.

by matting sail and paddle. Women and children handled smaller canoes with ease, often navigating the roughest water. If the canoe filled or capsized, its occupants emptied it, righted it, and climbed back in.

The waters of the sea, the rivers, and the Sound were the larders of the coastal Indians. From wood fibers and grasses the women twisted fishlines and wove nets; the men fashioned hooks and harpoons from wood, bone, and shell with amazing artistry. It was not necessary here, as in the interior, to preserve great quantities of fish, for there were always fish and crabs in the waters, clams and mussels on the beaches. At different localities the runs of fish varied seasonally. On the lower Columbia, from September to January, the natives caught an inferior grade of salmon. In February they fished for giant sturgeon on deep-set lines, and in the early spring they used scoop nets to dip up eulachon or smelts which they preserved by drying and stringing on a cord. The delicate flesh of Chinook salmon harvested from May to September was smoked over fires and packed in grass baskets lined with fish skin. Fish oil, a delicacy for flavoring berries and a cosmetic for hair and skin, was kept in gut or skin bags for individual use or trade.

The natives' diet, like their way of life, an early observer concluded, "neither secures them perpetual health, nor exposes them to any particular diseases . . . an Indian grows old over his smoked salmon just like a citizen at a turtle feast."

The land supplemented this seafood diet. For the diligent hunter armed with bow and tiny, sharp-headed arrows there were swans, geese, and ducks which migrated twice a year, or in mild seasons wintered on quiet waters. He could net snipe on the beaches and in the meadows; shoot or snare deer, wild pigeons, and grouse. His squaw combed huckleberries from bushes on burned-over hillsides and picked salmonberries, wild raspberries, and soapberries from the edges of the forests. If the camas did not grow locally, and if the ponds and lakes did not provide wapato, these bulbs were obtained by trade from neighbors. However, though roots, berries, and game meat were important foods, seafood was the staple of diet.

Rivers, bays, and inlets formed the dooryards and the principal highways. Villages clustered in cleared spots on rivers and streams and around quiet ocean bays and river mouths. As late as 1827 a visitor to the Strait of Juan de Fuca reported that from Tatoosh Island to Port Discovery he never lost sight of the smoke of village fires. The shores of the Columbia from its mouth to the Cascades were thickly peopled. Tidewaters of the Quinault, Chehalis, Yaquina,

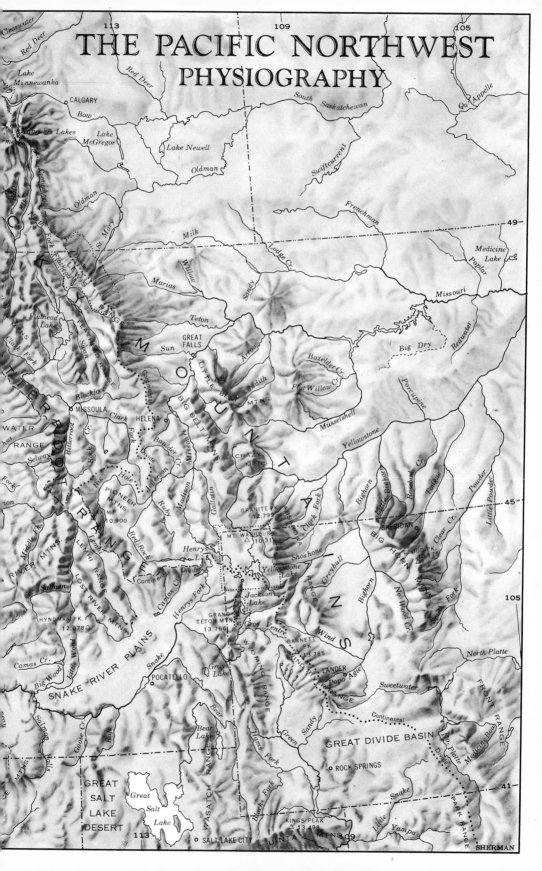

THE PACIFIC NORTHWEST
PHYSIOGRAPHY

Siuslaw, Umpqua and Rogue rivers were population centers, as were Neah Bay, Grays Harbor, and Willapa and Tillamook bays.

Dense forests inhibited land travel. The horse was unknown to the aborigines and relatively useless later in the culture. However, there were foot trails that joined sandy stretches of beach or led to berry patches in the hills, or followed up the swift shallow streams that cut through the Coast Range from the interior valleys; the Chehalis, Salmon, and Yaquina rivers provided such routes. A well-traveled road ran from Puget Sound to the Cowlitz River; another from the Columbia near St. Helens on the south bank into the Tualatin and Willamette valleys, where prairie grasses supported great herds of game. Thus a modest traffic in goods moved by land from seashore to valley, and from north to south.

The pattern of coastal life, modified somewhat in the valleys, prevailed from the coast to the Cascade Mountains. Along the Columbia River, coastal characteristics did not terminate so abruptly. But where the climate changed from wet and equably warm to dry with extremes of hot and cold, and the forests of the mountain slopes gave way to sagebrush, juniper, and grass, different cultures took over.

The Plateau People

For years students looked upon the Plateau culture as transitional between the Coast and Plains cultures. Recent scholarship shows that peripheral areas reflected but did not completely absorb neighboring influences. From the bend of the Fraser River south to the Great Basin, and from the Cascades to the Rockies, spread a pattern of living with its own individuality. This was more like the ancient lake dwellers' culture, elements of which persisted in spite of overlays of adapted customs. Southern Okanogans, Colvilles, and Sanpoils, for example, are believed to be representative of older levels. And Luther S. Cressman has advanced the theory that the Great Basin culture, strikingly illustrated in that of the Klamaths, was the source of the Columbia Plateau culture.

Three major linguistic stocks prevailed in the Plateau: *Shoshonean* in southeastern Oregon and Idaho; *Sahaptin* in northern Oregon, the southern half of Washington, and central Idaho; and *Interior Salish* in northern Washington, British Columbia, northern Idaho, and western Montana. Each language group had numerous dialects, though there were probably fewer than there were among the coastal Indians. Villages speaking a common tongue had a bond that was strengthened by intermarriage and the sharing of certain territories. These bonds were cultural and linguistic, not political.

14

Political organization varied.[5] Strictly local village autonomy was found among the Sanpoils, Southern Okanogans, and Teninos. There were loose bands of villages in interior British Columbia. Local autonomy with slight tribal tendencies was found among other peoples of the Middle Columbia area, while Kootenais, Flatheads, Coeur d'Alenes, Nez Perces, Cayuses, and Umatillas showed definite tribal characteristics. Among the latter group, however, were degrees of "tight" and "loose" tribal structures. The Umatillas were almost unique in that tribe and village were practically synonymous.

Heredity and personal achievement determined leadership in both village and tribe. Although possession of a large number of horses made a man rich, Plateau peoples did not put the same emphasis upon possession of goods as did coastal peoples, and social and political position was less clearly derived from wealth. An "aristocracy of merit" existed but was not a developed caste system. Slavery was uncommon except among those who had close trading relations with the coast.

Hides and basketry served the Plateau people, as wood and woven grass served coastal Indians, for containers and clothing. During the cold seasons, men and women wore skins and furs; in warm weather they wore loincloths, if anything. Bodies and clothing were adorned with bear claws, feathers, stone beads, and copper.

There was no common house type. Where villages were more or less permanently located, as at the Dalles of the Columbia, an ancient style of pit house was modified by the addition of a wooden wall, sometimes circular, roofed with mats or planks. These houses were large enough for two or three families. One interesting house type that showed environmental influences was reported in 1826–1827 by Peter Skene Ogden, the first white man to observe and comment on the Upper Klamath Indians. Their villages were built over water so deep that they used canoes to reach their houses. These "tents," as Ogden called them, were defensible log blockhouses set on foundations of stone and gravel with supporting poles sunk about six feet deep. "Indeed," he commented, "the construction of their Tents evince great ingenuity."

Seldom, however, could these people satisfy their food requirements in any one place; and so they moved as the seasons and food supply required. On the prairies they gathered roots, such as the camas; on the mountain slopes, berries; where deer grazed and buffalo roamed they hunted. Since they wintered wherever they found game for themselves and feed for their horses, their shelters were not designed

[5] Verne F. Ray, "Native Villages and Groupings of the Columbia Basin," *PNQ*, April 1936.

15

Native Peoples

A Bella Coola Indian house, British Columbia. John Boit wrote in Voyage of the Columbia, "*Every door that you entered was made in resemblance to a human or beast head, the passage . . . being through the mouth.*"

RIGHT. *Tlingit Indians of the northwest coast, photographed in 1962, their appearance little changed from that in the painting on page 101, done in 1858. Note, however, that the man standing center wears modern eyeglasses. Again John Boit writes of the Tlingits he saw in 1792, "They also wear European clothing on which they have sewed . . . buttons, thimbles, chain, money, pieces of shell, etc. On their heads they wear a shallow, wickerwork cap. . . ."*

LEFT. *A Nootka Whale House, Vancouver Island, holding wooden images of dead whales, and skulls and images of dead tribesmen. In this shrine were performed the rites essential to successful Nootka whale hunting.*

BELOW. *A southern Kwakuitl Indian village, Vancouver Island. Captain George Vancouver, in 1792, saw and wrote about villages much like this.*

Indian Encampment, Shoshone Village *painted by Albert Bierstadt in 1860. The Shoshones were wide-roaming horse Indians, at home along much of the Snake River and in the easterly Rockies.*

Root-Diggers *(detail) painted by Albert Jacob Miller. From his notes, "These . . . Snake Indians . . . are very poor, and subsist mainly on the roots of the earth . . . they are not permitted by the war-like tribes to hunt the Buffalo. . . ." Courtesy Walters Art Gallery, Baltimore. © 1951 Oklahoma University Press.*

One of our most valuable records of northwest Indians are the paintings of the Canadian artist, Paul Kane. Two of his works appear on this, three on the following page. ABOVE: Indian Camp Colville. *From the artist's notes, "Lodges of Chualpays . . . formed of mats on poles with space in which to hang salmon to dry."* BELOW. Interior of a Lodge. *"Of Clal-lums at Esquimalt, the largest buildings of any description among Indians, divided in the interior into compartments to accomodate 8 or 10 families."*

17

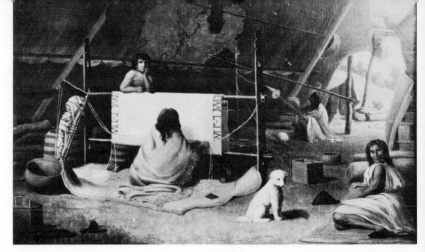

ABOVE. Clal-lum Women Weaving a Blanket. *The loom and blanket are easily seen. Also visible are the thread-spinning device* (right of loom) *and the head-flattening baby-carrier* (left), *wooden boxes, cooking utensils and woven baskets. The round-headed figures in the foreground are probably slaves.*

ABOVE. Medicine Mask Dance.

BELOW. Coffin Rock. *Here, in the lower Columbia, the Indians deposited their dead.*

ABOVE. Council in Bitterroot Valley, July, 1855 sketched by Gustavus Sohon, official artist for Governor Issac I. Steven's western expedition ordered in 1853–1856 by the United States War Department. This council, held at Hell Gate (Missoula, Montana) resulted in a treaty of peace with "Flatheads, Kootenay, and Upper Pend d'Oreille Indians." At councils similar to this the government also sought land cessions from Northwest Indians.

RIGHT. Nez Perce Indians on their reservation, about 1890. Alice Fletcher, left, an anthropologist of the period, helps in the allotment of reservation land to individual owners. It was hoped that private ownership of small plots would eventually make the Indians self-supporting.

Today's Indians take their place in today's communities. ABOVE AND CLOCKWISE. 4-H Range Club members, Warm Springs, Oregon, are responsible for the complete care of 30 blooded Herefords; farmers from the Umatilla Indian Reservation raise high quality grain; a Spokane Indian is deputy clerk, Federal Court House, Portland; a Snohomish part-Indian from Western Washington Agency is a secretary in a Portland administrative office; a Yakima, as Forestry Aid, scales logs at an unloading dock.

for permanent occupation. In some areas, grass mat lodges, or *wicki-ups*, were used. Kootenais, Flatheads, and some Nez Perces adopted the hide *tipi*, common among buffalo hunters of the Plains.

In the first half of the eighteenth century, the Shoshones acquired horses from the Southwest and distributed them to the peoples of the eastern part of the Plateau, and probably to the Plains Indians as well.[6] The horse was a factor of significant change in their traditional culture, for it permitted them to roam farther in search of food. The Nez Perces, for example, wintering in the Clearwater Valley in Idaho, crossed to the Beaverhead country in Montana, and followed well-worn buffalo trails to the Plains. From the natives there they may have derived their tribal organization, a late development which appears to have followed their acquisition of horses.

Mobility made possible wars farther afield. Shoshones, Paiutes, and Bannacks roamed over vast areas. Horse-stealing raids were to Plateau people what slave raids were to the Coast people, but they induced a kind of running warfare which not only developed rituals and techniques, such as the *coup*, but also cultivated a war spirit among horse-owning peoples. The horse was a status symbol for individuals and groups.

On the other hand, the horse also provided means for peaceable communication. Annual horse fairs attracted thousands of Plateau natives to meetings in the grassy valleys of the Yakima and Wenatchee rivers in Washington, and the Grande Ronde in Oregon. These were occasions for races, treaty-making, horse trading and exchange of other goods. Intermediary villages carried products of the coast, northern California, Montana—even pipestone from Minnesota—to these fairs.

Although the horse was important in their economy and the hunt was a means of livelihood, Plateau Indians were dependent also upon the rivers. Wherever a river was navigable, the Plateau dwellers plied it in dugout canoes made from pine logs but less skillfully constructed than the cedar canoes of the coast. But while the Coast Indians had access to seafoods at all seasons, the interior natives depended on salmon which in spring and late summer made their way to spawning grounds of headstreams. Failure of a salmon run meant disaster to these people, particularly to those in northern Washington and interior British Columbia.

Salmon were trapped in weirs, harpooned from rocky outthrusts at narrows, or dipped from pools at the foot of rapids and falls where they milled about trying to make the leap over obstructions. At the Dalles of the Columbia, now obliterated by The Dalles Dam, the In-

[6] Francis Haines, "Northward Spread of Horses to the Plains Indians," *American Anthropologist* (1938); *The Appaloosa Horse* (1951).

dians built fragile scaffoldings which extended over the swift, surging waters, for the choice sites were always where the current was strongest and the salmon were forced to pass close to the rocks to avoid it. At the end of the scaffold, teetering dangerously over the water, the fisherman plied his dip net. In 1812, Robert Stuart estimated that an experienced man could catch at least 500 salmon daily at this location.

For forty miles between the Cascades and Celilo Falls, the Columbia River turned and twisted through narrow channels with many rocky obstructions. Wishram, on the north shore, had been a permanent Indian village for centuries. A settlement at the site of the present town of The Dalles on the south shore was probably equally ancient. To it thousands of Indians trekked yearly to fish, to trade, and to gamble—which was another means of exchanging goods. According to Alexander Ross, one of the earliest white visitors, the Dalles was "the general theater of . . . roguery."

Native tobacco and slaves from northern California were brought to the fairs by central Oregon and Willamette Valley Indians. Eastern Plateau people came with horses, buffalo robes, pipestone, and pigments which they had traded or stolen from Plains people. The Spokanes were middlemen for stationary villages on the upper Columbia, and for Okanogans who traded with the coast via the Methow River. Yakimas, Klickitats, and Wenatchees crossed Chinook Pass to Puget Sound with articles from the Dalles, receiving in exchange dentalium, the *hiaqua*, since few coastal goods had value to Plateau people.

Geography and resources influenced the living patterns of Coast and Plateau peoples. Within their environments both developed means to break the hold of brute nature: language, song, religions, moral codes, commerce, and warfare. The contrast between Nez Perces and Chinooks or between Cayuses and Clallams was illustrated in physical appearance and social attitudes.

White men reacted unfavorably to Coast peoples, noting such characteristics as the artificially flattened heads and grossness of body. They were more favorably impressed with Plateau people, whom they described as tall, well formed, and with normal heads. They uniformly reported the Coast Indians to be immoral. The white men knew about, but did not respect, the Nez Perces', Flatheads', and Spokanes' strong feelings for family. Basic moral differences between the Coast and Plateau cultures can be suggested, if not explained, in the statement that the Chinooks succumbed early to white men's social diseases; the Yakimas and Nez Perces did not.

These, then, were the peoples of the Pacific Northwest. They lived well—some even abundantly—on the resources of the land. When the

21

white man came to exploit these resources he changed the patterns of their lives. Indians produced those goods for which ships first came regularly to the Northwest shores, and Indians provided a market for the white man's industrial output.

The cultures of whites and Indians were poles apart, and the values of each were incomprehensible to the other.

White man and Indian took toll of one another's lives, but the Indian took less than the white. The white man had to destroy the natives' ecology to build his own civilization.

CHAPTER
TWO

Spanish and English Explorers

THE SEARCH for wealth and power which brought Europeans to the New World in the fifteenth century eventually carried them to the northwestern corner of the continent. The ill-shaped pearls and small treasures of gold that Columbus found led his successors to the conquests of Mexico and Peru, and plundered riches only stirred imaginations to dream of "opulent countries" and of "pearls and riches on the coast of the South Sea." Quivira and the Seven Cities of Cibola were fabulous kingdoms, hovering mirage-like somewhere on the western horizon.

Map-makers at various times placed Quivira on the Missouri River, in the Colorado Rockies, in California, and eventually in the Northwest near a hypothetical inland sea. Spanish explorers of the Mississippi Valley and the great Southwest, at great cost in lives and suffering, corrected the map-makers with reports of crude Indian villages and impoverished pueblos. Obviously, then, Quivira lay farther to the west, near the shores of the great South Sea, or perhaps on the Strait of Anian which, it was believed, narrowly separated the northwestern coast of the continent from Asia.

So Spanish explorers turned to the great South Sea. In 1513 Balboa first looked upon the waters of the Pacific. Seven years later Fernão

Magalhaes (Ferdinand Magellan) and Juan del Cano revealed the terrifying extent of that sea on whose western edge they discovered the Philippine Islands.

Undertaking the conquest of the Islands in 1565, the Spanish learned by bitter experience that the prevailing winds south of the equator, which sped their ships to the Islands, made it impossible for them to return to Mexico by the same route. The aged monk Andreas del Urdaneta, once a navigator, charted a theoretical course which, when put to the test, proved that by heading north from the Philippines on the great circle, their sails would catch the westerlies and bring them to a landfall on the California coast (see map, Routes of Pacific Explorations). For the next two and one-half centuries Manila galleons crossed annually from Acapulco to the Philippines and returned by this long and hazardous route.[1]

In the meantime, Juan Cabrillo in 1542 cautiously explored the coast of Lower California, and his pilot, Bartolome Ferrelo, sailed north to the 42nd or 44th parallels. Continental shores did not turn to the west—there was only the immense and lonely sea. If the Strait of Anian existed, it lay further north than Ferrelo had voyaged.

From the start of the Philippine-Mexican trade, Spain's coastal explorations were limited to a search for harbors where her galleons might take refuge. Beyond this, she moved only to protect her claims when others threatened them.

SEARCH FOR A NORTHWEST PASSAGE

For Spain's rival, England, the North American continent lay athwart hopes for a short route to the Indies. If there were a passage through the continent—a Northwest Passage—her merchants would have a great advantage over Spain's.[2] The wish was father to the thought, and English ships in the sixteenth century intensively sought an Atlantic entrance. Martin Frobisher, John Davis, and William Baffin discovered the bays and straits named for them, and Luke Fox and Thomas James entered and explored portions of Hudson Bay (1631); but the Northwest Passage eluded them.

One persistent advocate of further exploration was Michael Lock (or Lok), a London merchant who had helped finance Frobisher's

[1] William L. Schurz, *The Manila Galleon* (1959).

[2] Glyndwr Williams, *The British Search for a Northwest Passage in the Eighteenth Century* (1962); Leslie H. Neatby, *In Quest of the Northwest Passage* (1958); Nellis M. Crouse, *The Search for the Northwest Passage* (1934).

and Davis' voyages in 1576 and 1585–1587. In 1596 Lock published a letter purportedly written by a Greek explorer in the service of Spain, Juan de Fuca, who claimed to have found the western opening of the Northwest Passage. By his account, in 1592 de Fuca had entered a broad inlet on the Pacific coast located between 47 degrees and 48 degrees north latitude, had sailed inland for more than twenty days, and found a land rich in gold, silver, and pearls, and a people who wore the skins of beasts. The Juan de Fuca story was a kind of fiction common to the day; but the legend of his voyage was perpetuated when map-makers put his strait in the latitude where, 200 years later, the strait leading into Puget Sound was discovered.

FRANCIS DRAKE AND SPANISH DEFENSES

Despite Lock's energetic propagandizing for Pacific exploration, the first English ship to enter the Pacific had other purposes. Francis Drake, having tasted the fruits of piracy with John Hawkins at Vera Cruz (1568), returned to the Spanish colonies in three successive raids (1570–1573). In 1577 he sailed in search of the route to the Moluccas, but instead entered the Pacific and looted undefended Spanish ports. While immediately profitable, his act was politically distressing to Anglo-Spanish relations.

Since Drake sailed north to some undetermined coastal point, it has been assumed that he sought the western entrance of the Northwest Passage, and because he took possession of the land at a California bay, that he was an agent of early English national interest in the Pacific. However, in "all his enterprises, booty seems to have been somewhere in sight."[3] There was no booty on the coast between the 38th and 48th parallels, the possible limits of his northern voyage. He found only a region where the rain was "an unnatural congealed and frozen substance," followed by "most vile, thicke and stinking fogges."

From this unpleasant climate Drake turned south again. Before his departure to circumnavigate the globe and return to England, he is supposed to have given the name New Albion to the northern California coast. This name later appeared on maps but was shifted to the shores of Oregon and Washington.

[3] Henry R. Wagner, *Sir Francis Drake's Voyage Around the World; Its Aim and Achievements* (1926), 212; *Spanish Voyages to the Northwest Coast of America in the Sixteenth Century* (1929).

Spanish loot inspired other English seadogs to emulate Drake, with the result that Spain was forced to take defensive action to protect her Caribbean colonies and ports and trade in the Pacific. Having dealt resounding punishment to English privateers in 1594, the Spanish government set moving the slow, cumbersome machinery of colonial administration to launch an expedition of discovery in the Pacific. In 1602–1603, Sebastian Viscaino and Martin Aguilar were commissioned to look for the city of Quivira and for harbors as far north as the 43rd parallel. Aguilar may have reached this latitude, but through an error of the Mexican historian, Torquemada, the "rapid and abundant river" noted by Aguilar at about 41 degrees north latitude was placed on the map at 43 degrees, almost at the location where the Columbia River was discovered in 1792. Thus the maps of the day, by accident and design, took on features approximating the truth.

But for more than a century and a half after Aguilar's voyage no vessel came with the purpose of exploring the Northwest Coast. Accidental landings cannot be wholly ruled out. Oregon Indian legends tell of white-sailed ships and of men who buried treasure on Neahkahnie Mountain. Finds of beeswax, marked with numerals and symbols as yet undeciphered, lend substance to tales of long-ago shipwreck and disaster.

From 1603 to 1769 Spain turned to South Sea voyages in search of an unknown continent which map- and myth-makers had projected; to the development of a Japanese-Philippine-Mexican trade, and to the protection of her established colonies. In 1763, as a result of the Seven Years' War, Spain acquired French Louisiana, an administrative burden but a hopefully comforting barrier between her mineral-rich provinces and aggressive English colonies to the east and north. Almost simultaneously, she began to occupy California, Russian expansion being the immediate cause of her renewed activity on the Pacific Coast.

RUSSIA IN THE PACIFIC

The eighteenth century was an age of tremendous energy. It was an age of enlightenment and of scientific interests, of imperial pretensions and of derring-do. Nations competed to advance the arts and sciences and their own interests. In some cases it was possible to serve both science and empire.

Peter the Great of Russia had ambitions not only to unify his country and to end her isolation but also to win a share in the riches of the East. By 1639, enticed by rich fur resources, Russian traders had undertaken the conquest of Siberia, had reached the Pacific, and had founded ports on the Sea of Okhotsk and Kamchatka Peninsula. Before his death in 1725, Peter drew up instructions for an expedition to search out an ice-free passage to China and India through the Arctic Sea, by which ships from Archangel could sail eastward through the polar regions into the Pacific. On Peter's map this passage was called the Strait of Anian. "In my last travels I discussed the subject with learned men and they were of the opinion that such a passage could be found," he wrote; and he continued: "Now . . . . we should strive to win for [Russia] glory along the lines of the Arts and Sciences."[4]

Vitus Bering, Martin Spanberg, and Alexei Chirikov were charged to locate the Pacific entrance to the passage. In 1728 Bering sailed from Kamchatka to 67 degrees north latitude, and following the Asiatic coastline through the strait which bears his name until it turned abruptly westward, he concluded that America and Asia were not far apart. A second expedition was authorized in 1732. Its public purpose was scientific inquiry; its private one, to acquire information about the geography and fur trade potentials of the North American coast. In 1741 the *St. Peter* and *St. Paul*, commanded by Bering and Chirikov, sailed from Kamchatka. Chirikov sighted the American coast on July 15, 1741, at about 57 degrees, but the loss of his small boats compelled him to return to his home port. Bering, in the meantime, sighted the coast on July 16, one degree farther north. He was forced to winter on Bering Island, where he and many of his crew perished. The survivors returned with sea otter furs, and within a decade Siberian traders, *promishlenniki*, were voyaging yearly to the Aleutian Islands and collecting immense quantities of fine furs.

SPANISH SHIPS ON THE NORTHWEST COAST

Three semiofficial Russian expeditions between 1765 and 1768 were interpreted by Spain as threats to her claims in the Pacific. Spain decided therefore to strengthen her position by settling Upper California and further exploring the Northwest Coast. Between 1769 and 1776 missions and presidios were established at San Diego, Monterey,

[4] Frank A. Golder, *Russian Expansion in the Pacific* (1914), 133.

San Gabriel, and San Francisco, and in 1774 Juan Perez was dispatched north to 60 degrees to explore and to take possession of the land. Perez was forced back at the 54th parallel, after scurvy had seriously weakened his crew. He reported that so far he had found no Russian settlements, discovered no ports, and taken possession of no lands. He described the western coasts of Vancouver and Queen Charlotte islands, and gave a vague description of Oregon and Washington shores. In recognition of his experience he was chosen in 1775 to pilot a second expedition of two vessels, the *Santiago* and the *Sonora*, under Bruno Heceta and with Juan Francisco de Bodega y Quadra second in command. They were to explore to the 65th parallel. Again the dread scurvy thwarted their plans, forcing Heceta to turn back at 49 degrees and Bodega at 58.

On July 14, 1775, the flagship *Santiago* anchored in the shallow bay under Point Grenville, and Heceta took possession of the land for Spain. At the same time Bodega anchored in the schooner *Sonora* probably near Cape Elizabeth, for fresh water supplies from the Quinault River. The landing party was attacked and massacred by Indians. To comemmorate the dead the nearby rocky island was named Isla de Dolores, the Isle of Sorrows, and the present Point Grenville (or Cape Elizabeth) received the name Punta de Martires.

Coasting south on August 17, Heceta came upon a large inlet which he named Assumption Bay in honor of the feast day on which he made his discovery. The northern headland he called Cape San Roque and the southern spit, Cape Frondoso. Currents and eddies in the bay led him to believe that he was at "the mouth of some great river, or of some passage to another sea." "Had I not been certain of the latitude of this bay . . ." he reported, "I might easily have believed it to be the passage discovered by Juan de Fuca, in 1592, which is placed on the charts between the 47th and 48th degrees; where I am certain that no such strait exists."[5] Heceta did not explore the bay. His depleted crew could not spare men for the longboat, nor had they strength to get up the anchor if it were dropped. The "Rio San Roque" appeared on subsequent maps, but Heceta failed to enter the Columbia River.

Perez, Heceta, and Bodega gave form to the shoreline, and names—few of which have survived—to many of its mountains, harbors, and bays. Their voyages entitled Spain to claim the original discovery of the Northwest Coast.

The Spanish did not pursue these discoveries. Their fear of Russia was allayed when it appeared that her traders were not attempting a settlement. It was the British who next challenged Spain.

[5] "Extract from the Report of Captain Bruno Heceta," in Robert Greenhow, *The History of Oregon and California* (1845).

North America, about 1719: *La Mer de l'Ouest* (The Western Sea). From a print in the Charles H. Carey Collection, Oregon Historical Library.

COOK IN THE NORTH PACIFIC

As we have seen, the English first entered the Pacific Ocean to prey upon Spanish treasure ships. In the following two centuries they sent expeditions of discovery into southern waters looking for the Unknown Continent and vying with the Spanish for possession of South Sea islands. British merchants secured a foothold in India and the East India Company pursued a rich trade with China. While their ships plied the long voyage around Africa, the Northwest Passage only intermittently engaged their attention.

In the mid-eighteenth century English interest was sharpened with the revival and popularization of an old tale of an apocryphal Spanish voyage. In this story, Admiral Bartolomeo de Fonte had coasted the North Pacific and entered a great waterway extending far into the continent. At the eastern end of the "sea of Ronquillo," he had met the ship of a Boston trader who had entered through a Hudson Bay inlet.

For those who in 1745 still believed in a practicable Northwest Passage, this tale confirmed the Juan de Fuca legend. A flurry of private explorers searched the shores of Hudson Bay and the ice-locked channels of Arctic waters, while influential voices demanded a government-supported exploration of the North Pacific.

In 1763, at the end of the war in which she acquired France's Canadian provinces, Britain embarked upon a new colonial policy designed to fit the American colonies into her imperial plans. While pursuing policies that led to the American Revolution and the breakup of her first empire, she was busy creating a new one in India. As befitted her imperial role in the Age of Enlightenment, Britain also engaged in exploration to serve the arts and sciences.

In 1768 Captain James Cook of the Royal Navy, privately subsidized in part, made his first voyage into the South Pacific to observe the transit of the planet Venus and to search anew for the Unknown Continent. Unfortunately, astronomical research was not advanced by his voyage and there was reason to doubt the existence of the Unknown Continent; but England now had a claim to New Zealand, Tasmania, and Australia whose coasts Cook mapped. A second voyage (1772–1775) proved conclusively that there was no other southern continent inviting occupation, and Cook's speculations as to the existence of Antarctic lands were left for a later century to prove.

Cook's two voyages to the Antipodes and the much enlarged world revealed by his reports, stirred men's imaginations. Even James Boswell, biographer of Dr. Samuel Johnson and London's literary set, "catched the enthusiasm of curiosity and adventure, and felt a strong inclination to go with him on his next voyage." Boswell was not alone in being "carried away with the general grand and indistinct notion of A Voyage Round the World."

It was Cook's third voyage, 1776–1780, that had historical significance for the Pacific Northwest.[6] Planned while the American colonies were debating their declaration of independence, it was inspired in part by "a desire to know as much as possible with regard to the planet which we inhabit," but primarily to satisfy public pressure for a thorough search for the Northwest Passage. The government offered a 20,000-pound prize for its discovery.

Cook was directed to proceed around the Cape of Good Hope into the Pacific, to cross from the Society Islands to the western coast of North America and to waste no time in exploration until he reached 65 degrees north latitude. His search was to concentrate about this parallel on the theory that there, if anywhere, could be found the western entrance of the Northwest Passage. If he failed, he was to continue into the Arctic through Bering Strait and look for an open-water polar passage. Such confidence was placed in Cook's competence that the Admiralty dispatched naval vessels to meet him in Baffin Bay.

On March 7, 1778, he sighted the Oregon coast at Yaquina Bay. Though his instructions did not require close examination of the area, he saw and named Capes Gregory (now Arago), Foulweather, and Perpetua. Haste and bad weather combined to make him miss the mouth of the Columbia River.

On March 22 at the entrance of the strait between Vancouver Island and the Washington coast, Cook sighted a cape which he named Flattery, with nice attention to meaning. Approaching, he said, "there appeared to be a small opening, which flattered us with the hopes of finding an harbour. . . . It is in this very latitude where we now were, that geographers have placed the pretended strait of Juan de Fuca. . . . But," he concluded, "we saw nothing like it; nor is there the least probability that ever any such thing existed."

His first landing was at Nootka Sound on Vancouver Island where he spent most of April repairing and rerigging his ships. Here, as elsewhere, his crew carried on a lively trade for furs which they used as bedding or to repair their worn-out clothes and which they bought

---

[6] James Cook and James King, *A Voyage to the Pacific Ocean . . . in 1776 . . . 1780*, 3 vols. (1784); James A. Williamson, *Cook and the Opening of the Pacific* (1948).

31

from the natives with any piece of metal or trinket. The Indians' eagerness for metal led them to dexterous thieving which, in spite of watchful guards, practically stripped the ship of ironwork.

For the remainder of the season Cook examined the coastline to the
north. On August 9 he passed through Bering Strait where, he said,
he reached the "hitherto unknown" western extremity of North America. Ahead lay the Arctic Sea, and at his right the frozen wastes of
North America. After a three-week search he concluded that there
was no passage here by which his ships could return home.

Cook was a great explorer and a great seaman. In the Pacific, he
charted the course for his successors. He discovered the islands which
he honored with the name of the Earl of Sandwich, first lord of the
Admiralty. The Sandwich (Hawaiian) Islands became a regular stopping place and supply depot for ships destined for the Northwest
Coast.

Cook had the advantage of new navigational instruments—the
chronometer and an improved sextant—that made possible accurate
determination of latitudes and longitudes. He proved a godsend to
sailors when he applied rules of sanitation to life at sea. In the four
years of his third voyage, only five men were lost by sickness, and
three of these had been ill when they left England. He used "sour
krout" and "portable soup" as preventives for scurvy and limited the
use of salt foods. He ordered his crews, when ashore, to vary their
diet with native foods, which at times the men found so nauseous that
it took "the joint aid of persuasion, authority and example, to conquer
their prejudices and disgusts." At any rate, his crew did not suffer seriously from the dread disease.

Cook's voyages became a training school for ambitious young seamen. Six names enrolled on the third voyage reappear in Pacific
Northwest history: Lieutenant George Vancouver was to be Cook's
principal successor in exploring the coast; Nathaniel Portlock and
George Dixon were to return in 1786, and James Colnett in 1787, as
pioneers in the fur trade; Corporal John Ledyard of the Marines was
to become a publicist for the Pacific fur trade area; and Joseph Billings was to lead a Russian expedition into the North Pacific and
eventually become a commodore in the Russian Navy.

Cook's third voyage proved to all but the most intransigent that
the navigable passage visualized by armchair explorers did not exist.
Subsequent search was more by way of justifying his conclusion than
challenging it. Not until the summer of 1954 did specially built and
powered vessels manage to break through the ice of the Arctic passage
between the Atlantic and Pacific oceans.

In Northwest history, Cook's name is usually associated with the beginning of the fur trade. Actually, the Russians in Alaska and, in small measure, Spanish garrisons in California had already been dealing in furs. Though Cook did not live to realize the trade's possibilities, his men did. Following his murder in the Hawaiian Islands in the spring of 1779, the *Resolution* and the *Discovery* returned once more to the Northwest Coast before sailing for China.

In China, the seamen were astonished to find that sea otter skins for which they had paid trifles were in high demand. One man sold his stock for $800. A few prime skins, clean and well preserved, brought 120 silver dollars each. This windfall led the crews to the verge of mutiny in their eagerness to return to the Northwest Coast. Captain Clerke noted in his official history that "there is not the least doubt . . . that a very beneficial fur trade might be carried on with the inhabitants of this vast coast," and some officers proposed to East India Company merchants that they outfit two small vessels to sail immediately. Within five years Portlock and Dixon were among pioneers of the "fur rush" to the Pacific Northwest.

Thus Cook's final voyage may be said to have closed one phase of maritime exploration and opened another. The first was concerned primarily with Spain's exploration to claim land, and Britain's to find a route to the Indies—the elusive Northwest Passage. The second period began when it was learned that the sea otter had value in world trade.

The men who followed Cook were principally interested in profit from Indian trade. With rare exceptions, subsequent discoveries and explorations were merely incidental. Traders translated legend into reality by finding the entrance to the Strait of Juan de Fuca and the Columbia River; the fur trade led to settlement of the Pacific Northwest.

CHAPTER
THREE

Maritime Fur Trade: International Rivalries

THE OFFICIAL REPORT of Cook's third voyage was published in 1784 and attracted as much attention if not more than the narratives of his earlier ones. "The extraordinary discoveries of . . . Cook," wrote a contemporary, "inspired all Europe with an enthusiastic desire of being acquainted with the parts of the globe still remaining unknown." It would appear that enthusiasm waxed great when the unexplored parts of the Pacific Northwest were reported rich in the sea otter fur so prized by the Chinese. By 1789, ships of France, Russia, Spain, Britain, and the new United States were in Northwest waters.

VOYAGE OF LAPÉROUSE

In 1785 Louis XVI of France personally helped plan an expedition of discovery into Pacific and Asiatic waters. Two ships, the *Boussole* and the *Astrolabe*, under Jean de Galaup, Count Lapérouse, were staffed with scientists and observers to search for "some river, some narrow gulf" which might communicate with Hudson Bay. But science was not the whole purpose of the voyage. Lapérouse was also in-

34

structed to examine the "possibility of establishing a colony or at least a factory [trading post] in a region not yet occupied."[1]

Lapérouse sighted the coast on June 23, 1786, near Mt. Elias at 60 degrees north latitude. He spent a month examining the vicinity and took possession of Port des Français (Lituya Bay), which he considered suitable and defensible. He then visited California to observe the strength and character of Spanish settlements and afterward crossed the Pacific to Macao where he tested the market with the sale of 1000 furs. At the end of September, 1787, Lapérouse put his Russian interpreter, Ferdinand de Lesseps, ashore at Kamchatka to make his way to Paris with reports and maps, while the commander explored the Yellow Sea and Malaysian shores.

Tragedy shattered the expedition. Twenty-one marines and officers had perished in a heavy storm while surveying Port des Français. Then sometime in 1788 the gallant Frenchman, along with his faculty of scholars and his crews, was lost with their vessels on an island in the Hebrides.

Reports carried home by de Lesseps, sole survivor of the voyage, did not encourage French colonial enterprise in the Northwest. Its trade did not seem a profitable substitute for that surrendered with Canada to the British in 1763. Nor could France, moving toward revolution at home, afford colonial expansion.

The French expedition brought reactions from other European powers, however. Official Russia had shown little interest in her traders' activities in North Pacific waters after the mid-1760s. In 1784, with no encouragement from the state, the Siberian merchant Shelikov established the first colony of a permanent nature on Kodiak Island. But reports of Cook's voyage had put this colonial outpost in new perspective and Catherine II had authorized a Russian voyage of discovery into the Pacific. In July, 1785, informed that Lapérouse's expedition was outfitting at Brest, she gave orders for Russians to proceed. The next month, Captain Joseph Billings, who had sailed with Cook as a common seaman, was in command of a Siberian Pacific expedition which would last nine years and accomplish little.

Spain, too, was roused to action, both with regard to the fur trade and the security of her claims in the Northwest. In 1784 a plan was submitted to the viceroy of New Spain to export California sea otter pelts to Manila for trade with China. The California trade was made a state monopoly under the Royal Philippine Company and the first cargo was exported in 1786.

Since the Perez-Heceta-Bodega expeditions of 1774–1775, Spain had

[1] *La Voyage de Lapérouse sur les Côtes de l'Alaska et de la California (1786).* Historical Documents, Institut Française de Washington, Cahier X (1937), xvii.

considered the Northwest Coast a legitimate possession on the basis of discovery and exploration. Further exploration north of 55 degrees in 1779 by Ignacio Arteaga and Bodega completed what was considered the necessary grounds for her claims to the whole region, and the next year the king ordered an end to voyages for exploration. But after Lapérouse's visit to California, the order was rescinded and the viceroy was informed "that the western coasts of Spanish American islands and seas adjacent should be more frequently navigated and explored."

In 1788 Don Esteban Jose Martinez and Lopez de Haro were sent to find out what the Russians were doing in the north. Martinez was less excited by what he saw of the Russians than by what he learned of British activities at Nootka Sound, a port he claimed to have discovered and named San Lorenzo nearly four years before Cook's visit there.

BRITISH TRADERS

Although their merchants congregated at Canton where Cook's men had sold furs so profitably in the winter of 1779, the British were relatively slow in getting into the Northwest fur trade. They were held up by two monopolies: the South Sea Company, which had sole rights to British trade in the Pacific, and the East India Company, with exclusive privileges over British trade in India and China. Only merchants licensed by the South Sea Company could trade on the Pacific Coast and only merchants licensed under heavy bond by the East India Company could dispose of their cargoes in China.[2] To trade without license laid ship and cargo open to seizure by "legal" traders, so that British merchants who ran this risk adopted the subterfuge of sailing under fictitious ownership and foreign flags.

The pioneer trader Captain James Hanna, probably a risk-taking independent, made two voyages in 1785 and 1786. By 1789, at least fifteen other British ships had been on the coast. It is possible that most of them belonged to Bombay and London merchants associated with Richard Cadman Etches and Company of London. Proposing to open a trade on the Northwest Coast and with Japan (whose ports were closed to westerners), Etches, under the name of the King George's Sound Company, obtained a five-year monopoly and licenses

[2] Dorothy Burne Goebel, "British Trade to the Spanish Colonies," *AHR*, January 1938.

from both South Sea and East India companies in 1785. But, as will appear, this arrangement was not wholly satisfactory.

James Strange, the second trader to arrive in the Northwest, probably represented Etches' company; there is evidence that he was also acting as an informal observer for the British government. With two vessels, the *Captain Cook* and the *Experiment*, under captains Laurie and Guise, Strange arrived at Nootka in June, 1786. He remained a month while the crews recuperated from scurvy and he traded with the natives. Before leaving the coast, Strange explored parts not seen by Captain Cook, and discovered an extensive body of water which he named Queen Charlotte's Sound.[3]

In the meantime, Etches dispatched from London the *King George* and the *Queen Charlotte*, under Captain Nathaniel Portlock and Lieutenant George George Dixon, both of whom had been with Cook's third voyage. They were elaborately outfitted with trade goods and "implements of husbandry" to establish several trading posts. In July, 1786, they were on the coast in the vicinity of Cook's River and until November, according to their testimony, carefully explored any northern inlet that might lead to the interior. After wintering in the Hawaiian Islands, they returned to the coast in March, 1787. Here, in the course of the season, they met Captains James Colnett and Charles Duncan in the *Prince of Wales* and the *Princess Royal*, Captain Charles W. Barkley of the *Imperial Eagle*, all probably employed by Etches, and Captain John Meares of the *Nootka*, at the time an independent.

Portlock and Dixon learned that somewhere south of King George's Sound the Spanish were making settlements, but they made none of their own. Having disposed of 2500 sea otter pelts at Macao, they returned to England in the summer of 1788, and explained that they had used their discretionary powers to decide against a settlement. This was indeed discreet, since none of their men volunteered to stay and man the posts.

Etches was indignant with Portlock for having failed his mission. Recognizing however that it would not be easy to persuade men to winter at such isolated places, he proposed that the government colonize the Northwest with convicts. The government did not respond. Neither did Etches abandon the trade. He and his partners were not satisfied with conditions of trade under their East India Company license. While he solicited influence to break the Company's monop-

[3] *James Strange's Journal and Narrative of the Commercial Expedition from Bombay to the Northwest Coast of America* (1928); William Beresford, *George Dixon, A Voyage Round the World* . . . (1789); "Four Letters from Richard Cadman Etches to Sir Joseph Banks," *BCHQ*, April 1942.

oly, his next ships were outfitted in foreign ports, sailed under other flags than the British, and disposed of their furs at Macao, a free Portuguese port on the China coast. Such was the arrangement for Captain Charles Barkley.

The Discovery of the Strait of Juan de Fuca

Barkley, accompanied by his wife and young son, left Ostende in November, 1786, in the British merchant ship the *Loudoun*, renamed the *Imperial Eagle*, and under the flag of a fictitious Austrian East India Company. Early in June he was at Nootka Sound, where he enjoyed excellent trade with the Indians. It was early in July in 1787 that Barkley made the discovery which gives him a special place in Pacific Northwest history. According to his wife's diary:

> . . . to our great astonishment, we arrived off a large opening extending to the eastward, the entrance to which appeared to be about four leagues wide, and remained about that width as far as the eye could see, with a clear westerly horizon, which my husband immediately recognized as the long lost strait of Juan de Fuca, and to which he gave the name of the original discoverer, my husband placing it on his chart.[4]

Barkley did not venture far into the strait. He found the natives on the north coast friendly and well disposed, but those on the south, where the shore was "like the Main," were "more of the Bandity kind." Among these people Barkley lost four men who went ashore with "too much confidence, and unarm'd." A search party burned the village in retaliation. A brief report on the voyage published in 1788 says that these murders occurred at 47 degrees 46 minutes north latitude. Thus Bodega's Isla de Dolores, renamed Destruction Island by Barkley, became a monument to two instances of Indian hostility.

Barkley traded some 4000 pelts, one of the richest cargoes of the time, which he carried to Macao in the winter of 1787–1788. In 1792 he returned to the Alaskan coast but not, so far as is known, to the scene of his major discovery.

Captain John Meares

Meares, under the British flag but unlicensed, first arrived on the coast in 1786, so late in the fall that he was forced to winter at Prince William Sound. In the spring twenty-three of the crew of the *Nootka* were suffering from scurvy—or, it was charged, from overuse of rum—when Portlock and Dixon gave Meares much needed assist-

[4] W. Kaye Lamb, "The Mystery of Mrs. Barkley's Diary," *BCHQ*, January 1942; F. A. Howay, "Early Navigation of the Straits of Fuca," *OHQ*, March 1911.

ance. However, as licensed traders, they forced him to leave under bond not to return.

But return he did, the next year (1788) with the *Felice* and the *Iphigenia* under William Douglas, both outfitted at Macao, flying Portuguese flags and nominally registered to a Portuguese merchant. At Nootka, on lands Meares later declared he had purchased from the local chieftain, his carpenters built a rough fort and put together the framework of a small schooner brought over in the *Iphigenia's* hold. In the meantime, Meares explored the coast.

Meares was neither modest nor reliable. He claimed discovery of the Strait of Juan de Fuca, but it is likely that he was using Barkley's charts in his report. He probably was first to enter Willapa Bay, which he named Shoalwater. At the approximate place where Heceta had found evidence of a large river, Meares reported, he had sailed into a large bay "with every encouraging expectation" but, finding no sign of a river, he named the bay Deception and the northern cape, Disappointment. He concluded, "We can now with safety assert, that . . . no such river as that of Saint Roc exists, as laid down in the Spanish charts." He accurately described the cape he named Lookout, now Cape Meares. Three Arch Rocks are probably his Three Brothers, and his Quicksand Bay may have been the entrance to Tillamook Bay.

In September Meares was again at Nootka where his schooner, the *North West America*, was launched and outfitted for trading. He then sailed for China in the *Felice* with furs and mast timbers.

It is possible that Meares had some affiliation with Etches on this second voyage. Whatever the earlier arrangement, a formal partnership was now undertaken by Meares, Etches, and others, as The Associated Merchants for Trading to the Northwest Coast of America, with Meares as spokesman for the group. In 1789, he sent out the *Princess Royal* under Captain Thomas Hudson, and the *Argonaut*, with Captain James Colnett. They carried the frame of another schooner, trade goods, and Chinese and Hawaiian laborers to occupy his so-called fort.

But when Colnett and Hudson arrived at Nootka they were surprised to find Don Esteban Jose Martinez, Spanish ships, and a primitive Spanish settlement.

TROUBLE AT NOOTKA SOUND

It will be recalled that in 1788 Martinez, sent north to investigate Russian activities, had come upon British traders. He was now ordered to return immediately to protect Spanish claims. Whether he subsequently exceeded his instructions is not clear, but it would appear from his own testimony that he understood he was to seize intruders.

On arrival at Nootka in May (1789) Martinez found Meares' *Iphigenia* and the schooner *North West America*. He seized Colnett and Hudson when they arrived in July, having sufficient proof in Colnett's papers and cargo that a fortified establishment was planned. On July 14th the *Argonaut* and the *Princess Royal*, along with their officers and crews, were taken to Mexico. A surprised viceroy eventually found reasons to release them in hope of avoiding an international incident. Colnett returned to Nootka and from there sailed for Macao.

The Nootka incident might have ended here, but as soon as Meares learned of the seizure of the vessels, he called loudly for government intervention, demanding over $500,000 indemnity for his company's losses.[5]

Although restitution was already being made in Mexico, Britain made an issue of the affair. The government was not anxious to unravel the thread of events at Nootka or to weigh the pros and cons. It wanted to provoke more general issues. Was the Pacific a closed sea for Spanish navigation, or was it an open sea with reciprocal freedom for subjects of both powers to fish and trade in its unsettled parts? Could claims to sovereignty be established simply on the grounds of discovery and the act of taking possession, or was occupation a requirement?

Madrid's first reaction was a stubborn insistence on sticking to the case at issue. It was soon made clear that what was really involved was Spain's system of exclusive trade within her empire. His Catholic Majesty called for aid from his ally, France. The British cabinet prepared for war by alerting its allies, Holland and Prussia. The Canadian colonies were advised to cultivate friendly relations with the United States, and the latter was cautiously approached to see if it would collaborate with Britain in the event of war. When Parliament voted a war budget, the Spanish, having vacillated between hostile gestures and apologies and finding their French ally at first dubious of Spain's legal position and then immobilized by revolution, decided in favor of peaceful settlement.

A convention signed at the Escurial late in October, 1790, averted

[5] *The Dixon-Meares Controversy*, F. W. Howay, ed. (1929); William R. Manning, *The Nootka Sound Controversy*, American Historical Association *Annual Report*, 1904; John Norris, "The Policy of the British Cabinet in the Nootka Crisis," *English Historical Review*, October 1955; Lennox Mills, "The Real Significance of the Nootka Sound Incident," *Canadian Historical Review*, June 1925.

war and gave the British all practical advantages. The British agreed to curb their subjects' "illicit trade with the Spanish settlements" and to forbid navigating or "fishing" (e.g., hunting sea otters or whales) within ten maritime leagues of any part of the coast occupied by Spain. Spain agreed to "restore" Meares' Nootka settlement and conceded British rights to fish, trade, and make settlements "in the Pacific Ocean or in the South Seas . . . in places not already occupied."

To effect restoration of Meares' establishment, both governments appointed commissioners to meet on the site. Spain was represented by the explorer Bodega, now commandant at San Blas, and Britain by Captain George Vancouver, a member of Cook's third expedition and currently prepared to sail for further exploration of the Northwest Coast.

Before the commissioners arrived at Nootka, the Spanish were busily remedying some errors of omission. Apparently Martinez had left a few settlers and priests at Nootka in 1789. These were reinforced and supplied in early 1790 by three vessels, under Lieutenants Salvador Fidalgo and Manuel Quimper, and Commandant Francisco Eliza. The ships carried provisions, including livestock, for settlements, and soldiers and artillery for fortified posts or *presidios*.

Thus was founded at Friendly Cove (Cala de los Amigos) on Nootka Sound a village reported to have fifty houses in 1792. The fort was "no great thing," but it had mounted cannon to protect an estimated population of 200 Spaniards and Peruvian Indians, all males. In 1792, Nunez Gãona, a fortified village of ten houses dressed up with gardens, was founded at Neah Bay on the south side of the Strait of Juan de Fuca.[6]

Nootka Sound was an international gathering place in the summer of 1792. Five Spanish, eleven English, two Portuguese, one French, and eight American vessels were anchored in its waters at one time or another. In August, Bodega and Vancouver met in Spanish quarters in Friendly Cove, compared maps and charts of their countrymen's explorations, argued their interpretations of the convention's terms, and glossed over irreconcilable differences with glittering social events. At one such momentous affair, the courtly Bodega entertained officers of all the vessels in port. "Fifty four persons sat down to Dinner," young John Boit noted with amazement, "and the plates, which was *solid silver* was shifted five times, which made 270 Plates."

There were no hard feelings between Bodega and Vancouver. Having finally, by joint efforts, defined and charted the island on which

[6] "John Boit's Log of the Second Voyage of the Columbia," in *Voyages of the "Columbia" to the Northwest Coast, 1787–1790 and 1790–1793*, F. W. Howay, ed. (1944), 411.

41

Nootka was located, they named it Quadra's and Vancouver's Island. (It is to be noted that Bodega assigned his matronymic in naming the island.) But in spite of amicable personal relations, the two could come to no agreement. Vancouver read his instructions to mean that the Spanish must surrender their settlement in order to "restore" that of Meares; Bodega understood that only the plot of ground where Meares' house had stood was to be delivered up. They agreed to notify their governments of the impasse.

After further negotiations in Europe, the Nootka Claims Convention was signed in 1793. Meares and his associates received an indemnity of $210,000, and Vancouver's and Bodega's dilemma was solved when Britain and Spain jointly agreed to abandon claims to exclusive rights:

> . . . the subjects of both nations shall have the liberty of frequenting the . . . port whenever they wish and of constructing there temporary buildings to accommodate them during their residence. . . . But neither of the said parties shall form any permanent establishment in the said port or claim any right of sovereignty or territorial dominion there to the exclusion of the other.

In 1795 other commissioners arrived to go through the forms demanded by the convention and to end the long-drawn-out dispute. By then the Spaniards had abandoned their settlements at Neah Bay and Friendly Cove. Thereafter English and American traders stopped only occasionally at Nootka and it was never again "occupied."

Domestic politics explain in part British belligerence in the Nootka controversy: the opposing viewpoints of "Big" and "Little" Englanders, jingoistic pressures in an election year, and merchants' clamor for free trade which meant freedom to trade with Spain's closed colonies. In winning its case Britain established a new principle of imperial sovereignty.

Spain interpreted sovereignty as a consequence of title; title was based upon prior discovery, exploration, and formal acts of possession. The power to exclude was inherent in a declaration of sovereignty. Britain, on the other hand, chose to interpret sovereignty as effective only when there was evidence of occupation. This meant, for all practical purposes, on-the-spot power to exclude. She did not assert that Meares' establishment at Nootka was evidence of English occupation. It was, rather, evidence that the Spanish were not there to prevent the occupation. Since the Spanish were not in a position to exclude, it followed that they had no exclusive sovereignty. By extension of this argument, the Northwest Coast was open to British commerce.

Having displayed belligerence to break down Spain's claims to exclusive sovereignty, the British government did not go on to establish its own. Despite pleas of Cadman Etches and his associates for state support in founding commercial outposts, the government gave them no direct encouragement and took no steps to build a case for British territorial dominion. Laissez-faire; laissez-aller. Great Britain, however, was alert to any circumstances which might jeopardize the principle it had threatened war to establish: that the region was open to the commerce of nations without prejudice.

During Spain's last two years as a contender for Northwest lands, her navigators diligently cooperated with the British in exploring and mapping the islands and coasts of southern Alaska and British Columbia. Between 1790 and 1793 Fidalgo made a detailed examination of the coast; Eliza charted the islands and channel from Caamano Bight into the Gulf of Georgia; Quimper explored Canal de Lopez de Haro and the entrance to Rosario Strait and mapped the northern shore of the Strait of Juan de Fuca to the site of Victoria, and the southern shore from Sequim to Neah Bay. He failed however to note the entrance to Puget Sound.

In the spring of 1792 Lieutenant Jacinto Caamano in the *Aranzazu* and Galiano and Valdes in the *Sutil* and *Mexicana* joined in the task of surveying the mainland shores of British Columbia and the Queen Charlotte Islands. Vancouver and Bodega also contributed to this work when they arrived in the summer.

VANCOUVER AND BROUGHTON

Reports of the Spanish explorations were not published for almost 175 years. On the other hand, those of Captain George Vancouver were in print a short time after his return to England, adding to the prestige of the British as explorers of the North Pacific.[7] They also provided grounds for Britain—when it served her purpose—to claim certain areas by virtue of prior discovery and acts of possession.

Vancouver's expedition, as originally planned in 1789, was intended to supplement the work of Captain Cook by examining the coast from the Spanish to the Russian settlements. His instructions were detailed and limiting. He was to search for a river or entrance to an inland sea which might yet provide a Northwest Passage. While he was to determine the direction and extent of all considerable inlets and mouths of rivers, he was "not to pursue any inlet or river

[7] *A Voyage of Discovery to the North Pacific Ocean . . . under the Command of Captain George Vancouver*, 6 vols. (1801).

43

further than it shall appear to be navigable by vessels of such burthen as might safely navigate the Pacific Ocean." He was to give special attention to the Strait of Juan de Fuca. The obvious purpose of his voyage was exploration that would facilitate Great Britain's commerce in the Pacific; his careful descriptions of natives, their habits and habitats, and surveys of anchorages and ports reveal the nature of British interests in the region.

Vancouver belonged to the best tradition of British seamanship. He was a cautious and skillful navigator, devoted in all respects to the "noble science of discovery." His official narrative reveals a determination to be accurate in geographical description and astronomical observation, and the reader almost comes to share his worry over two chronometers which would not stay synchronized.

Vancouver had learned from experience with Cook how important was the health of his men. He experimented with a diet of antiscorbutics—sauerkraut, "portable soup," wheat, malt, spruce beer, dried yeast, seed mustard, oranges, and lemons. His crew suffered no ill effects from their long journey through the South Atlantic and Pacific oceans.

Vancouver's flagship, the sloop of war *Discovery*, accompanied by the *Chatham*, an armed tender commanded by Lieutenant William Broughton, arrived on the coast south of Cape Mendocino on April 17, 1792. (In the summer the supply ship *Daedalus* joined them.) Vancouver identified capes and headlands mapped by his predecessors, changed old names for new, and added features others had missed. At noon on the 27th of April he came to an opening which he identified as Meares' Deception Bay. "The sea had now changed from its natural, to river coloured water, the probable consequence of some streams falling into the bay. . . ." But, "not considering this opening worthy of more attention," he sailed on to take advantage of a good breeze. So Captain Vancouver dismissed the entrance to the Columbia River. He was to return to the location in a few months with a changed mind, but being honest, he refrained from changing the original journal entry.

Two days' sail up the Washington coast, the *Discovery* hailed a ship—a "great novelty," as Vancouver put it, since no vessel had been sighted for eight months. This was the *Columbia*, an American vessel commanded by Captain Robert Gray. Vancouver sent off several of his officers to talk with Gray. They learned, among other things, that the Americans had been "off the mouth of a river in the latitude of 46 degrees, 10' where the outlet, or reflux, was so strong as to prevent his entering." "This," Vancouver concluded, "was, probably, the

44

opening passed by us on the forenoon of the 27th." If such a river or inlet should be found, "it must be a very intricate one, and inaccessible to vessels of our burthen."

Vancouver's instructions made the Strait of Juan de Fuca his principal goal. In the evening of the day he met Gray, Vancouver's ship anchored within the entrance of the strait. The next day, from a height of land at New Dungeness, Vancouver looked with immense satisfaction upon a landscape "almost as enchantingly beautiful as the most elegantly finished pleasure grounds in Europe." The official narrative reveals the writer's excitement as wonder on wonder unfolded. "I could not . . . believe," he wrote, "that an uncultivated country had ever been discovered exhibiting so rich a picture." From the snowy ridges on the eastern horizon, Mount Baker rose conspicuously, "remarkable for its height and the snowy mountains that stretch from its base to the north and south." Vancouver identified Meares' Olympus as a "very elegant double fork," and he named Mounts Baker and Rainier. Following the shoreline in longboats, his men came on continuous surprises: innumerable bays, harbors, inlets, and islands, large and small. An apparent headland was an island, and an island turned out to be a peninsula narrowly joined to the mainland. A long inlet resembled a monumental man-made canal so much that Vancouver named it Hood's Canal after the lieutenant who explored it.

In two months, Vancouver's ships made eighteen anchorages, while his men surveyed the extensive inland sea to which he gave the name Puget's Sound in honor of its chief explorer, Lieutenant Peter Puget. To the principal bays, inlets, and waterways, he gave names which in many instances still identify them—Cape Dungeness, Admiralty Inlet, Port Orchard, Port Discovery, Possession Sound, Restoration Point, Whidbey and Vashon islands, Deception Pass, Bellingham Bay, and Gulf of Georgia.

Exploration of the eastern shore of Puget Sound and the Gulf of Georgia and a long trip in a yawl to Jervis Inlet beyond the present Vancouver, British Columbia, revealed no entrance to a continental passage. But it was, indeed, a land well worth claiming for Great Britain.

> . . . The serenity of the climate, the innumerable pleasing landscapes, and the abundant fertility that unassisted nature puts forth, require only to be enriched by the industry of man with villages, mansions, cottages, and other buildings, to render it the most lovely country that can be imagined; whilst the labour of the inhabitants would be amply rewarded, in the bounties which nature seems ready to bestow on cultivation.

On June 4, 1792, the birthday of George III, at the site of the present city of Everett, Vancouver took possession of the land and named it New Georgia. He then proceeded through the inland passage between Vancouver Island and the mainland, rounded the northern tip of the island, and came to Nootka and his meeting with Bodega.

While negotiations were under way there, his lieutenants, James Johnstone and William Broughton, explored the island and mainland shores. At the end of August, Vancouver sailed north to Bentinck's Arm, turned out into the Pacific, and headed his ships south to that place where, the previous spring, he had noted signs of a river mouth but had not thought it worth investigating.

By the time his vessels hove to on October 19 he was better informed for he had learned from Bodega that the American trader, Robert Gray, had entered the river and named it Columbia's River.

Bodega had given Vancouver Gray's sketch of the river entrance but the British captain remained convinced that the river was unnavigable for a vessel of any size. What he had seen of the coastline south of the Strait of Juan de Fuca was a reasonable argument against "any safe navigable opening, harbour, or place of security for shipping. . . ." Therefore, he did not risk the 340-ton *Discovery*. He sent in the 135-ton *Chatham*, under Lieutenant Broughton, while he continued on to California.

The *Chatham* had a rough entry and Broughton's excess of caution was nearly disastrous; he anchored for the night in four fathoms of water and almost on the bar. "I never felt more alarmed & frightened in my life," a clerk confided to his journal. "The Channel was narrow, the water very Shoal, and the Tide running against the Wind . . . raised a Surf that broke entirely around us, and I am confident that in going in, we were not twice the Ship's length from Breakers, that had we struck on, we must inevitably have gone to pieces . . ."[8] The next day the *Chatham* cleared with only a shallow strike and entered the safe anchorage of a bay on the north bank. Here Broughton was surprised to find a fellow countryman, Captain James Baker in the small schooner *Jenny* of Bristol. Baker reported he had been in the river earlier in the year.

Broughton's orders were to explore the river and take possession of its tributary lands if it appeared that a claim to discovery and exploration could be supported. He spent three weeks on this mission. Having carefully examined the shores and principal streams of the wide tidal waters near the mouth, he proceeded upstream in the longboat. He placed on his map Baker's Bay, Young's River, Tongue

[8] "Columbia River Exploration, 1792," J. Neilson Barry, ed., *OHQ*, March 1932.

Point, Oak Point, Puget's Island, and Mounts St. Helens and Hood. Near the mouth of the Sandy River on the Oregon shore, opposite a sandy point on the north shore to which he gave the name Point Vancouver, he performed the ceremony of taking possession. Later, on behalf of their own claims and against the United States' claim of prior discovery, the British briefly argued the fine point that while Gray had discovered the saline bay, Broughton had explored the river and placed upon it the symbol of British sovereignty.

Vancouver's was the last significant northwest exploration by a European power. His extensive surveys and those of the Spanish had mapped the coastline and settled the century-old question of a Northwest Passage. To Cook's conclusions, Vancouver added "the complete certainty, that, within the limits of his researches . . . no internal sea, or other navigable communication whatever exists. . . ."

At the close of the eighteenth century, so far as national interests were concerned, the British appeared to have eliminated all other contenders for the region lying between the Russians in Alaska and the Spanish in California. The formal rite of taking possession had been performed at strategic locations; a hollow ritual if what the British had proved in the Nootka incident prevailed—that titles to unoccupied lands were hard to defend.

The search by sea for a Northwest Passage was concluded. But European interest in the Northwest had been stimulated by the discovery of new markets "for the productive labors of the civilized world" in trade with Indians. In ten years, from 1784–1795, British traders had harvested the greater part of the coast's produce. Vancouver's ships had scarcely left the northern waters when that trade fell into American hands.

CHAPTER
FOUR

Maritime Fur Trade:
The Americans in
the Northwest

BETWEEN 1785 and 1794 about thirty-five British vessels traded on the Northwest Coast; in the next decade there were nine, and between 1805 and 1814, three. This decline can be explained in part by the East India Company's iron grip on British trade in the Orient, but chiefly by the prolonged European wars which grew out of the French Revolution and affected British manpower and investment capital.

As British trade declined, Americans entered the field. Two vessels pioneered the New England-Northwest-Orient trade in 1788. At least fifteen ships followed in the next seven years, and there were seventy between 1794 and 1805.

Americans were free traders; their economy had no privileged corporations. A proposal to create one comparable to the East India Company for trading with the Indians was rejected in 1786 when the Continental Congress expressed the popular opinion that "commercial intercourse between the United States and the Indians would be more prosperous if left unfettered in the hands of private adventurers, than if regulated by any system of national complexion."

At that very time, the newly independent Americans found their postwar prosperity blighted. Business houses were failing, trade stagnated, and merchants complained of the "languor" of direct trade with Europe. But the French Revolution and then the Napoleonic Wars gave the United States an opportunity to enter a worldwide market, despite efforts of the warring powers to curtail neutral enterprise. In 1790 President Washington wrote to Lafayette of a developing trade with India and of ships profitably trading at Canton. It was furs from the Pacific Northwest that gave American merchants a commodity to trade in the Orient and helped to set the new nation's economy on its feet.

JOHN LEDYARD'S ''GREAT ADVENTURE''

The initial project to bring American ships into western waters never got out of the planning stage, yet it gave direction to the search for markets. Its originator was John Ledyard, a precocious New Englander born in 1751. His restless search for adventure—and for wealthy family connections to support him—had taken him to London, "hungering for fame." He had sailed in 1776 as a corporal of marines on Cook's momentous third voyage. Six years later, deserting the British navy, he returned to Connecticut and the following year published what purported to be his own journal of that voyage. He wrote enthusiastically of the richness and variety of sea otter pelts Cook's men had bought which "did not cost the purchaser six pence sterling," but sold in China for $100 or more.

Failing to interest American merchants in a trading voyage to exploit these resources, Ledyard went to Europe and in the capitals of Spain, France, and England, unsuccessfully sought financial backing for his scheme. In Paris he told his story to Thomas Jefferson, United States minister to France, who was immediately interested, having already considered exploring the West for reasons of state. With John Paul Jones, naval hero of the American Revolution, Ledyard worked out a plan in which they hoped French merchants would invest. It was practical, foreshadowing the pattern later used for large-scale trading enterprises. It called for

. . . two vessels . . . to proceed in company to the Northwest Coast, and commence a factory there under the American flag. The first six months were to be spent in collecting furs, and looking out for a suitable spot to establish a post, either on the main land, or on an island. A small stockade was then to be built, in which Ledyard was to be left with a surgeon, an assistant, and twenty soldiers; one of the vessels was to be despatched, with its cargo of furs, under the command of Paul Jones, to China, while the other was to remain in order to facilitate the collecting of another cargo during his absence. Jones was to return with both the vessels to China, sell their cargoes of furs, load them with silks and teas, and continue his voyage around the Cape of Good Hope to Europe, or the United States. He was then to replenish his vessels with suitable articles for traffic with the Indians, and proceed as expeditiously as possible . . . to the point of his departure in the Northern Pacific.[1]

They were soon discouraged. They learned that Portlock and Dixon had sailed from England for the Northwest. They "have actually sailed on an expedition which was thought of by Mr. Ledyard," complained Jones, "which I should suppose must interfere with, and very much lessen the profits of any similar undertaking by others." Also, the French government frowned upon the enterprise. Jones was informed that Spain would resent any enterprise encroaching upon its interests in the Pacific. Since France had already aroused Spanish suspicions by sending out Lapérouse, the French government apparently wished to avoid further complications by appearing to encourage Ledyard and Jones. Jones thereupon withdrew from the scheme.

Ledyard also gave up the idea of a trading voyage. He would win fame as an explorer of heroic dimension; he would go to the Northwest Coast and make his way alone to the sources of the Missouri and thence to "the shores of Kentucke." He found a patron in Sir Joseph Banks, president of the Royal Society of London and, by virtue of office as well as his own wide interests, a patron of world travelers and explorers. Through the assistance of R. Cadman Etches, Banks got Ledyard passage on a ship preparing to leave England for Nootka in the spring of 1786. But after Ledyard had outfitted himself at Banks' expense with a pistol, knife, hatchet, and some new clothes, he was vastly disappointed to learn that the ship was not permitted to sail. As an alternative, Ledyard decided to go via Russia and Siberia.

Ledyard's subsequent story is only remotely related to the history of the Pacific Northwest, but it serves to illustrate the complex interactions which make history. With Sir Joseph's letters of introduction to the right people, Ledyard went to Hamburg, Germany, then to

---

[1] Jared Sparks, *Life of John Ledyard* (1828), 155.

Sweden, with the idea of crossing to Russia on the frozen waters of the Gulf of Bothnia. In the middle of the Gulf, he found open water, so returned to Stockholm. In a second start he traveled into frigid lands in the Arctic Circle, rounded the head of the Gulf, and descended its eastern shore to St. Petersburg. There at the end of March (1787), with the help of Banks' friends, Ledyard was able to join a party carrying supplies to the Billings expedition in Siberia.

It will be recalled that in 1778–1779 Ledyard and Billings had been shipmates on Cook's flagship, the *Resolution*; Ledyard, a corporal of marines; Billings, a seaman. On November 13, 1787, Captain Billings was astonished to meet "Colonel" Ledyard 6000 miles east of St. Petersburg, at Yakutsk in Siberia, and was informed that Ledyard wished to cross with the expedition to the American continent "for the purpose of exploring it on foot."

It is interesting that as Ledyard was making his way to Yakutsk, Ferdinand de Lesseps, the sole survivor of Lapérouse's expedition, was en route from Kamchatka toward Yakutsk, with the dispatches, journals, and maps of the Frenchman's Northwest explorations. Their paths did not cross.

With Billings, Ledyard traveled to Irkutsk where the expedition waited for the ice to break up. But on a February evening in 1788 two hussars appeared at Ledyard's dwelling with orders to take him into custody and return him to Moscow for an inquiry. Ledyard evaded the inquiry and in the early summer was back in London at the door of his benefactor, Sir Joseph. Next he applied to the Society for Promoting the Discovery of the Interior Parts of Africa for a commission to explore that dark continent. Asked when he could start, Ledyard replied, "Tommorrow morning." In August Ledyard wrote Jefferson from Cairo that if he survived Africa, he would yet go "to America and penetrate from Kentuske [*sic*] to the Western side of the continent." The following January (1789) "mad, dreaming, romantic" John Ledyard was dead.

Others were to make the continental crossing of North America; others were to reap fortunes from Northwest Coast sea otter. In the year Ledyard died, Dixon and Portlock published accounts of their two-year voyage to that coast; Charles Barkley discovered the Strait of Juan de Fuca; Billings reached the Asian coast of the Pacific; and the Canadian Alexander Mackenzie was at Lake Athabaska planning the first of two expeditions which would earn him fame as the first to cross the North American continent. And as Ledyard lay dying of fever in Cairo, the first American vessels to the Northwest Coast of America were wintering near Nootka.

OPENING THE CHINA MARKET

Ledyard had pointed out the possibilities of the fur trade but his plans were premature. His countrymen had not yet explored the other angle of the trade—China. Robert Morris, who had rejected Ledyard's project in favor of a China voyage to see if Americans could compete with British dealers in Chinese goods, was one of several merchants who outfitted the *Empress of China* which sailed from New York in February, 1784. She carried a cargo of ginseng, wine and brandy, tar and turpentine, and $20,000 in specie, representing a total investment of $120,000. The liquors, tar, turpentine, and specie were traded in India for items in demand in China, such as lead, raw cotton, cotton cloth, and pepper.[2]

At Canton the Americans and their goods were well received, and the proceeds were invested in Chinese goods for the American market: tea, nankeens, chinaware, woven silk, and cassia, an inferior grade of cinnamon. The voyage returned a profit of 30 percent on the investment, only about one-tenth of what was reported on some later ventures, but sufficient to start a rage for East India voyages and speculations in East India goods.

The Americans made their profits by buying Chinese goods, especially nankeens, and selling them in the ports of Europe, in the West Indies, and in the markets of luxury-hungry Americans. The problem, however, was to find commodities with which to purchase Chinese goods. The only American product in demand at Canton was ginseng, which, badly prepared for shipment, brought a low price. Hence the larger part of a China investment had to be bought with scarce specie. In 1788, for example, four Canton-bound ships carried ginseng, India cotton, and "62 chests of treasure" probably amounting to $248,000. The Americans did not have enough specie to keep this up.

Captains Kendrick and Gray

Lack of specie and other high-value merchantable stock prompted six merchants to try Ledyard's idea of buying Chinese goods with furs from the Northwest Coast. They subscribed $50,000 to outfit two vessels.[3]

[2] Samuel E. Morison, *The Maritime History of Massachusetts, 1783–1860* (1921); H. B. Morse, *Chronicles of the East Indian Company Trading to China, 1635–1834,* 5 vols. (1926–1929).

[3] They were Joseph Barrell, Samuel Brown, and Charles Bulfinch, Boston, Crowell Hatch, Cambridge, John Derby, Salem, and John Pintard, New York.

Command of the 212-ton *Columbia Rediviva* was given to Captain John Kendrick, who had spent most of his forty-seven years at sea. Kendrick was impressive in size and courage. His ideas were bold and unconventional; he looked upon the Northwest as a theater for great deeds. "Empires and fortunes broke on his sight," wrote his clerk, John Howell. "The paltry two-penny objects of his expedition were swallowed up in the magnitude of his Gulliverian Views. North East America was on the Lilliputian, but he designed N. W. America to be on the Brobdignagian scale." Unfortunately Kendrick lacked the persistence and stability to execute his plans. It would appear that he was intemperate in habit and disposition, a poor trader, and not to be trusted with other people's property.

The consort of the *Columbia* was a 90-ton sloop, the *Lady Washington*. Like Kendrick, her 32-year-old captain, Robert Gray, had served as a privateer during the American Revolution. Gray had neither the colorful personality nor the special weaknesses of his superior. He was a hard man, strictly attentive to the "two-penny objects" of his business—to get sea otter skins and invest them in China goods.

The two vessels left Boston on September 30, 1787, heavily armed, carrying special papers issued by the Continental Congress, and a cargo of goods ill fitted for the Northwest trade.

In the first week of August, 1788, Gray approached Oregon's southern coast. On the fourteenth he dropped anchor in a bay, probably Tillamook. The Indians brought presents of berries and boiled crabs, and traded some otter skins while the crew took on wood and water. Two days later the apparently friendly situation was reversed in an instant. An Indian killed Marcus, Gray's Negro servant; the crew escaped to the ship and, with the changing tide, the *Lady Washington* sailed out of Murderer's Harbor. Since it was too late in the season for extended trade, the two ships wintered in Clayoquot Sound on Vancouver Island.

The next summer Gray and Kendrick were at Nootka when Martinez seized Meares' ships. Kendrick assured Martinez that he and Gray were at Nootka only to make repairs to their vessels, a standard excuse of mariners attempting to enter Spain's colonial ports. Martinez was not taken in by this subterfuge; he knew that the visitors' principal object was furs. He reported that he might have taken the Americans prisoners if his orders and his situation had permitted. Since they did not, he treated them as friends and, provisioning them from Colnett's stock, permitted them to trade on the coast on condition that they make no settlement.

Apparently Kendrick tried to keep up the appearance of being a neutral bystander. On the Fourth of July, the *Columbia* fired several salvos of thirteen guns to celebrate thirteen years of American independence, and at noon Kendrick entertained the Spanish priests, Martinez and his officers, and the English prisoners at a spendid banquet. "For his pretended intercession for my Vessel's release," Colnett reported that he gave Kendrick a gold watch, a gesture he regretted when he found that Kendrick had received favors from Martinez.

While the Americans were still at Nootka, troubles arose between them, probably because Kendrick had an idea of developing an independent trade between the Northwest Coast, the Hawaiian Islands, and China. Gray assumed command of the *Columbia* and Kendrick took the *Lady Washington* as his own ship. He sailed to China in the fall of 1789, used the proceeds from his cargo to rerig his ship, and subsequently made voyages only in Pacific waters. Two years later Kendrick and Gray met once more, but as rival traders.

At Macao, Gray sold his furs for something more than $21,000; at Canton, he took on a cargo of tea. In February, he sailed for Boston where he arrived in August, 1790, having made a complete encirclement of the globe in the course of his three-year voyage. Boston received the *Columbia* with a salute of thirteen guns. A crowd of people swarmed to the wharf to welcome her and to gawk at Gray's Hawaiian boy who had replaced the Negro, Marcus. But while patriots and the curious were pleased, the *Columbia's* owners were disappointed to find their investment barely refunded. According to the report that was circulated, the losses were charged to Kendrick whose reputation was "suspended between the qualifications of egregious knavery and incredible stupidity."

Gray, on the other hand, was taken into the partnership. Outfitted with a suitable cargo of blue cloth, copper, iron, and a knockdown keel and frame for a small sloop, he left Boston on September 28, 1790. A quick voyage brought him to the Pacific coast in June of the following year.

Gray wintered at Adventure Cove in Clayoquot Sound, an ideal spot both for protecting the ship and for assembling the sloop. A clearing was made on the shore and within a fortified log shelter were erected a blacksmith shop and a boat builder's shed. Two saw-pits were constantly in use to cut plank sheathing from logs towed to the spot. Adventure Cove had the appearance of a "young" shipyard, reported John Boit.

In March, 1792, the sloop, christened the *Aventure*, was hauled down the ways and supplied for a four months' cruise among the Queen Charlotte Islands under Robert Haswell, Gray's first mate. The *Columbia* was rigged, stowed, and made ready for sea again. But before it sailed on April 2, Captain Gray made his contribution to steadily deteriorating relations with the natives.

While the Indians in the Queen Charlotte Islands had already begun to take their toll of white men—Gray lost three in a fight with them—those about Nootka and Clayoquot had remained friendly until Gray's long stay wore out their hospitality. During the winter there were signs of increasing hostility; at the end of February, a critical threat of attack.

Gray chastised the Indians severely for their unfriendliness, much to the regret of young John Boit, who was ordered to carry out the punishment.

> . . . it was a Command I was no ways tenacious of, and am greived to think Capt. Gray shou'd let his passions go so far. This Village was about half a mile in Diameter, and Contained upwards of 200 Houses, generally well built for Indians, ev'ry door that you enter'd was in resemblance to an human and Beasts head, the passage being through the mouth, besides which there was much more rude carved work about the dwelling some of which was by no means innelegant. This fine Village, the Work of Ages, was in a short time totally destroy'd.

In April, Gray sailed almost to the California line, then hauled to the north to examine the shoreline for river mouths and bays which he might enter for trade. But squally weather and strong southerly currents kept the ship beating about for safe anchorages that were few and far between. In the vicinity of 46 degrees, 10 minutes north latitude Gray noticed evidence of a large river. The outflowing current was too strong to enter.

On April 27, a calm day, he anchored on the Washington coast in a shallow bay, abreast a village Boit called Kenekomitt, probably Neah Bay, where he traded a fine lot of skins. With a storm blowing up, the *Columbia* weighed offshore for the night. From this position next morning, Captain Vancouver's ships, the *Discovery* and *Chatham* were sighted.

It was then that Vancouver sent Lieutenant Peter Puget and Dr. Archibald Menzies to confer with Gray, particularly about the Strait of Juan de Fuca which, it will be recalled, was one of the prime objects of his exploration. As mentioned, Vancouver was not impressed with Gray's report of a large river to the south. After amenities were exchanged, he sailed on to his exploration of Puget Sound, and negotiations with Bodega at Nootka. Gray turned south once more on the chance that good weather would permit him to examine the coast more carefully.

On May 7, he saw an inlet "which had a very good appearance of a harbor." With the small boat signaling depths, the *Columbia* stood for the bar. A quick run between the breakers took her into a comfortable harbor which Gray called Bulfinch, but which the *Columbia's* officers named Gray's Harbor.

A large number of Indians put out in their canoes. Boit noted that their language was different from that of others they had met, and that "Without doubt we are the first Civilized people that ever visited this port. . . ." A brisk trade followed, but in the late evening the natives began to act hostile. In the moonlight, Gray saw their war canoes approaching. After several warning shots, he ordered a broadside on the nearest canoe, containing about twenty men, and "dash'd her all to pieces and no doubt kill'd every soul in her." But artillery fire seemed to have no damaging effect upon trade. The next day a number of Chehalis came to trade salmon, beaver skins, and otter for cloth, iron, and copper.

Toward sunset, May 10, 1792, the *Columbia* cleared Grays Harbor, her course set for the bay where Gray had seen signs of a river several weeks before. The next morning according to his official log:

> At four, A.M., saw the entrance of our desired port bearing east-southeast, distance six leagues; in steering sails, and hauled our wind in shore. At eight A.M., being a little to windward of the entrance of the Harbor, bore away, and run in east-north-east between the breakers, having from five to seven fathoms of water.

It was a fresh clear morning, the wind from the north. If Gray had not been so intent upon the progress of the pinnace that guided his ship over the bar, he might have noted that the river lay before him like a widening stream of silver in the morning sun; that the hills were flushed with the sunrise; that wisps of fog were caught in the trees that crowded close to the water's edge. If Gray had had the compulsions of a discoverer, he would have felt the thrill of his life as he ran into the broad estuary of the river about whose existence men had speculated so long. But he was a trader and whatever exploration he made was to find unspoiled Indians eager to exchange furs for beads and bright bits of cloth and metal.

The natives "appear'd to view the Ship with the greatest astonishment," reported John Boit, yet Gray's hope of a brisk trade in this previously unvisited spot was only partly fulfilled. The Indians traded cheaply enough: two salmon for a nail, four otter skins for a sheet of copper, a beaver skin for two spikes, and less valuable furs for one. But during his stay in the river, Gray traded only 150 sea otter, 300 beaver skins, and numerous others of less value. There was no reason to believe that this was a profitable stop for otter.

A short run upriver, jeopardized by sand bars, satisfied whatever curiosity Gray had about the river's course. There is no evidence that he thought it important. John Boit recorded that he ". . . landed abrest the Ship with Capt. Gray to view the Country." Modern scholarship has shown that three words "and take possession" were inserted at a later date and by a different hand. The fragment remaining of the official log of the *Columbia* says nothing about taking possession.

On May 20 Gray put out to sea. He returned to Nootka where he gave a sketch of the river's entrance to Bodega who later passed it along to Vancouver. From Nootka, Gray went to Canton where he sold his furs and bought a modestly profitable cargo of China goods. He dropped anchor in Boston July 29, 1793.

Gray's discovery later gave the United States a tenuous claim to these parts of the Northwest. But his chief contribution to history was his pioneering of the New England-Northwest-Canton trade which the sea otter made possible.

The Sea Otter

The fur of the sea otter was especially beautiful and highly prized by those who could afford it. A thick, fine underfur tipped to brown-black and sprinkled with a few long silver guard hairs gave a shimmering effect when moved by so little as a breath of air. The adult male pelt was about five feet long and twenty-five to thirty inches wide, that of the female somewhat smaller. A number of these carefully pieced together made royal robes for wealthy mandarins; tails and oddments were used for caps and for borders on elaborate gowns. Indians too valued the sea otter skin above all others; only chiefs could afford to wear robes made of them and two skins would purchase a slave.

These gregarious aquatic mammals (*Lutra enhydris marina*) were found only on Pacific shores where reefs or rocks gave them protection from storms and heavy surf, and where in floating beds of kelp they bore and raised their pups.[4] Some traders of uncommon sensibilities spoke of the animals as if they had personalities. They were friendly and fearless until they discovered that men were their enemies. Both

[4] Karl Kenyon, *The Seals, Sea-Lion, and Sea Otter of the Pacific Coast*, U.S. Department of the Interior (1955); Alan May, "The North Sea Otter," *Natural History*, June 1943; Adele Ogden, *California Sea Otter Trade, 1784–1848* (1941); Victor B. Scheffer, "The Sea Otter on the Washington Coast," *PNQ*, October 1940.

male and female guarded their pups from danger, and when they felt secure, gamboled and played with them in almost human fashion.

California, British Columbia, northern Washington, and Alaskan shores provided favorable habitats. The Oregon coast was, on the whole, unfavorable. Gray traded a few skins at Cape Orford and Tillamook Bay and only 150 in the Columbia River. Foster Dulles, in *The Old China Trade* (1930), estimated that between 1790 and 1812 Canton's imports from the "Northwest Coast of America" averaged about 12,000 skins a year. William Sturgis, who participated in the trade, says that in 1802 15,000 skins were carried to Canton, and he implies that this was a peak year both in number of ships and of furs. Probably less than half of these cargoes were marketed at Macao. The total number of skins taken from the Pacific Coast may have been as high as 200,000.

The sea otter pelt brought higher prices than any other fur in the China market. The top price of $100 for a complete skin paid to Cook's men in 1779, was bettered by Captain Hanna six years later, when he was said to have received $140 a pelt. In 1790 the price ranged from $25 to $45. Sometimes the market was glutted and the Hong merchants prohibited imports; in 1800 and 1804 there was a shortage and the price rose to $50. Using a rough estimate of 200,000 pelts and an average price of $30, the total value may have been about $6,000,000. Invested in Chinese goods that were sold in Europe, the West Indies, and the United States, the proceeds from the maritime fur trade were a stimulus to the American economy, and the foundation of several New England family fortunes.

The Schedule of Voyages

The great period of the Pacific Northwest maritime trade was from 1787 to the outbreak of the war between Great Britain and the United States in 1812, when it practically ceased. During these years the trade had so largely fallen into the hands of Boston traders that the Indians called all Americans "Boston men" to distinguish them from the British, "King George's men."

The small vessels engaged in the trade usually set out in the early fall, stopped at the Falkland Islands and at San Juan Fernandez, or some South American Pacific port, and with good luck reached the Hawaiian Islands the following spring. Refitted and replenished, they caught the prevailing winds to the Oregon coast.

After 1795 traders seldom visited Nootka. Their first stop was at Newettee on the northwestern promontory of Vancouver Island, or Kygarney (Kargahnee) on one of the Queen Charlotte Islands. According to John D'Wolf, in 1804–1805 this was "the best place of resort for ships on their first arrival, to obtain information for establishing a rate of trade."[5]

Most traders returned to the more congenial climate of the Hawaiian Islands for the winter. A few, particularly in the early days of the trade, wintered wherever they found a protected port and friendly Indians. Nootka had once been so favored and we have seen how Gray and Kendrick wintered in Clayoquot Sound. Apparently Puget Sound was seldom visited because the Indians had the reputation of being "bandity."

A second summer was spent cruising the northern islands or the California shores. In the autumn, the captain headed once more for the Hawaiian Islands en route to China where the furs were sold and the returns invested in Chinese goods. The voyage home was by way of the Cape of Good Hope, sometimes with leisurely port-to-port detours through the Mediterranean before continuing to the West Indies, then home to Boston or Salem.

THE COLUMBIA AS A PORT OF CALL

Although there were relatively few otter in the Columbia River it became a port of call and a few traders wintered in the river. Captain James Baker of the little 78-ton *Jenny* hove his ship into Baker's (Ilwaco) Bay shortly after Gray left the river in May, 1792. He was there again when Lieutenant Broughton arrived in October. The *Jenny's* sister ship, the *Ruby*, arrived in the spring of 1795 and Captain Charles Bishop, preparing to winter, planted a small sandy island with peas, beans, potatoes, radishes, mustard, cress, and celery seeds. When he returned in October, he found the potatoes plentiful and good but the "reddishes" had gone to seed, and with the exception of several bean plants, the rest of the garden stuff had disappeared.

In 1805, Lewis and Clark obtained from the Indians a list of thirteen traders who visited the Columbia; but the explorers' interpretation of the native rendering of these names makes most of them difficult, if not impossible, to identify. In 1813 Alexander Henry saw the names of traders carved on the trees at Cape Disappointment, giving him reason to suppose this harbor had been "much frequented" by Americans. The Indians' vocabularies reflected considerable contact with white men. Lewis and Clark reported that they used "many black-

[5] John D'Wolf, *Voyage to the North Pacific* . . . (1861), 18.

guard phrases" and common profanities with ease and had a vocabulary of such words as musket, powder, shot, knife, and file.

A commercial people themselves, the Chinooks of the lower river quickly adapted themselves to the white man's commerce. So long as he wanted what they had in abundance and did not value, and so long as there was no rival to bid up prices, trading was a simple matter. In the early days, a nail, a piece of iron or copper, castoff jackets, mirrors, or strings of thimbles bought prime otter skins. But those times passed quickly. Captain Bishop found the Indians of the Columbia considerably wiser than they had been three years before when Gray and Baker first opened trade. His journal tells that:

> . . . we expected of course from the Information we hitherto had of these People that with the choice goods that compose our cargo, we should have been able to procure them [furs] in ways of Barter readily and with ease, but our disappointment might be better conceived than expressed when after bartering and shewing them a great variety of articles for the whole day we did not purchase a single Fur. Tea Kettles, sheet Copper, a variety of fine cloths and in short the most valuable articles of our Cargo were shewn without producing the desired Effect, and in the Evening the whole of them took to their cannoes, and paddled to the shore, leaving us not more disappointed than surprized. . . .[6]

The next day the natives "began to set their own Price on the Skins which as may be seen from their behaviour yesterday was not moderate." On the third day, Bishop "broke trade," but not at prices he wanted.

In one interesting respect the Columbia River trade apparently differed from that of other coastal localities. Bishop found a local product of Chinookan handicraft, the *clamon*, valuable in trading for furs with other natives of the northern coast:

> . . . the best trade is the Leather War Dresses, articles to be disposed of, on other parts of the Coast, to great advantage, we procured such a Quantity, that at the least estimation is expected will procure us near 700 Prime Sea otter Skins. These dresses are made from the Hide of the Moose Deer which are very large and thick, this is dressed into a kind of White leather, and doubled, & is when properly made up, a complete defence against a Spear or an Arrow, and sufficient almost to resist a Pistol Ball.

When guns were put into the hands of the Indians, leather war dresses were useless and no longer manufactured.

[6] "Journal of the Ruby," T. C. Elliott, ed., *OHQ*, September 1927, 262.

By 1805, demands of both whites and natives had expanded. The traders brought guns, outmoded British and American muskets, powder, balls, and shot, brass kettles and pots, blankets, scarlet and blue cloth, sheets of copper, wire knives, buttons, beads, tobacco, sailor clothing, and rum. They took in exchange skins of all animals, dressed or undressed elk hides, packed dried salmon, and a baked breadstuff made from pounded wapato root.

At Kargahnee, ermine skins were highly prized by the natives. In 1804 shrewd William Sturgis imported 5000 ermine from Leipzig, worth less than 30 cents in the Boston market, and traded them to the Indians at the rate of five ermine skins for one sea otter. In one afternoon he bartered 560 prime otter, worth $50 a skin in the China trade.

Wherever competition was strong, as it usually was on the British Columbia coast, firearms were bartered, and as a result, the Indians became more hostile. Furthermore, they were encouraged to overkill furbearing animals so that the sea otter was practically extinct in the north by 1800.

California's shores had a rich supply but the Spanish prohibited foreigners from trading with their Indians. In 1805 Captain John D' Wolf, master of the *Juno*, while a guest of Governor Baranov at the Russian settlement on Norfolk Sound, invited his host to share in an expedition to California, using Kodiak Indians to hunt otter offshore in order to avoid Spanish restrictions. Baranov's superior, Baron Resanov, fearing to offend the Spanish because the Russians were dependent upon them for supplies, refused. In 1810 the Winship family of Boston, with enterprising leadership and large capital resources, enlarged on D'Wolf's plan. They contracted with the Russians to use Aleut hunters on the California coast, to supply the Russians with goods, and to market their furs in China.

To carry on such an enterprise, the Winships needed a depot in neutral waters, located midway between the Russian posts and the California hunting grounds. The Columbia River was such a site. It could be claimed as an American river since Lewis and Clark had wintered at its mouth in 1805–1806; it was navigable; and its shores could provide enough foodstuff to support the settlement and the Russians as well.

In late May, 1810, the *Albatross*, with supplies and livestock, arrived in the river, and Captain Nathan Winship chose a site some forty miles upriver on the south shore opposite present Oak Point, Washington. Some of the crew had started to hew logs for a fort, while others cleared a garden spot, when flood waters forced them to move their location a quarter-mile downstream. Work had hardly resumed when a massing of Indians signified trouble; the natives' repeated warnings that the white men should leave were finally heeded and the project was abandoned.

The Winships' attempt at settlement was significant not simply because it was the first effort to build an American post in the Pacific Northwest, but because enterprising merchants saw the Columbia River as a vital link in an enlarged commerce involving American seaports, Russian Alaska, Spanish California, the Hawaiian Islands, and the Orient. The Winships were pioneers by only a matter of months. Their idea, born of the maritime trade, was to become effective with the development of the land fur trade. When that happened, the Columbia River became the western depot of a trade that spanned the continent.

CHAPTER
FIVE

Continental Fur Trade and Exploration

DESIRE FOR FURS as well as proselytizing zeal moved the French to colonize the New World. In their search for pelts and souls, traders and black-robed fathers had penetrated the heart of the continent by the end of the seventeenth century. The Dutch at New Amsterdam were agents of Netherlands merchants engaged in the Indian trade. The Pilgrims' first export was a cargo of furs, and Massachusetts Bay Colony had hardly been settled when its traders began to expand New England along the shores of Maine. Colonists of Virginia, Pennsylvania, and the Carolinas had trade routes and outposts across the Appalachians before their settlements left tidewater. The Indian trade was one of the British colonies' principal enterprises, and efforts of the mother country to regulate it was a cause of colonial discontent. Dissensions among the colonies sometimes arose from competition for Indian markets.

The Indian trade was the primary wedge in a continental thrust. In the American colonies, settlers followed close upon the heels of traders, forcing them inexorably toward the unexplored, unmapped West. In Canada, the expansion of settlements was retarded by the policies first of French and then British trading companies. By the end of the seventeenth century, French *coureurs de bois* (unlicensed traders escaping the heavy hand of exclusive privilege) had pushed up the St. Lawrence into the Great Lakes country, the Old Northwest, and the Canadian Plains. By the close of the next century, Canadian "pedlars" competed with the British Hudson's Bay Company for the trade of the interior; by the beginning of the nineteenth century, British and American entrepreneurs contemplated a transcontinental trade. Such trade depended on practicable routes of communication; hence traders had to be explorers as well as merchants. Their travels led them to seek "eligible" rivers on the basis of a geography composed of rumored "facts" and whimsically devised fiction.

Joliet and Marquette discovered the Mississippi in 1673. A decade later LaSalle explored a fragment of its principal tributary, the Missouri. According to the Baron La Hontan's fictitious travels this "grand riviére des Esmourites" was navigable for 1000 miles; its source lay in a high but narrow "height of land" from which the waters leaped in a series of violent cataracts to the level plains. A short portage over the mountains led the adventurer to a westward-flowing river and thence to the great salt sea. So convincing was the legend that the Shining, White, Stony or Rocky mountains, the River of the West—even a great salt lake—were fixed ideas of geography before white men had seen any of them.

While the Hudson's Bay Company (HBC) sought openings into the continent from the shores of Hudson Bay, French traders from the St. Lawrence Valley entered the Canadian Plains by the Great Lakes and their peripheral network of lesser lakes and rivers. Pierre Gaultier, Sieur de La Verendrye, was licensed to trade at Lake Nipigon, where between 1726 and 1731 he learned from his Indian customers of great mountains to the west and a westward-flowing river. For more than twenty years he and his sons sought that river with almost fanatical persistence. They extended a line of posts to Lake Winnipeg and built a temporary trading house at the fork of the Saskatchewan. In 1738 their searches took them to the Upper Missouri. In 1742–1743, Verendrye's sons traveled up the river until they sighted mountains—probably the Black Hills—which they were "vexed not to be able to ascend" because of the hostility of the Indians.

The report of their journeys in the Missouri plains may have been the source of Major Robert Rogers' interest in the West. A Massachusetts colonial who had served in the British campaigns against the French, Rogers petitioned the British Crown in 1765 to support an expedition under his leadership "from the Great Lakes towards the head of the Mississippi and thence to the river called by the Indians Ouragon."

Nothing came of Rogers' project; but Jonathan Carver elaborated

Rogers' geography in his mythical travels, claiming that "the River Oregon, or the River of the West . . . falls into the Pacific Ocean at the Straits of Annian." Thus, before 1775, the La Verendryes, Rogers, and Carver had contributed to geographical speculation a Missouri-River-of-the-West route to the sea. Carver and Rogers also gave to history the word Oregon.

HUDSON'S BAY COMPANY TRADERS AND CANADIAN PEDLARS

At the conclusion of the Great War of Empire (1763) the St. Lawrence and Ohio valleys became part of Great Britain's extended New World empire under the administration of a colonial governor. But the vast Canadian region called Rupert's Land, drained by waters flowing into Hudson Bay, was open only to the HBC.

The Hudson's Bay Company was a chartered joint-stock company founded in 1670 under the title "The Governor and Company of Adventurers trading into Hudson's Bay."[1] In return for its monopoly of trade in a domain of royal dimensions, the Company was obligated to deliver to the king, on his visits to Canada, two elk and two beaver skins, and to search for the Northwest Passage. This it did only sporadically, when public pressure demanded. The Company's conservative but financially sound policies, set up by the Governor and Committee in London, were executed by factors and traders at the posts, manned by Orkney and Iroquois servants.

After the victory over the French, the Company's rivals were British subjects, Montreal merchants of Scottish blood who had emigrated to the New World after the war. These merchants formed partnerships with "pedlars" who traveled among the Indians to trade for furs. From time to time merchants and pedlars combined to reduce competition among themselves and to strengthen their position against the British-owned and managed HBC. In 1783–1784 one such fragile combination was organized under the name of the North West Company. It was reorganized in 1787 and again in 1804 under the same name.[2]

The North West Company was an association of Canadians; of Montreal merchants who purchased trading goods and marketed the furs, and of partners-in-the-field, or wintering partners, stationed at posts in

[1] E. E. Rich, *History of the Hudson's Bay Company*, 2 vols. (1958–1959).

[2] *Documents Relating to the North West Company*, W. Stewart Wallace, ed. (1934); Gordon C. Davidson, *The North West Company* (1918); W. Stewart Wallace, *Pedlars From Quebec* . . . (1954).

the interior or engaged in travels among the natives. At annual meetings at Michilimackinac or Fort William, which alternated with convivial reunions at Montreal, the partners settled accounts, divided profits, and set policies for the next year.

As old partners retired, energetic young men whose talents had been tested with responsibilities, were promoted to their places. This encouraged young clerks and traders and gave them a stake in the business. Especially it encouraged them to anticipate every move of their English competitors, and to extend the trade into the interior. In this they were supported by the services of skilled French Canadians as *voyageurs* or boatmen, who propelled canoes and *bateaux* and shouldered 90-pound packs of furs across portages. These were the laborers who moved the trade.

Scottish-born Alexander Mackenzie, one of the founders of the North West Company of 1787, was a pioneer both in exploration and in schemes for an enterprise of continental scope. He planned and carried out two amazing explorations. The first took him in 1789 to the Arctic by way of the river which bears his name.

His second expedition in 1793 brought him to the Pacific Ocean. He literally pushed his way up the Parsnip branch of Peace River to its headwaters in the Rockies. He portaged to a river which the Indians called Tacoutche Tesse, which we know today as the Fraser, but which he thought was the legendary River of the West. Forced to abandon its dangerous waters, Mackenzie crossed by Indian trail to the coast near Point Menzies. At Dean Channel he learned from the natives of the visit, only a month before, of Lieutenant Johnstone of Vancouver's surveying party. To mark the western terminus of his overland voyage Mackenzie used a mixture of grease and vermilion to paint on a rocky ledge the words: "Alexander Mackenzie, from Canada, by land, the twenty-second of July, one thousand seven hundred and ninety three."

His *Voyages*, published in 1801, is a classic narrative of adventure and exploration. He offered final and convincing proof that there was no Northwest Passage, no Strait of de Fonte, within the continent north of 50 degrees. The "immense ridge, or succession of stony mountains" through which he passed divided the waters of the Atlantic from those of the Pacific. "In those snow-clad mountains" he concluded, "rises the Mississippi if we admit the Missouri to be its source, which flows into the Gulph of Mexico; the River Nelson, which is lost in Hudson's Bay; Mackenzie's River, that discharges itself into the North Sea; and the Columbia emptying itself into the Pacific Ocean."

While his fundamental conclusion was correct, Mackenzie was in error in one important detail. When writing his book, he knew of Gray's discovery and Broughton's exploration of the lower Columbia. He assumed that the Tacoutche Tesse was the upper part of the same river. Therefore, he suggested that a continental trade could be developed using the Nelson, Saskatchewan, and Columbia rivers to connect with a terminal post at the mouth of the Columbia.

> . . . whatever course may be taken from the Atlantic, the Columbia is the line of communication from the Pacific Ocean, pointed out by nature, as it is the only navigable river in the whole extent of Vancouver's minute survey of that coast; its banks . . . [are] the most Northern situation fit for colonization, and suitable to the residence of a civilized people. By opening this intercourse between the Atlantic and Pacific Oceans, and forming regular establishments through the interior, and at both extremes, as well as along the coasts and islands, the entire command of the fur trade of North America might be obtained, from latitude 48 North to the pole. . . . To this may be added the fishing in both seas, and the markets of the four quarters of the globe.[3]

In 1802, Mackenzie proposed a company which would combine whaling with a land and sea fur trade and commerce with China. He urged the British government to provide protection for establishments at Nootka Sound, Sea Otter Harbor (at Dixon Entrance), and on the Columbia River. And he asked the government to force the East India and Hudson's Bay companies either to abandon their exclusive monopolies or to license the new company and cooperate with it in the Orient and in Canada.

His large view of the industry was not shared by either the government or his merchant associates in the North West Company. He withdrew from the company in 1799, and when he reentered in the organization of 1804 he had no immediate influence on policy. However, his *Voyages* had an influence far beyond expectations. It was read by Jefferson and carried by Lewis and Clark on their expedition to the Pacific Northwest.

LOUISIANA AND THE AMERICAN WEST

While the Canadians were advancing into the interior of the continent, the Spanish in Louisiana were trying to build up defenses

[3] Alexander Mackenzie, *Voyages from Montreal . . . Through the Continent of North America . . .* (1801), 401–402; *First Man West: Alexander Mackenzie's Journal of his Voyage to the Pacific Coast . . . in 1793*, Walter Sheppe, ed. (1962).

against their powerful neighbors. In acquiring French Louisiana (1763), Spain secured what she hoped was a broad protective belt for her provinces of New Spain, against British invaders. The presidios built in California after 1769 were expected to protect them from both Britain and Russia on the Pacific. But the Mississippi-Missouri boundary was unexplored and undefended. There Spain faced not only the British from Canada but, after the American Revolution, an energetic new nation with a continental orientation. In 1792, not only were the Americans poised on the Mississippi with eyes fixed on Spanish lands, but, it was reported, Canadian Nor'Westers, under François Larocque, were "established and fortified about fifteen days' march" from the Mandan villages on the upper Missouri.[4]

Spain's local officials therefore encouraged St. Louis merchants, with a monopoly grant, to form a syndicate for the purpose of exploring and garrisoning the upper river. (In the geography of the early fur trade, the Upper Missouri was that portion of the river above the mouth of the Platte, marked by the beginning of the open plains.) During the next five years the Company of Explorers of the Upper Missouri, or hardy independents associated with them, pushed beyond the Mandan villages of North Dakota to the waters of the Riviére Roches Jaunes, the Yellowstone.

But the interests of the syndicate were in trade; only incidentally in exploration or defense. Desperate colonial governors might plead for speedy help "to restrain the usurpations of the English," but Madrid was occupied with revolutionary Europe. Spain's empire in North America had lived out its term and was ready for the taking; with regard to Louisiana the question was only when, and by whom. Between 1790 and 1800 three potential takers emerged: the United States, Great Britain, and France.[5]

As early as the 1750s, Benjamin Franklin had pointed out the significance of the continental hinterland to whatever nation should possess it. But the principal architect of United States policy concerning the West was Thomas Jefferson. As private citizen and public officer his interest was both intellectual and political. He was curious about its geography, its inhabitants, its flora and fauna. As we have seen earlier, he encouraged John Ledyard's scheme because it might increase knowledge of the continent and promote American trade.

Jefferson was an expansionist but not an imperialist. He looked upon

---

[4] A. P. Nasatir, *Before Lewis and Clark*, 2 vols. (1952), I, 161; *Spain in the Mississippi Valley, 1765–1794*, Lawrence Kinnaird, ed., American Historical Association *Annual Report for 1945* (1949).

[5] R. W. Van Alstyne, *The Rising American Empire* (1960).

North America as a breeding ground for republican ideas and institutions, a home for the new nation's children, organized into independent states; and as a resource for their prosperity. His immediate concern however was to protect both the nation and the West from foreign powers hostile to republican ideology and institutions. He was sympathetic with the spirit that impelled Americans to trespass into the Floridas, to cross the Appalachians, and to infiltrate Spanish lands.

So long as the lands were in the possession of powers hostile to republican institutions, the West—the Mississippi Valley, the heart of the continent—was a threat to the nation and its future. The point of friction was the Mississippi River where the interests of American frontiersmen came into conflict with Spain over her vacillating policies concerning navigation of the river and transshipment privileges at its mouth. The long-range issue was the weakness of Spain and the strength of Great Britain.

Jefferson had been Secretary of State when the Nootka affair came to a head. At that time the first question to be dealt with was whether the United States should take part in a war in which a principal battlefield would be on the nation's boundaries if not across its territory. Washington and his advisors decided in favor of neutrality. But Jefferson took the opportunity to point out that, if Spain and Great Britain went to war, the odds were in favor of Great Britain. And if Britain should occupy Spanish territory, she would then reduce the Americans east of the Mississippi "by her language, laws, religion, manners, government, commerce, capital," and with her fleet on the Atlantic and her possessions in the interior she would encircle the United States completely. "Instead of two neighbors balancing each other, we shall have one, with more than the strength of both."

Jefferson's fears of Britain were not allayed in the 1790s, and his strong prejudices were shared by a large part of the West. American traders and settlers north of the Ohio were vigorously anti-British. The northern boundary at the headwaters of the Mississippi had not been defined at the conclusion of the Revolution; Canadian fur traders occupied the region and held the Indians completely in control. Hides and furs from American territory were drawn off to Montreal and, it was charged, American scalps decorated the lodge poles of Britain's Indian allies.

The year 1793 witnessed a new world crisis with repercussions in domestic politics. The course of revolution had led republican France to war with Great Britain. American sentiment divided sharply into pro-British and pro-French camps, with Jefferson leading the Francophiles. The inner core of his party was persuaded that the French

69

Republic would relieve the United States of both its bothersome monarchical neighbors, Britain and Spain, and would replace them as a strong and friendly republican ally. The plan was that

> . . . the Naval Forces of the [French] Republic should seize the Mouth of the Mississippi, declare that the Country belonged to them by right of Conquest and invite the Americans of the Western Country to take advantage of the freedom of Navigation. Then, if the Spaniards situated higher up the river molested the Vessels carrying the provisions conveyed by the Americans, the latter would have the right to repel Constraint and force by force. Thus, the Spanish Government would have no reason to complain of the United States having broken through inasmuch as the country would be reputed in the possession of the French Republic.[6]

While the French from the Mississippi delta attacked the British West Indies, the Americans would have a free hand in upper Louisiana and could rout the British from the Old Northwest if not from Canada as well.

It was this strategy that lay behind a project for exploring the West in 1793. That January, Jefferson, as vice-president of the American Philosophical Society at Philadelphia, suggested to the members that the society support an observer of western affairs who would explore the country along the Missouri and westward to the Pacific Ocean.

Two candidates were considered. One was 19-year-old Meriwether Lewis, an army lieutenant and close friend of Jefferson. The successful candidate was André Michaux, a man of mature years, famous as a world traveler and botanist, and an agent of Citizen Genêt, the French minister to the United States. The scientific objectives of the expedition were smothered in politics and plots; Michaux's "explorations" were limited and his politics unsuccessful.

With a shift of goals by the French revolutionaries from "liberty, equality, fraternity" to the guillotine and foreign conquest, American Francophiles lost their enthusiasm for France as a protector of the Republic. Further, with Europe involved in revolution and defense against a triumphant Napoleon, there was no immediate threat to United States security from Spain or Britain.

The Louisiana Crisis

Jefferson had hardly become president, in 1801, when he learned that by the secret Treaty of San Ildefonso in December, 1800, Spain had ceded Louisiana to France. He at once recognized this as a mat-

---

[6] André Michaux, "Journals of Travels in Kentucky, 1793–1796," in *Early Western Travels*, R. G. Thwaites, ed. (1904), III, 44–45.

ter of momentous importance to the United States. Circumstances were different than they had been in 1793, when French intervention in Louisiana would have given the Americans a republican neighbor. Napoleon, however, had destroyed the French Republic and his territorial policies were little different from those of the monarchs the revolution had expelled. He had, in fact, inherited his royal predecessor's colonial ambitions.

With Napoleon as its master, Louisiana could become not only a base for a French attack upon the British West Indies but for French conquest of North America as well. The tender issues of navigation of the Mississippi and of American rights of deposit at New Orleans could easily become a cause of war between the United States and her former ally, and Jefferson took the position that France and the United States could not remain friends when they met in so "irritable a position." Napoleonic France in North America would force the United States to become a maritime power and a belligerent in European affairs.

That Jefferson should contemplate an alliance with Britain and participation in a European war is evidence of the serious light in which he considered the cession of Louisiana. Reviewing the situation in 1803, he explained his own temper and that of his close advisors and Congress in these words:

> The exchange of a peaceable for a warring neighbor at New Orleans, was, undoubtedly, ground of just and great disquietude on our part; and the necessity of acquiring the country could not be unperceived by any. The question which divided the Legislature . . . was, whether we should take it at once, and enter singlehanded into war with the most powerful nation on the earth, or place things on the best footing practicable for the present, and avail ourselves of the first war in Europe, which it was clear was at no great distance, to obtain the country as the price of our neutrality, or as a reprisal for wrongs which we were sure enough to receive.[7]

Jefferson's cabinet agreed that if no arrangement could be made with Napoleon, the government should enter into conference with the British "to fix principles of alliance."

Yet a British alliance was not palatable to Jeffersonian Republicans, nor was Britain considered a disinterested party with respect to Louisiana. In September, 1801, when France and Britain were negotiating the short-lived Peace of Amiens, Secretary of State James Madi-

---

[7] Thomas Jefferson, *Works* (Federal edition), X, 20n. The reference to the "first war in Europe" is to the expected resumption of hostilities when the shaky Peace of Amiens collapsed.

son warned France that it was not in the interest of the United States "to favor any voluntary or compulsive transfer" of Louisiana from Spain to Great Britain as part of a price for the peace. In hope of removing the French threat peaceably, Jefferson asked the United States minister to Paris to find out whether Napoleon would sell the island of New Orleans and one, if not both, Floridas. In 1803, when the European peace was broken, the threat of British ambitions on the Mississippi loomed almost as large as Napoleon's. "The anxiety which Great Britain has shewn to extend her domain to the Mississippi, the uncertain extent of her claims, from North to South, beyond the Western limits of the United States, and the attention she has paid to the North West coast of America," Madison warned, "make it probable that she will connect with a war . . . a pretension to the acquisition of the country on the West side of the Mississippi. . . ."[8]

So Jefferson decided it was politic to establish an American defense against both France and Britain in the West. He set up a new Indian policy to win potential allies, garrisoned western outposts, and planned a military reconnaissance of the Upper Missouri where Canadian traders were established.

Lewis and Clark

In February, 1801, Jefferson had invited young Meriwether Lewis into his official family as his private secretary. Lewis had "knolege of the Western country, of the army & it's situation" which Jefferson thought might be useful to him. It will be recalled that Lewis had been considered as a leader for the American Philosophical Society's expedition in 1793. Therefore, when Jefferson decided late in 1802 that there was a pressing need for an exploratory expedition into the West, it was more than coincidence that Lewis, who shared Jefferson's concern about that area, should be so readily available.

In the light of Jefferson's designs for an Americanized continent and his distrust of British and French ambitions, this expedition can justifiably be considered a military reconnaissance. Knowledge of the interior's river systems was important; this was particularly so of the possible Missouri-River-of-the-West route. Long experience in frontier wars had taught Americans to appreciate Indians as allies—and as allies of the enemy. Their friendship depended upon accessibility to trading posts, regular supplies of goods, tactful flattery of influential chieftains, and the observance of elementary ideas of justice. The

[8] *Diplomatic Correspondence of the United States: Canadian Relations*, W. R. Manning, ed., 3 vols. (1940), I, 162; Mary P. Adams, "Jefferson's Reaction to the Treaty of San Ildefonso," *Journal of Southern History*, May 1955.

British had been successful in their Indian relations and their influence was spreading into the Upper Missouri. It was to win over the Indians, to get information about the rivers, and to prepare against a possible war that Jefferson originally projected the Lewis and Clark expedition.

Domestic politics and international diplomacy forced Jefferson to secrecy and devious explanations for his actions. He must be sure not to offend either France, with whom delicate negotiations were pending, or Spain, whose officials still controlled Louisiana, resented its cession to France, and were suspicious of everyone, particularly Americans.

Jefferson explained to the Spanish minister that the expedition "would nominally have the objective of investigating everything which might contribute to the progress of commerce; but that in reality it would have no other view than the advancement of geography." Privately, he noted that the "expiring state" of Spain's interest actually made Spanish reactions a "matter of indifference." On January 18, 1803, Jefferson presented "to the special Confidence" of Congress a message asking an appropriation of $2500 for the innocent purpose "of extending the external commerce of the United States," which he said, "while understood and considered by the Executive as giving legislative sanction, would cover the undertaking from notice. . . ." Thus is explained an expedition actually costing more than $50,000, military in personnel and supply, including no trained scientific observer nor any experienced Indian trader, but equipped for winning allies and reconnoitering a strategic area.[9]

However, Jefferson was not one to miss an opportunity to accomplish, with economy, more than one objective at a time. The expedition was also designed to gather data useful to science. Lewis went to Philadelphia where Robert Patterson and Andrew Ellicott taught him the mathematics and astronomy essential for surveying, map-making, and the use of instruments; Dr. Benjamin Barton helped him with botany and zoology and methods of preserving specimens. Dr. Benjamin Rush advised him on means of protecting the health of the men: they should wear flannel next to the skin in wet weather and shoes without heels; they should wash their feet in the mornings in cold water, and rely upon "opening-pills" for digestive troubles. Rush also helped formulate the questions Lewis might profitably ask the natives concerning their customs and economy.

In the meantime, in April (1803), unexpected good news arrived from France. Napoleon offered to sell the whole of Louisiana to the

[9] See *Letters of the Lewis and Clark Expedition with Related Documents, 1783–1854*, Donald Jackson, ed. (1962), 10–14, 419–429, 431n.

United States. For the sum of $15,000,000, paid largely in settlements of claims, the United States acquired a land area which more than doubled its territory.

One threat to national security had been removed, but another remained. The British traders still moved westward. And so the expedition was not canceled, nor was its original purpose changed. Albert Gallatin, Jefferson's respected advisor and Secretary of the Treasury, summarized the national purpose:

> The present aspect of affairs may, ere long, render it necessary that we should by taking immediate possession, prevent G[reat] B[ritain] from doing the same. Hence a perfect knowledge of the posts, establishments & force kept by Spain in upper Louisiana, and also of the most proper station to occupy, for the purpose of preventing effectually the occupying of any part of the Missouri country by G.B., seems important. With that view the present communications of the British with the Missouri, either from the Mississippi, or, which is still more in point, from the waters emptying in Lake Winnipec & generally in Hudson Bay, should be well ascertained, as well as the mode in which a small but sufficient force could best be conveyed to the most proper point from whence to prevent any attempt from Lake Winnipec.[10]

As sovereign of the Louisiana Territory, the United States had additional cause to seek information about Indian customs and trade and about the character of the country, its plants and animals. Lewis was "to explore the Missouri river, and such principal stream of it, as by it's course and communication with the waters of the Pacific ocean . . . may offer the most direct and practicable water communication across this continent for the purposes of commerce."

Early in July, Captain Meriwether Lewis set out for Ohio where he met his co-leader and old friend, Lieutenant William Clark. In December they were at St. Louis, where Lewis presented his credentials to the Spanish officials still in command. On December 20, 1803, the flag of Spain was for a brief moment replaced by the tricolor of France. Then it was lowered and, the ceremony of transfer having been carried out, the 15-starred flag of the United States was raised over Louisiana and "the heart of the continent." When the expedition got under way in May, 1804, it traveled from the mouth of the Missouri to the Rockies on American soil.

[10] *Ibid.*, 32.

CHAPTER
SIX

Americans and British
Cross the Rockies

THE SUCCESS OF the Lewis and Clark expedition depended upon its leadership, for which Jefferson had made wise choices. Twenty-nine-year-old Captain Meriwether Lewis was a man of some education; intelligent, reticent, and observant. "Whatever he should report would be as certain as if seen, by ourselves," Jefferson believed, and Lewis' journals justified the President's confidence.

The co-leader of the expedition, Lieutenant William Clark, thirty-three years old, was the son of a frontier family and younger brother of renowned George Rogers Clark. He was awkward with a pen but expert with a gun, experienced in Indian warfare and handling *peroques* and canoes. Even-tempered and patient, Clark was successful in negotiations with the Indians who called him the "red-haired chief, our brother."

A common background helped these men to work well together under Jefferson's instructions. Both were born and had lived a part of their lives as Jefferson's neighbors at Shadwell, Virginia. Both were army men and had fought in Ohio Valley Indian wars, Lewis as a young officer under Clark for several years. Because of red tape in the Corps of Engineers, Clark did not get a captain's commission before the expedition set out, but he was "Captain" Clark to the party. The two leaders were engaged in a joint enterprise, and a careful reading of their journals reveals how in personality and training they complemented one another.

The expedition was well equipped, carrying arms for defense and gifts for the Indians, a tested means of winning friendship. Every effort was made to provide helpful directions from reliable sources. The leaders had access to maps of men who had traveled the Missouri over its known length. At St. Louis they talked with Louis Labeaume, Manuel Lisa, Regis Loisel, and others, who gave the leaders "a good Deel of information." They carried Mackenzie's recently published *Voyages*.

It was a well-reported expedition. Jefferson urged all who could to keep records of their travels. Seven of the men complied, but only four of their journals have been found. Lewis' and Clark's voluminous accounts, read together in Reuben Gold Thwaites' edition, give a dimensional picture of the whole venture, and are a treasure-house of information about the country and the Indians.[1]

The party wintered at Fort Dubois on the Wood River not far from St. Louis, and setting out from there on May 21, 1804, arrived late in October at the Mandan villages. They set up winter quarters among the Mandans not only because it was late in the season, but also because this was a center of the Canadian traders' activities. Lewis advised the Indians to accept no more British flags or medals. He promised their principal chieftain a trip to Washington and emphasized the benefits they would receive from the Americans who now ruled the land.

The leaders exchanged courtesies with the Canadian traders, one of whom complained that "Captain Lewis could not make himself agreeable to us—he could speak fluently and learnedly on all subjects, but his inveterate disposition against the British stained, at least in our eyes, all his eloquence." But this was not a winter of social activities. As soon as the ice broke on the river, strenuous preparations were made to get the expedition under way.

When the expedition left the Mandan villages in April, 1804, it consisted of thirty-three persons, including one Indian woman and her two-months-old child. Sacajawea was the Shoshone wife of the interpreter Toussaint Charbonneau, who had purchased her from the Minnetarees. She was not a guide, for the route was new to her too. But when the expedition found her people on the Beaverhead River of western Montana she convinced her chieftain brother of the peaceful purposes of the party and persuaded him to supply much-needed

[1] *Original Journals of the Lewis and Clark Expedition*, R. G. Thwaites, ed., 8 vols. (1905).

horses. Occasional references to her in the leaders' journals reveal a woman adaptable and personable. Her child, Pompey, affectionately called "Little Pomp" in Clark's journal, is commemorated in Pompey's Pillar, a rocky outthrust on the upper Yellowstone River. With the exception of Sacajawea, Charbonneau, and York, Clark's negro servant, the expedition was a detachment of the United States Army on special service.

The party traveled by boat to the Three Forks of the Missouri, thence by foot up the Jefferson River through the Beaverhead country to the Continental Divide. Lewis was in advance of the main party, following an old Indian trail, when he discovered that the valley through which he was passing turned "abruptly to the west through a narrow bottom between the mountains." Now he "did not despair of shortly finding a passage over the mountains and of taisting the waters of the great Columbia this evening."

Four miles further on

> . . . the road took up to the most distant fountain of the waters of the Mighty Missouri in surch of which we have spent so many toilsome days and wristless nights. thus far I had accomplished one of those great objects on which my mind has been unalterably fixed for many years, judge then of the pleasure I felt in all[a]ying my thirst with this pure and ice-cold water which issues from the base of a low mountain or hill . . . here I halted a few minutes and rested myself. two miles below McNeal had exultingly stood with a foot on each side of this little rivulet and thanked his god that he had lived to bestride the mighty & heretofore deemed endless Missouri . . . we proceeded on to the top of the dividing ridge from which I discovered immence ranges of high mountains still to the West of us with their tops partially covered with snow. I now descended the mountain about ¾ of a mile . . . to a handsome bold runing Creek of cold Clear water. here I first tasted the water of the great Columbia river.

Lewis had crossed the Divide by Lemhi Pass and the rivulet from which he drank was one of the streams forming the Little Lemhi River. The Columbia lay beyond the snow-covered mountains in the distance.

By horse the company proceeded north along the Salmon River into the Bitterroot Valley, following a Nez Perce trail almost to Clark's Fork, near the present Missoula, Montana. They crossed the Bitterroots by Lolo Pass to the Clearwater. The trail was stony, steep, crossed by fallen timber. Game was scarce and it began to snow. "I have been wet and as cold in every part as I ever was in my life," Clark wrote in his journal: "indeed I was at one time fearfull my feet would freeze in the thin Mockirsons which I wore."

With the help of friendly Nez Perces on the Clearwater, the party made dugout canoes and continued to the Columbia River, reaching it on October 16. A month later, in a pounding rainstorm lasting several days, they camped near the sea on the north shore of the river.

From Cape Disappointment, they took their first look at the Pacific Ocean. According to Clark, it had been badly named: it "roars like a repeeted roling thunder and have rored in that way ever since our arrival . . . I cant say Pasific as since I have seen it, it has been the reverse." They then moved camp to the south side of the Columbia on the Lewis and Clark River, calling their primitive shelter of logs Fort Clatsop after the Indians of that vicinity. Here Clark marked the occasion by inscribing on a tree: "William Clark, December 3rd, 1805. By land from U. States in 1804 & 1805."

Christmas was celebrated in the incomplete stockade; the men exchanged gifts, fired salutes, shouted and sang. "We would have Spent this day . . . in feasting, had we any thing either to raise our Sperits or even gratify our appetites, our Diner concisted of pore Elk, so much Spoiled that we eate it thro' mear necessity. Some Spoiled pounded fish and a fiew roots," lamented Clark.

To make their monotonous diet palatable and to preserve food for their return journey, the men needed salt. A detachment was sent to the coast (at the present site of Seaside), where they erected a rock cairn, and managed to evaporate from three quarts to a gallon of salt a day. A whale cast up on the shore south of Tillamook Head was reported to Fort Clatsop, and a number of men were permitted to go with Clark to see it. Sacajawea, who had not yet even seen the ocean, was in the party, although it would appear that she had to argue for the privilege. "She observed that she had traveled a long way with us to see the great waters," wrote Lewis, "and that now that monstrous fish was also to be seen, she thought it very hard she could not be permitted to see either."

Through a dismal wet winter (Clark counted only six days of sunshine between January and the last week of March), the men hunted, suffered winter colds, food poisoning, and petty accidents, and counted the days until they could go home. Lewis and Clark worked over their maps and notes, talked with the Indians about their lives and customs, and the local topography, and planned the expedition's return route.

No one regretted the day, March 23, 1806, when Lewis turned their quarters over to the friendly Clatsop chief and the party dipped their paddles in the Columbia for the long trip home.

While at Fort Clatsop, Clark had noted in his journal: "There is a large river which falls into the Columbia on its south side at what point we could not lern; which passes thro those extensive Columbian Plains from the South East." On April 1 they camped near the mouth of that river. Using an Indian map drawn with charcoal on a piece of matting, Clark and seven men entered the many-channeled mouth of the Willamette River. From its magnitude, probably in spring freshet, he decided that it must drain "that vast tract of Country between the western range of mountains [Cascades] and those on the sea coast and as far S[outh] as the Waters of Callifornia." Subsequently, maps showed the "Multnomah" River's headwaters in 37 degrees north latitude and not far from Great Salt Lake. This error was not corrected until the late 1820s when it was proved that the Willamette had its source in the nearby Cascades.

THE RETURN JOURNEY

Arriving at the Bitterroot Range too early in the season, the explorers had difficulty crossing through the ice and snow that mantled Lolo Pass. Once again at their camp, Traveler's Rest in the Bitterroot Valley, the leaders separated, according to plan.

Lewis' road took him through Hellgate Canyon and up the Blackfoot to a divide by which he reached Sun River and the Great Falls of the Missouri, where the year before the party had left a cache of goods. With five men, Lewis then went up the Marias River, which proved not to have its source as far north as he "wished and expected." Although he believed that the watershed of the Marias was only a short distance from that of the Saskatchewan, he "lost all hope" of its extending to 50 degrees north latitude. This is a significant reminder that the original purpose of the expedition had been influenced by British interests in the Saskatchewan and by Mackenzie's great plan for a transcontinental trade having the "entire command of the fur trade . . . from 48 degrees North to the Pole."

The only Indian trouble on the whole journey occurred on the Marias, and evidently Lewis handled it badly. A small party of Piegans of the Blackfeet tribe attempted to steal the white men's guns and horses. One Indian was stabbed and a second was shot by Lewis, who left an expedition medal around the dead man's neck to inform the natives "who we were." It was later believed that this incident was played up by the Canadians to turn the Blackfeet against the Americans. However, it would appear that the Blackfeet were later enemies of all white men and even of other Indians who traded with the whites.

On July 28, Lewis rejoined the rest of his party at the mouth of the Marias and in the white *peroque* in which they had traveled up the Missouri the previous year, made a rapid trip downstream to the mouth of the Yellowstone where he was to meet Clark.

Captain Clark and his men, in the meantime, had retraced their route from Lolo Pass up the Bitterroot Valley, crossed the Continental Divide at Gibbon's Pass, and on July 8 found their cache and dugouts on the Jefferson River. Within three days they were at Three Forks. Here Clark divided his party. Some of the men went on to the Great Falls to join Lewis, while Clark, Sacajawea, Little Pomp, Charbonneau, John Colter and the rest traveled by horse across the Gallatin Valley to the Yellowstone River. The trip down this river, by dugout and bullboat in its lower stretches, was a pleasant one. Game was plentiful, the river was full and unobstructed, and the weather pleasant. In fact, there were so few hazards that Clark assumed that this was the route by which large *bateaux* could reach the heart of the mountains.

On August 12 Clark's party was reunited with Lewis and in a few days all arrived at the Mandan villages. It is fair to assume that they let it be known among the British and Indians that their mission had been accomplished and that Americans had reached the Pacific. As we shall see, the implication was that the northern and western boundaries of Louisiana had been defined by their exploration.

Before arriving at the Mandan villages the captains released John Colter to return to the mountains with two trappers who offered to share their outfit with him. They spent the winter of 1806–1807 on the tributaries of the Upper Missouri, ranging the valleys of the Yellowstone and Big Horn. Thus Colter became the first guide into the Yellowstone country and a pioneer of the American fur industry in the Rockies.[2]

On September 23 (1806), accompanied by the principal chief of the Mandans to whom Lewis had promised a visit with President Jefferson, the expedition arrived at St. Louis. "We Suffered the party to fire off their pieces as a Salute to the Town," wrote Lewis. "We were met by all the village and received a harty welcom from it's inhabitants. . . . I sleped but little last night."

Reporting the return of the expedition, Jefferson told Congress that the explorers deserved well of their country. Lewis served as governor of Louisiana Territory until his death in 1810. Clark was appointed Superintendent of Indian Affairs for Louisiana and then for Missouri Territory. For both men the offices were more burdensome than profitable. But the names of Lewis and Clark are indelibly fixed in Ameri-

[2] Burton Harris, *John Colter, His Years in the Rockies* (1952).

can history and the highways that today follow portions of their trails are continual reminders of their exploit. The completion of the journey without serious accident overshadowed the genuine hardships it had entailed. Although they discovered no easy mountain passes, and Jefferson's hope for a continental waterway was not realized, the explorers had passed safely through hostile Indian country and crossed the continent. That was an achievement in itself.

The explorers' reports covered plant, animal, and human life. Animal skins and Indian objects they had collected were displayed in the Indian room at Jefferson's Monticello and at Peale's American Museum in Philadelphia. Seeds and plants were consigned to a Philadelphia botanist for study and cultivation. A bitterroot plant leafed out, apparently died, then suddenly sent up a rosette of waxen flowers. It was appropriately named *Lewisia rediviva*. A flourishing specimen of snowberry moved Jefferson in later years to describe it as "singular as it is beautiful." More significantly, however, Clark's maps stimulated the already high interest in the trans-Mississippi West, an interest which did not stop at the Rockies, but contemplated the land "where rolls the Oregon."

AMERICAN TRADERS ENTER THE UPPER MISSOURI

Despite hostile Indians along the Missouri, traders and trappers were quick to follow the Lewis and Clark route.

Within the year after their return it was estimated that no fewer than 100 traders were licensed at St. Louis to go among the Indians of the Missouri country, and the number who did not bother with legal requirements may have far exceeded those who did. Several parties left for the Rockies early in the spring of 1807.

Among these was Manuel Lisa, merchant and trader, who had ambitions to control the Indian trade out of St. Louis and who had demonstrated his ability to get along with the warlike tribes.[3] From a number of sources he had heard that Indians of the Upper Missouri were trading with the Spaniards of New Mexico. Such a trade was known to Nor'Wester Larocque at the Mandan villages who, in 1805, reported the arrival of a Snake Indian whose people had met the Spaniards and traded with them. Lisa and his associates planned a trading system that would extend to the Missouri's headwaters and

[3] Richard E. Oglesby, *Manuel Lisa and the Opening of the Missouri Fur Trade* (1963).

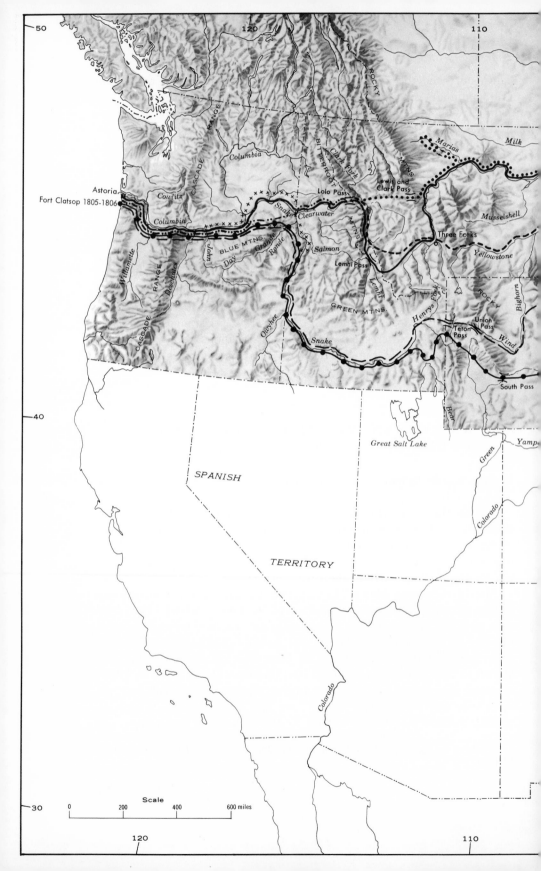

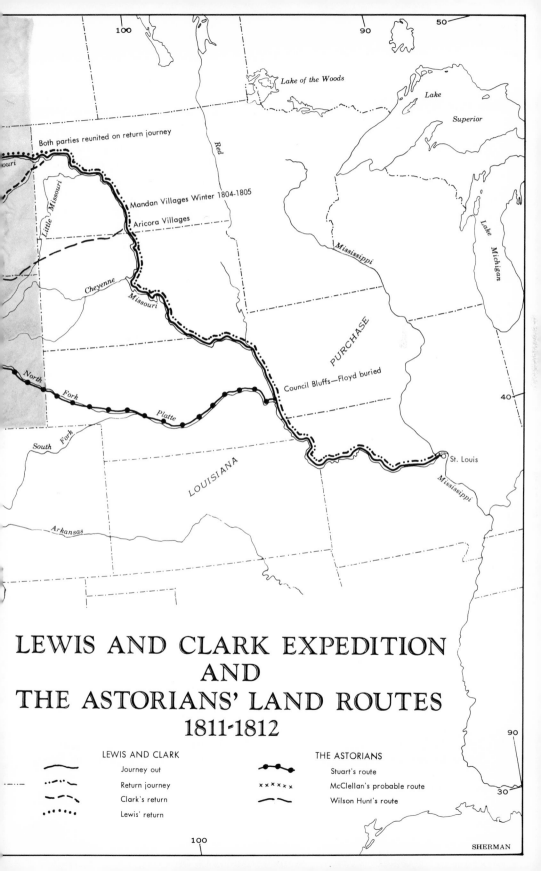

LEWIS AND CLARK EXPEDITION
AND
THE ASTORIANS' LAND ROUTES
1811-1812

LEWIS AND CLARK

Journey out

Return journey

Clark's return

Lewis' return

THE ASTORIANS

Stuart's route

McClellan's probable route

Wilson Hunt's route

SHERMAN

then, by a river as yet unknown to them but reported to flow south to Spanish lands, would connect with Santa Fé.

Lisa backed an expedition to Santa Fé in the summer of 1807. But before it started, he was on his way up the Missouri with a party including men who had been with Lewis and Clark, George Drouillard, John Colter, and probably John Potts. In July Lisa was at the mouth of the Big Horn where he built Fort Manuel (sometimes called Fort Lisa), and his men set out to trap the country and to invite the Indians to come to the fort to trade. It is possible that his haste was impelled by the report in St. Louis that British and American traders at Michilimackinac were forming a new company to trade on the upper river, and that a British party was moving to the headwaters of the Missouri.

NOR'WESTERS MOVE TO THE ROCKIES

The British traders were a party of Nor'Westers—representatives of the North West Company. The Montreal merchants kept abreast of all events in the world of commerce and diplomacy which might affect their interests; their wintering partners were equally alert to what was happening in any vicinity where they traded. At annual meetings they shared information from the marketplace and Indian country, and planned defense and attack on both fronts.

The company was well aware that the purchase of Louisiana would strengthen the American position on the Missouri and require some vital policy readjustments. They recognized that the Lewis and Clark expedition was a prelude to American expansion into the Far West, where already American trading ships were monopolizing the maritime commerce of the Pacific. Moreover, the North West Company's rival, the HBC, was strengthening its position on the Saskatchewan River, part of the Canadian highway to the sea. From 1804 to 1812, the policies of the North West Company were directed toward holding the Canadian Plains against the English company and securing footholds in the Far West against any competitor. In 1804, a bold move was made to establish the company in the Canadian Rockies.

Twenty-nine-year-old Simon Fraser was given the job of continuing Mackenzie's exploration and of establishing posts in northern British Columbia, then called New Caledonia. Following Mackenzie's route, he built Rocky Mountain Fort on the upper Peace River in 1805. Fort McLeod on McLeod Lake, Fort St. James on Stuart Lake, and Fort Fraser on Fraser Lake, were established during the next two years.

Americans and British Cross the Rockies

In 1808, with John Stuart, Jules Quesnell, nineteen *voyageurs*, and two Indian guides, he explored the "mighty river"—the Tacoutche Tesse which Mackenzie had presumed to be the Columbia. Like Mackenzie, Fraser found passage impossible for canoes, but he continued a grueling journey, mostly on foot, to the river estuary, near the present site of New Westminster. Observations of their latitude disclosed the disappointing fact that the river they had explored was not the Columbia; so Mackenzie's Tacoutche Tesse was named the Fraser.

In the meantime, across the eastern ridges of New Caledonia's mountains, one of Fraser's fellow Nor'Westers was wintering at the headwaters of the Columbia River. He too was temporarily a victim of the confusing mountain topography; he did not know that he had actually found the sources of the Columbia.

David Thompson

Trade brought David Thompson into the Northwest, but he is remembered today for his exploration of the Columbia River and his skill as a geographer and map-maker. The young Welshman entered the trade in 1784 as an apprentice, but after thirteen years with the HBC, he went over to the more aggressive North West Company. Various assignments during the next ten years acquainted him with the plains country from the Missouri to Lesser Slave Lake, and from Hudson Bay to the Rockies. In 1804 he was made a partner and in 1806 was assigned the task of developing the Nor'Westers' trade south of Peace River.

From Rocky Mountain House on the North Saskatchewan River, May 10, 1807, Thompson, accompanied by his wife and three small children, three men, and ten pack horses, set out for the mountains where he was to spend most of the next twelve years. A month later the party was in the "stupendous and solitary Wilds covered with eternal Snow . . . the collection of Ages and on which the Beams of Sun makes hardly any Impression." Here they waited fourteen days for the snows on the heights to melt.[4] Crossing these heights by Howse Pass, they came to the welcome sight of a ravine "where the Springs send their Rills to the Pacific Ocean," and followed the Blaeberry River, "a Torrent that seemingly nothing can resist," until June 30, when they reached a river where Thompson could report "thank God, we camped all safe."

[4] "The Discovery of the Source of the Columbia River," T. C. Elliott, ed., *OHQ*, March 1925; *David Thompson's Journals Relating to Montana and Adjacent Regions, 1806–1812*, M. Catharine White, ed. (1950); *David Thompson's Narrative of His Explorations in Western America, 1784–1812*, J. B. Tyrell, ed. (1916).

The river was the Columbia, though Thompson did not know it. Nor is this surprising when one examines a map of the region. It will be noted that the Columbia has its source in two lakes, lovely Windermere and shallow, reedy Columbia Lake. From them, the river flows north about 200 miles before it bends around the Selkirk Range to take up its long southwesterly course.

Thompson was looking for a river which flowed to the south and west, not to the north. Hence he turned his attention as soon as possible to the Flat Bow or McGillivray's River. This river, which we know as the Kootenai, had its source in a canyon near the Columbia's upper waters and not far from the mouth of Blaeberry Creek. It flowed parallel to, but in the opposite direction from, the Columbia, and within a few miles of it at Columbia Lake. The Kootenai then coursed south and east into northwestern Montana, reversed its direction and flowed north to Kootenai Lake, joining the Columbia above the 49th parallel.

Before the winter closed in, Thompson had explored the Columbia River to Columbia Lake and had traversed the two-mile portage to the Kootenai River. Had he not been concerned with building his winter quarters, trading with the Indians, and getting food supplies, he would have taken time immediately to "explore at least the Flat Bow Country, a[nd] by the Course of the large River, [to] determine whether it is the Columbia or not."

Thompson wintered at Kootenai House north of Lake Windermere at the junction of Tobey Creek with the Columbia. Indians from far and near came to trade and to seek an alliance with the white men against their traditional enemies, the Blackfeet. From them Thompson had encouraging news about the river he wished to explore. ". . . after drawing a Chart of their Country . . . from thence to the Sea, a[nd] describing the Nations along the River, they assured me that from this House to the sea a[nd] back again was only the Voyage of a Summer Moon. . . ."

However, it was not until early in 1811 that Thompson could embark on this Voyage of a Summer Moon. In the meantime his work as a trader took precedence over his yearning to explore. The Americans had arrived in the mountains.

COMPETITORS AND PATRIOTS

In August (1807), Indians told Thompson that about three weeks earlier forty-two Americans, including two or three men who had been with Lewis and Clark, had "arrived to settle a military Post, at the confluence of the two most southern a[nd] considerable Branches of the Columbia," and that they were preparing to set up a small advance post. "This establishment of the Americans will give a new Turn to our so-long-delayed settling of this Country, on which we have entered it seems too late," Thompson reported, "but, in my opinion the most valuable part of the Country still remains to us. . . ." If this were true, he must protect the trade of that country.

He learned that Flathead Indians who had been trading with him "had pitched away" to the American camp. To meet competition, it was necessary to hold the Indians with a regular and assured supply of the kinds of goods they wanted, so they could not be coaxed away by occasional opposition. It is in this light that we understand Thompson's distress over the "difficulty of getting Goods from Fort des Prairies, a[nd] the still more formidable poverty of the Country in Animals"—that is, horses with which to distribute goods from post to post.

The identity of these Americans has been a puzzle. One of the West's most informed historians, Dale Morgan, believes that there was an "obscure group of traders," among whom was one Charles Courtin, operating in the vicinity of Three Forks in the summer of 1807.[5] One tale has it that Courtin was killed by Indians on Clark's Fork in 1810. However, the possibility remains that these men were an advance group from Manuel Lisa's party, the only one setting out from St. Louis in 1807 which had the identifying features mentioned by Thompson: forty-two men, among whom were "two or three" former members of the Lewis and Clark expedition. The correspondence of the Americans, reported by Thompson, suggests that these men were

---

[5] *The West of William H. Ashley . . . Recorded in the Diaries and Letters of William H. Ashley and his Contemporaries, 1822–1838*, Dale L. Morgan, ed. (1963). There were other mysterious travelers in the Far West at an early date. In the early part of 1805, Louisiana Territory's Governor, James Wilkinson, said he sent an expedition to explore the Yellowstone River; he expected his party to return in late 1807. Who composed his party and what they did has not been discovered. However, an Anthony Bettay wrote Jefferson, January 27, 1808, that he had just returned from three years in the interior; that about 1700 miles from St. Louis, he had found a silver mine on the Platte River or one of its branches; had discovered an "eligible passage" across the mountains and a westward-flowing river, and a silk nettle which grew to about eight feet in height. The native nettle that reaches this size is found only west of the Rocky Mountains, especially in southern Idaho and northern Colorado. It is possible that the party of which Bettay was a member crossed the Divide about the same time as Lewis and Clark. This *may* have been the Wilkinson expedition. See *Territorial Papers of the United States*, Clarence E. Carter, ed., 26 vols. (1939–   ), XIII, 243.

experienced traders, under leaders both literate and informed on matters of American trade regulations.

The message Thompson received from the Americans was brought by two Kootenais who had had it from "a more southerly tribe." It was an open letter addressed to "the foreigners who may at present be carrying on a traffic with the Indians within our territories." Some of its contents were probably familiar to Thompson. Eight of the ten paragraphs were almost verbatim instructions on customs regulations for foreign traders in the Old Northwest.

The tenth paragraph, however, dealt specifically with the Far West and revealed a writer somewhat familiar with Anglo-American boundary issues and an expansionist whose zeal was not at the moment shared by the American government. It read:

> The new ceded Territories to the American States northward and westward of the Illinois, comprehend the Mississourie Red River and all the Lands westward to the Coast of California and the Columbia River with all its Branches; of which we have now taken Possession and on which we are now settled down to the Pacific Ocean; extending northward to about 50 Degrees north Latitude, according to the Boundaries settled at the Treaty of Peace, between the united States and the Court of Great Britain [sic], although it is by no means allowed here nor does any of our Expressions bear the Sense that, Great Britain has any special right to any of the Lands on the Pacific Ocean, or to the Commerce of any of the Rivers that flow into the said Ocean, all of which we shall comprehend as within our said Territories until some further Explanation takes place on this head between the united States of America and the Court of St. James.[6]

The message was dated July 10, 1807, from "Fort Lewis, Yellow River, Columbia," and signed by "James Roseman Lieutenant" and "Zachary Perch Captain & Commanding Officer." Thompson neither mentioned the missive in his journal, nor replied to it. He simply forwarded it to Rocky Mountain House.

About December 24 he received another letter, addressed this time specifically to "the British Mercht. Trafficking with the Cabanaws [Kootenais]." It informed Thompson that his failure to reply to the first letter was construed as "tacit disrespect," and that it was therefore concluded that Thompson did not properly "acknowledge the authority of Congress over these Countries, which are certainly the property of the United States both by discovery and Cession." Thompson was asked to submit "with a good grace" before military

---

[6] "Letter of Roseman and Perch, July 10th, 1807," J. B. Tyrell, ed., *OHQ*, December 1937, 393–394; T. C. Elliott, "The Strange Case of David Thompson and Jeremy Pinch," *OHQ*, June 1939.

posts were fortified and patrols sent out. This letter was dated September 29 from "Poltito Palton Lake" and was signed "Jeremy Pinch Lieut." Thompson privately characterized the writer as "one of these petty officers . . . [with] as much arrogance as Buonaparte at the head of his Invincibles." He replied that he was "neither authorized nor competent" to discuss boundary issues and that customs matters would be considered by all the partners of the North West Company.

Thompson's identification of his correspondent as military was only natural in the circumstances. However, research has failed to produce these names in army records; nor was there an army fort so far west. It must be inferred then that the names Roseman, Perch, and Pinch disguised the authors of a hoax, who depended upon military references for their authority. Their identity remains a mystery.

Thompson was not intimidated by the threats. With driving energy, he worked to win over the natives and to set up trading houses among them. Finan McDonald built a temporary depot near Kootenai Falls in 1808. In September 1809 Thompson selected the site for Kullyspel House on the eastern shore of Lake Pend Oreille. Saleesh House, near Thompson Falls on the Clark Fork River, was built the same fall. In 1810 or 1811 McDonald and Jacques (Joco) Finlay built Spokane House near the present city of Spokane. Not only did Thompson keep on the move through these parts of western Montana, northern Idaho, and eastern Washington, but he also made three arduous trips out of the country with packs of furs, returning with trading goods. In 1808 he left Kootenai House early in June, arrived at Rainy Lake on August 2, and was back on the Columbia in October. The next year he descended the Saskatchewan to Fort Augustus, and returning, crossed by Howse Pass to his post in thirty-five days. At the annual meetings of the partners in 1810 he was directed to go back to the mountains and explore fully the Columbia River.

There were several reasons for this. One was the Pinch episode; another, the activities of Manuel Lisa and his partner, Andrew Henry.

After his first trip to the mountains, Lisa became a partner and dynamic leader in the Missouri Fur Company. He had trading posts at the mouth of the Yellowstone and Big Horn; and Andrew Henry built a temporary house at the Three Forks of the Missouri, which he was forced to abandon under Blackfeet attack. Henry and his men crossed over the Continental Divide and, in 1810, established a winter camp on the northern fork of the Snake, near Elgin, Idaho. Although safe from hostile Indians, they were short of game and in the spring the party broke up. Some returned to the Missouri but others remained in the mountains and became the first of that "reckless breed of men" whose short lives were spent and expended in trapping the Rocky Mountain beaver grounds. Henry's Fort was only a winter encampment, but so far as we know for sure, it was the first American fur trade post west of the Divide.

Jeremy Pinch's and Lisa's enterprises, following so closely on the Lewis and Clark expedition, corroborated Canadian fears of American entry into the West. In the spring of 1808, Alexander Mackenzie was in London asking British government support for a Columbia River settlement on the ground that the Lewis and Clark expedition would provide the Americans with arguments for exclusive claims to the country between Spanish settlements and 50 degrees north latitude. He did not know that American traders were already moving west, but it is possible that he did know that there was already in the offing a major American venture to the Columbia. The Northwest had become part of fur trade politics and of the commercial rivalry which plagued American-British relations.

CHAPTER
SEVEN

Nor'Westers and
Astorians

THE FUR TRADE, which usually brought wholesale destruction to fur-bearing animals, was competitive, hence without regard for conservation. It demanded the continuous opening of new productive areas, which drove the trader westward. The Missouri, the Saskatchewan, and after 1811, the Athabaska rivers, were his highways to the Pacific Northwest. In the first decade of the nineteenth century, the trade was looking for outlets on the Pacific.

Between 1807 and 1813, the North West Company established its hold in the Pacific Northwest. The HBC challenged the Nor'Westers in the Saskatchewan and Athabaskan plains, but only once attempted to invade the Rockies. In the spring of 1810 Joseph Howse, with a party of seventeen, crossed over the pass used by David Thompson, followed Thompson's trail to Flathead Lake, and built a trading house near the present Kalispell, Montana. Trade was good, but Howse advised against further expeditions because of Indian troubles. The Nor'-Westers interpreted Howse's venture as evidence of their rival's intention to expand into the Rockies. For this and other reasons they petitioned the Board of Trade and Privy Council to restrict the HBC to its chartered lands and to grant their own company exclusive trade on the coast between 42 and 60 degrees.

As we have seen, the Nor'Westers were also threatened on the Upper Missouri. A more serious threat emerged in the ambitious plans of a competitor with whom they had had long experience in Wisconsin.

JOHN JACOB ASTOR

John Jacob Astor was a man of entrepreneurial talent.[1] Originally from Germany, he had emigrated to New York via London in 1784. Twenty years later he was the foremost fur dealer and one of the most successful merchants in New York. His career illustrates a capacity for large-scale planning and patient execution and fine dexterity in manipulating situations to serve his own interests. The Louisiana Territory encouraged plans for enlarging those interests. The blueprint for his ambitions projected a chain of trading houses between St. Louis and the mouth of the Columbia River; the establishment of posts at strategic locations throughout the interior of the Pacific Northwest; and a fleet to carry on Pacific coastal trade with the natives, supply Russian settlements, and connect with his already flourishing New York-Canton trade. This plan required that he eliminate competitors, or temporarily cooperate with them, whichever would soonest win him control of the American industry.

Astor incorporated the American Fur Company in 1808, but it lay dormant while he set up subsidiary, or regional, companies. For more than a decade he had dealt amicably with Montreal merchants prominent in the North West Company. Occasionally he bought from them furs and British goods which Indians preferred to those of American manufacture, and sometimes he carried Canadian furs to the China market. These mutually agreeable relations continued even when his traders were vigorously competing with the North West Company's men, and in spite of the suspicions of the Montreal merchants that Astor's interests were not wholly compatible with their own.

The Canadians found it especially advantageous to work with Astor in the Great Lakes area; through him, they could avoid United States regulations which applied to foreigners. Their relationship was formalized in a partnership when the South West Company was organized in January 1811.

What made the new company acceptable to the North West Company was a firm agreement that Astor's men would not intrude in the

[1] Kenneth W. Porter, *John Jacob Astor*, 2 vols. (1931).

trade of the Upper Missouri or west of the Rockies. This did not prevent Astor from forming a new company for this special purpose, nor did it stop some Nor'Westers from joining him.

In 1808 Astor had offered the North West Company a one-third interest in his projected fur company, to engage in the trade of the Far West. The wintering partners rejected the offer. But in the spring of 1810, when Astor was shaping his plans, it was understood, according to one North West Company merchant, that Astor was "to be conected with the N W Company to make settlements on the North West coast of America, to communicate with the inland N W trade."[2]

There were advantages for both Astor and the Canadians in such a connection. If need be, Astor was financially able to risk $500,000 in western establishments; he had vessels to supply coastal outposts and supplement the Indian trade by provisioning, and exporting furs for the Russians; and he had free access to the China market.

The North West Company, on the other hand, was struggling for survival with the HBC in the Canadian Plains; it had no ships in western waters, and was excluded from the China trade. However, it had one important advantage over Astor—a foothold in the Rocky Mountain trade. Furthermore, anticipating that growing tensions between Britain and the United States would lead to war, the Canadians hoped that the British government would intervene by erecting a military establishment on the Pacific coast.

In January, 1811, two representatives of the leading mercantile houses of the North West Company were in New York to complete the organization of the South West Company. There, at the same time, Astor tentatively agreed with three former Nor'Westers to form the Pacific Fur Company. Thus Astor's plans for a large-scale operation, including a land and sea expedition to the Columbia, were known to the Canadians. When his sea expedition sailed in the fall of the year, the Canadians notified their London agent, Simon McGillivray, who wrote Lord Liverpool, the Prime Minister:

> . . . I fear it may almost be too late to accomplish the object which the North West Company had in view, if they could have obtained the Sanction of His Majesty's Government in sufficient time. That object was to establish Settlements on the Columbia River, and so to secure the right of Possession to Great Britain before the arrival of the Americans.
>
> Still however this object might probably be accomplished and His Majesty's right to the Territorial possession of the Northwest Coast of America preserved, if one of His Majesty's Ships could immediately

[2] *Wisconsin Historical Collection*, XIX, 336–337.

be dispatched to take formal possession of and establish a Fort or Settlement in the Country. . . .

If the Plan which I have presumed to suggest should be adopted . . . the Northwest Comp would send an Expedition across the Continent to meet her, and to form trading Establishments under the protection of His Majesty's Fort; but unless they can obtain such protection, they cannot embark in their intended undertaking, and that Country and its Trade will be left to the possession of the Americans.[3]

The Nor'Westers were willing to gamble on their superior advantages and the possibility of war. Yet they were loath to jeopardize their position in the Pacific Northwest by a long and expensive trade war; nor could they ignore the possibility of having to cooperate with Astor if he became entrenched on the Columbia and the British government refused to help them.

One may therefore infer that in 1810–1811 the Canadians and Astor had a tacit agreement not to interfere with one another's trade. They may even have settled on spheres of interest in the New Northwest, as they had in the Old. This seems a reasonable explanation for Astor's venture, at an inauspicious time, into a situation of great risk. It must be kept in mind that Astor hated to lose money, and that he was not naive, though he sometimes pretended to be.

THE ASTORIANS

Astor's Pacific Fur was a joint-stock company. Of 100 shares of stock, Astor retained fifty, and thirty-five were assigned his partners. Fifteen shares were undistributed, but it was provided that when they were assigned, Astor would nominate four out of five three-share partnerships. Astor was to assume all risks for five years, with profits prorated among the partners. He was to have management of the concern for the first five years. Annual meetings of the partners were to be held at the Columbia River establishment and absent members were to vote by proxy. If the business proved unprofitable the company could be dissolved by majority vote at any annual meeting.

Five of Astor's nine partners had only recently severed connections with the North West Company. Alexander McKay had been clerk with Alexander Mackenzie's expedition to the Pacific in 1793, and a longtime partner in the company. Donald McKenzie, a chronically

[3] Arthur S. Morton, "Notes and Documents: The Appeal of the North West Company to the British Government . . .," *Canadian Historical Review*, September 1936, 310–311.

discontented young clerk related to Sir Alexander, and with two brothers and several other relatives associated with the company, resigned from its service in 1808. David Stuart was a cousin of John Stuart, who was in charge of the company's posts in northern New Caledonia. David's nephew, Robert, was relatively a newcomer to the trade. Duncan McDougall was a veteran Nor'Wester.

The Canadian Ramsay Crooks and Americans Robert McClellan and Joseph Miller had been associated with Astor's interests in the Wisconsin trade. In 1807 they were trading out of St. Louis, probably with some backing from Astor. Wilson Price Hunt of New Jersey, a newcomer to St. Louis the same year, possibly was also associated with Astor before the Pacific Fur Company was organized.

There was nothing petty in Astor's assault on the Northwest. He sent two expeditions. One was to cross by land and locate sites for a chain of posts. Originally it was intended that Donald McKenzie should share party command with Hunt, but before the expedition left winter quarters on the Missouri Hunt was given full charge and carried Astor's proxy. Placing Hunt in charge of the expedition was unfortunate since McKenzie was more experienced.

A second party was dispatched by ship to open a coastal trade and set up trading houses on the Columbia. Duncan McDougall was in charge of the sea contingent and was to command the chief post on the Columbia when Hunt was absent trading with the Russians or delivering fur cargoes to China.

The *Tonquin* sailed from New York September 8, 1810, and after a two-week stop at the Hawaiian Islands, arrived at the Columbia on March 22, 1811. By every report, Captain Jonathan Thorn was a martinet. Determined to enter the river despite a heavy sea, he ordered the chief mate and four men, none seamen, to sound the channel. The whale boat and its crew disappeared in the waves. Three more attempts were made and three more men lost—a sacrifice of eight lives, attributed as much to Thorn's unreasoning stubbornness as to the hazards of the Columbia bar—before the *Tonquin* crossed in.

Having surveyed the shores, McDougall chose Point George on the south bank for the site of Fort Astoria, and the men set about building their shelters. In the first week of June, the *Tonquin* left the river for summer trading along the north coast. There being no place as yet to store trading goods, the greater part of the year's supply remained in the ship's hold.

In August, Indians reported that the ship had been destroyed and the crew massacred. Actual details of what happened will never be known; but it would appear that Thorn antagonized the natives, whose reputation for treachery was widespread, and failed to take proper precautions against them. Nootka Sound is usually assumed to be the site of the disaster. However, it is more probable that the massacre took place at Newettee Harbor on the northern tip of Vancouver Island. Within six months the Astorians had suffered an appalling loss of life: eight men in entering the Columbia; at least twenty-seven with the *Tonquin*. The land party lost only two men, but it had other misfortunes.

At St. Louis early in September, 1810, Hunt was "preparing to proceed up the Missouri and prosue [*sic*] my trail to the Columbia." So reported General William Clark. But it was June 12 the following year when sixty-two men and the native wife of Pierre Dorion and their two children reached Council Bluffs, where reports of Indian hostilities on the upper river led Hunt to abandon boats, buy horses, and strike off across the Plains.[4]

The route lay generally to the southwest, and for some days the party traversed prairies of knee-deep grass. They followed the Big Horn to the Wind River, crossed its beautiful valley and reached the Grand Teton Range by an Indian road. Guided by three trappers who had been with Andrew Henry the previous winter, Hunt and his companions had no trouble reaching the Green River where they "were surrounded by mountains in which were disclosed beautiful green valleys where numerous herds of bison graze. . . ." Two weeks later, in a flurry of snow, they arrived at Andrew Henry's fort on the north fork of the Snake. Assuming the river to be navigable, they spent precious time making canoes, then embarked. Ten grueling days of portages, cordelling, and hazardous canoeing took them the amazing distance of 360 miles with the loss of only one man.

At Caldron Linn, the awesome character of the Snake was revealed. On October 29, from a precipitous cliff, Hunt looked down upon the river "full of rapids and intersected by falls from ten to forty feet high." But from where he stood, Hunt glimpsed only the crests of these falls: Shoshone, 212 feet high, and Twin Falls, 182 feet. The men abandoned their canoes.

The season was advancing, and the party still far from its destination. Supplies were exhausted, game was scarce, and the few Indians encountered were also short of food. Hunt sent Donald McKenzie and four men to the north in the hope of striking the main stream of the Columbia, while Robert McClellan and three men pushed ahead down the Snake Canyon.

Having cached their goods and distributed the scanty food supplies,

[4] *The Discovery of the Oregon Trail: Robert Stuart's Narratives of His Overland Trip . . . an Account of the Tonquin's Voyage . . . and Wilson Price Hunt's Diary . . .*, Philip A. Rollins, ed. (1935).

the expedition divided. Hunt's party, with Dorion's wife and children, kept to the left bank of the river; Crooks and his men tried the right bank. From the ninth of November until the sixth of December the two parties hugged opposite walls of the canyon parallel to, but out of touch with, one another. Two weeks later, starving and exhausted, they remet. Crooks, too ill to travel, was left behind with John Day and a *voyageur*, the three to make their way as best they could. Hunt and the others, leaving the "accursed Mad River" reached the lovely valley of the Grande Ronde on December 30. Here in the cold morning hours, Dorion's wife gave birth to a child. A week later in the Blue Mountains, the baby died.

On January 15, they came to the Umatilla River and friendly natives. A month's journey later (February, 1811) at Fort Astoria, Hunt found McKenzie, McClellan, and John Reed, from whom he had parted at Caldron Linn. Crooks and John Day, destitute even of clothing and having suffered terrible want and abuse from the Indians, arrived on May 11.

While the overland party was enduring these miseries, the men at Astoria faced troubles of another kind. McDougall was a poor leader in a situation calling for energy and firmness. Elementary health rules were ignored, and little was done to guard the men against diseases carried by Indian women. Attempts at discipline roused threats of mutiny. The loss of the *Tonquin* had reduced the Astorians' trading stock, and there were repeated rumors of Indian uprisings. Not until early July (1811) was it considered safe for David Stuart and a small party to set off up the Columbia on a trading expedition.

Stuart had not yet left when the Astorians had a surprise visit from David Thompson, on his long-anticipated exploration of the Columbia.

DAVID THOMPSON'S JOURNEY OF A SUMMER MOON

The North West Company, meeting at Fort William in the summer of 1810 and hearing details of Astor's project, concluded it must show its hand on the Columbia River, but without a display of hostility. Thompson was ordered back to the mountains. Forced by Indian troubles to seek a new route, he crossed the Rockies by Athabaska Pass, ascended to his post at the Columbia headwaters, and by way of the Kootenai, Clark's Fork, and the Pend Oreille, reached Spokane House. From there he proceeded to the falls of the Columbia (Kettle Falls) where his men built a large canoe. On July 3 (1811) Thomp-

Fur Traders

LEFT. Encampment of the Travellers on the Missouri *painted by Carl Bodmer about 1840. Vulnerable to Indian attack though it was, passage up the wide Missouri to the Far West offered some balancing advantages to the overland routes.*

ABOVE. Junction of the Yellowstone River with the Missouri *painted by Carl Bodmer. Here the great water highway into the west gave out and early travelers must proceed by land and lesser waterways.*

LEFT. The Rocky Mountains *painted by James Henry Warre. These towering mountains and forests became well-worked trappers' territory. By 1840, the best of the beaver streams were stripped clean.*

Fort George (formerly Astoria) *painted by James Henry Warre, the lonely outpost of the Astorians, chief depot of the North West Company and after the building of Ft. Vancouver, lookout station for the Hudson's Bay Company.*

LEFT. Chief Trader McDonald Descending the Fraser, 1828 *painted by A. Sherriff Scott. In 1825, Governor George Simpson traveled the Fraser River with Chief Trader Archibald McDonald and concluded, "I shall . . . no longer talk of it as a navigable stream."*

BELOW. Indians Threatening to Attack the Fur Boats *painted by Alfred Jacob Miller. For safety, fur boats sought night anchorage in midstream at the widest possible expanse of water. Courtesy Walters Art Gallery, Baltimore. © 1951 Oklahoma University Press.*

Caravan Enroute *painted by Alfred Jacob Miller. A trappers' supply caravan, laden with trading goods, moves up the Platte, headed for the annual rendezvous. Courtesy Walters Art Gallery, Baltimore. © 1951 Oklahoma University Press.*

Scene at Rendezvous *painted by Alfred Jacob Miller. From the artist's notes, "Here we rested over a month . . . encamping among . . . Indians . . . who assembled . . . to trade buffalo robes and skins for blankets, guns, ammunition, tobacco . . . Here the Trappers get their outfit, departing . . . for the beaver streams . . ." Courtesy Walters Art Gallery, Baltimore. © 1951 Oklahoma University Press.*

LEFT. Fort Vancouver *painted by James Henry Warre, was the "New York of the Columbia" to weary travelers. The Fort, across the river from today's Portland, was district headquarters for the Hudson's Bay Company.*

Fur Traders and Indians *sketched by Joseph Drayton in 1841 against the background of Fort Walla Walla, another Hudson's Bay Company trading post.*

LEFT. Fort Colville (on the upper Columbia) in the 1840s *(detail of diorama). Two men, center, bail furs for shipment; a man in the doorway brings more furs to be bailed. In addition to furs, some well-situated posts carried on farming and general trade.*

BELOW. Governor James Douglas Leaving Fort Langley after Proclaiming British Columbia a Colony, 1858, *painted by Franklin Arbuckle. Trapping trails gradually became migration trails; forts and trading posts were forerunners of cities, provinces and states.*

son set out with seven men, "by the Grace of God . . . on a voyage down the Columbia River to explore this river in order to open out a passage for the interior trade with the Pacific Ocean."[5]

At the mouth of the Snake, Thompson put up a notice which read:

> Know hereby that this country is claimed by Great Britain as part of its territories, and that the N.W. Company of Merchants from Canada, finding the factory for this people inconvenient for them, do hereby intend to erect a factory in this place for the commerce of the country around.

The next day Indians told him that a ship had arrived four months before. This was no surprise to Thompson, but his appearance at Fort Astoria five days later was indeed a surprise to the Astorians.

After a week's rest, during which he examined the river's entrance, Thompson left Astoria to return to the mountains. With him went David Stuart and eight Astorians who were to establish a trading post "somewhere below the Falls of the Columbia." At Celilo Falls Thompson pushed ahead of the rest and arrived at Spokane House on August 13. Stuart's slower-paced party reached the confluence of the Okanogan and Columbia rivers and there built Fort Okanogan. That Thompson was "cooperating" with the Astorians seems apparent. He knew the river; the Astorians did not. He must, therefore, have advised them as to the best site for a post.

OUTPOST ON A WAR FRONT

On his final trip on the Columbia, Thompson followed the full course of the river from its mouth to the source he had discovered four years earlier. He is remembered primarily as its explorer. But, contrary to long-accepted belief, he had not raced to the sea to get ahead of the Astorians. His mission was to study the feasibility of using the river as a waterway for the company's interior trade. Whether this trade would be in cooperation with Astor was decided in the spring of 1812, when the United States and Britain went to war.

Thompson was at Fort William for the annual meeting in the summer of 1812 when the proprietors decided to use the opportunity provided by war to oppose Astor. Donald McTavish was dispatched to England to arrange for a supply ship and convoy to come to the Columbia as quickly as possible. John Stuart, in charge of New Cal-

---

[5] "Journal of David Thompson," T. C. Elliott, ed., *OHQ*, March 1914, 57.

edonia, was directed to join his operations with those of Thompson and to meet McTavish's ship at the mouth of the Columbia the following spring.

Meanwhile, the Astorians' spirits rose when Hunt and his party straggled in, early in the spring of 1812, and when, several months later, the *Beaver* dropped anchor with trading goods and additional personnel. They were encouraged, too, by returns from Stuart's upper Columbia expedition. Stuart had left Alexander Ross in command of Fort Okanogan and had set up a new post, later known as Kamloops House, on the Thompson River. Returning to Astoria in the spring of 1812, Stuart brought evidence of rich trade possibilities in the northern interior.

At the partners' spring meeting, Donald McKenzie was assigned to lead a trapping expedition in the Snake River country, and John Clarke to establish a post near the North West's Spokane House. Robert Stuart was to carry reports to Astor overland, and Hunt was to conduct company business with the Russians.

Despite this flurry of energetic planning, two of the men, Ramsay Crooks and Robert McClellan, gave up their partnerships to return with Stuart to St. Louis, even though this meant repeating a journey they had barely survived a few months before. Their course led them to the Green River and through South Pass to the North Platte River, the route subsequently followed by mountain men and immigrant settlers. Although Andrew Henry's trappers had probably crossed South Pass, Stuart's party was the first of record to use this now famous gateway to the Oregon country. With some difficulty, they reached St. Louis at the end of April (1813) to find the United States at war with Great Britain.

Because of the war, and perhaps through unwillingness to risk a vessel on British-controlled sea lanes, Astor did not send out a supply ship in 1812. This put Hunt in a predicament. Leaving Fort Astoria that August, he had delivered to the Russians $56,500 worth of goods, receiving in exchange furs which he was to sell in China. Instead of returning to Astoria to pick up the Astorians' fur packs, Hunt proceeded to the Hawaiian Islands where, having sent the *Beaver* on to Canton to take advantage of a favorable market, he awaited vainly the arrival of the supply ship. In the end he had to purchase a vessel to get back to the fort.

Meanwhile, in January, 1813, the Astorians learned of the war, and of the expected arrival in the Columbia of a Nor'Westers' ship, the *Isaac Todd*, from England. When the vessel arrived, the Nor'Westers would have the advantage in trading stock, which was crushing news to the Astorians.

THE SALE OF FORT ASTORIA

But the *Isaac Todd* was delayed: Nor'Westers and Astorians were now equally embarrassed by lack of trading goods. The Astorians decided to abandon their enterprise and to dissolve the company, as their agreement with Astor empowered them to do, but for the winter to divide their trade with the Nor'Westers. For the record, they explained:

> The Ship Beaver was to have returned at the end of two months. Eleven months are now elapsed since she set sail. We have had no tidings of her since, and we have every reason to conclude that she must have either perished or taken her final departure from the coast. Another vessel was to have sailed about the usual time for our support, but after every due allowance, we need no longer expect her. We are now destitute of the necessary supplies to carry on the Trade, and we have no hopes of receiving more. We are yet entirely ignorant of the coast, on which we always had great dependence. The interior parts of the country turn out far short of our expectations. Its yearly produce in furs is very far from being equal to the expences the trade incurs, much less will it be able to recover the losses already sustained, or stand against a powerful opposition and support itself. In fine, circumstances are against us on every hand, and nothing operates to lead us into a conclusion that we can succeed.[6]

When Wilson Hunt, having finally procured a ship in Hawaii, reached Fort Astoria on August 20, he reluctantly agreed to the partners' decision, and turned again immediately for the Islands, this time to charter a vessel for removal of the Astorians and their stock. A few weeks later the Astorians learned that the *Isaac Todd*, whose arrival was expected at any moment, was accompanied by a frigate to seize the American establishment.

Astor's erstwhile partners now faced a new dilemma. All that remained of their venture was a limited supply of trading goods and a stock of furs. Nothing could be salvaged if the post were captured. So Duncan McDougall, on behalf of himself and his associates, Donald McKenzie, David Stuart, and John Clarke, agreed to sell to the Nor'-Westers "the whole of their Establishments Furs and present Stock . . . on the Columbia and Thompson Rivers."

No price had been agreed upon when, at the end of November (1813), the British naval sloop *Raccoon* arrived to fulfill "a duty to the North West Company." Captain Black took possession of the post, re-

[6] T. C. Elliott, "Sale of Astoria, 1813," *OHQ*, March 1932, 45.

named it Fort George, and left it in possession of the North West Company. Taking possession was an act of war which brought Fort Astoria into the peace negotiations that concluded the war.

So another surprise awaited Hunt on his return to Astoria in February (1814). The month of March was spent in bitter disputes between Astorians and Nor'Westers over inventories and prices, but the terms of sale were finally set. On April 4, the North West's brigade set out for Montreal, taking along those Astorians who wanted to leave at once. Alexander Ross, Ross Cox, Duncan McDougall, and several *voyageurs* chose to stay on as employees of the North West Company.

Hunt and three clerks, one of whom was Russell Farnham, proceeded in the *Pedler* to Sitka, Alaska, where they met Astor's vessel, *Forester*, whose captain had not dared to enter the Columbia after learning that the post had been captured. Farnham transferred to the *Forester* and was taken to the coast of Kamchatka. From there he crossed Siberia to St. Petersburg and proceeded to Copenhagen and London. In 1816 or 1817, he arrived in New York. This formidable journey was for the sole purpose of getting a more favorable price on the bill of exchange for $40,000 with which the Nor'Westers paid for the Astorians' furs.

Astor figured a loss of close to $160,000. He insisted that the true worth of the furs was two and a half times what he had received for them and that the trading goods were sold at only one-third of their value. The North West Company made no objection to the terms by which Astor had been bought out, competition removed, and their posts supplied, though the proprietors noted that, by the manner in which the bills of credit had been drawn, they lost at least 3000 pounds "owing to the rate of Exchange between Canada & England."

Astor at first blamed the war for his losses. Later he nursed the idea that he had been sold out by disloyal partners. This was not true. Astor had elected to take a large risk by competing with the Nor' Westers when war was imminent. His post was insufficiently supplied and mismanaged; the sale made the best of a bad situation. Had the *Isaac Todd* come when expected, the Nor'Westers would have held a compelling advantage over the Astorians and could have forced them out of the field with total loss. Failure of the ship to appear strengthened the bargaining power of the Astorians.

That Astor should be disappointed, even angered, by the failure of his company was natural. It appears, however, that his anger was directed at the Nor'Westers, over the low prices paid for his stock. "While I breath[e] & so long as I have a dollar to spend I'll pursue a course to have our injuries repair'd & when I am no more I hope you'll act in my place; we have been sold, but I do not despond," he wrote

Donald McKenzie in 1814. There seems to be no evidence that he blamed any of his associates for what happened, although he later cooled notably toward McKenzie, who had had little to do with the sale.

It may console those who consider Astor's loss a patriotic sacrifice to know that he actually suffered very little. The Treaty of Ghent reversed the decisions of the battlefield in the Old Northwest. Astor maintained his friendly relations with the Canadians, helping them circumvent trading regulations of the United States. In 1832, his American Fur Company, under the direction of Ramsay Crooks, captured the trade of the Missouri, and, two years later, of the Rockies as well. Although Astor did not live to enjoy a complete personal triumph, the American Fur Company achieved his goal—mastery of the trade of the mountains and the plains.

NOR'WESTERS AT FORT GEORGE

From 1814 to 1821, Nor'Westers controlled the fur trade in the Pacific Northwest. But the Montreal merchants' anticipations of making Fort George a major post in their continental trade were not realized. Like Astor, they had planned that the Columbia River post should be the principal depot for the trade west of the Rockies. Ships arriving annually from London would not only supply the trade of the interior, but would carry furs directly to the China market. However, the East India Company refused to allow North West Company ships to carry Chinese goods to England, and lacking this lucrative link in the trade, it was unprofitable to supply Fort George from London. In 1815, the company had to contract with Boston merchants to do its carrying.

Neither economy nor energy distinguished the administration of Fort George. Donald McTavish, the first governor, arrived on the long-awaited *Isaac Todd*, well fortified with luxuries, including a lively barmaid from Portsmouth, to compensate for an anticipated dreary exile on the Columbia. The presence of Jane Barnes complicated the internal affairs of the colony and created troubles with the Indians. Shortly after their arrival, McTavish drowned and Jane was shipped back to England via Canton.

In the view of a sharp-tongued critic writing in 1824, Fort George was "a large pile of buildings covering about an acre of ground . . . [with] an appearance of Grandeur and consequence . . . not at all suitable to an Indian Trading Post." Everything was "on too extended a scale except the Trade."[7] But to the men wintering under leaky roofs within its palisaded walls, their only contact with the outside world the annual express from Fort William and the supply ship, the fort was far from grand and life was dull, dreary, and lonely. The principal activities of some sixty-six men stationed there were hacking down the luxuriant growth of brush that encroached upon their garden, packing furs for shipment, and preparing and distributing goods for the interior posts—Fort Okanogan, Spokane House, Kamloops, Kootenay House, Fort Alexander, and Fort Nez Perce (Walla Walla).

In 1816 Donald McKenzie was sent back to the Columbia to take charge of the interior trade. The Astorians had not fully appreciated his talents, for he proved to be one of the North West Company's most successful traders and explorers. A man of huge stature, weighing over 300 pounds; tireless, fearless, and a skilled rifleman able to "drive a dozen balls consecutively at one hundred paces through a Spanish dollar," he was feared and respected by the natives. In four years he made three expeditions into the rugged Snake country.

In 1818 McKenzie built Fort Nez Perce as a trade center for the Nez Perce Indians and a supply depot for the vast area in which he explored and trapped. In 1819 he ascended the Snake River from the Clearwater to the Burnt River in a *bateau*, a feat not duplicated until modern times, and then with engine-powered craft. He initiated the trapping expedition, using company men as trappers instead of relying wholly on trade with the Indians. In his first outfit he took 55 men, 195 horses, 300 beaver traps, and a stock of merchandise, but no provisions, since he lived off the country. One hundred and fifty-four pack horses were needed to bring out his furs. In 1820–1821 he went out with seventy-five trappers, and returned without the loss of a man.

McKenzie embodied the dynamic enterprise which had once characterized the Nor'Westers as lords of the lakes and the forests in the Old Northwest and in the Canadian Plains, but he was frustrated by the apathy of his associates in the new Northwest. Enterprise was not a general characteristic of Nor'Westers at Fort George, but the days of the North West Company on the Columbia were numbered.

[7] Frederick Merk, *Fur Trade and Empire* (1931), 65; *New Light on the Early History of the Greater North West; The Manuscript Journals of Alexander Henry and David Thompson . . .*, Elliott Coues, ed., 3 vols. (1897); Alexander Ross, *Adventures of the First Settlers . . .; The Fur Hunters of the Far West*, Kenneth A. Spalding, ed. (1956); and Ross Cox, *The Columbia River . . .*, E. I. and J. R. Stewart, eds. (1957).

CHAPTER
EIGHT

An Interlude of Diplomacy

THE WAR OF 1812 had advanced the fortunes of the Nor'Westers over those of the Astorians: the Canadians were in control of the trade west of the Rockies, unchallenged by American competitors. However, in the negotiations which ended hostilities, the United States asserted claims to the region, and the Pacific Northwest entered the arena of Anglo-American controversy.

The Far Northwest was in no way connected with the complex issues which had brought the United States and Great Britain to war. In a most casual manner, the area entered into the negotiations which followed. But having become an issue of the peace, the region took on importance in the national interest.

Since Jefferson had opened the way for American expansion into the trans-Mississippi West, a subtle change of political attitudes toward this expansion had taken place. It will be recalled that Jefferson's continental policy aimed at protecting the new nation from hostile neighbors by any expedient means. He did not underestimate the drive of the American people toward territorial growth. It was, he held, "impossible not to look forward to distant times, when our rapid multiplication will expand . . . and cover the whole northern if not the southern continent, with people speaking the same language, governed in similar forms, and by similar laws." However, in his conception of the nature of the union—a federation of independent republics with a central government of limited powers—the function of the federal government was to defend but not to define the republics' interests. Although he was an ideological imperialist—that is, he would encourage republican institutions throughout the world as well as in the western hemisphere—Jefferson did not favor expansion that might breed imperial ambitions in the nation.

By 1812 his followers had departed from his strict constructionist views and become ardently nationalistic. The War Hawks whispered of their hankering to acquire Cuba and called for the conquest of Canada. The War of 1812 itself was, in large part, the expression of a militant and expansionist nationalism for which the federal government was the implementing agent. When the progress of the war established that Canada was securely British, it became federal policy to contain Britain within set boundaries, while losing no opportunity to extend American dominion. So it happened that while much of the peace negotiation was concerned with maritime matters—fisheries, impressment of sailors, trade, and navigation—boundary issues were a major problem, not easily solved. We shall concern ourselves here with only the western aspects of the problem.

After the purchase of Louisiana and completion of the Lewis and Clark expedition, Great Britain and the United States had tacitly accepted as their mutual boundary the 49th parallel from the Lake of the Woods west "as far as the respective territories" of the two powers extended.[1] This prudently vague statement allowed the British to assume the limit of the United States to be the Rocky Mountains. In the opinion of fur traders on the Missouri, however, there was no question but that the territory of the United States extended to the Pacific Ocean. Such was the assumption underlying Jeremy Pinch's ultimatum to David Thompson, and the one on which American statesmen acted in 1814 and for forty years thereafter.

Circumstances of domestic and foreign politics from 1790 to 1828 brought experienced diplomats into the State Department and then to the presidency, giving consistency to the nation's foreign policy. James Monroe and John Quincy Adams inherited the Jeffersonian principle of isolation from European politics and entanglements. They also inherited—or acquired—a strong conviction that national destiny made it incumbent upon the central government to anticipate the national interest. Both Monroe and Adams figured in the negotiations

[1] *Diplomatic Correspondence of the United States: Canadian Relations, 1784–1860*, William R. Manning, ed., 3 vols. (1940–1945), I, 278. Hereafter cited as *Canadian Relations*.

which followed the War of 1812; Monroe as Secretary of State and then as President, Adams as peace commissioner and then as Secretary of State.[2]

THE TREATY OF GHENT (1814) AND THE RESTORATION OF ASTORIA

Adams and his fellow peace commissioners had already received their instructions when Monroe, almost as an afterthought, reminded them that "the United States had in their possession at the commencement of the war a post at the Mouth of the River Columbia . . ." If it could be shown that this possession had been "wrested" from Americans in war, then this should be so stipulated in case the eventual treaty provided for reciprocal restitution of captured territories. Further, Monroe set up the position that the commissioners were to take if the question of western boundaries arose. The United States adhered to this position even though at times its demands were enlarged for bargaining purposes:

> On no pretext can the British Government set up a claim to territory, South of the Northern Boundary of the United States. It is not believed that they have any claim whatever to Territory on the Pacific Ocean. You will however be careful, should a definition of boundary be attempted not to countenance, in any manner or in any quarter a pretension of the British Government to Territory South of that line.[3]

The Treaty of Ghent did not take up boundary issues, except to provide for a commission to negotiate a settlement of the Maine boundary. The Pacific Northwest was not even mentioned. However the treaty contained a provision that "all territory, places and possessions . . . taken by either party" during hostilities, should be restored "without delay." As soon as the treaty was ratified (March, 1815), Monroe announced to the British attaché in Washington that Fort Astoria came under this provision. There the matter rested until 1817. Adams, by now Monroe's Secretary of State, while laying a groundwork for discussions of the Maine boundary as provided for in the treaty, abruptly requested the restoration of Astoria, and ordered

[2] Samuel F. Bemis, *John Quincy Adams and the Foundations of American Foreign Policy* (1949); Bradford Perkins, *Prologue to War: England and the United States, 1805–1812* (1961), and *Castlereagh and Adams, 1812–1823* (1964).

[3] *Canadian Relations*, I, 218.

special agent John B. Prevost to the Columbia to claim national authority and dominion with appropriate rites and symbols.

Fort Astoria was, in effect, doubly restored. While Prevost was delayed, awaiting British participation in the restoration ritual, Captain James Biddle of the *U.S. Ontario* appeared at Astoria in the late summer of 1818 and took possession of both shores of the Columbia. Two months later, after the surprised British government had given reluctant consent to Adams' demand, Prevost arrived on the British vessel *Blossom*. The British captain lowered the Union Jack and Prevost hoisted the Stars and Stripes. The Nor'Westers watched with interest and accepted with grace Prevost's concession that they could remain in charge of the post.

The British government protested this abrupt assertion of American claims. Adams blandly replied that the British had no authorized establishment on the Columbia and that they had "intimated no question whatever to the title of the United States" to Astor's settlement before the war. It had not therefore occurred to him that the United States' title was now "an object of interest" to Great Britain. He warned also that if it should ever become an object of serious importance to the United States, Great Britain would not find it either "useful or advisable" to resist.

Richard Rush, minister to London, probably did not submit verbatim to Lord Castlereagh Adams' ironical treatment of British territorial claims or his bold announcement that the Pacific Northwest fell within the United States' "natural dominion."

> If the United States leave her [Great Britain] in undisturbed enjoyment of all of her holds upon Europe, Asia, and Africa, with her actual possessions in this hemisphere, we may very fairly expect that she will not think it consistent either with a wise or a friendly policy, to watch with eyes of jealousy and alarm, every possibility of extension to our natural dominion in North America, which she can have no solid interest to prevent, until all possibility of her preventing it shall have vanished.[4]

The British argued ineffectually that Astor's post had been sold to the North West Company prior to its capture. They admitted that the Americans were justified in demanding return of the fort on the same principle by which Britain had demanded restoration in the Nootka controversy. But Castlereagh would not admit that consent to restoration settled the matter of sovereignty, and he requested further consideration of the boundary line between the two nations in the Far West.

[4] *Canadian Relations*, I, 268–269.

THE BOUNDARY ISSUE AND
CONVENTION OF 1818

Thus the Pacific Northwest boundary question appeared on the agenda of the commissioners' meeting called in the fall of 1818 to iron out other problems connected with the treaty.

Albert Gallatin and Richard Rush, the American commissioners, conceded that the United States did not have a perfect right to the country west of the Rocky Mountains, but they held that their country's claim was as good as Great Britain's. As to lands drained by the Columbia, they argued indisputable rights on the basis of discovery, exploration, and the settlement at Fort Astoria.

The British commissioners intimated that their government might accept the 49th parallel to where it crossed the Columbia River, and from that point let the river itself form the boundary—provided that the two powers held the river mouth in common ownership. This proposal was unacceptable to the Americans, since it would bring the British south of the 49th parallel. Facing other issues of greater immediate importance, after lengthy and fruitless discussion the commissioners agreed to a convention which postponed settlement of the Pacific Northwest boundary issue, and at the same time provided against its becoming a source of international friction.

It was agreed that the boundary between the United States and Canada should follow the 49th parallel to the Rockies but that

> . . . any such Country as may be claimed by either Party on the North West Coast of America, or on the continent of America Westward of the Stony Mountains shall . . . be free and open, for the term of ten years . . . to the vessels, Citizens and Subjects of the Two Powers; it being well understood that this Agreement is not to be construed to the Prejudice of any claim, which either of the Two High Contracting Powers may have to any part of the said Country; nor shall it be taken to affect the Claims of any other Power or State to any part of the said Country. . . .

In popular terms the Convention of 1818 has been known as the "joint occupation" agreement. But, as Samuel Bemis has pointed out, there was no such thing as joint occupancy. The convention simply meant that for ten years the region west of the Rockies was "free and open," without prejudice to either nation's claims or to those of other nations. This was essentially the method of conciliation Great Britain had found satisfactory in dealing with Spain in the Nootka controversy.

An Interlude of Diplomacy

There is no evidence to suggest that British statecraft considered colonization of the Far West. Not so with the Americans. The United States was an expanding nation; in its vocabulary expansion now meant colonization and ultimate absorption into the Union of lands which fell within its "natural dominion." Under the leadership of Adams, government took the initiative in establishing claims to such lands.

The Idea of Natural Dominion

Within six years after the acceptance of the Convention of 1818, Adams had eliminated two possible contenders to title in the Pacific Northwest. His 1819 Spanish "Treaty of Amity, Settlement and Limits" secured Spain's formal surrender of East and West Florida, areas already infiltrated by Americans. It also transferred to the United States the Spanish claims to all lands west of the source of the Arkansas River and north of the 42nd parallel to the Pacific. It was later argued that through this agreement, the United States succeeded to the original Spanish claims. The question was academic, but that Adams secured this provision reveals his determination to allow no ambiguities which might weaken the United States' case for an enlarged "natural dominion." He firmly believed that ". . . the remainder of the continent should ultimately be ours," although it was "very lately that we have distinctly seen this ourselves; very lately that we have avowed the pretension of extending to the South Sea." To Adams the United States and North America were "identical."[5]

THE RUSSIAN THREAT

The Russians were also possible contenders for title to the western shore. Although her nationals had settlements on islands off the Alaskan coast, Russia did not seem actively concerned with claims on the continent. In 1806 Baron Nikolai Rezanov, one of the organizers of the Russian American Company, had urged the establishment of a colony at the mouth of the Columbia River, where, he pointed out, his country "could attract population . . . and become strong enough to make use of any turn in European politics to include the coast of California in the Russian possessions."[6] Four years later, when Astor

[5] *Memoirs of John Quincy Adams*, C. F. Adams, ed., 12 vols. (1874–1877), IV, 438–439.

[6] Hubert H. Bancroft, *The North West Coast*, 2 vols. (1884–1886), I, 321.

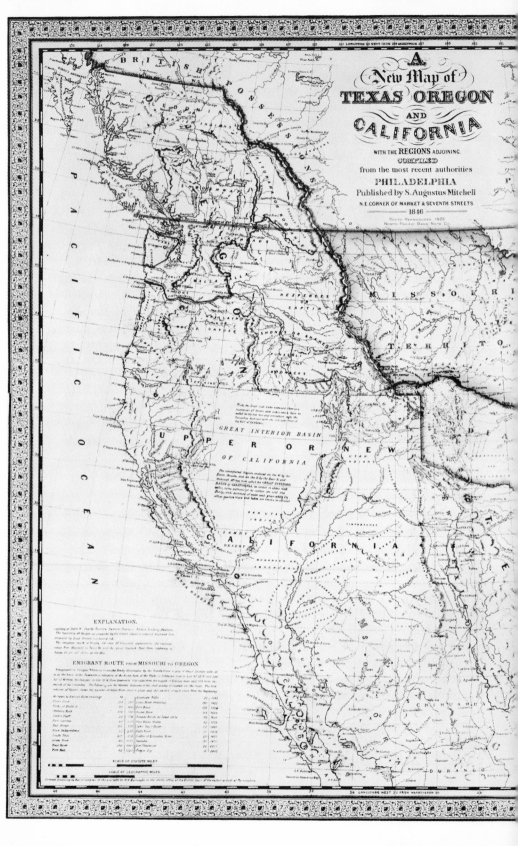

A
New Map of
TEXAS OREGON
AND
CALIFORNIA
WITH THE REGIONS ADJOINING.
COMPILED
from the most recent authorities
PHILADELPHIA
Published by S. Augustus Mitchell
N.E. CORNER OF MARKET & SEVENTH STREETS
1846

sought a contract to supply the Russian settlements from his projected depot on the Columbia, the Chancery at St. Petersburg informed Adams, then minister to Russia, that it would not object to trade between Russian colonies and the Astorian post, but that Russia's claims in America extended to the mouth of the Columbia. Adams was told that Russian maps "included the whole of Nootka Sound, and down to the mouth of Columbia River, as part of the Russian possessions." As he understood the situation, the Russian government was more interested in curtailing British commercial power by encouraging the Americans than it was in developing the naval power necessary to set up and protect colonies of its own.

However, in 1812, with the consent of Spain, the Russians founded Fort Ross on Bodega Bay in California, and later in the same year established a post in the Hawaiian Islands. This prompted Monroe to suggest in 1816 that the United States and Russia enter into a treaty to ensure their continuing amity in North America, and he proposed the 49th parallel as a boundary between their interests. The treaty was not pushed, but it is noteworthy that in his proposal Monroe ignored British claims in the area.

When Adams became Secretary of State, he suggested that the United States minister to Russia "observe attentively" the Muscovites' movements with regard to settlements on the coast. He did not believe that Emperor Alexander displayed "symptoms of the Passion which so vehemently prompted his ancestor Peter to make Russia a Naval Power"; nevertheless, he felt extreme caution was needed in dealing with him. As a leader of Europe's conservative reaction to the French revolutionary and Napoleonic eras, Alexander was intent upon restoring the Old Regime and undermining British power wherever possible. Thus to Adams, in 1818,

> . . . the whole System of Russian policy, as it bears on her Relations with Great Britain, with the European Alliance [the Holy Alliance], with Spain and the South American affairs, may require the most steady and attentive observation as it may link itself with objects of importance to the interests and welfare of the United States.[7]

Later in the same year John Prevost reported on his journey to the Columbia and his visit to California. The establishment of Fort Ross on Bodega Bay had dangerous implications. Not far distant was San Francisco Bay, a harbor "the most convenient, capacious and safe in the world." Spanish rule was weak, the population disaffected, and the harbor undefended. Prevost concluded that the Russians had in

[7] *Canadian Relations*, I, 275–276.

mind "early possession of this harbor and ultimately . . . the sovereignty of entire California." "Surely," he concluded

> . . . the growth of a race on these shores, scarcely emerged from the savage state, guided by a Chief who seeks not to emancipate but to inthrall, is an event by all to be deprecated. An event the mere apprehension of which I should think ought to excite the jealousies of the United States, so far at least, as to induce the cautionary measure of preserving a Station which may serve as a Barrier to a northern aggrandizement.[8]

In September, 1821, Alexander invited further suspicion when he issued a ukase excluding non-Russians from trading on the northern coast from Bering Strait to the 51st parallel and forbidding foreign vessels to approach within 100 Italian miles of the shore. Although this ultimatum had no force unless it was backed up by action, both the United States and Great Britain protested it. And although Russia had adopted the 51st parallel—two degrees above the line Monroe had earlier proposed—as the southern limit of her sphere of interest, circumstances had so changed in the intervening years that Adams could not be happy with the Russian position. While he would recognize Russia's rights to certain islands north of 55 degrees, he announced his nation's intention to contest any other nation's claim to continental territory.

These were years of harassment and worry for Adams. He was more ambitious for the presidency than he would admit. His succession to that office was being fought by men who seized any and every occasion to embarrass him. While Adams was negotiating with Great Britain over the northeastern boundary and fishing rights, his enemies tried to make it appear that he was sacrificing American rights in the Far Northwest. In Congress, Senator Benton from Missouri charged that "sovereignty of the Columbia" had been surrendered to Britain. Senator Lloyd of Boston protested that the State Department was not taking a strong stand against Russian interference with fishing rights in the North Pacific. In December, 1820, Senator Floyd of Virginia introduced a resolution calling for a congressional investigation of the settlements on the Pacific Ocean and for a report on the "expediency of occupying the Columbia." He introduced the so-called Oregon Bill again in 1821, and when the Russian ukase came up, Floyd demanded the transportation of artillery to the mouth of the Columbia to protect American interests. Again in February, 1823, he introduced a resolution calling upon the Committee on Military Affairs to make an

[8] *Ibid.*, I, 891.

appropriation to "take and retain possession of the territories of the United States on the Northwest Coast of America."

Senator John Floyd's cousin, Charles Floyd, a sergeant with the Lewis and Clark Expedition, had died on the Missouri; the Senator had known the Astorians Ramsay Crooks and Russell Farnham, and had become an ardent advocate of national expansion that would include the Columbia region. Adams charged that Floyd formed "gigantic projects upon crude and half-digested information" and was leagued with Clay of Kentucky and Benton of Missouri to undermine Adams' position.

Although exasperated, Adams wisely refrained from precipitous action. Early in 1823 Russia was in a mood to negotiate. When talks got under way, Adams informed Richard Rush, minister to Great Britain, with regard to the official United States position in the Northwest; he also clarified his own views for the benefit of his enemies in the Senate.

"It is not imaginable," he said, "that in the present condition of the world, *any* European Nation should entertain the project of settling a *Colony* on the Northwest Coast of America,"

> . . . but that the United States should form establishments there with views of absolute territorial right, and inland communication is not only to be expected, but is pointed out by the finger of Nature. . . . the American Continents henceforth will no longer be subjects of Colonization. Occupied by civilized Independent Nations, they will be accessible to Europeans and to each other on that footing alone, and the Pacific Ocean in every part of it will remain open to the Navigation of all nations in like manner with the Atlantic. . . .
>
> The application of Colonial principles of exclusion, therefore, cannot be admitted by the United States as lawful upon any part of the Northwest Coast of America, or as belonging to any European nation. Their own settlements there, when organized as territorial Governments, will be adapted to the freedom of their own Institutions, and as constituent parts of the Union, be subject to the principles and provisions of the Constitution.[9]

This principle of noncolonization was set forth in President Monroe's annual message to Congress in December, 1823: "The American continents, by the free and independent condition which they have assumed and maintained, are henceforth not to be considered as subjects for future colonization by any European powers."

The Monroe Doctrine had other ramifications with which we are not here concerned. But with regard to North America, it formalized

[9] *Ibid.*, II, 58, 64.

a long developing policy of American continentalism and exclusive sovereignty. This was not a policy Great Britain wanted to hear enunciated unilaterally by the United States at just that juncture, but because it in effect upheld the British position on Russian expansion in North America and in other respects supported Britain's views concerning South America, it was acclaimed as the New World's answer to the Old.

Adams moved swiftly, if not tactfully, to reach rapport with Russia, and a convention was signed in April, 1824. Russia consented to a southern boundary at 50 degrees, 41 minutes. Between this latitude and 49 degrees, it was agreed that both powers should enjoy free and equal navigation and commerce.

THE ISSUE OF SOVEREIGNTY

The issue of sovereignty was now limited to two contestants: Great Britain and the United States. In 1824 Richard Rush tried to attain some agreement in accord with Adams' stand of the summer before. He proposed an extension of the Convention of 1818 for ten more years, with the further stipulation that the British would make no settlements south of 51 degrees north latitude. Evidently Rush hoped that such demands would make the British fall back gratefully upon the 1818 American offer of the 49th parallel to the sea. However, the British commissioners took the position their predecessors had hinted at in 1818: they would accept the 49th parallel to where it intersected the Columbia and then the Columbia would be the boundary to the Pacific. The negotiations were inconclusive, but at least the "Oregon Question" was defined. It was a dispute for the territory, including Puget Sound, which lay between the 49th parallel on the north and the Columbia River on the south, between the ocean and the Columbia on the east.

Great Britain had followed with interest and not a little annoyance John Floyd's persistent efforts to create an Oregon territory. In December 1824 he had managed to get through the House a bill authorizing the President to occupy Oregon with a military post and to organize a government there. The bill failed in the Senate, but the prospect of its success prompted Richard Rush to warn his government that if it attempted in any way to exercise exclusive jurisdiction over both shores of the Columbia, even while keeping within the limits of 49 degrees north, "serious difficulties" with Great Britain would result. Furthermore, the report of a congressional committee, headed by Francis Baylies of Massachusetts, took such a belligerent tone in backing American claims that, according to Britain's Prime Minister, it had "almost the appearance of a Manifesto issued on declaring war."[10]

In this mood, Prime Minister Canning invited Albert Gallatin and Richard Rush to discuss the problem once more. Why he chose this time (1826) is difficult to explain. One possibility is that he wished to settle the controversy before the Americans, in Congress and at large, generated more heat about their rights in the Far West. Frederick Merk in *Albert Gallatin and the Oregon Question* (1950) has argued that Canning was forced to act because the HBC demanded clarification of the government's position before undertaking further development of its establishments. The company was acting on the assumption that the lower Columbia—that is, from the junction of the Snake westward—would be part of the boundary line. It was now suggested to Canning that this line be extended east along the line 46 degrees 20 minutes to the Continental Divide and thence north to where the Divide and the 49th parallel intersected.

As it happened, circumstances did not promise success for the negotiations. It took all the tact and diplomacy of aged Albert Gallatin, the United States special minister, to keep discussion alive. Futile concessions were made by each side. Gallatin's proposal was the perpetual free navigation of the Columbia south of 49 degrees. The British retreated to their former position in which the Columbia was the boundary, and offered to yield to the United States a small strip of shoreline, an enclave, on Puget Sound as compensation for the loss of that inland sea.

Two points were stressed repeatedly during the conferences: the British emphasis that they had no intention of colonizing the Oregon country and wished only to protect their right to trade there; and the equally repetitive assertion by the United States that it expected eventually to hold exclusive dominion up to the 49th parallel.

The outcome of weeks and months of discussion, terminating in August, 1827, was disheartening to the tired American commissioners. It was also distinctly anticlimactic. The Convention of 1818 was extended indefinitely, with but one change: either party could terminate it with one year's notice.

However, when Adams left the presidency in 1828, relations between his country and Great Britain were relatively harmonious. Much had been accomplished in his fourteen years of concern over the

[10] Quoted in Raymond Walter, Jr., *Albert Gallatin, Jeffersonian Financier and Diplomat* (1957), 335.

Pacific Northwest. He and his associates had, for all practical purposes, made firm United States claims to the Northwest from the Rockies to the Pacific, between 42 degrees and 49 degrees. The area of continuing dispute was, roughly, that part of Washington lying west of the Cascades. But the British had won something also. By accepting the Convention of 1818 and its renewal in 1827, they had kept the country open for the British fur trade.

CHAPTER
NINE

The Era of the Hudson's Bay Company

FROM 1814 to 1821, while diplomats labored to keep the peace between the United States and Britain, internal strife within the North West Company had weakened its operations. Merchant proprietors and wintering partners no longer worked in harmony. At the same time competition over the Athabaskan trade and in the Red River country had led to open warfare with the HBC. To end the scandalous situation, the British government stepped in to force a coalition of the rivals in 1821. The coalition was to run for twenty-one years, but by 1825 it was apparent that the HBC had absorbed its former rival.

The HBC remained intact as a joint-stock company but was enlarged by the addition of the North West Company's proprietors. It retained exclusive trade privileges in Rupert's Land. A royal grant of December, 1821, extended these privileges, rent free, to land outside the Canadian provinces and to the Pacific slope. By Deed of Covenant, the company agreed to abide by the terms embodied in an Act of Parliament (July, 1821) "regulating the Fur Trade and establishing a Criminal and Civil Jurisdiction within certain parts of North America." The company was charged to prevent trade in liquor with the Indians, to obey regulations for the improvement of Indian conditions, and to exercise jurisdiction over employees charged with criminal

122

offenses and over civil suits in which less than 200 pounds was involved. In cases where the sum was greater or the crime more heinous—manslaughter for example—the company was to bring the case to the courts of Lower Canada. It was not to trade in American territories or to exclude American traders from the region covered by the Convention of 1818.

All policy decisions rested with the Governor and Committee in London. Administration was placed in the hands of wintering personnel of Northern and Southern departments, each of which had a governor and council composed of twenty-five chief factors and eight chief traders. Wintering partners of the North West Company who chose not to retire were, with a few exceptions, assigned to administrative positions. In some cases it was difficult for old Nor'Westers who had fought the HBC so long and vigorously to enter meekly into this new order; but enter they did and in time their loyalty was unquestioned.

SIMPSON AND THE COLUMBIA DEPARTMENT

In Scottish-born George Simpson, trained in business practices, the Committee found so efficient a governor for the Northern Department that within several years he was sole head of the company in Canada and the architect of its policies. Through his personal friendship with Andrew Wedderburn, Lord Colvile, deputy governor and chief executive of the London Commmittee, he had the sympathetic ear of that body which, on the whole, followed his recommendations.

The independence of the wintering partners which had characterized the North West Company, was surrendered to Simpson's management. A new accounting system in the London office made it possible to keep track of sales and inventories; purchasing was centralized, and outfits for a year in advance of the trade were dispatched regularly. "Men of the Country," sturdy French Canadians, replaced imported Orkney men. Efficiency, in manpower as well as in provisioning and trading, was Simpson's objective. His word for it was economy.

Petty in dealings with subordinates, Simpson was nevertheless a man of large ideas, shared with, if not first promoted by, Colvile. The expansion of company enterprises in the Pacific Northwest was one of these ideas. Simpson's policies evolved from first-hand acquaintance with the region, to which he made two lightning-fast tours of inspection in 1824 and 1828, from recommendations of men who knew the land (and who were seldom given credit for their ideas), and from the ambiguities of the diplomatic situation.

The Convention of 1818 had provided for "free and open" trade in the Pacific Northwest for ten years. When Simpson toured the Columbia Department in 1824 he was confident that the convention would be renewed for another period; but he knew also that American trappers were once more moving toward the Rockies. He had to act quickly to protect the company's interests on both long-range and short-term conditions.

The Columbia Department extended from the Russian settlements to Spanish California; from the Rockies to the Pacific Ocean. Assuming that the Columbia River would eventually form the boundary between Canada and the United States, Simpson therefore adopted a policy of trapping out the lands that might go to the Americans. This procedure would serve two purposes: it would remove the chief attraction for American hunters, and it would forestall the settlers who seemed inevitably to follow hunters' trails. The vast, vaguely defined area known as the Snake River country, stripped of fur-bearing animals, would become a barrier rather than an inducement to American occupation. Furthermore, the largely untapped riches of the Snake country could carry the cost of developing the rest of the department until it was self-supporting.

Simpson immediately ordered a step-up in the conduct of the Snake River trapping expeditions. Initiated in 1816 by Donald McKenzie, they had been continued by able but unaggressive Alexander Ross in 1823 and 1824. Simpson replaced Ross with tough-minded, hard-driving Peter Skene Ogden.

Ogden was one of the few wintering Nor'Westers not taken into the coalition in 1821; but when Simpson had need for Ogden's particular qualities, he was brought in as a chief trader and assigned to the Snake country.[1] Ogden spent six harrowing years (1824–1831) exploring and trapping wherever he anticipated American intrusion. He traversed Idaho, northern Utah, and Nevada, where he discovered the Humboldt River; he explored central and southern Oregon and northern California. On his last expedition (1829–1830) his search for the mythical River Buenaventura led him to the Gulf of California. He was the HBC's outstanding explorer in the Far West.

For the rest of the department, north of the Columbia, Simpson planned permanent occupation. This meant reliance upon trade with

---

[1] *Ogden's Snake Country Journals, 1824–26*, E. E. Rich, ed., *HBS* XIII (1950); *Peter Skene Ogden's Snake Country Journal, 1826–27*, K. G. Davies, ed., *HBS* XXIII (1961); Gloria Griffin Cline, *Exploring the Great Basin* (1963).

the Indians at trading posts rather than upon roving bands of company trappers, and conservation rather than extermination of the beaver. New Caledonia, for example, was preserved through careful cultivation of the native trade. Here can be illustrated the distinguishing features of the trading post system.

The Post System of Trade

The fur trade had the same motivation as commerce generally: to satisfy the demands of people holding a valuable commodity which they would exchange to satisfy their wants. To increase their range of wants was profitable and was believed to be a civilizing agent. The HBC improved upon this maxim, as have others before and since, by limiting the opportunities to find satisfactions elsewhere—that is, by eliminating competition. The Indians consumed British goods and produced furs which supplied the London market; hence, a large part of the world's demand for fine furs. On the goods sold to the Indians, and on the furs they received, the company usually made a tidy profit.

A district trade was profitable when its returns in furs exceeded the cost of its outfit. In 1826 the formula for figuring costs of trading goods in the Columbia Department was prime cost plus a 70 percent markup, although 33⅓ percent normally covered all charges. In bartering with the Indians, traders had to set prices that would show a profit over the marked-up cost. Using the prime beaver pelt as the unit of trade, a trap, essential to conservation practices, cost the Indians of New Caledonia six skins. In 1833–1834, the cost of the outfit for New Caledonia district was 3000 pounds. The returns, at London prices, reached an estimated 11,000 pounds.

In order to increase the returns from their districts, traders adopted a credit system which tended to keep the Indians forever in debt to the company. Not until 1839 was this practice discontinued. Under monopoly conditions, the natives not only became increasingly dependent upon company posts for goods that had become essential to their living, but for foodstuffs as well. In time, the Indians' living leveled off to a subsistence standard and they became, in a sense, wards of the company.

Where new posts should be located and when old ones should be abandoned were questions decided by weighing practical considerations: potentialities of fur production; facilities for supply and communication; advantages in meeting or forestalling competition and/or opening new areas of trade; and, important to Simpson's economy program, conditions which made the posts self-sustaining in food. It

125

was also important that no major investments should be made in areas the company might lose when the boundary question was settled with the United States.

The company inherited from the North West Company four posts which might eventually go to the Americans. Flathead House was continued for a while as a supply depot for trapping expeditions into the Blackfoot and the Snake River countries and as an outpost against American competitors. Spokane House was a special object of Simpson's indignation when, in 1824, he found its people guilty of "an extraordinary predilection for European Provisions" whose cost made their diet like "eating Gold." It was abandoned in 1825 when Fort Colville was founded. Making few returns in furs, Colville was an important depot for the overland express; it produced fish in abundance, and by 1850 it was a granary for the northern interior posts.

Fort Nez Perce (Walla Walla) became the outfitting post for Snake River expeditions after 1826. The Nez Perces held the "Key of the River" from the Okanogan to the Dalles of the Columbia. They supplied horses for the Snake parties and were instrumental in keeping peace with warlike tribes to the south. Furthermore, this post was economical: in Simpson's Spartan opinion it could be supported by the river and a potato garden.

Fort George—old Astoria—produced neither furs nor food. It had a deepwater anchorage and seemed a logical site for the company's chief depot. But deep water was not especially important for ships of light draft, and American claims to the site were formidable. After Fort Vancouver was built (1824–1825) a man was kept at the old site to report arrival of company ships and as a lookout for American traders. In 1826 or 1827 the Indians pulled down the stockade and burned the buildings.

When Simpson was finally convinced that the Columbia was the only route by which interior posts could communicate with the sea— and it took a hair-raising voyage down the Fraser in 1828 to convince him that that river was not navigable—Fort Vancouver became the capital and headquarters of the department.

This palisaded outpost of empire, 100 miles inland on the north bank of the Columbia, was originally set on a bluff overlooking the river and a landscape "sublimely grand," to quote David Douglas, English botanist who first visited it in 1825. But a vista of river, valley, and "mountains covered with perpetual snow," eight-foot-tall stalks of wild lupine on the prairie, blue scilla on the riverbanks, or blooming salal with shining leaves touching up the shadowed edges of the forests—were not as gratifying to Simpson as fertile soil under cultivation or meadows grazed by herds of cattle.

126

Within five years, the farm at Fort Vancouver was supplying wheat, peas, barley, pork, and beef. Cattle and hogs were imported from California and the Hawaiian Islands, sheep from England. When their number was too great to pasture on the plains near the fort, the cattle were swum across the Columbia to Wapato (Sauvie) Island, across Multnomah Channel, and trailed over the hills to the Tualatin Plains. A neat vegetable garden, orchard, and vineyard produced abundantly under skilled Scottish gardeners. Apples grew so thick on the limbs of dwarfed trees that they looked like "onions fastened in rows on a string." To live at Fort Vancouver was to live well, and fish and wild game, staples of diet at many posts, were less the regular fare than additions to it.

The fort was removed from the bluff to the plain, nearer the river, early in 1829. By 1846 it was an enclosure, roughly 732 by 450 feet, surrounded by a high palisade of hewed logs fitted closely together and firmly buttressed inside. At its northwest and southwest corners bastions mounted several small cannon which, never used, were tributes to peace rather than symbols of war. Within the walls there were two courts around which were ranged one-story buildings housing officers and clerks, warehouses and workshops. Opposite the great gate stood the residence of the Chief Factor, and to its right, Bachelors' Hall, the common room for gentlemen and clerks.[2]

Over this "New York of the Pacific Ocean" Chief Factor John McLoughlin ruled.

DR. JOHN MCLOUGHLIN, CHIEF FACTOR

Born at Riviére du Loup, Canada, in 1784, McLoughlin was thirty-nine years old when he was appointed to the department. He had studied medicine in Quebec in the fashion of the time, and entered the service of the North West Company in which he became a partner in 1814. He bitterly fought the HBC in the Red River country and was one of the agents of the Nor'Westers when the coalition was arranged.[3] He was not easily reconciled to the new order, and some of his associates thought he was exiled to the Columbia because of his

[2] John Hussey, *The History of Fort Vancouver and its Physical Structure* (1957).

[3] W. Kaye Lamb's introductions to *McLoughlin's Fort Vancouver Letters, First Series 1825–1838*, HBS IV (1941), *Second Series 1839–1844*, HBS VI (1943), and *Third Series 1844–1846*, HBS (1944), E. E. Rich, ed.

partisanship. His exile, if such it was, made him the chief figure of Northwest history for almost a quarter of a century.

From their first meeting, Simpson appears to have disliked McLoughlin. En route to the Columbia in 1824, Simpson caught up with McLoughlin, who had a twenty-day start, and noted in his journal that

> . . . he was such a figure as I should not like to meet in a dark night in one of the byelanes in the neighborhood of London. . . . He was dressed in Clothes that had once been fashionable, but now covered with a thousand patches of different Colors, his beard would do honor to the chin of a Grizzly Bear, his face and hands evidently Shewing up that he had not lost much time at his Toilette, loaded with Arms and his own herculean dimensions forming a tout ensemble, that would convey a good idea of the highway men of former days.[4]

McLoughlin never became a dandy, but as Chief Factor of the Columbia River Department he was never again compared in appearance to a highwayman. Inclined toward corpulence, he impressed observers as a large man. He was often described as dignified and of courtly manner. His hair, prematurely gray but thick and bushy, framed a mobile face. His blue eyes could be kindly, but they could also grow icy, or flash with the temper he displayed on more than one occasion. To the Indians whom he ruled with a firm but just hand, McLoughlin was *hyas tyee*, a good chief. He was the "good doctor" to those missionaries and settlers who experienced—and happened to appreciate—his generosity.

But if Simpson was Emperor to some of his officers, McLoughlin was tyrant to those immediately under him. An able administrator where the trade followed the patterns of his earlier experience, and successful in carrying out Simpson's plans for agricultural development and diversified trade, he nevertheless suffered from the many demands made upon him. He was confident when dealing with Indians, whom he understood; but, subject to orders he considered inappropriate to local conditions, or with crises in his own personal life, he panicked, suffered from a nervous stomach, and exploded in violent tempers. His all-too-evident humanity does not detract from, but rather enhances, a character often portrayed in Olympian composure and granite serenity.

As Chief Factor, McLoughlin was expected to exercise discretionary powers as to appointments, outfits, distribution of personnel, and in all matters in which time and distance made it impossible to ask di-

---

[4] *Fur Trade and Empire: George Simpson's Journal, 1824–1825*, Frederick Merk, ed. (1931), 23.

rection from the Governor or Committee. It was his responsibility to see that policies broadly outlined by the London Committee, and more minutely by Governor Simpson, were carried out. This meant the economical administration of the Department and a profitable harvest of furs; establishment of new posts; supervision of personnel, numerous agricultural enterprises, the Indian trade, trapping expeditions, and a marine department; development of the region's resources other than furs, such as timber and fish, and opening of new markets for them; and the conduct of business with Russians in Alaska, with Californians, and with Americans.

Life at the Trading Posts

Fort Vancouver was the headquarters and nerve center of the company's business.[5] From here runners were dispatched with news and orders to outlying posts: to Colville, word that fifty horses were needed at Fort Nez Perce to outfit the Snake brigade; to Chief Trader Black at Fort Nez Perce, that an American trader had slipped up the river to the Dalles, and that Black was to reduce company prices temporarily; to John Work, leading a trapping party to northern California, that he was to meet Michel Laframboise and his men at the Umpqua; to William Connolly at Bear's Lake in northern Caledonia, that leather was needed at Fort Colville. To the fort came runners, bringing word of disasters: the Clallams at New Dungeness had attacked a party and killed two company men (1828); the *Isabella* wrecked at the mouth of the Columbia and her crew lost (1830); one of Ogden's *bateaux* had swamped at the Dalles and nine men drowned (1830); and—bitter news—McLoughlin's son John was murdered at Stikine (1842).

The fort hummed with the sounds of industry: the tinsmith fashioned utensils, the blacksmith beat iron into farm tools, coopers shaped casks for furs and salted salmon, carpenters strained their skill to build seagoing schooners. From early summer until late fall the tempo of life was strenuous. The annual ship arrived and goods had to be unloaded, checked, and assigned to outfits. Clerks worked from morning to midnight on annual accounts, checking and rechecking figures to show that the Department had not done too badly for the year. Furs had to be packed and ready when, in the fall, the sails stood fair for England again.

Trapping expeditions must be readied and set off; those returning

[5] *McLoughlin's Fort Vancouver Letters*, whole series; Narcissa Whitman's diary, letters in *First White Women Over the Rockies*, Clifford M. Drury, ed., 2 vols. (1963), I.

welcomed with salutes and cheers. The overland express must leave on schedule, carrying special mail and passengers to Red River, to York, to Montreal and civilization. Stiff hands of officers and clerks worked late to complete a message to family or to friends. ". . . send the old Heron, a few late news papers, to show what is going on in the old countries; with a letter, of at least two sheets, closely written, to make him knowing in what is going on in this," wrote Chief Trader Francis Heron. Inquiries about the progress of children at school, orders for goods and clothing, comments on fellow workers and on the company's affairs, fill in the human side of the business on which McLoughlin annually, officially and impersonally, reported to Simpson and the directors. The seventy pounds of paper in a dispatch box, carried painfully over portages and the Athabaska Pass, told of the hopes, worries, and loneliness of the Columbians.

Yet life at the fort was a welcome relief from long months in wilderness posts; it was heaven in retrospect for those who, in roofless camps of trapping expeditions, kept nightlong watches against Indians. The fort was where breeches and jackets of leather were changed for cloth. After the formalities of dinner with McLoughlin, at a polished table set with Spode and silver, the gentlemen smoked their long clay pipes, told stories of their adventures, or browsed among the books William Fraser Tolmie circulated as the Columbia Library. Life in Bachelors' Hall was a better life than that in the field, where hunger sometimes pinched so hard that the squaws scraped animal skins and boiled them for food, and the talk was of the chances of surviving another day.

Occasionally the fort had distinguished visitors. Thomas Nuttall spent almost a year (1834–1835) botanizing the region. David Douglas was an attractive person as well as a distinguished botanist. As a result of his two trips to the Northwest (1825–1827, 1830–1832) he introduced hundreds of northwestern botanical items to the scientific world. His name is familiarly attached to the native pine, mistakenly called in his honor the Douglas fir.

When the company's own employees assembled at the departmental capital they contributed an air of distinction too. The gentlemen of the officer class were required to have something more than trading skill and lore of forests and plains. Lack of education was a handicap; its possession was almost a guarantee of advancement. Doctors John Kennedy and Meredith Gairdner were graduates of Edinburgh, Dr. William Tolmie of Glasgow. At twenty-two, Gairdner was author of a comprehensive work on mineral and thermal springs. Tolmie's interests ranged from belles lettres to scientific farming. Trader Charles Ross was a classical scholar. Peter Skene Ogden was educated in the law. James Douglas (later to succeed Simpson as governor),

Dugald Mactavish, Alexander Anderson, Roderick Finlayson, and George Barnston, among others, revealed in their letters, journals, and histories the measure of literacy Simpson applied to men "tolerably educated."

Their regular assignments were seldom as pleasant as life at the fort. At Fort St. James on Stuart's Lake poor soil, easily exhausted, made gardening impossible. Usually fish were plentiful and quantities were dried and packed for other posts and for the Indian trade. "Where there are no gardens, the men have only dried salmon, as poor fare as civilized man subsists on in any part of the world," wrote one victim of too many years of it. Fort Fraser, on Fraser's Lake, stood in a valley open to the southwest and protected from the cold northeast winds; rich, sandy soil and a relatively long growing season produced potatoes, turnips, and other vegetables.

At Fort George in New Caledonia four acres of land were cleared and planted to wheat. "Pancakes and hot rolls were thenceforward to be the order of the day; Babine salmon and dog's flesh were to be sent 'to Coventry,'" rejoiced Trader McLean. But a late spring was followed by a cold summer, early autumn frosts. No pancakes. Even the natives suffered at Fort McLeod, which in Simpson's view was "the most wretched place in the Indian Country." Connolly, or Bear Lake post, and Babine were hardly better. Yet these six northern posts yielded a gross return of 12,000 pounds, 9000 pounds net profit in 1828, and were expected to do better the next year.

It took four months for the "voyage out" and return from northern Caledonia: by boat from Fort Vancouver to Okanogan, and by horse brigade—250 to 300 animals in the train—from Okanogan to Kamloops. Many animals died from the rigors of this trip over winding mountain trails. At Alexandria, on the Fraser River near the present Quesnel, the brigade was met by men from the north in their lightweight but sturdy swiftwater canoes, who carried the supplies back to Stuart's Lake, to be distributed to other posts by "large and small canoes, Horses, Dog sleds and Men's backs."

Fort Alexandria enjoyed a setting almost like that of Fort Vancouver. There was pleasant diversity of hill, plain, and wooded groves— and of food. No one complained of Fort Alexandria.

Coastal posts were required to live, so far as possible, on country provisions, fish, and game. In one case, much to Simpson's delight, consumption actually returned a profit. At Taku, located between Sitka and the Taku River, twenty-four officers and men were maintained on venison got at "so cheap a rate from the natives, that we absolutely make a profit in our consumption of provisions, the skin of the animal selling for much more than is paid for the whole carcass."

At Fort Langley, on the lower Fraser, 800 barrels of dried and salted fish were put up in 1846, of which more than half was sold in the Hawaiian Islands at $9 a barrel.

THE MARINE DEPARTMENT AND COAST FORTS

Fort Langley was built in 1827 to protect the company from American traders, who still came to the coast though the great days of the sea otter trade were over. In 1829 and 1830, the natives made the most of the presence of opposition and raised their demands. The effect spread into the interior where the Indians threatened to carry their furs to tribes who dealt with Americans and got higher prices. Between 1827 and 1829 two irritatingly persistent Americans, Captain John Dominis, the *Owhyhee*, and Captain D. W. Thompson, the *Convoy*, not only traded along the coast but had the temerity to enter the Columbia. As transients they were extravagant in trade, and "excited quite a sensation among the natives." Prices returned to the old rates only when the Americans left.

Simpson cherished the notion that company trading vessels would stop the Americans, and reduce the need for expensive coastal establishments. He appointed a cousin, Captain Aemilius Simpson, to head a marine department. The *Cadboro* arrived from England in 1827, to spend subsequent summers in the northern waters and winters in trading voyages to California or the Hawaiian Islands. The *Vancouver*, a 60-ton schooner, built in 1826 at Vancouver under great handicaps was hardly seaworthy and was used primarily on the lower Columbia. A better job was done on the 30-ton sloop, *Broughton*, launched the same year; but lack of skilled labor, iron works, and properly seasoned timber forced abandonment of local shipbuilding. In 1836 the pioneer paddlewheel steamer, *Beaver*, arrived under sail from England. Its two 35-horsepower engines and low draft would, it was hoped, enable the ship to enter coves and inlets where sailing vessels could not go. But its voracious appetite for fuel defeated Simpson's hopes. The Northwest's first steamer used sails in the early years of its long service in Pacific waters.

McLoughlin viewed the marine department with jaundiced eye, believing that permanent posts were less costly in the long run and made for better trade relations with the natives. Upon the death of Captain Simpson in 1831, McLoughlin took charge of the vessels and made them strictly auxiliary to new posts: Fort Simpson (1831 and 1834), Fort McLoughlin (1833), Stikine, and Taku (1840).

The annual supply ships which usually arrived in the Columbia in March, were under McLoughlin's orders while on the coast. The following season's trade and, in considerable measure, the morale of company personnel depended upon the safe arrival of these vessels and their cargoes. A disaster, such as the wreck of the *William and Ann* in 1829 and of the *Isabella* in 1830, seriously affected the trade, reducing outfits and upsetting the tight schedule for their dispatch to the interior. During their stay in the Pacific the vessels were used to distribute supplies, and they took on cargoes of lumber and salmon which were marketed in California, the Hawaiian Islands, or in South American ports on the return voyage to England.

EXPANDED ACTIVITIES: THE LUMBER TRADE AND FARMING

McLoughlin supported—perhaps anticipated—Simpson's ambition to expand the company's business to other commodities than furs. "We must avail ourselves of all the resources of this Country if we have to Compete for the trade of it with the Americans as we may depend [upon it] they will turn every thing they possibly can to account," he reported to the Governor and Committee in 1829.

A small water-powered sawmill, located about five miles east of Fort Vancouver, produced lumber for rebuilding the fort, employing six to ten saws and twenty-five men in 1838. McLoughlin and Simpson together, in 1828, selected a site at the Falls of the Willamette where, according to Simpson's enthusiastic report, "whole Forests of Timber can be floated into a very fine Mill Seat. . . . [and] Saws enough could be employed to load the British Navy." Timbers for a mill were cut at the spot in 1831, but the project was abandoned. An abundant supply of timber was one thing, but a market for lumber was another.

The first shipment of lumber to the Hawaiian Islands in 1828–1829 sold for $100 a thousand feet but the demand was spotty and unpredictable. Efforts to open a market in South America and California were not successful. The export trade in salmon, dried or salted, was disappointing. Not only was the demand light, but improperly preserved salmon spoiled on the voyage. It was no easy matter to develop the Pacific Northwest's resources.

Simpson, as had Astor before him, hoped to capture the carrying and supply business of the Russian American Company. Not only would this keep American traders off the coast, but British manu- factures could be sold with profit, and the HBC would have a market for surplus produce from its local farms. Here at least, the Americans could not underbid them. In 1829 Simpson made overtures to the Russian governor who, though attracted to any reasonable offer that would free his colony from dependence on irresponsible American traders, could not accept Simpson's terms. But when it established posts on the British Columbia coast, the company was in direct com- petition with Russian traders and in controversy over territory to boot. Their disputes were settled in 1839 in a commercial agreement by which the Russian American Company leased to the HBC a strip of its mainland coast extending from Mount Fairweather to Portland Canal. The Russians would keep the trade of Alaskan islands and offer no opposition to the HBC in the interior; in return the company agreed to sell the Russians agricultural products at stipulated prices.[6]

In 1838 the Puget's Sound Agricultural Company was formed, in part to supply the Russians. The HBC stockholders owned it exclu- sively and McLoughlin managed its affairs, but the PSAC was le- gally independent. It purpose was to establish "an agricultural Settle- ment with a view to the production of wool, hides, tallow, and other farm produce for the English and other markets, in the District of Country situated between the head waters of the Cowlitz Portage and Pugets Sound. . . ." But such activities were also a means of "prov- ing up" the company's claims (and Great Britain's) to the disputed region north of the Columbia. An agricultural settlement provided a stronger argument for occupation than a fur trading post.

Fort Nisqually, at the southern tip of Puget Sound, had been planned as a major trading post and farm when it was set up in 1833. Early hopes that the area would produce bumper wheat crops were dashed when it was found that the soil responded only if heavily fertilized. But heavy meadow grass fattened beef cattle, and after skilled husbandmen took over, a productive dairy farm was developed. In 1839, the Nisqually livestock industry was assigned to the newly formed Puget's Sound Agricultural Company and after 1841 sheep and cattle became the establishment's chief produce.

Plows broke the heavy sod at Cowlitz Farms in 1839. The turf re- sisted harrow and drag and the poorly prepared fields dried out in that unusually hot and dry summer. But two years later, 1000 acres

[6] "James Douglas and the Russian American Company, 1840," Willard E. Ireland, ed., *BCHQ*, January 1941, 65n; John S. Galbraith, *The Hudson's Bay Company as an Imperial Factor 1821–1869* (1957); *The Journals of William Fraser Tolmie, Physician and Fur Trader* (1963).

produced 8000 bushels of wheat and 4000 bushels of oats, barley, peas, and quantities of potatoes.

Agricultural development was handicapped by a shortage of labor. Indians were seldom reliable workers, and indentured employees of the company were unaccustomed to farming. To meet this problem the HBC settled six of its retired employees at Nisqually, and in 1841 sent out from the Red River, under James Sinclair, twenty-one families—116 men, women, and children—who crossed the Rockies with all their baggage. Seventy-seven of these persons, principally Anglo-Indian half-breeds, were located at Nisqually where they farmed on halves for the Puget's Sound Agricultural Company. Seven families were reluctant to accept these terms and were settled at Cowlitz Farms in a semi-independent status. To them were advanced seed, implements, and other supplies, but, except for their debts, they were outside the jurisdiction of the Puget's Sound Agricultural Company.

Thus western Washington was becoming a farming community. A similar change was taking place in the Tualatin and Willamette valleys in Oregon. Company cattle grazed on Tualatin prairies. In the Willamette Valley in 1833, at least eight families formed the nucleus of a growing Canadian population and gave the name French Prairie to their settlement. When they were joined by Americans, missionaries, mountain men, and settlers, a new chapter of Northwest history was in the making.

The HBC was both a deterrent and an aid to American occupation of the Oregon country. It fought the Americans as competitors in the Indian trade. By trapping out, it attempted to make the Snake River a barrier against American invasion and to preserve the northern region where British claims were strongest. On the other hand, by engaging in agriculture, by disciplining the natives, by maintaining posts at strategic locations, and by establishing routes of travel, it lessened the danger for venturesome Americans who did break through. While the company frowned upon any practices that made life easy for its rivals, it could not reject the stranger at its gates. John McLoughlin's humanity made Fort Vancouver an outpost of civilization as well as of empire.

CHAPTER
TEN

The American Rocky Mountain Fur Trade

FROM 1824 to 1846 the Pacific Northwest was a department of the HBC. As we have seen, the company hoped to discourage, if it could not prevent, Americans from getting a foothold in the region. But Americans—traders, expansionists, missionaries, settlers, and diplomats —continually reminded the company that the land was not yet Britain's.

After Astor's unsuccessful attempt, no organized American fur enterprise crossed the Rockies for nearly a decade. In 1822, General William H. Ashley and Andrew Henry tried to reinstitute trade on the Upper Missouri, using Lisa's system of permanent posts and trapping parties. When hostile natives forced them off the Upper Missouri in 1824, they led their hunters up the North Platte and into the Rockies.

For this area Ashley developed a new organization.[1] Abandoning the trading house, he resorted wholly to trapping parties. In midsummer he sent out hired trappers in groups, called brigades, to hunt the rivers and streams through the winter. In the late spring the brigades came in with their packs of furs, meeting their employer at some agreed place. This yearly rendezvous, usually in July in the valley of

[1] *The West of William H. Ashley*, Dale L. Morgan, ed., (1963), 4.

the Green River, at Bear Lake, or in Cache Valley, soon became a gathering place not only for employees, but also for free trappers and Indians from all over the Rocky Mountain region. At the height of the trade in the early 1830s, several thousand Indians assembled, and hundreds of white men came to purchase supplies and settle accounts with the "booshways" (bourgeois) or outfitters.

After business, pleasure. Sometimes two weeks were given over to lusty carousal, horse races, shooting matches, gambling. After recovering from their spree—stimulated by high-priced alcohol—the men separated for their year's assignments to the dangerous, lonely mountain country.

THE MOUNTAIN MEN

A mountain man had to survive both rendezvous and mountain life. Those who proudly carried the title were expert hunters and trappers, bear fighters and Indian killers. The occupational hazards were many. No fewer than ninety-four men were slain by Indians between 1823 and 1829. Few mountain men lived to retire to civilization and those who did had little more than scars to show for their years of hazardous toil.

Ashley and his successors, Smith, Jackson, and Sublette (1826–1830) and the Rocky Mountain Fur Company (1830–1834), were outfitters (and, at times, also leaders in the field) who supplied their indentured employees, free trappers, and Indian allies. Goods were priced to assure the outfitters a generous margin of profit. In 1826, gunpowder sold at $1.50 a pound; scarlet cloth, at $6 a yard; beaver traps, $9; and alcohol, illegal in the Indian trade but easy to transport and much in demand, was $13.50 a gallon. Free trappers received $3 a pound for beaver pelts. The wages paid hired trappers ranged from $120 to $600 a year, depending on the competition for their services. When accounts were settled the trapper usually was in debt for the goods he had purchased. It was estimated that from 1823 to 1827 Ashley brought in 500 packs of skins worth $250,000 at St. Louis. Figuring his annual investment (including costs of transportation) at a generous $20,000, the profit was in the neighborhood of $50,000 to $60,000 a year. The leaders, whether outfitters or partners-in-the-field, combined the talents of entrepreneurs, frontiersmen, and explorers. The names of William Ashley, Jedediah Smith, David Jackson, Tom Fitzpatrick, Jim Bridger, and the Sublette brothers, Milton, William, and Andrew, are associated with places and routes of travel as well as with sagas of adventure and commerce. They filled in the geographical details of the West and, in the process, linked the Mississippi Valley and the Rockies by well-traveled trails.

In 1824 Ashley's men crossed the Continental Divide. The next year Ashley explored the Green River, a principal tributary of the Colorado. Two years later he sent a howitzer along the North Platte route through South Pass, gateway to the West, and proved that wheels could travel to the mountains. In 1830, Smith, Jackson, and Sublette transported their supplies in a wagon caravan up to the pass. The road to Oregon was taking shape.

THE CLASH OF BRITISH AND AMERICAN TRAPPERS

Alexander Ross was in charge of HBC's Snake River expedition in the summer of 1824 when he met Ashley's brigade leader, Jedediah Smith and six trappers, and permitted them to travel with him from the Bear River to Flathead Post. Peter Skene Ogden later referred to "that damned all cursed day" which brought Americans into the region for which the HBC had not yet prepared a defense. On the Bear River the following May, some of Ogden's men took their furs and deserted to the Americans, who insisted that Ogden was trespassing on American soil.

The presence of American trappers west of the Divide kept Ogden almost continuously in the field. His American counterpart as explorer and leader of expeditions in the transmontane West was Jedediah Smith. Only twenty-three when he entered Ashley's employment in 1822, Smith became a partner three years later. His biographer, Dale Morgan, describes him as the outstanding field operator of the fur trade until his death in 1831.

In August, 1826, Smith led a party of men across the Mohave Desert to the California settlements. Unable to return with his full complement, he left most of them to hunt in the San Joaquin Valley, while he and two companions crossed the snow-covered Sierras, the desert Nevada plain, and survived to reach the rendezvous in Bear Valley. His 45-day exploit was followed by nine days of rest; then Smith was back on the California trail. His purpose was to join the party he had left behind and to "proceed further in examination of the country beyond . . . and along the sea coast." He was caught up in a fever of discovery. "I, of course, expected to find Beaver, which with us hunters is a primary object, but I was also led on by the love of novelty common to all. . . ."

His first venture had been a grueling one; his second was disastrous. Ten men were killed by the Mohaves. Arrived in California, Smith tasted Mexican prison fare before he was permitted to outfit and, in December (1827), to depart, presumably to return to the mountains. Gathering together the men who had survived the Mohaves and those who had remained in California the summer before, Smith headed north. His purpose was to explore and trap. He made good time until he essayed the almost impossible terrain of the Smith Fork of Trinity River and the lower Klamath. It took him six months to break out of tangled underbrush, densely forested mountains, and canyons to the coast. In late June, he crossed the 42nd parallel into Oregon country and on July 14 he was on the Umpqua River. While Smith and two of his men were scouting the way ahead, Indians caught up with his party and massacred all but one. Arthur Black escaped and made his way to Fort Vancouver. Smith and his companions, John Turner and Richard Leland, who had returned to the shocking scene and thought themselves the sole survivors, arrived at Fort Vancouver two days later, on August 10 (1828).

John McLoughlin, who had resented "to the utmost" the Americans' treatment of Ogden in 1825, now received his enemy with kindness, even generosity. He ordered an expedition to the Umpqua to salvage Smith's goods and to punish the Indians. Sir George Simpson, arriving on a tour of inspection, agreed to buy the recovered furs. The following summer, Smith and Black rejoined their fellow Americans at Pierre's Hole.

Sir George had no high regard for the Americans. The trappers were "generally speaking, people of the worst character, run aways from Jails and outcasts from Society . . . [they] acknowledge no master, will conform to no rules or regulations. . . ." The outfitters were "merely adventurers," and the leaders of the trapping parties were men who had been "common Trappers and therefore possess[ed] no influence."

Simpson anticipated no serious consequences from Smith's invasion of the company's domain. He believed Smith's experiences had convinced him that the geography of the West was a formidable deterrent to American advance.

> . . . the flattering reports which reached St. Louis of the Wilhamot [Willamette] Country, as a field for Agricultural speculation, had induced many people in the States to direct their attention to that quarter; but he has on his present journey, discovered difficulties

which never occurred to their minds, and which are likely to deter his Country-men from attempting that enterprise.

In the American charts . . . [the Willamette] is laid down, as taking its rise in the Rocky Mountains . . . and the opinion was, that it would merely be necessary for Settlers with their Horses, Cattle, Agricultural implements &c. &c. to get (by the main communication from St. Louis to S[an]ta Fee) to the height of Land in about Lat. 38, there to embark on large Rafts & Batteaux and glide down current about 800 or 1000 Miles at their ease to this "Land of Promise." But it now turns out, that the Sources of the Wilhamot are not 150 Miles distant from Fort Vancouver, in Mountains which even Hunters cannot attempt to pass, beyond which, is a Sandy desert of about 200 miles, likewise impassable. . . . And the other route by Louis's River [Snake], Settlers could never think of attempting. So that I am of opinion, we have little to apprehend from Settlers in this quarter, and from Indian Traders nothing. . . .[2]

Simpson would have been less sanguine had he read Smith's 1830 report to the Secretary of War in which he wrote encouragingly of a passable road to Oregon. Pack horses and mules were customarily used to transport goods and furs, but that spring he and his partners had pioneered a wagon train that included two lightweight wagons, ten five-mule-team heavy wagons carrying about 1000 pounds each, twelve head of oxen, and a milk cow. They had left St. Louis April 10 and arrived without mishap at the Wind River-Popo Agie junction on July 16. Buffalo provided more food then they could use, the passes and valleys were green, and the stock was easily fed. A few "pioneers" moved ahead of the caravan to cut down the banks of creeks and ravines over which the wagons had to pass; but otherwise, the route along the North Platte was open, level prairie with no obstructions. "The ease and safety with which it was done," Smith reported, "prove the facility of communicating over land with the Pacific Ocean."

Several of Smith's other observations suggest the interest Americans were taking in the Far West. Fort Vancouver, obviously a permanent settlement, was protected only by 12-pounders. The annual value of furs shipped from there would be more than $250,000 on the New York market. Company trappers had crossed the Divide, and were employing such destructive practices that the area would soon he exhausted of its fur stock. He concluded that the Convention of 1818 had given special privileges to the British and had enabled them "to take possession of the Columbia River, and spread over the country

[2] *Simpson's 1828 Journey*, 64, 66–67.

south of it; while no Americans have ever gone, or can venture to go on the British side."

So it was that reports of profits enjoyed by an ancient enemy, and of the potentials of a practically unknown land—reports that probably lost nothing in word-of-mouth repetition—lured new adventurers into the fur trade and roused a new interest in the Oregon country. In 1833 Chief Trader Francis Heron passed along the news that "upwards of 400" Americans were in the mountains in the winter of 1832. Astor's American Fur Company had established forts on the Upper Missouri among the Blackfeet: Fort Union on the Yellowstone, Fort McKenzie on the Missouri near the mouth of the Marias, and Fort Cass near the junction of the Big Horn and the Yellowstone. Its trappers trailed the brigades of the Rocky Mountain Fur Company, which succeeded Smith, Jackson, and Sublette in 1830, set up their rendezvous in the neighborhood of their rivals and paid higher wages and tariffs to entice their trappers away. The Rocky Mountain men were veterans in the trade, but the American Fur Company employees learned so quickly that by 1832 they were getting the upper hand.

Despite the decline in the trade, two new outfits appeared in the mountains that same year. Captain Benjamin Louis E. deBonneville was an inept adventurer; Nathaniel Wyeth proposed to be a rival of the HBC. A West Point graduate, Bonneville became interested in the fur trade while stationed on the frontier. He took two years' leave, ostensibly for the purpose of exploration, but actually his main purpose was to break into the fur trade. Instead, he was broken by more experienced competitors and withdrew, bankrupt, in 1836.

Bonneville has been called a "history-made" man, for Washington Irving's facile pen made his name famous. His travels were all within lands that had already been crossed and recrossed by the mountain men. But he did make a contribution to the history of the Far West. Jedediah Smith and his partners used wagons to transport goods to the mountains in 1830, but they did not go beyond South Pass, nor did they continue the practice. Bonneville, with his company of 110 to 120 men, took twenty light wagons through the pass to the Green River, thus opening another stretch of a developing western highway.

KELLEY, "PROPHET OF OREGON," AND NATHANIEL WYETH, COLONIZER

Although the West was still thought of as fur trading country, there was increasing interest in it as a land for settlement. Wyeth became interested in settling through Hall Jackson Kelley, a Boston school-

THE PACIFIC NORTHWEST
FUR TRADE AND MISSIONS

Qu'Appelle

113

109

105

49

Oldman

Poplar

Milk

Marias

TO FORT MANUEL
FORT UNION

Teton

FORT McKENZIE

Flathead
Lake

FORT
BENTON

Missouri

SALEESH HOUSE

AD

Swan

Fr.

Musselshell

FORT CASS

Lolo
Pass

ST. MARY'S

chsa

Selway

Gibbons
Pass

Yellowstone

THREE
FORKS

Jefferson

45

Salmon

Middle Fk.

Big

Hole

Rosebud Cr.

Tongue

Powder

Red Rock

Lemhi

Yellowstone
Lake

Shoshone

HENRY'S
FORT

Henrys Fk.

Jackson Lake

Bighorn

105

PIERRE'S
HOLE

JACKSON HOLE

Snake

Teton
Pass

Union
Pass

Wind

North Platte

Blackfoot

FORT HALL

FORT
BONNEVILLE

South Pass

Green

Bear

Hams Fork

CACHE VALLEY

FORT
BRIDGER

Blacks

Fork

FORT
LARAMIE

41

Great
Salt
Lake

OGDEN'S
HOLE

Missions

□ Protestant

△ Catholic

113

109

SHERMAN

teacher with a mission to propagate "Christianity in the dark and cruel places about the shores of the Pacific." Having read the Biddle edition of Lewis' and Clark's journals and talked with seamen and hunters, Kelley was convinced that the Oregon country must eventually become "a favorite field of modern enterprise and the abode of civilization."

Kelly devoted himself with uncommon persistence to its colonization. In 1829, he formed the American Society for Encouraging the Settlement of the Oregon Territory. Through circulars and pamphlets he preached that the Pacific Northwest was legitimately a territory of the United States, occupied by a foreign power whose grasp could be broken only by no fewer than "3,000 active sons of American freedom." Such a colony, "planned by Providence, made easy by Nature," would improve the moral condition of the Indians, open the continent to trade with the Orient, provide a refuge for the virtuous but unfortunate, and break the "bold and lawless spirit of enterprise" by which Great Britain held the land.

With few facts but fine imagination, Kelley built up an image of Oregon that became part of common thinking:

> Much of the country within two hundred miles of the ocean, is favorable to cultivation. The valley of the Multnomah [Willamette] is particularly so, being extremely fertile. . . . The Oregon is covered with heavy forests of timber. . . . The production of vegetables, grain, and cattle will require comparatively but little labor; these articles, together with the spontaneous growth of the soil, and the fruits of laborious industry, in general, will find a market, *at home*, and thereby comfort and enrich the settlers. Surplus staple articles may be shipped from their doors to distant ports, and return a vast profit in trade. Lumber, ship timber, &c. may be sent to the western coast of South America, the islands in the Pacific; bread stuffs, furs, salmon, and many articles of domestic manufactures, to the East Indies.[3]

It may have been Kelley's "flattering reports" that Simpson referred to when he spoke of American interest in the Willamette Valley, as a "field for agricultural speculation."

Although Kelley stirred a flurry of interest, particularly among New Englanders, few actually signed with him as colonists. Among those who did was Nathaniel J. Wyeth, a young entrepreneur who saw in the undeveloped West opportunity to satisfy his ambitions and repair his temporarily depleted fortune.

When Kelley's "immediate departure" had several times been postponed, Wyeth decided to form his own colonizing society. He or-

---

[3] *Hall J. Kelley on Oregon*, Fred W. Powell, ed. (1932), 73–74.

ganized the Pacific Trading Company, a joint-stock venture, whose participants could, for $40 expense money, join him in a commercial expedition to the Columbia. Wyeth planned to engage in the fur trade on so large a scale that the HBC would be forced to come to terms with him. Assuming that the joint occupation agreement with Great Britain would be terminated in 1838 and that Oregon would then fall to the Americans, he figured that his company would succeed to the monopoly. He intended to develop diverse industries to supplement the fur trade and carry some of the burden of costs. He reasoned, quite accurately, that it would be more economical to supply the fur trade west of the Divide from the coast rather than from St. Louis. Produce from the Willamette Valley, and preserved salmon, as well as valuable packs of furs, would fill the holds of his supply ships on their return to the Atlantic seaboard.

In the spring of 1832, Wyeth set out from St. Louis with a party of twenty-four, uniformed in coarse woolen jackets, pantaloons, striped cotton shirts, and cowhide boots.[4] They carried muskets or rifles, but they did not march to the notes of the bugle, as Wyeth had hoped they would. Desertions along the way at Pierre's Hole, where his party witnessed mountain life at its rawest, sadly reduced its numbers. Having cached his trading goods for want of horses, Wyeth continued with his eleven remaining men to Fort Vancouver, arriving practically destitute. McLoughlin, this "civilized man," received Wyeth kindly but gave him clearly to understand that hospitality did not mean encouragement in business.

Wyeth examined the mouth of the Columbia "with a view to the salmon business" and spent a few days looking over the Willamette Valley for a farm site. "I have never seen country of equal beauty except the Kansas country," he wrote in his journal, "and I doubt not [it] will one day sustain a large population." Here he found eight or nine retired HBC employees settled with their families, their prosperous gardens confirming his opinion that, if the country was ever to be colonized, this was the place to begin.

The Pacific Trading Company having been dissolved through attrition, Wyeth rehired two of his men to accompany him back to the States. The others found temporary employment with the HBC. John Ball, a New Yorker trained in law and a successful businessman who had joined Wyeth to fulfill an old dream of western adventure, taught school at Fort Vancouver during the winter of 1832–1833. In the spring, he and John Sinclair went to the prairie near the present Salem, where

---

[4] *The Correspondence and Journals of Captain Nathaniel J. Wyeth, 1831–6,* F. G. Young, ed. (1899).

they built a house, "the walls of which are the cylindrical fir and the roof thereof cyprus and yew," and with tools and seeds lent by McLoughlin, plowed and sowed. "Strawberries and other plants are in flower, and trees in leaf in April. By April 15 the camas are in bloom and plants of many kinds full grown." A month later strawberries were ripe, wild roses in bloom, deer and elk plentiful.[5]

But for all the richness of the valley and the grandeur of mountain peaks, Ball found strains of evil in the Garden: the natives were given to "falsehood and low cunning" and white men lived too close to the natives. "Fever and ague" burned out enthusiasm already weakened by loneliness. Ball and Sinclair sold their first crops to the HBC and left the country the following September.

Two other members of Wyeth's party, Solomon H. Smith and Calvin E. Tibbetts, a Maine stonecutter, became permanent settlers. Smith, a New Englander with some training in medicine and varied experience in business and fishing, succeeded Ball as teacher at the fort. Later he married an Indian woman and joined the Canadian settlement at French Prairie, where in 1834 he held school for his neighbors' children.

In the mountains, en route home, Wyeth made what he thought was a firm agreement with Tom Fitzpatrick and Milton Sublette of the collapsed Rocky Mountain Fur Company, to deliver trade goods to them at their next rendezvous. He seems to have formed a partnership with Bonneville at the same time. He returned to Boston, and organized the Columbia River Company with funds from the firm of Tucker and Williams and some financial assistance from Bonneville's backer, Alfred Seton of New York. In the summer of 1834 Wyeth was back in the mountains. But this venture was no more successful than the first. Sublette and Fitzpatrick announced that they were unable to continue in business, and refused to buy his stock. What Wyeth learned of Bonneville's dawdling winter activities did not encourage him or his men, thirty of whom were hired away from him. With 126 horses and mules, 41 remaining employees, and a large stock of goods, Wyeth had but one alternative: to set up a trading post in the hope that it might yet save his investment.

On the Snake River, near the mouth of the Portneuf above American Falls, Wyeth built Fort Hall. To celebrate its completion his men "manufactured a magnificent flag from some unbleached sheeting a little red flannel and a few blue patches, saluted it with damaged powder and wet it in vilanous alcohol." In Wyeth's opinion, the banner

[5] John Ball, "Across the Continent Seventy Years Ago," *OHQ*, March 1902, 103, 104.

made "a very respectable appearance amid the dry and desolate regions of central America."

When he reached the Columbia his supply ship had not yet arrived. When it did come the fall salmon run was about over and the half-cargo carried back to the States was not properly processed. Although his prospects were as dismal as they had been two years earlier, Wyeth put men to work on a farm at French Prairie. Another crew built Fort William on Sauvie (then called Wapato) Island at the mouth of the Willamette, which he planned to make the depot for his fishing enterprise. He had a few storehouses, some dwellings, and a blacksmith's and cooper's shop erected by October 6.

Misfortune dogged his efforts. The Sandwich Islanders he had imported as laborers deserted: "Our people are sick and dying off like rotten sheep of billious disorders," he wrote in September, 1835. In the mountains, Indians took the scalps of fourteen of his employees. In the spring of 1836 he decided to abandon the adventure. Courtney M. Walker was left in charge of Fort William which was soon abandoned, and a tenant, James O'Neill, took over the Valley farm. In June Wyeth left for the United States, having arranged to sell Fort Hall to the HBC.

Wyeth had attempted to enter the fur trade against heavy opposition and at the very time its fortunes were declining. He had neither the capital nor the experience to compete, on the one hand, with the well-entrenched HBC, or on the other, with the hardened leaders of the mountain men whom he described as scoundrels. His scheme of developing a Columbia River salmon industry for export trade was premature.

However, Wyeth helped open the road to Oregon. His idea of outfitting the mountain men appealed to McLoughlin. When Wyeth built Fort Hall, McLoughlin sent Thomas McKay to build Fort Boise; when Wyeth offered to sell his fort, McLoughlin bought it. When immigration began to move along the Oregon Trail, the British forts Hall and Boise became important stations on this long, barren stretch. Furthermore, the eight or nine Wyeth men who chose to remain in Oregon were the beginning of an American colony.

By the time Wyeth left the mountains in 1836, the era of fur trade was rapidly drawing to a close. Beaver were about trapped out and the mountain men were forced to work harder and range farther to find them. Then too, the market was greatly reduced when men began to wear silk instead of fur hats. The Indian trade was now securely held by the American Fur Company, which concentrated its dealings in hides and skins at forts Benton and Union on the Upper

Missouri. The last rendezvous was in 1840; thereafter most of the free trappers deserted the mountains. Some drifted to California and entered the horse and cattle trade of the Southwest; others came to the Willamette Valley and reluctantly, but of necessity, took up farming.

THE MOUNTAIN MEN TURN TO OREGON

Probably the first of these reached the Valley in 1832, when McLoughlin mentioned the arrival of a party of American hunters from California. The next group appeared in 1834, the year when McLoughlin politely welcomed Wyeth back to Vancouver. No welcome awaited Ewing Young and eight or twelve companions. Young was a tough product of the southwest frontier, whose career included beaver trapping, trading out of Santa Fe, and driving horses from California to Taos. His companions, with one exception, comprised a cross section of the "reckless breed of men," ranging from well-educated, energetic, and versatile Joseph Gale and steady Webley Hauxhurst down to roistering irresponsibles. The odd man of the party was Hall Jackson Kelley.

Having failed to launch his colonizing company in 1832, Kelley had undertaken the trip to Oregon alone, by way of New Orleans, Mexico, and California. In Mexico, it was said, he passed out religious tracts and was almost deflected from his Oregon destination by a new interest, a railroad between Vera Cruz and Mexico City. After numerous hardships he finally reached California and fell in with Ewing Young. According to his story, Kelley convinced Young and his companions of the desirability of living in Oregon. As they started for the Columbia, they were joined by some men who had horses which the governor of California claimed were stolen. The governor notified McLoughlin by way of a company ship then at Monterey that Young's party was composed of horse thieves.

At Fort Vancouver, Kelley and Young were coolly received. Kelley was obviously sick, physically and mentally. He was housed outside the fort until the next March (1835), when McLoughlin shipped him to the Hawaiian Islands. The following October Kelley returned to Boston on a whaling ship, convinced that he had been persecuted by the HBC. He became an even more zealous propagandist for American occupation of Oregon, and a bitter antagonist of the British.

Ewing Young and his companions moved into the Chehalem Valley

148

and built cabins, the nucleus of a small community of mountain men. The arrival of these rough characters almost coincided with that of a different type of settler. With Wyeth in 1834 had come a party of Methodist missionaries, Jason and Daniel Lee and their lay workers, Cyrus Shepard and Philip Edwards. Their aim was to civilize the wilderness. They were to accomplish what Kelley and Wyeth had failed to do.

The fur trade was over. Oregon's future lay in the plowed earth, in fields of wheat ripening under the August sun.

PART II

The American Colony in the Pacific Northwest

OVERVIEW

PART II *is concerned with the development of an American colony in the Pacific Northwest or, as it was commonly known, the Oregon Country.*

The first American settlers were a few mountain men and a small party of Methodist missionaries. In all, they may have numbered twenty-six in 1835. Five years later there were about 150; in the fall of 1843, 1200. By 1850, more than 13,000 settlers called themselves Oregonians.

The active founders of the colony were missionaries whose task of converting and civilizing the Indians was not to be accomplished in a brief visit. They brought families; they farmed, engaged in mercantile enterprises, taught schools, and organized a government. They advertised the country to attract the sober industrious settler who was American and Protestant; they succeeded better as colonizers than as missionaries.

The emigrants who followed mountain men and missionaries in 1842 were in the tradition of a free, mobile people. Oregon pioneers had roots in other times and places. Some were kin to the frontiersman of the eighteenth century; but within the type called "frontiersman" was a wide range of character: the rough individualists who fled to deeper wilderness when they saw the smoke from a neighbor's chimney; the lawless who sought the refuge of Indian life to escape the law's restrictions; and farmers building roads to hold them, as by lifelines, to their old homes and to bring church, school, and law and order to the new.

The frontiersman has been greatly romanticized. On the one hand is eye-gouging, cockadoodledooing, bear-killing Davy Crockett, who could ride a flash of lightning; on the other, the yeoman farmer with rifle in one hand and Bible in the other; or a pious Aeneas bearing his father on his shoulders and leading his son by the hand. Perhaps more realistically the frontier farmer was an individualist who was interested in political organization, about which he was surprisingly well informed. Though he was prone to engage in law suits, he had no respect for lawyers. Suspicious of the common law and learned judges, he preferred statutory law which he had a hand in making. He was versed in what he considered his natural rights. He was undramatic but not colorless; he was confident, practical, cautious, stubborn. Beyond a regard for his customary privileges, he had no feeling for history, but he held an exaggerated confidence in the future.

Above all, he was restless. He could not unharness his own team so long as he heard wagon wheels grinding ruts in a road to a new land. He identified himself with an expanding America. After all, he had pioneered other frontiers before he came to Oregon.

The decades of the forties and fifties witnessed a phenomenal migration. Thousands of settlers moved into new states, opened the Midwest, took the long, hard roads to Texas and California. It was, of course, a pleasant coincidence that in opening up the continent, a man was doing his patriotic duty while satisfying a restless drive and enhancing his own circumstances.

For Frederick Jackson Turner ("Significance of the Frontier in American History," 1893) the presence of "free" land explained American development, the character of the American people and their institutions. The physical environment determined what these people would be. Present explanations of the relationship of people to the frontier suggest man's persistent quest for the new Eden.[1] In America, "All Things Necessary to the Convenience and Delight in Life" were present; hence the new Adam, entering innocent into the Garden of the World—into Kentucky, Iowa, California—even into Oregon.

Oregon was described as a paradise of natural beauty with rich, well-watered valleys, mild climate, and excellent facilities for trade with the Orient. Some persons pointed out that much of the region west of

[1] R. W. B. Lewis, *The American Adam* (1955).

the Rockies was arid and untillable, mountainous and forested, but even they valued the rich valleys west of the Cascades though they had never seen them.

Whether the country was the New Eden, to be occupied because it was part of the United States' natural dominion, or because it was, remotely to be sure, "the hither edge of the frontier," it appealed to some people. Missionaries and emigrants already in Oregon, finding the country good, urged families and friends to join them. Their letters were published in Midwest weekly newspapers and quoted far and wide. "I was much opposed to coming as anyone could be," wrote one young woman after her arrival in 1846, "if I were back there and knew what I know now I should be perfectly willing to come. . . . It is an easy place to make a living."

Oregon may have invited some people because it was the gateway to the Orient; or because it was an easy place to make a living, to get free land, or to achieve freedom; but other places in one way or another also held out promises. Given alternative choices, why did a handful of people choose Oregon? It is possible that what was said about Oregon was heard only by those whose expectations could be satisfied nowhere else. Hence, what was said about Oregon was immensely important in determining who went to Oregon.

Asked in later years why they chose Oregon, men gave the answers expected of them: to save the souls of the Indians, to save Oregon from the British, to escape slave competition. But sometimes their anecdotes revealed more about their motivations than their studied answers. Old-timers told how in gold-rush days, immigrants arriving at Pacific Springs had to choose between the road to California, marked by a heap of glittering quartz, and the northwesterly road indicated by a sign bearing the words "To Oregon." Those who could read went to Oregon. Private letters and diaries reveal motivations. Young Charles Putnam wrote home from Fort Hall that he would go to Oregon because "the Aristocracy or respectable portion" of the companies in his train would go there. A wife, having arrived with her husband in time to qualify for land in her own right, was disappointed when her husband decided to work in a town. "Now," she wrote in her diary, "I shall be dependent upon a man for the rest of my life."[2] Thus we suggest that in this matter of determining why people chose Oregon, we add another category of possible explanations under the rubric "values."

Although in many respects emigrants to Oregon resembled those who chose other destinations, we assume characteristics that made them more responsive to Oregon's promises than to those of Texas, California, or Kansas. We suggest that settlers in Oregon found that it met their expectations and they reported it in terms—sometimes value terms—

[2] *Overland in 1846: Diaries and Letters of the California-Oregon Trail*, Dale L. Morgan, ed., 2 vols. (1963), II, 605. Unpublished diary of Lillian Rudd, copy in Oregon State Library.

that appealed to persons like themselves. In effect, they chose their own successors. This process, repeated over the decades, built a community which, though not entirely homogeneous, was distinguished from developing communities elsewhere, just as those communities were distinguished from one another.

Because Oregon was so distant, the road so long, and the investment in outfits so great, not everyone who wanted to go could do so. A 2000-mile journey by wagon was not lightly undertaken; it has been estimated that proper equipment cost from $800 to $1200. There was the added prospect of total loss of this investment—not easily acquired at a time when wages were less than $1.50 a day and Illinois lands sold for $3 to $6 an acre. To buy supplies at forts Laramie, Bridger, and Hall, took cash, and the prices were shockingly high: a dollar a pound for flour, coffee, sugar.

Would-be pioneers pored over maps that showed a "Great American Desert," stretching from the mouth of the Platte to the Rockies. A trail, outlined by Indians and fur traders, was cut into a road by the settlers' heavy wagons. The earliest wagon trains founds few hazards on the trail; grass and game were plentiful and the traveler could live off the country. But game was soon driven away, grass was consumed by the first companies to pass; hunger, dust and monotony cursed the latecomers. Indians were a continuous annoyance and a strain on taut nerves, though there were few attacks during the forties. Hostile natives—and cholera—beset travelers in the fifties. The South Pass was an easy highway across the Divide, but the Snake River country was barren, hot, dusty, and rough. Having survived so far, one was still a long way from the Willamette Valley.

Guidebooks by which pioneers plotted their journeys not only promoted emigration but gave practical advice. John M. Shively's Route and Distances to Oregon and California with a Description of Watering-Places, Crossings, Dangerous Indians, &c. &c. *was breezy, cheerful, and full of good sense.*

> *When the emigrants start to the sun-down diggings of Oregon, they should not fancy that they are doing some great things; and that they need military array, officers, non-commissioned officers, &c: all this is folly. They will quarrel, and try to enforce non-essential duties, till the company will divide and subdivide, the whole way to Oregon. When you start over these wide plains, let no one leave dependent on his best friends for anything; if you do, you will certainly have a blow-out before you get far.[3]*

The Elijah White party in 1842 took its cue for organization from the fur trade caravans. Captains were elected, pilots appointed, and a rudimentary military discipline enforced. The 1843 migration started with somewhat the same plan, but abandoned it for more democratic pro-

[3] *Overland in 1846,* II, 734.

cedures. *Travelers learned that the wagon train could not be expected to wait for the cow column, and so parties split into two sections, the fast travelers and the slow. Jesse Applegate's* Day With the Cow Column *is a classic description of a typical day. The routine was monotonous and the pace slow; yet dangers were ever present. Night watches stood over the wagon-encircled camp, where each evening some semblance of a social community appeared.*

> *. . . time passes; the watch is set for the night, the council of old men has broken up, and each has returned to his own quarter. The flute has whispered its last lament to the deeping night. The violin is silent, and the dancers have dispersed. . . . All is hushed and repose from the fatigues of the day, save the vigilant guard, and the wakeful leader who still has cares upon his mind that forbid sleep.*

In 150 to 180 days emigrants arrived at Whitman Mission or at the mouth of the Umatilla on the Columbia. Then, when some of the hardest traveling lay ahead, the pioneers were more or less on their own. The Columbia's shores were not hospitable to wagon travel, but where its walls closed in, wagons could trail the edge of the plateau to the Dalles. Here each family had to hire Indians and canoes, or make rafts to float them and their goods forty miles to the Upper Cascades and the portage trail. If they were fortunate they might be met by HBC bateaux or by earlier arrivals who came to help. Wagons were knocked down and loaded on the boats or floated down the river; the cattle were swum across to the north side and driven down an Indian trail through dense forest to Fort Vancouver, where the river had to be crossed again. In 1844 immigrants lost over half their stock in this grueling experience.

The next year, from the Dalles, an adventurous party followed an Indian trail through the Tygh Valley and around the rough slope of Mt. Hood. Their travail opened the Barlow Trail, for several years the principal highway into the Willamette Valley. But the trail, even when improved by a private road company, brought little joy to those who chose to follow it. Theodore Wygant in 1850 found it one of the most depressing stretches of his long journey.

> *For over eight days we struggled through snow, rain, mud and cold and witnessed suffering and despair among the poor emigrants, beyond anything we had before encountered—deserted wagons, hundreds of dead cattle mired in the mud, with only their backs sticking out,—cattle lying dead around wagons, with the immigrant families and their camp fires near, the people waiting for help to come to them from the Willamette Valley; such were the scenes that we passed through the Cascade Mountains, ourselves nearly all the time on foot, picking our way as best we could and driving our poor animals.*[4]

[4] Theodore Wygant, "Notes," typed manuscript, Reed College Library.

Descending Laurel Hill, wagons were chained to trees to keep them from running down the oxen. The worst stretch passed, the immigrants arrived at Toll Gate, where they paid five dollars for each wagon and ten cents a head for stock, in cash, note, or kind. In 1848, when settlers were better off financially, 56 out of 118 could not pay, and one "run like a turkey."

Few pilgrims approached the western shore by sea until after 1850. The first settlers were accustomed to land migration and to the covered wagon. Despite its inhospitable approach, the Columbia River route was the one most commonly used. In 1845, some parties attempted to reach the Willamette Valley by way of the Malheur River in central Oregon, and endured suffering and disasters before they gave up and turned north to the Columbia River route. After 1853, the Malheur route to the Deschutes and across the mountains to the Willamette Valley was sometimes used. In 1846 Jesse Applegate undertook to lead a party across northern Nevada and California into southern Oregon. After three months of intense hardship the party finally reached the Valley, where they vented their wrath on Applegate.

Arrived in Oregon, the emigrants were frustrated by the slow processes of diplomacy which delayed settlement of the boundary issue and the organization of a government. Despite their enterprise and spirit of aggrandizement, these men were sticklers for legal forms when it suited their purpose. They abided by decisions of state which their own actions made inevitable: the union of the Oregon country with the United States. The same token respect for law impelled them to build a temporary government in the pattern of the one they had known in the States, and most of them looked forward to the day when the boundary issue could be settled and political union with the nation assured. Yet independence of spirit and self-assertiveness led them to resent the restrictions of territorial status and to agitate immediately for the sovereignty of statehood.

The inhabitants of the Oregon country faced the problems of reconciling anticipations of economic opportunity with the realities of their situation. Their prosperity came from the happy accident of gold discoveries, first in California, and then in the Pacific Northwest itself. In their first few years as territorials they had to fight their most serious Indian wars, suffer the depredations of the lawless elements who followed mining frontiers, and reach out, by ship and rail, for closer contact with the nation and the world.

In 1838 and 1840, a few Americans in the Willamette Valley petitioned Congress to consider their plight as colonials, remote from their parent country and faced with dangers magnified by isolation. Forty years later, the state of Oregon and the territories of Washington and Idaho were on the eve of victory over isolation. A transcontinental railroad was approaching and town builders anticipated cities where only villages existed. Optimism, which encouraged Americans to devastate forests and till deserts, to build wagon roads and railroads through uninhabited country, prevailed in the Pacific Northwest. It had been optimism, too, which brought the missionaries into Oregon in the 1830s to found an American colony in the Far West. We turn now to the early years of that colony and to the trials which forged its character and outlined its future.

CHAPTER
ELEVEN

Missions
and Missionaries

Piety was not an outstanding virtue of fur traders. Among the mountain men, the Bible had a place along with Sir Walter Scott's works, Byron's poems, and Jane Porter's *Scottish Chiefs* as popular reading matter in winter camps. But a praying man such as Jedediah Smith was an oddity.

Religious teaching was part of the education of most of the gentlemen of the HBC, but so were the skeptical philosophies of the eighteenth century. When conflicts between orthodoxy and the new science were argued in Bachelors' Hall, the chances were that deistical or agnostic views would be advanced along with those of the Anglicans, Calvinists, and Catholics. As a rule French-Canadian employees were Catholic.

The company was obligated by its 1821 license to provide for the moral improvement and religious instruction of the Indians. As a gesture of compliance, Simpson ordered that divine services be read on Sundays. At Fort Vancouver, the Sabbath was strictly observed. Work ceased for the day and a bell summoned the inhabitants to hear the reading in French of the scriptures and a "Penser y Bien."

However, Dr. William Fraser Tolmie, a devout young Scottish Calvinist assigned as trader to Fort Nisqually, was shocked to find that business there continued as usual. He closed the store wicket and summoned the Indians for religious teaching. The post clerk's "Journal of Occurrences" reported that in one lesson Dr. Tolmie "explained the creation of the World, the reason why Christians and Jews abstained from work on Sundays; and had got as far as the Deluge in sacred history" when he was requested to stop because the Indians "could not comprehend things clearly."

Pressed by critics at home, who seized on the fact that the usual procedure was merely to give lip service to religious teaching, the Governor and Committee in London sent out an Anglican chaplain, Herbert Beaver, who with his wife Jane, arrived at the Columbia in 1836. The peculiar affinity of Beaver's name with the trade did not help adapt him to its crudities and complexities. Strongly anti-Catholic, he found to his "utter grief and astonishment" that he was "in the very stronghold of Popery," which he promptly assailed. Interpreting his appointment to mean that he was to form "without forcing the consciences of Men . . . a Christian, a Protestant, and a Church of England Congregation," he began his work in the schoolroom. Since the majority of the pupils were from Catholic families, McLoughlin feared the consequences of instruction based on the Church of England catechism. After one week, Beaver was relieved of schoolroom duties.

On one occasion, Beaver accused McLoughlin and other officers of living in sin because their marriages lacked formal religious sanction. The enraged Chief Factor promptly caned him. The Beavers returned to England after twenty-six months of bitter controversy. James Douglas, McLoughlin's colleague, in explaining the affair to the Governor and Committee, summarized for them the qualifications of a clergyman for the heterogeneous community of the Company's western district: "A Clergyman in this Country must quit the closet & live a life of beneficent activity, devoted to the support of principles, rather than of forms; he must shun discord, avoid uncharitable feelings, temper zeal with discretion, illustrate precept by example, and the obdurate rock upon which we have been so long hammering in vain will soon be broken into fragments."[1]

The "obdurate rock" of religious controversy was not removed from the Oregon country with the Beavers' departure. It was already there when Douglas described his ideal cleric.

---

[1] "The James Douglas Report on the 'Beaver Affair,' " W. Kaye Lamb, ed., *OHQ*, March 1946, 28; *Reports and Letters of Herbert Beaver . . .*, Thomas E. Jessett, ed., (1959).

THE METHODIST MISSION SOCIETY: JASON LEE

Between 1820 and 1840, an upsurge of religious awakening coincided with the accelerated movement of American people to the West. Missionary societies were formed, or their attention redirected, to work among Indians and in pioneer communities. In 1832 the (New York) *Christian Advocate and Journal* carried an emotion-charged story of four Indians—Nez Perces or Flatheads—who had come to St. Louis, seeking the "whiteman's Book of Heaven." This was interpreted as a Macedonian cry of heathens seeking Christ, and it inspired societies and individuals to answer the call.

One of the first to respond, Jason Lee volunteered to take on the assignment for the Mission Society of the Methodist Episcopal Church. In June, 1833, he was formally dedicated to the task of setting up a mission among the Flatheads. His nephew, Daniel Lee, also an ordained minister, was appointed Jason's colleague. With lay helpers Philip L. Edwards and Cyrus Shepard and Courtney M. Walker, a nonprofessor, the Lees joined Wyeth's expedition to the West in 1834.

Jason Lee, born in 1803 of New England parentage, was a powerfully built, slow-moving man of tremendous endurance. He was devout, practical, and friendly, but lacked the firmness his responsibilities required. He was received hospitably by Dr. McLoughlin, who invited him to hold services at the fort. Lee's first preachings were to an astonishingly heterogeneous congregation: English, French, Scottish, Scotch-Irish, American, Indian, Hawaiian, Indian half-breed, and three Japanese survivors of an unintentional trans-Pacific voyage, whose wrecked junk had been found on the coast in 1833.

McLoughlin strongly advised Lee to give up the idea of a mission among the Flatheads. The long history of the tribe's wars with the Blackfeet, which made their country dangerous even for traders, was but one argument. In addition, the Flatheads' nomadic habits would make it exceedingly difficult for the missionaries to support themselves in such isolated country, let alone to instruct and to convert their charges to a "civilized life."

Lee did not decide quickly or easily to locate in the Willamette Valley. He yearned to know "the identicle [*sic*] place that the Lord designs."[2] Probably the determining factors in his decision were the advantages of the Valley for the missionaries' survival and independence, and the prospects for its colonization by Americans. True, few

[2] Jason Lee, "Diary," *OHQ*, December 1916, 398.

Indians remained in the Valley. Four years of influenza epidemics (1829–1832) had practically wiped them out. On the other hand, as Lee reported to the Mission Society, the Willamette was "so situated as to form a central position from which missionary labors may be extended in almost every direction among the natives and those emigrants who may hereafter settle in that vast and fertile territory." His choice was a beautiful prairie spot on the southern edge of the French-Canadian settlement, ten miles north of the present site of Salem and near a village of thirty Indians, a "filthy, miserable company" contentedly subsisting on camas roots.

On Sundays, Lee preached to his French neighbors; on weekdays he and his helpers worked against time to build a mission house and plant crops. Before their shelter was properly roofed, the first Indian pupils arrived. In the next four years, Lee reported a total of fifty-two admissions. Of these eight died, some ran away, others were removed by their parents. Epidemic influenza and other diseases spread through the school, further weakening the missionaries' tenuous hold upon the natives and seriously undermining their own health.

But Lee sent back such an encouraging report of his first year's labors that in 1836 the Mission Society sent thirteen more men and women to help him. This enabled him to establish a station at the Dalles of the Columbia, where the Indians had permanent villages and gathered annually in great numbers for the fishing season.

As superintendent of an expanding mission, Lee was forced to spend more and more time in providing for its physical needs. At the end of the third year, he noted in his journal that the "main object I have kept in view has been the Glory of God in the salvation of souls." But the spring of his spiritual strength was drained: ". . . the *filling up*, the *Filling Up*, there is the difficulty," he cried.

Despite spiritual weariness, Lee had great plans for his Oregon mission. These included a number of new stations among the Indians, a campaign to redeem Catholics, and the recruitment of respectable, Protestant, American settlers. In 1838 he went East to present his ideas before the Society. So successfully did he arouse the enthusiasm of its members and of the congregations he addressed, that $100,000 was subscribed to send back with him the Great Reinforcement of fifty persons, thirty-two adults and eighteen children. On the ship *Lausanne* they brought a stock of goods to set up a mission store, as well as tools and equipment for the enlarged mission family and the proposed new stations.

No sooner had the passengers disembarked in the spring of 1840 than they were dispersed to build new missions. John H. Frost, Daniel

Lee and their families were sent to the Clatsops at the mouth of the Columbia, where they built their first house near Point Adams. Later they rebuilt on the grass-covered sand dunes of Clatsop Plains. Dr. John P. Richmond and his wife went to Fort Nisqually, the first Americans to reach that area tacitly assumed to be British. Alvin F. Waller and William H. Willson located at the Falls of the Willamette.

The Willamette Mission remained Lee's headquarters, where he was assisted in supervisory duties by David Leslie and Gustavus Hines. Here no fewer than twenty-five adults—ministers and laymen—farmed several hundred acres, pastured herds of horses and cows, and taught the eighteen or nineteen children of their own families and a varying number of Indians. There was a sharp contrast between life at the new stations and at the Willamette Mission where, in the words of one disgruntled newcomer, "the Mission family live better than they would at home."

The Dalles station ranked second in conveniences and probably first in the size of the Indian population it sought to Christianize. In the fall of 1841 Jason Lee preached at a camp meeting where he reported 130 were baptized and 500 took the sacrament. But the Indians showed few signs of permanent conversion. They were neither humble nor grateful for Christian teachings, and they expected to be paid for attending worship. One November day in 1843, the missionaries, watching an eruption of Mt. St. Helens, were inspired to sing joyfully, "How awful is our God." The Indians failed to comprehend the lessons their teachers read into such a phenomenon. Their white teachers struggled not only to keep the natives under their influence but also to keep up their own courage.

John Frost at Clatsop Plains found the Indians had "no correct knowledge of the relation they sustain to God, as rational and accountable human beings, nor of the future state as a place of retribution." A modern scholar has suggested that Christianity failed to take hold among the Clackamas Indians of the Willamette Valley because they were unable "to conceive any universal principle of power, force, or deity."[3] The same reasoning may account for the failure of northwestern Indians in general to respond to Protestantism. This religion's world view was the antithesis of their own; and the abstractions of theological doctrine could not easily be translated into a language that dealt with things rather than ideas.

Wherever they located, the missionaries were overwhelmed by a sense of futility. A paltry number of Indians occasionally attended

[3] Melville Jacobs, "A Few Observations on the World View of the Clackamas Chinook Indians," *Journal of American Folklore*, September 1955, 289; Daniel Lee and J. H. Frost, *Ten Years in Oregon* (1844), 233.

Frost's services, and on many Sundays the missionaries preached to congregations composed only of each other. Disheartened by the Indians' indifference, gross habits, and materialism, the newly arrived missionaries were further discouraged by what they considered misrepresentations of the task to which they had been called. "Instead of thousands [of Indians] I have found but a few hundreds," wrote John Richmond from Nisqually, "and these are fast sinking into the grave. Extinction seems to be their inevitable doom, and their habits are such that I am fearful that they will never be reached by the gospel." Another complained that there were already too many missionaries in the field. Jason Lee's nephew, Daniel, concluded: ". . . the Church has been led to an improper estimate upon the prospects of Christianizing and civilizing the natives . . . and must now realize . . . disappointment."

The days of the Methodist Mission were numbered. Conflicts over secular and spirtual needs led to a rebellion against Lee's leadership. Dr. Elijah White, a recruit of 1837, carried complaints to the Society already disturbed by Lee's failure to return financial statements covering the funds at his disposal. In 1843 the Society suspended Lee who the next spring left for the East, never to return.

George Gary was sent out in 1844 to "ascertain . . . whether the mercantile, agricultural and mechanical operations" were necessary to the operation of the Mission, and to dispose of properties, dismiss personnel, and to give the Mission "as far as practicable, a strictly spiritual character." His findings led him to close the Mission and sell its properties. This decision has been variously interpreted. It suggests that the Board was reversing its policy of 1838, which through generous financing had enlarged the opportunities for secular activity, and that it was only now understanding the full implications of its activities. It also unfortunately suggests that there was something unethical in the secular activities of the Mission. This last interpretation has been the basis of a common criticism of the Oregon Methodists. It overlooks the fact that the original intention of the Board was to Christianize and civilize. These objectives were inseparable; the secular basis of the civilizing process could not be ignored. The missionaries did not come, as had Joseph Williams, to preach and to see the country. They came to establish themselves on the land and to mold the inhabitants to their concept of civilization.

The Mission Society considered this a long-range process. It agreed to pay the return transportation of the missionaries only after ten years of service in the field. Cultivating the land, raising herds of cattle, building grist and saw mills, buying and selling goods, were necessary activities of a people who intended not merely to survive a short time, but to root themselves in the country. McLoughlin was realistic when he reported that "the formation of a Colony of the United States Citizens on the banks of the Columbia . . . [was] the main or fundamental part" of the missionaries' plans. If such had not been their intention, they would not have placed so much emphasis upon recruiting married couples or upon encouraging the addition to their ranks of marriageable women teachers. Nor would they have been so zealous in efforts to bring "the right kind of people" to Oregon and discourage elements incompatible with their social ideals.

THE WHITMANS AND THE SPALDINGS

Some of the same problems afflicted other missionary efforts. Not only did secular activities vie with the spiritual but also work with the natives was difficult and discouraging. Most reluctant to concede the hopelessness of the task were the Whitmans and the Spaldings, sent out by the American Board of Commissioners for Foreign Missions (ABCFM).[4] In 1834, the Board, representing Congregationalist, Presbyterian, and Dutch Reformed membership, commissioned Samuel Parker and Dr. Marcus Whitman to survey the Oregon field. The next year, at the fur traders' rendezvous, Parker and Whitman talked with Flatheads and Nez Perces, whose eagerness to be taught deeply stirred them. Whitman returned east to raise money and recruits for a mission.

In 1836, Whitman, his recent bride, Narcissa, Henry Harmon Spalding and his wife, Eliza, and layman William H. Gray, attached themselves to a fur traders' caravan to the mountains. They traveled with wagons and drove a small herd of cattle. The heavy wagon was abandoned at Fort William (Laramie) when its slow progress threatened to put the missionaries too far behind their mounted guides. Spalding's light wagon, cut down to a two-wheeled cart, was taken through to Fort Boise, the first vehicle to go so far on the western trail.

On September 12 (1836), McLoughlin welcomed the tired travelers to Fort Vancouver. There is no record of what cheerful tidings Mrs. Beaver or Mrs. William Capendale, wife of the post farmer recently arrived from England, offered Narcissa Whitman and Eliza Spalding, first white women to make the continental crossing. But

[4] Clifford M. Drury, *Henry Harmon Spalding* (1936); *Marcus Whitman, M.D.* (1937); *Elkanah and Mary Walker* (1940); *A Tepee in his Front Yard* (1949); *Diaries and Letters of Henry H. Spalding and Asa Bowen Smith . . . 1838–1842* (1958).

Charles M. Russell was a working cowboy for fifteen years before he became "the cowboy artist." He loved and painted the northwest—country, Indians, animals, history—with special vividness. ABOVE. Lewis and Clark Expedition. Individual fur traders had preceded these explorers to the Yellowstone but their great expedition beyond the Rockies turned national attention to the Far West. BELOW. Father de Smet's First Meeting with the Flathead Indians. The Flatheads liked the preaching of "the Missionary of the Mountains." Many became converts.

BELOW. From the original Methodist Mission established by Jason Lee on the Willamette in Oregon, other missionaries founded missions among the Clatsops, at Willamette Falls, at Ft. Nisqually and here at the Dalles of the Columbia.

ABOVE. Cataldo Mission, in Idaho's northern panhandle, was built by Father Ravalli and Indians in the 1840s. Said to be Idaho's oldest extant building, it has been restored as an historical site.

ABOVE. Smith, Jackson, Sublette Expedition, 1830 *painted by William Henry Jackson. This lively, cheerful fur traders' caravan, headed for western Wyoming, was the first to travel with wagons on the Oregon Trail to the Rockies.*

BELOW. *Dr. John McLoughlin, called the "Father of Oregon," welcomes the Whitmans and the Spaldings to Fort Vancouver in 1836. The wives were the first white women to cross the Great Plains. (Detail from the rotunda mural, Oregon State Capitol Building).*

ABOVE. Oregon Trail *painted by O. E. Berninghaus. The Trail was two thousand miles long from Independence, Missouri to the Willamette Valley, Oregon. A few settlers' wagons rolled west in 1841. The Great Migration of 1843 made it necessary to set up a provisional government in the Willamette Valley.*

RIGHT. An Emigrant Camp, Oregon Trail *etched by S. Sartain exudes an almost garden-party charm. No doubt there were occasional camp sites like this but vast stretches of the Trail were treeless and dusty, water holes hard to find and often contaminated and Indians almost always annoying if not actually hostile.*

The long journey finished at last, a roof to live under was of prime importance. Neighbors often helped to raise the new cabin.

BELOW. *In the 1840s when the wagons started over the Trail, not many carried a camera! By the late 1870s, cameras were not uncommon but the great wagon trains would soon become a rarity.*

ABOVE. *Oppenheimer Mill, 1859, was built 6 miles south of Colville. After the settlers' cabins came the little crossroads communities. . . .*

. . . and Burnt Ranch, RIGHT, *on The Dallas-Canyon City Road, shows that frontier rawness was beginning to disappear by 1885.*

while their husbands located mission sites, the missionary wives enjoyed McLoughlin's hospitality, the luxury of a variety of fresh foods, and the "foreign" atmosphere of the fort where French was the common tongue.

In her first letters home, Narcissa Whitman described her adventures and the congenial life of the fort. She invited others to follow, but advised that "if anyone wishes to come by land (& by the by it is the best for health & the cheapest) let them send all their outfit to Oahu by ship & take only the suit they wish to wear & a few changes of undergarments, packing their provisions only & they will make an easy pleasant trip & less expensive than we made.... *We see now* that it was not necessary to bring anything *because we find it all here.*"

Despite McLoughlin's warning that he would have trouble with the Cayuses, Whitman chose to settle among them at Waiilatpu, "the place of the rye grass," at the junction of Mill Creek and the Walla Walla River, about twenty-five miles east of Fort Walla Walla. A crude house was built and occupied by November, 1836. "We shall not have access to as many Indians at first as Brother Spalding," Whitman reported, "but in the end I think as many will be benefited by this station as that. We have far more good land for cultivation here than there—probably more than at any place in the upper Columbia."

The Spaldings located in the present Idaho on a small prairie where Lapwai Creek flowed into the Clearwater. They were among friendly Nez Perces, who had shown promise of adaptability to Christian discipline, and who, under the Spalding's influence, developed a reluctant interest in an agricultural way of life. The Whitmans' experience with the Cayuses was different. Although they spoke the Nez Perce tongue and were closely bound to them through intermarriage, the Cayuses soon revealed themselves as proud, arrogant, and troublesome.

In the fall of 1838 a small reinforcement of helpers made it possible to set up several other stations. Unlike the Methodist mission which functioned under Jason Lee as the single responsible head, the American Board's missionaries formed a self-directing group, who decided policies and made station assignments in annual meetings. The membership was marked by a great diversity of personalities. Strong-willed, egotistical William H. Gray, a layman artisan, continually agitated for a mission of his own. Timid, complaining Asa Bowen Smith, scholar and linguist, was stationed with his wife at Kamiah until they were intimidated by the Indians. Before he left the Oregon country in 1841, Smith devised a practicable alphabet which Spalding used in printing a Nez Perce text of the Book of Matthew. This pioneer publication was made possible by the gift of an old press from the Hawaiian mission. Elkanah Walker and Cushing Eells, with their wives, were sent to Tshimakain, "the place of the springs," on the trail between forts Colvile and Walla Walla and about twenty-five miles northwest of the present city of Spokane. Mary Walker, a woman of high intelligence and spirit, recorded her sense of futility in a lengthy and fascinatingly candid diary, where one catches the echoes of disharmony which too often blemished the annual meetings.

There were several reasons for conflict between the Whitmans and Spaldings. Their sympathetic biographer, Clifford Drury, has advanced a possible explanation for their unhappy relations. A rejected suitor for Narcissa's hand, Spalding had questioned her fitness for missionary work, and before her marriage to Whitman had declared he would not go on a mission of which she was a member. This old wound was reopened from time to time and had to be cleansed with Spalding's repeated confessions of guilt, and temporarily healed with promises to forgive and forget.

Spalding was a man of great physical energy, who gave himself unremittingly to his heavy task. He soon became convinced that the spiritual salvation of the Nez Perces, as well as their physical survival, demanded that they abandon their traditional hunting economy and become settled farmers. His emphasis on the secular aspects of missionary work was not always approved by his co-workers. Spalding was thin-skinned but quick to criticize; and, one is inclined to believe, jealous of the more aggressive, positive Whitman.

Whitman though a frail man, was also energetic, decisive in his views, and impatient with his colleagues who did not share them. Driving himself unmercifully, he developed a productive farm, built and operated a grist and pit-saw mill, and attempted to supply the other stations. He worked assiduously as physician to the suspicious natives, and often rode hundreds of miles to care for his fellow missionaries. Though not an ordained minister, he preached and taught, and within the mission family assumed a leadership that was perhaps needed, but not specifically constituted in its organization.

Eliza Spalding, plain in appearance, hiding her emotions even from her private diary, was better educated than her husband. She was a skillful teacher, and probably more secure in her religious convictions than was Narcissa Whitman. Narcissa's letters reveal an intense, emotional woman whose real calling was to be mistress of a well-ordered Christian home. She had a gift for describing her reactions to the people and things that harassed her days, but despite her prayerful efforts, she could neither accept the Indians, nor understand her fellow workers. Ten years at Waiilatpu—the burden of running a large household, taking care of sick and hungry Indians and immigrants, teaching

171

school, and rearing orphaned children—these make her occasionally sharp tongue understandable to us. It was not always so to the other missionaries who had their own problems. The heartbreak of her two-year-old daughter's death by drowning, the lonely forebodings of her own death, and the tragic conclusion to her life, have endowed Narcissa with a saintliness her immediate contemporaries would not have recognized.

The differences between the Spaldings and Whitmans reached a climax in the winter of 1839–1840. Spalding wanted more emphasis on changing the pattern of the Indians' material lives; Whitman saw no hope for the Indians except as they were submerged in a superior civilization. Whitman would encourage white settlement; Spalding would postpone it, if possible, until the Indians were ready for it. Complaints from Smith, Gray, and Whitman reached the Board, which in 1840 ordered Spalding's dismissal. Gray and the Smiths were to return to the States, Lapwai and Waiilatpu were to be closed, and the Whitmans were to remove to Tshimakain.

By the time these orders were received in the fall of 1842, a fresh reconciliation had taken place, and receipt of the unhappy orders from home strengthened the newly forged bond of harmony. To persuade the Board to rescind its orders, and to report the latest developments in mission affairs and prospects for the future, Whitman decided to return east even though the season was late and the journey hazardous.

The cause he had to plead had taken on new meaning in the fall of 1842 when more than 100 emigrants stopped at Waiilatpu on their way to the Valley. A greater migration was promised in 1843. To abandon the station at this time was to abandon the settlers and the Indians who would need the missionaries' help more than ever. The importance of Waiilatpu was pointed out in Elkanah Walker's statement that if the Board felt a mission should be abandoned, it should be Tshimakain "with far less disastrous consequences both as respects white settlers and the natives."

In the East, Whitman talked with government officials about Oregon, and convinced the American Board that it should continue to support the existing missions. He preached Oregon to audiences already smitten with Oregon fever, and he helped guide the wagons of the Great Migration of 1843 across the trail he had first traveled seven years before.

Upon his return Whitman turned Waiilatpu into a provision center, rest station, and hospital for the immigrants of the following three years. In late November, 1847, the last covered wagons had hardly disappeared down the river road when the Cayuses turned on the Whitmans and their crowded household in a fury of butchery and crowned Narcissa and Marcus Whitman's labors with martyrdom.

INDEPENDENT MISSIONARIES AND CATHOLICS

In 1839 McLoughlin reported that there had "arrived a new order of missionaries styled 'Self Supporters,' to bewilder our poor Indians already perplexed beyond measure by the number and variety of their instructors." Some of these independents became permanent settlers, resorting to farming as a necessity. Some passed through the country in search of the proper setting for a utopian community.

Sixty-four-year-old Joseph Williams traveled to Oregon and back to Indiana in 1841–1842, part of the time journeying alone, because he wanted "to preach to the people . . . and . . . to the Indians, as well as to see the conutry." He was shocked by the profanity and "deistical" thinking of the nonreligious people he met. He disapproved of the missionaries' secular activities, though they fed and clothed him. In the light of his personal interpretation of the command "to go and preach," he was grieved "to see some of them so high-minded, and doing so little in the cause of God," and he feared they had "lost the spirit of their station, and . . . [had] turned their attention too much to speculation."

If they were aware of such criticism from fellow Protestants, the missionaries bore it with Christian fortitude. They were less tolerant of Catholic priests. Two years after Jason Lee had set up his mission on the edge of French Prairie, the French Canadians asked for priests to instruct them in their old religion, and McLoughlin forwarded their petition to the Bishop of Quebec, asking for the establishment of a church.

The HBC's London Committee expressed strong doubts about the wisdom of allowing priests to enter the Willamette settlement, feeling that the field of missionary labor was limited and that activities of Protestants and Catholics in the same locality might lead to Indian troubles. On the other hand, McLoughlin argued that the presence of priests might prevent the American missionaries from acquiring influence over the Canadians. Reluctantly the company gave permission for priests to go to Oregon on condition that they set up no mission south of the Columbia River. Within a year after their arrival in November, 1838, this condition was removed and Governor Simpson ordered McLoughlin to facilitate their mission.[5]

Father François Norbert Blanchet came from a family distinguished in its service to the church and had already proved his abilities when the Bishop of Quebec appointed him Vicar General of the Oregon Country. He and his assistant, Father Modeste Demers, were instructed to "withdraw from barbarity . . . the Indians . . . and to tender services to the wicked Christians who had adopted there the vices of the Indians and live in licentiousness and the forgetfulness of their duties." The priests' work was primarily among the French Canadians. They founded Mission St. Francis Xavier in the Cowlitz Valley, where Demers was in residence when not on missions to Walla Walla, Colville, and Okanogan. Father Blanchet was stationed at French Prairie, the largest parish, where in January, 1839, St. Paul's mission was dedicated in a moving ceremony. In 1842 St. Joseph's school for boys was founded; and two years later six sisters of the Congregation of Notre Dame de Namur founded a convent and school for girls nearby.

In December, 1843, the Oregon mission was made a vicarate apostolic with Father Blanchet as Bishop. While in Europe to raise funds and enlist workers for his vineyard, he was elevated to Archbishop, and Oregon was made an ecclesiastical province. The seat of the province was located at the Falls of the Willamette (Oregon City) where, on a nearby prairie, the church of St. John the Apostle was erected in 1846. Father Demers was consecrated Bishop of Vancouver Island, and the Archbishop's brother, A. M. A. Blanchet, Bishop of Walla Walla.

Missionary work among the Indians of the interior was the task mainly of Jesuit Fathers. The Indian delegation to St. Louis in 1831 which had started the Protestant missionary movement was succeeded by no fewer than three other delegations of Flatheads asking for "black robes" to teach them. Catholic Iroquois employed by the North West Company had taught the Flatheads and some Nez Perces about prayer and about the black-robed men who taught how to pray. Two Iroquois, among the last of these native lay missionaries to the Rocky Mountains, went to St. Louis in 1839, where their entreaties won from the Bishop of St. Louis promise of a mission the next spring.

The man chosen "to sound out the disposition of the Indians" was Father Peter John DeSmet, a 39-year-old Belgian who had been serv-

[5] William N. Bischoff, S. J., *The Jesuits in Old Oregon* (1945), 4.

ing in pioneer Missouri.[6] Traveling to the mountains with the fur caravan of 1840, Father DeSmet was met at the rendezvous by a deputa-
tion of Flatheads who escorted him into their country at the headwaters of the Missouri. Everywhere he found encouraging evidence of
the Indians' desire for teaching. After reporting back to St. Louis, he
returned to the mountains the next year with Fathers Point and Men-
garini and three lay brothers, to begin the arduous labor of converting
the Indians, and combatting "the avarice and cupidity of civilized
man," the "abominable influences of frontier vices," and the "Apostles
of Protestantism."

Mission St. Mary in the Bitterroot Valley was founded in 1841 and
the next year Mission of the Sacred Heart was established among the
Coeur d'Alenes. Reinforcements of priests and lay brothers, recruited
in both Europe and North America, extended the work of the mother
missions. St. Ignatius (Spokane), founded in 1844, has had the longest
continuous history. St. Francis Xavier (1884), in the Willamette Valley
near St. Paul's, was intended to serve as headquarters for the order,
but its distance from the interior posts and the decline of the French
population in the Valley caused it to be abandoned in 1852.

By 1850, five Jesuit and two Oblate missions were operating in the
Northwest. Although the California gold rush opened a new field, and
some of the fathers were sent there to set up missions, the work of the
Jesuits among the Northwest Indians was not abandoned. Their persistence resulted partly from their organization and concentration on
a single goal. They had the advantage of working with the relatively
unspoiled tribes of the interior, and they tailored their expectations to
the capacities of these people. They did not require examination in
problems of doctrine; they asked of their converts only the simplest
expressions of faith. These expectations so differed from those of the
Protestants that where the latter often labored to convert their tens,
the Jesuits labored to hold a few of their thousands of converts to
their Christian duties.

In some areas where both Protestant and Catholic missionaries
worked, as among the Spokanes and Nez Perces, sectarian distinctions confused the Indians and undermined whatever progress the
missionaries might have made toward teaching common Christian concepts of deity. The Catholic Ladder, a visual teaching aid devised by
Father Blanchet and systematically used by the Jesuits, was adapted
by the Spaldings to tell the Protestant story. Both versions graphically
illustrated the damnation awaiting converts to the other's faith. If

[6] William L. Davis, S. J., "Peter John DeSmet: the Journey of 1840," *PNQ*,
January, April 1941; April 1942; January, April 1944.

continuous missionary service were the final test for success of the two religions among the Indians, the laurels would go to the Catholics.

After the Whitman massacre the Protestants withdrew from the interior. But while their work among the natives declined, Protestant churches in the Willamette Valley multiplied and flourished. According to DeMofras, who visited the Valley in 1841, 600 persons attended Father Blanchet's services at St. Paul's. In 1847 his priests had an estimated 1200 parishioners. By 1850, however, the Catholic community in the Valley had begun to disperse. In the course of the next decade many French Canadians sold their lands to Americans and moved away, some following the gold rushes to California, to southern Oregon, and to Montana.[7]

PROTESTANTS VERSUS CATHOLICS

The Protestant missionaries' experiences proved to them that Oregon's future belonged to the white men, and they intended that these should be Americans. Nor is it surprising that they also expected them to be and remain Protestant.

The first half of the nineteenth century saw the emergence of a strong American nationalism; frontier people were expansive and aggressive, proud and sensitive, inexperienced with and hence suspicious of foreigners. They were traditionally anti-British; they were also traditionally anti-Catholic. The era that formulated "Manifest Destiny" also waged a "Protestant Crusade." Religious fervor moved both Catholic and Protestant, but Protestants believed they were fighting a holy war against the increasing numbers of Catholic foreigners in the United States and against the church's enlarged activities. The elements necessary for a Protestant Crusade were present in the strong prejudices of the Oregon missionaries, even before the Catholic priests arrived in 1838.

It is impossible to believe that when Jason Lee went east in 1838 to lay plans for an expanded mission endeavor, he was unaware that Catholic priests were on their way to Oregon. One must suspect that he used this as a strong argument for increasing the mission's resources. The men and women who came in the Great Reinforcement were as much bound to save souls from Catholicism as they were to save them with a Protestant doctrine. The circulation of anti-

[7] Robert C. Clark, *History of the Willamette Valley, Oregon*, 3 vols. (1927), I, 231. *The Golden Frontier: the Recollections of Herman Francis Reinhart, 1851–1869*, Doyce B. Nunis, Jr., ed. (1962), 80–81.

Catholic tracts, the controversy over the character of marriage rites performed by ministers and priests, aroused strong feelings among men who otherwise did not take religion seriously. Anti-Catholic sentiment, while gentlemanly and moderate compared with its expression in the East, was sanctioned by political and economic circumstances of the Willamette community. Inextricably woven into the fiber of that community were national as well as religious antipathies. Rightly or wrongly, the HBC was associated with Catholicism as well as with British interests.

The missionary era of Pacific Northwest history, from 1834–1843, was not one of spiritual activities alone. It was a period of colony building, but a colony in which religious elements were important. The influence of these formative years persisted in the development of that part of the Northwest later organized as the State of Oregon.

The Problem of Law
and Order:
A Government for
the Colony

As COLONISTS and religious workers, the missionaries were concerned with the civil and moral life of the community developing in the Willamette Valley. In 1838 the HBC had jurisdiction over British subjects, including its own employees and twenty-three retired French Canadians who had settled in the Valley. The Americans, eighteen "stragglers from California, etc.," and ten Methodist clergymen and missionaries, including six women, were outside United States jurisdiction, and hence outside the law. Jason Lee and John McLoughlin were in effect keepers of the peace, through persuasion and their economic positions. Together they "wielded the entire influence over this small population," according to Elijah White, who disapproved of the dyarchy.

ECONOMIC INFLUENCE OF THE HBC AND MISSIONS

Until 1838, Fort Vancouver was the settlers' only source of supply. Lacking cash, they could exchange surplus wheat, deer hides, fur pelts, or labor, for company goods. McLoughlin was obligated to protect the company's interest, hence he must trade for the company's profit. However, he was also generous by nature, advancing goods on credit to the destitute and needy, and thus causing himself considerable trouble with his superiors.

The Mission too had an economic influence through cash and credit with the HBC. The small reinforcement of mission workers in 1837 brought much-needed cash and briefly energized the economic life of the settlement. According to James Douglas, the mission was the "life and soul" of the American colony, and "dispensed bounties with a liberal hand." Even $500 laid out in labor and farm stock gave an "extraordinary impulse" to industry and raised the prices of goods, especially of work horses which formerly brought two pounds and now sold for five or six.

Lee and McLoughlin erred in deciding not to help Ewing Young and his companions in 1834. In retaliation for what they termed Mc-Loughlin's "tyrannizing oppressions," Young and Lawrence Carmichael set up a distillery, using equipment salvaged from Wyeth's abandoned Fort William. Indians, French Canadians, and mountain men suffered continuous thirsts, but whiskey was dangerous to the peace and specially to Indian-white relations. The company had controlled distribution, using it only to meet competition. The missionaries were opposed to liquor on principle. Young's enterprise threatened the objectives of both company and Mission.

To meet this threat, Lee organized a temperance society, which, with McLoughlin's financial help, offered to reimburse Young for expenses already incurred if he would abandon his still. Young agreed not to manufacture liquor but proudly refused the money. Fortunately a means of reconciling him with the community was at hand.

At this time (December, 1836), the American brig *Loriot* arrived in the Columbia, bringing William A. Slacum, commissioned by President Jackson to examine and report on coastal settlements of whites and their attitude toward the United States. In talks with the settlers Slacum learned of their great need for cattle, an important item in any frontier economy.

While McLoughlin would lend the settlers animals from the company's growing herd, he could not sell them. There were cattle on

California's "thousand hills" that could be bought cheaply enough, but the problem was to get them to Oregon. Ewing Young was the man for the job. The Willamette Cattle Company, financed largely by the Mission and McLoughlin, was organized January 13, 1837. Two weeks later eleven settlers, including two Canadians and Philip L. Edwards of the Mission as treasurer of the company, sailed passage-free on the *Loriot*. The following October the party, under Young's expert leadership, returned safely with 630 of the 830 head of cattle they had bought.

Young's success in this venture enhanced his community status. Respectability came with wealth. Within a few years Young not only had growing herds of cattle but also a sawmill and small store. Other settlers, by owning cattle, gained a degree of independence from the company.

Successful handling of the distillery episode and the organization of the cattle drive demonstrated the effectiveness of Lee's and McLoughlin's cooperation. But in matters of civil order, such as prosecution of crimes, neither had legal jurisdiction over the Americans. On one occasion Lee and his colleagues had assumed authority and held a court in a murder case. However this kind of action could prevail only with the tacit consent of the Americans. Mulling over their experience in the winter of 1837–1838, the missionaries concluded that their prospects would be enhanced if the "right kind" of people could be encouraged to settle in Oregon, and the "wrong kind" discouraged. It was then that Lee decided to go East and ask the Mission board to expand the Oregon Mission and equip it for the colony's physical as well as spiritual needs.

Slacum had apparently encouraged Lee to believe the United States government was not indifferent to developments in the Far West. Hall Jackson Kelley's impassioned writings and numerous petitions to Congress had kept alive an interest in Oregon. Senator Lewis Linn of Missouri, like Senator Floyd of Virginia before him, had agitated for occupation of Oregon, establishment of a military post there, and free land for settlers. If Congress could be moved to act, the boundary issue resolved, and sovereignty of the United States established, a territorial form of civil government would follow.

Lee carried to Congress a petition composed by Philip Edwards and signed by thirty-six of a possible fifty-one settlers south of the Columbia River. Nine were French Canadians, the others almost equally divided between members of the Mission and unattached Americans. The petition asked the United States government to "take formal and speedy possession," since a stable government would attract desirable settlers. So far, the colony had functioned without courts or laws, relying upon the HBC and moral influence. This could not continue with immigration increasing and dependence on the company diminishing. "We are anxious when we imagine what will be—what must be—the condition of so mixed a community, free from all legal restraint, and superior to that moral influence which has hitherto been the pledge of our safety."

A "good community" would not emigrate to a country known as lawless. "We can boast of no civil code. We can promise no protection but the ulterior resort of self-defense," the petitioners confessed. They asked:

> By whom, then, shall the country be populated? By the reckless and unprincipled adventurer . . . by the Botany Bay refugee; by the renegade of civilization from the Rocky Mountains; by the profligate deserted seaman from Polynesia; and the unprincipled sharpers from Spanish America?[1]

Direct but brief reference was made to a need for regulating Indianwhite relations, with an oblique reference to the British. The petitioners could not "suppose so vicious a population could be relied on in case of a rupture between the United States and any other Power." According to James Douglas, the petitioners, in asking for aid from the United States, revealed their natural bias. However, he doubted that their appeal would attract much attention unless it was "in accord with the tide of public feeling" in the United States.

The tide of public feeling was at low ebb. Although Congress was aware of the Oregon problem, for reasons of domestic politics it was in no mood to raise an issue with Great Britain. Texas and California were problems too; the abolitionist movement was fomenting sectional antagonisms, and a severe depression had set in. Senator Linn presented Lee's petition to Congress, together with a bill to occupy Oregon, but Lee was refused permission to address Congress and the bill was tabled.

Lee was more successful with the Mission Society and the public at large. In church pulpits and on lecture platforms he helped generate "Oregon Fever." As we have seen, the Society raised about $100,000 to support the Mission.

Douglas, acting chief officer of the company in McLoughlin' temporary absence, looked "with much anxiety" to the immigration that might be attracted by the "overcharged" picture of the country's importance. He suspected also that the missionaries intended to engage

[1] "The Oregon Memorial of 1838," Cornelius J. Brosnan, ed., *OHQ*, March 1933, 74–77; C. J. Pike, "Petitions of Oregon Settlers, 1838–1848," *OHQ*, September 1933.

directly or indirectly in trade, an event that he wished could be averted since the company would have to take the field against them. If it did it might be accused of persecuting the Americans and arouse their government. Douglas' fears were justified. The missionaries did engage in trade. The new steward or business manager of secular affairs, George Abernethy, moved the mission store to the Falls of the Willamette where it sought the patronage of settlers in Tualatin Plains. But the company did not have to take the field against the Mission. It did not have to: the mission store depended upon the HBC for supplies. The monopoly was not broken, but the seed of competition had been planted.[2]

GROWTH OF THE COLONY

With the Mission's Great Reinforcement of 1840, the American colony had grown to about 150 persons. In the fall of 1839 and the spring of 1840 the first secular immigrants arrived in response to Lee's advertisement of the Oregon country. Led by Thomas Jefferson Farnham, fourteen men had set out from Peoria, Illinois, in 1839. Only seven arrived in Oregon, the others having abandoned the venture along the devious route from the South Platte to the Colorado Rockies and the Snake. At about the same time, several independent missionaries —Harvey Clark, Alvin T. Smith, and Philo B. Littlejohn—crossed the mountains with their families and a party of mountain men as guides.

Their leader was Robert "Doc" Newell, who, with his brother-in-law, Joseph L. Meek, seven other men, three Indian women and several children, drove "with some little difiquilty" two heavy wagons from Fort Hall to Fort Walla Walla. Recognizing that he and his party had opened a new stretch of the road to Oregon, Newell proudly noted in his journal: "This is to be remembered that I, Robert Newell, was the first who brought waggons across the rocky mountains . . . up to this 19th day of April 1841." The newcomers settled in the Tualatin Plains near Ewing Young and his friends, swelling the number of ex-mountain men to thirty or thirty-five.

The itinerant preacher Joseph Williams did not find the American secular society elevated in tone. But old-timer James O'Neill, a former Wyeth man, thought otherwise.

[2] Arthur L. Throckmorton, *Oregon Argonauts: Merchant Adventurers on the Western Frontier* (1961).

. . . the white people live without any forms of law; but in general are very honorable in paying their debts, and give notes and bonds. They have no sheriffs, constables, fees, nor taxes to pay. They profess to be very hospitable to strangers, and kind to one another. No breaking each other up for debts. Here are no distilleries, no drunkeness, nor much swearing. They seem, indeed, to be a very happy people.[3]

This was a rosier picture of the community than the Methodist missionaries or McLoughlin admitted. Some of the mountain men, like Newell, settled down as farmers and did their part to maintain peace and order. Others farmed as necessity dictated, consumed "blue ruin," gambled, and on Sundays gathered to run the *correr el gallo,* a cruel horse race for possession of a live greased goose or chicken, and quarreled among themselves. But George W. Ebbert and Caleb Wilkins, who had thought to be "kings" in a little domain of freedom were surprised to find themselves subjected to a civilizing process.[4]

The harmony that marked Lee's and McLoughlin's relations was dissipated when the Mission entered the mercantile business, and when in 1841 some of the Mission group settled on McLoughlin's land claim at the Falls of the Willamette. The claim controversy stirred a furor that embittered McLoughlin's relations with the Americans for the remainder of his life.

Nor were the mountain men, as a rule, amicably disposed toward McLoughlin or the company. In the mountains the HBC had been a competitor in the fur trade; in the Valley, it was a monopoly, its officers "aristocrats," and whether mountain men labeled themselves Jacksonian Democrats or Clay Whigs, they opposed what the company stood for.

A strong feeling of American versus British was developing. In 1839 a British naval squadron under Captain Edward Belcher had arrived in the Columbia. Belcher's visit was primarily for the purpose of investigating the HBC–Russian relations on the Stikine River and surveying the Columbia River bar, its channels and inner anchorages, in anticipation of increased trade between the company and the Russian colonies in Alaska. But to the Americans his presence meant that the British planned to seize the Oregon country. Furthermore, it was bruited about, and with truth, that the company planned to strengthen its claims north of the Columbia by colonizing the Cowlitz Valley.

According to Thomas Farnham, several Americans asked him why the Oregon colony was neglected by the United States; why foreigners

[3] Joseph Williams, *Narrative of a Tour . . . 1841–42* (1921), 57.
[4] George W. Ebbert, "A Trapper's Life in the Rocky Mountains & Oregon," microfilm copy of Bancroft interview (1878) at Oregon Historical Society.

were permitted "to domineer" over them, drive traders from the country, and reduce them to dependence. He suggested another petition to Congress, and offered to present it to that body when he returned East. The so-called Farnham petition was composed by David Leslie of the Mission, signed by sixty-seven citizens of the United States or persons who expected to become citizens, and represented the views of a restless secular community.

The petition described the settlers as exposed to the attacks of savages and "others that would do them harm," and elaborated on British efforts to hold the country north of the Columbia. It stated that theft, murder, infanticide, and other crimes were increasing at an alarming rate, and that the people's only means of protecting themselves, other than by force of arms, were "self-constituted tribunals, originated and sustained by the power of an ill-instructed public opinion." It asked for "the civil institutions of the American Republic"; prayed for "the high privileges of American citizenship; the peaceful enjoyment of life, the right of acquiring, possessing and using property; and the unrestrained pursuit of rational happiness."

This petition was no more successful than the less elaborately stated one of 1838. On January 8, 1841, Senator Linn introduced a joint resolution of Senate and House, to occupy, settle, grant lands, and extend certain laws of the United States to the Oregon country. Again, Congress took no action.

THE BEGINNING OF LOCAL
SELF-GOVERNMENT

At the time Linn was introducing his resolution, the Oregonians were facing a problem which required immediate solution. Ewing Young died, leaving properties, but apparently without heir. Jason Lee and his friends were prepared for this contingency. After the funeral on February 17 (1841), Lee addressed the mourners on the matter of disposing of Young's estate, making it clear that such a situation might arise again. The settlers were urged to organize for this purpose of law, and further, for "the better preservation of peace and good order." After some discussion, the settlers agreed to the appointment of a committee of seven to draft a code of laws.

So far, considerable harmony apparently prevailed in the meeting. But when Lee proposed a list of offices and the slate of candidates to fill them, there was less agreement. His proposal called for a governor, a supreme judge with probate powers, three constables, three road commissioners, an attorney general, clerk of court, public re-corder, treasurer, and—somewhat ironically—two overseers of the poor. A bare majority approved the offices; but some settlers, suspecting that they were being rushed into an organization, moved to adjourn until the following day, when a larger attendance could further con-sider the matter.

There must have been a great deal of coming and going, of talking and listening, that evening. On the next day, February 18, 1841, a full meeting of the inhabitants held a referendum on the actions of the day before. They now approved only those offices necessary to handle probate cases and offenses against the peace. They elected a sheriff and three constables and Dr. Ira L. Babcock as judge with probate powers to act under the laws of New York. They drew the line firmly at creating the office of governor, but they approved a committee, headed by Father Blanchet, to draft a civil code and to report to an assembly on June 1. When that day came, Father Blanchet announced that the committee had not met.

The scanty minutes of the June meeting show that the majority of settlers did not want to set up a hierarchy of officers, and were doubt-ful whether an organization was necessary. Since Lee had sparked the whole idea, its rejection was evidence that the influence of the Mission was waning. From Father Blanchet's lack of cooperation it was apparent that the company and the French Canadians did not subscribe to it. But the settlers did elect Dr. William J. Bailey to re-place Blanchet, and directed the code committee to confer with Mc-Loughlin and Lieutenant Charles Wilkes about the advisability of or-ganizing a government.

Wilkes, commander of the United States Exploring Expedition of 1838–1842, entered the Columbia with two vessels in the summer of 1841. In his short stay he found no reason for alarm for the security of the settlers' lives and property. So far as he could tell, the Americans were "orderly, and some industrious, although they are, with the ex-ception of the missionaries, men who have led for the most part dis-solute lives." He did not encourage the settlers to organize.

Despite Wilkes' opinion, the idea of at least a minimum of govern-ment was slowly taking hold. For one thing, proceeds from sales of Young's estate, eventually amounting to more than $3000 in promis-sory notes, were common property of the community, and evidence that a community of a limited nature existed in fact.

Between 1841 and 1843 new circumstances gave further reason to consider organizing. In 1841, the HBC sent out twenty-one families from the Red River in Canada to settle in the Cowlitz Valley. Enticed by more fertile pastures and prospects of greater freedom, some of them began gradually to move down into the Tualatin and Willamette valleys. In 1842, a party of 114 Americans, led by Elijah White and Lansford W. Hastings, arrived from the States.

This important immigration was the first major result of the Oregon fever, generated in part by Senator Linn's bills which would reward settlers with grants of free lands, and in part by the rhetoric of expansionist orators on lyceum platforms and at "Oregon Meetings." For instance, in 1841 Tilghman Howard urged his fellow citizens of Bloomington, Illinois, to occupy Oregon. That it was not a part of the United States should not deter one immigrant from going. "A colony could protect and govern itself until the general government should be driven by a sense of duty, and from a regard to the interests of the United States, to protect the people."

The new arrivals brought word that Senator Linn had again, in January of 1842, introduced a bill to force settlement of the boundary issue. It would extend the laws of the United States to lands south of the 49th parallel and grant immigrants a section—640 acres—of free land. The prospects of its passage were so favorable that hundreds of people were gathering in Missouri preparatory to moving to Oregon in the summer of 1843. To the settlers it was now a question of how to protect their claims from the prospective immigrants.

The importance of this question cannot be exaggerated. Only the sovereign state could grant titles; the settlers already in Oregon had no legal rights to the land. They were few in number and held their lands by occupancy and mutual consent. But this was a frail defense against the anticipated overwhelming number of newcomers seeking land. Faced with this problem, the Oregonians also had reason to worry about an Indian uprising.

Elijah White had returned to Oregon with a presidential appointment as Indian agent for the territory, anticipating a provision of the Linn bill authorizing the President to appoint agents for territory west of Iowa. When the bill failed to pass, White's office was wiped out, but this was not known in Oregon until the fall of 1843. Meantime, White bustled about on his official duties.

At the Whitman mission the Cayuses had grown increasingly impudent. While her husband was East in the winter of 1842–1843, Narcissa Whitman was so frightened by one ruffian that she took refuge with the Methodist missionaries at the Dalles. During her absence the Waiilatpu mill was burned.

White tried to keep the interior Indians peaceable by imposing white men's methods upon them. In a series of conferences with the principal Nez Perce chieftains (but unfortunately failing to reach all the Cayuse chiefs), he prevailed upon them to accept eleven funda-

186

mental laws regulating their conduct toward white men. He urged them to choose a head chief who would be responsible for enforcing the laws; but he failed to realize that their social structure did not allow this kind of united action and that the concept of responsible power was foreign to them. The Nez Perces attempted the impossible and failed.

But rumors of Indian restlessness in the interior created fears and suspicions in the Valley. Unfortunately, White was tactless, officious, and ambitious. His methods of dealing with the few natives that lived by petty thievery on the outskirts of the settlement were decried as arbitrary, costly, and futile, and he was charged with using his office to build a political career in the colony.

TENDER ISSUES OF POLITICS

Thus with missionary influence waning and hostility toward the HBC growing, with the settlers excited about their rights in the land and fearful of Indian troubles, a climate of opinion was formed in favor of a government. Two alternatives were presented. The settlers might set up an independent state, as had the Texans, and claim the land in their own right. Or they could form a temporary government to preserve the peace and their land claims until the boundary issue was settled and the Unites States extended its jurisdiction over them. In either case, their working relations with the HBC had to be defined. Two parties emerged, the Independents and the American. The Independents wished to go it alone and form their own republic. Lansford W. Hastings, a somewhat volatile and ambitious man who had become McLoughlin's legal advisor concerning his disputed land claim, was apparently one of the chief instigators of the movement.

The American Party had two factions: the Moderates and the Ultras. The latter, opposed to McLoughlin, the company, and everything British, would risk any action that might bring the United States to assert its rights in Oregon. In the Ultras' eyes, the Moderates were sycophants of a foreign power because they took the position that American sovereignty could be established only when Congress should terminate the Convention and settle the boundary problem and that, in the meantime, for their own security the Americans had to cooperate with McLoughlin.

Outside the American groups were the French Canadians, torn by anxiety over their own land claims, distrustful of the Americans, and dependent upon the company. They took their lead from McLoughlin.

For personal and company reasons McLoughlin encouraged the Independents; for the practical reason of keeping the peace, he depended upon the influence of the Moderates.

In the winter of 1842 the Pioneer Lyceum and Literary Club, sometimes called the Willamette Falls Debating Society, provided a forum for public discussion of these views. On one occasion Hastings proposed a resolution to the effect that it was "expedient for the settlers on this coast to establish an independent government." The affirmative won. But when it was rumored that some of those who favored independence also expected to assume power in the state, a second debate affirmed that it would *not* be expedient to form an independent government "if the United States extends its jurisdiction over this country within four years."

Discussion gave over to action in the early spring of 1843, when some settlers met at the home of William H. Gray to discuss the specific problem of protecting their herds from wolves, as well as other more general matters. They decided to call a general assembly of the inhabitants to meet at Joseph Gervais' house at Champoeg on the first Monday in March. The second "wolf" meeting brought a large turnout. The settlers amiably agreed to a voluntary tax for wolf bounties and to a committee to administer it. Then, according to Gray's account, he made a plea for an organization to protect them from dangers "worse than wild beasts" that threatened their lives. He offered a resolution to form a committee that would take "measures for the civil and military protection of the colony." This was approved and a committee of twelve was appointed to draw up a report on organization.

The committe reported to a gathering of settlers on May 2, 1843, Dr. Ira Babcock presiding. The report proposed an elected government of three rudimentary branches; a judge, a legislative committee, and an executive committee of three persons; it proposed division of the country into counties with elected officials. It also proposed organization of a militia.

The motion to accept the report was rejected. According to the minutes of the meeting, "considerable confusion existing in consequence," the settlers by acclamation voted to divide "preparatory to being counted; those in favor of the objects of this meeting taking the right, and those of a contrary mind, taking the left. . . ." In Gray's later version of the affair, which mountain man Joe Meek corroborated, Meek stepped into the yard, drew a line across the dirt with a stick, and cried in his notably loud voice, "who's for a divide? All for the report of the committee and organization follow me."

The minutes state that "a great majority being found in favor of organization, the greater part of the dissenters withdrew." Tradition says that fifty Americans and two Canadians lined up for the report of the committee and fifty French Canadians against it. This dramatically close vote is justifiably disputed; the number of French Canadians at the meeting was smaller than has been claimed. Furthermore, some of the Americans were opposed to the committee report though not opposed to organization of a government. The issue that created confusion was not merely that of organizing a civil state, but rather of accepting the committee's whole report which also called for the raising of a militia.

Between the first and second wolf meetings there had been considerable public discussion of what was involved in measures for military protection. To some realists the military emphasis was an invitation to trouble considering the fact, as Robert Newell later recalled, that in the whole country there were "63 Americans and 400 British subjects and 15,000 Indians." George W. LeBreton, a partisan American and recorder of the skimpy minutes of the meeting, defined the divisive issue in a private letter written in December 1843:

> The Canadians generally at the instigation doubtless of the Officers of the HB Company refused to join in these measures stating that they would be protected by the compy and that it was the "Bostons" only that the Indians intended to make war upon. . . . Dr. McLoughlin understanding that Dr. White the Sub Indian Agent intended to call upon him for a supply of arms & ammunition that the Inhabitants might have the means of defending themselves wrote a Letter to Dr. White stating that he should refuse to supply him with such articles if called upon . . . his motives might have been good to prevent excitement and believing there was no danger &c. The American part of the population proceed[ed] to organize themselves. . . .[5]

The dissenters having withdrawn, the rump assembly adopted the committee report and elected nine persons as a legislative committee, instructing them to form a code of laws and to report it July 1 to the citizens assembled at Champoeg.

A GOVERNMENT RATIFIED

A rollicking celebration marked the Fourth of July, the westerners' favorite holiday. The next day the inhabitants of the Valley gathered in a solemn conclave of democracy, presided over by Gustavus

[5] LeBreton to Caleb Cushing, December 1, 1843, in Cushing Papers, Library of Congress.

Hines. The legislative committee reported a code derived from the laws enacted at Iowa's first territorical session in 1839 and from the Ordinance of 1787 for the Territory North of the Ohio River, a basic document for organization of American territories. The Iowa code was used not simply because, as has been suggested, someone happened to have a copy of the "Little Blue Book." It is reasonable that Elijah White had with him a copy of the laws he was expected to administer as Indian agent under the Iowa Territory agency and White was a member of the code committee.

In details the Oregon code varied only slightly from its model. But in two major instances it was tailored to the special desires of its framers. An article on lands, the longest in the document, allowed the Mission a township (six square miles). All persons obeying the laws, and including the missionaries as individuals, were to be sustained in their possession of 640 acres (one section) if they recorded metes and bounds, improved the property within six months, and resided on it within a year. Especially palatable to the voters was the omission of a taxing power. Voluntary subscriptions and fees were to support the government. Men were eligible to vote and hold office after six months residence. The code also authorized election of a major and three captains to form rifle companies. (It is interesting that the militia was not called up until March, 1844, after a fracas in which a drunken Indian killed George LeBreton. The company drilled three times and dispersed when the question was raised as to who was going to pay them.)

After adoption of the code, the settlers elected the executive committee: David Hill, Alanson Beers, and Joseph Gale, and a supreme judge. The code committee was carried over as the legislative committee until the next election when a new one was chosen. It is worthy of note that the jurisdiction of the new government was assumed to extend to the Russian settlements at 54° 41′. (See map of counties, page 233.)

The government was provisional; that is, it was to serve until a permanent government was established. Whether this would be independent or under the American system was ambiguous, but the appointment of a committee to report the organization to Congress supports the notion that it was to serve until Congress organized the Oregon Country as a territory. In this step, taken in July, 1843, the Independent Party suffered a setback; it had already lost one of its leaders. Lansford Hastings left in May with a party of fifty-three for California where, it has been said, he hoped to win immortality by revolutionizing the Mexican province.

THE IMMIGRATION OF 1843 AND THE CODE REVISION OF 1844

The 900 or more immigrants who arrived that fall came primarily from Missouri, Illinois, and southern Ohio where Senator Linn's Oregon bills had popular support. Congress' failure to pass the 1842 measure had vastly disappointed them. Nor were they pleased with the government they found in Oregon. McLoughlin reported that some were "disposed to set up an independent State because if the Country becomes a Territory of the United States they will be so remote from the seat of Government." On the other hand, some ardent proponents of American rights wanted to force an immediate settlement of the Oregon issue on the spot and in favor of the United States. In short, the newcomers fell easily into the categories of sentiment already present in the colony.

Almost at once they were at variance with the old settlers, agitating for revision of the land laws and for a stronger, more aggressive government. Since they controlled, by weight of numbers, the election of the legislative committee which sat in June, 1844, they were able to implement their wishes. In revising the code, they dropped the word provisional and thereby prevailed upon the French Canadians to join despite their fear that a stronger state might be more costly and might more successfully reflect American antagonism to them. The Mission claim was reduced to a square mile and a tax schedule set up. It called for a 50-cent poll tax, and a tax of one-eighth of one percent *ad valorem* on "all merchandize brought into the country for sale, improvements on farm lots, mills, pleasure carriages, clocks, watches, mules, cattle, and hogs." This was blatantly discriminatory against the old settlers and especially against the HBC. But it was the revisionists' ace card: any person refusing to pay taxes was excluded from the protection of the laws of Oregon.

A test case arose almost immediately. In February, 1845, Henry Williamson and several companions erected a log hut almost at the gates of Fort Vancouver and posted a claim stated in a venerable old rhyme:

> Meddle not with this house or claim
> For under is the Master's name.

Only through the good offices of Elijah White, Gustavus Hines, and Jesse Applegate, was Williamson prevailed upon to move. But Mc-

Loughlin had had warning that the new colonists were less amenable than those of former days.

Each fall's immigration changed in some measure the character of government and heightened the political temper of the community.[6] The immigrants of 1843 had been rambunctious and independence minded; those arriving in 1844, adding perhaps 1200 persons to the colony and bringing its total to about 2500, were confident that Oregon would soon become part of the Union.

Congress in the winter of 1843–1844 had considered giving notice to Great Britain of termination of the Convention. In May, 1844, the Democratic Party nominated James K. Polk for President on an expansionist program that called for occupation of Oregon. The immigrants of that year undertook to make the local government conform more exactly to American precedents and prepare the way for the American system.

The legislative committee, sitting in December 1844, prepared a number of bills introducing specific changes in the code which were referred to the people and ratified at the June 1845 election. The executive committee was abolished and the office of governor created; the judiciary was reformed, the legislative committee was designated a legislature, and counties were organized. Anticipating ratification, the inhabitants of Clackamas, Yamhill, Tualatin, and Champoeg held county conventions and nominated candidates for offices. George Abernethy, former steward of the Mission and a merchant at Oregon City, was elected governor.

Because existing official documents are not helpful in analyzing the organization of June, 1845, the account of James W. Nesmith, successful candidate for Supreme Court Judge, assumes special importance:

> We have five organized counties [Clackamas, Champoeg, Yamhill, Tualatin, Clatsop], the Gov., Judge, Sheriff, Recorder, Attorney, Treasurer and Assessor are State officers and operate for the whole, and hold two courts in each county annually; the Justices [of the Peace] form the inferior courts. We have a Legislature composed of thirteen members who have now just commenced their annual session at this place [Oregon City] which is the seat of *Government*.
>
> . . . I received the nomination of the Champoeg Convention and ran for [Judge] . . . at the election which took place on the first Tuesday of the present month at which I received the unanimous vote of the whole Territory happening to be on all tickets, two of which I

[6] The 1844–1845 codes can be found in *The Frontier Experience: Readings in the Trans-Mississippi West*, Robert V. Hine and Edwin R. Bingham, eds. (1963).

send you . . . were *printed* for Champoeg County. They are the first tickets printed in Oregon. . . .

The question of adopting a constitution was before the people at the late election, but was rejected. . . .[7]

In the spring and early summer of 1845 a crisis had developed in the relations between Great Britain and the United States over Oregon, and war appeared imminent. Informed of the situation, thoughtful colonists recognized that a very unpleasant local situation could develop. The American community now outnumbered the British; but a British naval vessel was in the Strait of Juan de Fuca and two British army observers had come to look over possible defenses of British interests.

At a critical moment, Jesse Applegate emerged as a statesman. A Missouri farmer of more than ordinary intellectual attainment and widely read, Applegate had captained the "cow column" of the 1843 immigration. He was notably a Moderate in Valley politics. Realizing that the community could not defend itself against lawless elements while weathering the international crisis, he proposed a means for British subjects and American citizens to live together without violence while their home governments made vital decisions of war or peace. McLoughlin assented to Applegate's suggestions, feeling that he could no longer "oppose a general union of the inhabitants" since to do so might incur individual suffering and disturb "the peaceful relations of our respective governments and [drag] them into a ruinous war."

The local government was now redefined as a "compact of certain parties, British and American . . . to afford each other protection in person and property to maintain the peace of the community and prevent . . . crime." Fundamentally, the intent was to associate by concensus the two populations affected by threat of war and to provide for a peaceable transition to whatsoever might ensue from resolution of the Oregon Question.

The compact carried two conditions which made it possible for the British to cooperate: it did not affect the allegiance of the parties, and the tax law was revised and discriminations against the British removed. Furthermore, Vancouver County was organized north of the Columbia River where British interests were located. As members of the compact, the British could now take up lands on the same terms as

---

[7] *OHQ*, December 1912, 380–381; Mirth Tuft Kaplan, "Courts, Counselors and Cases: The Judiciary Department of Oregon's Provisional Government," *OHQ*, June 1961.

Americans, run for office, and vote. The agreement was formalized by the legislature at Oregon City, August, 1845.

A month after adoption of the compact the wagons of 3000 immigrants rolled into the Valley. They brought news that the boundary issue between Great Britain and the United States was on the verge of settlement. But whether that would be in peace or war, still remained unclear.

CHAPTER
THIRTEEN

The Oregon Treaty and the National Design

GOVERNMENT had evolved in the colony because the Americans had no protection for their persons and property. In land under United States sovereignty protection would have been provided by Congress. But under the terms of the conventions of 1818 and 1827, the colonists were in a political vacuum, and they had taken steps to fill it.

Albert Gallatin had pointed out to the British in 1826 that American settlers were in the habit of "carrying laws, courts, justices of the peace" with them. There was an "absolute necessity on our part to have some species of Government."[1] Americans were capable both of great lawlessness and great discipline. Discipline prevailed in Oregon.

This was evident in 1845. Highly charged with anti-British sentiment that had been building up in the States, the immigrants nevertheless accepted the government they found in Oregon and with few exceptions obeyed its elementary laws. The compact takes on significance when one considers the situation in which it functioned. It pre-

[1] *Canadian Relations*, II, 569.

195

vented incidents which might have led to a war that neither Great Britain nor the United States wanted.

Although between 1831 and 1842 the halls of Congress and country schoolhouses had occasionally reverberated with militant declarations of American rights in Oregon, the boundary question was not raised on the diplomatic level. And after the renewal of the Convention in 1827 Britain showed no official interest in Oregon until the United States began to assume military postures in 1842. From the end of the Napoleonic Wars to the mid-nineteenth century, Conservative and Whig governments tried to insure prosperity (and their own political security) with a foreign policy geared to peace. A century ahead of the United States in economic development, Great Britain was not attempting to add territories to her dominions. British capital tended to flow to areas with resources to feed her industries and markets for her manufactured goods. The Pacific Northwest did not attract investment capital. It was a private preserve of the HBC, its economy primitively extractive and its resources, like the wants of its inhabitants, limited.

However, no government hoping to remain in office could easily surrender lands to which the nation had what it considered unquestionable rights. British claims to western Washington, disputed with the United States since 1818, were strengthened twenty years later when the HBC and the Puget's Sound Agricultural Company began to develop farming settlements north of the Columbia. This area also had military value. If and when British colonies developed in western Canada, the Columbia River and the Sound were outlets for more than HBC trade and the Sound was ideal for a naval base.

But in 1838 there was no strong sentiment to commit the nation to HBC interests, and after the 1837 revolts in Upper and Lower Canada, the future relations of Canadian colonies to Great Britain were debated. On the one hand, Britain must bear her colonial burdens if she intended to remain a first-class power; on the other, there might be advantages in a "kindly and gentle separation."[2]

The Governor and Committee of the HBC feared the government would surrender western Washington to the United States by default, if not by outright concession. They urged national as well as their own private interests, but so coolly were their arguments received that they began to look for a new site for their principal depot. In 1842, a site on Vancouver Island was chosen against the day when Fort Vancouver would have to be abandoned. There was reason to believe that day was not far distant. The Webster-Ashburton Treaty (1842) had ended the

[2] E. E. Rich, *History of the Hudson's Bay Company*, 2 vols. (1958–1959), II, 720.

long dispute over the Maine boundary; Oregon had not been brought up in the negotiations because it was not considered as important as other matters. With Lord Aberdeen in the Foreign Office, the company had no friend at court.

THE AMERICAN POSITION, 1827–1842

The American attitude toward the Oregon country was relatively uncomplicated. In 1827 the State Department had claimed to 50 degrees 40 minutes, offered to compromise at the 49th parallel to the sea, but refused further compromise. The nation's natural dominion in this quarter had been defined. The American people were peaceably cultivating new lands and creating new states. Oregon was remote; until the mid-thirties it was known only through reports of fur traders. Although a few enthusiasts agitated for its occupation, serenely confident in their burgeoning national strength and promise of a rosy future, neither people nor government felt compelled to force what would, in time, fall naturally into their hands. Providence had decreed to the republic a "mission" and had made clear its "manifest destiny."[3]

The rhetoric of the day assumed a single identity and unity of purpose for the American people. However, to the affirmation of national unity was posed the prospect of sectional division. The needs of new segments of the economy for a laissez-faire climate, the unresolved constitutional problem of relative powers of states and the nation, and, most dramatically, the stepped-up attack upon slavery, affected almost every issue of domestic policy. For example, debates on central banking and corporate monopolies, tariff and free trade, internal improvements and disposal of the public domain, and even upon the paths that expansion might take, were affected by the slavery issue. "Thirty-six thirty," the compromise line of 1820 which tried to balance the power of North and South, free state and slave, lay athwart the promise of the Union's future. So too did some aspects of maritime and continental rivalry.

American expansion, as suggested earlier, was invited by an unoccupied continental domain. Although most Americans thought of themselves as simple yeomen, their actual performance showed a profound regard to commercial opportunities as well as for fertile

[3] Julius W. Pratt, "The Origin of 'Manifest Destiny,'" *American Historical Review*, July 1927; Frederick Merk, *Manifest Destiny and Mission in American History* (1963); Albert K. Weinberg, *Manifest Destiny* (1935).

prairies.[4] The predominantly farming areas of the South and Mid-west opposed policies favorable to that of commercial New England, but they did not want to jeopardize their own chances to build prosperity on the same foundation.

New England pioneers had been in the vanguard of settlement in the Old Northwest. Sectionally, New England was oriented to the sea. Her ships entered the Pacific to open the American fur trade with China, and they did not withdraw when that trade declined. In 1841, it was reported that $40 million, largely American capital, was invested in Pacific whaling fleets. Since 1822 a naval squadron had been assigned to protect commerce with China (and anticipated the opening of Japan), India, South Sea and Hawaiian Islands, and California.

New England wanted Pacific Coast ports for her commerce. So, in the forties, New England Whigs with clear conscience supported questionable operations to acquire California while opposing, on principle, the annexation of Texas because it was a slaveholding state. They could remain indifferent to expansion if its objective was the Oregon Country, with only one good harbor; they could be highly excited about expansion into California, because it had three. On the other hand, southern Democrats and Whigs for the same reasons were just as eager to acquire California, and just as indifferent to Oregon which was situated north of 36°-30' and beyond the area of potential slave expansion.

Norman Graebner has argued that ". . . the expansion of the United States was a unified, purposeful, precise movement that was ever limited to specific maritime objectives. It was the Pacific Ocean that determined the territorial goals of all American presidents from John Quincy Adams to Polk." Maritime mercantile interests "provided more than a contributing motive to American expansionism" and "determined the course of empire." The "goal of American policy was to control the great harbors of San Francisco, San Diego, and Juan de Fuca Strait."[5] This provocative but extreme statement helps to explain the politics of American expansion in the decade of 1836–1846; it does not fully explain its complexities.

Whether the continent was to be possessed by a unified people, or by sectional confederations, each attempting to realize its own national destiny, was not clear in the forties. But common fear that some

[4] Richard C. Wade, *The Urban Frontier; The Rise of Western Cities, 1790–1830* (1959) demonstrates a thesis applicable to the Pacific Northwest.

[5] Norman A. Graebner, *Empire on the Pacific: a Study in American Continental Expansion*, copyright 1955, The Ronald Press Company, vi.

part of the West might fall to hostile foreign powers temporarily drowned the sounds of belligerent sectionalism. As in 1800, the potential bogey was Great Britain. The specter grew when it appeared that Britain in the Pacific Northwest might connect with the Republic of Texas or with Mexico and the remnant of Mexican rule in California, thus creating a "foreign" confederacy to block the American march to the Pacific and commerce of the western sea. Thus the confrontation of the United States and Britain was over a larger issue than simply a Pacific Northwest boundary line.

In the closing days of President Jackson's second term, American settlers in Texas had revolted from Mexico and set up a republic recognized by the United States, Great Britain, and France. Texans and their friends in Congress wanted annexation to the United States, but the ugly question of extending slaveholding territory made it politically inexpedient for Democratic administrations to openly favor this.

Jackson anticipated ultimate annexation of Texas—provided, however, that the struggling republic was not strengthened by its own territorial expansion and foreign aid. Both contingencies were present: Britons were investing in Texas bonds and lands, while Texans made feeble but meaningful gestures toward the Pacific. Texas' successful revolt had demonstrated Mexico's weakness; California was ripe for the taking. As with Spain's Mississippi Valley possessions in 1800, the question was who would move first, the United States, Texas with the aid of Britain, or Britain by negotiation with Mexico.

Jackson made a gesture to avoid the alienation of California when he sought, unsuccessfully, to buy lands around San Francisco and Monterey bays. He revealed concern for western defenses when he sent navy purser William A. Slacum to investigate Pacific Coast settlements and to "gather useful information." Slacum's report emphasized, among other things, the strategic military importance of Puget Sound and San Francisco Bay, and indicated the nature of the administration's interest in the Far West.

THE WILKES EXPEDITION

Van Buren, Jackson's successor, inherited another information-gathering project. The United States Exploring Expedition was authored in 1836 for a comprehensive survey of the whole Pacific. When the expedition sailed two years later, its commander, Lieutenant Charles

199

Wilkes, was instructed to examine especially "the territory of the United States on the seaboard" and "the coast of California, with special reference to the Bay of St. Francisco. . . ."

The ostensible scientific purpose of his coastal survey was to learn whether speculations about a navigable river entering the Pacific through southern Oregon or northern California were justified. The myth of the Buenaventura had been disproved by Jedediah Smith, Peter Skene Ogden and others who had traveled the coast since 1826. To complement Wilkes' sea search, Captain John C. Fremont was dispatched overland in 1843 for the same purpose. Fremont's report revealed a national interest in "a new road to Oregon and California," and in the "unexplored regions east of the Cascade mountains between the Columbia and the Sacramento" rivers. Implicit in both Wilkes' and Fremont's reports was the notion that the Oregon country and California had more in common than geographic contiguity.

Wilkes arrived in the Northwest in 1841 and spent several months examining Puget Sound and the Columbia and its settlements. Having lost one of his ships, the *Peacock*, on the Columbia's uncharted bar, he thought this river overrated, but he wrote glowingly of Puget Sound harbors and urged that they never be surrendered in boundary negotiations. A party of his men under Lieutenant George F. Emmons followed the fur traders' trail via the Willamette Valley to the Sacramento. A geologist, an artist, and several botanists justified the scientific purpose of the journey; their hardships "were more than compensated by the information . . . furnished in relation to the southern section of Oregon," notably the difficulty of moving a large party across the Siskiyou Mountains.

After a cursory inspection of the shores of Oregon and northern California, and a careful examination of California ports, Wilkes found interesting possibilities in the chaotic political situation of the Mexican province. He concluded that upper California would soon be lost to Mexico:

> It is very probable that this country will become united with Oregon, with which it will perhaps form a state that is destined to control the destinies of the Pacific. This future state is admirably situated to become a powerful maritime nation, with two of the finest ports in the world—that within the straits of Juan de Fuca, and San Francisco.

His tour took him, among other places, to the Pacific islands and Singapore. In each instance, his report stressed commercial possibilities and, in the case of the Hawaiian Islands, lack of defensive facilities.

THE MAKING OF A CRISIS

Evidence mounted to show that the HBC also was interested in Pacific commerce in connection with its trade in Oregon. In 1833 it had an agent in the Hawaiian Islands and employed an English resident in California. In 1841, McLoughlin's son-in-law, William Glen Rae, was sent to Yerba Buena (San Francisco) to manage a company store and his purchase of land and the best house in the village suggested that the company was there to stay. In 1843, it was rumored that Sir George Simpson and others had purchased California properties valued at 15,000 pounds; the next year that McLoughlin had asked Mexico for an extensive grant of land on the Sacramento River, and had promised to settle it immediately. From 1842 to 1845, persistent reports came from Mexico City that Great Britain was trying to buy California.[6] However, such rumors ascribed to the government projects of private investors who carried little weight in the Foreign Office.

If Britain was not in the market to buy, the United States was. According to John Quincy Adams, in 1842 Secretary of State Daniel Webster was willing to withdraw claims to territory north of the Columbia River if Britain would use her influence in Mexico to facilitate purchase of California by the United States. A sacrifice of eight degrees north of the Columbia would be more than compensated with Mexican territory that included San Francisco and Monterey harbors.

Webster's maneuver fell through, in part because of an embarrassing incident. Commodore ap Catesby Jones of the Pacific fleet, hearing reports that Mexico and the United States were at war, "seized" California to prevent the British from doing so. For twenty-four hours in October, 1842, the American flag flew over Monterey; it was run down when Jones learned, with chagrin, that his act was premature. It must have appeared to the British that the Americans were trigger-happy. The Foreign Office could congratulate itself that the Webster-Ashburton Treaty (1842) had resolved the long-standing dispute over the Maine boundary and the slave trade through amicable compromises. Since Webster appeared indifferent to the Oregon country, Lord Aberdeen immediately proposed new negotiations over its boundaries. But Webster left office in 1843 and was succeeded after a brief interval by John C. Calhoun, who responded, pro forma, with the old arguments for the American claims to the region drained by the Columbia.

[6] *The Larkin Papers*, George P. Hammond, ed., 10 vols. (1951–1964), II, 67, 140–141, 205.

When Calhoun was candidate for the Democratic nomination for President in 1844, he championed the annexation of Texas for sectional reasons. To his radical followers in the South, this was appealing. "With Texas," the *Charleston Mercury* crowed, "the slave states would form a territory large enough for a first rate power and one that under a free trade system would flourish beyond any on the Globe— immediately and forever."[7] Calhoun's chief rival for the nomination, Martin Van Buren, evaded the Texas issue; both ignored Oregon.

But Oregon enthusiasts, small in number and usually Democrats, were not to be ignored. In the summer of 1843, more than 100 met at an "Oregon Convention" in Cincinnati. They held that the nation's rights from the 42nd parallel to "54 degrees 40 minutes north latitude" were unquestionable; that the territory should be organized, and military posts established on the Oregon Trail.[8] In the following winter, Oregon advocates introduced into Congress bills to give notice to Great Britain that the United States intended to terminate the Convention of 1827 and to assert its rights to all of Oregon. Their language was intemperate. "Our object is not to bring on war," proclaimed Senator David R. Atchison of Missouri, "it is to occupy the land we are entitled to; and if war follows our doing so, why, let it come. Before we yield an inch by negotiation, let our common country sink—let all be lost."

From the politicians' angles, the campaign of 1844, both within the Democratic Party and between Democrats and Whigs, was waged over numerous local issues and control of political machines; but the situation shaped up so that a candidate unburdened by outright commitment to slavery, and who could side-step divisive domestic questions and capitalize on expansionist fervor could win popular approval.

Tennessee's James Knox Polk was such a candidate. He had a simple program: "Let Texas be reannexed, and the authority and laws of the United States be established and maintained within her limits, as also in the Oregon Territory, and let the fixed policy of our government be, not to permit Great Britain or any other foreign power to plant a colony or hold dominion over any portion of the people or territory of either." Polk's election was interpreted as an expression of the "will of the States and the people" for annexation of Texas. And the will of the people was affected by a joint resolution of House and Senate, signed by Tyler on March 1, 1845, three days before his term expired.

Such alacrity after so many years of delay cannot be explained

[7] Quoted in Chauncey S. Boucher, "The Annexation of Texas and Bluffton Movement in South Carolina," *MVHR*, June 1919, 15.

[8] C. S. Kingston, "The Oregon Convention of 1843," *WHQ*, July 1931.

wholly by the election returns. An important spur to action was a much-reported and not altogether groundless rumor that Britain was trying to arrange a treaty between Mexico and Texas in which Texan independence would be guaranteed by Great Britain and France. Such a guarantee was, of course, a defense of Texas against the United States as well as against Mexico. This so-called "interference" produced an indignant reaction toward Britain which not only cleared the way for the annexation resolution but provided impetus for a direct thrust at Great Britain through Oregon.

It was not so clear that Polk's election was a mandate of the people for the "reoccupation" of Oregon. Nor was it immediately clear what Polk meant by "the Oregon Territory." In the negotiations opened in 1842, Webster, Abel P. Upshur (during his few months as Secretary of State), and Calhoun had each lengthily proved the United States' claims to the 51st or 54th parallels and offered to compromise at the 49th. British negotiators had as lengthily and laboriously refuted the proofs and, as formerly, held out for western Washington, offering as compromise an enclave on Puget Sound. But Aberdeen's position was less firm than that of his predecessors. Early in 1844 he proposed to the harassed Prime Minister, Robert Peel, a settlement on the 49th parallel, provided that the Americans would make two concessions:

> . . . that if the line of the 49th degree were extended only to the water's edge, and should leave us possession of all of Vancouver's Island, with the northern side of the entrance to Puget's Sound; and if all the harbors within the Sound, and to the Columbia, inclusive, were made free to both countries; and further, if the river Columbia from the point at which it becomes navigable to its mouth, were also free to both. . . .[9]

"This," he argued, "would in reality be a most advantageous settlement." And Edward Everett, United States minister to London, reported informal talks which showed that Aberdeen was trying to find in this formula a way of "saving the national honor." However, the House of Representatives, smarting from the Texas crisis, passed a bill authorizing the President to notify Great Britain of intent to terminate the Convention and to provide for the organization of the Oregon Country into a territory. The Senate failed to act on the bill, but so much anti-British sentiment had been aroused and the situation was so highly inflammable that, as Aberdeen pointed out, termination might be followed by "a local collision" in Oregon which could lead to war.

[9] *Treaties and Other International Acts of the United States of America*, Hunter Miller, ed., 7 vols. (1931–1942), 25.

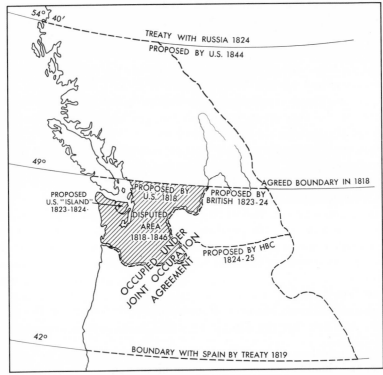

OREGON BOUNDARY NEGOTIATIONS

Polk's inaugural address (March 4, 1845) did not moderate the situation. He slapped British hands for interfering in Texas and asserted American rights to all of Oregon, declaring it his duty to use all constitutional means to defend those rights. In the face of congressional belligerence and Polk's apparently stern commitment, the London *Times* called for "resolute determination" from the British and the dispatch of a naval squadron to the Pacific Northwest. The government's response was not impressive. The 50-gun *America* was sent to the Strait of Juan de Fuca and Lieutenant William Peel traveled to Fort Vancouver (September, 1845) to reassure British subjects of "firm protection for their rights." *HMS Modeste* appeared in the Columbia on a second annual visit in September 1845, and was stationed off Fort Vancouver for the next eighteen months. Officers and crew added a note of gaiety to social life and burdens to Mc-Loughlin's office, but they did not show signs of hostility to the Americans—or to the British who were coexisting peaceably under the compact. Sir George Simpson persuaded the government to send two young officers of the Royal Engineers, Lieutenants H. J. Warre and

M. Vavasour, to plan defenses along the Canadian border and at the mouth of the Columbia River. Their mission, disguised as a tour of private persons for sport and scientific inquiry, was useless; by the time London received their report, the crisis had been resolved.

"FIFTY-FOUR FORTY OR FIGHT"

Events moved rapidly after Polk's inauguration. He had made a public announcement for "all of Oregon"—that is, from the 42nd to the 54th parallels; in July, his Secretary of State, James Buchanan, offered to settle at 49°, the old line of compromise, without further concession. Unfortunately, Sir Richard Pakenham rejected the proposal without referring it to his government. Polk, disregarding Buchanan's advice, then withdrew the offer and refused further discussions despite the chastened Pakenham's efforts to keep them open. In his first message to Congress (December, 1845) Polk brilliantly reviewed the long history of the Oregon Question but omitted reference to the fact that Aberdeen was willing to accept the 49° line with slight reservations. Polk now asked Congress for authority to give notice of termination of the Convention.

Polk wanted a "naked notice," even though it might lead to war. Much to his surprise, the Senate had lost the strong anti-British feeling which so powerfully moved it a year before. It debated the wording of the notice and argued the line of "54—40" versus "49." It was during these two months of debate that the slogan "54—40 or fight" became popular with Polk's supporters and with advocates of expansion at any cost. Such a clamor was raised and so much passion generated in party journals that one waggish editor suggested reducing the matter simply to "P.P.P.P.—Phifty-Phour Phorty or Phight."[10]

The Senate was not about to fight; Aberdeen's government did not want war. As Edward Everett reported from London, Aberdeen was willing to make further sacrifices to keep peace, but there was a point beyond which no administration could go and "if the United States proceeded, while an amiable negotiation is in progress to put an end to the Convention of joint occupation and to appropriate to themselves the territory in dispute, war was inevitable."[11]

A certain comic aspect appeared in the situation. Seeking to protect his government's position, Aberdeen wanted to know how the

[10] Edwin A. Miles, " 'Fifty-Four Forty or Fight'—an American Political Legend," *MVHR*, September 1957, 306.
[11] *Canadian Relations*, III, 920.

Senate would word the notice of termination before he made his offer of compromise; the Senate delayed in hopes of learning what
Aberdeen would offer; Polk, on whom, constitutionally, the whole
matter rested, hoped the British government would be overthrown
before it was realized that the Senate and the Foreign Office were in
close agreement on basic terms.

In London, Edward Everett, and his successor Louis McLane,
discussed informally the terms of agreement. In Washington, Pakenham and Buchanan formally negotiated by day and passed on to senators news of their progress at evening social affairs. Baffled by a Senate
attitude which he thought prejudicial to American interests, and anxious to get to the real business of his administration—war with Mexico
—Polk did a thing unprecedented in American history since the first
fumbling days of the new government. In effect, he surrendered responsibility for negotiation to the Senate. In April he submitted a
draft of a tentative treaty. The Senate approved its terms and immediately adopted a resolution of termination in language that would
cause Great Britain no serious embarrassment. Then the formal document, a treaty in the strictest sense but referred to as a convention
during these strange maneuvers, was signed June 15, 1846, and ratified on the 19th.

According to Daniel Webster, "the remarkable characteristic of the
settlement of the Oregon question by treaty is this. In the general operation of government, treaties are negotiated by the President and
ratified by the Senate; but here is the reverse—here is a treaty negotiated by the Senate, and only agreed to by the President."

THE GROUNDS FOR CONCILIATION

" 'Phifty Phour Phorty or Phight' has now phortunately phallen to
phinal phlat phooted phixing at 'Phorty nine' without the 'Phight'
against a phoreign phoe," cried one editor.[12] Except for a few ex-
tremists, most Americans probably did not care. In the spring of 1846
the overriding public interest had shifted from war with Britain over
Oregon to the occupation of California and a quick victory in Mr.
Polk's war with Mexico.

Annexation of Texas was credited to Tyler's otherwise inept administration; Polk fixed on California as his prime goal. Oregon had been
of secondary importance, but it was an excellent issue on which to

[12] Miles, *op. cit.*, 307.

test the British attitude toward the United States' probable war with Mexico. When Buchanan had argued that, because of the danger of war with Mexico, Polk should be more tactful in treating with Britain, Polk piously declared that "we should do our duty towards both Mexico and Great Brittain [*sic*] and firmly maintain our rights, & leave the rest to God and the country." Buchanan answered that he thought "God would not have much to do in justifying us in a war for the country North of 49°."[13] Great Britain had shown no appetite for an American war. Polk's militant expansionism was successful; he encouraged revolt in California while United States troops massed on the disputed border between Texas and Mexico. When late in May (1846) he decided for war with Mexico, the Senate had already decided for peace with Great Britain. One might conclude that settling the Oregon issue was expedient for Polk and the United States.

It was also expedient for Great Britain. Peel's government faced crises in the empire—famine in Ireland, war in India. At home, repeal of the Corn Laws and other issues revealed its insecurity. His government even fell for a brief time in December, 1845.

Credit must be given to Edward Everett for his role in working out the dilemma in which Polk had placed Aberdeen. Although formal negotiations were carried on in Washington, Everett and Aberdeen could talk informally and frankly in London. As early as December, 1843, Everett had suggested that the United States "depart from the 49th parallel, as to leave the whole of Quadra & Vancouver's island to England. . . ." Aberdeen's September 1844 proposal for a complete withdrawal from western Washington, was a response to this.

THE OREGON TREATY OF JUNE 15, 1846

The treaty was brief, consisting of four articles. I. The boundary was extended westward along the 49th parallel "to the middle of the channel which separates the continent from Vancouver's Island; and thence southerly through the middle of the said channel, and of Fuca's Straits to the Pacific Ocean"; provided, however, that navigation of the channel and Straits south of 49° "remain free and open to both Parties." II. Navigation of the Columbia River from the 49th parallel to the sea was to remain "free and open to the Hudson's Bay Company and to all British subjects trading with the same. . . ."

[13] *The Diary of James K. Polk*, M. M. Quaife, ed., 4 vols. (1910), I, 1–12.

British subjects with their goods and produce were to be treated the same as citizens of the United States. III. "The possessory rights of the Hudson's Bay Company and of all British subjects who may be already in occupation of land or other property, lawfully acquired . . ." were to be respected. IV. Properties of the Puget's Sound Agricultural Company were confirmed to the company, provided, however, that "in case . . . the situation of those farms and lands should be considered by the United States to be of public and political importance, and the United States' Government should signify a desire to obtain possession of the whole or . . . part," the property should be transferred at an agreed evaluation.

British hope that "all boundary questions once arranged . . . [Britain] might live on brotherly terms with Jonathan" was not fully realized in 1846. Two provisions of the treaty plagued the relations of John Bull and Jonathan for another fifteen years. One of these affected the HBC properties.

The company was not happy with the treaty. According to its historian, E. E. Rich, the boundary sacrificed a trade with an average annual profit of over 40,000 pounds from Fort Vancouver and other posts in the surrendered territory. By the American interpretation, Article II, which allowed "free and open" navigation of the Columbia, conceded to the company access to its inland posts only; it did not grant "equal footing" with United States citizens in the inland trade. Furthermore, confusing the company's charter with its License of Exclusive Trade which expired in 1859, the United States took the position that at the same date the company's right of access terminated. Without this the value of its possessory rights guaranteed by Article III was so much diminished.

That the company retained possessory rights at all was derived from McLoughlin's firm stand against American interlopers on company properties north of the Columbia during the critical days of 1845. "Possession by right of prior occupation" accounted for treaty Articles III and IV which allowed the company to recover its investments in posts and farms of the Puget's Sound Agricultural Company.

Simpson estimated the value of these properties at 100,000 pounds or $500,000, and he was willing to deal with the United States for this price, but negotiations through a "contact" broke down. By 1853 the value of the properties and trade had markedly declined. American settlers were encroaching upon the pastures around Fort Nisqually. Custom duties on imported goods made it impossible for the company to compete with American merchants. Simpson became increasingly anxious to sell, and probably would have accepted the State Department's offer of $300,000 in 1855, but the Senate refused to agree to it. Four years later the United States claimed that the term of the company's license having run out, its possessory rights had also expired. The General Land Office ordered surveys of company lands in Washington Territory and "to the great satisfaction of the settlers" opened some 33,000 acres on the lower Columbia. Fort Vancouver, occupied by the United States Army since 1850, was included in a military reservation, and the last vestiges of the company's long occupation were removed in 1860.

Such infringements on the Treaty of 1846 brought protests from the British Foreign Office, and with the crisis of the Civil War approaching, the Secretary of State made conciliatory gestures. It was 1863, however, before the United States entered negotiations. In that critical Civil War year, with the prospect that Great Britain might recognize the South as a belligerent, Lincoln's Secretary of State, William Seward, agreed to a joint commission to determine the reimbursement for the company under Article IV of the treaty. American and British commissioners and pleaders worked on the case for five years, and it is notable that they did not have to call in an umpire before reaching a decision. In September, 1869, they awarded the company $450,000 for its rights and $200,000 for Puget's Sound Agricultural Company holdings. Payment was made between 1860 and 1871. It took twenty-five years to settle this problem arising from the treaty. It took as long to conclude another dispute which was aggravated by the first.

The Oregon Treaty had defined the boundary line as "the middle of the channel" separating the continent from Vancouver Island. However, there were two channels, Canal de Haro, which lay nearer the island, and Rosario (or Vancouver's Channel) nearer the mainland. To which channel did the treaty refer? Between the two lay the San Juan Islands. While the line was still at issue, these islands were presumed to be in a neutral situation. The HBC had set up a sheep ranch on the largest and by 1852 its agents were having trouble with a few Americans who had settled there. When an American killed a company pig, a crisis developed. American troops occupied the southern part of San Juan Island, while British warships hovered offshore. In 1860 the two powers agreed that the island should be jointly occupied by troops to keep the peace. For twelve long years the Pig War remained a cold war.

In 1871, having arrived at a peaceable conclusion of the company's possessory rights in Oregon, both powers agreed to arbitrate their differences over the channel line. Emperor William I of Germany was chosen arbiter. The decision of his experts favored the Americans and the Canal de Haro became the boundary line. The San Juan Islands became a United States possession, the British evacuated, and peace reigned along the 49th parallel.

Both of these matters could have easily been settled within a short time after the Oregon Treaty was signed in 1846, but the United States was busy with the Mexican War, the conquest of California, and the bitter controversy over slavery. These domestic problems also delayed territorial organization for the citizens of Oregon.

CHAPTER
FOURTEEN

The Winter of Discontent and the Cayuse War

IN NOVEMBER, 1846, welcome news of the treaty arrived. Oregonians now expected that they would soon come under federal administration and that many of their problems would be solved. In December a bill to organize Oregon Territory was introduced in Congress. The measure might have passed with a minimum of debate, but Oregon's future was tied into sectional controversy. Congress argued for two years whether slavery would be allowed or prohibited in the proposed territory.

Meanwhile the government devised by the settlers in 1845 continued to operate. "Weak in resources, transient in purpose, and primitive in its machinery and devises," it coped as best it could with problems that might have overthrown a stronger state.[1] Indeed, common recognition of its temporary nature may explain its survival. But at all times and in all places local politics seethed and factions formed

[1] F. G. Young, "Financial History of Oregon," *OHQ*, December 1906, 360–361.

and reformed on issues exacerbated by economic frustrations, political ambitions, and worry over land titles.

In spite of increased immigration between 1845 and 1847, the economy showed few signs of improving. While there was no shortage of staple foods, there was a lack of goods, cash, and markets for the Valley's abundant produce. This kind of poverty, general among settlers, created discontent. The bedrock needs of each year's new immigrants were of another kind and bred uglier moods. The "old" settlers who occupied the choice lands, were town proprietors and merchants with power to give or withhold credit and were objects of special envy, resentment, and suspicion.

By 1846, between 8000 and 9000 persons (excluding Indians) lived in the Oregon country.[2] About 7000 were immigrants from the United States, of whom 2000 to 3000 had arrived within the year. Two-thirds of the total white population was located south of the Columbia River in the northern part of the Willamette Valley.

OREGON CITY: METROPOLIS OF THE OREGON COUNTRY

Incorporated by the legislature in 1845, Oregon City was the capital and only town that warranted the name. Its location made it commercially important. The falls provided power for mills. A crude ferry on the Willamette connected with roads to the Yamhill and Tualatin valleys. After 1845 the Barlow Road brought immigrant trains directly to the town. A portage road around the falls made it possible to move goods and people by small boat to the upper Valley. Although ships seldom could come up to the townsite, cargoes were lightered to shore from deep water.

Oregon City was hardly more than a clearing in the forest in the early months of 1843. Three years later the town had a population of about 500 persons, a "splendid" Catholic church and a "neat" Methodist one, two saloons and a weekly newspaper, the *Oregon Spectator*, which published its first issue on February 5, 1846. Along the narrow ledge on the east side of the river and on the rocky heights above

[2] Neil M. Howison, "Report on Oregon, 1846," *OHQ*, March 1913, 25. Lieutenant Howison was detailed by Commodore Sloat of the Pacific Squadron to examine affairs in Oregon during the early months of the 1846 crisis with Great Britain. He arrived in the Columbia in mid-July. When he attempted to leave in September, his schooner, the *Shark*, was wrecked on the bar. His report contains excellent material on the Willamette settlement.

were about seventy-five houses, some being shops as well as dwellings. According to the *Spectator* the town had two blacksmiths, coopers, and cabinet makers, four tailors, two hatters, two silversmiths, and "other artisans," a tannery, two grist mills and two sawmills, one with a power-driven lathe.

The owner of the Imperial Mills was the town founder, Dr. John McLoughlin, who had retired from the HBC by the spring of 1846. His later years in the American community were neither happy nor prosperous, although he was probably the richest man in the country. His anguish over the death of his son John at Fort Stikine in 1842—which, he claimed, was a murder that Sir George Simpson refused to prosecute—and other disagreements with his superiors had hastened his retirement from the company and the loss of special emoluments of his office. He valued his properties at Oregon City at $500,000 in 1849, but his early gifts of lands to the missionaries had led to an invasion of his holdings by persons who contended that McLoughlin held them on behalf of the company. Disputes over land titles embittered his relations with the Americans. Under the terms of the land laws applied to Oregon when it became a territory he was, in effect, dispossessed. In 1862, five years after his death, the State of Oregon made some restitution to his heirs and cleared disputed titles to Oregon City lots.

George Abernethy was the leading American entrepreneur. Former steward of the Methodist Mission, he was a principal figure in the Mission party, and governor of the colony from 1844 to 1849. When the Mission was closed in 1844, he had bought out the store he had managed since 1840. For $20,000 he took over settlers' notes to the amount of $30,000 and assumed Mission liabilities of $10,000. On the notes he collected 10 percent interest; on his debt to the Mission Society, payable in annual installments of $2000 in specie, he paid six percent. Thus capitalized with gifts originally intended for religious work, he was able to buy out the Island Milling Company, its saw and grist mill and lathe. In 1848 he built a saw mill at Oak Point on the north bank of the Columbia. By 1849 he initiated direct credit transactions with a New York firm and from this beginning emerged "the pattern of trade between Oregon merchants and New York wholesale houses which prevailed until the first continental railroad was completed in 1869."[3]

However, all was not smooth sailing for storekeeper Abernethy, and only grim determination helped him to survive the lean years when it was difficult to collect on settlers' notes and more difficult to raise the

[3] Arthur Throckmorton, *Oregon Argonauts*, 101–102.

cash to pay off his debts to the Mission Society. If he had hopes of becoming sole retailer to the American community, he was disappointed. In 1842, Captain John H. Couch, representing the firm of J. P. Cushing and Company of Newburyport, Massachusetts, set up a store, and was followed the next year by Francis W. Pettygrove. This disposition of Americans to enter trade led McLoughlin to set up a branch of the HBC at Oregon City in 1844. Chief Trader Archibald McKinlay was in charge of the business when the treaty of 1846 made it inconvenient for the company to trade under its own name, and the firm became Allan, McKinlay and Company, known locally, however, as the company store.

Pettygrove flourished as a merchandiser. Within two years he had a granary at Champoeg where he captured the custom of the upper Valley; he had a second store at Portland where he and his family resided, and he supplied his brother-in-law, Philip Foster, who had a store at Eagle Creek where the Barlow Road came out of the mountains. Pettygrove was well capitalized, and his situation was bettered in 1845, when McLoughlin bought a partnership for his son David for $20,000.

TRADE AND WHEAT

Pettygrove also had better shipping connections than were available to either Couch or Abernethy. Couch was supplied from the Hawaiian Islands by Captain Avery Sylvester, who made three trips in eighteen months during 1844–1845. In the same interval Pettygrove received two shipments of goods directly from New York as well as several from the Islands. The HBC stores were well stocked by the annual supply ship from England. But between 1843 and 1848, only six American trading ships entered the Columbia directly from the United States.[4] The significance of this fact can best be pointed up by a comparison of the Oregonians' situation with that of the Californians. In 1843 the non-Indian population of California was probably about 7000 persons, roughly what Oregon's would be in 1846. In that year forty-three vessels—whalers and traders—were on the California coast. In 1844 and again in 1845, fifteen vessels of the "trading fleet proper" entered ports with cargoes. Between 1841 and 1845, an estimated sixty-nine vessels from the Atlantic Coast and the Hawaiian Islands were in trade with California. After the American conquest,

[4] *Ibid.*, 57. To Throckmorton's list should be added the *Raymond*, 1847, which stocked Captain Nathaniel Crosby, Jr.'s store at Portland.

150 vessels entered California ports between April 1847 and October 1848.

The California market, civil and military, made demands to which traders were quick to respond; an estimated $250,000 worth of goods was imported in 1846. California also had export commodities with which to make purchases. Oliver Larkin estimated that exports for the same year consisted of 80,000 hides and almost 2,000,000 pounds of tallow (for the New England shoe industry), 10,000 to 15,000 bushels of wheat, 10,000,000 feet of lumber, 1000 barrels of brandy and wine, 200 ounces of gold, and soap and furs to the value of $30,000.

Oregon's prairies produced wheat in abundance. A first year's sowing seeded second-, even third-year crops, without retilling. For many settlers boiled wheat was the principal food; roasted, it was their substitute for coffee and tea. It was the chief item in business transactions and its market price was the nominal price in exchange for all goods and services. However, the purchasing power of a bushel of wheat depended on market demand, and this was limited. In 1843, Captain Sylvester reported a "very dull" trade with settlers on the Columbia "not because they did not want my goods, for they were in want of everything but provisions, but because they had nothing to give me in return." In 1844 he took to the Islands, on consignment for Foster, 29,000 shingles, seven barrels of salmon and two barrels of peas for which Foster received, net, $200.75.[5] The next year, he loaded 50,000 feet of lumber at H. H. Hunt's mill, above Astoria. Evidently sales in the Islands did not warrant his return for more. But in January 1847, Pettygrove sent to California a cargo of lumber, salmon, beef, potatoes, butter, cheese, cranberries, turnips, cabbage, onions, and flour. The flour, costing $6 a barrel in Oregon, sold for $15. This was the beginning, modest as it was, of the Oregon-California trade in produce, which, with the gold rush, put the Oregon economy on its feet.

Until the opening of the California market and the regular arrival of trading ships, the HBC was the principal buyer of grain, supplementing its own farm produce with purchases from settlers to fill its contract with the Russians in Alaska. In 1842 a company agent bought wheat at Champoeg for 60 cents—in 1846 for 62½ cents—an Imperial bushel on orders paid in goods at Fort Vancouver.

The company provided the Americans with a market, but it was not an effective agent in keeping consumers' goods at competitive prices. Joel Palmer, an immigrant of 1845, wrote with great candor and without sparing the feelings of his countrymen.

[5] "Voyages of the *Pallas* and *Chenamus*, 1843–45," *OHQ*, September 1933, 268; December, 1933, 361.

. . . the fact is, the prices were much lower before these American merchants went into the country. . . . Their mode of dealing is to ask whatever their avarice demands, and the necessities of the purchaser will bear. And not being satisfied with an open field, they have petitioned the Hudson Bay Company to put a higher price upon their goods, as they were selling lower than the American merchants wished to sell.[6]

The company acceded to the merchants' request, and sold to Americans at their countrymen's prices and to its own people at lower prices.

The Cash Shortage

With the exception of the missionaries, the first settlers had no cash and little need for it. Immigrants between 1842 and 1847 arrived practically destitute. Their capital was in wagons and outfits; their reserves were spent along the way to replenish supplies. What remained had to go for immediate wants. Because the HBC offered a greater variety of goods of quality and often at more favorable terms than American merchants, anyone with a coin in hand bought at its stores. As a result, the coin that came into the country was automatically drained off into the company's strongbox. For example, the first money that entered Oregon in quantity was a barrel of silver dollars sent to Fort Vancouver in 1846 to pay the monthly wages of the *Modeste's* crew. By the end of the month, the money was back in the barrel again. Cash that did not go to the company just as automatically went into the safes of American merchants, instead of circulating. Hence almost all transactions were by barter or on credit.

It was not always easy to distinguish between the two. Abernethy found he could not do custom milling; specified amounts of wheat or flour were deducted as grinding fees at his mill. If credit was advanced, repayment was often made in kind. The Widow Brown cobbled shoes and was credited on Foster's account books. If an individual performed services or sold goods to a merchant, he received an order redeemable in whatever goods the merchant had on hand. For legal services, Peter Burnett was paid with an order for $49, and with it was able to purchase only brown sugar at 12½ cents a pound.

Merchants carried heavy accounts of debts owing them. Abernethy purchased the Mission's $30,000 worth of settlers' notes. At Fort Vancouver in the spring of 1844, McLoughlin had $29,330 in unpaid accounts, and Couch about the same amount. It was estimated that in 1846 3000 persons were indebted to the HBC, 1000 to McLoughlin, and 500 still had unpaid notes with Abernethy.

[6] Joel Palmer, *Journal of Travels . . . 1845 and 1846; Early Western Travels*, XXX, 217.

By 1845, the economic situation was so desperate that the fall session of the legislature attempted to make practically every product of the land—"wheat, hides, tallow, beef, pork, butter, lard, peas, lumber, at their current values" as well as "available orders" on merchants—legal tender for payment of taxes and debts. Governor Abernethy vetoed the measure on grounds that it was "inconvenient." As he pointed out in his veto message, no person would sell without a contract designating "how and in what manner he would receive his pay."

The next year, 1846, the legislature passed the "fundamental legal tender act of early Oregon" which made gold and silver, treasury drafts, approved orders on solvent merchants, and "good merchantable wheat, delivered at such places as is customary for merchants to receive it," lawful tender for the payment of taxes and judgments rendered in the courts. Sheriff Joe Meek testified that when he collected taxes he had greater need of a warehouse than of a wallet. The act, however, was discriminatory against merchants and indirectly worked genuine hardships on new immigrants who had no stock of wheat and little cash. But under the law, merchants were forced to take wheat in payment of debts even when some cash was coming into the country. A public notice in the *Spectator*, December 24, 1846, signed by Jacob Hoover, uncle of a future president, shows an immediate effect of the law:

> I hereby give notice that my note, in favor of either John McLoughlin, or the Hudson's Bay Company—I do not now distinctly remember which party—dated in October, 1845, will not be paid unless the payment is compelled by law, as the payment of said note in "good merchantable wheat" has been refused at the granary at Linton.

As a consequence, all credit transactions were slowed and the use of a two-price system was accelerated. In the first issue of the *Spectator*, Pettygrove advertised goods available at his "Red House" store at Oregon City and his newly opened shop down river at the site of the present Portland. Hardware, farm implements, dry goods, clocks, and cane-seat chairs suggest that the wants of the settler were not on the lowest level of sustaining life. These items were sold at reduced prices for cash. Thus the economic situation was aggravated: large demand and short supply of goods made prices high; but the price of wheat, the settlers' principal currency, remained reasonably uniform and low because of the limited demand for it. With the nominal price of exchange based on wheat and the real price based on coin, the merchant, by using a two-price system, forced a greater difference between real and nominal prices. In 1846, some goods were offered one-third lower for cash; the next year, 50 percent lower. In short, coin that found its way into circulation commanded a premium while surplus wheat piled up in the merchants' granaries.

As a dealer in crops, wholesaler and retailer, and as a banker in extending credit, the frontier merchant served a vital economic function; but his role was not always appreciated. Because the HBC was the largest dealer in wheat; because it, like the American merchants, acted as a banking institution in expanding or contracting credit; and because it was British, it drew the greatest disapproval, especially when it reached the limit of its market demand and restricted its purchases of wheat. The surplus in 1845 was estimated at 50,000 bushels of grain or 10,000 barrels of flour. When the company refused to buy, settlers interpreted this as a measure to beat down the customary price and to increase its profits. It was charged that the company made a clear profit of $74,000 on an investment of $24,000 worth of merchandise, and it was argued that "if justice were done . . ." at least $50,000 of this profit "would be in the hands of our farmers."

The settlers made several efforts to reach out for a new market. In 1841, former mountain man Joseph Gale headed a group of farmers who built the *Star of Oregon*, and without a seaman among them, sailed to California where they sold both cargo and vessel and invested the proceeds in cattle. A "Friend to Fair Trade" in 1846 suggested that farmers engage in shipping for themselves and at a meeting in April the next year citizens were called upon to cooperate in the business of exchanging products in order to meet the "present oppression upon the producers by mercantile extortion." But it was not until 1848, when the possibilities of the growing California market were manifest and shipping facilities already beginning to improve, that a group of Clatsop Plains farmers took independent action. Inexperienced at shipbuilding and navigating, they nevertheless built a two-masted 40-ton schooner, loaded it with their butter, bacon, eggs, and potatoes, and sailed for the south where they sold both ship and cargo at a profit.

THE POLITICS OF DISCONTENT

The dreary wet months of 1846–1847 were Oregon's winter of discontent. Immigrants, whether graziers from Clay County, Missouri, or Yankee peddlers on the make, had inherited the attitudes of Jacksonian democracy with regard to privilege and monopoly in politics and economics. "Monopoly" was the cry raised against Oregon merchants, but also against men who held sections of the best prairie land, townsites, river frontage, and offices in government. Often these were one and the same person. The first editor of the *Spectator*, William G. T'Vault, charged that he was dismissed not, as alleged, because of his bad spelling, but because his views differed from those of the Oregon Printing Association, principally Governor Abernethy. "The political sentiments here avowed," T'Vault explained in his valedictory editorial, "were at war with some of the present aristocracy of the land."

In 1845, two attempts had been made to challenge the local landed aristocrats. One was by Henry Williamson, when he built a cabin at the gates of Fort Vancouver; the other, when eccentric young Charles E. Pickett staked out a mile-square claim on lands the missionaries claimed at the mouth of the Clackamas River. Pickett built a cabin and planted a garden, which, according to his biographer, "was indeed a stubborn determination for social good that led him to the first manual labor of his two-year stay in Oregon." In the fall of the next year, a self-appointed committee composed of Asa L. Lovejoy, settler on the Portland site; Morton M. McCarver, who with Peter Burnett was trying to build a town at Linnton; T'Vault and two others, proposed at a public meeting that the legislature petition Congress to disallow claims already occupied at certain strategic locations. It was recommended that the Falls of the Willamette and adjacent land for a mile in each direction, forts Vancouver and Nisqually, Peter Skene Ogden's claim at the mouth of the Columbia on the north shore, and the portage site near the Dalles of the Columbia "be reserved for internal improvements" and the claimants reimbursed with "floating claims."

This "unwarrantable, unjust and obnoxious effort" to make reserves of "townsites, water falls, capes &c. that have been settled for years" was viewed "with indignation and contempt" by other inhabitants. But even those who promoted legalized claim-jumping were not happy when squatters moved in on their own lands. So great was this threat that in the spring of 1847 public meetings were held in protest against trespassers and squatters, and 150 men signed a resolution not to vote into office anyone who took part in such activities.

At the root of the land problem was the community's insecurity as to title for individual claims. No one knew what policy Congress would adopt when it set up a territorial government—whether the government would accept the provisional land laws, or erase claims to lands already occupied. No one knew whether the land he occupied would be declared public domain and subject to sale at public vendue or to claim by prior occupancy under preemption laws. Yet despite confused titles, towns were promoted, mapped, and lands were sold. The buyer had no guarantee except the integrity of the seller, who could do no more than promise to fulfill his contract when titles were cleared.

If on the one hand there was evidence of confidence between buyer and seller, on the other there was overt suspicion of the privileged who thought their positions might influence congressional policy—the HBC through the treaty, Elijah White through a temporary connection with the federal government, Abernethy who was suspected of ambitions to succeed himself as governor of the new territory, and missionaries generally because they claimed to be the solid, stable, respectable element. Pickett damned them all as "vulgar, tin-peddling, shaving, picayune, upstart Yankee and Cockney canaille." He made public his comments in Lyceum meetings; he printed them on rubbed-down cedar shingles which he posted on trees for all to read. In the handwritten pages of his "Flumgudgeon Gazette and Bumble Bee Budget: a Newspaper of the Salamagundi Order and Devoted to Scratching and Stinging the Follies of the Times," under the name of "Curltail Coon, Editor," he lambasted his enemies: the missionaries, teetotalers, legislators whose "varied evolutions, manoeuvring, marching, countermarching, double dealing, and tangling up of affairs" had created the legal tender act, and politicians—generally as well as specifically—Morton McCarver (the "big brass gun"), White, and Abernethy.[7]

Of the politically ambitious, there was no lack. By the fall of 1847, wrote George L. Curry, new editor of the *Spectator*, "it would appear really that some of our good fellow citizens have lost their wits and are running mad for office." Petitions recommending favorite sons of one county were condemned by other county conventions who had their own candidates. One faction drew up a memorial asking Congress to make sure that no local person should be appointed to any important office because of local rivalries. Legislative sessions were given over to such in-fighting and vituperation that editor Curry was asked not to report it for fear of disturbing the peace. Charging censorship, he resigned; not, however, before passing on to the community one tidbit of real news. J. Quinn Thornton, a friend of the Abernethy faction, was reported to have left on a ship for the Hawai-

[7] Lawrence C. Powell, *Philosopher Pickett* (1942); "Flumgudgeon Gazette in 1845 . . .," *OHQ*, June 1940.

ian Islands; actually, he had changed ship and sailed for the East.[8] He was carrying political recommendations to the President and Congress with credentials from Abernethy testifying that he was a spokesman for all Oregonians. According to Curry in the November 11, 1847, *Spectator*:

> Some will have honors whether or no, and we understand that one of our distinguished functionaries has gone to the States in two ships —that another . . . started in the height of desperation in a Chinook canoe . . . to head off the one on board of two ships—that one of the members of the late "Yamhill Convention" intends crossing the Mountains on snow-shoes and is sure of being in at the death—that we ourselves had gone thither, in as much as we were absent. . . . Well, really, we might have gone had we found ships, canoes, or snow-shoes disengaged.

Such was the situation when the legislature began its winter session, December 7, 1847. The next afternoon a messenger arrived with the startling news that the Cayuse Indians had attacked the Whitman mission and massacred its inhabitants.

THE CAYUSE WAR

If there was little light and sunshine in Oregon's political scene in 1846–1847, there was less in 1847–1848, when the government faced its severest test and one for which it was least prepared—an Indian war.

The Valley Indians had been so depleted in numbers by influenza epidemics in 1830–1833 and so debilitated by disease and starvation in the next decade that they were more an annoyance than a threat. Those in the interior, however, were numerous and of a different character. The Cayuse had shown serious hostility toward the missionaries, who early realized they were existing on a thin edge of security.

---

[8] Thornton had made himself immensely unpopular by his attacks on Jesse Applegate, charging that Applegate had deliberately subjected the 1846 immigrants to unnecessary hardships on the Applegate trail. The community took sides in a quarrel that led to such incidents as the one indicated in the following broadside: "To THE WORLD!! J. QUINN THORNTON, Having resorted to low, cowardly and dishonorable means, for the purpose of injuring my character and standing, and having refused honorable satisfaction, which I have demanded; I avail myself of this opportunity of publishing him to the world as a reclaimless liar, an infamous scoundrel, a black hearted villain, an arrant coward, a worthless vagabond and an imported miscreant, a disgrace to the profession and a dishonor to his country. JAMES W. NESMITH. Oregon City, June 7, 1847."

221

The deep-rooted cause of the Whitmans' troubles lay in their inability to understand these people whom they conscientiously sought to help. They were harsh when the natives broke the white man's moral code or ignored rights of privacy and possession, concepts the Indians did not comprehend. On the other hand, they were meek when subjected to indignities the Cayuses would not tolerate. When Marcus Whitman was slapped by a native, he turned the other cheek. When he found an Indian stealing from his garden, he whipped the pilferer.

Aware that tribal medicine men often paid with their lives when their patients died, Whitman nevertheless tried to cure the Indians' illnesses. Immigrants who stopped at Waiilatpu from 1845 to 1847 were sick with diseases from which white men ordinarily recovered but which brought death to the Indians in epidemic numbers. The Indians believed they were being deliberately poisoned, and as lodge after lodge sent up the death chant, even those who had been friendly to the missionaries wavered in their loyalty. Panic fed on rumor, agitated by half-educated natives who also spread the word that their ancient way of life, their hunting grounds, and their freedom were menaced by the immigrants.

On November 29, 1847, the mission was attacked. First victims were Marcus and Narcissa Whitman. In all, fourteen whites were murdered, two died of exposure, and forty-seven, of whom thirty-seven were children, were taken captive. The Spaldings, with the help of the Nez Perces, escaped from Lapwai to the Valley. The Walkers and Eellses remained with their faithful Spokanes until spring.

All fury spent, the Cayuses were willing to surrender their captives and negotiate peace to avoid a retaliatory war which, Ogden assured them, would mean their extermination. But a tense situation prevailed among the interior Indians who feared the Americans perhaps more than the Americans feared them. The settlers naturally dreaded a general uprising; a fear that did not lessen with rumors that the Walla Wallas, Nez Perces, and Yakimas were allied with the Cayuses, and that the Molallas and Klamaths were ready for the warpath.

At first report of the massacre, the legislature called for troops. By the end of December a company of militia was at The Dalles. With less alacrity, a regiment of 500 men was enlisted. These men were reluctant to leave their homes, which might also need protection, and there was some quibbling about appointments of military commanders. A real dilemma arose as to how the government could finance the war. Apparently the legislature did not consider a tax increase; it merely called for voluntary subscriptions. In order to arm and provision the troops, Abernethy, Applegate, and Lovejoy gave personal pledges to the HBC. Expenses of the war reached $175,000, of which $2,885.02 was contributed in cash. Individuals gave goods and personal notes. Commissary-general Joel Palmer bought goods if cash was at hand, gave due bills, or commandeered wheat from those most able to spare it. However, orders, due bills, and loans had greater value than under ordinary circumstances, since it was assumed that the federal government ultimately would pay the costs of the war.

Related to the problem of raising troops and sending them into the interior was the question of objectives and the means by which they could best be accomplished. Former mountain men, HBC officers (although they generally remained aloof), and a few Americans believed that the militia should be used for the limited purpose of capturing the Indians responsible for the massacre. Robert Newell, for one, strongly urged a peace commission to proceed in advance of the troops, reassure friendly Indians of the white men's peaceful intentions, and negotiate with the Cayuses for the surrender of the guilty. On the other hand, certain influential men, in some cases unacquainted with Indians and Indian warfare, wanted a war of retaliation if not of extermination.

Abernethy—his qualities of political leadership at no time more evident—appointed a peace commission composed of Joel Palmer, Robert Newell, and Henry A. G. Lee. No better appointments could have been made. On the other hand, the legislature appointed Cornelius Gilliam to command the troops. By mid-January, Gilliam was en route to the interior. Abernethy's orders instructed him to confer with the commissioners, but Gilliam did not approve of the commission or its purpose. The commissioners soon found that they could not depend upon him to abide by his agreements, and that he could not, or would not restrain hotheads among his men. It was agreed one day that the commissioners should go ahead of the army to avoid frightening the friendly bands. The next day the commander ordered the army to accompany the commission.

Time was of the essence if the peacemakers were to prevent disaffection among all the natives. To Gilliam, the secret of success was to strike before the Indians combined or slipped away into the mountains. He believed that the commissioners were deliberately stalling the army; on the other hand, the commissioners were privately convinced that Gilliam and his supporters wanted battle and had no regard for justice in dealing with the Indians, innocent or guilty.

Robert Newell's journal gives a running account of events after the troops left the Dalles. On February 24, skirmishes at Umatilla Springs: "The murderers were verry eager for battle those not guilty kept off." One Cayuse was killed, six wounded. The next day, "the friendly Kayuses done all they could to avoid battle but could not." One chief was killed. At Walla Walla the Indians "wishes to be at peace." Yellow Serpent was "a friend." At the ruined mission, the peacemakers learned that hostile Indians hovered in the hills: "The Commissioners have no chance to arrange with the Indians as we are short of provis[ions] and time. Our Col. is quite hasty." On March 4, the commissioners talked with the Nez Perces again. "Col. Gilliam left the council in a huff, and declared he has come to fight and fight he will. . . . Most of the officers and men of the Army are disposed to adhere to what the Commissioners say . . . but the Col. is altogether against them, and no unity apparent among them." On the eighth the Nez Perces agreed to see the Cayuses and "tell them our intentions also to perswade the inocent to ceparate from the guilty." The next day, a party including a peaceful chief and two Cayuses appeared for a parley. They refused to give up two men whom the commissioners believed guilty, but would surrender five whose guilt was less clear. Gilliam was willing to pass up these if the Cayuses surrendered Joe Lewis, a half-breed troublemaker. Under these circumstances Newell concluded that the peace commissioners had done as much as they could.

However they had accomplished something. The murderers were isolated from the other Cayuse bands. One more battle was fought on the Touchet River and when the much-sought Cayuse killers fled to the mountains the war was over. A year after the outbreak, Abernethy summarized the conclusion of the six months' campaign:

It is true that the Indians engaged in the massacre were not captured and punished; they were however driven from their homes, their country taken possession of, and they made to understand that the power of the white man is far superior to their own. The Indians have a large scope of country to roam over, all of which they were acquainted with, know every pass, and by this knowledge could escape the punishment they so justly merited. In view of this the troops were recalled and disbanded early in July last [1848], leaving a small force under command of Captain Martin to keep possession of the post at Waiilatpu, and a few men at Wascopam [the Dalles]. . . .[9]

[9] *Spectator*, February 6, 1849. In the fall of the same year, the Cayuses, as the price of peace, surrended to Governor Joseph Lane five of their number who were brought to Oregon City and held in a temporary prison on Abernethy Island. In May 1850 a grand jury sat for nine days and returned true bills against the Indians who were arraigned for trial. The community, however, was not of one mind with regard to these particular Indians' guilt. Every effort was made to carry out legal formalities and demonstrate the rule of law. Judge Orville C. Pratt presided over the court and Amory Holbrook, territorial attorney, prosecuted.

The Winter of Discontent and the Cayuse War

The Cayuse war was not a war in the sense of sustained military action. The Cayuses were trying to avoid the consequences of their deed. The Americans, at best, were trying to catch up with the guilty and enforce recognition of the law against murderers; at worst, they wanted to draw the blood of any native. The HBC's officers remained neutral; war was not their method of getting along with Indians, but they were alert to the worsening of Indian-American relations.

This was evident in the Valley. It was reported that with the men of the Valley off to war, the Molallas became increasingly impudent and offensive. The Klamaths, who traveled the Klamath Trail to the Silverton country to camp with the Molallas, appeared to be agitating against the whites. Frightened by their presence, the settlers ordered them out of the country; when they appeared reluctant to move, in early March, (1848), the whites attacked their camp. In two days of sporadic fighting, thirteen Klamaths were killed and one wounded. One white man was wounded. The Battle of the Abiqua, named for the river on which it took place, has been variously interpreted. Apparently contemporaries were reluctant to talk about it; some who did called it a skirmish in which several squaws and noncombatants were murdered by the whites. Frances Fuller Victor reported in *Early Indian Wars in Oregon* (1894) that the settlers who recalled the incident, were "ashamed of their easy victory." On the other hand, Robert Down, in his *History of the Silverton Country* (1926), concluded that the battle was the result of a justifiable effort of the settlers to expel a dangerous group of Klamaths.

TERRITORIAL ORGANIZATION

News of the Whitman massacre had no sooner arrived than the legislature set up a committee to petition Congress for immediate territorial organization. This interesting document was composed by Peter Burnett, who would shortly become California's first governor, George L. Curry, former editor of the *Spectator* and later Oregon's fourth and last

Kintzing Pritchett, territorial secretary, Major Robert B. Reynolds, and Captain Thomas Claiborne of the United States Rifle Regiment acted for the defense. All but one of the accused pleaded guilty, so the defense had to rest on the question of whether the court at Oregon City could pass on a crime committed outside its jurisdiction and before the establishment of the territorial government. The jury reached a decision without leaving the courtroom. The five Indians were publicly hanged within the month.

territorial governor, and L. A. Rice. It dwelt less on the colony's Indian danger than on its anomalous situation:

> Embarrassed as we were, and finding by actual experiment that a resident and civilized people could not exist without government of some kind, however imperfect, we were forced, as a community, to organize a temporary system of laws for the preservation of peace and order. . . . In organizing and putting in operation our plans of temporary government, we were met by, and had to overcome, great and serious difficulties. That it is, with even the same means, much more difficult to administer a mere temporary system of laws, where all is new and fluctuating, than a regular and permanent one, is a truth so sensible and apparent as not to need illustration. No people can, or will, be contented and happy under a government where all is painful suspense and uncertainty. . . .

Furthermore, it stated a philosophy of rights inherent in citizenship under the government of the United States. ". . . We have acted under the firm conviction that there exists a mutual duty between our government and all its citizens; and that, while we owe and observe a most willing allegiance towards the United States, we have a right to claim their protection and care. Our forefathers complained that they were oppressed by the mother country, and they had a just right to complain. We do not complain of oppression, but of neglect. Even the tyrant has his moments of relaxation and kindness, but neglect near wears a smile. . . ."[10]

Apparently there was unanimity with regard to the petition. But there was none within the legislature or without over recommendations that might accompany it concerning land laws and appointments to the new government. According to the one cynical observer, Oregon's politics in the winter of 1847–1848 were "filthy party strife," to promote the Democratic Party. While there was, no doubt, strife of this nature, the use of national party labels was an error. The large majority of the Oregon population were Democrats, if for no other reason than inheritance. But there were no organized parties as such and the strife was rooted in local antagonisms.

The legislature chose Joe Meek to carry the petition to Washington. With nine companions, this colorful mountain man crossed the Rockies in the early spring of 1848 and arrived in St. Louis in the record time of two months. In the meantime, J. Quinn Thornton, who it will be remembered had already sailed for Washington with the Mission party's recommendations for office, arrived at the capital before Meek. But "Old Joe," distant cousin of President Polk, made both himself

10 "Petition of Citizens of Oregon," *PNQ*, January 1949.

and the news of the massacre conspicuous. Congress was pressured into action, and a bill to organize the territory was introduced. It passed by a narrow margin and was signed by Polk on August 14, 1848. The following March Governor Joseph Lane declared the territorial government in operation and the first phase of colonial experience ended.

The "provisional period" is one of great interest for students of American institutions and character. In circumstances complicated by national, racial, religious and economic conditions, a people with limited experience in state building had worked out problems as they arose despite deep-rooted antagonisms. Their methods had served their forefathers on earlier frontiers—the public meeting, the newspaper, the legislative hall. They had developed a proud independence and a sense of accomplishment which was exhibited in a memorial addressed to the Congress shortly after Oregon had achieved territorial status. Acknowledging "that providential care which had guided them to their present enviable and prosperous condition," Oregonians presented to Congress, not the supplicating hand of a people asking favors, but the "hand of kinsman and friend" seeking their rights. In this frame of mind, the American colony in the Far Northwest began its territorial experience.

CHAPTER
FIFTEEN

Territorial Government and Problems: Oregon

TERRITORIAL ORGANIZATION was the United States' solution to the problem of governing peoples outside the boundaries of the states. The Ordinance of 1787, devised to take care of the region north of the Ohio River, was the model legislation and contained the feature which by providing a terminal date for colonial status distinguished the American colonial system from all others.

The organic act by which Congress created a territory outlined the offices and procedures for its government. When the population of a territory qualified it to elect a congressional representative and to support a state government, and when other conditions were met, the territorial legislature applied to Congress for an enabling act permitting the territorials to draw up a constitution. After the constitution was ratified by the territory and Congress had passed an admission act, the territory took its place as a state on equal footing with others in the Union. To far-off Oregonians, territorial status was a prelude to statehood and to the sovereignty which pre-Civil War political theory held inherent in statehood.

Under territorial organization the federal government provided protection for immigrants and settlers; the army moved in with garrisons and mounted riflemen wherever trouble brewed. Longstanding (and often disputed) policies concerning internal improvements prevented the government from building roads for civilian needs, but it could be expected to construct territorial roads for military purposes. Aids to navigation and commerce, such as lighthouses and harbor improvements; the establishment of ports of entry, customhouses, and mail service, all were welcomed by territorials not only for their direct services, but because they brought money into areas starved for a circulating medium. So did the construction of territorial buildings—legislative hall, penitentiary, the inevitable insane asylum—while the location of the capital and government buildings raised land values in the fortunate communities chosen for them. The machinery of government was supported by federal moneys. Federal salaries for territorial officers, *per diems*, and mileage for legislators and jurors, relieved local tax budgets. These were some of the advantages territorials could look forward to.

Of most importance to Oregon's settlers, however, was the provision Congress might make with regard to land. Only the federal government could treat with the Indians for cessions of lands. Once they passed into the federal domain, official surveys substituted township and range for the old method of designating boundaries by familiar but impermanent features of the landscape. After surveys were made, the public domain was offered at public auctions (vendues); preemption laws permitted prior occupants to buy 160 acres at fixed minimum prices before public sale. Oregonians, however, had assumed grants of 640 acres of free land and the provisional government's land laws had been based on this assumption. Hence, it was a matter of extreme concern to the settlers whether Congress would recognize these laws when it organized the territory.

THE OREGON TERRITORY ORGANIC ACT, 1848

The Organic Act which created Oregon Territory was similar in many respects to acts which had constituted other territories. It provided for a governor, three judges, an attorney, and a marshal, appointed for four-year terms by the President with the consent of the Senate. The territorial secretary was appointed for five years and, to assure administrative continuity, assumed the duties of governor when the latter was absent from the capital. The supreme court, composed of the chief justice and two associates, was convened annually. There were three judicial districts in which the resident judges held court, and the several courts, supreme and district, had original and appellate, chancery and common-law jurisdiction. Justices of the peace, locally elected, acted in limited cases. The territory was represented in Congress by an elected delegate serving a two-year term; he spoke for his constituents and advised on legislation affecting them, but had no vote.

Every white male inhabitant (excepting federal military personnel on duty) who was twenty-one years of age or over, and a resident of Oregon in 1848; who was a citizen of the United States or had declared, on oath, his intention to become one, and had taken an oath to support the Constitution of the United States and the Organic Act, was qualified to vote in the first election. Thereafter, the territorial legislature was empowered to define qualifications of voters and elected officers.

Legislative authority was vested in a territorial assembly consisting of a council of nine, serving three-year terms, and a house of at least eighteen (and a maximum of thirty) elected annually. The governor was given no veto power over legislation, but all acts passed by the legislature were subject to congressional approval. The powers of the legislature with regard to debts and finances were limited.

Several special features marked Oregon's Organic Act. One was the section applying the Ordinance of 1787 to the Territory, thus implicitly prohibiting slavery. A second was in the provision for support of public schools. The Land Ordinance of 1785, establishing a survey system for the nation's western lands, reserved section 16 of every township for the maintenance of schools. In the case of Oregon, however, the amount of land was doubled and sections number 16 and 36 of each township were reserved for this purpose. For this unique generosity to Oregon Territory, Thornton claimed credit.

The Act stipulated that laws in force under the provisional government should continue to operate until changed by the territorial legislature. However, as customary, Congress recognized Indian rights to the land and, until these rights were extinguished, could make no regulation respecting its disposal. Hence the provisional land laws were declared null and void—with one exception: title to 640 acres occupied as missionary stations among the Indians were confirmed to the societies to which the stations belonged. In this matter too Thornton's influence was evident.

On March 2, 1849, Oregon's first territorial governor, Joseph Lane, accompanied by United States Marshal Joe Meek, arrived in Oregon City. The next day, Governor Lane declared the Territory organized and in operation. Before the year was out the people had chosen a legislature, a council, and a delegate to Congress. The principal task of the first delegate, Samuel R. Thurston, was to persuade Congress to give Oregonians the land law they had anticipated under their provisional government.

THE DONATION LAND LAW, 1850

Assuming the surrender of Indian title to their lands, Congress on September 29, 1850, passed "An Act to Create the office of Surveyor-General of the public lands in Oregon, and to provide for the survey, and to make donations to settlers of the said public lands." Under this law, commonly known as the Donation Land Law, a half-section, or 320 acres, was granted to every male settler (including American half-breeds) over the age of eighteen who was a citizen or declared his intention to become one before December 1, 1851, and who had occupied and cultivated his land for four consecutive years before December 1, 1850. If he married by December 1, 1851, his wife was granted a like amount of land to hold in her own right.

This took care of the claims of settlers in Oregon before December 1850. For those settling between December 1, 1850 and December 1, 1853, who were white male citizens twenty-one years of age or over, 160 acres were granted. If married, their wives were entitled to a like amount. An amendment of February, 1853, extended the act to immigrants arriving as late as December 1, 1855, and permitted claimants to patent after two years' occupancy and payment of $1.25 per acre. The original act also granted lands to the territory for the support of higher education; two townships of land, one north and one south of the Columbia River and west of the Cascades, were to be selected after a survey of the region and were to be dedicated to the support of a territorial university.

The law also settled the question of the disputed Oregon City land. It was charged that Delegate Thurston here exercised his influence to defraud McLoughlin and benefit the American "junto of aristocracy."[1] The law affirmed possession of Abernethy Island to the "Wallamet milling and trading companies"—that is, to Abernethy—but the rest of McLoughlin's claim was put at the disposal of the legislature for the endowment of a university. All lots sold or granted by McLoughlin before March 1849 were confirmed to the purchasers or donees.

The Oregon Donation Land Act had several interesting effects. It recognized women's part in pioneering by allowing wives the uncommon privilege of holding real property in their own names. A minor consequence of the double allotment for married couples was an in-

[1] *Spectator*, March 20 and May 1, 1851.

creased number of marriages. Since single adult women were as scarce in Oregon as in other frontier societies, very young girls suddenly became marriageable and soon were wives. Almost half the claimants were married in Oregon. More significant was the long-range effect of the act upon the economy of the Willamette Valley. The size of the grants isolated the settlers, impeding the growth of towns and the diversification of occupations, industry, and crops, and increasing a characteristic tendency of pioneers toward provincialism and localism.

Furthermore, the land law did not immediately clarify land titles. It applied to "unoffered" public domain—that is, unsurveyed lands not subject to public sale. Its purpose was to protect qualified settlers until they had filed their claims and taken patents (titles), after which time the remaining lands, having been surveyed, came under general laws regulating the sale of the public domain.[2]

In providing for a survey the law stipulated that where the land was "deemed unfit for cultivation," only township lines were to be run; otherwise only such lines were to be surveyed as were "necessary." The initial survey (1851) set up the Willamette Meridian and base lines, and plotted townships and ranges for the most heavily populated areas. These were a necessary beginning. Field surveys of sections within townships were proposed for 1852 and 1853. Also necessary—very necessary—were surveys of individual land claims, if settlers were to get title or patent. The settlers' requests for surveys constituted the definition of "necessary" in this case.

Oregonians filed their entries in the provisional government's land office until federal offices were opened in Oregon City (1855), Roseburg (1860), La Grande (1867), and The Dalles (1875). However, since the law did not require them to complete title within a specified time, claimants delayed asking for surveys. In 1856 only 750 claims had been surveyed and 800 examined, platted, and approved. The next year the Secretary of the Interior reported that "not having been empowered to hasten the surveys of private land claims, . . the work [of surveying] in many townships goes on tardily, because settlers still withhold their requests for surveys." Consequently, land was held for the most part under "inchoate, imperfect rights," and since surveys were necessary before public sale, no public lands were offered in Oregon Territory until 1862.

The land offices received entries from 3134 persons qualified to re-

---

[2] The Preemption Act of 1841 allowed settlers after twelve months' occupation of surveyed land to purchase 160 acres at $1.25 an acre before public sale. The law was modified to permit preemption of both surveyed and unsurveyed lands and extended to Oregon and Washington territories in 1854.

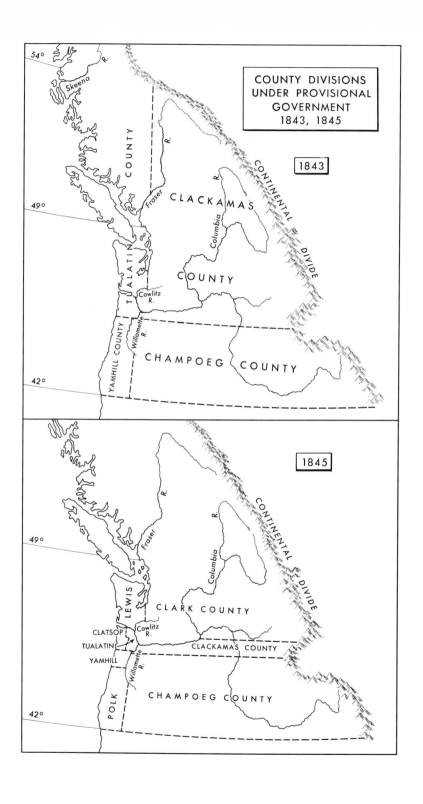

COUNTY DIVISIONS
UNDER PROVISIONAL
GOVERNMENT
1843, 1845

1843

54°

Skeena R.

49°

TALATIN COUNTY

Fraser R.

CLACKAMAS

Columbia R.

COUNTY

Cowlitz R.

YAMHILL COUNTY

Willamette R.

CHAMPOEG COUNTY

CONTINENTAL DIVIDE

42°

1845

49°

Fraser R.

LEWIS

Columbia R.

CLARK COUNTY

CLATSOP

Cowlitz R.

TUALATIN

CLACKAMAS COUNTY

YAMHILL

Willamette R.

POLK

CHAMPOEG COUNTY

CONTINENTAL DIVIDE

42°

ceive sections (or half-sections) by virtue of residence in Oregon before December 1, 1850. This is a surprisingly low number out of the possible 8000 or more adults in the Territory by this date. No fewer than 5000 immigrants had arrived in the fall of that year. Probably 25,000 to 30,000 persons entered Oregon Territory before the Donation Land Act expired (1855). However, under the original and amended provisions of the law, only 7437 claims, covering 2,500,000 acres within Oregon's boundaries, were eventually patented, and north of the Columbia, 1018 patents withdrew 300,000 acres from the public domain.[3]

Since it has been assumed that the purpose of immigration to Oregon was to acquire free land, we would expect a larger number of entries. It is also interesting that few original claimants retained the lands they filed upon. This may have been because of the fluidity of the American frontier settlement, but it also suggests that many claimants were speculators on a small scale. In any case, a study of 100 square miles of the richest farmlands in the Willamette Valley showed that before the end of the nineteenth century, two-thirds of the donation land claims had passed out of the hands of original entrants and their descendants.

Not all who entered claims patented them, and in some cases—how many is not known—patentees were not original occupants. If a qualified person wished to claim lands already occupied, he paid the occupant for his "prior rights," and then filed as original claimant. For example, in March, 1850, Baptist missionary Ezra Fisher bought for $5000 Samuel H. Barlow's 640-acre claim and then filed an original entry. This suggests a meteoric rise in prices which can be explained in part by competitive demand from immigrants who wanted land but not just any land that was unclaimed, and hence preferred to buy rather than take a donation grant. The price suggests speculation and the availability of capital for investment—in others words, a boom in real estate.

GOLD BUILDS PROSPERITY

The desperate economic situation of the late forties was relieved by the discovery of gold, first in California and later in the North-

[3] Data processed from Genealogical Forum of Portland, *Genealogical Material in Oregon Donation Land Claims*, 3 vols. (1957–1963); Robert C. Clark, *History of the Willamette Valley*, 3 vols. (1927), I, 405–409; Charlotte Shackleford, "Donation Land Claims," in *Building a State: Washington, 1889–1939* (1940), 410–446.

west. In 1849 more than fifty vessels entered the Columbia to take on wheat, farm produce, and lumber, for some 100,000 Californians who could pay handsomely for Oregon exports. At first middlemen profited, but competitive buying raised prices for producers. Wheat shot up from 62 cents to $2 a bushel; lumber rose to $30 and then to $80 and $100 a thousand board feet. Granaries were emptied and farmers who stayed home and women and children who farmed while their men went to the mines, accumulated tidy fortunes. As early as January, 1849, the *Spectator* reported that $400,000 in dust had reached Oregon.

Even after speculative buying stopped and Oregon commodities had to compete with eastern and South American imports, continuing evidences of prosperity appeared in farm improvements, merchants' inventories, and the growth of towns. Merchants profited beyond their highest hopes, and in an inflated market old debts were erased but still with profit to the creditors. This paradox was possible through dealings in gold dust.

Gold dust was the medium of exchange. This was not a perfect medium, however; the quality of dust varied and it was not easy to set a par value. Oregon's merchants were not hesitant to profit by transactions in which they put their own prices on it. For example, dust quoted at $16 an ounce in California was worth only $11 or $12 in goods in Oregon. The same gold paid the merchants' suppliers at the San Francisco quotations, i.e., $16. But such manipulations, too long pursued, were hazardous. A stable currency was preferable in the long run.

Early in 1849, the Oregon legislature had attempted to stabilize the price of gold by establishing a mint. Organization of Oregon Territory put an end to this encroachment on federal powers. But a group of citizens, among them George Abernethy, organized the Oregon Exchange Company and privately minted $5 and $10 pieces, using crude gold bought at the uniform price of $16 an ounce. Since the content of gold in crude form was 8 to 12 percent higher than in standard federal minted coins, the Oregon mintage rapidly went out of circulation. The exchange ratio between dust and coin soon leveled off. In 1854, a federal mint was opened in San Francisco and the Pacific Coast was supplied with metallic currency more than adequate for its needs. The discovery of gold in southern Oregon in 1851 kept the economy geared to a high pitch of prosperity. A temporary abatement in 1854–1855 shook the whole region, but spirits were restored by new discoveries of gold in Washington Territory, British Columbia, and Idaho.

The economy of Oregon Territory prospered on mining and its demands. But it was also benefited by immigration. Between 1850 and 1855, 30,000 to 35,000 persons came into the Territory, boosted the sale of lands, and increased the demand for goods and services. Homes, new mills, small shipyards, local markets as well as suppliers of the mines required some diversification of products. As the economy flourished, town sites were "puffed" and proprietors and promoters vied with one another to build the biggest, best, and fastest growing city in the country. A speculative fever was quickly reflected in the local papers where proprietors touted the advantages of their respective sites. Nathaniel Crosby and Thomas H. Smith, proprietors of Milton City, advertised that they would give to every head of family two town lots, to single men, one lot, if they would build upon the properties within six months. The proprietors would supply building materials on credit. To anyone that would built a grist mill, they offered mill site and land. They projected a railroad to the Yamhill Valley, and advertised a "Brilliant chance for investment!" In 1855 Milton City was county seat of Columbia County, but shortly afterward it was swept away by a flood. Its projected railway ran only as advertising matter in the *Oregon Spectator*.

Elijah White, Alonzo Skinner, and Joseph D. Holman laid out Lancaster City (renamed Pacific City), across the Columbia from Astoria. John Adair, a proprietor of Astoria, was not anxious to see a rival across the river and in February, 1850, complained to Samuel Thurston:

> I have been informed of a speculation started by Dr. White, formerly a sort of Indian agent in Oregon, which promises to assume a rather portentous form. It is no less than the building of a new city in Baker's Bay to which he proposed to transfer the port of Entry and everything else . . . Dr. White has started a new town there with the name of "Lancaster City" and sundry good folks above her have taken shares therein. . . . As yet there are only one or two Indian grog shops on the ground, but what may not puffing and petitioning do. Baker's Bay may well set itself up as a rival to Portland . . .[4]

White's "puffing and petitioning" had, by November of 1850, reached such proportions that Astoria's few inhabitants were seriously alarmed. When Lancaster's proprietors had brought from San Francisco a number of buildings, including a knocked-down hotel, and invested an estimated $100,000 in the location, Astorians managed to have the townsite taken over by the United States government as a military reservation.

[4] John Adair Letters, Oregon Historical Society.

Other towns had happier histories. Milwaukie, founded in 1847 by Lot Whitcomb, grew to be something of a rival to Oregon City, having about 500 people in 1850. Both were eclipsed by the growth of Portland, which frustrated the ambitions of other towns as well. Peter H. Burnett and Morton M. McCarver had hoped to tap the Tualatin Valley by means of the old HBC cattle trail across the hills, but it was impassable by loaded wagons, and Linnton did not flourish. Rainier appeared for a short period to be the coming town on the Columbia, claiming to be the head of deep-water navigation; but like Linnton, St. Helens, and Milton City, it lacked easy access to the Valley hinterland.

That William Overton's claim, twelve miles down river from Oregon City, would ever outstrip the territorial capital in size and importance was believed only by the owner, who in 1844 wagered $500 on its future. Asa L. Lovejoy and Francis Pettygrove took up claims just north of Overton's, where a narrow forested shelf sloped gradually to the Willamette, drained by an alder-lined creek fed by springs and streams from canyons in the hills behind it. In 1845 they platted their lands and flipped a coin to name the site. Portland won over Boston.

Oceangoing vessels could reach Portland. What the town needed was settlers and a hinterland from which to draw cargoes for the ships. In 1850, the inhabitants of the village sent a river boat to the Cascades to divert newcomers from the Barlow Road and Oregon City. At the same time they tried to find a practical route over the hills into the Tualatin Valley. A community enterprise carried on through 1851 to 1853 finally completed a corduroy road up Canyon Creek with the result that heavily laden wheat wagons could reach Portland from the Tualatin Plains and the Yamhill settlements. Portland then had the two principal requirements to make it a city: access to a productive hinterland and deep-water navigation.

DISSATISFACTION WITH TERRITORIAL STATUS

Prosperity gave inhabitants of Oregon Territory confidence in their future. But it did not reconcile them to territorial status. While they welcomed its advantages, they quickly grew restless with its drawbacks.

Congress appropriated funds which determined the kind and extent of improvements and help that the Territory could receive. What

Plowing virgin ground. The 8-horse team testifies that it was hard, hard work. Today there are about 127,000 farms in the three states.

RIGHT. *80,000 sacks of wheat await shipment down the Columbia, 1899.*

BELOW. *Vast wheatfields were threshed with greatly increased speed by the "very lastest improvement in mechanized farming." Wheat still is the leading agricultural crop in Oregon and Washington.*

RIGHT. *Stock-raising, an important part of northwest agriculture to the present time, could furnish plenty of excitement. A man, center, has just been bested by a bull and on-looking companions are ready to hightail it over the fence.*

ABOVE. *Sheep-shearing demanded great skill and additional "hands" during the season. Shearing competitions sometimes enlivened an otherwise monotonous routine. Idaho is a leading state in the marketing of lambs and produces about 10-million pounds of wool yearly.*

LEFT. *No rain, no crop, no farm. From early times, settlers in many locales found it necessary to irrigate arid land. But individual effort was frequently inadequate.*

BELOW. *In 1941, the great Grand Coulee Dam was completed and, after 1945, controlled water distribution in the Inland Empire.*

Grand Coulee not only produces power but makes the desert bloom.

Irrigation creates pasture land from dusty flats. Contrast this with the corral squared out of the desert, preceding page. Of Idaho's 33,000 farms, 25,000 are irrigated.

Washington is the chief apple-growing state in the nation though fruit is not the state's chief crop. A portion of Washington's 51,500 farms are new orchards made possible by irrigation from Rocky Reach Dam.

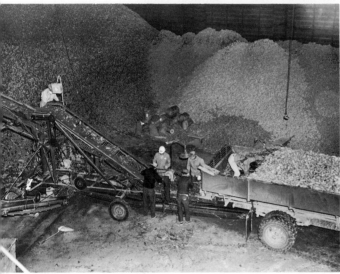

Thousands of irrigated acres of potato plants...

...yield tens of thousands of tons of potatoes.

Some of the best of Oregon's 42,500 farms are in the Hood River Valley BELOW. *Could the migrants trekking the Oregon Trail possibly have had this vision of a Land of Milk and Honey?*

the territorials expected and what they got were often at variance. Bureaucratic red tape and apparent indifference of the Treasury Department toward the time and space separating Oregon from the national capital, delayed payment of territorial vouchers. Military protection for immigrants on the Oregon Trail and for the settlers was slow to materialize. Territorials resented their ineligibility to vote in national elections, and they especially resented the imposition of appointed officers.

The territorial officers, appointed by the President under the patronage system, were exposed to criticism they did not always deserve. But territorial records support charges that appointees were often incompetent, absent from their duties, and willing to exploit their offices for financial as well as political ends. In a number of cases, officers were locally unpopular simply because they were "foreigners," that is, they had not previously been residents of the Territory. It was charged that they were "usually obscure strikers, who do the dirty work of parties, and being sent out as governors, assume pro-consular powers, and endeavor to 'mould public sentiment' into sending them to Congress."[5]

In 1848, Polk had rewarded a faithful Indiana Democrat of favorite-son rating with the governorship of Oregon Territory. Joseph Lane was a "foreigner" but his reputation as a general in the Mexican War, his partisanship, and his personality pleased Oregonians. His term as governor was short, but his influence in local politics was of long duration. The new governor arrived in Oregon City on March 2, 1849. Two days later, his appointment expired with President Polk's presidential term, but Lane carried on the duties of his office, including the important one of superintendent of Indian affairs, until his successor arrived. In a short time he built up a strong political machine—the Salem clique—supported by the vitriolic pen of Asahel Bush, editor of the *Oregon Statesman* (1850). In 1851 Lane was elected territorial delegate and served until 1859 when he resigned to become the vice-presidential candidate on the Breckinridge ticket of the southern extremist party in the campaign of 1860.

Abraham Lincoln, President Tyler's candidate to succeed Lane, refused the offer. The tenure of John P. Gaines, Tyler's second choice, was short and filled with contention. Everything was against him. He was a Whig, while Oregonians were Democrats; he was dignified— pompous according to his enemies—and a marked contrast to the easygoing frontiersman, Joe Lane. In less than a year Gaines was at

[5] Quoted in Earl Pomeroy, *The Territories and the United States: 1861–1890* (1947), 88.

swords' points with the majority of Oregonians. Controversy over the location of the capital, a common cause for quarrels in territories, left the governor sitting in Oregon City on his constitutional principles. Two judges and one legislator whom Gaines declared the legal assembly remained with the governor while other legislators convened at Salem under the watchful and gleeful eyes of the Democratic machine.

Gaines' successor, John W. Davis, was a Democrat, but he survived only nine months of attack and invective in the best of Oregon's uninhibited newspaper style. The editor of the Whig *Oregonian* (founded in 1850 to counter partisan *Statesman*) explained that local Democrats would not accept Davis because "he had neither driven his team across the plains nor been to the mines."[6] Probably the real source of opposition lay in the Salem clique's fear that the new governor might diminish its power or that of Joe Lane, who had influence in Washington, D.C., even though he was a nonvoting delegate, and who demonstrated his strength when he secured the appointment of local politico George L. Curry to the governorship in 1854.

No charges of corruption or venality were pressed against Oregon's territorial governors, but the first chief justice and associate fulfilled the worst expectations of cynics. It was the duty of the judges, sitting with a quorum of two, to compose the supreme court of the Territory. They were required to live in assigned districts to hold district courts. One judge found it inconvenient even to reside in the Territory and never appeared. Chief Justice William P. Bryant was euphemistically described as "in reduced circumstances" when he arrived in Oregon in 1849. When he left the following November he was well off financially. In the six months he was in the Territory he held two terms of his district court and one two-day term of the supreme court. He purchased interests in the disputed McLoughlin land claim at Oregon City, for which title could be adjudicated only before his own court. He continued to hold the office and draw a salary for a year and a half after he had left the Territory.[7]

The third district position remained unfilled until 1851. After Bryant's departure, Orville C. Pratt (second district) was the only supreme court judge in the Territory for almost a year. He added nothing to the dignity of the bench, and, like Bryant, missed no opportunity to improve his own fortune. Private business and political interests often took him from the Territory. When present, he was a center of controversy and political machination. He quarreled with his asso-

[6] *Oregonian*, August 5, 1854.

[7] Sidney Teiser, "The First Chief Justice of Oregon Territory: William P. Bryant," *OHQ*, June 1947. For Teiser's other studies of territorial judges see *OHQ*.

ciate William Strong and with Bryant's successor, Chief Justice Thomas Nelson, and brought so much confusion into the judicial processes that the courts suffered in prestige. In the capital controversy, Nelson and Strong concurred with the governor's position which they held to be constitutional, but Pratt moved to Salem with Democratic partisans. Ruling that he presided over the legal court, he used his office to play an injudicial role in politics. On the happier side, in filling Bryant's unexpired term, Nelson stood out "as a preeminent exemplar of judicial dignity and independence in an atmosphere of political animosities." Strong, who became a permanent resident in Oregon, enjoyed an unblemished reputation.

Bryant and Pratt were symbolic of the evils to which a territory could be subjected when its highest offices were party spoils and offered opportunities for aggrandizement. They are also prime examples of "absenteeism" which plagued more than one territory. One year after Oregon Territory had been organized, the editor of the *Spectator*, noting that Pratt, the Territory's only judge at the moment, was in California and that the governor and other officers were out of the capital on Indian business, was "forced to conclude" that Oregon had no civil government. For this there was "no remedy . . . but in the erection of a State Government and the elevation of our own officers."

The 1850 legislature considered but failed to act upon a resolution calling for a convention to write a state constitution. It did, however, ask its congressional delegate to work for a change in the Organic Law that would permit Oregonians to elect their own governor and secretary of state. Absenteeism and "foreigners" in high offices were traditional subjects of complaint among territorials; disaffection was common to thwarted local politicians. But in this far western corner of the nation, a fundamental concern for the right of self-determination underlay party and personal conflicts. The idea that men had a right to determine for themselves the kinds of institutions under which they would live was prominent in men's minds during the sectional conflicts of the fifties. For Oregonians, slavery was an academic question, but territorial status was not, because, according to a member of the legislature, it was "repugnant to the true spirit of our Constitution" which intended that men should govern themselves.

Jesse Applegate, called by his contemporaries the "sage of Yoncalla," often raised his voice on behalf of principles. In this case, he compared the disenfranchisement of American citizens in a territory to that of British colonials, and advocated immediate application of the principle of self-determination, not only to the whole Oregon Territory but to a part of it as well. He recommended that Congress divide the Territory, set up a new territory in the north, and "restore to the people of said Territories their political rights, by allowing them to adopt their own form of Government—to choose their own officers— as a body politic, to have their voice in the councils of the nation. . . ."[8]

In speaking for organization of the region north of the Columbia, Applegate was recommending a step toward the independence of that area's inhabitants from the domination of the Willamette Valley. And this is what the settlers in the north wanted.

[8] *Oregon Statesman*, December 16, 1851.

CHAPTER
SIXTEEN

Washington Territory and Indian Troubles of the Fifties

IN THE SPRING OF 1845 John R. Jackson, a naturalized American of English descent, settled in the Cowlitz Valley at Jackson Prairie. In the late summer, Michael T. Simmons and several companions located at Tumwater, where they were joined by four families. This American movement into the area north of the Columbia had been one reason for McLoughlin's decision to enter into the Compact of 1845.

At its August session that year the legislature created Vancouver County comprising all the area north of the Columbia and approximately along the line of the 46th parallel to the Continental Divide. In the December session, Cowlitz Valley and the area lying west of the trail to Nisqually was set off as Lewis County, and Vancouver was renamed Clark County.[1]

---

[1] James Douglas and Charles Forrest of the HBC, and Simmons were elected Judges, and John Jackson, Sheriff, of Vancouver County. They served both counties after the division.

Settlers moved slowly into the northern counties even after the boundary settlement in 1846. Among the early comers were Sidney Ford and Joseph Borst, who located on Ford Prairie in the Chehalis Valley. Edmund Sylvester joined Simmons and his friends near Tumwater, and Levi Smith built a cabin at Chambers Prairie on the site of the present Olympia. In 1849 Marshal Joe Meek reported 304 inhabitants, probably two-thirds of whom were employees of the HBC. Lewis County was so thinly populated that in order to fill the panels of grand and petit juries for the trial of Indians accused of murdering Leander Wallace, Meek had to draw jurors from Clark County. Apparently a large immigration moved north of the river in the next twelve months, for the 1850 census showed a population of 1049. Three years later an estimated 4000 persons were scattered in small villages on the eastern and southern shores of Puget Sound and over the prairies of the Cowlitz. Pettygrove had founded Port Townsend, and the Terrys, Hortons, and Yeslers had laid the foundations of Seattle.

Several factors accounted for the relatively slow growth of population north of the Columbia. One was the Puget's Sound Agriculture Company's continuing control of the better lands. The Willamette Valley, with its settled conditions, growing villages, and greater conveniences, attracted men with families, and Valley settlers encouraged reports that north of the Columbia the land was poor and the population representative of the crudest elements of the frontier.

INDEPENDENCE FROM OREGON, 1853

A sense of deep frustration moved the citizens north of the river, and a handful of men, among them Judge William Strong, began to agitate for division of the Territory. They first proposed the matter at a Fourth of July meeting, 1851. A "convention" of a dozen men organized the movement and, on November 25, 1852, some of the inhabitants assembled at Monticello (the present Longview) and drew up a memorial to Congress, requesting the creation of the "territory of Columbia." In the next session of the Oregon territorial legislature, Isaac N. Ebey and Francis Chenoweth from Clark and Lewis counties, had a rare opportunity to influence the balance of power in a legislative squabble. According to Judge Strong's recollections, they used it to get the legislature's approval of the Monticello memorial. The memorial listed the reasons for the divorce: Oregon Territory was too large to form a single state and division was inevitable. The capi-

EMPIRE OF THE COLUMBIA

tal at Salem was an exaggerated 500 miles from the main population in the north, and the Willamette Valley inhabitants "having a majority of voters . . . controlled the Territorial Legislature and kept from them [residents in the north] the benefits of congressional appropriations." The "great and important focus of commercial interest" of the proposed territory would concentrate on Puget Sound. Because of their geographical positions, the residents north and south of the Columbia "would always rival each other in commercial advantages . . . [and] as they now are and always have been, be actuated by a spirit of opposition."[2]

Joseph Lane presented the memorial to Congress in February, 1853, arguing for it in terms of the nation's defense against "any foreign aggression," and the encouragement of emigration to the Far West. There was no real opposition to the creation of Columbia Territory. Congress questioned whether the population of the proposed territory was large enough to justify organization. To this Lane answered that "the population . . . will be quite as great as that of the whole of Oregon at the period of its organization." (The 1854 census reported 11,154 inhabitants.) The only change in Lane's bill substituted the name Washington for Columbia, though it was pointed out that this would create confusion with the national capital.

Several factors may help to explain the ease with which the Washington territorial bill moved through Congress. Credit must be given to Oregon's delegate Joseph Lane, who was influential in the Democratic Party. There was some suspicion of British intentions in colonizing British Columbia, and Puget Sound's importance as a naval base and commercial *entrepôt* had been much emphasized a decade earlier. But probably a determining factor was the national interest in a railway route to the Pacific. At the time Lane introduced the territorial bill, Congress was debating appropriations for surveys of transcontinental routes. Both private and political interests were promoting a northern route to Puget Sound as an alternative to southern and central routes.

On March 2 (1853) President Millard Fillmore signed the bill creating Washington Territory. The news was received in the new territory with the firing of guns and celebrations. "No longer in the hands of go-betweens, we have become 'a people' within ourselves," exulted the *Columbian's* editor. " 'Progress' is our watchword. Our destiny is in the keeping of God, the National Government, and our own judgment. . . . So, *nous verrons*."

[2] "Memorial," in *Readings in Pacific Northwest History: Washington, 1790–1895*, Charles M. Gates, ed. (1941).

248

WASHINGTON TERRITORY'S ORGANIC CODE

Washington Territory was defined as the lands bounded by the Canadian line on the north, the Rocky Mountains on the east, and on the south by the Columbia River to where it intersected the 46th parallel near the mouth of Walla Walla River. What is now southern Idaho remained a part of Oregon Territory until 1859 when it was added to Washington Territory.

The Organic Code by which the new Territory was governed for thirty-six years differed in no essential from that of Oregon Territory. Laws already in force were to be continued until repealed or modified by the legislature.[3] The same provision was made for the support of common schools. The Donation Land Law was applied to the new Territory, but as amended July 17, 1854, it excluded from entry townsites and lands suitable for trade and commerce, extended preemption privileges to surveyed and unsurveyed lands, and provided two townships for university purposes.

Governor Isaac Ingalls Stevens arrived in Olympia November 25, 1853, and on November 28 called for elections; the new Territory was organized. Political life was not dull. The Territory had its Democratic machine, the Olympia clique, and uninhibited editors of partisan newspapers such as the (Olympia) *Pioneer and Democrat* and *Puget Sound Courier*, who gave Washington's politics a flavor comparable to that provided for Oregonians in the *Oregon Statesman* and *Oregonian*. There was perennial and bitter controversy over the location of the capital, the penitentiary, and the insane asylum. There were Indian scares and an Indian war, and it was charged that partisanship was involved in handling these crises. Fortunately, the first governor was an expert in the game of politics.

Stevens had the personality and talent to create a following among Washington's individualistic citizenry, despite an articulate opposition. A West Point graduate originally from Massachusetts, he overcame the handicap of not being a frontiersman by a successful military career in the Corps of Topographical Engineers during the Mexican War from which he emerged a major general. Like many army men, Stevens supported General Franklin Pierce for the presidency. For his

---

[3] The territorial legislature immediately set up a commission to prepare a statutory code eliminating some confusions inherited from Oregon statutes. Arthur S. Beardsley, "Compiling the Territorial Codes of Washington," *PNQ*, January 1937, 4.

political services and in recognition of his training and manifest abilities, Stevens was rewarded with the concurrent offices of governor of Washington Territory, superintendent of territorial Indian affairs, and leader of the Northern Pacific Railroad survey.

The Pacific railroad surveys (1854–1861), of which there were five, were intended to ascertain practicable routes for railroads to the Pacific. They were extremely important not only because they encouraged hopes for transcontinental communication, but also because they contributed accurate information about the West.

Stevens' explorations were confined to the area between the 47th and 49th parallels. One of his assistants, Lieutenant George B. McClellan, explored the Rocky Mountain and Cascade passes. But both en route to Puget Sound and in the course of his duties as governor and superintendant of Indian affairs, Stevens became thoroughly familiar with the eastern part of the Territory, which he called "the Great Plains of the Columbia," and which he maintained would support a farming population. His enthusiasm for the Territory and his championship of the northern railroad route that would open it have been interpreted as merely a desire to promote his own political interests. Such an attitude ignores Stevens' integrity as "a practical geographer of uncommon stature."[4]

Stevens, the politician, managed to build in Olympia a powerful clique which, in the words of his opposition, was guilty of "perpetuating a political dynasty which stinks in the nostrils of all honest men." Nevertheless, Stevens was engaged in more than politicking. As superintendent of Indian affairs, he made treaties with numerous bands of restless Indians; as commander of the territorial militia and governor, he fought with the people, the army, and the Indians. Stevens inherited a situation which had already plagued Oregon's governors.

To understand the Indian Wars of the 1850s we must consider the background issues. Under the Donation Land Law settlers had their choice of land from the public domain; but the federal government could not legally dispose of that domain until Indian titles to it had been extinguished. The United States had inherited from Britain the principle that the Indians held primary right, and, accordingly, treated with the Indians' headmen as if they were sovereigns with power to transfer their rights. Having ceded the lands—in legal theory the condition of their sovereignty, but in reality the condition of their "natural" freedom—the natives became the United States' Indian problem.

[4] Donald W. Meinig, "Isaac Stevens: Practical Geographer of the Early Northwest," *Geographical Review*, October 1955.

Experience had shown that the Indians did not easily assimilate with white society. In the first quarter of the nineteenth century, the government therefore chose to remove them, by force when necessary, to locations remote from settlements where, it was believed, time and education would eliminate their barbarities. In his first message to the Oregon territorial legislature, Governor Lane summarized the prevailing enlightened view concerning the Indians' predicament, and proposed the customary solution. The white man's "arts of civilization" doomed the Indians to "poverty, want and crime," and the natives would best be served by being removed to "a district remote from settlement." Such a district was the vast, open country east of the Cascades, then considered of little value to white men.

By the Indian Treaty Act of 1850, Congress authorized a separate office of Superintendent of Indian Affairs for Oregon and a commission to negotiate treaties with Indians. The commission, headed by ex-governor John P. Gaines, had made six treaties with Willamette Valley bands when its authority was transferred to Anson Dart, the recently appointed superintendent. With the aid of Henry H. Spalding and John Parrish, former missionaries, Dart concluded thirteen treaties, ten of them in council at Tansey Point with the Indians living near the mouth of the river and two with Clackamas living in the Valley. For a total of $91,300 to be paid in ten annual installments, in clothing, flour, groceries and other goods, and small amounts of money, the Indians surrendered an estimated 6,000,000 acres of land. But poor and reduced as they were, they refused under any circumstances or for any consideration to move east of the Cascades.

Considering the distinctive patterns of life that had evolved in the two environments, coastal and plateau, and the hostilities of the peoples toward one another, it is not difficult to understand the Indians' position. Dart provided in the treaties that each village or band, therefore, should reserve certain portions of its ceded land as its permanent home. This, however, was not in accord with national policy. The Commissioner of Indian Affairs in Washington, D.C., found in Dart's treaties "novel provisions, the practical operation of which could not be foreseen." He submitted the treaties to the Senate without recommendations, and that body, having learned of the settlers' opposition to the "novel provisions," failed to ratify. After futile efforts to explain to the Indians why the government did not fulfill its part of the treaty obligations, Dart resigned from the superintendency. His successor, Joel Palmer, was not appointed until March, 1853. Meanwhile, Indian trouble broke out in southern Oregon.

TROUBLES ON THE ROGUE

By 1850, settlers and miners were moving into the Umpqua and Rogue valleys. The Rogues were notoriously predatory; the miners, sometimes irresponsible and often aggressive, shared the frontiersman's common belief that the only good Indian was a dead Indian. In the summer of 1851 the Rogues (joined at times by Klamaths and Coquilles) attacked travelers and settlements, with heavy loss of life and destruction of property. After a bloody battle between volunteers and natives, ex-governor Lane and Joel Palmer negotiated the Treaty of Table Rock (September, 1853) which was ratified by the Senate less than a year later.

The Rogues and the Cow Creek band of Umpquas ceded their lands, the Rogues receiving annual payments totaling $60,000 (less $15,000 deducted to indemnify settlers for their losses); the Cow Creek band, $11,000 in money installments and $1000 in clothing for the headmen. One hundred square miles in the vicinity of Table Rock was reserved for the Indians' temporary use, and the Indians reluctantly agreed to move to a permanent reservation when one should be provided. Siletz reservation for the southern and central Coast Indians was created by executive order in 1855, but before it was set up and the Rogues removed, sporadic outbreaks of violence continued, caused mainly by the whites' wanton murder of Indians who strayed off the temporary Table Rock reserve. In October, 1855, thirty volunteers (most of the Rogue wars were fought by volunteers) attacked a camp of Indian noncombatants, killing old men, women, and children. Futile efforts were made in council to quiet the Indians' anger. In the spring of 1856, a two-day battle forced the main body of Rogues to sue for peace, and the following year they were removed to Siletz. The few who refused to move were treated as outlaws, run down, and shot.[5]

The Donation Land Law which in effect encouraged the whites to occupy lands not yet ceded by the Indians had paramount importance in the Indian-white conflicts of the 1850s. But two other conditions contributed to this unhappy situation. Because of cultural differences, whites and Indians valued the land for basically different reasons. To the white settler, land was a personal, transferable possession to be used as its owner wished. To the Indian, land was communal property sanctified by traditional holding. It was also valued

[5] Charles H. Carey, *A General History of Oregon Prior to 1861*, 2 vols. (1936), II, 564.

by the Indian for what it produced naturally to sustain life and customs.

A settler on the Rogue River recalled that prior to the outbreak of hostilities the Indians, "in loud, angry tones" had demanded that the pioneers leave because, among other misdeeds, they were "frightening the fish away from the streams. Already there were fewer elk and deer in the forests, fewer ducks and geese in the marshes, fewer berries in the woods, because of our presence." Further, a Rogue warrior is reported to have said: "This is my country; I was in it when those large trees were very small. My heart is sick with fighting, but I want to live in my country."[6]

Such statements—and they can be multiplied by the score—may reveal more accurately the sentiments of Indian interpreters and apologists than those of the Indians themselves. But reduced to realistic and unromantic terms, the Indians' cause was the preservation of their livelihood and way of life. Those of the Willamette Valley and the lower Columbia and Cowlitz Valley, for example, had to all practical purposes surrendered their heritage when they first allowed white men to settle among them. The treaties which formalized an accomplished fact also formalized the American settlers' promises that the United States would pay for the lands. Fulfillment of these promises was long delayed. Watching the white men build cabins, set snake rail fences, kill off game so that cattle might graze and gardens grow, and having no token of the government's good faith, the Indians assumed that nothing was to be done for them. It was natural that their already fragile confidence in the settlers' or agents' promises should give way to animosity.

Oregon's western Indians made the establishment of reserves in their native habitat a condition of cession. But interior bands, with few exceptions, could not easily define a particular area as their own. Since no one area supplied all their needs, most of the Indians east of the Cascades assumed their lands to be those where, without conflict with neighboring bands, they hunted, gathered berries, dug camas roots, fished, or grazed their horses. The Yakimas, however, were noteworthy for an unusually strong conviction of exclusive possession. The value placed by interior Indians on their lands could not be translated into white men's terms. "Suppose you show me goods, shall I run up and take them?" asked Chief Peu Peu Mox Mox of the Walla Wallas. "Goods and earth are not equal. Goods are for using on the earth."[7]

[6] Agnes Ruth Sengstacken, *Destination West!* (1942), 121; Frances F. Victor, *The Early Indian Wars of Oregon* (1894), 407.

[7] Reported in Hazard Stevens, *Life of Isaac I. Stevens*, 2 vols. (1900), II, 45–46.

THE SUMMER OF TREATY MAKING—
THE WALLA WALLA COUNCIL

When Isaac Stevens arrived in Washington Territory in the fall of 1854 only one Northwest Indian treaty—Table Rock—had been concluded and ratified. The governor's task as superintendent of Indian affairs was to negotiate for land cessions from Nebraska to the Pacific.

The same act which authorized him to do this gave Joel Palmer power to negotiate with the Indians of Oregon. Although land was a primary objective of negotiation, it was also important to get the Indians off the land they ceded. On the basis of his experience with the Rogues, Palmer recommended essential points of Pacific Northwest Indian policy: the Indians were to be confined to reservations, preferably remote from settlements; their reservations and lives were to be protected from the greed and degrading influences of the whites; on the reservations, the Indians were to be governed by law in their relations to one another, and were to have the help of missionaries and teachers. Palmer's recommendations were transmitted to Congress in February, 1854, with a request for speedy action because of multiplying signs of Indian hostility. Through the winter of 1854 and the following summer, Stevens and Palmer, each in his own territory or working together, labored to effect settlement with the Indians. By January 1855, Palmer secured a treaty with the confederated bands of the Willamette Valley, which now was ratified by the Senate. It provided for a reservation (actually set up in 1857) at Grand Ronde in the foothills of the Coast Range. Palmer also negotiated with the confederated bands of central Oregon who agreed to a reservation at Warm Springs, but this treaty was not ratified until 1859.

Stevens first negotiated with the Nisquallys, Puyallups, and other bands living at the head of the Sound. Although the treaty (December, 1854) was unpopular with the settlers because it allowed numerous small reservations close to settlements, it was ratified by the Senate within four months. However, his treaty with the Duwamish, Clallams, Makahs and related bands and villages—and important treaties with the interior bands—were not ratified until four years later. One explanation for the Senate's delay was the outbreak of hostilities almost on the heels of the Walla Walla Council (1885).

In May, 1855, Stevens and Palmer faced the greatest test of their skills when they met with the most powerful, numerous, and independent Northwest Indians near the site of the Whitman massacre eight years before. It was reported that 6000 Indians appeared at the Walla Walla Council before it concluded.

254

Stevens was in a hurry; the Indians were not. Peu Peu Mox Mox protested that "we require time to think quietly, slowly." But the Indians' time was running out. (Two years later, Peu Peu Mox Mox was taken hostage and killed when he tried to escape.) Cayuses, Walla Wallas, Umatillas, and Yakimas showed their hostility; the Nez Perces remained the most friendly throughout the three long weeks of negotiation. Reluctantly, however, in separate treaties, the chiefs of these principal bands all ceded their lands and agreed that, within a year, they would move to reservations within the ceded areas.

The Walla Wallas were to receive a total of $96,000 in cash to be distributed annually over a 20-year period; the Yakimas and the Nez Perces each $200,000 (less $60,000 advanced for removal expenses) on the same terms. In some cases, special gifts and housing were awarded headmen. The Yakimas had fishing rights reserved for them on the Columbia. The government was to set up agencies on the reservations with schools and other aids. Each treaty provided that, at the President's discretion, individuals would be allowed allotments of reserved lands; also that the use of liquor would be forbidden on the reservation. The government retained the right to build public roads across the reserved lands; otherwise, it was stipulated that the reservations were for the exclusive use and benefit of the Indians, and that no white man except Indian Department employees would be permitted to live upon them without permission of the tribe, the superintendent, and the agent.

The Nez Perces retained the Wallowas and the upper Grande Ronde Valley and much of central Idaho. The Yakimas contemplated with resentment the reduction of their lands to a small part of the Yakima Valley. Misunderstandings, perhaps unavoidable in some cases, resulted from the Walla Walla Council. Some bands claimed they had been present but that their chiefs had not signed the treaties. Some who had not been at the Council at all, notably the Spokanes, found themselves in an anomalous position as "nontreaty" Indians.

The ashes of campfires were still warm, peace pipes hardly cooled, when ominous reports were heard. Gold discoveries at Colville started a small rush of miners across Yakima lands. Believing they had been betrayed, the Yakimas turned on the whites who crossed their boundaries. Six miners and Indian Agent A. J. Bolon were killed. In October (1855) Major Granville O. Haller with a company of regulars was repulsed with losses when he tried to enter the Yakima Valley, presumably to inquire the reasons for Chief Kamiakin's hostility.

The treaty-making summer was followed by three years of war. Conflicts broke out almost simultaneously on the Rogue, which we

255

have already discussed, and east and west of the mountains in Washington Territory.

THE WAR IN THE PUGET SOUND COUNTRY

It was reported that Leschi, a Nisqually chief, spurred on by the Yakimas, was behind acts of violence and cruelty of which Puget Sound Indians were "heretofore judged incapable."[8] Cabins were burned, cattle driven off, travelers ambushed. Frightened people took refuge in blockhouses hastily erected or converted from church, barn, or schoolhouse. The volunteer militia was hard pressed to catch up with marauding Indians who vanished mysteriously after a raid. Strangely, some settlers continued to live peaceably while their neighbors' cabins were burned and the occupants murdered. Suspected of helping the Indians, they insisted that they had escaped attack because they were "neutral."

There was no such word as neutral in Stevens' vocabulary. The governor ordered the inhabitants of western Washington into blockhouses where they could be protected—or kept under surveillance. When five men refused, Stevens declared martial law and arrested them for trial by a military court. Chief Justice Edward Lander, on duty with the volunteers, left his post to open his court to *habeas corpus* proceedings. When two of the prisoners were still held in military custody—although Lander had proved the civil court was functioning—the judge ordered Governor Stevens arrested for contempt. The governor retaliated by having Lander arrested and imprisoned on the charge that he had absented himself from military duties without leave. This dilemma was finally resolved in a unique fashion. When Lander was released he laid a fine on Stevens, who thereupon pardoned himself.[9] Although he was censured by the legislature for declaring martial law, Stevens' popularity survived the incident and in 1857 he was elected delegate to Congress by a vote of 986 to 549.

Less amusing was the conflict between the governor and settlers on one hand and General John E. Wool and the regular army on the other—a conflict which handicapped the prosecution of the war. Commandant of the Pacific military district with headquarters at San Francisco, Wool agreed with many regular army men that in most instances settlers were responsible for troubles with the natives; and

[8] "Seattle's First Taste of Battle, 1856," *PNQ*, January 1956, 6.
[9] Edmond S. Meany, *History of the State of Washington* (1909), 197.

that the army's duty was as much to protect Indians as whites. Wool explicitly charged that the Northwest troubles were fomented by whites who hoped to relieve their depressed economy in 1854–1855 with army expenditures. He blamed Stevens for not prohibiting settlers from entering ceded lands before treaties were ratified and for failing to remove the natives to an Indian country. Wool further made himself unpopular in 1856 by ordering the interior closed to settlers until Yakimas and other disaffected Indians were confined to their reservations.

The governor, as spokesman for the settlers, denied the general's charges and countered with some of his own: the army refused to protect settlers, and its officers were incompetent to do so. The subsequent Civil War records of George McClellan and Phil Sheridan suggest they were not incompetent on the battlefield. The Oregon and Washington legislatures, expressing a common lack of confidence in Wool, petitioned for his removal from the Pacific command.

There was some reason for the army's contempt for volunteer militias, their inexperienced command, lack of discipline, and the short terms—three to six months—of enlistment. The volunteers did a great deal of marching; the larger objectives of war were lost sight of, and sometimes military skirmishes were hardly distinguishable from vigilante actions.

General Wool was relieved of his command in 1857 and Brigadier General Newman S. Clarke succeeded him. Thus far, the Yakimas had been the militants, raiding settlements and attacking small parties of travelers in the Yakima Valley. In the spring of 1856, Yakimas, Klickitats, and a sullen group of Cascades Indians attacked settlers at the Cascades of the Columbia. For the moment the Yakimas escaped unpunished, though their chief, Kamiakin, was also suspected of building an alliance with the Colvilles and Spokanes. When, in the spring of 1858, miners at Colville became fearful of an uprising, Colonel Edward J. Steptoe was ordered to Colville to protect them. He was stopped near Rosalia by a large party of Spokanes who warned him not to cross the Palouse country. His retreat to Walla Walla was harassed by a series of running battles, as a result of which Colonel George Wright was ordered to the interior.

While Major Robert Garnett reduced the natives remaining in the Yakima Valley, Wright, with more than 500 men, advanced against combined forces of Yakimas and Spokanes. By his skillful deployments at Four Lakes and Spokane Plains he convinced the enemy they had no chance to win and further fighting meant their extinction. This was brought home to them in a hard way when Wright rounded up and slaughtered 800 or 900 of their horses and destroyed their caches of winter food. As the Indians surrendered, summary justice was dealt a quota of ringleaders from each band. Qualchin, a young Yakima warrior accused of murdering an Indian agent, was sent word that his father Owhi would be hanged if he did not come to Wright's camp. "Qualchin came to me at 9 o'clock," Wright reported, "and at 9¼ A.M. he was hung."[10]

The war on Puget Sound was over by 1857, the Yakima War in 1858. Washington Territory had had a baptism of blood. The wars had mixed effects upon the Pacific Northwest, and especially upon Washington Territory. They created among the whites an unpublicized civil war in which lines were drawn between families with Indian blood—such as French Canadians—and those who did not, and between spokesmen for the Indians' rights and the sworn enemies of barbarous redskins. Time did not easily erase these lines. The wars increased army expenditures, and circulation of the scrip with which volunteers were paid was advantageous to farmers and merchants alike. Stevens reported the issuance of close to $1,000,000 in scrip redeemable by federal appropriations. This was not an insignificant sum in a frontier economy. Wages went up. Farm help in the Willamette Valley in 1857 was getting $50 a month plus room and board; mechanics and carpenters earned $3.75 to $5 a day.

On the other hand, in Washington the wars halted enterprises that would have profited the community. Capital and labor were diverted from new productive ventures to rebuild and restock farmsteads. Immigration of a much desired kind—sturdy farmers with families, innovating men, and builders—was curtailed, postponed, or deflected to Oregon, whose territorial days and territorial trials were about over.

[10] John Mullan, "Topographical Memoir of Col. George E. Wright's Campaign," *Sen. Ex. Doc. No. 32, 35th Cong. 2d Sess.*, 69.

CHAPTER
SEVENTEEN

Oregon Statehood,
Organization of the
Idaho Territory, and the
Last of the Indian Wars

THE MOVEMENT for statehood which had originated almost simultaneously with Oregon's organization as a territory, arose from discontent
with a system which Oregonians believed reduced them to a position
of colonial subjection. Self-determination was a principle of government made increasingly popular by territorial experience.

From 1850 to 1854 the statehood issue was largely confined to legislative debates on resolutions calling for a constitutional convention. In
the latter year the question of a convention was first submitted to
the voters and rejected by a majority of 869. It was also defeated in
the next two annual elections, but by so narrow a margin that Delegate Lane introduced the necessary bill to enable Oregonians to proceed to statehood. The bill was not even considered by a Congress
distraught over bleeding Kansas.

The vacillations of Oregon voters on the statehood issue were in part a result of local party politics. While both Democrats and Whigs wanted statehood, their enthusiasm waxed or waned according to party expediency. Whigs, a minority party, were reluctant to support a statehood movement if it meant that the Salem clique would dominate state politics as it had the Territory's. Democrats vociferously championed statehood for Oregon when in 1851–1852, a national Whig administration imposed a Whig governor.

As long as the Oregon Democrats remained firmly cohesive they did well; the clique could even survive Whig administrations. But its high-handed practices bred within the party rebellious factions which were only awaiting an opportunity to throw the rascals out and put themselves in command. The emergence locally of the nativist Know-Nothing Party was more an anti-Salem revolt than the anti-Catholic, anti-foreigner movement it was in the East.[1] It was scotched when the clique put through the legislature a *viva voce* voting measure to ferret out the party's secret membership.

Rebellion also brewed in southern Oregon, a stronghold of Democrats. The miners would not take dictation from Salem; their economic interests lay with northern California and San Francisco rather than with the Willamette Valley and Portland. At one time they proposed to secede from Oregon Territory and unite with northern California to form a new territory. In 1861 a new twist appeared in southern Oregon's intransigence—a movement to secede from the United States and create an independent, slaveholding republic with Joe Lane at its head. The movement died aborning. Thus the question of Oregon's statehood was a matter of principle, of local politics, and of national crisis. By 1857, local issues were almost subordinated to the issue dividing the nation.

Actually, slavery was an academic question in Oregon. Although many of the early settlers were of southern origin, they were not of the slaveholding class. Later some claimed that they had left their southern homes because they were opposed to slavery for moral or economic reasons. The records indicate that a greater number of Oregonians were anti-Negro than anti-slavery. The 1844 sessions of the legislature had prohibited slavery, excluded free Negroes and mulattoes, and provided for the removal of those already in the colony. The 1845 Compact simply prohibited slavery; but some slaves were held and some free Negroes remained in the community. (In 1846 Neilson estimated thirty; the 1850 census reported 207 "free colored," a cate-

[1] Priscilla Knuth, "Nativism in Oregon," Reed College *Bulletin*, Armitage Essays, January 1946, 24.

gory which no doubt included some Hawaiians.) The Oregonians' negative attitudes toward slavery, however, led pro-slavery forces in the United States Senate to defeat an Oregon territorial bill in 1847, and when a bill did squeak through Congress the next year, it was without direct reference to this issue.

Yet, in spite of an apparent commitment against slavery—and Negroes—the Oregonians would support slavery in principle if outside elements tried to dictate to them on this matter. Asahel Bush, editor of the *Statesman*, pointed out in 1857 that if some abolitionist society were to attempt to "abolitionize" Oregon, it would become a slave state. "Such is the temper of the Oregonians; they want no outside interference."

The Democracy, as old-time Jacksonians called their party, split wide open on the slavery issue. Supporters of Stephen A. Douglas' principle of popular sovereignty by which a territory could determine for itself whether its constitution would be slave or free formed a National Democratic Party. Northern Democrats who would take no stand that would rend the nation apart in civil war joined a Union Party. Southerners who held that Congress could not constitutionally interfere with slavery and was obligated to protect property in slaves made up a third group which claimed to be the true Democratic Party.

Oregon Democrats were in a deep dilemma. Many citizens in theory were sympathetic with the South, but they found Douglas' position appealing. The clique demanded "party regularity" above all. Since chances were few that Oregon would ever attract slaveowners, the state would be "free"; therefore, the Oregon Democrats should take their stand with the South, slavery, and states' rights.

It was difficult for Oregonians, as it was for citizens in the whole country, to find a party refuge in those troubled days. Many Democrats realized that they were no longer at home in the party of Jefferson and Jackson. Whigs had nowhere to go. "The Whigs are all dead out there—they call themselves the *Republican* party—which means negro worshippers," wrote old-line Whig David Logan. "I can't go the Locofocos and I'll see the Republicans to the Devil before I'll vote with them. I don't know what I am exactly, but any thing but an abolitionist."

Civil war in Kansas, the position of the incoming Buchanan administration with respect to slavery in the territories, the Dred Scott decision which in effect refuted the principle of popular sovereignty and supported the position of the southern diehards, forced Oregonians to a decision irrespective of party or factional affiliations. "If we are to have the institution of slavery fastened upon us here, we desire the people resident in Oregon to do it, and not the will and power of a few politicians in Washington City," wrote editor Thomas Dryer of the *Oregonian*, a former opponent of statehood, and a Whig in the process of becoming a Republican.[2]

THE OREGON CONSTITUTION

Under threat of limits to their rights of self-determination, Oregonians went to the polls in June, 1857, and by a vote of 5938 to 1679 favored a constitutional convention and sovereign statehood. Ignoring the fact that Congress had not passed the enabling act to authorize this step, they were asserting their independence.

The citizens sitting in the convention in August wisely avoided argument on slavery. They wrote a constitution without reference to the matter and, submitting it to the voters for ratification, added a schedule of three questions: "Do you vote for the constitution?" "Do you vote for slavery in Oregon?" "Do you vote for free Negroes in Oregon?" The results were an interesting revelation of Oregon opinion: the constitution was approved 7195 to 3125; slavery rejected, 7727 to 2645; and free Negroes excluded, 8640 to 1081.

In essence, what the Oregonians had done was to act upon the principle of self-determination, or popular sovereignty, Douglas' solution for the problem of slavery in the territories. However, consistent with their traditional party affiliation, in June, 1858, the voters proceeded to elect as their governor, John Whiteaker, and senators Delazon Smith and Joseph Lane, pro-slavery states' rights Democrats. If this election was an assertion of Oregon's convictions, it also was an indication of the diminishing strength of the Salem clique. A narrow margin of 943 for its candidates showed it was losing ground. The vote in the presidential election of 1860 was even more revealing of the breakdown of party regularity: Candidates John C. Breckinridge, running with the clique's strong man, Joseph Lane as vice-president, polled 5074 votes, Stephen A. Douglas, 4131. With the Democrats thus split, Lincoln and the new Republican Party, firmly committed to exclude slavery in territories, and with a platform of projects such as government supported railroads and a homestead bill, won Oregon with 5344 votes.

[2] Robert W. Johannsen, *Frontier Politics and the Sectional Conflict: the Pacific Northwest on the Eve of the Civil War* (1955).

In adopting a constitution and electing state officers, Oregonians assumed that statehood was an accomplished fact. Congress was not to be rushed in this manner, however. Oregon must remain a territory until properly admitted into the Union. The prospect it soon would be was indeed dark in 1858. Republicans and anti-slavery forces were against admitting a state which had consistently been Democratic, even though at the same time it was aligned among the "free" states. Republicans therefore united with pro-slavery Democrats, who did not want another non-slave state. It took a fragile coalition of moderate Democrats and fifteen Republicans to pass the Oregon Admission Act, which was signed by President Buchanan, February 14, 1859.

Oregon's future political temper was faintly foreshadowed in its constitutional convention debates. It was a state pulled between conservative and innovative political attitudes. An appeal was made that "here upon the Pacific Coast . . . we ought to go by the reason of things, and not go so much by precedent." But the prevailing opinion was voiced by a delegate who held that "if he was sent here to form a new Bible he would copy the old one . . . to make a hymn book, he would report an old one—they are better than any he could make."

Except for one minor article on the judiciary, there was nothing in this constitution not to be found among American state constitutions of the time: those of Indiana, Iowa, and Michigan were the principal models.[3] If the convention distinguished itself in any major respect it was in a penurious thriftiness which burdened a few ill-paid officials with multiple duties. In its economy-mindedness, in its provisions limiting state and county indebtedness, and regulating banks and corporations, the constitution expressed the sentiments of a farming people who remembered the panic of 1837 and the ensuing depression, and who had no understanding of, or desire to share in, the emerging industrial economy of the day. Judge Matthew P. Deady spoke for the convention and Oregonians generally when he said:

> We have an agricultural community, and the domestic virtues incident to an agricultural people; and there is where you look for the true and solid wealth and happiness of a people. . . . In the manufacturing countries power, political and otherwise, is in the hands of capitalists; there are many people dependent on them, and dependence begets servility. . . . I am not in favor of such a state of things here.

The constitution of 1857 served Oregon without amendment until 1902.

[3] Helen Leonard Seagraves, "The Oregon Constitutional Convention of 1857," Reed College *Bulletin*, Armitage Essays, June 1952.

NORTHWEST POLITICS

Politics in the new state were influenced by the Civil War and by the rapid rise of the Republican Party. Loyalty to the Union drew War Democrats, Republicans, and old Whigs into a loose coalition, the Union Party, in 1864. The state Democratic convention of that year condemned the rebellion but asserted the principles of the 1798 Kentucky-Virginia Resolutions, that states had the right to nullify federal legislation. The Democrats were defeated in the state elections. The next year a special session of the legislature ratified the Thirteenth Amendment and in 1866 a large majority of the regular session ratified the Fourteenth Amendment, both measures of Radical Republican reconstruction.

Although the power of the Salem clique had been broken, the Democratic Party revived by 1868, recaptured the senate and adopted a resolution to rescind Oregon's assent to the Fourteenth Amendment. This futile gesture indicated that the Democracy had not succumbed to the Republicans and their Portland machine. Between 1862 and 1885, Oregonians elected three Democratic governors, six senators, and seven representatives; three Republican governors, three senators, and six representatives.

As a territory, Washington could participate only vicariously in national elections through the election of its delegate. Isaac Stevens, delegate since 1857, was chairman of the Democratic national committee for Breckinridge and Lane but after Lincoln's nomination he worked diligently to prevent secession.[4] On the local scene, Stevens lost control of his party to the faction supporting Douglas and a vague kind of Unionism.

Republican strength grew remarkably, and with the Democratic split elected William H. Wallace delegate. The Democrats recovered in 1863, to elect George E. Cole. But thereafter, with two exceptions in each case, the voters continued to elect Republican delegates and the presidents appointed Republican governors. Though the appointees did not as a rule add prestige to the territorial system, party patronage built a following strong enough to keep the Territory in the Republican camp. After eastern Washington had a voting population, politics became almost as strong a divisive factor as the Cascade Mountains and agitation for the creation of a new territory was an immediate consequence.

[4] Robert W. Johannsen, "National Issues and Local Politics in Washington Territory, 1857–1861," *PNQ*, January 1951, 22.

THE NORTHWEST GOLD RUSHES

In 1860, while Oregon was getting the feel of "flying with her own wings" as her state motto asserted, the Pacific Northwest had become a mining frontier. As surface mining declined in California, miners moved from northern California to the Rogue River country where, by 1851, a modest gold rush was under way. Jacksonville became the capital of the mining district, Scottsburg its transportation center, and Marshfield a port of entry. In the next several years, as prospectors pushed across the Cascades, strikes were reported on the Santiam and John Day rivers, and in 1854–1855 substantial discoveries were made on the upper Columbia in the vicinity of Colville. These brought hundreds of miners into the region, whence they spread into Canada, where rich discoveries were made on the Fraser River.

By 1858 the Fraser rush was reminiscent of early days on the Sacramento. Thousands of Californians came by boat directly to Victoria; a lesser number arrived in Portland and Seattle and thence proceeded overland to avoid as much as possible the dangers of Fraser River trails. At the peak of the rush all normal activities ceased temporarily; soldiers deserted their posts, sailors their ships, and farmers their plows, to try their luck on the golden river. Miners had to be fed, and every settlement on the waters of Puget Sound suddenly entertained notions of becoming the great supply center for the northern mines. Fleets of sailboats and sternwheelers carried passengers and goods to Victoria, and herds of cattle and strings of pack horses moved north through the Cowlitz, Yakima, Wenatchee, and Okanogan valleys to supply the mushrooming camps. Rich strikes in the Caribou district brought a repeat performance in 1862. Even after the boom days were over, farmers and ranchers still found a profitable Canadian market. In 1866, the United States customs office at Little Dalles reported $507,479 worth of goods exported over the line. Of this sum nearly $350,000 was in livestock, beef cattle, sheep, and pack animals.

When Oregon was admitted to statehood, Washington Territory was enlarged to include all the remaining part of the old Oregon Territory, a portion of Wyoming, all of present Idaho, and that part of Montana not included in Nebraska Territory. Except for its fur trade and missionary activities, its well-traveled section of the Oregon Trail along the Snake, and its Indian problems, this part of the Territory east of Cascades had shared little in the events which had affected western Oregon and Washington.

Eastern Washington was the land of Nez Perces and Blackfeet, as contrasting in temperaments as the land itself, sharply divided between the barren and forested, the clear and open plain and the walled-in, rugged valley. Secular settlement was begun in the 1840s when several old mountain men settled near Lapwai Mission; Mormons from Utah tried to colonize Lemhi Valley in 1854. Old Fort Walla Walla was abandoned in 1855, but a scattering of settlers remained. Indian wars and closure by military order discouraged movement into the country except that of a few miners in the Pend Oreille country in 1858. The next year, Lieutenant John Mullan began construction of a military road from Walla Walla across the northern part of Idaho to Fort Benton on the Missouri. When rich gold deposits were found on the Clearwater in 1860, the interior was practically in a state of nature. It lost its innocence within a year.

One of the principal gold regions of eastern Washington (now western Montana) was in the Jefferson Basin and Gallatin Valley, organized as Missoula County in 1860.[5] Jefferson Basin, resort of early fur trappers, was known as the Bannack district where the names of such creeks as Grasshopper, Stinking Water, and Alder Gulch became synonymous with rich placer and quartz diggings. In 1863, the 17-mile length of Alder Gulch's gravel bars was reported to have 10,000 miners and on its steep banks were four "cities" famous in mining history: Virginia, Nevada, Central, and Summit. Gallatin Valley showed its gold-bearing quartz veins in Last Chance Gulch, and Helena became a permanent settlement to serve other equally famous camps.

The principal mining area of what is now Idaho lay between the Coeur d'Alene and Salmon rivers in Nez Perce country. E. D. Pierce found color on the Clearwater and within a year, the Salmon River district, as it was sometimes called, had thousands of men working at Pierce, Elkhorn, and Oro Fino placers. "Fabulous Florence" had a brief, brilliant, and remarkable rich moment of greatness beginning in 1863. In 1862, the Boise Basin was reported to have richer deposits than the gravel bars and ravines of the Salmon district; at the same time miners found new reason for excitement on Oregon's John Day and Powder rivers.

Walla Walla was the hub for important trails to Washington Territory's mining camps: the Mullan Road, completed in 1860, was hardly

---

[5] William J. Trimble, *The Mining Advance into the Inland Empire* (1914); Merrill D. Beal and Merle W. Wells, *History of Idaho*, 2 vols. (1959); Merle W. Wells, *Rush to Idaho*, Bulletin No. 19 (1963), and *Gold Camps & Silver Cities*, Bulletin No. 22, Idaho Bureau of Mines and Geology (1963); D. E. Livingston-Little, *An Economic History of North Idaho, 1800–1900* (1965).

more than a pack trail, but thousands of miners traveled it to Missoula, the Bitterroot and Blackfoot rivers, and to Helena and its famous gulches; trails up the Clearwater led to the camps of the northern part of the Salmon River district; and the old emigrant trail was traveled in reverse to Boise Basin, Centerville, Placerville, and Bannock City (Idaho City).

Columbia River boats from Portland to Wallula or Lewiston are reported to have carried 15,000 men in 1861, 24,500 in 1862, and 22,-000 in 1863. Since these were figures for only one route and it is known that miners moved by other routes as well, it is not unreasonable to assume that the mining population of eastern Washington Territory at the height of the gold rush was somewhere around 75,000. However, nothing was more fluid than a gold-rush population, which could melt away like spring snows. One day a gravel bar might have 10,000 miners working it, and tent and dugout "cities" scattered around it. In a month or two only a few Chinese might remain, patiently working over the same rock that had been skimmed by their impatient predecessors.

The Mining Camp

A voluminous literature describes the life of western mining camps. The romantic stories of Bret Harte, the humorous sketches of Samuel Clemens and J. Ross Browne contain no more distortions than sensational penny dreadfuls. Letters and diaries reveal sensitive, hardworking, law-abiding young men trying to make their stake in a hard way. Bawdy houses and whiskey palaces were part of the raw frontier, as were highwaymen and professional bad men, claim jumpers and vigilante committees, hangings and shootings. While law was not absent, it was directed toward objectives different from those of a stable society.

In the gold camps of the Northwest, as elsewhere, the miners themselves organized their first governments. These were district associations whose purpose was to define the extent of claims and the minimum requirements for holding and protecting them. The miners elected claim recorders and judges whose qualifications usually were some knowledge of mining and mining law, and whose jurisdiction was limited to these matters.

The Washington territorial legislature organized new counties in the mining districts. Spokane County (1860) included all of eastern Washington from the Columbia to the Continental Divide and south to the Clearwater. Missoula, Shoshone, and Walla Walla counties were hewed out of this vast region by 1863. Voting precincts were vaguely defined. Sometimes miners voted, but they were underrepresented in the territorial legislature, and the county officials they elected found it difficult to administer laws that applied more appropriately elsewhere in the Territory. Administration of civil and criminal codes depended upon the demands of constituencies as well as upon the efficiency and integrity of elected officers. The miners got as much law as they wanted, even though in the early days judicial proceedings were obstructed by lawyers and judges unfamiliar with territorial statutes and unable to get copies of them. Common law and equity were not easily applied by an untrained and uninformed judiciary. "I had a copy of Blackstone and two six-shooters. My administration was very successful," Joaquin Miller said of his judgeship at Oregon's Canyon City.

If in their mores the mining districts offered a sharp contrast to the agricultural communities of the western part of the Territory, the miners' political views were even more dissimilar. During the war years, western Washington was Unionist, strongly tending toward Republicanism. The mining camps had their Unionists, but they also had their southern sympathizers and Democrats were in the majority. Many miners from both sides in the Civil War had come to the mines to escape military conscription, but they gallantly defended their homelands and causes with toasts, torchlight parades, and fist fights on Saturday nights.

For western Washington Republicans, it was a matter of concern that eastern Washington's Shoshone, Missoula, and Walla Walla counties, outnumbering the western counties in population three to one, were strongly Democratic. Hence it is not surprising that the movement for the division of Washington Territory originated with Olympia Republicans.

CREATION OF IDAHO TERRITORY

Assuming that separation was desirable, there was still the puzzling question of how to divide huge sprawling Washington Territory. To draw a line at the Cascades would reduce it to a small province in which Olympia and Vancouver could fight unendingly for the capital. If on the other hand, division was made at a line extended from the northward course of the Snake, then Lewiston, with chances of becoming the capital of the proposed territory, was willing to cooperate with Olympia for separation. However, Walla Walla, flourishing as the center of the vast inland empire, was dead-set against division; it was, it claimed, the natural site for the capital of Washington Territory undivided.

The mining region itself was, on the whole, opposed to separation. While western Montana was supplied from Fort Benton on the Missouri or by freight trains from Salt Lake, Idaho was wholly dependent upon Oregon. It was feared, not unreasonably, that as a territory Idaho's economy would remain tributary to Portland and its political life be dominated by Oregon's Republicans. Remaining a part of Washington Territory, but given proper representation in its legislature, the mining area might better its condition. But the principle of self-determination so recently championed in Oregon and western Washington was not to be allowed in the case of Idaho.

A bill to create Idaho Territory was presented to Congress. Modified to please western Washington, supported by Olympia's Delegate William H. Wallace and Oregon Congressman John R. McBride, (both rewarded with offices in the new territory), the Idaho bill was passed by Congress and President Lincoln signed it March 4, 1863, in the darkest days of the Civil War. Civil War politics helped Idaho to become a territory.

> In Congress the Radical Republicans and Lincoln both were receptive to schemes for the admission of new states and the creation of new territories. Additional western states might serve to offset the return of Southern Democrats to Congress in case the North should win the war. The Republicans were aware that without additional Western support, they would be able to retain control of the federal government only with great difficulty. . . . Thus the distraction of the Civil War actually encouraged, rather than disrupted, the Olympia Radical Republican movement for purging the politically hostile Idaho miners from Washington territory.[6]

The Territory of Idaho—"a geographical monstrosity"—included areas which later became the states of Wyoming, Montana, and Idaho, and was the last oversized territory created in the north.

The Organic Code recognized the Nez Perce 1855 treaty reservation, which meant that Lewiston—which wanted to be the capital—and Florence and other Clearwater mining towns located on the reservation were excluded from the Territory until the treaty was revised. A new treaty was negotiated in June, 1863, but a number of bands having little confidence in government promises to exclude whites from their reservation refused to sign. These nontreaty Indians lived

[6] Merle W. Wells, "The Creation of the Territory of Idaho," *PNQ*, April 1949, 117.

precariously but peacefully among the whites until 1877. On the other hand, under Chief Lawyer the treaty bands moved to a much reduced reservation and with remarkable patience waited four long years for the Senate to ratify and the government to perform its obligations. Not until 1867 did Lewiston become legally a part of the Territory of which it had been the controversial capital since 1864.

Idaho's Organic Law differed in only two major provisions from that of Washington Territory. Slavery was prohibited, and the governor was given veto power which could be overruled by a two-thirds vote of the Council and Assembly. Since the legislature was sometimes irresponsible and rarely of the same political party as the governor, territorial politics were lively to say the least, and Idaho's experiences illustrate the worst features of the system.

Although the population was predominantly Democratic—Copperhead, according to Radical Republicans—federal patronage was used with little restraint to build up the Republican Party and to reward with office the hungry faithful in Oregon and western Washington. Senator John H. Mitchell from Oregon "endorsed candidates on a baldly political basis, intervened in departmental channels, and, together with certain colleagues from the Pacific Coast, exercised a sort of guardianship" over both Washington and Idaho territories. Idaho was a "political dependency of Oregon," a contemporary testified, and to reward political and personal services, men unacceptable in Oregon were billeted upon the Territory.[7]

Officials were commonly absent, voluntarily or otherwise, and there were more acting governors than commissioned ones. The struggle between President Johnson and a hostile Congress affected the careers of the President's appointees, two of whom were charged with malfeasance, suspended, and later restored. The integrity of honest and competent men was impugned, making it a risk of political fortune to accept office in the Territory.

However, few of Idaho's officers were model public servants.[8] The first governor, William H. Wallace, formerly Washington Territory's delegate, had worked hard to create the territory he expected to use as a stepping stone to higher preferment. Three months after he declared the Territory organized, and with no apparent regard for the difficulties of setting up and administering so large a territory and so heterogeneous a population, he ran for delegate, was elected, and left his duties to an inept and greedy secretary of the Territory.

[7] Earl Pomeroy, *Territories and the United States: 1861–1890* (1947), 67.

[8] Merle W. Wells, "Clinton DeWitt Smith, Secretary, Idaho Territory, 1864–1865," *OHQ*, March 1951; W. Turrentine Jackson, "Indian Affairs and Politics in Idaho Territory, 1863–1870," *PHR*, September 1945.

270

Caleb Lyon, Wallace's successor, had a first term disturbed by a violent struggle for the capital between Republican Lewiston and Democratic Boise. The victory of Democrats did not make life easy for Republican appointees, not even when Lyon upheld President Johnson against the Radicals. The governor's career came to an abrupt conclusion in the spring of 1866. The Secretary of State quietly absconded to Hong Kong with $41,000 of territorial funds; Lyon left soon afterward with $46,000 of Indian funds. Two years of territorial history in which Idaho "was looked upon only as a theater of speculation and as a place for temporary residence where . . . rapid fortunes might be acquired" gave David W. Ballard of Oregon reason for "perplexing doubts and misgivings" when he was appointed governor. In his four years (1866–1870), Ballard was once suspended from office and was engaged in such bitter feuds that he deserved laurels, at least for persistence. His was a party administration—Radical Republican—but the legislatures with which he had to work were Democratic; the third session had only one Unionist in it. Ballard's first message contained a politely couched but unpopular recommendation that its members cease raiding the treasury to supplement their *per diem.* "By the God," exploded one legislator, "I do not believe the house will submit to it, for the governor to say we shall act thus and so. . . . We didn't elect him governor. He is no part or parcel with us."

Ballard was also handicapped by continuous interference from Republican factions in Oregon, each of which sought to control appointments in Idaho. By the end of his term Ballard had worn away much of the territorials' antagonism toward him, and, though defeated when he ran for delegate in 1870, he was endorsed by Idaho papers for having conducted his office with dignity under extreme provocation. His successors' problems were not so much involved in national politics, but President Grant found it difficult to locate a man to take the governorship. No fewer than five were offered the commission before he found Thomas W. Bennett, who served from 1871 to 1875. David P. Thompson of Portland held office one year, 1875–1876, and Mason Brayman for the following four years. Between 1880 and 1885, four appointments were made and three of the appointees served fragmentary terms.

Obviously Idaho had small success in attracting and holding dedicated public officials. Local problems and politics did not encourage hope for a smooth political career. The earliest legislatures were headstrong and irresponsible and "not much experts at making laws." The first code, adopted "in much haste and with much less consideration than its importance demanded," according to Ballard, was not printed until after the second legislature had met because the territorial funds had been stolen. But ignorance of the code did not deter the second legislature from passing new laws, creating some "perplexing discrepancies."

Legislators and executives were seriously handicapped both by their failure to receive moneys appropriated by Congress for territorial purposes, and by their failure to safeguard those they did get. As of December 1, 1866, the Territory had outstanding warrants for $87,957 and no funds. Local tax money was hard to raise from the 3480 taxpayers. Yet with heady pride the legislature appropriated $100,000 to pay for a capitol building.

Test oaths were a continuing problem in Idaho politics. In 1862 Congress passed a measure requiring persons elected or appointed to public offices in areas under federal administration to swear that they had not countenanced or encouraged the Southern cause. The legislature passed a bill excusing local officers and administrators from the requirement though this meant the withholding of federal appropriations for the Territory. When Ballard vetoed the bill on the ground that territorial legislation could not be in contradiction to congressional legislation, the measure was triumphantly passed over his veto. In later years, Idaho Republicans revived test oaths to purge the voting lists of Mormon Democrats.

Added to these troubles was the enduring controversy over location of the capital and division of the Territory. In 1864 the easternmost part of Idaho was withdrawn to form part of Montana Territory and with it went a large part of Idaho's population. Four years later the organization of Wyoming Territory left Idaho with its present southern boundary. Divided into two parts by its mountainous topography, the territory was still a geographic monstrosity. The greater part of the population was in the south, where Boise clamored for the capital. When her friends captured the state seal and archives, Lewiston countered with a movement to unite the northern part of the territory with Washington.

During tempestuous political controversies, fundamental problems of law and order were neglected. Little was done to organize defenses against serious Indian attacks in the southern part of the Territory. During Lyon's and Ballard's administrations, highway robberies, murders, and lynchings perpetrated by white men were widespread. Failure to convict the few lawbreakers brought to trial led to the organization of vigilante committees who took the law in their own hands.

Nevertheless, by the end of the 1860s Idaho Territory began to settle down to a more placid existence. The census of 1870 reported

15,000 white residents, hardly more than the number of men in Alder Gulch seven years before. The placer mines had given over to quartz mining and the human flotsam of the first era had drifted off to Colorado or Nevada. Ranches stocked the small but fertile valleys, and settlers were beginning to raise more wheat than their local market could use.

THE LAST OF THE INDIAN WARS

During most of the sixties, miners, packers, stockmen, and immigrants in central Oregon and southern Idaho were harassed by the Snakes (a name applied generally to Sahaptins, Paiutes, and other bands of natives in the southern part of the interior). The Snakes began to raid the herds of peaceful natives on the Warm Springs Reservation in 1859, but their guerrilla war with army, volunteers, and citizens dates from July, 1860, when they attacked Captain A. J. Smith's exploring expedition just east of Harney Valley. This provoked a short but intense campaign in charge of Colonel Enoch Steen. Typically, however, in this war Steen and his men caught or killed very few of the enemy. Just after the men returned to barracks at Fort Dalles in September, a group of Snakes killed immigrants on the Oregon Trail near the Oregon border. The outbreak of the Civil War delayed army action against the natives until the spring of 1864 when Brigadier General Benjamin Alvord laid out a campaign for the Oregon militia. But for various reasons the Snakes were not defeated until after General George Crook and the regular army took over late in 1866. Through the next year and a half, using Indian auxiliaries, a winter campaign, night marches, and more or less continuous harassment, Crook found, surprised, caught, and defeated enough of the small number of Snakes to bring the war to an end by 1868.

In 1870 the Bureau of the Census tried to arrive at the "true" Indian population by enumerating those living on reservations, those who were nomadic, and those living in severalty (that is, "out of tribal relations," on land granted for individual use). The total for Oregon and the territories was 31,705, of whom 22,871 were on reservations, and some 6500 nomadic. However, reservations east of the Cascades, set aside by the 1855 treaties, had been so large and the white population so small that the Indians, whether in treaty or nontreaty bands, continued to live much as they had for the past fifty years. As the number of settlers increased, so did the pressures upon the Indians. Making no distinction between treaty and nontreaty Indians, the settlers took the land for their own, using force if fraud did not succeed; they resented Indian occupation of so much country that they now found valuable, and demanded that the government reduce the reserves and remove the Indians from settled areas. The Indians, with no other recourse, since the government had failed to protect them, turned to the teachings of their prophets or the leadership of rebellious young warriors.

As in 1855, the interior Indians were still deeply attached to their lands, and in the seventies this attachment was sanctified among most eastern bands by the revival of the Prophet cult, a native religion which stressed the theme that the earth must not be cultivated. Smoholla, the most influential of the prophets, was reported to have said that "those who cut up the land or sign papers for land will be defrauded of their rights and will be punished by God's anger." Thus when policy dictated the removal of all Indians to reservations, the issue was not simply one of clearing the land for white settlers, but of violating the Indians' religious feeling.

The government proposed early in the 1870s "that the Indians should be made as comfortable on and as uncomfortable off their reservations as it was in the power of the Government to make them; that such of them as went right should be protected and fed and such as went wrong should be harassed and scourged without intermission." The government no longer requested Indians to move voluntarily to the reservations; it ordered them to go, and used military force if they refused.

Although the condition of Indians off the reservation was made "as uncomfortable as possible," the government failed to provide for them when they were on the reserves. Despite attempts at reform during Grant's administration, incompetence, corruption, and the unwillingness of Congress to appropriate adequate funds made chaos out of Indian administration. Bands willing to settle down to farm on the reserves had no implements, stock, or even adequate food until their farms produced. Agents at Fort Hall agency repeatedly ordered the Bannacks to the hunting grounds in order to avoid starvation, thus negating the more humane intentions as well as the political expediencies of the reservation system.

The causes of conflict—specific grievances, distrust, fear that engendered desperation—were generally present. The several Indian wars of the 1870s had much in common. The first was the Modoc War of 1873. Settlers' demands for removal of the Indians around Klamath Lake had led to the establishment of Klamath Reservation in 1864. Some of the Modocs led by rebellious young Keintpoos, "Captain Jack," left the reserve, repudiating their treaty, and went to Lost River, which they asked be given to them as a second reservation. After characteristic indecision and delay the government denied the request and gave newly appointed Superintendent T. B. Odeneal orders to remove them "peaceably if you can, forcibly if you must." The attempt of a completely inadequate detachment of soldiers to carry out the order led to war. It took six months for raw troops, often under incompetent officers, to reduce the Indians.

The Modoc war is most notorious for the murder of General Edward R. S. Canby and peace commissioner Dr. Eleasar Thomas in northern California on April 12, 1873.[9] Two weeks later a 64-man patrol under Captains Evan Thomas and Thomas F. Wright was ambushed on Hardin Butte and twenty-five of the patrol were killed before the Indians withdrew. A second ambush, May 10, led to a reversal of fortune. Defeated, the Modocs split into several groups, each trying to escape on its own. Relentlessly pursued, even in the rugged lava beds around Mt. Lassen, the Indians were captured or surrendered individually or in small groups. Resistance collapsed after the capture of Captain Jack on June 1. Those who had participated in the murder of General Canby and Commissioner Thomas were tried; four, including Captain Jack, were hanged.

The seeds of the Nez Perce war of 1877 were germinating at the same time and in the same causes that produced the Modoc war. As with the Modocs, the Nez Perce tribe was divided into bands—those who supported the treaties of 1855 and 1863 and those who renounced them. When in 1861 miners and settlers moved into Nez Perce Reservation and laid out the town of Lewiston within its boundaries, the government negotiated a new treaty (1863) with some of the chiefs. The government claimed that the headmen who relinquished three-fourths of the 1855 reserve signed for the entire tribe. Old Chief Joseph and other nonsignatory chiefs hotly denied the government's position and Joseph and his people continued to live in the Wallowa Valley of northeastern Oregon.

In the summer of 1876 Assistant Adjutant General H. Clay Wood, in a special report on the Nez Perce, concluded that "the Nez-Perces, undoubtedly, were at liberty to renounce the treaty of 1855 . . . the Government having violated the treaty obligations," and that "the non-treaty Nez Perce cannot in law be regarded as bound by the treaty of 1863; and in so far as it attempts to deprive them of a right of occupancy of any land its provisions are null and void." Nevertheless, the government acceded to the demands of Oregon's governor, and upon the recommendation of a special commission including Gen-

<hr>

[9] Keith A. Murray, *The Modocs and Their War* (1959).

eral Oliver O. Howard and Nez Perce Agent John B. Monteith, ordered the Wallowa Nez Perces, now led by young Chief Joseph, to remove to the Lapwai Agency.

The Indians were to be on the reserve by the middle of June. This meant rounding up their huge herds of half-wild cattle and horses and moving them and all their other possessions across the flooded Snake and Salmon rivers within a month. It is evident from recent studies that the Indians intended in good faith to obey the government orders.[10] However, in revenge for some personal grievances a group of young warriors made a quick foray at Cottonwood. Neither the settlers nor General Howard had expected the Indians to leave without resistance; when news arrived of the depredations Howard considered them the first sign of a major outbreak. He took prompt action and probably transformed a minor outbreak into a full-scale war.

The Nez Perces' flight from White Bird Canyon over Lolo Pass to their final defeat in the Bear Paw Mountains has been well chronicled. The popular view has held that Chief Joseph masterminded the long retreat, a march of desperation for the Indians and a humiliation to the army and frightened settlers. Francis Haines suggests that the Indians were divided in their councils and that Joseph had little to do with either retreat or military operations. As they considered the war to be a personal dispute between Howard and themselves, the Indians' first intention was simply to escape from Howard's jurisdiction and join their friends, the Crows. Escape to Canada was decided upon only at a much later date. Whatever the interpretation, the consequences were indisputable. The Nez Perce war cost about $930,000 and the lives of 127 soldiers, mostly regulars, and 50 civilians. Of their 191 fighting men and 450 women and children, the Indians suffered 151 killed and 80 wounded.

A leader of the Bannack scouts, Buffalo Horn, whom General Howard employed during the Nez Perce war, led a large band of Bannacks in a major outbreak in the summer of 1878. In this case, the ineptness and inefficiency of the Indian Bureau was a major cause of trouble. From the time they signed the Fort Bridger Treaty (1868), many of the Bannacks had expected to settle peaceably on the reservation. However, wholly inadequate supplies for their annuities of food, clothing, and implements had to be shared with Shoshones who were moved to the reservation. Repeatedly, the Fort Hall agents sent the bands under their jurisdiction back to the hunting grounds because they could not provide for them.

[10] Francis Haines, *The Nez Perce* (1955); Merrill D. Beal, *I Will Fight No More Forever: Chief Joseph and the Nez Perce War* (1963).

After a buildup of tension and unrest in 1877 and the spring of 1878, a large party of Bannacks raided Big Camp Prairie. About 150 troops led by Buffalo Horn and Egan moved toward the Malheur Reservation to meet dissident Paiutes under Oits. They then moved north to the Columbia in the hope of enlisting other dissidents. Defeated at almost every turn by regular and volunteer forces, the Bannack band was broken up and scattered by the end of July, 1878.

An arduous campaign was then waged against a renegade band of Sheepeater Indians in what is now Valley County, Idaho. After two months spent chasing the elusive Indians, the officer in command of one detachment of soldiers could only report: "The country is so rough that animals cannot be got through it at all—Most of our horses and mules have given out and have been shot."[11] The Sheepeaters were captured in September in a last-ditch campaign led by Lieutenant Edward S. Farrow. This ended active resistance on the part of the interior bands.

Even after their final subjugation in war, individuals and bands left their reserves to wander aimlessly among the frontier communities. Settlers continually clamored for further reductions of the reservations while they expropriated Indian homestead farms outside them. In the 1880s the Indians were gradually forced to accept the reservations as the limits of their freedom; conflict ceased, and the aboriginal possessors of the land were left with little hope of finding a place in the new owners' society.

The Indian troubles were in part responsible for eastern Washington's and Idaho's slow growth in population. Yet western Washington, which escaped the wars, also stagnated. In the decade, 1870–1880, when Idaho added about 17,000 people, Washington increased by 51,000 and Oregon by 83,000. Both territories complained that because they lacked transportation facilities, settlement was discouraged and their economies retarded. For this they blamed selfish machinations of Oregonians who lived in Portland, the Pacific Northwest's one metropolis.

[11] Quoted in Ray H. Glassley, *Pacific Northwest Indian Wars* (1953), 246.

CHAPTER
EIGHTEEN

Portland: The Web of Commerce and Culture

MIGRATION TO the Northwest had diminished in the late 1850s, and despite the mining rushes there was a relatively slow increase in permanent settlers in the 1860s. The Civil War directed migration from farm lands to cities where industry competed with agriculture as one attraction for a mobile people. While the Homestead Act and war demands for farm produce encouraged agricultural expansion into the Midwest, beyond Kansas migration dwindled to a small trickle.

During the postwar decade Idaho and Washington experienced a greater rate of growth than did Oregon, but in actual numbers, more immigrants located in Oregon than in the territories. Between 1870 and 1880 Oregon's population increased from 90,922 to 174,768; Washington's from 23,955 to 75,116, and Idaho's from 14,999 to 32,610.

Portland was a village in a clearing with 821 residents in 1860. In 1870, its population approached 10,000. Washington's largest towns were seats of counties that could boast no more than 2488 in Thurston County, 1709 in King, and 6801 in Walla Walla. Ten years later Multnomah County, including Portland, had one-third as many inhabitants as all of Washington, only 7000 fewer than Idaho, and Washington Territory still had no town of more than 4000 population.

Compared with San Francisco, Portland was a mere village. The Bay City was the terminus of the first transcontinental railroad, completed in 1869, and was in size, transportation facilities, capital, resources, and enterprise, the commercial capital of the Pacific Slope. Portland was tributary to San Francisco in commerce, finance, and transportation; but, in turn, the Pacific Northwest was tributary to Portland for the same reasons.

Portland has been appropriately described as the "city that gravity built."[1] Down the Willamette flowed the produce of the Valley; down the Columbia came the immigrants and the riches of Idaho mines and the interior's wheat fields. California ships brought goods to Portland for distribution to the Valley and for transshipment on sternwheelers up the Columbia.

THE OREGON STEAM NAVIGATION COMPANY

By 1860 competition on the Columbia forced small rival boat companies to merge. The Oregon Steam Navigation Company (OSN) was organized just in time to profit from the gold rush to Idaho. Within a year, it carried an average of $400,000 a month in gold to Portland; transported 10,500 passengers and 6290 tons of freight. In 1862, despite a winter in which even some waters of the Columbia froze over, the company moved 24,500 passengers and 14,500 tons of freight.

From all sources, passengers, freights, mail contracts, and treasure shipments, the company profited handsomely. In the twenty years of its history (1860–1880) it paid a conservatively estimated $4,600,-000 in dividends. The small steamers, sailboats, and barges which had formed its first working capital were quickly replaced by powerful and elegant sternwheelers. By 1880, the company owned twenty-six vessels and had invested more than $3,000,000 in its facilities. It also had a monopoly on traffic on the Columbia.

The key to its success was its control of the portages at the Cascades and at The Dalles, now a bustling village at an old Indian site. In 1862 the company built a six-mile railroad at the Cascades on the Washington shore and a fourteen-mile road running from The Dalles to beyond Celilo Falls. Thereafter, despite efforts to dislodge it, the company had the river's traffic securely in hand. On the Willamette River, the company capitulated to the People's Transportation Com-

[1] Glenn C. Quiett, *They Built the West* (1934), 339; Randall V. Mills, *Sternwheelers up Columbia* (1947).

pany in 1862–1863, surrendering an unprofitable run to its rivals on condition they stay off the Columbia.

The men chiefly responsible for the OSN were Captain John C. Ainsworth and Simeon G. Reed of Portland, and Robert R. Thompson, originally of The Dalles. This triumvirate, sole owners of the company's stock after 1867, built the concern into a $5,000,000 enterprise by plowing profits back into improvements and reaching out for a continuously expanding area of traffic. They drew the interior trade to Portland by combining land and water routes where necessary. At Wallula, pack and wagon trains took their cargoes over the Walla Walla-Spokane-Colville trail to the little Dalles of the Columbia. There the *Forty-Nine*, under Captain Leonard White, the ostensible owner, ran to the head of Upper Arrow Lake and tapped the trade of Caribou and Kootenai mines. To compete with the St. Louis-Fort Benton route on the Missouri, the company's Oregon and Montana Transportation Company carried cargo and passengers from White Bluffs overland to Lake Pend Oreille where the *Mary Moody* ran from the lower end of the lake to Cabinet Rapids on Clark's Fork. Here a portage connected with the *Cabinet* which ran to Thompson Falls, and the *Missoula* continued to the mouth of the Jocko. Thence, by wagon, shipments reached the mining camps of Helena.

From Umatilla Landing on the Columbia four stagecoach lines ran to Old's Ferry on the Snake, where in 1866 the *Shoshone* was built at a cost of $100,000. Her run was to the mouth of the Bruneau River where it was expected to intercept the Salt Lake City-Boise traffic. But when the *Shoshone* failed to pay its way, it was brought down the surging canyon of the Snake to Lewiston by two intrepid company employees.

The cost of building and navigating boats on such remote waters was greater than any revenue they earned, but it was part of a necessary overhead to prevent competitors from drawing off some of the heavy payload that traveled from Portland to eastern Oregon, Washington, Montana, and Idaho. From San Francisco and Sacramento, Wells Fargo Express overland stages and express lines tapped the mining districts and Ben Holladay's Overland Mail fanned out from Salt Lake City to Alder Gulch, the Boise Basin, and even The Dalles.

Few people had affection for the OSN, primarily because it occupied a monopoly position. Inhabitants of western Washington felt a special antagonism toward it because, they charged, it diverted immigration to Portland and inhibited the growth of the Territory. Since there was no road between Puget Sound and the Columbia where immigrants reached the river, the frustrated territorials took up picks and axes to build one from Steilacoom to Walla Walla. Portlanders thereupon sent agents to meet immigrant companies and advise them that the route was impassable. The first to try it almost starved before they were rescued. Unused during the Indian wars, the road remained no more than a trail.[2] In 1869 Governor Alvan Flanders pointed out that Oregon had been granted more than a million and a quarter acres of public domain for military roads.[3] When the Territory sought similar appropriations, it was said that Oregon influence intervened.

Attempts to challenge the OSN on the Columbia were unsuccessful. Washington capital was insufficient to meet so powerful an opponent; underfinanced local companies were easily bought out after a taste of rate war. In 1864 the legislature chartered the Washington Transportation Company to build a railroad at the Cascades and asserted the power of eminent domain to condemn OSN lands and portage road. Washingtonians hailed with joy this move to fight the "unscrupulous monopoly," and OSN efforts to stop it in the territorial legislature and courts were defeated. In the end, the company won, but only by persuading Congress to disapprove an act of the territorial legislature. Simeon Reed, OSN vice-president and manager, gleefully pointed out that it would be a " 'bitter pill' for our friends in W. T. and hereafter the Legislature of that Territory will be reminded that there is a 'power above them.' "

Thwarted in their attempts to compete with the OSN and Portland, Puget Sound communities had to content themselves with their fine harbors, their lumber exports, and their trade with British Columbia. For this last, yards at Seabeck, Port Ludlow, Utsalady, and Port Madison were building firstclass vessels by 1876. Both shipbuilding and lumbering were financed by California capital which made Seattle and Port Gamble the chief export towns. Of thirty-seven sawmills in the Territory, producing about 130,000,000 board feet of saw lumber, twelve on the Sound cut more than 117,000,000 feet which went chiefly to South America and Australia; but total value of all territorial exports in 1875 amounted to $759,000 and of this slightly more than half was in commodities shipped to British Columbia.

In the interior the OSN was no more popular than in western Washington. It was blamed for the high prices miners had to pay for flour, bacon, beans, and whiskey. The slow growth of farming population in the interior was attributed to the company's exorbitant rates. Sometimes the company was blamed undeservedly. It had an expensive transportation system. In the 401 miles between Portland and

[2] Blanche B. Mahlberg, "Edward J. Allen, Pioneer and Road-builder," *PNQ*, October 1953.

[3] *Messages of the Governors of the Territory of Washington*, Charles M. Gates, ed. (1940), 152.

Lewiston, at low-water seasons cargoes had to be handled fourteen times; between Portland and points above The Dalles, at least ten times under any conditions. Because there was no timber near the river east of The Dalles, wood for engines that consumed fifty cords in the upriver trip had to be transported to fueling stations. The company followed the rate policy common to all transportation companies and charged all the traffic would bear.

Neither did Willamette Valley towns or farmers have any affection for the OSN—or for Portland either. When the OSN surrendered the Willamette River to the People's Transportation Company, the triumphant antimonopoly company immediately adopted monopoly rates, made possible, it was charged, because the OSN cooperated. Ben Holladay's Oregon and California Railroad promised competition that would force rates down, but the promise was never fulfilled. In 1878 the Valley had two competitive railway lines and three steamship companies, but a cargo of wheat shipped by rail from Eugene to Portland cost $6.00 a ton, exactly what the OSN charged on the Portland-Wallula route.

Portland was the only outlet for Valley produce, and Portland commission merchants controlled the market. In 1872 Corvallis welcomed a charming southern colonel, T. Egenton Hogg and his prospectus for a Corvallis-Yaquina railroad which was to give the upper Valley an outlet to the coast and was eventually to become a link in a transcontinental, the Corvallis-Eastern. Hogg almost created a seaport out of tidebound Yaquina Bay; but the Corvallis-Eastern ended a few miles up the slopes of the Cascades. Valley farmers remained subject, but still unresigned, to Portland's dominant mercantile position, and Portland became the West's chief wheat export city.

In 1867 a Valley shipper timidly entered the foreign export trade with a cargo of wheat for Liverpool. By 1875 Portland's wheat fleet rivalled Seattle's lumber draggers in number and outstripped the value of exports by approximately 50 percent. Ten years later the interior was sending to Portland three times as much wheat as was formerly shipped from the Valley.[4] Thus the economy of the interior was tied so closely to Portland's foreign export trade that not even railroads could break the bond.

In 1872 Portland was reputed to be one of the richest towns of its size in the United States, a reputation so firmly fixed that statistics could not shake it. Wealth came from transportation, banking, merchandising, and real estate, and Portlanders who made money plowed it back, cautiously and profitably, into their businesses. Banks and

[4] Dorothy D. Hirsch, "Study of the Foreign Wheat Trade of Oregon, 1869–1887," Reed College *Bulletin*, Armitage Essays, August 1953.

private lenders would take few risks when their money in safe investments earned legal interest of 12 percent, with a 5 percent bonus in addition. If a quarter of a million dollars were available in 1872, it could readily have been invested at 17 percent.

There were no large industries in the city or in the state. An iron furnace and several casting plants comprised its heavy industry. Oregon shipbuilding activities were modest. About the same number of ship carpenters, riggers, and calkers were employed as in Washington. In 1874, a shipyard on Coos Bay built the largest sailing vessel yet constructed on the Pacific Coast, the 186-foot, 1118-ton clipper *Western Shore*, which broke all coastal records for speed. In 1876 the Oregon Shipbuilding Company was incorporated, the first of any magnitude, using Portland capital almost exclusively. But so provincial was Portland's enterprise that the city fathers rejected a Maine shipbuilder's offer to build a yard on the Willamette if encouraged by the gift of a waterfront site. No tycoons had emerged as yet in the lumber industry. Portland's mills produced little more than the growing community could consume. The city lived on its hinterland.

In 1875, the *City Directory* listed six wholesale grocers, four banks, ten brokerage firms, twenty commission houses, and eleven corporations, of which eight were engaged in some kind of transportation. The interests of commission merchants, dealers in farm machinery, and general merchandisers as well as bankers and transportation people were interrelated. Robert R. Thompson, one of the founders of the OSN, and Henry W. Corbett of the California Stage Company and a banker were also hardware merchants. Captain J. C. Ainsworth, president of the OSN, was connected with construction companies that built the western portion of the Canadian Pacific Railroad and the Northern Pacific branch between Tacoma and Portland. He too became a banker. Simeon Reed and William S. Ladd were general merchants before they became boat owner and banker. In partnership they also operated seventeen farms in the Willamette Valley. Broadmead, 7000 pastoral acres in Yamhill County, was a showplace among Valley farms. The owners imported purebred stock to upgrade sheep, beef, and dairy cattle, brought in managers experienced in the latest scientific methods of farming, and experimented with grain and grass seeds, soil drainage, fertilizing, and the newest inventions in farm machinery.

Oregon's agriculture needed the encouragement of gentlemen farmers who could afford experimentation. Willamette Valley farmers had easily fallen into patterns of farming and husbandry that had comfortably supported pioneers, but were ill suited to new competitive situations. To encourage scientific agriculture, private subscribers instituted a State Agricultural Society in 1860. While annual fairs there-after displayed the rural arts from seeds to silos and quilts to quince jellies, only a handful of innovators saw virtue in purebred stock and selective breeding, quality seed and diversified farming. North-west farmers learned slowly, even from experience. The livestock that survived the hard winter of 1861–1862 provided a nucleus for herds and flocks which by 1876 had far outgrown local demands.[5] But sur-pluses and assets were again wiped out by the calamitous winters of 1880–1881 and 1887–1888. Farmers, clinging to the delusion that win-ters were consistently mild, were not prepared to feed or water their unsheltered herds.

Farmers were badly hit by the 1873 depression. It did not help their frame of mind when gentleman farmers bought their lands at de-pressed prices, and as in the case of Ladd and Reed, enclosed a half-mile of track for training their racing horses. While farmers languished in hard times, however, residents of the city of Portland were experi-encing a real estate boom that sent prices up 20 to 25 percent in older parts of town and 50 to 100 percent in new additions.

A SHOW OF CITY ELEGANCE

Many of Portland's more prosperous families were of New England origin and their eastern connections were useful in building their for-tunes. The economic and social influence of the Portland dynasties significantly outweighed their strength in numbers, and gave the com-munity such tone that it was often described as a New England village transplanted to the West. Actually, this was less true of Port-land than of Salem or Forest Grove, and later of Walla Walla, where the climates were less commercial and the village aspects more real than fancied. Portland combined qualities assumed to be characteris-tic of New England with those of a rugged and recent frontier.

By the late 1870s the business district lying parallel to the Willam-ette River was lined by brick structures with cast-iron facades of fluted columns and Corinthian capitals or with narrowly arched street floors surmounted by second and third stories carrying the traditional "orders" of architectural decoration. Side by side with these manifesta-tions of the classical revival were evidences of the West's eclectic taste for sharp-arched neo-Gothic windows pointing to late Renais-

[5] J. Orin Oliphant, "Winter Losses of Cattle in the Oregon Country 1847–1890," *WHQ*, January 1932; "The Cattle Trade from the Far Northwest to Montana," *Agricultural History*, April 1932.

sance mansarded roofs. Next to a well-proportioned brick structure, marked only by a modest brass plaque, crouched a frame building with the familiar flat false front carrying its identification in story-high lettering.

Between Ankeny and Pine, on First Street, were the shops and better stores. When daytime din of heavy drays rumbling over the cobblestones ceased, the night reverberated with the quick beat of high-stepping horses and the whir of carriage wheels approaching the New Market Theater and the more respectable avenues of Portland's night life. At this location in 1888 Olin Levi Warner placed his lovely masterpiece, the Skidmore fountain, endowed by a pioneer businessman for the refreshment of "men, horses and dogs."

Desire that the city be beautiful was evident from the first years, when, as the residential district spread from the river toward the hills, park blocks were laid out and planted to elms. Substantial but not elaborate homes were set in large fenced yards, unimaginatively landscaped, and monotonous in design and approach. The prevailing style of the sixties was the "Gothic Cottage" made popular through widely circulated carpenters' handbooks. In the seventies, sophisticated tastes preferred the Italian villa and French Second Empire styles.[6] The occupants of these houses lived well, entertained with the opulent menus of the day, and put on enough airs to distinguish them as the local aristocracy. As wealth accumulated, a must for social leadership was the tour of European capitals and the purchase of private art collections. Simeon Reed made two such tours and spent $20,000 on second-rate Munich-school oils of tediously sentimental themes. The Ladds, Corbetts, and Failings brought back to Portland fine pieces of oriental art and some superior examples of the modern schools.

A perennial shortage of domestic help plagued Portland housewives when even their Irish maids deserted them to marry. In the seventies the Irish comprised the largest foreign-born group in Portland; but within a decade, "China boys" became the laundrymen, gardeners, houseboys, and chefs for the well-to-do. Seldom did a ship come in from the Orient without bringing 300 to 400 Chinese laborers. Their first destination was the railroad construction camp or the mines, but when the depression following the panic of 1873 halted railway work, they congregated in Portland or in Astoria where they worked in the salmon canneries. In 1880 Clatsop and Multnomah counties had more than 4000 Chinese—almost 1000 more than were in the whole of Washington Territory.

[6] Marion D. Ross, "Architecture in Oregon 1845–1895," *OHQ*, March 1956.

CHURCHES AND SCHOOLS

The New England influence was probably most noticeable in Oregon's churches and schools. According to Samuel Bowles, editor of the *Springfield Republican* and editorial mouthpiece for Jay Cooke's Northern Pacific Railroad, the residents of Portland kept Sunday with almost as much strictness as Puritanic New England, "which can be said of no other population this side of the Rocky Mountains at least." By 1872 the *City Directory* listed fourteen Protestant churches. Oldest and largest of three Methodist edifices was the Taylor Street Church, founded in 1851 by James H. Wilbur, who cleared land and cut timbers for the first frame structure. Father Wilbur, as he was called, served several pastorates and spent eighteen years as Indian agent on the Yakima reservation. The pastors of the Congregationalists' two churches, George H. Atkinson and Horace Lyman, had both been sent to Oregon in 1847 by the American Home Missionary Society. Atkinson was the father of Oregon Territory's public education bill, and Lyman was one of the founders of La Creole Academy (Rickreall) in Marion County, the short-lived Montville Institute in Linn County, and Pacific University at Forest Grove.

The First Presbyterian Church was organized in Portland in 1854 but no church was built until 1865. J. Lapsley Yantis, its pastor, divided his services between the Portland congregation and one at Calypooia, eighty miles up the Valley. Under the pastorate of Aaron Ladner Lindsley, First Presbyterian grew to be one of the city's largest churches. Between 1867 and 1886 Lindsley not only served the local church but also established missions among the Indians of the Northwest and Alaska, and organized no fewer than twenty-one other congregations of the denomination.

The first American Episcopal priest, St. Michael Fackler, arrived in Oregon in 1847. Trinity Episcopal parish was organized in 1851, and three years later Thomas Fielding Scott, missionary bishop of Oregon and Washington, dedicated the first Episcopal church building on the Pacific Coast, an unusual accomplishment for a denomination not popular or common on the frontier. On the other hand, Baptist missionaries were active early in Oregon, but it was not until 1872, twenty-two years after the first organization, that a church was built in Portland. The 1880s witnessed the largest growth of this denomination, particularly in Washington Territory.

Portland's colony of Jews organized a congregation in 1858 and three years later started construction of Temple Beth Israel which when completed in 1888 had a seating capacity of over 700. A second congregation, Ahavai Sholom, was organized in 1872.

A rough chapel built in 1852 served the city's few Catholics until 1862, when the Irish began to arrive and Archbishop Blanchet moved the seat of the diocese from Oregon City to Portland. Two years later he dedicated a procathedral, and twenty years later he saw completion of the Cathedral of the Immaculate Conception. His death in 1885 brought to a close forty-seven years of continuous association with Oregon's church history.

This record was equaled only by that of Thomas Lamb Eliot, who in 1867 assumed the pastorate of "liberal Christians" organized the year before in the First Unitarian church. Son of a pioneer Unitarian minister in St. Louis, Eliot, "the conscience of Portland," was highly effective in molding public opinion toward needed social and educational reforms. After serving as pastor of the Church of Our Father from 1867 to his retirement in 1893, Eliot continued to serve the community in others ways until his death in 1936.

Eliot and other churchmen before him were the advocates and builders of educational institutions. They had good soil in which to work, for the Northwest had a high literacy level. The 1870 census reported only 2609 Oregonians unable to read in a population of 78,711 ten years of age or older. Washington had 1018 in 17,585, and Idaho Territory, 3293 in 14,999, who by census definition were illiterate. There were full- or part-time schools in nearly every Oregon settlement. Portland had a "free school" in 1851, and five years later its first public school was opened with John Outhouse (pronounced Othus) as teacher. A free secondary school was established in 1889 but only after twenty years of bitter struggle was tax support for public high schools finally achieved in less prosperous districts. To encourage improvement and standardization of public schools the legislature in 1872 had set up the office of State Superintendent of Public Instruction and a State Board of Education.

In Portland private academies, Protestant, Catholic (St. Mary's was founded in 1854), and Hebrew and German schools, served those who wanted religious or language education not offered in public schools. In 1861 Bishop Thomas F. Scott opened Spencer Hall at Milwaukie; in 1869, it was succeeded by St. Helen's Hall in Portland where many of the young ladies who would be mistresses of Portland's finer homes were educated. Founded in 1851 by the Methodist missionary James H. Walker and supported largely by Presbyterians, Portland Academy and Female Seminary was formally incorporated in 1854, discontinued in 1878, and reopened in 1889. The new Academy was a great

Fishing

ABOVE. *Salmon fishing at a Chinook village. So plentiful were the fish that a winter's supply could be caught in a few weeks.*

LEFT. *Drying racks preserved fish in ample supply. Lewis and Clark ". . . saw stacks of dried fish packed in woven baskets. . . ." The predominantly fish diet of the coastal Indians was varied by wild plants, berries, roots, seeds and nuts. Berries were dried or preserved in fish oil.*

A whale chase off Cape Flattery. The Indians developed large canoes and specialized harpoons for hunting sea otter and whales. The prestige attached to the hunt —equipment, hazards, bravery—seems to have been more valued than the meat or furs.

Robert Stuart, with the Astorians in 1811, watched the grandfathers of these Indians fish in the same place, in the same manner. The place is Celilo Falls, Oregon; the manner is by large dip-net (and looks to be fine sport).

A Columbia River fish wheel was a large revolving double wheel, turned by the current, which scooped up the fish passing beneath in boxlike wire nets. Such efficient mechanisms led to the depletion of fish runs.

BELOW. *Astoria's Butterfly Fleet of yesteryear. Today's diesel boats are bigger and better, faster and fuller—but not so beautiful.*

The first fish cannery on the Columbia, Cowlitz County, 1866. Flimsy and bleak as it was, it helped launch today's multimillion dollar salmon industry. During 1965, the total catch of five salmonid species for the entire Columbia River was 8½ million pounds.

The salmon are running! After a successful program of conservation in cooperation with Canada, the United States purse seine fleet again fishes for sockeye near Point Roberts, Washington.

LEFT. *The purse net is half on the stern of the seiner, half in the water, a set being made around a school of salmon. . . .*

. . . and successfully. The holds are full. A tender will unload and conveyor belts will take the fish directly into the cannery for processing.

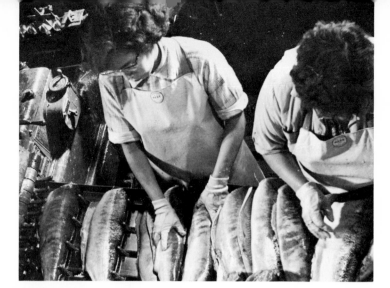

ABOVE. *In the cannery, women inspect each salmon just before it is cut into can-sized segments by a machine called the "Iron Chink."*

LEFT. *Filled cans are arranged on racks to be taken to retorts for cooking.*

BELOW. *Fish for future runs must be assured. At the hatchery near Bonneville Dam, salmon fingerlings thrive on a nutritionally-controlled liquid food.*

success, offering a curriculum usually found in the last two years of high school and the first two years of college. The Academy goaded the public schools to higher standards before it surrendered to them in 1916.

Portland had no monopoly of religious instruction or general education, or for that matter of a New England inheritance. The capital city, Salem, also wore the mantle of culture. Willamette University represented the culmination of a long struggle to make the Methodist Mission school, the Oregon Institute, something more than an elementary academy. In Forest Grove, Mother Tabitha Brown's orphanage grew into the Congregationalist Pacific University under the direction of the Reverend John S. Griffin, and with the masterful teaching of classicist Sidney H. Marsh.

Practically all of Oregon's institutions of higher learning had their roots in church schools. Some academies designed to serve local needs for secondary education or to implement some doctrine had brief histories. The Baptists founded institutes at Corvallis (1856) and West Union (1858); the Disciples of Christ opened Bethel Institute (1855) which merged with Christian College to form Monmouth University (1864). Presbyterian Albany Academy was founded in 1858, and the same denomination's Corvallis College, chartered by the territorial legislature in 1858, became Oregon Agricultural College (1885) when the church relinquished control. It was partly supported thereafter as a land-grant college under the Morrill Act of 1862.

A state university had been projected when Oregon became a state and received land grants for purposes of higher education. The small income from the land fund, and the relatively large number of private academies already in existence, discouraged any notion of building one until the seventies, when the legislature appropriated $100,000 for the purpose. A struggle over the location was resolved when the city of Eugene raised money to start Deady Hall on the present campus site. In 1876 the University opened to a handful of students.

Oregon's resources for support of education were limited; its school land funds were stolen or mismanaged, and while the public might profess a devotion to learning, taxpayer and private donor were less concerned with cultural development than with economy. The struggles of academies and colleges to keep going were heroic, and a surprising number survived. They provided a modest education for ambitious young men and women, and after 1870 the majority of Oregon's most respected members of bench and bar, the medical profession, and school staffs had their training at these institutions.

In 1885 the governor of Washington Territory reported twenty-five institutions "of the higher order," but few that warranted the description. The legislature provided for a state university in Seattle, which in 1861 offered an elementary curriculum. Its first president, Asa Mercer, was an energetic prophet of Puget Sound's great future, and is perhaps best remembered as the man who imported the "Mercer girls" to add a touch of feminine gentility to the Territory's bachelor population.[7] Mercer accomplished more in the field of publicity than in higher education. In 1873, Governor Ferry reported that for lack of financial support the University was one in name only and he recommended appropriations that would enable it to establish and maintain a curriculum "equal at least to that provided in first-class seminaries and academies."

Two years before the University opened, the legislature incorporated Walla Walla's Whitman Seminary (1886), which was reorganized in 1883 and incorporated as Whitman College. Among its original trustees were Elkanah Walker, Henry H. Spalding, and Cushing Eells, men whose personal histories gave special meaning to this memorial to the Whitmans. Its founding also marked the end of an era for the city which supported the college and guarded its standards. Walla Walla had changed remarkably from a rowdy rendezvous for miners to a prosperous farming town as sedate and proper as New England's Concord which it sought to emulate.

LITERATURE, AESTHETIC AND APPLIED

Pioneer generations that had neither time nor money for much formal learning nevertheless placed great value on books. Almost every pioneer home had some; the Applegate family was perhaps unusual for its collection of political and philosophical works. The spirit that created a circulating library at Oregon City in 1844 did not wane as the years passed. A library group formed in Portland in 1850 had a life of six years, but the Library Association organized in 1864 with a board of directors drawn from the city's leading citizens has had a continuous history. Starting with donations of $2611, and supported by an initiation fee of five dollars and quarterly dues of three dollars, it had a collection of 9872 volumes by 1880, and the annual report of that year showed that the number of volumes loaned was 18,208.

Oregonians were not masters of belles lettres. Margaret Jewett Bailey's *Grains: or Passages in the Life of Ruth Rover, with Occa-*

[7] Delphine Henderson, "Asa Shinn Mercer, Northwest Publicity Agent," Reed College *Bulletin*, Armitage Essays, January 1945.

sional Pictures of Oregon, Natural and Moral (1854) shocked and titillated the community with its autobiographical implications. This "realistic" novel fascinated the curious, who tried to ferret out the real-life identity of the villainous missionary; it was dismissed by a reviewer who declared that "to call it trash would be impolite," and who considered "an authoress" simply another affliction for Oregonians already "castigated by . . . unjust laws—poor lawyers and worse judges—taxes, and no money."

Despite their inadequacies, Oregonians were prolific writers. The *Oregonian* received more literary manuscripts—"public lectures, poems, &c."—than its first editor cared to print. Newspapers, however, were most authors' only outlets and by combing their pages one discovers the products of native talent, often anonymous, often concerned with local events. "Josh," for example, told in the Jacksonville *Oregon Sentinel* how the Goddess of Health advised him to find health and food for thought in the "dark, embrowned woods" where streams were "alive with the swift darting trout." But Irony came and reported

> . . . If you go to the woods,
> You needn't take fish hook or gun.
> For Edgerton's Party caught all of the trout,
> And slaughtered the last, last deer.
> And drove all the bear beyond the McCloud,
> There'll be no more hunting this year.

Flora McClure's moral tale, inspired by the hard winter of 1880, concluded:

> And thus it is, from year to year,
>   Some farmers live without a fear
> That rains will come, till they are here;
>   Then buy their feed when feed is dear;
> And lose half of their stock at last;
>   But never profit by the past.

Joaquin Miller, Indiana-born Cincinnatus Heine Miller, had a varied and colorful career in Canyon City and Portland, where his second book of verses, *Joaquin et al.*, was published in 1869. The next year he moved to the more receptive intellectual atmosphere of California, "where passion was born, and where blushes gave birth" to his songs of the South. Sad Sam Simpson (1845–1900), on the other hand, spent all but his first few years in Oregon, writing verses for the most part unfortunately imitative of the worst romantic verbiage of the times. However, an original note occasionally came through the purple passages; for old Oregonians, at least, his "Beautiful Willamette" had a nostalgic appeal:

> From the Cascades' frozen gorges,
>   Leaping like a child at play,
> Winding, widening through the valley,
>   Bright Willamette glides away;
>   Onward ever,
>   Lovely River,
> Softly calling to the sea,
>   Time that scars us,
>   Maims and mars us,
> Leaves no track or trench on thee.

If Oregon's literary art was imitative, its political writings and newspaper style were original and often unrestrained. Pickett's *Flumgudgeon Gazette* made merry with the politics of the 1840s. William L. Adams, an ordained Campbellite minister from Plainsville, Ohio, carried on the tradition with *Breakspear—a Melodrame entitled Treason, Stratagems and Spoils* (1852) which caricatured Democratic factions of the next decade in a manner thought devastating at the time. As a newspaper editor Adams was a practitioner of the "Oregon Style" which characterized not only his own paper, the old *Spectator* revived as the *Argus* (1855), but the Whig-Republican *Oregonian* and the Salem clique's *Oregon Statesman* as well. *Statesman* editor Asahel Bush, was "Ass of Hell" in the pages of the *Argus*, which in turn was the "Air Goose" to Bush. Bush on one occasion wrote that Thomas J. Dryer's *Oregonian* was a "complete tissue of gross profanity, obscenity, falsehood, and meanness," whose editor seldom spoke the truth, "even by mistake." Without naming his enemy, Dryer, in a vocabulary reminiscent of a Mississippi riverman's, gave notice:

> Strayed, stolen, lost, absquatulated, mimeloosed or run away, one . . . formerly editor, proprietor, printer, compositor, pressman, roller boy, extra seller, libeler, item gatherer, affidavit maker, slanderer general, and "pimp" generalissimo of a small, cheap paper called the _____.[8]

This was the style that gave notoriety to the founders of Oregon journalism. Those who came after them and were responsible for the thirty-five newspapers in the state in 1870 spoke more quietly as a rule. An occasional paper, like the tabloid *Bee*, owned by W. S. Chapman after 1878, strained both good taste and the laws of libel to the point where a State Press Association was organized to provide a code

[8] George S. Turnbull, *History of Oregon Newspapers* (1939), 84.

of ethics for the profession and to agitate, which it did successfully, for stronger state libel laws.

In 1860, Henry L. Pittock bought the nearly defunct *Oregonian* and hired Harvey W. Scott as editor. Scott had crossed the plains in 1852, graduated from Pacific University, and at the age of twenty-seven was reading law and acting as part-time librarian for the Portland Library Association. From 1865 until 1910, except for five years when W. Lair Hill was editor, Scott was the highly literate, even scholarly, spokesman for Portland—in most cases for its conservatism and its Republican Party. Seldom was the reader at a loss to understand where the *Oregonian*—that is, Scott—stood on an issue. Although in the seventies twenty papers, dailies, weeklies, and monthlies, began publication in Portland, *The Morning Oregonian* was ritualistically to Portland what the *Evening Transcript* was to Boston. Harvey Scott was opposed to "crack pot" ideas such as free silver, woman suffrage, and free public high schools. His sister, Abigail Scott Duniway, was Oregon's leading suffragette and editor of the *New Northwest* (1871–1887). An able writer and lecturer, Mrs. Duniway seldom saw eye-to-eye with her brother. She survived his disdain as she did showers of eggs and other missiles when she spoke for her cause before hostile audiences.

Frances Fuller Victor (1826–1902) was the Northwest's other professional woman writer. After having written the two-volume *History of Oregon* (1886–1888) for Hubert Howe Bancroft's multivolume *History of the Pacific States*, she made Portland her home where she corresponded for local and San Francisco newspapers and wrote *The Early Indian Wars of Oregon* (1894) and several promotional books. Her best-known work was *The River of the West* (1870), a history of pioneer Oregon woven around the life of Joseph L. Meek.

MUSIC AND THE THEATER

Music and the theater had a part in Oregon's cultural life. There was, of course, the background of folk singing, campfire songs, and church hymns common to the frontier. Pianos and portable organs graced early parlors. The first musical organization was something out of the ordinary on the frontier. Aurora, half-way point between Salem and Portland, was founded in 1857 by a German society which had separated from its mother colony in Bethel, Missouri, and under the patriarchal leadership of Dr. William Keil, continued in Oregon the Rappist tradition of mysticism and communitarianism. Concerts by these music-loving Germans introduced Oregonians to classics presented with professional competence. The performers were first instructed by a university-trained schoolmaster and polished by the sharp-eared, sharp-tongued Meister Heinrich Carl Finck. Finck's son, coached in music by his father and in the classics by Aurora's Professor Wolff from Gottingen, entered Harvard in the sophomore class and became a music critic in New York and Philadelphia.[9]

The musical standards and tastes of Aurora were shared by a large part of Portland's German community, numbering 1600 in 1880. *Liederfests* at the Turn Verein may have been the origin of the Handel and Haydn Society. In its first concert in the spring of 1879, the society gave the premier performance of Dudley Buck's *Legend of Don Munio* specially orchestrated by the composer for the limited number of local musicians. To round out an ambitious first season, a full orchestra and chorus performed *The Messiah* at a reception for ex-President Ulysses S. Grant, one of Portland's more famous visitors.

Theater—using the word to include elocution recitals and General Tom Thumb's midgets as well as drama—was popular in mining camps and frontier towns. Portland had variety troupes and minstrel shows as early as 1856, and a theater building in 1858.[10] At the old Stewart Theater, the Oro Fino, and the Adelphia, Portlanders wept over *East Lynne* and *Camille*. But the theater of which the city was most proud was the New Market, built by Alexander P. Ankeny, merchant and shipping magnate turned speculator in the arts. At the grand opening in 1875, James A. Hearne played *Rip Van Winkle* before the local diamond horseshoe.

THE PROPER OREGONIANS

"Oregonians," remarked Samuel Bowles in 1869, "have builded what they have got more slowly and more wisely than the Californians; they have . . . less to unlearn; and they seem sure, not of organizing the first state on the Pacific Coast, indeed, but of a steadily prosperous, healthy, and moral one—they are in the way to be the New England of the Pacific Coast." As the city grew it did not wholly lose this atmosphere. In many ways, it remained a village. But even as villages have their seamier sides of life, so had Portland.

[9] John E. Simon, "Wilhelm Keil and Communist Colonies," *OHQ*, June 1935; Robert J. Hendricks, *Bethel and Aurora* (1933).

[10] Alice Ernst, *Trouping in the Oregon Country: a History of Frontier Theater* (1961).

With the development of maritime commerce, once respectable boardinghouses and residences at the north end of First Street became sailors' rooming houses, and saloons and bawdy-houses gave the North End a reputation and a clientele that flourished with the years. Shipmasters filled crews with the drugged or drunk, "shanghaied" by professionals. When fancy ladies strolled from their haunts to parts of town frequented by genteel ladies, the latter lowered their parasols to exclude the intruders from their vision; and when Ben Holladay drove by in his carriage accompanied by a lady who did not "belong," proper ladies peeked very cautiously indeed to avoid acknowledging his bow.

But spreading out across the Willamette to East Portland, Lents, Alberta, and St. Johns, the inhabitants did not have to crowd together in unwholesome districts. Modest homes, gardens, and orchards dotted the landscape as forests receded. Spring still comes to Portland in a burst of bloom from cherry and apple trees planted eighty years ago. From its origin a homey town, not robustly friendly but amiable; cautious in its enthusiasms, reluctant to peer very far out from under its ruffled parasol, Portland was Oregon—conservative and, in most circumstances, contented with itself. And this was perhaps natural.

As an American colony, the first settlements of Oregon laid out the pattern of the future. Measured sobriety, thrift, and the caution of the commercial elements combined with agricultural provincialism and tradition to create a conservative community. However, Oregon's conservatism was not reactionary; it did not fight change. It welcomed separation from elements which disturbed its way of life, as it had done in encouraging the separation of Washington. Oregonians did not reject anything new simply because it was new—a Maine-owned shipyard or Abigail Duniway's suffrage agitation—without a reasonably polite hearing.

Portlanders took their politics, business, and morals seriously but not uncomfortably. They voted Republican as a rule, but until the end of the century there was no incident to arouse political antagonisms among nonprofessionals. Neither business nor politics kept city leaders from sharing in civic duties, holding offices, or serving on commissions to develop a water system and a street railway. The rich supported the city's cultural life, philanthropies, and churches. But the elite did not admire extravagance or ostentation. William S. Ladd replied to his farm manager's letters by turning the paper upside down and writing between the lines. Simeon Reed, lacking formal dress to attend the opera in Paris, had his wife pin back the tails of his Prince Albert coat to simulate the proper garb.

The state's principal citizens and wealthiest men might, on occasion, align themselves in rival camps and battle over railway franchises or land grants; they might finagle laws to get more than their share of the public domain, or to squeeze out a competitor; they might buy juries or legislators, and turn their eyes from others' fraud and corruption. But seldom did an individual emerge to notoriety or prominent infamy, or strain after power without regard for public opinion. On the whole, Portland's citizens were "proper Oregonians." Their virtues and their vices were suspended in a narrow middle range.

PART III

A Period of Transition

OVERVIEW

THE 30-YEAR PERIOD *from 1880 to 1910 was a time of transition for the Pacific Northwest. In 1880, it was still an isolated frontier which attracted relatively small numbers of settlers, found little use for its rich natural resources, and maintained its commercial contact with the rest of the world by sea. By 1910 the population of Oregon, Washington, and Idaho totaled more than 2,000,000, the economy was closely interlocked with that of the rest of the nation, and the general level of growth compared favorably with that of other sections.*

The completion of northern transcontinental railways, ushering in a new day of easy and rapid transportation, was largely responsible for population growth. Thousands of immigrants came West "by the cars" who would never have attempted the voyage by schooner around the Horn, or ventured to cross a continent by long and weary marches. Trains carried agricultural produce, lumber, and minerals to markets hitherto out of reach.

Yet much more was involved in the transformation of the region than simply the means of travel. Far-reaching developments taking place in the country as a whole made living conditions very different from what they had been ten or twenty years earlier. Large-scale production, which revolutionized many lines of manufacturing, gave big business a new interest in exploiting the natural resources in the West, and placed a correspondingly higher value upon them. Giant corporations with tremendous working capital and centralized management brought the frontier, however remote, into the orbit of their control. The man-made environment of steel and stone that appeared so suddenly in the nation's cities was something new in Portland, Oregon, as well as Portland, Maine.

Railroads (and telegraph lines which accompanied them) were particularly important in the Pacific Northwest because they linked the region with older states that were themselves undergoing profound economic and social change. The far western frontier was doubly transformed: once by the physical conquest of distances, and again by new forces which were immediately brought to play upon it. Industrialism and urbanization had special implications for these newer sections of the country that stood so near to the pioneer stage of history. On the one hand, their development was greatly accelerated; on the other, concentration of population and economic power in the East sometimes worked against the kind of dispersion that was essential for the long-range development of the Pacific Coast.

The years of transition were marked by an exuberant optimism. This generation knew the excitement of the region's first big boom since gold rush days. Boosters enjoyed a field day, beating the drums of progress in the ears of listening Americans everywhere. Colonel Nicholas Owings, who had been a secretary of state and head of the Immigration Bureau in Washington Territory, set the tone in an interview for a popular magazine. Washington, he insisted, had more and better timber than the Baltic. It was better dairy country than Holland, raised better hops than New York and better grain than any other state in the Union. It had the grandest harbor in the world, and would assuredly be the center of American trade with the Orient. "Here on Puget Sound," he declared, "is the future seat of the western empire of wealth."

Owings was a professional booster and his language was undeniably extravagant. But the statistics of the eighties encouraged extravagance. Oregon, Washington, and Idaho received three times as many new settlers in the eighties as in the seventies. Farmers doubled their production. Cities arose as if by magic in a few years' time.

Northwesterners denied that their growth and expansion were speculative, and that they were heading for an inescapable "bust." They were just "growing up with the country." Nevertheless they were lifted high by a wave of national prosperity, and when the wave passed they were becalmed. In the general panic of 1893 and the depression years that followed, the stream of immigration largely disappeared, the flow of investment slowed to a trickle, and the Pacific Northwest had intimate experience of hard times. Prosperity returned with the Yukon gold rush which brought unprecedented opportunities in the outfitting trade to the Puget Sound cities and to Portland. In the decade from 1900 to

1910 the fine art of boosting reached a climax in Portland's Lewis and Clark Exposition in 1905 and Seattle's Alaska-Yukon-Pacific Exposition in 1909.

Much of this era's growth was achieved, not by shouting and display, but by careful analyses of the region's economic opportunities under conditions of modern industrialism. Tough problems in production and marketing had to be solved. Despite the new railroad connections, conditions of competition were often unfavorable. Railroad carrying costs were higher than they were elsewhere, and the advantages of established industries in other parts of the country curbed the development of new ones in the Far West. Of necessity, the region developed around its material resources and caught up with other sections only as the economies of production made it possible, and as local trade increased with the growing population.

This was a time of change in political life. Washington and Idaho, having languished in territorial status for a quarter-century and more, drew up constitutions and were admitted as sovereign states in the Union. Delegations from the Far West appeared in Congress with votes to parlay for their constituencies. The Northwest's political parties became more full-bodied and more complicated as they represented both agricultural areas and urban populations. The Pacific Northwest went "radical" for reform, and in the first decade of the new century led all other regions in the speed with which its states adopted progressive legislation.

Society was profoundly affected by the development of urban civilization in the Pacific Northwest. To be sure, the number of cities of more than 100,000 population could be counted on the fingers of one hand. But in these few areas, an urban way of living developed, and the rich (and the sordid) features of urban culture were accentuated and disseminated. Change from frontier to city civilization took place with unusual abruptness, and experiences which in older places extended over several decades were compressed into the space of a few years. The technician and professional expert found a community sufficiently large and diversified to support his craft. The artist found discriminating patronage; science and learning were stimulated and nourished by the multiplication and improvement of schools and colleges. With an end to physical and intellectual isolation, provincialism diminished, if it did not disappear.

It would be a mistake to think that living in Seattle or Portland was like living in Boston or Chicago. Frontier characteristics were still discernible, since it took time to build institutions equal to those of older states. But cities enriched the interests and activities of people in the Northwest just as they did elsewhere, and civilization came to be much the same in essential qualities, whether in the valley of the Columbia or on the Atlantic Coast.

Such is the setting that gives special meaning to the events of the

303

latter years of the nineteenth-century and the first decade and a half of the twentieth. It would be hard to magnify the differences which set off the beginning of the period from the end, or to exaggerate the rapidity with which important changes took place. In point of time, a single generation spanned the years of transition. In quality and conditions of living, the Pacific Northwest of 1914 was part of a new and forward-looking world. These chapters in the history of the region tell how the modern Northwest came into being.

CHAPTER
NINETEEN

Beginning a New Era: The Magic of the Steel Rails

OF ALL THE AGENCIES that contributed to the development of the American West, none was expected to work greater magic than railroads. The idea of a transcontinental line linking New York and Chicago with the Pacific Coast created tremendous excitement in men's minds. Whether the dream was of a great commerce with the Orient or of peopling new frontiers, transcontinentals stirred imaginations long before they were built.

George Wilkes, one of the earliest promoters of a transcontinental, thought of the railroad as a means of putting the United States on the "short route to Asia." "The riches of the most unlimited market in the world would be thrown open to our enterprise, and . . . our commerce would increase till every ocean billow between us and the China seas would twinkle with a sail. . . . We should become the common carrier of the world for the India trade."

If Wilkes saw sails on the sea, others saw cultivated fields and new cities on the far western horizon. Westerners pictured the railroad

305

threading its way through a vast interior without rival in beauty and resources. Over it would pass a constant flow of wealth from rich farms to the seaboard, where cities would spring up to rival Boston and New York. "This," insisted the Oregon booster who penned the prophecy, "is no fancy picture, but simply words of truth and soberness."

The story of surveying, financing, and constructing the transcontinentals is one of combined private enterprise and government aid on a national scale. Local groups along proposed routes sometimes took an active part in efforts to build roads. Territorial and state legislatures incorporated railroad companies or memorialized Congress to aid lines that held national charters. Mass meetings were staged and local capitalists promised to raise money. But the roads were built largely by outsiders, and while Jay Cooke might speak of Oregon capitalists Ladd, Ainsworth, and Reed, as "our Western Associates," eastern bankers shouldered the main responsibility and called the tune. During the latter half of the nineteenth century railroading was no longer an enterprise that western communities could undertake for themselves. If the frontiers of the Far West were to be linked by rail with the rest of the country, it was because captains of finance had their own reasons for doing it. Those reasons were not public altruism.

To settlers of the Far Northwest it seemed that the railroads were infinitely slow in building. The first surveys had been made before the Civil War. Isaac I. Stevens laid out a route between St. Paul and Puget Sound while en route to Olympia in 1853 to take up his duties as Washington's first territorial governor. Rivalry among advocates of northern, central, and southern routes, another instance of the 1850s' sectional controversy, stalled congressional decisions. But the Republican platform in 1860 made its bid to Westerners: ". . . a Railroad to the Pacific Ocean is imperatively demanded by the interests of the whole country . . . the Federal Government ought to render immediate and efficient aid in its construction." And Republicans in power made good their promises. The Union Pacific and the Central Pacific were chartered in 1862 and the Northern Pacific in 1864. During the Civil War, capital, labor and materials for building were unavailable. But the means of financing them was embodied in their charters.

LAND-GRANT RAILROADS

The basic legislation laid down the terms for construction and finance, and stated the government policy of "efficient aid." All three lines were land-grant roads; that is, they were subsidized with lands from the public domain. Each was to receive a 200-foot-wide right of way and sections of public lands to help finance construction. The Northern Pacific's charter originally provided ten alternate sections per mile in states through which it passed and twenty sections per mile in territories. If sufficient lands were not available within this primary grant, other sections could be selected as lieu lands from a secondary zone which reached back from the tracks another twenty miles. Additional funds were to be raised through stock sales and, for the Union and Central Pacific, through government loans. These were in the form of 30-year bonds for $16,000 to $48,000 per mile of track laid, depending on the topography of the land. With this kind of assistance the two companies began construction in 1866.

The Union Pacific pushed the laying of rails with such energy that by May, 1869, the line following the Platte River route extended from Omaha to northern Utah. At the same time the Central Pacific under the vigorous direction of the "Big Four," Leland Stanford, Collis P. Huntington, Mark Hopkins, and Charles Crocker, forged eastward from Sacramento through the mountains of California and Nevada. On May 10, 1869, the two lines met at Promontory Point, Utah; the gold spike was hammered home and a consignment of tea started eastward from the Pacific Coast as a token of anticipated overland trade with China and Japan. The next morning the first transcontinental passengers from the East crossed over the "last tie."

The Northern Pacific did not get started so expeditiously. Its charter provided generous grants of land in the territories but not government loans. Jay Cooke, financial genius who had successfully handled public sales of government bonds during the war, took over the job of financing the road on a commission basis. He prevailed upon Congress to extend the secondary zone of lieu lands to thirty miles on each side of the road, and to authorize the company to issue, for every mile of track laid, $50,000 in bonds secured by the land grant and other properties. Cooke's widespread enterprises met disaster in 1873, but by that time, the eastern division of the Northern Pacific was finished from Duluth, Minnesota, to Bismarck, North Dakota. At the other end of the road, Cooke's "Western Friends" had laid a stretch of track from Kalama on the Columbia River to Tacoma on Puget Sound.

The building of the Kalama-Tacoma section resulted from a change in the original plan. According to the charter, the main line of the road was to run from Clark's Fork by way of Spokane Falls to Ainsworth at the junction of the Snake and Columbia rivers, up the Yakima River, and across the Cascade Mountains to Puget Sound. A branch was to follow the Columbia from Ainsworth to Portland. In 1870, the charter was amended to permit the main line to follow the Columbia, and the route over the Cascades thus became the branch. This change was made at Cooke's request. He had bought controlling stock in the OSN which was not only a profitable business but also had a 20-mile portage railroad on which he could immediately issue $5,000,000 in bonds. The new route favored Portland's continuing preeminence and increased the Northern Pacific's land grant to include alternate sections along the Columbia River and through the Cowlitz Valley. By building this section the railroad earned 2,000,000 acres of timber estimated to be worth $100,000,000.

The choice of Tacoma as the terminal city was made in the face of a spirited counter effort by the people of Seattle, who offered both land and cash as inducements to bring the railroad to their community. Seattle was somewhat older and larger than Tacoma, but this very fact worked against it, since its possibilities for land speculation were less promising than were those at the infant settlement on Commencement Bay. Having chosen Tacoma, the Northern Pacific brought tracks in at water level and built wharves to serve ships that plied the Sound or took on cargoes for the ocean trade. The St. Paul and Tacoma Land Company, many of whose investors were associated with both the Northern Pacific and the OSN, pushed the sale of lands and speedily brought the government of the town under its control. For a number of years the Kalama-Tacoma road went no farther than Tacoma, leaving other towns on the sound to be served by steamer. Thus, despite great expectations, until 1883 the Northern Pacific did not provide a transcontinental connection for Washington Territory and remained nothing more than draftsman's lines on most of the map of the Pacific Northwest.

The disappointed people of Washington demanded that lands reserved for the Northern Pacific be returned to the public domain. As matters stood, the railroad could not perfect its title to the reserved land or sell it except as it was earned through construction, public lands could not be taken up in areas reserved for the railroad's lieu land selections, and the alternate odd-numbered sections lying within the limits of the grant—as mapped by the railroad—were withheld from settlement. In the case of earned lands, the railroad company deliberately delayed taking final steps to secure title in order to escape taxation. The grant was never recaptured, and popular resentment against the Northern Pacific became so strong that the company was viewed almost as the archenemy of the public.

Washington's economic progress depended upon the completion of the Northern Pacific Railroad; Oregon's geographic position was such that it could contemplate several railroad connections. The Northern Pacific line down the Columbia River was one, but equally important were proposals (1) to build up the Columbia and Snake rivers to a junction point on the Union Pacific, (2) to cut across the Cascades and join the Willamette Valley by rail with the Central Pacific at a point in northern Nevada, and (3) to cross over the Siskiyou Mountains from the Rogue River Valley to the Sacramento and a connection with the Central Pacific. All these proposals were feasible, but most Oregonians felt compelled to choose among them, not realizing that three of the four lines would be completed between 1883 and 1888.

To inhabitants of the Willamette Valley, railroad projects had local as well as transcontinental importance because they would offer competition for river boats and, it was hoped, cut the costs of transportation and open up fertile farmlands otherwise lacking in service. Early surveys proposed to link the upper Valley with northern California, drawing off trade to San Francisco; but some Oregonians, notably those of Portland, preferred a line that would run up the Valley, cut across the mountains and join the Central Pacific in northern Utah, thus avoiding the San Francisco magnet of trade. However, no one opposed a Valley railroad; rather, many were eager to get their fingers in the building of one. For a time Valley projects were enmeshed in a web of promotional rivalry and financial intrigue.

Not one, but two Oregon Central Railroads were incorporated; one by a group of Portland capitalists and citizens of the west side of the Willamette River; the other, by men whose interests lay on the east side. Congress authorized a grant of 5,000,000 acres in the Willamette, Umpqua, and Rogue valleys to subsidize a road, but left it up to the state legislature to decide which company was to receive it. The west side company was the first to organize, but the east side one with great fanfare and celebration began actual construction. At this point, Ben Holladay, the big man of California's overland express and coastal shipping who probably had a hand in the situation from the beginning, offered to take over the east side company if he were assured that it would get the land grant. The legislature was pliable to the Holladay party. The west side company having been disqualified on a legal technicality, the east side road received the grant. The losers were indignant, but most of them were also astute; they eventually sold their assets to Holladay on the best terms they could get.

The Oregon Central and its land grant became a part of Holladay's Oregon and California Railroad and by September, 1870, the tracks reached Salem. A year later, trains rolled into Eugene. By the end of 1872, service extended to Roseburg. There the Oregon and California rested for more than a decade.

Cooke was bankrupted in 1873; Holladay fared better for a while. He brought Willamette River steamboats under his control, and his uncompleted railroad served as a feeder to the water routes. Farmers who had supported Holladay because they hoped competition between rails and river boats would bring down freight rates were shocked to find they still had to pay "all the traffic would bear" and the Valley was still dominated by Portland.

The European and Oregon Land Company was both a land sales office and a colonizing agency for the Oregon and California Railroad. From its offices in San Francisco and New York it offered land at moderate prices to encourage sales. But these were disappointing; so too were the road's revenues. Local agriculture was inadequate to sustain it; much of the land grant was covered with virgin timber not yet wanted in the market. Mines in southern Oregon which were expected to bring in large revenues failed to produce. Bondholders, oversold on the O&C's prospects, became increasingly disgruntled.

The Valley and Oregon as yet had no transcontinental connection. Efforts to get one—several if possible—nevertheless continued. One company proposed to connect with the Union Pacific via the Columbia and Snake rivers; another, promoted by B. J. Pengra who had been the front man for the west side road in the Oregon Central scramble, sought a connection with the Central Pacific at Winnemucca, Nevada, which would open up the Klamath region. Both companies applied for land grants, but Congress by the mid-seventies had become skittish about public criticism of its openhanded generosity for western railroads and there seemed little prospect of a forthcoming grant.

HENRY VILLARD

The answer to the Northwest's quest for a completed transcontinental connection came from an unexpected source. German-born Henry Villard had only an academic knowledge of railroad finance when he first came to Oregon in 1873 to represent German bondholders in Holladay's O&C Railroad.[1] Immediately enthusiastic about the possibilities of the region's economic development, he took over the O&C on behalf of the investors, and after acquiring Holladay's Willamette River steamers, he purchased for $5,000,000 the OSN, which had been recovered by its original Portland owners after Cooke's bankruptcy. These holdings Villard combined with Dr. Dorsey Baker's short line railway from Wallula to Walla Walla to form the Oregon Railway and Navigation

---

[1] James B. Hedges, *Henry Villard and the Railways of the Northwest* (1930); Henry Villard, *Early History of Transportation in Oregon*, Oswald Garrison Villard, ed. (1944).

Company. Villard's share in this operation was carried by the Oregon Improvement Company, a holding company through which he also proposed to develop the region's iron and coal resources to build a steel industry.

By the time Villard had these plans laid out, he had built a railroad up the Columbia; in November, 1882, Portland had unbroken service to Walla Walla's wheat fields and Villard had found a way to make the OR&N a part of a transcontinental line. In 1881, skillfully concealing his purpose, he approached a group of eastern bankers and investors, asking for $8,000,000 to use as he wished. With this fund, usually referred to as the Blind Pool, he bought stock in the Northern Pacific until he had enough to demand representation on the board of directors. After a short and violent struggle Villard gained control of the board and became its president.

Persuaded that once the rails were laid the Pacific Northwest's rapid economic development would more than repay the tremendous capital outlay, Villard pushed completion of the Northern Pacific. From 1881 to 1883 crews moved like armies across plains and through mountains, extending the rails into country formerly traveled only by pack animals. Engineers simultaneously pressed forward from both terminals. From Glendive, Montana, they carried the line up the Yellowstone Valley, through Bozeman Pass to the headwaters of the Missouri, and through Mullan Pass to the Little Blackfoot River. From Wallula on the Columbia River gangs of Chinese laborers toiled on a right-of-way across the plateau to Lake Pend Oreille and Clark's Fork. Tunnels were bored through mountain barriers. Bridges spanned the rivers, and trestles carried track over ravines. On Clark's Fork, men strained to penetrate dense forests which presented "a solid rampart of trunks" and turned broadest day into "somber twilight." In the winter thousands of men struggled through deep snow to clear the grade and lay track. At some points in the gorge whole mountainsides were blasted into the canyons below.

The trains were soon running from Portland to St. Paul. Villard drove the traditional gold spike at Independence Creek sixty miles west of Helena on September 8, 1883. As his special train moved west, villages, towns and crossroads held celebrations. At Portland the city fathers, business firms, and private citizens vied with one another in lavish decorations, pageants and parades. At Tacoma, where an immense triple arch spanned Pacific Avenue, hours of oratory and feasting filled the days and nights. Seattle, sulking over neglect, nevertheless entertained its guests at an immense barbecue and clambake. It was an irony that while Villard was receiving encomiums in the Northwest,

311

his enemies within the board of the Northern Pacific were finagling the stock to remove him from the presidency. But the Northwest finally had a transcontinental railroad.

The people of Puget Sound were encouraged by the completion of the Northern Pacific main line, but far from satisfied. The route by way of Portland placed them at the mercy of that city. Tacoma demanded immediate construction of the Cascade branch which would give it a direct route across the mountains, down the Yakima Valley to Ainsworth and the main line. The Oregon and Transcontinental, Villard's holding company, now controlled by Northern Pacific's Elijah Smith, resisted the Tacoma promotion. Meanwhile, Seattle citizens were loudly indignant over the Northern Pacific's refusal to build northward to their city, and Arthur Denny, one of the city's founders, threatened that if the Northern Pacific did not, Seattle would build its own railroad.

Seattle's struggle to become a railroad terminus is an important and illuminating chapter in the city's history. The townspeople did attempt their own railroad despite Villard's warning that this would be suicidal. There was something at once bold and amusing in the way they organized to win by energy and "indomitable spirit" what was not to be had by congressional largesse or Wall Street legerdemain. The idea that a railroad could be built by calling out the community to dig a roadbed was indicative of spirit, if not of practicality.

The town did not stop with a pick and shovel brigade—it had adventures with large-scale promotion and financing. Two railroad companies were formed—the Seattle and Walla Walla, and the Seattle Lake Shore and Eastern. The Seattle and Walla Walla represented local enterprise. The Lake Shore and Eastern was organized originally by local people, of whom Thomas Burke, an enterprising young lawyer, and Daniel H. Gilman were the leaders. But it was launched with the express intention of finding in the East investment capital that would not demand control of the enterprise. Gilman managed to raise enough funds in New York to undertake construction. Organization and financing was patterned after that of the transcontinentals. The company would issue stocks and sell bonds; a construction company (preferably composed of Seattle men) would take assets of the road in payment for building. So far as possible, both railroad and construction companies would dodge the problem of raising cash by depending upon the credit of the contractors who did the actual work.[2]

Just where the railroad was to go was vague: from Seattle east into the Cascades, where it was believed there were iron deposits; across the

[2] Robert C. Nesbit, *He Built Seattle: a Biography of Judge Thomas Burke* (1961).

312

mountains to some point in eastern Washington, and perhaps through the Rockies and across the plains to a terminal in Iowa. Unfortunately the promoters' visions exceeded their ability to perform. Burke was fertile in ideas if not in expedients. He outlined the possibilities of the road so persuasively that presently the directors were, like Stephen Leacock's plumed knight, "riding off in all directions" but arriving nowhere. One section of track penetrated the Cascades and stopped. Another ran west from Spokane toward Okanogan and stopped. A third started bravely north from Seattle toward Bellingham and stopped. What was built was poorly done; the eastern investors became increasingly unhappy with the whole enterprise.

In 1890 the Lake Shore and Eastern was purchased by the Northern Pacific. Although it had primarily a nuisance value, its history illustrates the ambitions of western promoters and the misuse of eastern capital. The promoters seem to have lost little or nothing, but they failed to win much either. In later years, Burke had a career of local usefulness to James J. Hill, who was to provide the answer to Seattle's prayers for a railroad.

The years 1883–1893 saw the main network of transcontinentals completed except for the Milwaukee line. In 1884 the Oregon Short Line, which had been proceeding from its junction with the Union Pacific at Granger, Wyoming, northwest through the Snake River Valley, met the tracks of the Oregon Railway and Navigation Company at Huntington, Oregon. And Idaho, which previously had exported principally gold, began to ship out cattle and fine horses by the carload. By 1889 farm produce and lumber to the value of $9,500,000 moved over the "Short Line." In 1887 the Northern Pacific had finished its Cascade Division through the Yakima Valley and Stampede Pass to Puget Sound. That same year the Oregon and California, now a part of the Southern Pacific system, closed the gap between Roseburg and San Francisco. Thus Tacoma had one direct route to the east, and Portland had two to the east and one to California. With the completion of the Great Northern Railway in 1892, Seattle became a full-fledged western terminus.

THE GREAT NORTHERN RAILWAY

The Great Northern illustrates how a complex of local lines could be made strong by knitting them together into a single system. Unlike the Northern Pacific, the Great Northern was not a land-grant railroad.

James Jerome Hill and his Scottish Canadian associates started out with several short lines in Minnesota and North Dakota, and moved toward Winnipeg and a connection with the Canadian Pacific. The St. Paul-Minneapolis and Manitoba was a well-built line, serving fine agricultural country, and under good management it developed a modest but profitable traffic. By 1886 Hill was ready to project more ambitious plans. He promoted the Montana Central, which was built between Helena, Great Falls, and Butte. In 1887, Hill's road from Minot, North Dakota, joined the Montana Central, and tapped the Rocky Mountain copper mines.

The final step was to complete the section between Helena and Puget Sound. Again Hill supported local efforts, this time in Seattle, Everett, Fairhaven, and Vancouver, British Columbia. In 1889–1890 the Seattle and Montana Railroad carried its line from Seattle north to Everett and thence up the Skykomish River. Tracks were laid by other local companies between Vancouver and Fairhaven, and between Fairhaven and Everett. In 1889, under the name of the Great Northern, Hill merged the lines into one system. On January 6, 1893, the last spike of Seattle's transcontinental was driven home at the tunnel mouth on the west slope of the Cascades.

The Great Northern was built without benefit of land grant or federal loan. Other transcontinentals went into receivership during the lean nineties; but Jim Hill's road paid dividends. Management, like the original construction, was conservative, efficient, and energetic. By 1900, the Great Northern had swallowed up the Northern Pacific in everything but name; by 1902, Hill, with J. P. Morgan's backing, made a bid for a larger empire and ran afoul of Edward H. Harriman who controlled the Union and Southern Pacific lines. The war of the giants ended when they combined to form the Northern Securities Company. This holding company was dissolved by court order in 1904, but "Empire-builder" Hill's Great Northern had become a part of Morgan's banking empire.

Not all small lines grew into or were absorbed by large ones. The construction of feeder lines in the Northwest distributed the benefits of the transcontinentals over the greater part of the region, but the success of these short lines depended largely upon local conditions. Port Townsend derived no benefit from a Tacoma connection. Similarly, transverse feeder lines which cut across the Willamette Valley proved disappointing. The Oregon and Southeastern, affectionately called Old Slow and Easy, was "a homely short line that meanders up the valley of the Row River a matter of twenty miles and finally bogs down in the middle of nowhere." The Corvallis and Yaquina Bay Railroad, "the frustration route," found everything perverse and never achieved the dream of its promoters.[3] Most of the small lines in the Northwest failed or became capillaries in the regional distribution system.

The railroads did not revolutionize the region's economy or change to any remarkable degree its patterns of trade.[4] But completion of the transcontinental arteries did give life to a first-class boom.

[3] Randall V. Mills, *Railroads Down the Valley; Some Short Lines of the Oregon Country* (1950).

[4] Robert W. Fogel, "A Quantitative Approach to the Study of Railroads in American Economic Growth; A Report of Some Preliminary Findings," *The Journal of Economic History*, June 1962; Leland H. Jenks, "Railroads as an Economic Force in American Development," *The Journal of Economic History*, May 1944.

CHAPTER TWENTY

The Boom of the Eighties

THE BOOM that followed completion of the Northern Pacific Railroad was in part a consequence of the migration of farming populations to new agricultural areas in the Puget Sound country and eastern Washington and Oregon. It was also an urbanization movement which brought west thousands of people seeking new opportunities in the rising cities. This influx was further stimulated by accelerated exploitation of the region's chief natural resources.

People were probably the most significant initial factor of growth since they were both producers and consumers. In 1880, the Pacific Northwest, through immigration and natural increase, had 132,500 more heads to count than in 1870. In the decade of the 1880s, the increase was almost a half-million. Washington alone added 275,000 persons. Governor Miles C. Moore reported the arrival of 95,000 immigrants in the two years 1887–1889, a number greater than the entire territorial population had been in 1880.

Hardly less impressive was the census report of a fourfold increase in true values of real and personal property to a total of one and a half billion dollars, and again, Washington accounted for half of this increase. Since "true value" was a "fair selling price" in the opinion of local persons presumably familiar with trends, Washington's jump from $62,000,000 to $760,000,000 in ten years is a useful indicator of boom conditions. The Territory's assessed valuation of property and value of manufactures also stood ten times higher in 1890 than in 1880, a rate of growth unequaled in any other state. During this same decade, the sum of debts incurred in Washington increased 3253 percent, the largest increase in the nation and affording an interesting comparison with Oregon, where indebtedness increased 173 percent.

THE PROGRESS OF AGRICULTURE, 1880–1890

The Sound country had never been considered good for farming. Bitter experience taught that soil which supported evergreen forests did not easily produce wheat. In 1880 there were fewer than a thousand farms between the Sound and the Cascades, and townspeople of western Washington ate flour and provisions imported from Portland and beef from Ellensburg and eastern ranges. Yet bottomlands of river valleys were fertile. Between 1888 and 1890 Puyallup hop ranches increased from 500 to 5000 acres, yielding one to four tons per acre. To the north, as La Conner tidelands were diked, oats and hay were grown with great success and some farmers raised vegetables which, because of superior size and quality, sold for seed at fancy prices. These were the exceptional producers, but they attracted wide notice. Eighteen hundred new farms were established between the Sound and the Cascade Mountains within ten years, and crop values increased by nearly $2,000,000. This expansion was modest compared with that of the wheat lands across the mountains, but because of their specialties, high per-acre yields, and nearness to emerging cities, the Sound counties assumed new importance in agriculture.

The building of railroads up the Columbia River and through the Walla Walla and Palouse country had the same tonic effect that the Erie Canal had had in New York and Ohio half a century earlier. In ten years some 2,500,000 acres of agricultural land were opened in Idaho, the Columbia Basin, and Wallowa district of Oregon. Six hundred thousand acres were put in cultivation in the Snake River Valley of southern Idaho. By 1890 nearly 15,000 new farms had been established, and the value of their produce sold was 40 percent of the total for the three states. Here was a development that revealed the new Northwest's agricultural potential. Acre for acre, wheat harvests ran higher in the Palouse than in Dakota's famed Red River Valley; potato yields were greater than Maine's. Topsoils several feet deep produced repeated crops of grain, and needed nothing more than alternate-summer fallow. Failures were almost unknown and early settlers who paid $5 to $10 an acre had no great difficulty paying their debts and putting money aside, though they had little capital to start with.

In the Palouse country, farmers plowed the steep slopes, precariously perched on horse-drawn gang plows. Twenty mules or horses were needed to pull harvesters or headers. In the Umatilla area, where gentler grades permitted, the steam combine was introduced in the late 1880s. In the Inland Empire, agriculture was commercial from the beginning, and successful farmers were those equipped with improved machinery, who used the large-scale methods that had proved efficient in California and the Midwest. Farming the "Golden Land" was a different operation from that of the first Northwest settlers whose crude single-share plows turned the soil of small prairies and narrow valleys.[1]

Where plows and harvesters invaded, open ranges disappeared. But there was ample grazing in the more arid and inaccessible parts of the Columbia Basin and in eastern Oregon where steers roamed at large for most of the year. Ben Snipes and his partners ranged cattle from the Yakima Valley to the Columbia. Feudal lords acquired vast acreages in southeastern Oregon through range warfare, purchase, preemption, and abuses of federal land acts designed for small settlers. The small settlers gave up.

In 1872, Peter French and Dr. Hugh J. Glenn moved from northern California into Harney County and built the famous "P" Ranch on the upper Blitzen River. Henry Miller and Charles Lux, also California ranchers, extended their holdings in the same area in 1883. As the "LF" ranch expanded, Miller "could travel from the Kern River in California up through Nevada, to the Malheur River region and not spend a night off his land."[2]

Cattle from eastern Oregon and Washington stocked Montana and Wyoming ranches. In 1880, 170,000 head were driven from Pacific Northwest states into Wyoming; from there to the Black Hills of the Dakotas or to Kansas markets. The drives from eastern Washington followed the Mullan Road to Montana; from eastern Oregon herds moved to stock Snake River Valley ranches. But the principal market for beef was found in Portland, Puget Sound towns, and San Francisco. Harvey Scott, noting that cattle production in populated areas of the Midwest was 25 percent greater than on western ranges, predicted that in the Pacific Northwest the stock business of the future would be very different from that of the past. "There will be no great roving bands, no gigantic 'round-ups,' no big annual drives; but there will be more and better cattle for market each fall, and they will yield a larger aggregate profit than formerly."

Stock men of the Inland Empire took pride in their horses, too. It was said that 100,000 horses in Yakima's Horse Heaven country bore

[1] Giles French, *The Golden Land: a History of Sherman County, Oregon* (1958).

[2] George F. Brimlow, *Harney County, Oregon, and its Range Land* (1951), 177.

Ben Snipes' brand. Pendleton sent riding horses and draught animals to farm and city alike, and developed breeds for every purpose from racing to hauling streetcars. The continuing annual roundups at Pendleton and the Ellensburg rodeo recall these early days when the two towns built their reputations on their horses.

Willamette Valley sheep men crossed the Cascades where they found pastures for bands of 1500 to 12,000 head, and, in good years, made 100 percent profits. Welsh-born John Griffith Edwards had fought the cattle barons in Wyoming before he moved into Wasco County and took over the famous Hay Creek Ranch—"the greatest Merino breeding station in the world"—where 50,000 animals grazed.[3] In later years buyers from all over the world came to select rams from his flocks of Rambouillet.

Herders bitterly contested with cattle ranchers for control of ranges, and were forced to drive their flocks to the higher feeding grounds well up in the mountains. Eastern Oregon's Harney Valley became an important sheep area, and in 1890 Umatilla, Morrow, and Crook counties together reported 572,000 head. Many Washington bands wintered on the Snake River and summered in Idaho mountains. Others from south of the Snake went to the Blue Mountains; those in central Washington to Colville or to summer ranges in the Coeur d'Alenes.

In five years of the early eighties eastern Oregon doubled its wool clip, from 3,800,000 to 7,700,000 pounds. Although the western Oregon product generally was considered of better quality than that of the interior, the eastern production far outstripped the western in quantity. One hundred thousand sheep were sheared near Sprague in 1889. Numbers of animals were driven to Montana, and the railroads carried them in double-decked cars. The sheep industry declined in importance with increased settlement. However, 10,000,000 pounds of wool were shipped through Pendleton and The Dalles in the early nineties and at the end of the century Pendleton was the chief primary market for wool in the United States.

But the 1880s were also hard years for stockmen. The winter of 1880–1881 was cold and no provision had been made to feed range animals. In 1884–1885 the worst snow storm in Pacific Northwest history destroyed whole herds, and a Wasco County rhymester lamented:

> If I can make enough in time,
> To take me out of this cold clime,
> You bet your life I'll stomp away
> From Oregon and the John Day.[4]

[3] Phil F. Brogan, *East of the Cascades* (1964), 111; E. R. Jackman and R. A. Long, *The Oregon Desert* (1964).

[4] French, *op. cit.*, 85.

Eastern Washington and Montana bore the brunt of the snows in 1886 and 1887, and cattle raising no longer held its early promise for those who had to start from scratch.

Nor did agriculture in general remain as substantially important to the economy as other enterprises. According to the federal census, in 1880 Oregon's farms represented nearly half its total assessed wealth; ten years later they constituted only 27 percent. Washington's farms declined from 31 to 14 percent of that Territory's assessed valuation. In Idaho the figure remained unchanged at 18 percent. One explanation suggests the unstable character of an agricultural boom. For example, Northwest production of wheat increased steadily, but not spectacularly, from about 11,000,000 to 18,000,000 bushels between 1880 and 1890. Export of wheat rose sharply in 1881–1882 when about 10,000,000 bushels were exported, and dropped to almost half that amount by 1885. In the last two years of the 1880s exports were less than production at the beginning of the decade. The Northwest produced more wheat than it could market, and the indebted marginal producer could hardly make it in a competitive and fluctuating world market.

Another explanation of the decline in the importance of agriculture is found in the increased exploitation of natural resources and rapid growth of cities. The new importance attached to the resources is illustrated in the development of the lumber industry of western Washington.

LUMBERING AND THE LUMBER TRADE IN THE EIGHTIES

Paul Bunyan, hero of the logging camps, scarcely showed his strength in Washington until the eighties; then suddenly he became an amazing giant. Hustling to keep up with the whining saws, which in 1884 consumed 1,000,000 board feet a day, he hewed down the forests along the shores of Puget Sound and inland up the river courses. Pope and Talbot mills at Port Ludlow and Port Gamble rafted their logs from Hood Canal and the western shore of the Sound. Seattle and Tacoma were both mill towns. One hundred and sixty million board feet were cut in 1880; a decade later the harvest passed the billion mark. Southwest of Olympia in the Satsop and Chehalis districts, magnificent forests fell to the axe and were brought down to tidewater mills by logging railroads. Only half of Thurston County's original stand of timber remained in 1890.

Here was an industry with a plentiful supply of cheap raw materials for which under boom conditions there was a thriving market. Standing timber cost but a third to a half of the average cost for the country as a whole, and while the value of sawed lumber was correspondingly lower, the margin of profit was still sufficiently large to attract capital for plants.

The average mill in Oregon in 1890 was a $25,000 plant. At Port Blakeley near Seattle a new mill boasted engines of 3000 horsepower and saws that handled 150-foot logs and cut 300,000 board feet in a day. Operating figures for the lumber industry in Washington as a whole ran ten to fifteen times larger than they had a decade before. Logging camps and mills represented a $20,000,000 investment, delivered a $15,000,000 annual product, and supported 10,000 men on a $4,000,000 payroll in 1890.

Lumbering in the Northwest was wasteful. Stumps were cut twenty feet from the ground because the butt was shaky and full of pitch. Much good wood was left on the ground. At the mills, huge double-bladed rotary saws at every turn converted a half inch of log into sawdust and raised mountains of slabs and mill ends to be burned. Logs and timbers were cut at random lengths, without regard for standard grades and dimensions. As better and more powerful machinery was introduced, some of these practices were corrected. The donkey engine doing the work of many oxen could snake great logs out of the woods with less destruction of young growth. For large logs, the band saw proved more efficient and less wasteful than the rotary type. It was only as stumpage values increased that there was real incentive to develop methods that utilized the entire tree. Little regard was shown for conservation or planned cutting until demands of the trade increased and the forests began to shrink.

Northwest lumber had long been rather like Robinson Crusoe's pile of gold; there was lots of it but it was worth little since there was so little opportunity to use it. The railroads did not appreciably change this situation, but they did enlarge the local market and enable shipment of substantial quantities of lumber to the Plains states.

California remained the lumberman's best customer, and coastal shipping rose to nearly 200,000,000 board feet in 1883–1884 and to 323,600,000 in 1889. Foreign exports also increased. Scores of square-riggers sheltered in the protected harbor at Port Townsend while their captains negotiated for cargoes at mill ports on the Sound. One hundred and forty-eight vessels, registered in a dozen different countries, made up the Sound's lumber fleet. Norwegian barks cleared for Melbourne, and Chilean ships carried rough lumber to Valparaiso. American ships weighed anchor at Port Blakeley, bound for Buenos Aires, Boston, Honolulu, Brisbane, or Shanghai. Swedish vessels left for London; British ones for Adelaide and Sydney. Some cargoes amounted to 1,000,000 feet of lumber and were valued at $10,000 to $20,000.

However, these were the exceptions; ordinary cargoes ranged from $1000 to $6000 in value and many were small, worth only a few hundred dollars. The export trade was not, therefore, as valuable as the number of participating ships would suggest. Lumbering was geared mainly to domestic markets and only the surplus found its way to foreign ports. Lumber amounted to little more than $1,000,000 in a $15,000,000 export trade.

However, domestic trade accounted for the significant gains. In Washington, where cargo mills had been cutting only one-tenth of their product for home consumption, firms like Stetson and Post of Seattle began producing entirely for local needs. A boom in building accompanied the influx of immigrants and the mills were quick to respond. Treasury officials estimated that this local trade exceeded the California trade in 1885 and doubled it in the next five years.

The development of the lumber industry in the area tributary to Portland resulted from increasing trade with the Midwest. Experimental consignments to Denver, Salt Lake City, and Omaha grew to shipments amounting to $5,000,000 a month, with a single mill sending as much as 26,000,000 feet to these cities of the Rockies and High Plains. Favorable railway freight rates gave Oregon an advantage over Puget Sound in commerce with these points, and for a number of years Oregon claimed this market as hers exclusively, save for the cedar shingles which Washington sent to Colorado, Utah, Iowa, Illinois, and Ohio. But shipping rates, shifting and unpredictable, worked as often against the Northwest as for it. Portland's trade with Denver was highly sensitive to changes in the Union Pacific rate level, and Puget Sound found it difficult to supply the Montana market because of rates that favored St. Paul even though that Midwest city was much farther away. Rail charges spelled the difference between success and failure, and bitter struggles were waged between rival communities and different sections to secure revisions in their favor. Even with this wider, more complex pattern of competition, the trade of the Northwest with the interior increased encouragingly. Northwest lumbermen might have to share their new markets with producers of southern pine, but their own production grew in gratifying fashion, and became the foundation of a trade to be expanded in the future.

INDUSTRIAL MINING

When surface and placer mining gave over to quartz mining a new era began in the industry. A class of professionals specialized in prospecting for quartz veins and their discoveries, worked only long enough to hold the claim and to sink shafts deep enough to show strike and dip, were sold for development. In Idaho and western Montana and sections of eastern Washington where mining had languished since the middle sixties, new machinery and large-scale processes of extraction and reduction revived the industry and made it a principal enterprise.

Mining engineers succeeded the prospector and hit-and-miss miner of the old days. Experts examined the fields and ledges, developed hydraulic machinery to exploit more stubborn placer fields, or built shafts, elevators and tunnels along the richest veins. Elaborate stamp mills and concentrators handled complex ores, separating gold, silver, and lead, for no marketable minerals were ignored. Miners used steam drills as well as picks and shovels. They lived, not always happily, in company towns and toiled for wages that were not always commensurate with their labor and its hazards.

The problems of the new era can be illustrated in the story of Bunker Hill and Sullivan, two famous lead-silver mines at Wardner, Idaho. In 1885 an old prospector, Noah S. Kellogg, working up Milo Gulch, found ironstone outcrops, and his companion, Phil O'Rourke, found "Glittering Galena," evidences of the ores. These discoveries immediately brought Kellogg into litigation with men who claimed half interest as grubstakers. The claimants won, and James Wardner, one of the victors, worked the surface for the choicest ores. Lacking capital for stamp mills and concentrators, he prevailed upon the Helena Concentrating Company to provide machinery which brought enormous profits to them but practically none to the other owners. At this time (1887), Wardner asked Simeon G. Reed to buy them out. It was learned afterward that Wardner had "prepared" the mine for Reed's inspection by exposing a high-grade deposit and removing the low-grade ore. Twenty-one feet of lead ore on the surface sold the mines.[5]

Reed invested close to $500,000 in the Bunker Hill and Sullivan Concentrating and Mining Company, capitalized at $3,000,000. In 1887, the operating profit was $29,000; in 1891, the deficit, $130,000. Reed was plagued by labor troubles and mismanagement; in 1894 he sold to a British syndicate which through the reports of the famous mining engineer, John Hays Hammond, was aware of the mines' potentials. Between 1894 and 1900, the net assets of the company rose to more than $4,000,000, and $750,000 was paid in dividends when it was sold to Donald O. Mills of New York City. The mines at Wardner have been consistently profitable producers ever since.

By 1900 mining was too expensive an operation for local capital to handle, and only incidental profits accrued to the communities in which

[5] T. A. Rickard, "The Bunker Hill Enterprise, Part III," *Mining and Scientific Press*, January 24, 1920.

A prospector heads into the Rockies. Prospecting was usually a lonely business.

Placer or surface mining was any method of getting gold-bearing ore out of sand, gravel, or loose rock. RIGHT. A Chinese uses a rocker to wash gold out of stream gravel. Chinese worked over abandoned stream bars since they were prohibited from taking up claims.

Mining

In lode or quartz mining, rock brought to the surface had to be crushed to extract the ore. The arrastra, of Spanish origin, was a simple, crude crusher. The wheel, rotated by water or horse power, drags stones over the ore in a circular, rock-lined pit.

BELOW. A gold dredge, Idaho City. This was the most elaborate method of washing ore out of stream gravel and sand.

324

LEFT. *Miners at the Trade Dollar Mine, Silver City, Idaho. At extreme right,* the man standing with a dinner pail is William D. Haywood, soon to be secretary of the Western Federation of Miners and later a founder of the Industrial Workers of the World. ABOVE RIGHT. *Labor unrest troubled a number of major lode mining districts at the turn of the century. The Bunker Hill and Sullivan concentrator at Kellogg was destroyed by dynamiting.* LEFT. *Federal troops were sent to maintain martial law.*

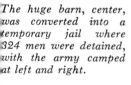

The huge barn, center, was converted into a temporary jail where 324 men were detained, with the army camped at left and right.

LEFT. *Warren, Idaho, in the Salmon River mountains, was originally a placer mining town. Lode mining kept the town going after the initial boom. When gold was discovered in Idaho in 1860, gold seekers poured in, towns grew up overnight and often became ghost towns almost as rapidly.*

Bullion Mine, Idaho, 1884. Today, the annual incomes from minerals in Oregon, Washington and Idaho are respectively $68½, $81 and $86 millions. These minerals include industrial (sand, gravel, and crushed rock) and base metals (lead, zinc, copper, gold, and silver).

Silver City, Idaho, 1895, at the height of the later mining boom when the Trade Dollar and Black Jack lode mines tunneled into Florida Mountain. The Morning Star Mine, upper center, was an important early producer.

Sluicing, another placer mining operation. The water flow is so gigantic that the men directing it are hardly visible.

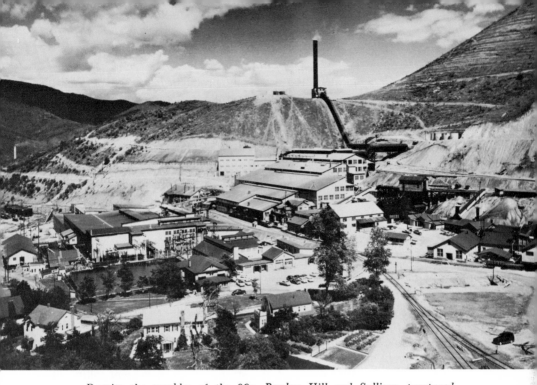

Despite the troubles of the 90s, Bunker Hill and Sullivan prospered. This electrolytic zinc plant at Kellogg, about 1940, is only one of several major installations. An estimated two billion dollars worth of wealth has come from this district. BELOW. The Anaconda Company's Berkeley Pit at Butte, Montana. Upper left, the new copper concentrator now located close to both open pit and underground mining will reduce production costs and extend the life of the mine indefinitely. The new concentrator can treat 42,000 tons of ore a day.

the mines were located. Returns from products extracted at Wardner in 1889 were $17,344,600; the payroll for 4500 men employed was $3,300,000.

URBAN EXPANSION

Farming, lumber, and mining underlined, each in its own way, the importance of natural resources to the development of the Pacific Northwest. More significant perhaps was the vigorous growth of cities. In some respects this growth stood out in sharp contrast to the scattering of population over wide farm areas, and to the increase of exploitative industries which did not draw a heavy population. How much farms, mills, and mines contributed to the rapid growth of cities is difficult to determine. The towns' speculative expansion, having little connection with the development of regional resources, was a clear manifestation of the boom spirit of the times. On the other hand, the lively growth of these communities was part of a strong urban movement taking place all over the country. The trend was as definite in frontier areas as in older industrial sections. The number of cities was indeed small; such was the pattern throughout the trans-Mississippi West. Nevertheless, the rise of Seattle and Tacoma on the Sound and of Spokane in the Inland Empire shifted the balance of metropolitan centers in the Northwest to one considerably more decentralized and complex than that of the earlier period of Portland's preeminence.

Bearing in mind the census bureau definition (used until 1950) of "urban"—cities and unincorporated places having 2500 inhabitants or more—the importance of urban growth, 1880–1910, is demonstrable. During the eighties, Oregon's city dwellers increased from 14.8 percent of the total population to 26.8 percent. By 1900 the figure had risen to 32.2 percent; in 1910 it was 45.6 percent. In Washington the percentages were even more striking. The population in 1880 was 90 percent rural. Ten years later, when the state was admitted to the Union, it was 35.6 percent urban, and by 1910, 53 percent. This meant that migration to Oregon and Washington during these years was to a surprising degree an urban movement.

Statistically, one in five of Oregon's newcomers (1880–1890) could be found in Portland and 41 percent in the urban counties, Multnomah and Marion. Three urban counties in Washington (King, Pierce, and Spokane) received half of the new population, and the three cities, Seattle, Tacoma, and Spokane, gained one of every three new residents

328

in the Territory. Thus while rural counties received their thousands, cities counted their tens of thousands. Portland jumped from 17,500 to 46,385. Seattle, with 3533 persons in 1880, was nearly as large as Portland in 1890 (42,837). In the same decade, Tacoma enjoyed a similar growth (1098 to 36,006) and Spokane, scarcely more than a village of 350, emerged as a lively center of nearly 20,000.

Visitors reacted in different ways to these rough, flourishing communities. In 1888 John Muir spoke of Seattle and Tacoma as lively, progressive, and aspiring places, young and loose-jointed but "fast taking on the forms and manners of old cities, putting on airs, some would say, like boys in haste to be men." A year later Rudyard Kipling commented on the way Portland men fought tooth and nail for wharf and rail projects, and worked their lives out for what they considered the city's rightful preeminence. "All this is excellent and exactly suitable to the opening of a new country, but when a man tells you it is civilization, you object." At Tacoma, the British author found a scene of feverish activity, and apparently shared the sentiments of a friend who told him that "they are all mad here, all mad. A man nearly pulled a gun on me because I didn't agree with him that Tacoma was going to whip San Francisco on the strength of carrots and potatoes." Kipling stopped briefly at Tacoma, then escaped to Victoria "to draw breath." An American city at the height of a boom was too much for him.

The transition from wilderness to city produced some odd contrasts. In Portland, one could sit in a mahogany-panelled barroom, complete with telephone and clicker, and a half hour later be in the depths of a forest (and for that matter one can still do this today). Tacoma's streets were likely to end abruptly in a 15-foot drop and a patch of blackberries. Telegraph and light wires clung precariously to hastily erected poles. Everywhere was the raw smell of fresh sawdust.

Fire played its part in bringing about change. Kipling, arriving in Seattle only a few weeks after much of its business section had been burned out, spoke of the "horrible black smudge, as though a Hand had come down and rubbed the place smooth." Seattle rose twice in a short space of years: once in the jerry-built wooden structures so characteristic of frontier towns, the second time in buildings of stone and cement.

The new cities had electric lights and gasworks, five-story business blocks, and streetcars nosing their ways about the hills. Portland was said to have the nation's first long distance transmission of electricity when in 1890 it tapped power generated at Oregon City falls to run an electric streetcar up Washington Street.

Compared with California's, the Pacific Northwest's economy was underdeveloped. Its principal industries were extractive, adding little value by manufacture; other manufactures were small enterprises producing for home markets. But the Northwest was not as stifled by lack of capital as had been many older frontiers. Gold mines had built some fortunes that were retained for investment and not wasted wholly in conspicuous consumption. Europeans and easterners invested in lands, mines, and railroads and not all of their moneys were siphoned back to eastern financial centers. San Francisco was the West Coast's money center and California capital was available to Northwest entrepreneurs, especially to those dealing in commodities like lumber that were needed in California. Some Northwesterners were thrifty and they ventured their savings, cautiously to be sure, in safe local enterprises. Earl Pomeroy points out that "if the Western economy sometimes seemed colonial, some of its greatest monopolies were home grown."[6] Such, for example, was the Oregon Steam Navigation Company. But, also, as Pomeroy indicates, the "simple agrarian democracy" of the 1840s had had its day, and forty years later organized economic power was evident everywhere; Portland's leading families—Corbetts, Ladds, Failings, for example—were in trade, banking, transportation, real estate, and, on occasion, in milling, mining, and farming.

The Northwest's commerce and industry which utilized the natural resources of the region expanded largely in response to the needs of the growing population. Portland produced lumber and wood products, "beer and buggies, and bricks and biscuits." By 1890, manufacturing plants in the city added about $13,000,000 in value to the raw materials used. Flour milling was a million-dollar industry, more important to the city than its sawmills. Four railroads poured into Portland's lap the products of mines, forests, and farms, as well as manufactured goods from the East. Portland's rail shipments to the Sound amounted to $750,000, coastwise trade to nearly $5,000,000, and foreign export trade to $6,600,000, 80 percent of it in wheat and flour.

Major lines of manufacturing in Seattle were those related to construction and to foods and clothing. Lumber mills and slaughterhouses, foundries, carpentry and masonry work, canneries and flour mills employed half of the labor force and turned out half of its manufactures. The city had a dozen sawmills by 1890 and nearly as many sash and door and furniture plants. Her manufacturers produced soda crackers and canned salmon; soda water, ice, and cigars; pumps, stump-pullers, and donkey engines; heavy castings, brass machine work, and iron ornaments that added a touch of elegance to residences and shops.

[6] Earl Pomeroy, *The Pacific Slope; a History of California, Oregon, Washington, Idaho, Utah, and Nevada* (1965), 85–86.

TABLE I

Persons Engaged in All Manufacturing, 1880–1890

	1880	1890
Washington	1,147	20,366
Oregon	3,473	18,798
Idaho	388	774
California	43,693	83,642
United States	2,732,595	4,712,622

Source: "Census of Manufactures," Bureau of the Census, 1890. These figures are comparable to each other but not comparable to data from later censuses because of changes in coverage.

Tacoma claimed more lumber-working plants than any other city on the Coast, and more wholesale drygoods, hardware, and grocery establishments than either Seattle or Spokane. Here were located the Northern Pacific Railroad shops, a smelter—the city's bid for importance in heavy industry—and grain elevators of 2,000,000 bushels capacity. Alert to the importance of linking rail and water transportation, Tacoma made much of the network of steamship lines which served other Sound communities twice daily and had San Francisco sailings twice weekly. Wharfage and handling services were provided at one-third the rates charged at Portland, and towing, pilotage, and lighterage costs were a tenth of those on the Columbia. Through these competitive advantages Tacoma sought to challenge Portland's supremacy in the grain trade. Forty-four cargoes, worth nearly $3,000,000, were shipped from Tacoma to England in 1888–1890.

Spokane's rise was meteoric, but businessmen there stoutly insisted theirs was no mushroom growth since it had the strength of a rich surrounding country. The city enjoyed natural advantages. Its waterpower resources were estimated at 150,000 to 215,000 horsepower capacity, and Edison Electric soon installed what was said to be the largest incandescent light plant west of the Rockies. Spokane's strategic location as a rail center and crossroads of stage and wagon routes enabled it to tap the wealth of Palouse grain fields and Coeur d'Alene mines, and gave it a commanding position as a marketing and distribution center for the northern intermountain territory. The general development of this area supported the city, to which twenty villages in the wheat belt to the south looked for equipment and supplies. Several thousand miners in the Idaho mountains had to be fed. This explained the rapid increase of Northern Pacific rail receipts, which soon reached $200,000 a month, and contributed to a $10,000,000 total in transactions for the city's 590 business establishments in 1889. With wool and flour handy for processing and ample supplies of lumber at St. Joe and Coeur d'Alene, Spokane had reason to explaim exuberantly, "Anything can go here with the surrounding country building up."

The boom affected some smaller towns too. Centralia grew in two years from a village of 600 to a trading center of 3000 and thought of itself as the future "great inland metropolis of Western Washington." Ellensburg enjoyed a short period of real estate promotion with schemes for capturing the trade to the Okanogan country and establishing an iron and steel industry that would make it "the Pittsburgh of the West."[7] Port Townsend developed grandiose ideas from the small furnaces at Irondale, and dreamed of a navy yard and seaport seventy miles nearer the ocean than the "overgrown towns" up the Sound.

There was a vast difference, however, between speculative expansion and growth solidly supported by population, resources, and competitive advantages. Astoria, for example, had ambitions equal to those of any booming town. It was ideally located for deep-water navigation and surrounded by rich stands of forest; yet it failed to show significant growth. Rough terrain made the forests inaccessible and there was no hinterland of rich farmlands. The town had no railroad connection until the nineties, and it could not compete with Portland for the grain trade of the interior. While the leading cities attracted the greater population and industry, the smaller ones stabilized as secondary trading centers, their dreams of greatness not destroyed, the realization only postponed. It was in this mood of exuberance and optimism which ignored danger signals that Washington and Idaho moved toward statehood.

[7] Samuel R. Mohler, "Boom Days in Ellensburg, 1888–1891," *PNQ*, October 1945.

CHAPTER
TWENTY-ONE

The Statehood
Movement in
Washington and Idaho

WASHINGTON, Montana, and the two Dakotas were admitted to the Union by the Omnibus Bill of 1889. Idaho and Wyoming came in under separate enabling acts passed by Benjamin Harrison's Republican Congress the following year. Each of these territories had a distinctive history, although Washington's was linked with Oregon's until 1853. Territorial government in Idaho and Montana was a natural consequence of the gold rush to the northern Rocky Mountains a decade later, while the early settlement of the Dakotas and Wyoming was part of the movement to the High Plains after the Civil War. Yet, however varied the circumstances of their first development, the territories experienced a common boom growth stimulated by the completion of transcontinental railroads. Each territory gained rapidly in population, and the need for state government increased proportionately. Conversely, expansion in population and economic development promised greater revenues to support state governments.

Territorials felt that statehood was too long deferred. The people of

333

Oregon had won statehood without railroads, as had half a score of other territories earlier in the Mississippi Valley. The general rule was that a territory must contain enough people to elect a representative to the lower house of Congress under the federal ratio (125,000 in 1870), but there had been exceptions. The people of Washington, and to a lesser extent those of Idaho, expected to achieve statehood quickly and easily. To their great disappointment, decades passed before it was won.

STATEHOOD FOR WASHINGTON

In the meantime, territorials reiterated the old themes of dissatisfaction.[1] Washington's territorial courts suffered no scandals involving the integrity of its judges, though they were, as in other territories, politically self-conscious and motivated. But after Stevens' term expired in 1857 some odd characters sat in the governor's chair; three followed in rapid succession between 1857 and 1861; then, between 1866 and 1872, three others sampled the Far West and departed. The problem of absenteeism became so serious that Congress imposed salary deductions for absences without good cause.

Taking the vote for territorial delegate as an indication of local party strength, it would appear that only three times in thirty-six years was the appointed governor not of majority preference. Yet "foreigners" were no more acceptable to Washingtonians than they had been to Oregonians. A correspondent to the *Puget Sound Herald* in 1860 referred to Henry M. McGill, secretary of the Territory and acting governor at the time, as a "stranger, recently exported from the political rubbish floating about Washington [D.C.]." After 1872, four local residents, Elisha P. Ferry, Watson Squire, Eugene Semple, and Miles C. Moore, were appointed governors and served faithfully and well. But these happy instances did not fully placate the territorials. The system, according to Orange Jacobs, Washington Territory's delegate, was "in direct conflict with the sentiments of the American people and the genius of our government."

The citizens had a measure of autonomy in the election of territorial legislators; but here too there were grievances. The legislature was

[1] Earl S. Pomeroy, *Territories and the United States, 1861–1890* (1947); Wilfred Airey, "History of the Constitution and Government of Washington Territory," unpublished thesis, University of Washington, 1945; Keith Murray, "Movement Toward Statehood in Washington," unpublished thesis, University of Washington, 1940; Mary W. Avery, *History and Government of the State of Washington* (1961).

required by its organic act to meet annually, and members were reluctant to give so much time to public affairs. In 1869 Congress permitted biennial sessions, which were then given largely to haggling over the location of public buildings and quarreling with the governors. The lawmakers had broad powers and sometimes contested successfully with governors for control of local patronage. On the other hand, their bills were subject to congressional disapproval and, after 1866, to gubernatorial veto. Congress seldom intervened directly, and only once—in the controversy with the OSN—did it disapprove a western territorial bill. In 1874 governors were empowered to appoint such local officers as school superintendents, auditors, and treasurers. Washingtonians protested vigorously; their remonstrance was heeded and the measure repealed.

Of primary importance in agitation for statehood were the political temper of the Territory and the ambitions of its leaders. Idaho and Washington wanted to escape the influence of Oregon's well-oiled machine. The citizens of each territory, according as they were Republican or Democrat, yearned to share federal goodies distributed to their fellow partisans in the states. But sometimes the admission of a territory hung upon whether its voting habits were agreeable to the party in power.

Statehood was prerequisite to the solution of certain practical problems. Designated lands did not become fully available for educational purposes until a territory was admitted to the Union, and other land grants from the public domain and availability of proceeds from sales of federal lands also depended upon admission. Private titles in tidelands were uncertain, and boundaries between territories remained subject to change by Congress, making dismemberment a real and present danger. Federal appropriations were niggardly, and would doubtless remain so until congressional representatives acquired the political lever of voting power. Population and investment capital could be expected to increase when the national government expressed confidence in an area by granting statehood. Territorial government was, then, an acceptable form of administration only so long as a small population, with insufficient means of its own, found advantage in having the federal treasury pay most of the bills.

Subdividing territories as they became more populous was, of course, a long-standing practice. Washington had once been part of Oregon Territory and Idaho a part of Washington. Idaho lost territory to Montana in 1864 and to Wyoming four years later. On the whole there was little opposition to dividing large, sprawling territories into smaller ones, but in the Inland Empire and the Rocky Mountains the pattern of future state boundaries was not yet clear. The logic of economic geography did not necessarily apply in state-making, and there were no final

335

answers so long as territorial boundaries could be drawn and redrawn at will in Washington, D.C. Statehood would bring a final decision, for the federal constitution protected each state against division except with its own consent.

Such questions were hotly debated. Who could say whether the Walla Walla country should be part of Washington, rather than of Oregon, as Oregonians proposed in 1858? Did the Idaho Panhandle relate more naturally to eastern Washington, or to the mining districts of western Montana? The transfer of Walla Walla to Oregon was viewed by the rest of Washington Territory as outright dismemberment. In Walla Walla itself some sentiment favored the shift; the area was oriented toward Portland by the Columbia River and growth might come more quickly in union with Oregon.[2] Annexation of the Idaho Panhandle to Washington was reasonable and met less resistance. For a time southern Idaho acquiesced and the proposal seemed likely to go through.

If population was the first requirement for statehood, Washington Territory badly needed both Walla Walla and northern Idaho. In 1878 Washington, Idaho, and Wyoming combined could hardly claim a population large enough to entitle them to one representative in the lower house of Congress. However, Congress had made several exceptions to the usual 125,000 minimum; Oregon, Nevada, and Nebraska had all come into the Union with fewer inhabitants.

Washington's First Constitution, 1878

The territorials thought a good case could be made for Washington's admission for reasons of political expediency. The Republicans had barely edged into national power with the disputed election of Rutherford B. Hayes. The citizens of Washington Territory had been strongly Republican since the Civil War, so it would be to the national party's advantage to garner far western votes against the reviving Democracy in the East.

A measure calling for a convention to draw up a state constitution was passed by an unimpressive majority of 4000. In December, 1877, Delegate Orange Jacobs asked Congress for an enabling act to admit Washington as a state as soon as a constitution was written and ratified. Without waiting for Congress to act, the convention assembled at Walla Walla in the summer of 1878.

The constitution there prepared reflected western agrarian views on governmental reform and the fifteen delegates' inexperience in public

[2] C. S. Kingston, "Walla Walla Separation Movement," *WHQ*, April 1933; Merle W. Wells, "Territorial Government in the Inland Empire; the Movement to Create Columbia Territory, 1864–1869," *PNQ*, April 1953.

administration and fiscal matters. The proposed document contained a number of unworkable provisions intended to prevent corruption and the domination of government by private corporations. If a legislator had a personal interest in a bill he was required to declare his interest and abstain from voting. Since treasurers might profit from their office, they were limited to a single term. To prevent watering and inflating stocks, corporations were restricted to issuing securities for labor, services, money, or properties actually received.

In matters of public finance, the convention was so dominated by rural ideas of economy that it failed to consider future requirements of a developing country. Salaries were fixed at low figures. Public indebtedness was limited to $100,000 at any one time and was to be paid off on a ten-year schedule. No state debt was to be contracted for internal improvements. Cities were limited to debts not exceeding 3 percent of property valuations, and no greater amount than could be paid off in twelve years with a 12-mill tax.

In October, 1878, the proposed constitution was referred to the people and, in a very light vote, approved, 6462 to 3231. The legislature then formally memorialized Congress for admission. But Jacobs' request for an enabling act never got out of congressional committee, and the legislature's memorial was ignored. The reasons can only be conjectured. One may have been the opposition from Walla Walla and Portland to a constitution that assumed retention of Walla Walla within the new state. A Walla Walla editor spoke of annexation to Oregon as releasing "our beautiful valley from its death embrace with Puget Sound." Admission of Washington Territory would not be a boon to the Democratic Party in Congress. The strength of Republicans and Democrats was almost in balance. The Republicans controlled the House by a slender margin and Democrats hesitated to grant statehood to a territory that showed every indication of voting Republican.

Statehood Movements of the 1880s

During most of the 1880s, the question of statehood continued to involve Washington and Idaho jointly. The proposal to annex the Idaho Panhandle to Washington appeared regularly in most of the enabling bills introduced into Congress and found favor not only in Washington but in Idaho as well. Separation from southern Idaho appeared to be in the interests of inhabitants of the Panhandle and the real question seemed to be whether the mining communities should join Washington or Montana. Statehood for Idaho as a whole appeared unlikely because of its slow population growth and the raging controversy over Mormonism and the Mormons' political influence in the

337

southern districts. Separation and annexation were thus matters of geography and politics. But the chief obstacle to admitting new states was still the effect this would have on the balance between Republicans and Democrats in Congress. Democrats had been loath to admit Washington Territory in 1878; now with Cleveland and the Democrats at the helm of state, Republicans became equally reluctant.

Montana and Dakota territories, like Washington, aspired to statehood, and the prospect of eight or ten new senators and even half as many representatives appearing in Congress at once raised questions as to their political alignments. Since the Cleveland Democrats controlled both houses by only slender majorities, practical politics plainly counseled a policy of delay. Congress devoted considerable time to lengthy speeches and debates in which the issues (though not the politics) of division, annexation and admission were fully discussed—and no action was taken.

The Democratic dam went out in 1888. Benjamin Harrison defeated Cleveland and the Republicans established clear majorities in both houses of Congress for the first time in ten years. Since it appeared more than probable that most of the new states would be Republican, the lame duck Congress passed an omnibus admission bill and Cleveland signed it on February 22, 1889, a peculiarly appropriate date. The Omnibus Bill, so-called because it included Montana, the Dakotas, and Washington, authorized each territory to elect delegates to a constitutional convention in the summer of 1889, and in the fall to hold elections on ratification and candidates for state and national offices.

The conventions and the constitutions they drew up had so much in common that they were reported and analyzed as a group by observers of the day.[3] The majority of delegates were fairly young men, recent immigrants, fairly well-to-do, well educated, and representative of a wide variety of occupations and enterprises. The constitutions revealed no well-defined symptoms of agrarian radicalism, but their attitudes toward corporations plainly indicated a reform mood, including numerous safeguards against political corruption and economic centralization— generally considered the greatest threats to genuine self-government.

In their zeal to protect society from these evils, the conventions of 1889 and 1890 wrote some of the longer constitutions in American history. Skeptical of the honesty of public officials and fearful of the sinister influence of lobbyists, they multiplied stipulations and provisions, seriously confusing the nature of a constitution with the processes of legislation and administration, and making statutory law a part of their

[3] John D. Hicks, "Six Constitutions of the Far Northwest," *Mississippi Valley Historical Association, Proceedings*, IX, 1917–1918; Frederic L. Paxson, "Admission of the Omnibus States," *Wisconsin Historical Society Proceedings*, 1911.

constitutional law. The constitutions made general pronouncements on corruption and monopoly which were meaningless unless implemented by statutes. On other points they were so specific as to lead later to embarrassment and circumvention.

Washington's Constitutional Convention, 1889

Such general observations can be illustrated in the convention which met in Olympia on July 4, 1889. The delegates—many had lived in the Territory less than fifteen years and only a few had been members of the 1878 convention—represented a wide cross-section of the society: farmers, stockmen, editors, merchants, bankers, a mining superintendent, several physicians, a couple of teachers, and a preacher. But more significant than diversity of occupation was the considerable number of young lawyers and a smaller but important group of men with political and economic experience. J. J. Browne of Spokane and H. G. Blalock of Walla Walla were among the wealthiest men in the Territory; J. B. Hoyt, manager of the Seattle Dexter Horton Bank, who was elected chairman, had served as speaker of the lower house of the Michigan legislature, as governor of Arizona Territory, and as a supreme court judge in Washington Territory. George Turner of Spokane had headed the Alabama delegation at three national Republican conventions. C. H. Warner of Colfax was chairman of the territorial Democratic committee. Politically, the convention numbered forty-three Republicans, twenty-nine Democrats, and three Independents.

Washington's constitution was modeled on familiar patterns.[4] The writers drew heavily from the constitutions of Oregon and Wisconsin and adopted California's provisions for a court system. W. Lair Hill (a specialist in constitutional law and editor of the *Oregonian* from 1872 to 1877) proposed a framework which was used as a basis for formulating the Washington document; polite consideration was given to the work of the 1878 convention.

The resulting document demonstrated westerners' distrust of authority. It curtailed the patronage power of governor and legislature by making elective the offices of judges and of chief administrative officials, including the secretary of state, auditor, treasurer, attorney-general and superintendent of public instruction. The consequence was divided executive power. Furthermore, the delegates showed considerable distrust of elective officials in clauses that limited their freedom of action, attempted to guarantee their good behavior, and added a means of removing them from office altogether.

In the light of nationwide criticism of legislative corruption the legis-

[4] Avery, *op. cit.*, 317–322; James L. Fitts, "Washington Constitutional Convention of 1889," unpublished thesis, University of Washington, 1951.

lature in particular was the target of constitutional restraint. A legislative session could not exceed sixty days. It could not incur a public debt exceeding $400,000 or allow municipalities to undertake obligations larger than 5 percent of the value of their taxable property. However, the debt could be increased an additional 5 percent for water, light, and other utilities (Art. VIII, Sec. 6). Thus the way was opened for municipal ownership of utilities.

The state was not to lend state moneys to any individual or company, or subscribe to the stock of any corporation. Maximum salaries were set for judges, the governor, and administrative officers. The principal of the common school fund was to remain "permanent and irreducible." No money was to be expended for religious worship, exercise, or instruction. Lotteries were forbidden. No private or special legislation was to be enacted on any of eighteen different subjects, all enumerated in detail. As one delegate remarked, "If . . . a stranger from a foreign country were to drop into this convention, he would conclude that we were fighting a great enemy, and that this enemy is the legislature."

The members of the convention shared the farmers' concern over the growing power of trusts and monopolies. A general antimonopoly clause, phrased in general terms, was accepted without debate (Art. XII, Sec. 22). Railroads were prohibited from making discriminatory charges, issuing free passes, and consolidating competitive lines. The legislature was authorized to establish reasonable maximum rates for transportation of both passengers and freight (Art. XII, Sec. 18), but after much discussion of a proposed railroad commission the convention rejected the committee report and no such commission was established for fifteen years. Despite a general disposition toward reform, the constitution was essentially a compromise between regulation by and freedom from state interference.

During the fall of 1889 the electors of each territory covered by the Omnibus Bill voted favorably on the constitutions that had been referred to them, and chose their officers. Early in November each certified to President Harrison that its new government was ready to assume authority. The President thereupon issued formal proclamations declaring them to be states in the Union—North and South Dakota on the 2nd of November, Montana on the 8th, and Washington on the 11th.

The inauguration of Washington's state government was celebrated with pomp and ceremony. On November 18 exultant citizens lined Olympia's streets to watch pioneers and notables with bands and drum corps, foot soldiers, and cavalry parade to the Capitol grounds. Polished orations emphasized the significance of the occasion. Miles Moore, last territorial governor, gave his valedictory and Elisha P. Ferry, the state's first elected governor, saluted the legislature and the people in his inaugural address. Statehood, he said, "is the consummation of hopes long deferred yet ever renewed. It is the accomplishment of the result for which they [the pioneers] had waited with anxious solicitude, and which they now welcome with joy and satisfaction." The boom of cannon closed the ceremony, marking the end of the old regime and the beginning of the new.

IDAHO BECOMES A STATE

Although Idaho and Wyoming were not included in the Omnibus Bill, these territories also held constitutional conventions during the summer of 1889. Though Idaho's population numbered only 117,225, it was believed that the same party considerations that had favored the Omnibus states might also serve it. It was expedient that Idaho take advantage of the situation, and at once. Its internal politics revolved around the separatist movement which would annex the Panhandle to either Montana or Washington. Northern Idaho to all appearances preferred to go with Washington, and was supported by the Republicans in Boise as well as in Lewiston. However, a faction trying to defeat annexation made its bid for solidarity on other grounds—the disenfranchisement of Democrat Mormons in the southern part of the Territory.

A bill to annex the Panhandle to Washington was before congressional committees on territories when Nevada's Senator William M. Stewart proposed that southern Idaho be annexed to his state. This resolution of Idaho's boundary issues, embodied in a bill which divided Idaho between Washington and Nevada, had reached President Cleveland's desk for signature into law in February 1887 when Idaho's territorial governor, Edward A. Stevenson, asked for a delay. Southern Idaho was strongly opposed to annexation to Nevada and it was hoped that the completion of the Idaho Central Railroad would be a factor in bringing northern and southern Idaho into more harmonious relations and break the strength of the Lewiston separatist movement. In 1888 the House committee on territories rejected a bill for Washington-North Idaho unification. In the Territory itself Republican-inspired sentiment moved reluctantly toward admission as a state rather than toward dismemberment.[5]

[5] Merle W. Wells, "Politics in the Panhandle," *PNQ*, July 1955; "The Idaho Admission Movement, 1880–1890," *OHQ*, March 1955; Herman J. Deutsch, "The Evolution of Territorial and State Boundaries in the Inland Empire of the Pacific Northwest," *PNQ*, July 1960.

Without a congressional enabling act or authorization from the territorial legislature, Governor Stevenson started the machinery for election of delegates to a constitutional convention on his own initiative. On July 4, 1889, seventy-two delegates assembled at Boise. Their handiwork, more a code than a constitution, resembled that of Washington in general stipulations. The delegates pointed out to business and taxpaying elements of the population that the proposed constitution was "conservatively progressive." To reduce costs of government they set ceilings on state salaries and put county officers on a fee basis, claiming that state government would thus actually cost less than had the territorial regime.

But the convention embodied in its fundamental law some uncommon provisions. The state was given control over water rights and irrigation reservoirs and ditches, the provision stating explicitly the principle of public and beneficial use. Reflecting the sensitivity of mining districts to the new character of their industry, the constitution prohibited child labor in mines, authorized the legislature to create boards of arbitration for settlement of labor disputes, and provided for a lien law (Art. XIII, Secs. 6, 7). It also established an eight-hour day on all public works.

The constitution also contained a provision which, in effect, disenfranchised a large segment of the Democratic electorate and made the new state firmly Republican. Mormons in Idaho were strongly Democrat; they were also extremely unpopular because of their religion, clannishness, and the highly successful economic enterprises capitalized by their church.[6] In January, 1889, the territorial legislature had passed a test oath bill which prevented Mormons from voting. Although the proposed constitution guaranteed religious liberty, Article VI, section 3 disqualified for voting, jury service, and civil office persons who lived in a "patriarchal, plural or celestial marriage" or contributed "to the support, and or encouragement" of any society teaching such practices.

On its submission to the people, the constitution was approved by 12,398 persons, rejected by 1773. There were grounds for doubt about some of the returns—in one instance more ballots were cast than there were voters—and there were procedural irregularities. In one county the Mormons abstained from voting; in other counties, apathy may explain small voting totals. "Considering the serious obstacles which the promoters of statehood had to overcome," says Idaho's historian Merle Wells, "[the vote] certainly was remarkable, if not excessive."

In the spring of 1890 Congress took up a bill to admit Wyoming and Idaho. In either a benign or a disinterested mood, it ignored Idaho's

[6] Merle W. Wells, "Origins of Anti-Mormonism in Idaho, 1872–1880," *PNQ*, October 1956.

failure to secure an enabling act, and overlooked reported irregularities in choosing convention delegates and in ratifying the constitution. The House committee on territories reported a majority in favor of admission, despite a minority report calling attention to the invasion of civil rights in the article disqualifying Mormons.[7]

On the eve of Independence Day, 1890, President Harrison signed the bill which formally admitted Idaho and Wyoming into the Union. The last vestiges of territorial vassalage in the Pacific Northwest (save for Alaska) were gone. Political history there would henceforth be the history of sovereign states.

[7] The minority argument was against disenfranchisement for a crime until the fact of guilt had been ascertained by court judgment. The majority report accepted the provision because it implemented on the state level a federal law against polygamy. In *Watkins* v. *Idaho* (1947), the Idaho supreme court upheld disenfranchisement of persons adhering to plural marriage.

CHAPTER
TWENTY-TWO

Discontents of the
Eighties and Nineties

"The old settler finds himself in the midst of a strange, new age, and almost incomprehended scenes," said Washington's last territorial governor in his valedictory address. Old settlers were still present, but their number was overwhelmed by those largely responsible for the prosperity with which Washington entered statehood—that "superior class of settlers" who had brought with them "ample means" for their relocation. They had also brought scars from their experiences as farmers in the Midwest.

There were times when the fabulous American prosperity faltered, leveled off, or fell sharply. At such times—whether 1873 or 1886—some segments of the economy—labor for example—suffered more than others. One in particular—agriculture—on each occasion showed less resilience for recovery and less ability to hold its own, even in good years.

For the industrial laborer, real wages (the purchasing power of his dollar) had increased notably since 1873; but technological changes, competition of European immigrant labor, and the adjustments and readjustments of market prices created unemployment such as the country had never known before. In spite of expanded production the farmer's realized income had steadily declined since the 1860s. He sold in an

344

unprotected market; he bought in a protected market; he borrowed when money was cheap, paid his debts when it was dear. Improved transportation enabled him to sell in a wider market but it was more highly competitive and costs took a large percentage of his revenue. Even in prosperity the difference between total earnings of labor and capital, of agriculture and industry, seemed to justify David A. Wells' gloomy prophecy of 1869, that in America, the land of plenty, the rich were getting richer and the poor, poorer. In the next three decades, though industrial labor and agriculture each had its own grievances, their common demand, even if the phrase was not yet in their vocabularies, was parity of income with other sectors of the economy. Labor shifted its emphasis from demands for better working conditions to insistence on shorter hours and higher wages; farmers, to demands for regulation and control of interests they believed inimical to their welfare.

The shock of recognition that all was not well in his tight little world revived for the farmer *bêtes noires* of the Jacksonian era—monopolies, banks, and special privileges; now, however, they came under the names of "corporations," "trusts," and "vested interests." To fight the ogres, farmers moved, perhaps not so innocently as one might assume, toward doctrinaire agrarianism with its simple solutions: change the power structure and redistribute the land—or its equivalent in modern terms, the national income.[1]

What may appear surprising was the farmer's effort to hold on to the myth of his peculiarly noble way of life while his every complaint dispelled it. The farmer was in part a victim of tradition and of his leadership. His leaders were not usually dirt farmers, but businessmen, editors, and politicians who capitalized on agrarian discontent, not with evil intent but from traditional bias. Repeatedly the farmer was told that he was the backbone of the social structure and the defender of the moral life in a moral universe. So not unlike his agrarian prototypes in other times and places, in a crisis the American farmer justified himself and his actions in strong moral commitments and convictions. For every Henry Adams who felt that the moral universe had been shattered, and for every realist for whom it had never existed, tens of thousands of Americans believed there had always been and always would be a moral order, but that for the moment society was out of its proper relation with it. The farmer's task was to set the times aright.

Thus to protests against the Establishment was added the dimension of a moral crusade. The single tax, prohibition, Coxey's Road Bill, free

---

[1] John R. Rogers' *Homes for the Homeless* (1895) contains a "surprisingly modern account of the Gracchi and their attempted land reforms," according to Russell Blankenship, in "The Political Thought of John R. Rogers," *PNQ*, January 1946.

and unlimited coinage of silver, women's rights, regulation of railroads, direct government, all became basically moral issues moderating the intensity of the drive toward fundamental economic and political change, and in some instances diverting it entirely.

ORGANIZATIONS OF PROTEST: FARMERS

Protest became organized through local movements and national federations. Trade unions joined to form the National Labor Union (1866) which collapsed in the ugly days of violence in the mining and railroad industries during the seventies. The Knights of Labor, opposed to trade unionism, grew phenomenally, to 700,000 members in 1886. Its contention that, "when bad men combine, the good must associate, else they will fall, one by one, an unpitied sacrifice in a contemptible struggle," made Knights of farmers who had become city workers. Momentarily at least, the goals of industrial labor and the farmer were as one: "To secure the toilers a proper share of the wealth they create."

Granges of the Patrons of Husbandry (1866) proliferated in the Midwest and, concentrating on legislation to regulate the railroads, were successful in some states. The Farmers' Alliances, the National Farmers or Northwestern Alliance (1880), and the Farmers and Laborers Union or Southern Alliance (1884), enlisted millions of members and worked through thousands of clubs on programs of education, legislation, cooperative purchasing and marketing, and local problems. By the end of the eighties, the Alliances were pressing toward political organization; a movement which reached a climax in 1892 with the formation of the Peoples' Party, or Populists, under a distinctly agrarian program.

Against this summary background we place the Northwest's malcontents—one might as well say the West Coast's, since California had its share of troubles. Many farmers who moved west in the late eighties had enjoyed good crops and prices in 1883 and 1884, followed by three years of disastrously low prices. Therefore when in 1888 wheat rose an average of 24 cents a bushel, debt-free farmers could liquidate and move to the city or to a new promised land. Some chose to come to the Pacific Northwest. However, moving did not erase memories or change attitudes acquired during the hard times of the two preceding decades, and it is possible that because these farmers were immigrants their discontent was greater and their protest more charged with emotion.

346

The people of the Pacific Northwest joined their voices with those of national labor and farm groups and reformers. The Patrons of Husbandry were active in the early seventies. Although membership declined nationally, the number of Granges in Oregon—eighty-six with 3140 members in 1891—was higher than it had been a decade earlier. The Farmers Northwest Alliance in 1891 had 183 units in Washington alone. Oregon was invaded by the Southern Alliance which within a year had as many members as did Northwestern.

The Southern Alliance operated through secret societies, with rituals and paraphernalia, and excluded Negroes. When it entered politics, it chose the Democratic Party, hoping to make it its own. The Northwestern Alliance objected to secrecy and to the exclusion of Negroes, of whom it had no great number anyway. At first it held to the expediency of working with established parties, but later took the lead in forming an independent party. The Southern Alliance focussed on solutions to specific problems and local situations; the Northwestern, though militant toward the "encroachments of concentrated capital and the tyranny of monopoly," was more strongly attracted by ideological schemes and one-shot social panaceas.[2]

No love was lost between the two organizations, but despite jurisdictional quarrels they agreed upon common enemies. "The power of trusts and corporations has become an intolerable tyranny, the encroachments of the landgrabbers have almost exhausted the public domain, and the corruption of the ballot has rendered our elections little less than a disgraceful farce." Railroad rates were high because of monopoly. Taxes on farm lands were heavy because, through political connivance, other kinds of property failed to carry their share of the tax load or escaped taxation altogether. Money was scarce because banks of issue, "the pawnshops of American liberty," had arrogated to themselves financial controls which rightfully belonged to the government. Land was scarce because designing politicians had allowed railroad companies and speculators to appropriate the public domains.

A convention of Grangers, Alliances, Knights of Labor, and Prohibitionists met at Salem in September, 1889, and came out for:

1. prohibition of the manufacture and sale of intoxicating liquors;
2. a national monetary system "by which a circulating medium in necessary quantity shall issue direct to the people without the intervention of banks";

[2] Fred Yoder, "Farmers' Alliances in Washington—Prelude to Populism," in State College of Washington, *Research Studies*, September–December 1948; Gordon B. Ridgeway, "Populism in Washington," *PNQ*, October 1948.

347

3. transportation corporations should be regulated "to prevent unjust exactions and discriminations against persons, places or products";
4. a governmental land system that will restore to the public domain all unearned land grants, restrict settlers to the possession of 160 acres and corporations to no more land than necessary for the conduct of their business;
5. impose residence requirements and a test of knowledge of American institutions as conditions of naturalization and suffrage for foreigners;
6. trusts and combinations for maintaining artificial prices to be held a conspiracy against the common welfare, and punished accordingly;
7. a prohibition on the issuance of nontaxable bonds.

Since Prohibitionists were militant, represented a cross section of public opinion, and dextrously turned every opportunity and movement to their own ends, it is not surprising to find them lending their voices to the convention's demands and getting their plank in the convention's platform.[3] The Knights of Labor were no doubt responsible for the fifth resolution, but then anti-foreigner sentiments were not exclusively those of labor. The Knights were strong in small communities where farmers were only part-time laborers; parochialism as well as economic competition was a component of such racism as existed among agrarians and laborers.

Unions in Industry

The lumber and mining industries had unions in Washington in the early eighties; in 1885 Tacoma had a labor mayor, R. Jacob Weisback, and the next year Seattle Knights of Labor helped to form a "people's party" to elect labor sympathizer W. H. Shandy as mayor. The ten-hour day was in effect in the mills, an eight-hour day in the mines. Wages of both industrial workers and unorganized farm laborers were higher in the Northwest than in other areas where their employers' products had to compete.

But labor's relative well-being bred antagonisms. Some large-scale farmers, mills, and mine owners hired Chinese who worked longer hours for smaller wages. In September, 1885, Chinese employed in a Squawk Valley hop yard were fired on, three were killed and three wounded. Four days later, miners burned Chinese quarters at Coal Creek. The

[3] Norman H. Clark, *The Dry Years: Prohibition and Social Change in Washington* (1965).

348

next month, a crowd ran the Chinese out of Tacoma. Seattle was threatened with riots of such seriousness that Governor Squire exhorted the people to keep the peace; President Cleveland issued a proclamation, and United States troops were sent to preserve order. In February, 1886, Mayor Henry L. Yesler declared martial law in Seattle. Before troops arrived, the Home Guard escorted the Chinese to a waiting ship for deportation. Peace restored, martial law was lifted. Leaders of the anti-Chinese riot were prosecuted but the few convictions were overturned in appeals to higher courts.

In Portland, where labor was weak and not easily aroused, serious trouble was averted. Harvey W. Scott's editorials tried to please everyone and reflected his readers' ambivalences. He spoke forthrightly against rioting, asserting that Chinese labor was necessary for work Occidentals would not do; on the other hand, he demanded that Orientals should be excluded from the country as an inferior race with customs and mores inimicable to American society.

Other incidents in Washington mingled the race problem with agitation against corporation labor policies. In the fall of 1888 the Northern Pacific Coal Company, a subsidiary of the railroad, imported forty-eight or fifty Negroes to work its Roslyn mines, for longer hours and lower wages than local miners were receiving. To protect the Negroes against anticipated troubles, the company hired an escort of forty-one guards from the Thiel Detective Agency in Portland. Governor Eugene Semple ordered the guards arrested and, in his report to the Secretary of the Interior (1888), ascribed major importance to the incident:

> The system by which corporations or rich individuals claim the right to maintain a standing armed force to overcome opposition to their schemes is one that has grown up within the last twenty years, and constitutes a serious menace to our free institutions. These so-called "detective agencies" are almost exactly on a par with the societies of "High Binders" amongst the Chinese, mere organized bodies of ruffians, offering, for hire, to become the instruments of the rich and strong for the oppression of the poor and weak.

Troubles began at the Newcastle mine on the eastern shore of Lake Washington in 1886 with a feud between the Knights of Labor and the Miners Union. Apparently, but not certainly, the Knights' fifty or fifty-eight "discordant" members went out on a strike in which the 150 or 200 Union members refused to join. In early January the two groups clashed, one man was killed and possibly nine injured. After local officers had restored peace, the company refused to take back the trouble-makers, and, claiming threats of property damage, imported another

349

army of guards, this time deputized by United States Marshal T. J. Hamilton on the grounds that they were to protect the mails and post office located in a company-owned building. Again Governor Semple was outraged, and asserted that enforcement of the law rested with local legal officers and, in the last resort, with the governor's office.[4]

Idaho miners were drastically affected by technological changes. New machinery turned miners into shovel men, and forced them, if they were not to suffer wage reductions, to demand that all underground workers be paid the same. But wages fluctuated with prices of ore, and men laboring in tunnels and shafts of western mountains found that their pay envelopes varied with quotations on ore at New York. Managers for absentee owners ruled with heavy hands, without regard for the men's safety or welfare. Miners reacted much as did American wage earners elsewhere. So Idaho, still a frontier, produced some of the most militant labor organizations in America. Coeur d'Alene mining towns, where in 1892 the men were prominent in forming the Western Federation of Miners, witnessed instances of violence and martial law which put them in a class with Homestead and Pullman.

Miners staged armed demonstrations and used dynamite; owners used spotters and provocateurs, imported strikebreakers and Pinkerton detectives.[5] In the spring of 1899, affairs came to a climax when the miners commandeered a train to carry them to Wardner, where they blew the Bunker Hill concentrator to bits with 3500 pounds of dynamite. Governor Frank Steunenberg immediately appealed to President McKinley, and 500 federal troops were sent to the Coeur d'Alene area. Seven hundred or more miners were arrested and imprisoned in a bullpen under atrocious conditions. Repeated protests eventually brought an investigation and withdrawal of the troops, and after six months, release of the prisoners. Meanwhile state officials inaugurated a system of permits for mine employment which required applicants to renounce allegiance to the Federation. It was years before the union regained its strength; but memories of 1899 perpetuated hatred and suspicion to breed further conflict at a later time.

While labor moved to strong-arm unionism, the farmers turned to politicking. To change the power structure and redistribute wealth, something more than tracts and lectures and something less than armed marching men was called for. To win Democrats and Republicans to their side appeared as a hopeless task; both were part of the corrupt Establishment.

[4] "Trouble in the Coal Mines, 1889: Documents of an Incident at Newcastle, W.T.," *PNQ*, July 1946.

[5] *Report of the Industrial Commission on the Relations and Conditions of Capital and Labor Employed in the Mining Industry* (1901).

POLITICAL CORRUPTION

In the Pacific Northwest, evidence of corruption was at hand. To protect their interests, powerful corporations—railroads, timber companies, and utilities—built their political fences shrewdly, distributing campaign funds where they would put their spokesmen into high office. Judge Henry McGinn recalled that the Northern Pacific did not hesitate to spend $30,000 to elect a United States senator. John H. Mitchell, Senator from Oregon for twenty years and wheelhorse of the Portland Republican machine, was legal counselor for both the Oregon and California Railroad and the Northern Pacific. He was reported to have remarked, "Ben Holladay's politics are my politics and what Ben Holladay wants I want." Joseph N. Dolph, another Oregon senator, was also vice-president of the Oregon and Transcontinental Company and hence was linked not only with the interests of every important railroad in Oregon and Washington but with timber and mining interests as well. State legislators bought by the railroads were vigilant in warding off public scrutiny of freight rates, and in defeating every effort to establish effective regulatory agencies.

Oregon in particular suffered a succession of unhappy experiences with venal officials and land-hungry speculators that all but destroyed popular confidence in the state government. Governor George L. Woods certified The Dalles Military Road as completed when actually it was an oxcart trail, and through the audacious swindle the road company secured 500,000 acres in the best part of the John Day Valley. The Oregon Central Military Road, like The Dalles Military Road, was originally intended to provide access to the Idaho mines and force a reduction in the OSN rates on the river. No wagon road was completed, but a land grant of 850,000 acres of public domain went into private hands with no benefit to the public. In all, Oregon road grants—2,500,-000 acres—nearly equalled the acreage taken up in settlers' donation grants.

Under the Swamp Land Act, federal lands were given to states to encourage reclamation of tidelands and marshes. Southern and eastern Oregon land, where the nearest water was at least thirty feet below the surface, was surveyed and sold as swamp. Governor William Thayer himself was an applicant for 100,000 acres. Ignoring or nullifying provisions of the law, he allowed Henry C. Owens to acquire and contract to sell more than 1,000,000 acres to which he had no claim beyond the act of filing. The guardians of public peace and private property were so negligent that farmers in Baker County organized a protective association to prevent speculators from dispossessing them.

An Oregon logging camp, 1900. Clearing the virgin forests for space in which to build the camp was a logging operation in itself.

RIGHT. *The logger's life was rough and tough.* BELOW LEFT. *The I.W.W. achieved some improvements in camp conditions. This dining hall boasts "gracious lumber camp living."* BELOW RIGHT. *Safe hijinks on a windless day!*

Skidding a fir log out to the point of transport. The twelve oxen and eight men were soon to be almost entirely replaced by the donkey engine. Compare the cut-over area to the later picture showing to-day's model methods in which slashing is removed.

LEFT. *Logging trains carried timber to mills or to the nearest river to begin a longer journey by water.*

RIGHT. *A Benson log raft, so named for its inventor, Simon Benson, ready to be towed down the Columbia. It may be towed all the way to a mill in California.*

A sawmill and lumber yard, early 1900s. In 1860, the United States lumber industry centered in Pennsylvania; in 1870, Michigan; in 1910, the South. Since 1920, however, it has shifted to the Pacific Northwest, where the States rank among the first 10 producers of softwoods as follows: Oregon first; Washington fourth; Idaho sixth.

RIGHT. Today's "safe and economic cut." It can be done by one man, the saw almost at ground level. Gone is the enormous stump waste.

BELOW. A pulp and paper mill floats its raw material in close-by waters for easy storage and access. A mid-Columbia River hydroelectric plant 200 miles away provides power for the mill.

ABOVE. *A Norwegian ship, standing by at Coos Bay, Oregon, takes on a load of lumber. Piles are stacked and numbered, loaded by carrier and boom.*

ABOVE. *A diesel tractor has just finished the log harvest from this designated area—a model of strip cutting and systematic cleaning of the forest floor. The tractor has hardly moved out of sight before the "chopper" appears, to drop millions of seeds on the 500,000-acre St. Helens Tree Farm in western Washington.*

RIGHT. *Millions of hardy seedlings get a sturdy start in an industrial nursery. They will be transplanted to forest lands, under the direction of foresters. A new tree crop is planted as a mature one is harvested.*

Oregon school lands were exploited without consideration for the purpose for which they were intended. State officials had shown amazing lethargy and negligence in surveying and locating sections 16 and 36 from which the schools were to receive the revenues. As a result, much of this land, distributed in individual townships, was taken by private purchasers or claimants—or sometimes included in Indian or military reservations. Under the terms of the federal grant, in such cases where sections 16 and 36 were taken, the state could appropriate lieu lands from the national domain within the state. In 1887 Oregon legislators were made aware of their school lands and promptly passed a law to dispose of them. It was a law that encouraged fraud. It authorized general sale at $1.25 an acre; and in cases where sections 16 and 36 or parts of them had been taken up, the purchaser himself could select the lieu land. Thus he might choose from the best in the domain—providing he could identify the original section or base for which it was substituted. Since the identification, "naming the base," could only be made by persons with access to land office records, land office personnel could levy tribute systematically from all purchasers; there were instances where officials named the same base for a number of purchases and collected a gratuity on each occasion. The land-ring scandals did not reach a climax until after 1900, but the game and the players were well known before the law caught up with them.[6]

Corruption and fraud, then, were charges that could be documented against individuals in public offices as well as against corporations. If these conditions were to be remedied, it was apparent the physicians were not to be the men who ran the Democrat or Republican parties.

FORMATION OF THE PEOPLE'S PARTY

At election time Grangers had usually cast their votes for Republicans or Democrats, depending upon their position on issues the Grange considered important. For some years it preferred a campaign of education and debate to win over the major parties. The Alliances used the same procedures, and as a result of the two organizations' efforts, many citizens were becoming acquainted with the general tenor of agrarian thought and with such issues as prohibition, the single tax, woman suffrage, and free silver.

At the Salem Convention in 1889, the Knights of Labor and Pro-

[6] Stephen A. D. Puter, *Looters of the Public Domain* (1908); Lincoln Steffens, "Heney Grapples the Oregon Land Graft," *American Magazine*, October 1907; F. G. Young, "Sale of Oregon's Lands," *OHQ*, June 1910.

hibitionists, who had already organized a party polling 2700 votes in Oregon in 1886, formed a coalition under the name Union Party. Both of Oregon's major parties took notice of this, and for good reason; in the elections of governor and representatives to Congress, the Republicans did not have safe margins of victory.

Unorthodox Sylvester Pennoyer, Democratic candidate to succeed himself as governor, quickly read the trend of the times and enlisted on the side of some limited reforms; he declared his opposition to tax-free bonds, supported the Australian ballot, and purposed to look into administration of the State Land Board. He won the support of the Union Party. Pennoyer also took advantage of a split in the Republican Party and appeared on an Independent-Republican ticket. His election with a plurality of 5000 votes may have encouraged the idea of a third party in Oregon. In Washington, Alliance leaders in 1891 debated the wisdom of such a move. G. D. Sutton, president of the Northwestern Alliance, strongly opposed a third party, believing that the Alliance would dissolve in political discord and fanaticism if forced to contend with "all the antagonistic elements which are continually crowding to the front of the third party movement." E. B. Williams, vice-president, voiced exactly opposite views. He saw no hope of obtaining reforms through the old parties, both of which for twenty years "have legislated against us and in favor of our enemies." There must be no more bending the knee and begging the politicians to hear the farmers' prayers. "Let us," he urged, "act for ourselves, and be our own leaders. We know that we have the power. Why not use it."

While the local leaders were thus divided, the organizations' national leaders were moving toward independent political action. Delegates from the Northwestern and Southern Alliances held a national convention at Cincinnati in May, 1891, and with great pressure from representatives of the Middle Border and Western states, decided upon a platform and national party candidates for 1892. In the Pacific Northwest, the Alliances fell in line. Sutton stood his ground, found few supporters and was finally forced out of office. Third-party proposals simmered in the local Alliances through the winter and spring of 1892, and by campaign time most of the rank and file favored an independent ticket.

The People's, or Populist, Party came to life at a lively convention in Omaha in 1892. Ignatius Donnelly's oft-quoted platform preamble was a rousing indictment of American society:

> We meet in the midst of a nation brought to the verge of moral, political, and material ruin. Corruption dominates the ballot-box, the Legislatures, the Congress, and touches even the ermine of the bench. The people are demoralized; most of the States have been compelled

to isolate the voters at the polling places to prevent universal intimidation and bribery. The newspapers are largely subsidized or muzzled, public opinion silenced, business prostrated, homes covered with mortgages, labor impoverished, and the land concentrating in the hands of capitalists. The urban workmen are denied the right to organize for self-protection, imported pauperized labor beats down their wages, a hireling standing army, unrecognized by our laws, is established to shoot them down, and they are rapidly degenerating into European conditions. The fruits of the toil of millions are boldly stolen to build up colossal fortunes for a few, unprecedented in the history of mankind; and the possessors of these, in turn, despise the Republic and endanger liberty. From the same prolific womb of governmental injustice we breed the two great classes—tramps and millionaires.

The platform was an agrarian manifesto calling for (1) a subtreasury system or its equivalent to provide a "safe, sound, and flexible" legal tender; free and unlimited coinage of silver and gold at the ratio of 16 to 1; an increase in the amount of circulating medium to not less than $50 per capita; and a graduated income tax; (2) government ownership and operation of railroads, telegraph and telephones, "in the interests of the people"; and (3) the reversion of lands held by railroads, other corporations, and aliens to the national domain for occupation by actual settlers. These were matters upon which westerners and southerners could agree. The lengthy resolutions of "sentiment" were devised for general appeal but those with political connotations meant more to westerners than to southern or midwestern delegates. To restore "the government of the Republic to the hands of the 'plain people,' with which class it originated," the party recommended (1) the Australian ballot, (2) the initiative and referendum, and (3) the direct election of United States senators.

The new party found a ready response in the Pacific Northwest. Local Populist clubs were formed and state conventions drew up platforms and slates of candidates. General James B. Weaver, the party's candidate for president, stumped the region; Kansas' Mary Ellen Lease, famous for her exhortation to farmers to "raise less corn and more hell," was introduced to a large audience in Portland by Abigail Scott Duniway, Oregon's leading feminist. Though the dominant voice of the press continued to be Republican, a score or more of newspapers, some new, came out for Populism.

Populists showed up surprisingly well in their first national campaign. Weaver won 56,650 votes, or about 30 percent of the total vote, in the three Northwest states, while Republican Benjamin Harrison carried Oregon and Washington by a margin of little more than 8000 votes in each state. In Idaho, where Democrats supported Weaver, Populist electors won by easy majorities.

Yet the Populist vote in itself was merely a minority vote. Only four Populists were in the Oregon legislature in 1893 and ten in 1895, most of them from rural counties in the southwest part of the state. The party drew from Republican strength in Multnomah and other normally Republican counties, and from Democrats in Democratic counties like Jackson and Linn; but it failed to gain control in any of the more populous districts. In Washington, Populists captured eight seats in the 1893 legislature and twenty-three seats in 1895, but they ran third behind the Democrats and fell short of the votes necessary to put through any of their reforms. In Idaho they equaled or slightly exceeded Democratic strength; in Oregon they ran well ahead of it. But in no three-cornered contest were they able to dent Republican solidarity. Republican governors controlled the state capitols and Republicans made up the congressional delegations. Idaho's Populist candidate A. J. Crook was a strong contender for a Senate seat, an indication that the legislature was more than warm for Populism, but the machine prevailed and veteran Republican George Shoup was elected. In the congressional election of 1894 Populist James Gunn beat his Democratic rival, but trailed 3000 votes behind Republican Edgar Wilson. It appeared that if the Republicans were to be turned out of office and a new order instituted, Populists must either make substantial gains in their own right, or they must settle for some kind of alliance or "fusion" with the Democrats and agree upon a single ticket.

The idea of fusion produced as much anguish and difference of opinion among Populists as had the question of founding a third party in the old Farmers' Alliances. "True" Populists, to whom Populism was a way of life promising a kind of salvation, insisted on maintaining the independence and integrity of the party, following the economic program and the evangelical spirit of the Omaha Convention, and holding aloof from political bargains. Their strategy assumed that in time dissidents from the major parties would be converted to Populism and march behind its banners.

Fusionists, on the other hand, would bargain to serve the cause. Free silver Democrats and Republicans could join hands with Populists, an unnatural alliance but expedient for vote-getting. "Politicians," it was said, "do not want the Omaha platform, they would rather rattle around in Silver, which is a very small reform and a convenient hobby for politicians to ride on." Furthermore, if Populists could benefit by fusion, so too could Democrats, who had had neither platform nor office for a long time. Alliance of Populists and Democrats therefore was mutually useful. There was a touch of irony in the fact that while a restless urge on the part of rank and file Alliance men brought about the establishment of the Populist Party, its founders were led into entanglements which soon destroyed their organization. The Democrats took over; claiming to be the party of the people whom they would not have crucified on a cross of gold.

In the Northwest decision to fuse or not to fuse depended upon the balance of party strength in a given state, and on the degree to which its Republicans or Democrats were amenable to Populist demands. In Washington, Populists gained in numbers between 1892 and 1896 while the Democrats weakened. In Oregon, on the other hand, the Democratic Party was moving toward reform, and an old-line Democrat was considerably torn in 1894 by the difficulty of supporting Cleveland and Pennoyer simultaneously. State Democratic conventions declared for free silver, direct government, income tax, and banking reform, all of which were Populist planks. A current saying was "Scratch a Western Democrat and you find a Populist." From such a situation it was only a short step to developing the "Popo-crat" who figured so conspicuously in the campaign of 1896.

DEPRESSION AND POLITICS

The virulence of politics in the nineties can partly be explained by the region's economic situation. Hard times came knocking at western cabin doors where people had thought to avoid the sound.

Taking wheat prices as a crude index of farm income, we find that what was happening nationally was also taking place on the West Coast. There was a downward trend of prices, though Pacific exports, estimated roughly at one-third of annual production, were increasing (see Graph XI, p. 626). The sharpest drop in the average price of wheat for the entire United States and for the West Coast came in 1894. Of the three northwest states probably Idaho was hardest hit. Wheat which sold for 82 cents in January, 1892, brought 36 cents in September. Prices of farm truck—potatoes less than two cents a pound, eggs 10 cents a dozen—reflected the loss of purchasing power when mines closed or drastically cut employment. Banks and business houses "collapsed like paper houses in a rainstorm" and Idaho's distress spread to Spokane, its financial and commercial center.[7]

On the other side of the picture, with the exception of Idaho, the

[7] William J. Gaboury, "The Stubborn Defense: Idaho's Losing Fight for Free Silver," *Idaho Yesterdays*, Winter 1961–1962.

inhabitants of the Northwest were relatively prosperous compared with those of other agricultural areas. In 1890, although one in every four Washington farms was mortgaged, fewer homes and farms were mortgaged and the encumbrances were less heavy in the Pacific Northwest than in Kansas or Minnesota. So far as we can tell, foreclosures were rare; perhaps less than one percent of the total number of mortgaged properties. On the other hand, in Kansas where interest rates had shot up from 8 to 18, 24, and an occasional 40 percent, 11,000 farms were foreclosed between 1889 and 1893—before the real depression had set in. A thorough study of tax delinquencies in the Northwest would probably reveal that small-time speculators let go of nonincome properties but that few developed properties reverted to the state.

Though the number of bank failures was high—five closed their doors in Spokane and fourteen out of twenty-one in Tacoma—failures were not abnormal. The shrewd, thrifty, well-established businessman sat out the depressed years while marginal enterprises went under. The risks were always great in a restricted, undiversified economy; in times of distress they were magnified. Many men were unemployed; in 1894, breadlines formed and city charities were hard-pressed to care for the needy. Nevertheless it appears that employment did not so much decline as fail to increase at the earlier rate. Wages in the Northwest lumber industry remained higher than in Wisconsin and Minnesota. The average wage for farm labor in Washington dropped from $37.50 a month in 1891–1892 to $29.74 in 1894, but a hired hand in the Northwest was still better off than his counterpart in Minnesota, who received $26 in 1891–1892, and $24.82 in 1894.

The gay nineties obviously were not years of booming prosperity, but the Northwest's reactions to hard times were out of proportion to the actual situation. Hence, one might conclude that the discontent expressed in politics and public protests had deeper roots than immediate economic stringencies. In this respect the phenomenon called Coxey's Army, viewed in the context of Populism and labor disorders, is significant. In 1893, Jacob S. Coxey, a businessman of Massillon, Ohio, proposed two measures to relieve national distress: a $500,000,000 federal roads project to provide jobs for the unemployed, and a federal non-interest-bearing bond bill to subsidize public construction. In order to impress upon Congress the need for such work projects, Coxey proposed a march of the unemployed upon the nation's capital; an idea probably suggested by westerners who had already begun local "marches." However, while Coxey had specific demands—the proposed relief projects—the workers who formed "armies" in California, Oregon, and Washington had no particular programs, only the idea that government should do something. A commander of a Los Angeles contingent

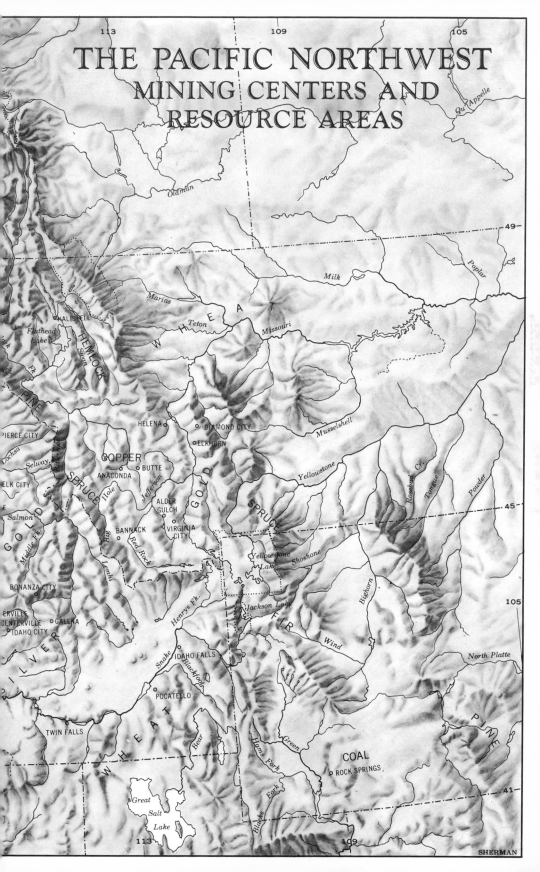

THE PACIFIC NORTHWEST
MINING CENTERS AND
RESOURCE AREAS

Qu'Appelle

113   109   105

Oldman

49

Milk

Poplar

Marias

W   H   E   A   T

Teton   *Missouri*

Flathead
Lake   *Skull*   HEMLOCK   *Musselshell*

KALISPELL

FR.

PINE

PIERCE CITY   HELENA   DIAMOND CITY

Lochsa   COPPER   ELKHORN   *Yellowstone*   *Rosebud Cr.*   *Tongue*   *Powder*

Selway   ANACONDA   BUTTE   SPRUCE

ELK CITY   SPRUCE   *Jefferson*   45

Salmon   *Big Hole*   ALDER   GOLD   SPRUCE

GOLD   *Middle Fk.*   GULCH   *Yellowstone*   *Shoshone*

BANNACK   VIRGINIA   Lake

Red Rock   CITY   *Bighorn*

BONANZA CITY   *Lemhi*

ERVILLE   *Henrys Fk.*   FIR   *Wind*

CENTERVILLE   GALENA   *Jackson Lake*

IDAHO CITY

SILVER   *Snake*   IDAHO FALLS   105

Blackfoot   North Platte

POCATELLO

PINE

TWIN FALLS   W   H   *Bear*   *Green*   E   A   T   COAL

Hams Fork   ROCK SPRINGS

Great
Salt
Lake   41

Blacks Fork

113   109

SHERMAN

put the matter in a nutshell. If Congress did not know what to do for the unemployed,

> we will tell them there are millions of acres of desert land in the West that would be fertile if irrigated. For the unemployed workingmen in that portion of the country we will ask an appropriation large enough to get employment to the hundreds of thousands there. While our State [California] raises an abundance of fruit and grapes every year, they rot because there are not people enough there to consume them; while the poor in the East go hungry because private monopolies want so large a profit on operating railroads that we cannot ship them. The Australian Government owns and operates its own railroads, and so should the American Government.[8]

A company of the Industrial Army was recruited in the Portland Plaza blocks, rallied by parades and marathon speeches. "We do not want charity, but we ask for employment," F. W. Phelan of the American Railway Union was quoted as saying. "It is the duty of the government to take care of its subjects in times like these. All other governments do so, but so far the United States is not preparing to meet the emergency. We shall march to the national capital and lay our grievances before Congress." Some 400 men were enlisted in Portland; in Seattle, similar demonstrations won over about 1500. The *Oregonian* news columns reported that the men were "orderly, sober and in sober earnest." Editorially, however, they were "vagrants," and to the Army's challenge —"We are starving in the midst of plenty. Why?"—editor Scott replied:

> It is easy to tell why. . . . these men did not make the most of their opportunities. . . . And though they were getting the best wages ever paid, they were dissatisfied and wanted more. Through their unions they forced their demands for wages. . . . Their political demagogues told them they ought to get still more, . . . Then, when employment could no longer be had, great numbers of these men . . . found themselves destitute, and forthwith began to accuse and denounce society and government for conditions resulting from their own imprudence.

Probably the most unusual feature of the western armies' brief history was their habit of stealing trains. When refused transportation, the Oregon army—following the example of James Hogan's company in Montana—seized a train at Troutdale, a few miles out of Portland, only to be captured by regular army troops east of The Dalles. Returned to Portland, the prisoners were greeted by cheers from a friendly crowd. Fifty-two of the leaders were brought to court and defended by prominent attorneys. After expressing their regret over the episode, they were

[8] Donald L. McMurry, *Coxey's Army, a Study of the Industrial Army Movement of 1894* (1929), 139.

released; the federal troops left extra rations for the marchers and departed. Reduced to about 300, the marchers reached Idaho in early May and stole another train. At Boise, the Portland group disbanded. Some of Seattle's army under "Jumbo" Cantwell rode the rails in small groups, a few reaching Washington, D.C. With the arrest there of Jacob Coxey, the whole movement petered out.[9]

The complaints of the Coxeyites pointed up a characteristic of western discontent: The industrial age was too complicated for workmen to survive by individual efforts. What in the next decade was called "social justice" required that government act in economic crises. Farmers and workers were as much a part of the nation as were trusts, corporations, gold bugs, and other special interests. This was the underlying theme in the campaign of Bryan versus McKinley in 1896.

THE ELECTION OF 1896

The presidential election of 1896 brought the fusion issue to a climax. In Washington farmers who converged upon Ellensburg, by wagon, bicycle, and afoot to attend the Populist state convention, were generally considered the strongest middle-of-the-roaders and opposed to fusion. Yet the convention quickly turned to negotiations with Democrats and Silver Republicans meeting at the same place and time, and decided upon fusion. Although Democrats and Silver Republicans announced their own platforms in language "as noncommittal as good politics could make it," they had a common ticket with Populists like John R. Rogers, C. W. Young, Neal Cheatham, and Robert Bridges. As a result, Populists laid claim to the chief state offices, while Democrat James Hamilton Lewis and Silver Republican Wesley C. Jones were nominated for Congress.

In Idaho free silver was the issue. William E. Borah, who was just making a name for himself as orator and politician, expressed the attitude of the majority of Idaho Republicans when he claimed that true Republicans were Silver Republicans. These men walked out when the Republican national convention declared for the gold standard; only a minority of Idaho organization men remained regular and worked for McKinley, though reluctantly. As one of the latter put it, "I am for silver but I don't know exactly where I am at."

Borah and his followers easily accepted fusion with Democrats and Populists. Their Republicanism had a liberal streak; they had earlier declared in favor of woman suffrage, a federal department of mines,

[9] Herman C. Voeltz, "Coxey's Army in Oregon, 1894," *OHQ*, September 1964.

postal savings, and the right of labor to organize. So Silver Republicans, Democrats, and Populists had no difficulty in working out a slate that united them for Bryan and for Democrat Frank Steunenberg as governor. The silver votes were split in the contest for congressional representative, and Borah consented to run against both regular and fusionist candidates. Everyone knew that the gold bugs had no chance and any one of them who agreed to run for office was greeted as "another lamb for the slaughter."

Bryan carried Washington and Idaho. In Washington, fusionists carried all of the eastern counties except Klickitat, and every county between the Sound and Cascade Mountains from Olympia to the Canadian border. In several other counties the vote was extremely close; there was a tie in Clark County, a margin of only ten votes in Lewis, twenty-five in Island, and twenty-six in Kitsap.

Oregonians were somewhat ambivalent. The distribution of Bryan and McKinley votes followed a pattern of economic alignments. Twelve counties switched from Republican to Democratic. But McKinley carried fifteen counties lying in a broad band along the northern seacoast and the Columbia River, and in the lower valleys of the Willamette, the Deschutes and John Day rivers. These counties, the state's wealthiest and most productive, remained safely Republican despite some defections.

McKinley led in Oregon by 2117 votes, but he carried Multnomah County by 5371. As elsewhere, the Republicans owed victory to their effective control of the populous centers. It was charged that the Portland machine committed the crudest kind of fraud, importing rascals from San Francisco to vote at more than one polling place. Jonathan Bourne protested that Bryan actually carried Oregon only to have the victory snatched from him by Republican repeaters. The traffic in ballots helped to elect McKinley, but it aroused resentments which contributed to a demand for political reforms.

The aftermath of 1896 was as significant on the local level as the election itself. Strangely enough, the situation most promising for reform proved to be the most disappointing. In the states where Populism and fusion won, the fruits of victory were not realized. In Washington, Governor John Rogers and his Populist supporters controlled both houses of the legislature. Rogers urged comprehensive legislation but achieved only a small part of it.

The very strength of the Washington Populists led to their undoing. Inexperienced in government, heady with their recent victory, lacking leadership and self-discipline, they failed to agree upon and carry through a program. Populist legislators had the votes to send one of their number to the United States Senate, but they could not agree on a candidate because so many Populists had personal ambitions of their own. After a week of balloting the choice fell upon George Turner who, though "sound" as an enemy of the railroads, was more Jeffersonian than Populist and too much the judge and wealthy mine owner to be a true "man of the people." The Ellensburg platform had committed Populists to a number of specific reforms, but Populist legislators quarreled over patronage; the 1897 session ended with scarcely a half-dozen measures approved beyond those that the Republicans themselves agreed to.

Governor John R. Rogers of Puyallup was a man of ability. An intellectual lately turned reformer, he had been active in the Union Labor Party in Kansas, and a member of the Farmers' Alliance. He had published several tracts and pamphlets, even a piece of fiction, in the vein of agrarian reform. Elected to the legislature in 1892 as a Populist, he had a good record there and was especially recognized for his sponsorship of school finance legislation. Yet in 1897 Rogers was not the leader of his party. Before the 1896 election, M. P. Bulger of Tacoma, chairman of the state executive committee, assumed the position of quarterback and attempted to call the plays. After the victory Frank Baker, the new state chairman, claimed the right to dispense patronage. Rogers was governor because he had been a compromise candidate, acceptable as second best by the supporters of C. W. Young and H. N. Belt. Whatever Rogers' personal qualities, they were not sufficient to give him preeminence either in the art of conciliation or in the tougher methods of party boss.

So Rogers lectured the legislature on the dangers of factionalism to no avail, and many Populist bills died aborning. A tax measure intended to shift the burden from home owner to the "great properties," provided only for modest exemptions and some changes in the manner of collection. Bills to establish maximum freight rates and create a railroad commission were defeated in the senate through the combined opposition of Republicans and ten of the fifteen Populist members. A bill that looked toward the direct election of United States senators died in committee. An attempt to set up a program of industrial insurance was wholly inadequate. Despite repeated Populist demands for economy in government new state agencies were created—a bureau of labor, a road commission, and a commissioner of horticulture—which, though worthy, cost money. The Seattle *Post Intelligencer* accused the legislature of being a "riotous, incoherent tempestuous irresponsible assemblage of men."

The spirit of reform all but disappeared when gold was discovered in the Klondike; the stubborn issues of democracy and public policy suddenly became unimportant. The two issues that came before the people, the single tax and woman suffrage, were defeated. Republicans won handily in the elections of 1898 and 1900, and Populist voters, chastened by defeat and disillusionment, again sought affiliation with one or the other of the old-line parties. Rogers won reelection, but as a Democrat. Populists could no longer claim Turner as one of their own. Reform was not dead, but the Populists as a party had lost the opportunity to vitalize it.

Oregon followed another course entirely. The Populists had not enjoyed the numerical strength they had in Washington; they accepted the status of a minority, and after the eclipse of the organization many returned to Democratic or Republican folds. But both major parties acknowledged in some degree the strength that the third party had mustered. One Republican leader put the matter bluntly: "I have a lot of Pops in my district and I have to do something to keep them happy." Corruption and fraud could no longer be ignored.

During the last decade of the nineteenth century, Oregon took steps to clean up elections. These were, however, merely the first steps toward a major political reformation. In the Pacific Northwest, as in the West generally, reform was not the product of hard times; it was the accomplishment of a new decade of prosperity.

CHAPTER
TWENTY-THREE

Recovery and the New Prosperity–1900-1915

By 1897 the national economy was showing signs of emerging from the depression and entering an era of prosperity. Within four years increased production of gold cheapened the monetary standard; technology and entrepreneurial talent coupled with astonishing accretions of investment capital increased manufacturing production; while immigration swelled both the labor pool and the consumer market.

Some of these factors indirectly eased hard times in the Pacific Northwest. As we shall show in a later chapter, heavily capitalized corporations in the lumber industry turned their sights on the coastal forests. Cheaper money and rising prices enabled would-be emigrants to dispose of their properties and move westward. Thousands came to the Northwest in the last of the great mining rushes and the last great migration of agricultural peoples.

THE YUKON AND NORTHWEST MINING

The stampede to Klondike gold fields and the beaches of Cape Nome provided the greatest excitement the West had experienced since Oro

Fino and Virginia City. Alaskans had been mining quietly for some years, but in the summer of 1897 the Yukon burst into the headlines. In July, Seattle newspapers reported the arrival of steamers from the north with million-dollar cargoes of nuggets and dust. Within a few weeks coastal steamers were jammed with strangers bound for Dyea and Skagway, where the rugged mountain trails left the coast, climbing steeply over dangerous passes to the lakes and riverways that led to the placer grounds of the interior.[1] "Stranger things than fiction happen here every day," wrote Arthur Perry from Dawson City: $495 in one pan, in another $800 worth of dust. The first season's digging netted one miner $112,000, another $94,000. Perry listed twenty-two who made from $12,000 to $50,000 apiece during one winter.

Such success stories were reported in the newspapers and in promotional pamphlets distributed by the thousands. Even the United States Geological Survey put out a map of Alaska with GOLD in brightly colored letters over large areas of the territory, and a description of the routes by which they might be reached. "Clondyke is almost a household word," declared the Seattle *Post Intelligencer*. "In every city, town and hamlet on the Pacific Coast little else is talked of and people are preparing to go north by the very first means of transportation they can encounter."

A great deal happened in Alaska that did not merit such exuberant publicity. Hardships and failure were common; the great majority of prospectors made a bare living and might have made it easier at home. Poverty and privation were as much a part of the Yukon rush as a $500 pan.

The total output of the placers could only be roughly estimated, for there was no adequate system of reporting it. It was said that the United States Assay Office at Seattle received $18,000,000 worth of gold by the end of 1900. Statistics of production for the Territory of Alaska gave a total of $17,800,000 for the years 1897–1900. The annual yield did not pass $10,000,000 until after 1904, when industrial methods were more generally used. The Canadian figures for the Klondike districts report gold to the value of $95,000,000 mined in British territory by 1900.

Gold in such quantities stimulated business throughout the Pacific Northwest. Prospectors not only found treasure but spent it. En route to the mines, they paid dearly for transportation, subsistence, and supplies. It may have cost nearly $1000 to reach the Yukon properly equipped to begin digging. This money, together with a great deal of

[1] Charles M. Gates, "Human Interest Notes on Alaska and the Yukon Gold Rush," *PNQ*, April 1943.

the gold that was mined, passed quickly from hand to hand and produced far more business than output of gold alone. As usual on a mining frontier, money was made from miners as well as from mines.

This fact was not lost on Seattle's businessmen. In less than a month during the summer of 1897 merchants sold goods worth $325,000; for several years thereafter Seattle's direct interest in outfitting and supply was heavy indeed. Goods awaiting shipment to Alaska lined the sidewalks and every available steamer was pressed into service. Moran Brothers rushed completion of a dozen river boats for use on the Yukon. Anticipating a continuing trade with Alaska (and increasing trade with the Far East as a consequence of the Spanish-American War and American expansion into the Pacific), the Northern Pacific Railroad spent $1,000,000 improving its Puget Sound waterfront facilities.

Since other West Coast ports were competing for the Alaska trade, Erastus Brainerd, Seattle's publicist, left no stone unturned in advertising the city as the best outfitting center and point of departure. Partly because of its location and partly as a result of energetic promotion, Seattle established itself as the fastest growing city in the Northwest.[2]

The contribution of Oregon and Washington mines to the development of the region is a mere footnote to Alaska's. Profits, such as they were, came more from such industrial materials as coal, sandstone, and later, gravel. Even iron was a disappointment. Local belief that there were rich minerals in the Cascades induced some investments that encouraged speculation. But the truth was that Oregon and Washington had few if any bonanza deposits. Those explored were found to be relatively small, with low-grade ores, the veins faulted and hard to follow.

Idaho continued to be a major source of metal ores. Gold, however, was no longer the principal product, dropping from 90,500 ounces to 50,000 between 1901 and 1916, its annual value ranging from $1,869,000 in 1900 to $1,035,000 in 1910. Silver, zinc, and lead now superseded gold in importance. By 1917 Idaho's mountains had yielded $400,000,000 in minerals, of which a quarter was in silver, and more than half in lead. The mining industry had already shown strong trends toward industrialization and consolidation; with the turn of the century these were accelerated. And still Idaho's production of mineral riches contributed little to its own economic development or to that of the region. Reduced to ingots, the metals moved east to feed the nation's ravenous metal industries.

2 Jeannette P. Nichols, "Advertising and the Klondike," *WHQ*, January 1922; Jonas A. Jonasson, "Portland and the Alaska Trade," *PNQ*, April 1939.

THE NEW IMMIGRATION

Mining failed also to contribute to Idaho's growth in population, yet
between 1900 and 1920 the state shared in the largest immigration to
the Northwest up to the 1940s (see Graph I, p. 621). In 1900–1910
the net growth by in-migration reached nearly 1,000,000 persons. This

TABLE II

*Growth in Population and Percent of Increase over
Preceding Census, 1900–1920*

	1900	1910	1920
Washington	160,871	623,887	214,637
Percent increase	45.0	120.4	18.8
Oregon	95,832	259,229	110,624
Percent increase	30.2	62.7	16.4
Idaho	73,224	163,822	106,272
Percent increase	82.7	101.3	32.6

was the era of the nation's last great internal movement of agricultural
peoples, profoundly affecting Oklahoma, Florida, and Montana, as well
as the Far West. The places of birth of the Northwest's new residents
confirm their agricultural origins: Washington's came principally from
Illinois, Iowa, Wisconsin, Missouri, and Minnesota; Oregon's from
Missouri, Iowa, and California; Idaho's, from Utah. Furthermore,
unlike previous migrations to the Northwest, this was composed of
older people looking for opportunities to recreate in new and more
favorable circumstances ways of life they had treasured elsewhere.

Certainly there were channels of communication spreading the news
that wages in certain western industries were higher than they were in
the Midwest. For example, in 1890, 75.5 percent of the planing mill
employees in Washington earned $50 or more a month; of their coun-
terparts in Minnesota and Wisconsin, only 16.7 and 34.5 percent received as much. Some immigrants came to escape the conditions they
felt were responsible for their hardships during the nineties; others to
escape midwestern extremes of weather, with winter colds and summer
droughts, as the correspondence files of Oregon real estate promoters
in the era indicate. It is interesting that the urge to move to the Pacific
Northwest was also stimulated by reports from persons who had visited

Portland's Lewis and Clark Exposition in 1905 or Seattle's Alaska-Yukon-Pacific Exposition in 1909.

Since it was costly to move and resettle, we can assume that recovery from the depression had so far advanced that the new immigrants were able to bring to the Northwest some capital for investment. In the later 1880s, Portland Board of Trade studies found that two-thirds of the married men arriving in Oregon had an average of $2500 in immediate resources and the other third had $1000. It is not likely that immigrants in 1900 were less well provided. On a conservative estimate it is probable that newcomers brought into the Northwest at least half a billion dollars in a decade.

The Pacific Northwest had never courted penniless immigrants. Responsible businessmen and state agencies encouraged only those who could fit into the region's narrowly structured economy. Beginning in the 1870s, promotional literature reiterated a constant theme: artisans and laborers might find jobs, but much employment was seasonal. The demand for "clerks, bookkeepers, salesmen and bartenders" was limited. Forty-five years later, Oregon still advised that no laboring man without capital should leave an established home to come to the Northwest.

If the Northwest had little to offer skilled or unskilled laborers, it did have land for farmers, and private and railroad land companies that wanted to sell it. Their advertising painted the Pacific Northwest as the "mecca of the homeseeker and investor. A land of promise and opportunity, where the soil, climate and all conditions are unsurpassable for the successful pursuance of varied industry." Much was made of roses blooming in January, strawberries gathered in December. Pictures of "typical" thousand-acre farms, sleek dairy herds in knee-high pasture, fat sheep on endless rangeland, and intensively cultivated orchards laden with fruit illustrated the brochures. And promising markets were implied:

> . . . in addition to markets in the Orient, Oregon prunes bring top prices in France and other countries; Oregon apples in England, Germany, France and other markets. Oregon butter comes in for a big share of outside trade, large shipments being made to Alaska.

Another inducement held out to agricultural people in the Northwest was the opportunity to homestead 160 acres of public domain for relatively little cash outlay. By the terms of the Homestead Act (May, 1862), qualified persons could file on 160 acres of unappropriated land for a fee of $10. Residence or cultivation for five years was required before a patent would be granted. One of numerous amendments made proof of residence and cultivation necessary, but another permitted commutation at $1.25 per acre, the minimum preemption price for public lands.

Initially intended to perpetuate the existence of a yeoman farmer class, to satisfy the demands of Midwesterners for a share of the public domain, and to encourage settlement along the routes of the transcontinentals, the Homestead law was, as it has been described, an "incongruity" in the pattern of American agricultural development. In the Northwest it was especially so. The size of the unit was inappropriate for efficient farming in the interior, and its intent was defeated when it was applied to the forested regions in the West. But "free land" was attractive and railroads which sold their sections at $2.50 an acre for reasons of their own encouraged would-be homesteaders by offering them special tours at low rates to look over the landscape before investing in it. Such practices account, in part, for the large number of Minnesotans who moved into Washington via the Great Northern during the first decade of the century.

FARMING, 1900–1915

So the farmers came to the land of promise. As a result, farms came to represent a larger fraction of the estimated wealth of the area in 1910 than they had in 1890. Nearly one man in four of those gainfully employed was engaged in some kind of agricultural or animal industry. There were as many in agriculture as in all lines of trade and transportation put together, and more than twice as many as were employed in the extractive industries of logging, fishing, and mining. If the sawyers and lumber mill workers were counted with the extractive industries, there was one man on the farm for every man in manufacturing of any kind, from bakery to smelter.

Farm values increased nearly 300 percent, three times the rate of growth recorded by the nation as a whole. For the State of Washington alone this meant a gain of $500,000,000, a figure that put this state in the same class with Kansas, Nebraska, and Illinois. In 1910 Washington's average farm was worth nearly $11,000 compared with a national average of $6444.

In 1900 it was still possible to buy land in the wheat belt for $7 to $10 an acre; a decade later prices were four times higher and irrigated land in Yakima and Chelan counties brought $126 to $146 an acre. Farmland in the valleys back of Seattle and Tacoma were priced fully as high, while those around Portland rose to $228 an acre. The day of cheap land was over.

For those who had established themselves early, rising values brought substantial gains, but for others who came later farming was an enterprise that required a considerable investment and put them under a heavy indebtedness. On the whole, however, the farmer's financial position was favorable in 1910, for increased property values more than offset his debt. Although one farmer in three had a mortgage on his place (the figure had been one in five several years earlier) and average indebtedness had risen from $1300 to $2000, this debt represented only 22 percent of the value of the farm. The Washington farmer had an equity of 7000 dollars in his property, higher than that in any other state except Nebraska.

Depression experiences had exploded the myth of the independent farmer. The highly commercialized nature of agricultural operations had brought him into a complex network of marketing and distribution. Ships and railroads served for transport, but many agencies had a part in storing the crops and getting them to the consumer. Sometimes these functions were handled by middlemen while the plowman stayed in his field. Increasingly, however, farmers came to study the problems of shipping and merchandising for themselves, developed those products that could be sold most readily, and even began to manage their own storage and selling problems on a cooperative basis.

To achieve high productivity at low cost put a premium on scientific and technical studies, most of which were done at agricultural experiment stations supported jointly by the state and federal governments. One of Enoch Bryan's interests as president of the State College of Washington was to reorganize its experiment station for a more effective program. But farmers as a rule were slow to change their ways— and the ways of farming in the Northwest were considerably different from those of Iowa and Illinois.

At first glance it would seem that the region was still a single-crop economy. In Washington where wheat represented 44.5 percent of the value of all crops (1910), dependence on this one commodity was greater than in any other state except North Dakota. In the three Northwest states cereals comprised 46.5 percent of the total value of crops; for Washington the figure was 54.1 percent. Yet a comparison of grain farms with those of other regions and with other types of farms shows that if Washington farmers put 40 percent of their improved land into grain, so did those of Kansas and Nebraska, Iowa and Wisconsin, even Ohio and Delaware.

Production of wheat was matched by that of cattle and of forage crops, fruits, and vegetables. Hay and forage in 1910 were worth twice as much in dollars as wheat had been ten years earlier, an indication that cattle raising and dairying were substantial enterprises. Oregon's

375

fruit growers contributed 40 cents in farm income (1910) for every dollar that came from the wheat fields. The vegetable gardens of the Northwest accounted for 8.1 percent of total crop values, whereas the national figure was only 7.6 percent. In the general ratio between the different kinds of agriculture, the Northwest mirrored the national economy remarkably well. The region put a slightly smaller proportion of improved land into grain, a somewhat larger proportion into forage, and slightly more into vegetables, than did the nation as a whole. Any conclusion that the local economy was out of balance should be qualified by the recognition that, in degree of diversification, here was the nation in miniature.

Wheat and Grains

Of all the varieties of husbandmen in the Northwest, those operating on the most princely scale were the wheat farmers. Some of these men could drive their harvesters in a straight line for five miles without leaving their own property. In the Palouse hills wheat farms averaged (in 1910) 384 acres in size; in Adams county, 775 acres, representing a capital investment of more than $20,000.

Experimentation was essential to develop the varieties of wheat best suited to the Inland Empire. W. J. Spillman, agriculturist at Pullman, Washington, worked on special hybrids that would bring a good yield and develop the stiff straw necessary for a fairly long harvest season. Little Club spring wheat and Turkey Red winter wheat were raised successfully, and in areas with sufficient rainfall a farmer might harvest a crop of wheat and one of oats or barley in the same year. It was reported that the more successful growers returned the value of their farms in a single year; that they stored one-half to two-thirds of their crop in their own warehouses, and with all their bills paid, could laugh at the wheat market. Whitman County alone produced $10,000,000 worth of wheat in 1909.[3]

The picture of the wheat grower laughing at the market may have been true in the best of good times, but it hardly applied to wheat farmers generally. North and west of the Palouse were the largest farms, though not necessarily the best ones. In this area the soil was not too rich, and meager rainfall forced operators to learn dry farming. Failure and disappointment were frequent. The wheat farmers paid dearly for

[3] Donald W. Meinig, "Environment and Settlement in the Palouse, 1868–1910," unpublished thesis, University of Washington, 1950; Oliver Baker, "Columbia Plateau Wheat Region," *Economic Geography*, April 1933; William E. Leonard, "Wheat Farmer of Southeastern Washington," *Journal of Land and Public Utility Economics*, January 1926.

transportation. In Kansas, served by competitive railroad lines, farmers paid only 3.6 cents a bushel to haul their grain to the nearest shipping point; the Washington farmer paid twice as much. Freight to Liverpool cost the Northwest shipper 16.8 cents a bushel, ten cents more than his Kansas competitor paid. Transportation costs also prevented Minneapolis millers from buying grain in the Far West. Ironically, Walla Walla wheat shippers paid five to ten cents a bushel more for transportation to Chicago than to England. The Northwest did compete with Kansas in the Liverpool market even though the net value of Northwest wheat at the farm might be eight cents a bushel lower; but only the superior productivity of fresh fertile soils made this possible.[4]

In such circumstances grain farmers usually contented themselves with selling their crops to large exporting houses in Portland and accepting prices that were determined by market conditions in England and the Orient. If the price was favorable, 80 cents or more, wheat usually went to England as grain. If the price fell lower, it was milled in Portland or Tacoma for shipment to the Orient. Of the several port cities, Portland was the most favored; nevertheless, for several years during the 1900s export trade from Puget Sound was as large or larger (see Graph XI, p. 626).

Ranching and Dairying

In the Northwest, the progress of intensive farming was accompanied by the stabilization of livestock and sheep raising and a rise in the dairy industry.[5] Of the various kinds of domestic animals on the farms of the region, horses, still the principal agricultural power tool, remained of greater value than all other animals combined. Since western beef could not compete with eastern, 1,000,000 cattle were fattened on grass or other forage in the Kittitas Valley or Blue Mountains to serve the growing markets within the Northwest. Slaughterhouses in Oregon and Washington did a $21,400,000 business in 1909, compared with $6,400,000 ten years earlier. Wool production leveled off at about 38,000,000 pounds for the region, Oregon and Idaho each reporting approximately 2,000,000 sheep of shearing age.

The chief change in ranching stemmed from grazing conditions. The

[4] A. Berglund, "Wheat Situation in Washington," *Political Science Quarterly*, September 1909.

[5] Dexter K. Strong, "Beef Cattle Industry in Oregon, 1890–1938," *OHQ*, September 1940; Todd V. Boyce, "History of the Beef Cattle Industry in the Inland Empire," unpublished thesis, State College of Washington, 1937; Frederic S. Hultz, *Range Sheep and Wool in the Seventeen Western States* (1931); Frederic V. Coville, *Forest Growth and Sheep Grazing in the Cascade Mountains of Oregon* (1898).

open range was largely gone, and though great acreages still remained in the public domain, by 1910 most of this land could be used only under federal regulations set up to prevent overgrazing. However, Congress seemed to work at cross-purposes, on the one hand toward a policy of land management; on the other, toward encouragement of the abuses it sought to remedy. In 1909, it doubled allotments under the Homestead law for arid grazing lands, on condition that one-fourth of each 320-acre allotment be cultivated. In 1916 the livestock industry was further encouraged by increasing allotments to 640 acres. Yet in the same period (1890–1910) nearly 48,000,000 acres, mainly in the Cascade and Blue mountains, were made national forest reserves.

In creating the Blue Mountain reserve in 1906, the government took a major step not only in preserving range lands but also in stopping range wars. These had begun in 1896, and spread through central Oregon wherever sheepmen contested with cattlemen for precious stands of grass. According to a spurious report couched in bitter irony, ranchers of Crook County organized "on the aggressive lines of sheep shooting":

> . . . If we want more range we simply fence it in and live up to the maxim of the golden rule that possession represents nine points of the law. If fencing is too expensive . . . deadlines are most effective substitutes and readily manufactured. When sheepmen fail to observe these peaceable obstructions we delegate a committee to notify offenders, . . . "You are hereby notified to move this camp within twenty-four hours or take the consequences. . . .
>
> These mild and peaceful means are usually effective but in cases where they are not our executive committee takes the matter in hand and being men of high ideals as well as good shots by moonlight, they promptly enforce the edicts of the association. . . . Our annual report shows that we have slaughtered between 8,000 and 10,000 head during the last shooting season and we expect to increase this respectable showing during the next season providing the sheep hold out and the governor and the Oregonian observe the customary laws of neutrality. . . . We do not justify . . . [a threat of murder] except when flock owners resort to unjustifiable means in protecting their property.[6]

Under federal administration a system of permits on a lease basis allowed grazing of sheep and cattle in separate areas with numbers of animals strictly controlled to prevent overgrazing. The law was evaded whenever possible, sometimes with the connivance of state officials. But ranchers, overlooking the important facts of a limited market and

[6] Quoted in Allen Hodgson, "History of the Ochoco National Forest," manuscript in office of Ochoco Forest Supervisor, 1913.

competition from large cattle companies which owned private range lands, blamed federal laws for their declining prosperity. The "government" is no more popular among Northwest ranchers in the mid-sixties than it was at the beginning of the century.

Despite their vicissitudes, Oregon wool-growers continued to have economic importance as well as a picturesque quality. Basques brought from the northeastern Pyrenees to eastern Oregon and southern Idaho were famed for their skill with sheep, and they made sheep-raising not only an enterprise but a way of life. In the Kittitas Valley and the Snake River country also, sheep-raising was an important undertaking.

Dairy herds doubled in size and the dairy industry emerged as an important specialty. By 1910 dairy farmers owned 444,000 milch cows, and delivered 146,000,000 gallons of milk and 37,000,000 pounds of butterfat annually. They prospered most in the valleys of western Washington and Oregon, especially where urban markets were fairly accessible. In Washington, the chief dairy counties were Snohomish, Skagit, and Whatcom; in Oregon, Lane, Linn, Washington, Clackamas, and Tillamook.

Truly impressive production records were made on some of these farms. In Washington, C. W. Orton of Sumner more than doubled the amount of milk from each of his cows, simply through carefully controlled feeding and good management. Charles Eldridge of Chimacum took a world's record with a cow that gave 3555 pounds of milk in a single month. One of the most modern establishments in the Far West was Fred Stimson's Hollywood Ranch with its herd of purebred Holsteins, across Lake Washington from Seattle. Specialized dairy farms in western Oregon were much the same. A typical one in Tillamook County included fifty-three acres of bottomland, thirty-six animals and, together with house, barn, and machinery represented an investment of $32,790.

Bulletins published by agricultural agencies emphasized the opportunities awaiting those who would reclaim cutover timberlands, and described in some detail the way this might be done. One emigrant from the Midwest settled forty acres of logged-off land, put dairy cows on it, and in a short time built it up from a $1000 investment to a $10,000 asset. "I make more here in the summer in one month out of cream," he declared, "than I did all year in Kansas. Hurrah for Washington." But this was not a common experience; it took years to turn stump land into pasture, and many stump ranchers remained close to subsistence living.

The growing market for fresh milk, cream, and butter in nearby cities nevertheless did much to encourage the dairy farmer, and the establishment of condensed milk plants and cheese factories gave him

379

other outlets for his produce. Carnation built a plant at Kent in September, 1899, and by 1906 canned milk from Washington (half of which found its way to Alaska) was a half-million-dollar item. In Coos County, Oregon, cheese factories turned out 124,586 pounds in 1909.

In Tillamook County the manufacturing and marketing of cheese was much improved by the organization of dairy and creamery associations, which standardized grades and consolidated merchandising procedures. In 1899 the Tillamook Dairy Association was organized as a cooperative. After a few years of financial difficulty it proved its worth and by 1916 all but two factories were functioning for the benefit of their farmer members. In 1909 the Tillamook County Creamery Association began operation. Factories were enlarged, improved, and inspected; and a cooperative selling agency served sixteen of the larger factories, handling through its central office 90 percent of the output of the county. While prices in New York and Wisconsin tended to govern those in Oregon, it was possible nevertheless to get a good return for the western producers.

Fruit Growing

As wheat dominated the agricultural scene in Walla Walla, Umatilla, and the Palouse, and cattle and sheep the eastern Oregon and mountain grazing lands, fruit-growing was the field of great promise in several of the lesser river valleys in central and western Oregon and Washington. In the Hood River and Rogue River districts, where apples had been grown since the 1850s, growers developed commercial orchards and shipped carloads of Yellow Newtons and Spitzenburgs to New York City. In the Wenatchee, Okanogan, and Yakima valleys, apple "ranchers" achieved unsurpassed productivity. Oregon and Washington produced 622,000 barrels of apples in 1890; in 1917 the figure was ten times as large. Washington, the number one producer among all the states, was then putting on the market 20 percent of the total commercial crop for the entire nation. This development came partly in response to marketing opportunities opened up by the railroads. By 1910 four to six boxes moved to the East for every one to the Coast.

Early successes spurred the planting of thousands of new trees, and drove land values sharply upward until orchard lands, acre for acre, were the most expensive agricultural properties one could buy. First-class fruit lands favorably situated around Medford, Oregon, brought $250 to $500 an acre in 1912. In Okanogan a few years later improved apple land was worth two or three times that much. Wenatchee bearing orchards were priced in 1914 at an average of $1925 per acre, while Oregon orchards brought returns of 10 to 15 percent on investments of $4000 an acre. Some growers reported yearly returns ranging fom $800 to $2000 an acre. Such figures stimulated speculative land-jobbing where conditions were not always suitable for orchards. Seattle promoters, for example, encouraged farmers to plant apple trees in Columbia Basin areas wholly unsuited to commercial crops.

Although chambers of commerce might paint a rosy picture of profits, those who became deeply involved in an orchard enterprise found that it not only called for a considerable investment of capital but required close attention to technical details. The average apple ranch in 1914 covered 11.4 acres, of which 6.5 acres were usually in orchard. Even this operation represented an investment of some $20,000, and approximately one-third of the farmer's operating costs were interest charges on his capital debt. Size was limited, too, by the amount of work involved in the care and cultivation of the trees, which the owner and his family found it best to do themselves. There were a few large orchards, but for the most part apple-growing was not entrusted to hired help or tenants.

Careful husbandry was the secret of success. The soil had to be conditioned with plow and harrow, enriched with mulch or manure. In irrigated areas furrowing or "creasing" was necessary to carry the water to each individual tree, and a monthly schedule of watering was followed from May to August. Pruning and thinning trees called for skill and good judgment. Spraying involved four different treatments, extending from the dormant period of early spring until the end of the summer. Harvesting in the fall season required extra help. Pickers, at the rate of $2.50 per day, loosely filled fifty to eighty boxes in a ten-hour stretch. The fruit was then sent to a packing house, where it was sometimes individually wrapped as in the case of apples, tightly packed in boxes and stored in specially constructed quarters until shipped to market.

Many commercial orchards owed their existence to improvements in artificial refrigeration. Prior to World War I such installations could handle only a small part of the crop; much of the fruit was moved to eastern storage, and the remainder put into local "common storage" houses. But with organization of packing houses and cooperatives, methods of handling fruit were improved and storage plants and refrigerator cars developed by the railroads enabled the apple grower to move his crop to larger market areas and preserve it for sale throughout the year.

The Yakima County Horticultural Union was organized in 1902 as a joint-stock corporation including both growers and middlemen. In 1913 a group of local packing associations in the same general area established the Yakima Valley Fruitgrowers Association. This nonprofit organization developed cold storage facilities and carried on marketing activities, mainly through fruit brokers. By 1921 the Wenatchee District Cooperative Association had 550 members in twenty-one local units. The real development of centralized marketing followed World War I, but the foundations were well laid in earlier years.

Soft fruits and berries, vegetables both for market consumption and for seed, and flower bulbs were specialties concentrated for the most part in the most fertile sections of western Washington and Oregon and in irrigated districts of central Washington and southern Idaho. These farms developed an amazing productivity. Idaho potato growers raised 179 bushels to the acre, the highest output in the entire United States, and so profitable that four-fifths of the irrigated land under cultivation in Idaho was given to this one crop. Hops were raised in Puyallup and Yakima until first local and then federal prohibition laws ruined the market. Sugar beets were introduced in Idaho and in the Yakima Valley.

Wagons, moving to the town's canneries from five and six miles out in the country, oozed a rich fragrance on hot summer days, when berries—blackberries, raspberries, strawberries—became the leading horticultural crop around Puyallup, where growers were leagued in a cooperative association of 1500 members. Early shipments were expressed to the nearest markets or moved in refrigerator cars to Spokane and western Montana. Long-distance shipping as far east as Minneapolis was possible only with the most careful handling, inspection, and grading; berries of poor quality went to local canneries.

Truck gardens fed the population of neighboring cities celery and asparagus, sweet corn and onions, lettuce, peas, and tomatoes. The vegetable seed industry dated back to the middle eighties when A. G. Tillinghast established seed gardens near La Conner. In 1912 Charles Lilly built up his market through national advertising and encouraged other farmers to specialize in growing produce for seed. This led a few years later to the organization of the Skagit Valley Seed Growers Corporation with 100 farmers under contract to supply Lilly with top-quality products. Cabbage seed built many a fine mansion on La Conner flats.

George Gibbs of Whatcom demonstrated the feasibility of growing flower bulbs in the Northwest. Out of his efforts grew a branch of specialized agriculture which in later years reached national prominence. Climate and soil alike were suitable for bulbs in a few highly localized areas, notably around Bellingham, Lynden, Woodland, and Puyallup, where the earth was a well-drained sandy loam and where rainfall was adequate and distributed throughout the year. Farmers in these areas imported from Europe their starter bulbs—narcissus, hyacinth, and tulip —which in three to six years of hard work produced for sale. Most of the product was used in the greenhouse forcing trade, with sizable shipments going to Chicago and New York.

. . .

Northwest farmers made a living—some a good one, others a poor one. Newcomers faced some of the same hazards that had destroyed their predecessors in the 1880s. In *Honey in the Horn* (1935) Harold L. Davis chronicled the failure pattern of 1900:

> Below them was the Looking Glass Valley, all open grassland among old orchards and caved-in houses and blackened remnants of haystacks. . . .
>
> Once Looking Glass had been a rich locality, with six big heavy-set ranches running cattle on the open grass, each making its proprietor ten times as big an income as he needed to live on. The cinch was too good to last. The valley, along in 1890, had attracted some three hundred industrious colonists, who divided the open grass-country between them and set out to make it pay as big for them as it had for the original exploiters. Since it was only good for pasture, it went right on paying the same as usual, with the difference that, instead of giving six ranchers ten times too much apiece, it gave three hundred ranches about one-fifth enough. The colonists lived for a few years by borrowing, and when they could borrow no more they all got up and left, and the mortgagors took their land and offered it for sale for the amount of their loans, with accrued interest. That was more than anybody could afford to pay, and more than it could ever be made to pay off. So, as a demonstration of the way capital operated in developing agriculture, the valley remained tied up tight, without any colonists and also without the six ranches it had supported to start with.

"Work," said a character in Allis McKay's novel about Wenatchee Valley settlers *They Came To a River* (1941), "Make a place for yourself here by your labors. There is room in this valley for every man who isn't afraid to spend himself." The land fulfilled its promises only to those who mastered it.

CHAPTER
TWENTY-FOUR

Water for a
Thirsty Land

THE SOIL of the Pacific Northwest was not easily mastered. By modern classifications of land capacity, 23,000,000 of the 157,000,000 acres within the three states are of cultivable quality, ranging from very good (596,000 acres) to fairly good (8,300,000 acres); 121,000,000 acres range from "well suited" to "fairly well suited" for grazing or forestry, provided great care is taken to protect soil and vegetation; and 11,500,-000 are "not suited for grazing, forestry, or cultivation."[1]

The limitations of the land became apparent with the influx of farming population. In 1913 Governor Ernest Lister of Washington complained that if he had to place even a thousand new farming families, he would be at a loss to tell them where to find reasonably priced land ready for the plow. If agriculture was to thrive, it would be because men found new ways to carry water to the areas still open—the desert.

The first white men to pass through the Inland Empire had remarked upon its cheerless wastes, hills seamed and slashed by dry ravines, plains smoking with dust, and soil baked and brittle. For a people who sought grassy valleys and well-watered plains for settlement, the plateau was

[1] *Atlas of the Pacific Northwest Resources and Development*, Richard M. Highsmith, Jr., ed. (n.d.).

384

a godforsaken country. It was barren and unyielding, save to cattle-men whose animals could subsist on bunch grass.

The generation of 1900, however, saw more promise in this land. The possibilities of bringing water from a mountain stream to an orchard or garden encouraged farmers to dream of man-made oases with vege-tation as lush as that in Iowa or Virginia. The soil was fertile and the snows of the mountain ranges held the necessary moisture. In the middle valley of the Columbia and its tributaries, farm lands were screened from rain clouds by the Cascades and river channels were deeply carved below the valley floor, but here too, water was to be had if practicable ways could be found to distribute it.

The varied topography, with its many levels of difficulty, enabled farmers and ranchers to begin with the easy problems and progress to the more technical and costly. Individual farmers started with short improvised ditches at Bloomington and Canyon Creek in Bear Lake County, Idaho; in the Methow and Okanogan valleys in central Wash-ington, or in Jackson and Josephine counties in southern Oregon. Some-what later, private companies raised money to finance more ambitious projects, including canal systems which would serve as much as 200,000 acres (near Boise) and reservoirs that would hold the spring runoff for use during summer months. By 1914, planning and construction had progressed to the point of reclaiming whole valleys, with agencies of the United States government directly behind the projects.

Irrigation was first applied to going concerns. Cattlemen in the Harney Basin irrigated for forage crops. Apple growers in the Hood River district increased the output of existing orchards and developed larger ones through irrigation. But for the most part, irrigation was the magic by which wholly new garden areas were created in places previously desolate and uninhabited. It was a dramatic and spectacular demonstration of man's power to alter his environment, his agricultural environs no less than his cities.

Success was mixed with failure. Walla Walla wheat farmers and others who tilled their fields trusting to the summer rains were skeptical of the complicated management and elaborate routine that irrigators found essential. The question of water rights led to stormy disputes and protracted litigation under laws that were sometimes inadequate or defective. But while the problems were many and perplexing, irrigation held such promise that farmers became wedded to it. The paradox of irrigation was that while it stimulated individual initiative and fed upon private speculation, it was actually ill suited to both. The benefit a farmer or a small company might realize from constructing and operating an irrigation system was limited. Repeatedly, such small undertakings failed. Successful reclamation of the land required a collective, institutional approach, as the Egyptians had learned 6000 years before. The individual might prosper once the land was watered, but the task of watering called for social action. Sometimes this action was taken by organized water users, and sometimes it came through governmental measures which made larger funds available and provided more certain and equitable protection to individual claims and interests.

IRRIGATION BY PRIVATE ENTERPRISE

The first big advances in irrigation came during the boom years at the turn of the century. Some 385,000 acres were reclaimed in the 1890s in Idaho alone—an expansion that trebled the extent of irrigated land and brought the total area served to 600,000 acres. By 1902 Oregon farmers were irrigating 440,000 acres. Development in Washington was more limited, but here, too, three farms were irrigated in 1900 for every one that had been in 1890. By 1909 in the region as a whole, 30,000 farms totaling nearly 3,000,000 acres were served by canals and ditches at a total cost of $70,000,000.

The major part of this expansion was the result of private enterprise. Investors and speculators were attracted by the prospect of increased land values, for desert lands worth $5 an acre or less brought many times that amount when watered. In 1909, 90 percent of the irrigated acreage in Oregon and 75 percent in Idaho was classified under private operation. Individuals and partnerships were responsible for 59.8 percent of Oregon's irrigated lands. Cooperatives accounted for 43.9 percent in Idaho.

This was possible because the first undertakings were the simplest and were done at comparatively low cost per acre. In 1905 half of Oregon's irrigation was achieved by temporary dikes and dams that simply forced spring flood waters over plowed fields. After an average initial cost of $16.25 per acre, the average annual charge for maintenance and operation was only 69 cents per acre. The farms thus served were on valley lands bordering secondary streams; the higher bench lands and extensive tracts lying along the major rivers could only be reached by elaborate canal systems or expensive pumping operations. These required more capital and stronger organizations for successful management.

For a while considerable reliance was placed in commercial companies. Corporations were demonstrating their strength in many fields; by issuing stocks and bonds they could raise the necessary capital. While comprehensive planning was not feasible by individual or local effort, large systems under a single management would be efficient and economical. Land owners would benefit and operators would profit.

These expectations seemed reasonable, and a number of commercial concerns were formed. In 1890 the Payette Valley Irrigation and Water Power Company operated one of the largest systems in Idaho. The Ridenbaugh Ditch, operated by the Boise City and Nampa Canal Company, was fifty miles long and watered 25,000 acres. Several large ditches were constructed in Umatilla Valley, including one near Irrigon, controlled by the Oregon Land and Water Company and another owned by the Maxwell Land and Irrigation Company which served the bench lands near Hermiston. The summer flow of the Umatilla was so thoroughly diverted in 1909 that the river was left dry at three different places. The Klamath Falls Irrigation Company delivered water to 2000 acres of farmland, and in the Yakima Valley the Washington Irrigation Company built the Sunnyside Canal, an extensive system irrigating some 36,000 acres of land north of the river between Parker and Prosser.

Despite these instances of commercial companies' success, their accomplishments as a group were not impressive compared with those of other operations. Oregon's commercial companies provided water for only 11.3 percent of the total irrigated land, while in Idaho the figure was only 3.1 percent. To be sure, they were able to finance somewhat larger systems and to lead their canals to less accessible locations beyond the reach of other private ditches. Nevertheless they encountered many difficulties, and their experience soon demonstrated the weaknesses of the commercial type of enterprise in irrigation.

The corporations were of two types, both with shortcomings. Some were land and water companies that combined irrigation with land speculation. Profits were derived from increased land values. The companies' interests usually did not extend beyond the acreage they owned, and ended when the land was sold. Sometimes the service was good, as in the case of the Washington Irrigation Company. Sometimes it was poor, construction flimsy, and maintenance woefully inadequate. Whatever their policies, the companies held a limited, short-term view, whereas the needs of the water users called for comprehensive, long-range programs.

Other corporations, attaching value to the water and not to the land, trafficked in water rights, selling a perpetual right for perhaps $10 per acre, with an additional maintenance charge. Presumably these companies had a more enduring interest in the water service, and were free from the burden of heavy investments in land. They were, however, trading in claims to which titles were not always clear, and which had to await court settlement in an indefinite future. Moreover, they were

387

dealing with landowners whose positions were often stronger than their own. The land had many owners, the canal but one. Dry land could be bought at low prices, and land speculators could afford to wait years for water if in the end they might get it more cheaply. Saddled with heavy construction costs, the canal company must realize quick returns or face bankruptcy. A number of companies failed and saw their water systems transferred to the men who owned the land.

FEDERAL AID: THE CAREY ACT

The Carey Act, passed by Congress in 1894, was designed to give commercial companies more security and protection. The federal government did not deal with the corporations directly. Tracts of land were transferred from the public domain to the jurisdiction of the states if the states would see that they were reclaimed. The states then signed contracts with individuals or commercial companies to construct and operate the necessary systems.

This was the second attempt by the federal government to encourage the reclamation of arid areas in the West. The Desert Land Act (1877) had permitted an individual to purchase public lands in 640-acre tracts, 25 cents down at time of filing, and $1.00 an acre in three years if in that time he had put eighty acres under irrigation. In 1891 evidences of fraudulent transactions led Congress to cut the size of the tract in half. By 1910, 800,000 acres in Idaho and Oregon had been taken up under this act. But no provision was made for supervision and no machinery was set up to allow private entrepreneurs to reclaim larger tracts utilizing the means of corporate management and bonding. The Carey Act was an extension of the earlier policy, and the philosophy behind it was much the same. The differences concerned mainly the adaptation of federal land policy to the requirements of large-scale private financing and construction.

In matters of administration the Carey Act left most of the responsibility to the states. A state taking advantage of the act must apply to the United States for grants of lands, submitting a map and plan of development in support of each application, and set up an agency under whose direction the improvements would be completed and administered. The states undertook to examine each proposed plan for feasibility and adequacy of water supply, and to manage the sale of lands to settlers. No lands were to be leased or disposed of except for reclamation and settlement, and not more than 160 acres could be sold to one person. Idaho and Washington accepted the provisions of the act in 1895, and

Oregon in 1901. Idaho and Oregon both assigned the task of supervision to the State Engineer since he was the officer charged with listing and certifying water rights.

When the states applied for specific grants, the plans and proposals in the applications were drawn up by the companies, and the contracts subsequently concluded between the companies and the states stipulated the terms under which water rights would be provided and sold. The price of water rights was governed by the cost of constructing the system, at estimates that often proved to be too low. The companies were given a measure of protection in that the state sold the land only in conjunction with water rights, and after 1896 the cost of canal construction was made a lien upon the lands benefited by it. Thus assured of a return on their investment, irrigation companies borrowed from banks and financing agencies and sold bonds to pay for construction.

Idaho made a very good thing of the Carey Act: three-fourths of the land irrigated under this law was situated within its borders. The Twin Falls South Side project, encompassing 240,000 acres, was highly successful and served as a model for others. Between 1904 and 1911, thirty-five requests were processed, which taken together contemplated the irrigation of 2,000,000 acres in the Snake River Valley at an estimated cost of $66,000,000. By 1912 a third of that amount had actually been spent. The Twin Falls North Side Land and Water Company submitted proposals covering 200,000 acres, and sixteen other companies signed contracts for canals serving from 12,000 to 112,000 acres each. Financial reverses in 1913 slowed development and for several years little was done. Achievements fell far short of goals; nevertheless Idaho Carey Act projects in 1917 covered at least 868,000 acres, of which 456,000 were productive.[2]

Except in Idaho, the Carey Act was generally considered a failure. The State of Oregon selected 432,203 acres and signed several contracts with private companies operating in the Deschutes Valley, but none was successful or important. In Washington no projects were approved, though the Washington Irrigation Company pressed for one in the Yakima Valley. The reasons for failure were partly technical and partly administrative; engineering was imperfect, surveys were often inadequate, construction costs were underestimated, and once water rates were established they could not be increased. The states gave the projects little supervision and paid too little attention to the adequacy of the water supply. As for the settlers, some got too little water and others too much. Their unfortunate experiences gave the projects a bad name and discouraged the sale of Carey Act lands. Even when the act was

[2] Mary G. Lewis, "History of Irrigation Development in Idaho," unpublished thesis, University of Idaho, 1924.

amended (1901) to extend the period of repayment, the financial burden was heavy both for settlers and companies, and it became increasingly evident that additional government aid was necessary. Furthermore, there was pressing need to clarify the legal status of conflicting water rights and to establish in each state some procedures by which outstanding claims could be reconciled and recorded.

WATER RIGHTS

Issues at law were thorny where they touched water rights. There was no uniformity among the states as to a valid basis of such rights and for some years there was no way of determining from public records how much water was subject to valid claims and how much remained unappropriated. At first Oregon and Washington followed the common law of riparian rights, favoring landowners along the banks of the streams, and made no provision for diversion of water to be consumed in the process of irrigation. This principle was modified later, partly by court decisions and partly by state legislation, to conform to the doctrine of appropriation for beneficial use. Under this doctrine, priority of application for actual use established a right over another claimant who could not prove that he already used the water for beneficial purposes. However, claims by appropriation could be made for lands situated back from the stream as well as for those along the banks, provided it was practicable to irrigate them by canal. The conflict of overlapping claims, based on the two principles—riparian and beneficial use—inevitably led to confusion and litigation.

The constitutions of Washington and Idaho both had provisions which declared that the application of waters to irrigation should be deemed a public use, a principle which Oregon recognized by statute in 1891. Washington also included a clause permitting condemnation of land to secure right-of-way for an irrigation canal. Idaho asserted the power of the state to regulate and control the distribution of water, defended the right of individuals to divert unappropriated water, and outlined principles to govern distribution when the supply was inadequate for the full needs of all claimants. In all three states, however, there remained the further problem of maintaining administrative jurisdiction over filing and certifying claims based on appropriation.

The practical importance of this problem became evident as engineers began to measure the water flow of rivers used for irrigation. The success of an irrigation system hinged on its capacity to satisfy the legal claims of the dependent water users. At first state laws in Washington and Oregon required merely a posting or filing of claims which gave notice of intended diversion and indicated the amount of water to be appropriated. No proof of actual use was called for, and no state agency was empowered to limit claims to the amount of water actually available in the river. In 1905 a little figuring revealed that known water claims in the Yakima Valley considerably exceeded the total flow of the river. Obviously not everyone was taking his allotment of water, but any irrigation system ran the danger of embarrassment if all claims had to be supplied at once. Similarly, filings in five eastern Oregon counties totaled 810,025 second feet, or enough water to cover the entire area each year to a depth of twenty-three feet, which was patently absurd. The total recorded claims for water in Oregon amounted to fifty times the low-water flow of the Columbia River.

Some action was necessary to regulate and police the filing of claims to water rights. Following the Wyoming system, Idaho declared that the rivers belonged to the state and that water rights must be acquired from the state. The system adopted required that improvements must be completed within a stated period of time and that an applicant submit proof of actual use of the water claimed. The state engineer then issued a certificate defining the amount of appropriation. He also assisted the courts by making surveys in cases where preexisting claims were in process of adjudication. However, his powers were limited, since he could act only in disputes before the courts. Because many claims could only be resolved in court, much confusion persisted. Nevertheless, Idaho made such progress that by 1909, 55.5 percent of the area irrigated was covered by either a court adjudication or a state permit.

In 1909 Oregon enacted a regulatory law which put control of water rights on much the same basis. The state engineer, previously without any real authority, now became a key figure. Persons seeking water rights must apply to him, must begin work within a year thereafter, complete the improvement within five years, and demonstrate beneficial use. Since water rights acquired by purchase from canal companies were limited by the main source of supply, provision was also made for the definition of rights acquired prior to 1909, through a Board of Control composed of the state engineer and several division superintendents, upon petition by water users. Decisions and awards of the engineer and the Board became matters of permanent public record.

Washington enacted its water code in 1917, establishing a comprehensive system of adjudication and state control administered through the newly created office of hydraulic engineer. The code provided for the recording of water rights, both previously existing and subsequently established, and the means of adjusting conflicting rights and supervising the operation of irrigation works. The engineer and courts shared in this procedure, which culminated in the issuance of certificates of rights and included a thorough investigation of all diversion dams, canals, and measuring devices.

THE NEWLANDS ACT

Improvements in state procedures governing water rights did much to give users legal security, but it was also imperative that a steady supply of water be assured. Provisions of law and administrative regulations were of little use if the water supply was limited to the fluctuating flow of rivers that ran full or flooded in the spring and went dry in the summer. Any program of real expansion must look toward impounding water in large reservoirs, constructing diversion dams higher up on the rivers, and building long canals to serve plateau and bench lands lying well above stream beds. Such a program went beyond the capacities of individual and private enterprise. It was doubtful that it could be realized by state sponsorship. Because of the close connection of reclamation with the administration of the remaining public domain, and because a new conception of land management was developing, aroused in part by John Wesley Powell and his disciples in the United States Geological Survey, there were good reasons why Congress should further commit the federal government to the aid of irrigation. With the passage of the Newlands Act in 1902, Uncle Sam became directly involved in the reclamation business.

Three main purposes governed the reclamation program under the Newlands Act: (1) to plan and construct major improvements by means of a federal agency; (2) to design and carry out each project so as to provide maximum benefits for the entire area in which it was located; and (3) to make federally financed projects self-liquidating. This last was to be done by charging costs against the lands they served, and eventually by transferring ownership and management of the canals (though not the dams and reservoirs) to associations of water users. No one knew at the time by what specific means these ends could be accomplished, but in the ensuing years all three objectives were consistently pursued.

The United States Reclamation Service, created for these purposes (it became the Reclamation Bureau in 1923), was charged with the development of all federal projects except a few on Indian reservations. Reclamation Service engineers made detailed investigations to determine the costs involved and the conditions that must be met to satisfy federal requirements; the Service controlled all expenditures from the

Reclamation Fund and supervised the construction and operation of dams, canals, and other improvements.

The Reclamation Fund, as established by the Newlands Act, was fed and replenished out of revenues received by the United States from the sale of public lands in the thirteen western states and three territories where projects were to be built. It was stipulated that the major part (51 percent) of the sums "covered into the fund" from a particular state should be expended in that state, while the remainder might go to projects situated in any one of the states. In this way each state was assured a proportionate share of the benefits, while at the same time there was sufficient latitude in fund distribution to allow planning on a national scale and to permit the construction of improvements too expensive to be built with funds from one state alone. The Reclamation Fund was a revolving one with expenditures for the construction of projects to be repaid by water users over a 10-year period as the land became productive. By the end of 1903, revenues of $5,800,000 were available from land sales in the three states of the Pacific Northwest.

Although the largest revenues had come from Oregon, serious difficulties stood in the way of large undertakings there. The pattern of land ownership was unfavorable because the federal domain in the extensive arid areas was cut up by wagon road grants and swampland selections. The water supply was generally limited, since the streams flowed from lower, rather than the preferred higher, mountain areas. Basins that might have served for storage purposes were already held by cattle ranchers. The Deschutes was perhaps the best river for irrigation, but its flow had been largely appropriated by various Carey Act corporations. The situation in Washington also was unfavorable. In the Palouse Valley and the Big Bend of the Columbia large areas were suitable for irrigation, but costs were prohibitive and probably would continue so for some years. In the Yakima Valley problems of land ownership, water rights, and previous development seemed to make federal action impracticable. Numerous small reservoirs could be built in the Okanogan country but no system of any size. Idaho offered some of the best opportunities but here again work already under way made it difficult to know how the federal government should proceed.

FEDERAL PROJECTS

Despite these obstacles, six Reclamation Service projects were approved —Umatilla and Klamath in Oregon and Okanogan and Yakima in Washington. In Idaho the Boise-Payette projects were enlarged and a begin-

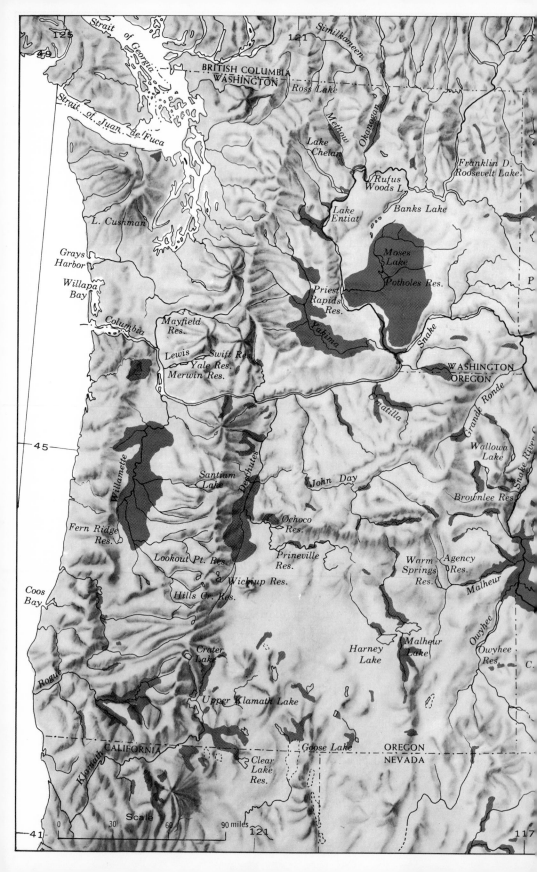

THE PACIFIC NORTHWEST
IRRIGATION AREAS

113

109

49

Milk

Nelson Res.

Marias

Teton

Missouri

Fort Peck Res.

Noxon Res.

Flathead Lake

Hungry Horse Res.

Clark Fk

Swan

Canyon Ferry Res.

Musselshell

Lochsa

Selway

Bitterroot

Yellowstone

rwater

Salmon

Hole

Jefferson

Madison Res.

MONTANA

WYOMING

45

Middle Fk.

Big

Lemhi

Red Rock

Lima Res.

Hebgen Res.

Yellowstone Lake

Shoshone

ascade Res.

Island Park Res.

Buffalo Bill Res.

Bighorn

Arrowrock Res.

Henrys Fk.

Jackson Lake

Boysen Res.

Boise

Magic Res.

Snake

Blackfoot

Wind

Bruneau

Blackfoot River Res.

American Falls Res.

L. Walcott Res.

Bear

Hams Fork

Green

IDAHO

UTAH

Blacks Fork

Flaming Gorge Res.

Great Salt Lake

113

41

109

SHERMAN

ning was made on the Minidoka project in the central Snake River Valley. By 1909, 125,000 acres of arid land were watered by facilities of the United States Reclamation Service.[3]

The underlying secret of the Service's success was its recognition of the fact that its program would assuredly fail if federal projects were located only in unoccupied and undeveloped areas. In some of the most promising locations limited irrigation was already being done under private enterprise, or in some instances under the Carey Act. Such efforts deserved support, and the Reclamation Service lent itself to meaures of mutual effort as well as to wholly new projects.

Both Oregon projects were developed in areas where irrigation was already practiced. The Umatilla project was in the vicinity of Stanfield and Hermiston, where several private companies were operating and three-fourths of the land was privately owned. Cold Springs Reservoir, completed in 1908, was filled from the Umatilla by means of a diversion dam and feed canal leading from a point south of Echo. The facilities were of permanent construction, with concrete dams and cement-lined canals. Costs of $60 per acre were assessed against lands which, with the advent of water, were valued at three or four times that amount.

The Klamath project was also located in an area long served by private canals. Here an elaborate plan was worked out to water 187,000 acres. It called for storage reservoirs at Clear Lake and Miller Creek (Gerber Reservoir), several diversion dams on Lost River, and a network of canals to irrigate land south of Klamath Falls and to control the flow into Tule Lake in northern California. However, the plan required that large private holdings be subdivided and sold in tracts of not more than 160 acres before government water would be made available to them. By 1912 the Main Canal, Clear Lake dam, Lost River diversion dam, and many of the distribution structures had been completed.

In Washington a modest development, consisting of two storage reservoirs on Salmon Lake and Salmon Creek near Conconully, a diversion dam on the lower waters of Salmon Creek, and distribution canals, served some 7700 acres lying west of the Okanogan River in the vicinity of Omak, devoted primarily to fruit-growing. In the Yakima Valley private and commercial development of irrigation had already gone so far that the Reclamation Service at first saw no prospect of carrying out construction there. The Washington Irrigation Company not only had extensive landholdings in the center of the valley, but had a bill before the Washington state legislature which would allow it to use Lake Cle Elum for storage. Should Cle Elum and the other mountain

---

[3] United States Bureau of Reclamation, *Reclamation Project Data* (1948).

lakes come under private control, this would seriously jeopardize plans for comprehensive development of the entire valley under federal auspices. Federal engineers were dubious of success so long as appropriations for water rights were known to be excessive. They were willing to recommend a federal project only on condition that outstanding water rights be reduced to a realistic figure, and that the Washington Irrigation Company sell its water system—though not its lands—to the United States.[4]

The federal demands precipitated a lively political flurry in Yakima Valley where Wesley Jones of Yakima and A. J. Splawn of Cowiche led the drive for the Service's program, with Colonel William W. Robertson, editor of the Yakima *Republic*, aiding their cause. The private reservoir bill was defeated, and the Washington Irrigation Company finally accepted the government terms. The reduction of water rights was accomplished by an energetic campaign up and down the valley to persuade applicants who had filed for excessive appropriations to scale them down.

Early in 1906 the Sunnyside and Tieton units of the Yakima project were under way. The Sunnyside project required only improving and enlarging an existing canal and reconstructing the diversion dam. The Tieton development involved building a diversion dam on the Tieton River and a canal system to water 27,500 acres between the river and Ahtanum Creek west of Yakima. Reservoirs were established at Lake Cle Elum, Bumping Lake, Lake Kachess, and Lake Keechelus. These facilities guaranteed an adequate stream flow throughout the year and allowed for construction of canals leading to the higher benches and lands in the upper valley. The Yakima project was intended ultimately to serve 450,000 acres in south-central Washington. Expenditures through 1910 amounted to $3,500,000.

Reclamation Service projects in Idaho required equally complex negotiations and even more ambitious planning. The development of bench lands between the Boise and Snake rivers was undertaken in response to petitions from local irrigators who had found the improvement of higher elevations too much for them. It required incorporating a number of existing canals into the project system. Agreements concluded with landowners and canal companies gave the Reclamation Service adequate control, while recognizing individual property rights and making a firm commitment to supply water in the future. In some instances water users formed associations and worked out contracts with the Service to repay the project costs. Contracts were signed with several local irrigation districts, such as Pioneer, Riverside, and Nampa-Meridian. Only as

[4] Calvin B. Coulter, "Victory of National Irrigation in the Yakima Valley, 1902–1906," *PNQ*, April 1951.

these arrangements were perfected could the Reclamation Service proceed with construction.

The Boise project featured in particular the Boise River diversion dam southeast of the city of Boise and the Deer Flat reservoir southwest of Nampa, together with low-line and high-line canals. These facilities were well advanced toward completion by 1910. The construction of Arrowrock Dam, a tremendous concrete, arch-gravity type of structure 354 feet high from river bed to crest and 1150 feet long, created a reservoir of 286,600 acre-feet capacity. Finished in 1915, Arrowrock was the first of a series of huge storage basins that gave reclamation in southern Idaho greatly increased potential.

The Minidoka project differed from others in that irrigation in this locality was a new venture. The plan adopted by the Reclamation Service included a storage dam on the south fork of the Snake River at Jackson Lake in northwest Wyoming and a general-purpose dam on the middle Snake River near Minidoka. The latter installation served for diversion, storage, and the generation of hydroelectric power. A gravity canal system led from the dam to Acequia, Rupert, Heyburn, and Paul, while the lands south of the river around Burley and Delco, some of which lay above the gravity canals, were irrigated by a pumping system.

The burden of watering the land had fallen on the federal government. The Reclamation Service remained the farmers' friend even when, in later days, farmers viewed other government agencies with suspicious eyes.

CHAPTER
TWENTY-FIVE

Harvests of the Forest
and the Sea

THE TRAVELER to the Far West distinguished its landscape, not only for snow peaks and sagebrush range, fertile valleys and checkerboard fields of wheat, but also for the depth and extent of year-round green forests and the numerous waters teeming with fish. Forest and fish were important to the region from the time of its first settlement. Both lumbering and fishing took on new significance at the turn of the century.

The Northwest's forests, including those of western Montana, cover about 93,000,000 acres. The Ponderosa, often called the western yellow pine, prevails east of the Cascades at dry timberline heights. Spruce from the west coastal ranges did not come into commercial use until World War I. But Douglas fir (or Oregon pine), the predominant forest type from the coast to the summit of the Cascades, was first in commercial importance and has remained preeminent.

The greatest growth of Douglas fir occurs during its first seventy-five years. At twice that age the tree has reached approximately maximum size, in good soil averaging 190 feet in height and thirty to forty inches in diameter at breast height. The mature tree produces a soft, fine wood; second growth, or immature wood, has a coarser grain and dark heart of summer wood. Both are strong and durable without being heavy, and are used for structural purposes such as frame constructions, building forms, bridge and trestle timbers, railway ties, pilings, and ship building.

By 1887 the assault on these forest giants was under way. Twelve years later the *Pacific Lumber Trade Journal* proclaimed lumber king, since all but seven of western Washington's big towns were dependent upon their big trees. In 1914, 55 percent of the payrolls of the Northwest were derived directly from the industry. Output of camps and mills represented 38 percent of the value of all manufactures and the capitalized value of the forest lands was estimated at slightly over $1,000,000,000.

The tremendous expansion of the United States economy had created a great market for timber products and with the virgin stands of the East and Midwest cut over by the mid-eighties, the Far West (and South) became an important source of supply, attracting eastern capital to its exploitation. With the increase in operations and under the pressures of speculative gain, important changes took place in the pattern of timberland holdings.

Usually small operators bought timber from private lands and cut freely on the public domain, undisturbed by public protest except as it threatened to make government fussy about trespass. Operators of large mills and improved machinery required a dependable supply of logs and found it feasible to own timberland. The California firm of Pope and Talbot had long cut from their own holdings; men like Ben Healy of Wisconsin first appeared in Washington's forest industry as an absentee owner, but some became active in management of mills and camps. Chauncey W. Griggs and his son, Everett, from Minnesota purchased 80,000 acres from the Northern Pacific, founded the St. Paul and Tacoma Lumber Company, and were soon among the state's most prominent lumbermen.

In 1900 Frederick Weyerhaeuser announced purchase of 900,000 acres from the Northern Pacific at $6 an acre. This was but a beginning. In a short time his holdings were estimated at 2,000,000 acres, and according to a contemporary "pretty much everything outside of the government forest reserve is tributary to Weyerhaeuser. He may not own it, his name may not appear as record anywhere, but it is under his domination. Such is true of Oregon's great forest lands also." With Weyerhaeuser's first purchase a wave of buying was set off that had no parallel in the history of the region, perhaps of the nation. Prices soared to unheard-of levels and speculators, large and small, turned a pretty penny trading on the general advance in values. A tract bought in 1899 for $10,000 was sold ten years later for $110,000. In Idaho a large tract purchased for $240,000 in 1901 resold in 1909 for $2,500,000.

There were less expensive ways of acquiring land. The federal government was generous with the public domain; land laws governing its disposal were designed primarily to help settlers get cheap, even free, land for farming; but the laws were used to build vast empires of timberlands, often with the connivance of public officials. A recent immigrant to Seattle wrote home to Norway that

> The large sawmill companies naturally want to buy up all forest land that is now held at $1500 to $5,000 per 160 acres, depending on the stand of timber and its location. The government does not sell land, but turns it over to those who either are or will become dwellers on the land; . . . according to laws affecting timber claims—and the companies may later buy from those who have "proved up" such claims. . . . One quickly receives papers on timberland, and if one does not have to live on it, it becomes very quickly an easy way of earning money for people of all classes.[1]

Dummies and false entrymen filed 106-acre claims under the Homestead law or the Timber and Stone acts. They immediately commuted the residence requirement by paying $1.25 an acre, and transferred title to a lumber company at cost, receiving $50—or sometimes less— as a fee for their services. In other cases homesteaders, often women, filed for land, piled up a few boards to represent a cabin, and put a potted plant beside it—thus establishing proof of residence and cultivation—and waited out the five-year period. It was an easy way to pick up cash and it became easier as one grew adept at multiple filings. This required cooperation of land office officials, who provided it for a fee.

Timberland frauds in Oregon led to scandals. The United States Attorney General appointed Francis J. Heney a special prosecutor to conduct investigations involving prominent citizens, a United States senator, and land office officials, which led to some convictions.[2] Wagon and military road grants facilitated the concentration of private holdings, and the failure of the state to patent its school lands meant that much valuable timberland which might have been administered by the state was taken up by private claimants instead. Huge federal grants to the Northern Pacific and Oregon and California Railroad formed the basis of some of the largest privately owned timber holdings. Though instances of large fraud shocked the people of the Pacific Northwest and elsewhere, and had political repercussions in Oregon, the "looting of

[1] Kenneth O. Bjork, *West of the Great Divide* (1958), 449; Richard Lillard, "Timber King," *The Pacific Spectator*, Winter 1947; David M. Ellis, "The Oregon and California Railroad Land Grant, 1866–1945," *PNQ*, October 1948.

[2] Stephen A. D. Puter, *Looters of the Public Domain* (1907).

the public domain" was but an episode in the development of the industry.

Naturally, increased demand for lumber and new transportation facilities were responsible in some measure for both trading in lands and expansion of mill facilities. While buying and selling of stumpage was closely identified with the operation of mills, the early high margin of profits in timberlands came from speculation and rising land values rather than from the demand of lumber mills themselves.

The distinguishing feature of the new regime was the great concentration of ownership over vast acreages of forest lands. In 1913 the Weyerhaeuser Timber Company alone held 26.1 percent of the privately owned standing timber in Washington; Weyerhaeuser and the Northern Pacific Railroad together owned 45.7 percent; Weyerhaeuser and Southern Pacific owned 22.4 percent in Oregon. The Northern Pacific owned 29.8 percent of the private timberlands in Montana. Twenty percent of the privately owned timber was in small acreages (1000 to 2000 acres) of less than 60,000,000 board feet each. Thus while three large owners controlled 237 billion board feet of standing timber, 17,000 small owners held 205 billion feet.

Because of the small size and often inaccessibility of their holdings, small operators found it difficult or impossible to log them efficiently. "Gyppos," contractors for logs or small mill operators, moved camp continuously to new areas of easy cutting and hauling, and contributed as much to the devastation of the forests as they did to the hazards of the men who worked their gear, "Haywire from the cookhouse to the tail block," which meant in loggers' language "no damn good at all." For large operators land ownership was viewed rather as a capital expense—in some circumstances a burdensome one. Meanwhile, the business operated under sharp fluctuations in volume and price that seem only remotely connected with land values or ownership.

The general trend in production was sharply upward between 1890 and 1905. The region as a whole attained peak production for the pre-1917 period in 1913, with a total cut of 7.46 billion feet (see Graphs XIV, XV, XVI, pp. 627, 628). The mills were highly mechanized establishments, a far cry from those that had been the pride of the Far West a short time before. In logging camps too, new machines and tools handled the heavy timber with speed and precision. Old-timers might smile when Sol Simpson of Simpson Logging Company sold his oxen, shifted to horses, and then to donkey engines to do his skidding. The newfangled ideas soon proved their worth and were widely adopted. Logging railroads were pushed farther into the mountains and at Polson's railroad camp, Grays Harbor, the fleet of locomotives with potbellied, topheavy stacks called attention to the new importance of the steam engine. Before 1911 skidding was done on the ground. After that, spar pole and high lead rigging were commonly used. Huge spools of wire were delivered at the camps to be spun into rigging that hung like monstrous spider webs against the sky. Here was indeed a bold demonstration of power, when two men set the choker on a turn of logs, stood back and watched them lifted like matchsticks and carried, dangling, to a loading area 200 yards below on the mountain slope. High-line logging made it possible to cut on rough terrain where no ox or horse could skid logs.

Problems of Production

As early as 1904 the productive capacity of the mills was expanding faster than the market. Although output figures increased for several years thereafter, the mills frequently operated only five days a week, took several winter weeks off for repairs, or closed down altogether. In 1917, William B. Greeley estimated that the output of the mills was only 62 percent of capacity.

There was no single national or world organization to keep prices uniform and reasonably steady, as was the case with sugar, wheat, and other commodities. Lumber prices varied as much as 50 percent in one year, and the fluctuations were practically impossible to anticipate so that production might be adjusted to them. Once operating at a given level, the mills developed a momentum that made them less sensitive to market conditions. Transportation costs, ever a large factor for the Northwest mills, narrowed their market and often prevented them from shipping to places where they might otherwise have competed successfully. A company might cut to excess in order to pay land taxes or interests on its debts, or to take advantage of a slight rise in price.

Common problems forced this highly competitive industry to common action. Local associations formed in the nineties on the Sound and in Portland proved short-lived. But soon after 1900 stronger associations were formed, such as the Oregon Lumber Manufacturers Association and the Pacific Coast Association whose strength was mainly in Washington. While these groups did not always share the same interests, particularly in the matter of railway rates, they combined in 1911 to form the West Coast Lumbermen's Association. By the beginning of World War I the Association included companies producing 90 percent of the lumber output of the Pacific Northwest, and was established as the principal agency of the industry.

Mutual agreement was necessary, mainly with regard to prices and the establishment of uniform grades of specified types of lumber. Grading assured quality, and the fixing of standards was of prime importance in selling to markets elsewhere in the country. When it came to setting prices there was more than a hint of "restricted competition," which manufacturers defended on grounds that "cutthroat" competition was wasteful and price stabilization desirable for the industry as a whole. The Association published standard price lists with the explicit understanding that Association members would, so far as was practicable, use them. After 1906, when trust-busters sounded an alarm, the published prices became reports of "prevailing prices." Although not enforced as openly as before, they continued to exert much the same effect, since loyal members were unlikely to sell for less than the list price.[3]

Trade associations did much to bring order into both production and marketing of Northwest timber products but they did not extend the tight controls characteristic of monopolistic operation. Competition was too complex to be eliminated or managed by any group of producers. Wood products had to compete with an ever-growing number of substitutes, and rival products—steel, cement, or asbestos—limited the per capita consumption of timber and forced salesmen to aggressive action in maintaining their markets. Western mill owners watched their costs closely, lest they be shut out by producers of southern pine. Large owners, despite economy and efficiency, were never free from competition from small establishments that had less indebtedness and lower overhead. Thus, while the ownership of timberlands was highly concentrated, production of lumber was not. The West Coast Lumbermen's Association cut down competition but never created a true monopoly.

The enterprise of the lumber companies, effective in solving technical and marketing problems, did not reach to the area of liberal labor policies. The attitude of the employer toward his wage hands was probably no different from that in other industries. Logging operations, however, were seasonal, marked by long hours, absence of a uniform wage scale, and deplorable living conditions. In the early twentieth century private enterprise felt little responsibility for the laborer's welfare and the lumber operator, facing stiff competition, paid no more than he had to in wages and spent a bare minimum on camp living quarters. If challenged, he replied that he could afford no more, and that the logger wouldn't know what to do with a clean camp if he had one.

This argument sometimes seemed reasonable. The logger was not fastidious; usually he was a transient, a drifter with no dependents. If he "threw a wingding" (lost his temper), "threw the rope over the top" (worked so carelessly as to endanger another's safety), or "played Arab" (not on the job when needed), or "threw the book away" (disregarded

[3] John Cox, "Trade Associations in the Lumber Industry of the Pacific Northwest," *PNQ*, October 1950.

orders)—the yell "Draw your pay" from the "rawhider" (a driving boss) "tramped" him and sent him back to Portland or Seattle skid roads. A short spree, "antigodlin'," (off the straight and narrow path) gave him a repertoire of new "bunkhouse fables" (stories about a spree), but, his belly "hollow as a coon leg," the transient logger tied his bed roll on his shoulders and looked for another "rat's nest" (duty camp), another rawhider, and another "stomach robber" (cook).[4]

As time went on, other sorts of men appeared in the camps. Some were ambitious, able young fellows who through hard work soon rose to higher positions. Others were stump ranchers who turned to logging to supplement meager incomes. To regular loggers "farmers" meant "unskilled men," and "farmer laydowns" were "easy logging shows." In some areas, particularly in Willamette Valley foothills and around Centralia, Washington, farmers made up as much as 75 percent of the logging crews. Since neither transients nor farmers considered their jobs permanent they took little interest in camp or labor conditions.

On the other hand, among the loggers were some men of American, French-Canadian (Canuckers), or Scandinavian stock, who had followed the industry from Maine to Wisconsin, to Minnesota, and to the Northwest, just as their employers had. Accepting the life of a migratory worker for a time, such a man nevertheless looked forward to marriage, home and family. Sometimes—though rarely—he married first and brought his wife to the camp or found a place to live in a nearby town. The real logger took pride in his special skill and, wage earner though he was, he took an almost proprietary interest in the industry. It was this last group that was ready to make personal sacrifices to improve general wage levels and living conditions. These were the men who formed unions, organized strikes, and battled with the companies. The drifters might be the radicals, but the steady loggers, like the shingle weavers in the mills, were the backbone of the organized labor movement among timber workers.

NORTHWEST FISHERIES

While whistle-punk, topper, dog tripper, and choke-setter attacked the forests, other men in the Northwest grew callouses netting the harvest of rivers and the sea. Salmon had through the centuries been a staple of the Indians' diet. The first settlers could by their own efforts take all

[4] Walter F. McCulloch, *Woods Words; a Comprehensive Dictionary of Loggers Terms* (1958).

the fish they could use or they could buy from Indians choice Chinook at 25 cents apiece. In 1867 the Hume brothers, who had found fishing the Sacramento River more profitable than mining, built a salmon cannery on the Columbia, and the next year, Captain John West followed suit. By 1881 some thirty canneries represented a capital investment in plant and boats of more than a million dollars, and turned out a pack of 530,000 cases, valued at $2,600,000, according to local reports.

Some 4000 Chinese prepared the fish for the cans, a skilled cutter handling 1600 fish in a day, for which he was paid $1 to $1.50. While an unwritten law decreed that a Chinese would be shot on sight if caught fishing, he was the common laborer in the canneries and relatively safe in the chinatowns of Astoria and Portland, even during the tense days of anti-Chinese riots in the late seventies. Cannery work and fishing were seasonal because the prime run of the preferred salmon migrated up the Columbia to the spawning ground from April to August. The canneries employed 2500 to 3000 fishermen, most of them Scandinavians and Finns who lived at Astoria, Ilwaco, and Cathlamet, and worked in lumber camps or farmed in off-seasons. Cannery operators supplied boats and gear on rigid lease terms which discouraged independent fishermen and competition.

The fisherman's work was hard and hazardous, and barely provided a living when he worked with a leased boat in a noncompetitive situation. His rental was taken out of his catch, for which he received, in good times, as much as 65 cents a fish. When fishermen refused to rent, preferring to use their own boats, canneries refused to buy their fish. Only a strong association of fishermen could battle the canneries.

The boat in common use was an open, flat-bottomed, 26-foot craft, sloop-rigged with a centerboard, easily manned by two men, using set or drifting nets. The mesh of the gill net was of such size as to catch the salmon by the gills and drown them while letting other fish slip through. As the name implies, a set net was fixed in position before the tide ebbed and removed about an hour after it turned. The drift net was staked at the shore end, laid out with large corks and allowed to move with the current. Seining was a different operation from gill netting and required fewer boats and more power. From one boat corked nets of finer mesh than gill nets were laid out to a second boat which remained stationary while the first moved in a circle away from shore and against the current back to the stationary boat. The net lines were then pulled tight and the catch hauled to shore. Off Astoria, in the middle of the five-mile-wide Columbia, was shoal water where, at the proper turn of the tide, men and horses appeared to walk on the waters, as they pulled in their 100- to 400-fathom-long seines.

Growth of the Columbia River salmon fishery industry must be credited largely to the use of more efficient gear. The waters of Bakers Bay on the Washington shore were dotted with pound nets. Fixed in position, these nets acted as a kind of fence that guided salmon into an enclosure or pound where they could be taken more easily. Oregon fishermen continued for the most part to use gill nets, put out from small boats, but these nets too were larger and more numerous each year, until observers declared that when the fish were running the nets overlapped and choked the river from bank to bank. Steamboat captains were forced either to change their schedules or shut off their engines to avoid fouling their propellers.

Boat fishermen resented fixed gear that entangled them and forced them out on dangerous waters of the bar. Ilwaco pound men met gill netters from Astoria with guns. Each group organized its own association, published its own story, and appealed to its legislature or to the federal government for protection; this kind of interstate altercation and competition made the fishing industry difficult to control.

Upriver, between the Cascades and Celilo Falls, where Indians had fished from ancient times, white fishermen installed fish wheels, which dipped continuously and virtually pumped fish out of the river. Mounted sometimes on scows, sometimes on permanent foundations, the wheels delivered 20,000 to 50,000 fish in a day. Owners of fish wheels became vested interests, highly defensive of their sites, for there was rarely room for more than one wheel at a good location. Most of them were on the Oregon side of the Columbia, but Washington had a few. Though sharply criticized, these devices were not outlawed in Oregon until 1927 or in Washington until 1935.

Robert Hume, Innovator and Entrepreneur

The salmon industry had not been profitable so long as the output depended upon local or San Francisco markets. However, by 1872, shipments were made to Australia, China, and South America. The Hume brothers found the most profitable outlet for their large pack in Great Britain, and Robert D. Hume captured that market for himself almost exclusively. After a few years on the Columbia, he made the Rogue River the center of his activities and by the end of the century he owned a town, Wedderburn, a sheep range, pea farms and pea cannery, newspapers, mills, a fish cannery, ice and cold storage plant, a can manufacturing plant of his own design, and ships to carry off his annual pack. His monopoly of the Rogue River industry was so complete that he withstood three attempts by the powerful Alaska Packers Association to invade his domain. Obviously no independent fisherman could work the Rogue which Hume claimed as his own.[5]

Probably Hume's greatest contribution to the industry was not appreciated until long after his death in 1908. In 1878 he began artificial salmon propagation, and by this means assured himself of a continuing annual run. He was years ahead of his contemporaries who as late as 1895 understood little about the peculiar migratory habits of the salmon and made little effort to learn.

Northern Fisheries: Puget Sound and Alaska

Compared with Columbia River canneries, early fishing enterprises on the Sound and the coast were small. Two young men from Maine established a fishing station at Tacoma, shipping their catch to Portland and San Francisco. Several companies of Italians and Austrians, Greeks and Portuguese, worked out of Seattle, taking mostly halibut, rock cod and mackerel. Jackson and Myers ran a cannery for a time at Mukilteo, later at Port Blakeley. A Port Madison herring fishery owned by J. P. Hammond employed, during the winter months, a dozen men of varying nationalities. With catches selling in Portland and San Francisco for five to eight cents a pound, nobody made much profit. Census takers in 1880 reported a trade worth only $181,372.

With the advent of new populations and new capital, however, the fisheries grew rapidly into one of the area's biggest businesses, and Puget Sound fishermen delivered a $5,500,000 product in 1902. In 1908 Washington ranked fourth in the United States in value of fish products, surpassed only by Massachusetts, New York, and Virginia. Just before World War I, Washington alone turned out $20,000,000 worth of fish and shellfish, harvested by 8500 fishermen. Another $10,000,000 worth of salmon was caught and sold by British Columbians. The Alaska fisheries, most productive of all, sent 4,000,000 cases of canned salmon to world markets. Pacific Coast canneries alone could more than encircle the world with their tins, and provide four pounds of salmon annually for every man, woman, and child in the United States.

On Puget Sound, as on the Columbia, there were runs when great numbers of Chinook moved in through the Strait and San Juan Islands on their way to spawn in the Fraser or Skagit rivers. Other salmon stayed in the Sound and could be taken at almost any time between May and November. Fishermen were busy most of the year, and they devel-

[5] Gordon B. Dodds, *The Salmon King of Oregon; R. D. Hume and the Pacific Fisheries* (1959).

oped improved gear, some adapted to the seasonal runs and some to trolling which could be carried on at various times and places.

At the approaches to the Fraser, such as Point Roberts, San Juan Island, and Birch Bay, the sockeye salmon followed favorite passages, at which the fishermen set up permanent seines, or traps, which functioned in much the same ways as the pounds of Bakers Bay. Costing several thousand dollars each, the traps delivered rich catches with a minimum of effort during the migratory seasons. Like the fishing wheels, they were criticized for their very efficiency; nevertheless, in 1915 some 600 licensed traps were operating in Washington waters.

Sockeyes swept through the border waterways in schools which alert fishermen detected and captured with purse seines, which sometimes enclosed schools of nearly 1000 fish. This popular method of fishing led to the development of specially designed boats. Powered by gasoline (in recent years, by diesel) engines, the 60- to 80-foot boats had a capacity of fifteen to twenty-five tons and took a crew of five to seven men. In 1912, approximately 100 were operating on Swiftsure bank, off the southern shores of Vancouver Island. Purse seines and traps accounted for the greater part of the catch on Puget Sound, but from 1912 on, motor trolling boats began to share in it. Experienced operators who knew where the best feeding grounds were cruised over a wide area, chiefly offshore, that was not reached by other types of boats. Trollers thirty to sixty feet in length were identified by tall poles which stood vertical on both sides of a central mast, until lowered to carry the lines into the water. Although the first commercial trollers failed to reach the greater depths haunted by large salmon, and though they hooked and injured many fish without landing them, they rapidly improved their methods and found a permanent place in the industry. Larger boats were built, longer and heaver lines used, and considerable ingenuity was shown in multiplying the number of hooks and staggering them at different depths. In later years, Alaskan offshore trollers working beyond the three-mile limit put as many as twelve lines, each with thirty hooks, in the water simultaneously, using a system of in-hauls and power reels. Scandinavians and Finns were expert trollers and the most independent fishermen in the business. Selling entirely to the fresh-fish or mild-cured market, they got premium prices for their catch, and had no association with the canneries. Competition was tough, and many boats made small profits; sometimes none. Still, there was a living in it, and the independent boat owner with his "swivelneck" companion who worked for 20 percent of the catch, became a familiar sight along the Oregon and Washington coasts.

In varieties of salmon caught and in essential techniques of fishing and canning, Alaska fishery was much like that of the Columbia River and Puget Sound. Gill net boats operated in Bristol Bay, purse seiners and traps in the central and southeastern districts. Types of gear depended on local conditions and were improved as experience dictated. The same forces of organization were felt, and the canneries controlled the area, much as they did farther south.

Salmon canning began in Alaska with experimental ventures by the Alaska Commercial Company in 1887–1888. The first product was shipped to San Francisco, where the possibilities of northern fishery were soon recognized. In the next years, canneries were established in such numbers that the Alaska pack rapidly outstripped that of the Columbia and the Sound.[6]

Early in this period the industry suffered severe growing pains. Competition to get the fish was intense—far more so than on the Columbia. Alaskan natives were shunted aside by cannery workers who came from California and the Sound. As the best trap locations were discovered, rivalry led to acts of violence. One group dammed the streams and even destroyed the traps set by another. In the mad rush for fish, little or no thought was given to the question of ultimate depletion. In these hectic years, a good trap location might change hands at $20,000 to $90,000 though the trap itself had cost but $5000 to build.

Organization of the Canning Industry

Before 1893, most of the canneries were owned and operated by partnerships or individuals such as Robert Hume. Plants were small, and since they used little machinery, many were moved from place to place in search of more favorable fishing conditions. The next decade saw rapid change which, while it increased profits for the larger and more successful canneries, forced some smaller ones out of business. The "iron chink," developed in 1903, and other machines for making, filling, and soldering the cans, made the Chinese laborer obsolete and increased productive capacity, until a day's turnout soared to several thousand cans. Canning cost per case was reduced, but mechanization put a premium on high capitalization and demanded a large supply of fish for survival. The marketing problem loomed in an entirely new light. Despite improvements in transportation, overproduction soon glutted the markets with consequent ruinously low prices. Out of this situation came the big packing associations.

The trend toward combination and consolidation was apparent in

[6] Otis B. Freeman, "Salmon Industry of the Pacific Coast," *Economic Geography*, April 1935.

the early 1890s. Individual cannery owners first formed cooperatives and set up marketing policies and restricted production in an effort to stabilize prices and profits. These steps led to a more thorough reorganization in 1892, with the formation of the Alaska Packers Association by a merger of 90 percent of the canneries operating in Alaska. Individual companies surrendered their plants in return for capital stock in the Association and accepted a single unified management. A number of canneries were closed, competition was abated, and production was held at profitable levels. From the start the Association was a financial success, controlling, between 1893 and 1910, a half to three-quarters of the total pack of Alaska salmon. Libby, McNeil & Libby and Pacific American Fisheries, Inc., in turn, acquired a number of canning firms and established themselves as the other big operators in the Alaska trade.

The same trend toward consolidation was reflected in the British Columbia Packers Association and the Columbia River Packers Association, both of which were formed shortly after 1900. These organizations functioned much as did the Alaska Packers, though they never produced more than a quarter to a third of the total pack. The British Columbia Packers by 1914 were producing 280,000 cases annually; the Columbia River Packers, about half as much. From 1900 to 1920 the Alaska Packers Association alone produced well over a million cases a year.

However, nothing like a complete monopoly was reached in the salmon fisheries, and for a long time the operations appeared to become more competitive, rather than less. Size and financial strength were advantageous, but in the period of rapid expansion new techniques and the militancy of the fishermen's unions temporarily saved the industry from domination by any one group.

Nevertheless, big business methods were important in many ways. Marketing was handled through agents and brokers, and was ever more closely related to the food companies which served as outlets. Wholesale firms were established in San Francisco, Seattle, and Vancouver, with storage facilities to permit distribution throughout the year.

North Pacific Halibut and Shellfish

The advent of transcontinental railroads, declining yields of Atlantic fish banks, and improved methods of refrigeration account largely for the rapid rise of the Northwest halibut fishery in the early part of this century. A few schooners put in at Port Townsend and Victoria during the 1870s and 1880s, with fish for transshipment to San Francisco.

411

With refrigerated transportation, shipments could be made to the East Coast and Pacific halibut was sold even in Gloucester. By 1915 the industry was handling an annual catch of 66,000,000 pounds.[7]

The first western shipments, crudely packaged and poorly iced, arrived in miserable condition, failing to earn their express charges. Eastern fishermen resented competition from the western boats, and New England dealers spoke disparagingly of the "worthless 'California' halibut." High carrying costs, sometimes as much as $1.25 a hundred, put a heavy burden on the western shipper, while the distribution setup required him to ship to New York even though his fish might eventually be sold in the Midwest.

Nevertheless, the decreasing Atlantic yield encouraged western fishermen. Halibut prices went up and competitive conditions became more favorable. The larger firms with better trade connections established themselves on Puget Sound and began operating fleets of boats. Some were eastern firms like the New England Fish Company (a group of Boston dealers operating out of Vancouver, B.C.) and the International Fisheries Company which operated a branch at Tacoma. Among those who entered the trade at Seattle, the strongest firms were the San Juan Fish & Packing Company, Seattle Fish and Cold Storage Company, and Chlopeck Fish Company.

Halibut, a bottom fish, feed in forty to sixty fathoms of water, and the fishermen's gear was designed to put as many hooks as possible on the bottom. The common unit of gear was a ten-line skate, consisting of a hemp ground line 500 fathoms long with hooks set on five-foot cotton branch lines or "gangings" spaced nine feet apart. Two men handled these skates from a dory, setting them in strings two to six skates long, anchored and buoyed with an identifying flat at each end of the string. Several strings, set parallel to each other, extended either along the edge of the bank or across it.

Life on the halibut boats was not for weaklings. It took considerable skill to set and run the skates without fouling them, from dories bobbing like eggshells on rough seas. Crews of larger boats ran two to three skates an hour during a day's fishing—arduous exertion in itself. Nor was the day's work done when the fish were pulled into the boat. The catch, running from 100 to 1000 fish, must be transferred from the dory to the larger boat, there to be cleaned, iced, and stored in the hold. Once loaded, the boat headed for home port or for the nearest cold storage plant, where its cargo was unloaded and forwarded to market. Men on the schooners usually fished on shares with the boat taking a third of the catch.

[7] William F. Thompson and Norman L. Freeman, *History of the Pacific Halibut Industry*, International Fisheries Commission, Report No. 5 (1930).

While dories and basic gear remained much the same, important improvements appeared in the attendant boats. The larger companies soon turned to steamers, buying boats specially designed for the trade. Schooners continued to use sail under favorable conditions, but they now carried auxiliary engines which made them independent of the weather. Both types of vessels were easily recognizable by their nests of dories carried either amidships or on the stern deck.

Before 1910 nearly all the halibut fishing was done off Cape Flattery and Swiftsure and on the inner banks along the coast of British Columbia and southeastern Alaska. Summer fishing centered mainly in the southern waters. In winter, small boats stayed in port while steamers fished the Alaskan grounds. From 1910 on the catch began to taper off, necessitating a search for new grounds that drove the boats into deeper waters and farther north and west along the coast of Alaska, beyond Cape Spencer. Success here staved off for a time the threat of depletion, and for several years before World War I halibut fishermen were more concerned about overproduction and declining prices than about exhaustion of the fishing grounds. The disappearance of the fish from Puget Sound and the nearer banks was a danger signal but its full import was not yet realized.

Shellfish, the Northwest's third fishing specialty, did not compare with salmon and halibut in economic importance, yet they supported a sizable industry which attracted wide attention. Willapa Bay, long famous for its oysters, had been exporting them to San Francisco since the early 1850s, and was still the most productive spot. Other tidal areas at the head of Puget Sound and to the north in Whatcom, Skagit, and Jefferson counties, were also productive. Soon after 1900 Easterners invested considerable capital in the industry. In 1908, oysters, together with crabs and clams, brought returns of some $460,000. By 1915 the shell fishery was a million-dollar industry, but by that time harvests were thinning and it appeared that the beds which had produced so abundantly were on their way to extinction. Experiments were begun to find means of restoring and maintaining the beds. In 1907 more than 100 carloads of eastern oysters had been transplanted as seedlings in the Willapa and Puget Sound districts; transplanted stock did well, but the problem remained of how to breed oysters locally. By 1915 Professor Trevor Kincaid of the University of Washington had some success in overcoming this difficulty.

Most oyster beds were managed by commercial corporations on privately owned lands. As early as 1907 proposals were made that certain beds at Willapa Harbor, Shelton, Oyster Bay, Port Orchard, and Hood Canal be maintained as public lands, and the remainder offered to the highest bidders in tracts of not more than fifty acres each. When the State

413

of Washington surveyed and platted the tidelands, it established extensive reserves for oyster beds, principally on Hood Canal. Commercial oystermen were critical of this step, declaring that for proper cultivation the reserves needed improvement calling for greater expenditure than the state would be willing to make. For the preservation of the industry, state and private owners had to learn to work together. The advantages of cooperation and far-sighted planning for the harvests of the land and the sea had to be learned the hard way.

Pioneers had said that "when the tide is out, the table is set." Their successors found in the waters and forests not just food and shelter, but two important industries to complement the agricultural economy. Fishing declined in importance, but the forests became the foundation of the region's economy.

CHAPTER
TWENTY-SIX

Building the Cities

ENERGY, MONEY, AND PEOPLE went into the creation of a new urban setting for the Pacific Northwest. By 1910 the percentage of population living in towns of 2500 or more was slightly larger for Oregon and Washington than it was for the country as a whole, but the region had only three cities by census definition (see Table XI, p. 611).

In twenty years Seattle, Portland, and Tacoma had accumulated populations of between 100,000 and 250,000. Their skylines were completely altered. New subdivisions circled the business districts in ever-widening rings of residential neighborhoods. By World War I old landmarks were gone and the urban face was different. Capital was poured into construction. After the big fire of 1889, Seattle put $13,000,000 into rebuilding the heart of the city. Between 1903 and 1906, $33,000,000 went into more pretentious structures, a million-dollar railway station, an equally costly courthouse, high schools, and churches. In one year (1908–1909) Spokane put nearly $15,000,000 into new buildings; railroad companies spent $20,000,000 in Tacoma alone. In less than a decade (1907–1914) construction in Portland and Seattle totaled over $200,000,000.

City building attracted investment capital which, applied generously, provided employment for a large segment of the region's new popula-

4l5

tion. And city building was part of the promotion by which new population was enticed to the Northwest. Popular magazines extolled the beauties and opportunities in the rising cities. Chambers of commerce and railroads turned out a flood of pamphlets, both purely tourist pieces and informative bulletins filled with solid factual data. But the biggest and most dramatic promotions were the Lewis and Clark Centennial Exposition in Portland (1905) and the Alaska-Yukon-Pacific Exposition in Seattle (1909).

Both these fairs were in the grand manner. At Portland's Guilds Lake pretentiously columned halls housed displays from every state in the Union and many foreign countries. A pleasantly simple but monumental structure of huge native logs (destroyed by fire in 1964) dramatized western forests and forest products. Congress appropriated $1,000,000 for the coining of Lewis and Clark commemoration gold dollars and $1,700,000 for the United States building which, surrounded by pools and fountains, was the hub of radiating avenues of halls and rose-lined promenades. Nearly 2,000,000 paid admissions met expenses and returned a 21 percent profit to stockholders. Portland was publicized throughout the land and those who watched the development of the city during the next few years were satisfied that their advertising had paid off handsomely. Continuing in the mood of public spirited promotion, in 1907 Portland's citizens instituted the first of its annual June rose festivals.

Olmstead Brothers of New York drew the preliminary plans for the development of the University of Washington's 250-acre campus into a site for Seattle's A-Y-P Exposition. Several million dollars went into landscaping, roads, and buildings which were later adapted by the University for its own permanent use. Towers, obelisks, arches, flying buttresses, and classical colonnades replaced natural groves; cascades and fountains in formal design focused all eyes upon a superb view of Mt. Rainier. Exhibits said to be valued at $50,000,000 represented national and foreign cultures as well as the region's industries and resources, from mining to dairying and from fisheries to forests.

No one doubted that what the cities were spending on themselves was an investment in a rosy future. Portland put $6,000,000 into a municipal water system bringing the waters of mountain streams from Bull Run Reservoir thirty miles away. Seattle and Tacoma probed the Cascades, exploring problems of sanitation in watersheds and the preservation of forest cover. Seattle laid 428 miles of sewers through tunnels and over hills to an outlet on the Sound to discharge in deep water regardless of tidal ebb and flow.

In Spokane residents pointed with pride to the Monroe Street bridge, a monolithic arch of reinforced concrete, 281 feet long, which in design and construction was considered a major accomplishment of the time. Portland debated the building of a bridge across the Willamette to replace one of its numerous ferries for so long that the trials and difficulties were rehearsed in a ballad, each stanza ending with the plaintive refrain:

> They're going to build, I feel it yet,
> A Bridge across the Will-a-mette.

Once the Morrison Street bridge was completed (1885), other million-dollar projects were undertaken more easily, and the city was released from its confinement between river and west hills to spread out on the east-side plain.

Seattle's most ambitious projects were regrades. The city's prosperity of the moment rested on a narrow shelf of level land along the vital waterfront; but industrial developments and railroad stations and yards required large stretches of flatland. City Engineer R. H. Thomson, technically imaginative and politically resourceful, convinced the voters that their city could not long prosper clinging to the side of a hill.

So Seattle moved its hills into the sea. Little rock was involved, so hydraulic cannon assaulted the steep slopes with millions of gallons of water while huge, specially designed wooden conduits carried both water and dirt to a new location.[1] Ten million cubic yards of earth were sliced and sluiced to make embankments or to raise tideflats which previously had been several feet under water. New land emerged for what is now the principal industrial section of the city. Grades of some streets were reduced by fifteen to twenty-five feet. At the corner of Fourth Avenue and Blanchard Street the level was lowered 107 feet. The old Washington Hotel, perched on top of Denny Hill, was dismantled, the hill cut down, and a new Washington Hotel arose on the spot. In Tacoma the Northern Pacific improved the flats at the mouth of the Puyallup River, drawing the city still farther away from the site of the old town on the Point. The techniques used were less dramatic than those of Seattle, but the facilities necessary for a growing metropolis were skillfully carved from the difficult natural contours.

Seattle debated whether private or public funds could better provide accommodations for rail and water terminals. It was charged that the railroad's private wharves, enjoying monopoly positions, demanded too much in fees and spent too little on facilities. Hiram Chittenden, a leader in port development, declared that monopoly on the waterfront discouraged wholesome growth; Populist Robert Bridges insisted that

[1] *That Man Thomson*, Grant H. Redford, ed. (1950); Arthur H. Dimock, *Preparing the Groundwork for a City: the Regrading of Seattle, Washington* (1928).

waterfront terminals should be public intermediaries between land and water carriers and controlled by neither. The controversy was resolved in 1911 with the creation of a Port Commission, an independent agency. Within five years the commission issued $5,750,000 in bonds to finance comprehensive improvements: at the mouth of the Duwamish, four piers with 5000 linear feet of berthing space; at Hanford Street and nearby, a grain elevator of 500,000 bushel capacity and cold storage plants; and the Central Waterfront Terminal at the foot of Bell Street, with 1200 feet of berthing and a six-story warehouse of 300,000 cubic feet capacity. At Smith Cove a huge double pier extending nearly half a mile into the water, with a gantry able to lift 100-ton loads, was designed specially for the lumber export trade. Salmon Bay terminal served the fishing fleet with sheltered moorage, 195,000 square feet of open wharf space, and nearly thirty square city blocks under roof.

In 1910 Portland chartered a Commission of Public Docks to construct and maintain water terminals. Earlier the state legislature had created the Port of Portland (1891) as a municipal corporation charged specifically to maintain and improve harbor facilities. In twenty-five years the Port spent nearly $7,000,000 on services that materially strengthened the city's competitive position in ocean commerce, nearly half the revenues being used to deepen the Willamette within the confines of the city. By 1904 the Port had a dry dock in operation and four years later coaling was provided at competitive costs. For a number of years it supplied towing and pilotage, sometimes at a loss, in order to offset disadvantages of the long upriver voyage.

Portland had other problems peculiar to a river port. Since the Oregon Railway and Navigation Company had become a link in a transcontinental and had absorbed the vital portages at the Cascades and The Dalles, river boats no longer traversed the upper Columbia. Portlanders now felt the pinch of monopoly other Oregonians had experienced from the OSN. Uniting efforts to beat the railroad monopoly, eastern Oregon communities and Portland prevailed upon Congress to appropriate funds for a boat canal at the Cascades and a canal and locks at The Dalles. Whether they were used or not, these "aids to navigation," merely by being there, forced the railroads to reduce their rates. This was to Portland's advantage with regard to upper river traffic. But as oceangoing vessels increased in size and draft, the city found its future also hinged on improvements at the Columbia bar and the depth of the Columbia's and Willamette's channels, which were under federal jurisdiction. In 1884 the United States Corps of Engineers had built a jetty four and a half miles long at the south entrance to scour out a channel. Between 1903 and 1913 the original jetty was extended three miles and during the next four years a north jetty was constructed, giving the bar channel a mean depth of thirty-seven feet.

The Engineers also built stone and pile dikes and revetments on the main courses of the rivers and dredged out the bars that formed in the runoff of spring freshets, thus maintaining a controlled depth of twenty-six feet (at mean low water) on the Columbia, and of thirty feet on the Willamette as far as Portland. (In 1963 a project calling for a depth of forty feet at bar and in the main channels was assigned to the Engineers.)

While these public improvements were being made, private construction multiplied the number of stores, office buildings, and residences. Property values rose rapidly, attracted investment capital, and contributed to still further improvement. Assessed property values in Portland increased from $44,000,000 in 1902 to $144,000,000 three years later and to $234,000,000 by 1907.

Owners of the Central Building, advertising for prospects, claimed that land values in Seattle's "Inner Business Circle" had advanced 25 percent a year from 1900 to 1907. Here, they said, was a "mine of ever-increasing values and ceaseless dividends." Tideland tracts picked up for next to nothing sold at fantastic profits. "Get the tideland habit," urged Charles Bussell, "it will make money for you while you sleep."[2] Speculative increments were both incentives for and results of multi-million dollar investments in public and private building.

The new hotels, stores, and office buildings bore few signs of parochialism. Many of the designers and builders were trained in eastern schools, and while few were innovators, many exercised discriminating taste. Seattle's 42-story L. C. Smith Building was one of the tallest commercial structures in the nation outside the city of New York. Designed by Gaggin and Gaggin of Syracuse, it would have graced any urban center. The Metropolitan Tract was a model "city within a city," its modern medical office buildings the work of New York architects.

The business blocks in downtown Portland were less imposing but not without quality. The Union Station (1894) and the Portland Hotel (begun in 1883, finished in 1890) were designed by McKim, Mead, and White of New York, who sent out William M. Whidden and Ian Lewis to supervise construction of the hotel. Both men stayed to design and build the City Hall, County Court House, the Arlington Club, and the Good Samaritan Hospital. Albert E. Doyle's scholarly taste was apparent in his adaptations of traditional styles: the classical in the United States National Bank, Renaissance in Multnomah County Li-

[2] Charles B. Bussell, *Tide Lands, Their Story* (n.d.).

brary, and Elizabethan Tudor in Reed College's two halls. Few public or private buildings could be termed peculiarly western or regional in character.

Business encroached upon old residential streets while new residential areas spread further into the wilds. Seattle churches sold their downtown corner lots at substantial profits and erected new buildings in locations presumed to be safe from invasion by commerce. Homes in the path of expansion were razed or, if they stood fast, became isolated landmarks of a bygone age, surrounded by masses of commercial masonry. If the ratio of home owners to renters remained unusually high in the Northwest, it was because new subdivisions were continually opening up. In Portland, old communities on the east side of the Willamette River, St. Johns and Lents, were incorporated into the city and farmlands became the Rose City, Ladd, Hawthorne, and Laurelhurst additions to the city. Regal-sized lots were platted in some subdivisions; in others, thirty to forty foot frontages showed a strange penuriousness when hundreds of acres within city limits were undeveloped. One might buy lots for $3000 "on the heights" with spectacular views of Mounts Hood, St. Helens, or Rainier. These were the aeries of the wealthy. But a newcomer could buy according to his taste and pocketbook and he could avoid heavy assessments and still own his home.

City planning came late and expensively to older urban areas that were forced to battle entrenched interests in order to abolish slums, build rapid transit and highway systems, and if possible, to protect human privacy. The new cities of the Far West, with dreams of unlimited future greatness, could barely conceive that they too might benefit by planning. But in a period of affluence and under pressure from the few who had perspective, in 1911 and 1912 Seattle and Portland took steps to acquire land for parks and playgrounds, plan scenic boulevards, and to think about grandiose schemes for future building.

Portland's park blocks were laid out in the sixties. In 1871 the council purchased 100 acres above a reservoir on the west side and over the years developed Washington Park. Donald Macleay's gift of forest acreage later moved the city fathers to take over adjacent tax delinquent lands and to purchase others for Forest Park, containing 3600 acres in 1965 and anticipating an eventual addition of 2000 more acres, all kept in the natural state. Seattle's acquisitions began with donations of scattered tracts of land by a few public-minded citizens. John C. Olmsted of the New York firm of Olmsted Brothers was employed to recommend a long-range plan of park development. His reports (1903–1908), the basis of the present park system, won voter approval for a $1,500,000 bond issue for land acquisition and improvement. By 1909 Seattle had five public playgrounds and fourteen parks ranging from formal gardens to simple lawns—and forest glens and narrow ravines preserved in their natural state simply for the views they afforded, or complex picnic areas with swimming and boating facilities. Olmsted's recommendations made Seattle aware of its many natural advantages and inspired a substantial start toward a parkway that would one day circle the city in a scenic belt fifty miles long. Portland also employed the Olmsted firm and voted a million-dollar bond issue to build Terwilliger Boulevard, designed by E. T. Mische to open the southwest section of the city hills and offer a scenic view of the environs.

Edward Bennett's Portland plan (1911–1912) called for a web of radial boulevards extending from the downtown commercial districts into peripheral residential areas, a majestic civic center in the heart of the expanded city, and parks situated high on the hills to command sweeping views of the whole development. Virgil C. Bogue, another Olmsted planner, who had a part in the reconstruction of Tacoma's and Seattle's waterfronts, prepared for Seattle a plan more pretentious than Portland's. Bogue thought the focal center of the future Seattle—the principal railroad depot and civic buildings in the grand manner—should be located where central and arterial highways would make it accessible from various sections of the city. Tunnels would pierce the hills to reach the waterfront or more distant neighborhoods to the east; a funicular railroad along Virginia Street would handle traffic up the steep bluff from the shoreline. Bogue's plan disregarded projects already under way which tended to center the mercantile and civic buildings farther south where, for the most part, they have remained. Bennett disregarded Portland's reluctance to act with decision on civic matters. Bogue asked too much, even of a people who dreamed great dreams and carried out a surprising number of them; Seattle was not prepared to think of pushing tunnels through hills or under the waters.

THE ARTS

The pursuit of progress in these regards left little time for cultivating taste or contemplating creatively the human conditions, but culture had its devotees in the Far West at the turn of the century. Theater usually meant vaudeville.[3] John Considine's People's Theater in Spokane ignored the state law of 1895 which prohibited employment of women in bars and theaters; when convicted, Considine paid his $500 fine and opened more theaters. In partnership with New York's Tammany boss, Tim

---

[3] Eugene C. Elliott, *History of Variety-Vaudeville in Seattle from the Beginning to 1914* (1944).

Communities

RIGHT. *Fort Nisqually, Washington, sketched by a nameless artist, was a Hudson's Bay Company trading post and farm established in 1833. Many of today's towns and cities throughout the Northwest had beginnings as unpromising.*

The striking growth of one of the Northwest's finest cities, Portland: ABOVE LEFT. *In 1852, enough forest had been cleared for a few houses and stores.* ABOVE RIGHT. *In 1871, the forest has further receded and Portland can muster a parade.* BELOW. *Today's handsome city.*

Fort Boise, originally a military post, was chartered in 1874 as Boise, probably taken from the French words les bois. *Said to have the largest colony of Basques in the United States today, Boise is the capital and largest city in Idaho, population about 35,-000. From the Capitol Building,* center, *an avenue extends through a portion of Boise's business district.*

LEFT. *Crowning the State Capitol Building at Salem, Oregon, is the heroic figure of the pioneer who settled the west. Numerous interior murals commemorate great events in Oregon's history. Salem, on the Willamette at the site of a former Methodist mission, now has a population of about 66,000.*

BELOW. *Beautiful Olympia and the Capitol Building of Washington cluster at the southernmost tip of Puget Sound. Its population is about 19,000.*

The University of Washington began more than 100 years ago as the Territorial University of Washington and is the oldest state university on the west coast. BELOW LEFT. *As it appeared in 1920.* BELOW RIGHT. *The University today has an enrollment of about 27,000. In addition to the usual academic colleges, it has a professional school in urban planning, a Far Eastern and Russian Institute and a Fisheries Research Institute.*

The University of Idaho, in Moscow, was founded as a land grant college in 1889. It has an enrollment of 5200, conducts a joint program in atomic engineering with the National Reactor Testing Station in Idaho Falls and the Hanford Graduate Center in Richland, Washington.

The University of Montana, Missoula, was founded in 1893. Its enrollment is about 5400. It operates experiment stations in forestry, wildlife and conservation.

RIGHT. *A strong attachment to education was evident in the Northwest from the first settlements. School was important and children got there!*

BELOW. *That attachment continues to operate today in some of the best school systems in the country. Here, a pilot program in group piano instruction helps children learn the piano faster and more confidently.*

Sullivan, he built a circuit which sold for $4,000,000 in 1914. Alexander Pantages' Crystal Theater in Seattle likewise grew into a vaudeville circuit which extended from the Yukon to San Francisco and rivalled Considine's in showmanship and featured stars. Portland's Mayor George L. Baker got his start in the Fourth Ward's rough politics through his popularity as a vaudeville impresario. His successful stock company, the Baker Players, gave Portland its own "legit" and promoted Baker's political popularity.

But the Northwest was also occasionally host to distinguished artists and received them well. Mark Twain, Mischa Elman, and Madam Schumann-Heink were sellouts wherever they appeared. Seattle's 1916 concert season included Walter Damrosch with his great orchestra; the Boston National Opera Company, and the Ballet Russe with Nijinsky and Lopokovic. Portland supported its own symphony orchestra and in 1920 Jacques Gerskovitz organized and conducted the first Junior Symphony in the country. Seattle's musicians under the leadership of Harry West organized a symphony in 1903; four years later it was sponsored by the Seattle Symphony Society and with maestros Michael Kegrize and Henry K. Hadley, it achieved great box office successes.[4]

The Portland Art Association (1892) housed sepia prints and plaster casts of Elgin marbles in the city library until the generosity of Henry W. Corbett, William B. Ayer, and Mrs. William S. Ladd provided the Association with its own building. Despite severe financial limitations, the first curators, Henrietta H. Failing for a short time and Anna Belle Crocker for many years, tried to make the museum a creative center. Its educational program led to the founding (1909) of the Museum Art School under Henry Wentz. The Association found it no easy task to convert Portlanders to the changing art forms and styles of the early twentieth century. The controversial New York Armory Exhibit was brought to Portland in 1913 and Marcel Duchamp's "Nude Descending a Staircase" enraged a number of local citizens. While some Oregonians owned excellent examples of French and American Impressionists which they lent to the Museum, showings of Braque, Derain, and Picasso upset some of the trustees and cost the Association dues-paying members. The desire "to learn to criticize in the sense of discerning, to sift out, as we can, what is there:—and to be willing to be criticized; to have the will to seek impersonal reality" encouraged both Museum and School to endure public scorn and indifference and to survive a crippling paucity of funds.[5]

[4] Edward Sheppard and Emily Johnson, "Forty Years of Symphony in Seattle, 1904–43," *PNQ*, January 1944.

[5] Anna Belle Crocker, *It Goes Deeper Than We Think* (1946), 71.

In Seattle the Washington State Art Association, founded in 1906—it had 2000 members in 1912, 800 of whom were lifetime members at a fee of $100—assembled and exhibited art treasures, and promoted, unsuccessfully, the construction of a museum and auditorium in the Metropolitan tract. Nevertheless, first in the public library and then in rented quarters, it exhibited the works of John LaFarge, Alma-Tadema, and other traditionalists. Paintings and sculpture by Henry Levy and Leon Bonnat became part of a growing permanent collection. Shows of Persian rugs, Chinese ebony furniture, Oriental jade, and Japanese color prints commanded wide public interest and attracted as many as 40,000 viewers in a year.

No local Edward Hicks emerged to paint Peaceable Kingdoms; the Northwest's untutored folk artists labored over representations of Mounts Rainier and Hood, woodland sketches, or copied ruined castles and foreign scenes for county fair blue ribbons. But E. Frere Champney and Paul Gustin, John Butler and Roi Partridge gave the Northwest some claim to distinction and recognition in Chicago, New York, and London museums. Butler's "Mask of Pan" was hailed as a "high water mark in the artistic life of Seattle." Photographs by Imogene Partridge and by Edward Curtis, famous for his portrait studies of Indians, won acclaim far beyond the region.[6]

Self-taught Homer Davenport (1867–1912) bridged the gap between art and politics as editorial cartoonist for the *New York Journal*.[7] Born in Silverton, Oregon, Davenport joined the Hearst chain to illustrate the Hearst position on national and international affairs. In *The Country Boy* (1910) he wrote sensitively and with poignancy of his childhood in the valley village of his birth.

LITERATURE AND HISTORY

The quality of local belles lettres was not notably improved with the new century, although there were some exceptions. Versatile, nonconformist Charles Erskine Scott Wood (1852–1944) who practiced law in Portland, was a talented watercolorist and sensitive poet. One of the self-conscious imagists of the period, he was Oregon's chief contributor to the "new poetry."

[6] Adele Ballard, "Seattle Artists and Their Work," *Town Crier*, December 19, 1914 and December 16, 1916; Seattle *Museum Auditorium Monthly*, I, January 1912.

[7] "Editorial Cartoons by Homer Davenport," foreword by Roy P. Nelson, *Northwest Review*, Spring 1962.

Never have I found place or season without beauty:
Neither the sea, where the white stallions
Champ their bits and rear against the bridles;
Nor the desert, sitting scornful, apart,
An unwooed Princess, careless, indifferent.[8]

In *The Poet in the Desert* (1918) Wood protested man's inhumanity to man and gave testament to Nature and the natural right of the individual to

come out from the haunts of men;
From the struggle of wolves upon a carcass,
To be melted in Creation's crucible
And be made clean.

. . .

I know that Freedom is Nature's ordinance.[8]

The ironical humor and radical views of his *Heavenly Discourses* (1927) written for *The Masses* confirmed Portland conservative opinion that Wood was at heart, if not an anarchist, at least a communist like his friend John Reed. Reed (1887–1920), son of a wealthy Portland family, educated at Harvard, was a journalist for the *American Magazine, New York World*, and *Metropolitan Magazine*, and covered Villa's revolt in Mexico, the Paterson and Ludlow strikes in this country, and the war in Europe.[9] His friendship with leaders of the Russian Revolution and his participation in the organization of the Communist Party in the United States made him locally infamous. His *Ten Days that Shook the World* (1919) and his burial in the Kremlin shook the placidity of Portland and the Northwest.

The literary life of the Pacific Northwest was handicapped by an ill-advised cult of parochialism. Herbert Bashford, editor of San Francisco's *The Literary West*, in 1902 called for "the strenuous intellectual life rather than the strenuousness of financial speculation in the whirlpool of trade," and urged regional themes to breathe freshness and color into American letters. "Better far a quatrain on a California redwood or a Washington fir than a dozen epics founded on the musty legends of yore."[10] Charles Brinkley's Seattle, "lusty, sordid, wrapped in gray," grew in poetic vision to "marble and a thousand masts as one Pointing

[8] Reprinted by permission of the publisher, The Vanguard Press, from "Collected Poems of Charles Erskine Scott Wood." Copyright, 1929, 1949, 1957, by Sara Bard Field.

[9] Edwin Bingham, "John Reed and Charles Erskine Scott Wood," *PNQ*, July 1959.

[10] *The Literary West*, August 1902.

aloft." But alas, landscape and local color were not adequate substitutes for talent. Ella Higginson, muse of Bellingham, saw life, sweet, wholesome, and as uncomplicated as a flower in her garden. Frederick Homer Balch's *The Bridge of the Gods* (1890) was filled with pious sentiment and romantic Indians.

Eva Emery Dye (Oregon City) found subjects for fairly discerning historical tales in the Lewis and Clark expedition (*Conquest*, 1902), and the fur trade (*McLoughlin and Old Oregon*, 1900, and *McDonald of Oregon*, 1906). The writing of history was more avocation than profession for most Northwest authors and was largely inspired by their own experiences: John Hailey's *Idaho* (1910), Harvey W. Scott's *History of Portland* (1916), Herbert Hunt's *Tacoma* (1916), and Nelson W. Durham's *Spokane and the Spokane Country* (1912) presented in some detail the authors' home environments. Clinton Snowden's *History of Washington* (1909–1911) and William D. Lyman's *History of Old Walla Walla County* (1918) were more valuable for factual detail than as explanations of events. Edmond S. Meany's *History of the State of Washington* (1909) breathed local patriotism and Joseph Schafer's *History of the Pacific Northwest* (1905), a summary account, scarcely suggested the scholar who would later edit the Wisconsin Historical Collection. His colleague at the University of Oregon, bold Frederic G. Young, made important scholarly contributions to the *Oregon Historical Quarterly*.

The major work and one of the few to come out of the region that had significance in the broader field of American history and politics was J. Allen Smith's *The Spirit of American Government* (1907). His critical analysis of the Constitution of the United States was a new approach, anticipating some of Charles Beard's conclusions and influencing his University of Washington colleague, Vernon Parrington, in the formulation of his economic interpretation of literary schools and personalities. Smith's work created a small furor among citizens who preferred their history, like their art, to follow tradition.

In this summary treatment of the Northwest's intellectual world, two men almost forgotten in the field of science deserve mention. Thomas Condon (1822–1907) was a Congregationalist Home Missionary who rode circuit from The Dalles through valleys tributary to the Columbia. There his amateur interest in geology and paleontology became an absorbing vocation. On the upper Crooked River, he collected fossil cretaceous seashells; in the John Day Valley, fossils of Pliocene camels and three-toed horses. In the sixties Condon was corresponding with leading scientists and supplying The Smithsonian Institution and Museum of Natural History with specimens of his exciting finds. He was appointed to the faculty of the University of Oregon when it opened in 1876, and he organized his researches into a distinguished pioneer geological work, *Two Islands and What Came of Them* (1902).

Thomas Jefferson Howell (1842–1912) was brought from Missouri to Oregon when he was eight years old. With six months' formal schooling and some help from his doctor-father, he educated himself while he farmed on the Clackamas. In 1877 he started a herbarium and ten years later had a catalog of 2152 species and 227 varieties of plants. Without funds to publish, he borrowed type, hand-set it into pages which he carried by foot, a few at a time, to Portland to use a power press. By this painfully arduous procedure, extending over six years, he printed his *Flora of Northwest America* (1903).

EDUCATION

Schooling was more easily available by the turn of the century. Washington's Barefoot Schoolboy law (1895) initiated the principle of state support for local school districts, specially beneficial to rural areas.[11] But probably the most noteworthy gain was in the establishment of high schools offering programs distinct from those of elementary schools and undergraduate levels of university work. With encouragement from the perennial debate over the quality of the school, Portland and Seattle systems were standardized and operated under annual budgets of $2,000,000 or more. The public schools of 1914 were far superior to those of ten or fifteen years earlier, and attendance, encouraged by state laws, increased. But much remained to be done to serve the growing numbers ready for higher learning.

Four of Washington's five private colleges were small institutions of academy rank in 1910. Whitman College, however, had a strong faculty and offered instruction in classical subjects to 100 students. On the other hand, state schools were entering a period of rapid growth. President Enoch Bryan built the State College at Pullman into an institution which in 1910 had almost 1000 students, boasted not only an agricultural experiment station and curricula in engineering and mechanical arts, but also had a general program in the liberal arts. The University of Washington in 1895 moved from its ten-acre campus in the heart of Seattle to a spacious one on the outskirts of the city over-

[11] Frederick E. Bolton and Thomas W. Bibb, *History of Education in Washington* (1935); U.S. Works Progress Administration, *History of Education in Portland, Oregon* (1937).

looking Lake Washington. In 1910 it had 1700 students. Under presidents Frank P. Graves, Thomas Kane, and Henry Suzzallo, despite internal dissensions, troubles with politically appointed regents, and growing pains in general, the undernourished university emerged to full accreditation.[12] By 1914 a strong faculty of nearly 200 persons was available to 3300 students. Besides classical subjects, the University offered professional fields such as forestry, engineering, law, and teacher training. The overlapping of subject interests and competition for state funds sparked sharp rivalry and bitterness between university and state college, but in time each school found its place and professed cooperation on academic, if not on athletic grounds.

Oregon and Idaho tried to build higher education on meager budgets. The University of Idaho opened at Moscow in October, 1892, with one unfinished building in the middle of a plowed field, a faculty consisting of the president and one professor, no students, no library, and no laboratories. In ten years time enrollment reached 140, and by 1914 four separate colleges, in arts and sciences, agriculture, engineering, and law, enrolled 438 students. The regents having declared that "Proper teaching cannot be done unless it is intimately associated with that other great fundamental expression of University life—research through which the bounds of knowledge are extended," a goal was defined. It could be achieved only when the community which paid the bills understood its significance.

Oregon was slow to appreciate the complexities and costs of higher education. The State College at Corvallis with 592 students in 1910 was the largest and strongest institution in the state, having the most popular support. Stressing technical and agricultural education, it adapted its curriculum to the needs of rural populations and resource industries. It had, for example, a first-class school of forestry. The University at Eugene had 311 students in 1910 and grew slowly, partly because of its location in the upper Valley, which was already oversupplied with private institutions and the State College, and partly because the ideal purpose of a university was no better comprehended in Oregon than in Idaho. Despite an attractively winning president, Prince Lucien Campbell, and a loyal faculty particularly strong in social sciences, the University subsisted on an annual appropriation less than that of Nevada, Idaho, or Montana universities. In 1907, it was almost entirely cut off through pressures on an economy-minded legislature that was appalled at requests for operation and expansion funds.

Even normal schools, it was said, provided "too much literary educa-

[12] Charles M. Gates, *The First Century at the University of Washington 1861–1961* (1961).

431

tion . . . and not work enough to furnish a supply of milk, eggs, and butter, pork and beans."[13] The communities which harbored teachers' colleges, Monmouth, Ashland, Weston, and Drain, quarrelled so bitterly among themselves for meager state appropriations that the legislature in 1909 withdrew support from all. A year later, the voters, with a choice of restoring one or more, chose Monmouth (now Oregon College of Education) as the state's one normal school.

Despite their parsimony, rural Oregonians sent their offspring to college. In 1910 there was one college student for approximately every 400 persons in the Willamette Valley, which boasted six private colleges as well as the University and State College. Portland, which had no institution of higher learning, had only one college student for every 1000 persons. Seattle sent 423 of its youth to the University there, 30 to colleges outside the state; Portland sent only 97 students to Eugene and 75 to schools outside Oregon. It was largely Portland's lack of facilities for higher education that led to the establishment of Reed College.[14]

Amanda Wood Reed, childless widow of Simeon G. Reed, was encouraged by her pastor, Thomas L. Eliot, to found The Reed Institute. Her only stipulation affecting the $1,500,000 endowment was that the Institute be located in Portland and that it be nonsectarian. After a study of the region's educational facilities, the General Education Board of New York recommended to the Institute's trustees that they found a four-year "high quality" college of arts and sciences. The dynamic first president, Massachusetts-born William Trufant Foster gathered together a small faculty of able young men and women representing the country's leading institutions. The college welcomed its first class of fifty students in 1911 in temporary quarters. The following year it moved to its own campus and admitted its second class.

[13] Quoted in John C. Almack, "History of Oregon Normal Schools," *PNQ*, June 1920, 131; Henry D. Sheldon, *History of the University of Oregon* (1940).

[14] Wallace K. Buttrick, "Report to the General Education Board of New York" (1910). Ms. in Reed College Archives.

CHAPTER
TWENTY-SEVEN

Commerce of the Cities

WHILE cultural and educational standards were related to the development of urbanity in the Pacific Northwest cities, commerce, banking, and rudimentary manufacturing were the bases of their prosperity and the essential factors in the region's extractive and agricultural industries. With the greater utilization of raw resources and the boom in building, these economic institutions expanded along with the cities in such close interaction that one can hardly say whether commerce, banking, and manufacture created the cities, or vice versa.

Trade was concentrated largely in metropolitan centers; but exchange of goods was increasingly complex. Portland was still pre-eminent in the wholesale trade, claiming to be the distribution center for a territory of 250,000 square miles, doing $200,000,000 worth of business in 1908. Tacoma imported from eastern and California merchants and no less than 225 drummers brought to the city a wholesale trade of $50,000,000 in 1909. Treating the whole Inland Empire as a tributary, Spokane jobbers fought to make their city a supply center for farmlands and mining districts. Its location on the Northern Pacific Railroad, near the wheat fields and mines, did much to spur its growth, but these advantages were in some measure lost when the railroad set higher freight rates on eastern goods shipped to Spokane than on goods to terminal cities on the Coast.

For twenty years the merchants of the Inland Empire protested this discrimination, demanding of the Interstate Commerce Commission that

433

rates from Chicago be no higher to Spokane than to Seattle and Portland. On 14 percent of the items enumerated in the Spokane rate case against the Northern Pacific Railroad the rates were high enough to cover shipment of the goods from Chicago to Puget Sound and back to Spokane. On the remaining items 70 percent carried smaller differentials. The railroads argued that their rate schedules were justifiable exceptions to regulations under the Interstate Commerce Act because the railroads had greater competition at the coast terminals. Only by demonstrating that little real competition actually existed did Spokane traders finally (1917) win rate revisions and the trade of the territory around them.[1]

Spokane's dissatisfaction was not with high rates but with discriminatory ones. By the beginning of the twenties, the Pacific Northwest had reluctantly been forced to accept heavy freight charges. The region's railroads were expensive to build, maintain, and operate. Freight shipments originated at great distances from distribution centers. The roads did not attract freight to an efficient point of available capacity. Shipments from West to East were of low-value, high-bulk goods, such as wool, wheat, and lumber. East-West traffic was in high-value, low-bulk commodities, and the long trains snaking across the plains and double-engined through the mountains were made up largely of empty cars.

Ocean commerce, coastal and foreign, remained vitally important to the coastal cities. Even after the Yukon rush was over, Seattle's trade with Alaska remained highly profitable. For several years before World War I it represented 25 percent of the city's domestic commerce, and 16 percent (in value) of all waterborne traffic, foreign and domestic, moved to and from Alaska. In 1895 Tacoma and Seattle, competing for ascendancy on the Sound, shared a foreign trade of $5,000,000, of which three-fourths went to Tacoma; eight years later $100,000,000 was divided almost equally between the two ports. Between 1909 and 1914 Seattle's trade with China and Japan averaged some $30,000,000 annually, and its total trade reached $56,000,000 in 1914. Seattle was the nearest to a "free" port on the Pacific. In costs of wharfage, pilots' fees, towing, and moorage, ships entering San Francisco paid an average of $1153; Portland's average was $490 and Seattle's only $176. But Portland maintained primacy in grain shipments, sending to foreign markets 13,000,000 bushels in 1909.

Portland with its old local firms such as Ladd and Tilton, branches of the Bank of British Columbia, and the London and San Francisco Bank, had long been the chief Northwest banking center. In Washington and

---

[1] Douglas Smart, "Spokane's Battle for Freight Rates," *PNQ*, January 1954.

Idaho no corporate banking was permitted until late in the territorial period, but private bankers like Dexter Horton in Seattle and Levi P. Ankeny in Walla Walla had built up considerable businesses in their own communities. To meet local agricultural and commercial demands, the bank was as vital an enterprise in small communities as it was in the cities.

Between 1889 and 1909 bank assets for the region as a whole increased from about $32,000,000 to $355,000,000, or from $42 to $251 per capita. This was a most important advance, for it meant that the region's economy had outgrown its earlier limitations. At the beginning of the century per capita resources of the Pacific Northwest were less than in any other section of the country except the South. Ten years later they were surpassed only by New England and the Middle Atlantic states; with assets of $175 per capita Idaho was better off than the Plains states as a group with $161.

During the decade of expansion bank deposits in the Northwest mounted far beyond the demand for loans, and the banker's problem was no longer one of attracting money to meet the needs of an enlarging business community, but rather of finding investment outlets for surplus savings and reserves. In a word, the region had advanced from debtor to creditor financing as had older sections of the country. The establishment of new banks expanded credit. Between 1900 and 1915 the combined number of state and national banks increased sixfold, until in the latter year 792 banks were serving the area. At the beginning of World War I state banks, averaging $300,000 in capital resources, outnumbered national banks, averaging $1,200,000, by 575 to 217.

The rapid increase in the number of state banks shows the grass-roots character of the region's banking. But its real strength was in large city banks, state or national, which were five- to twelve-million-dollar enterprises. In 1909 six Spokane and Tacoma banks had resources of $35,800,000 and four Seattle national banks held $38,000,000, while sixty-four national banks in the smaller towns had total resources of $35,200,000. Four Portland banks had about as much strength—$32,000,000—as did sixty-eight banks outside the city.

The metropolitan banks filled important functions as central banks for others, especially smaller ones. For example, when city banks accepted funds from correspondent institutions, which had more in deposits than they could profitably put to work in their own communities, they served as investment outlets and increased credit where it appeared to be most needed. At the same time the metropolitans protected themselves by placing reserves with still larger banks, perhaps in Chicago, San Francisco, or St. Louis. In 1909 national banks in Portland carried just under $3,000,000 in balances with reserve agents and $4,130,000

435

with other national and state banks. Seattle banks carried a much larger sum with reserve agents—$5,700,000—but only $3,300,000 with other national and state banks. This would suggest that Portland continued to be the financial capital of the region even after its primary position had been challenged by the new cities of the north. The banks of Washington's "big three," Tacoma, Spokane, and Seattle found the demands of their own communities greater than the demands of Portland or its city banks.

MANUFACTURING

By census definition, manufacturing is the processing of goods, usually aided by machinery, for wholesale markets. Appearances and certain kinds of statistics suggested that the Pacific Northwest was a thriving manufacturing area. For example, Seattle's lumber mills with their towering chimneys belching smoke and flame gave parts of the city the appearance of a factory community. Moran's shipyard, expanded to build the battleship *Nebraska*, possessed all the heavy equipment and machinery commonly found in such establishments at Charleston or Portsmouth. Swift and Company's packing plant was a $3,000,000 installation, employed 500 men, and could handle 500 cattle and 2500 hogs and sheep daily. Flour mills and lumber plants lined the waterfront. The huge Wheeler-Osgood sash and door factory gave Tacoma (so far as one plant could) the sights and sounds of industry.

Manufacturing output and payrolls doubled between 1900 and 1914. In 1910 Portland claimed 2000 establishments representing a combined capital of $30,000,000, and occupation for 25,000 persons. For the region as a whole, manufactured goods exceeded farm crops in value. In the cities, one man in three of the gainfully employed was engaged in some manufacturing or mechanical occupation (see Graph XIII, p. 627).

By 1914 the manufacturing interest of the Northwest was adding $168,000,000 annually to the value of its raw materials (see Graph XII, p. 626). "Value added"—that is, the sale value of a product minus the cost of the raw material but including the cost of labor—is a fairly good measure of the productivity of industry, although it should be noted that, in the long run, the meaning of "value added" may be distorted by changes in the real value of the dollar. However, a comparison of the Northwest's value added by manufacture with that of other regions shows its relative insignificance as an industrial area. For example, the value added by manufacturing in Detroit and Pittsburgh amounted to

$400 to $500 per capita; in Portland, Seattle, and Tacoma the figure was $157. The capital invested in manufacturing in the Pacific Northwest looked like pin money when measured against industrial capital in the East or Midwest. The Northwest had $4.29 in farming for every dollar invested in manufacturing.

Western boosters took it for granted that diversified manufacturing, like commerce, would move freely into any newly populated section and could be expected to develop without difficulty. But the turn of the century witnessed far-reaching changes in the geographic distribution of manufacturing throughout the nation. Cheap transportation over long distances directly affected the location of industries. Some manufactures such as steel and garment-making concentrated where resources, markets, and cheap labor were available, and, by exploiting economies of scale, dominated the entire national market. Established concerns in heavily populated areas had telling advantages over new ones in sparsely peopled areas.

Economists have formulated complex equations to describe the relation of industrial development to location of markets.[2] What concerns us here is that manufacturing, contrary to what Northwest boosters believed, did not automatically gravitate to new communities. It is important, therefore, to look at the industrial profiles of these far western cities; what were the principal lines of manufacturing, and what others, though of less individual importance, contributed significantly to local payrolls.

The main manufactures were those related to the region's natural resources. The secondary ones were for the most part oriented toward the local market. Production in which supplies and costs of raw materials, labor, and transportation were higher than elsewhere, rarely developed locally. There was small prospect of building a steel industry in the West when Pittsburgh could fill the national demand cheaper than the West could.

Dreams of a Steel Industry

But men dreamed of a steel industry in the Pacific Northwest because they had exaggerated notions of the region's coal and iron resources. Oregon had a scattering of low-grade coal deposits and coal was Washington's most important branch of mining. Deposits of bituminous and subbituminous grades were opened up in the Roslyn area east of the Cascades, at Newcastle and Black Diamond near Seattle, and at Puyallup and Carbonado near Tacoma. Seattle had shipped coal to California for

[2] Edward J. Cohn, Jr., *Industry in the Pacific Northwest and the Location Theory* (1954).

some years and looked forward to more of this trade with the expansion of population and industry along the coast. For a decade production increased steadily, rising to 3,000,000 tons in 1903. In 1913, coal mining was a $10,000,000 business, but output was no greater than ten years earlier. Wider use of fuel oil and importation of higher grades of coal from Wyoming narrowed the market for the local product.

Both states had some iron ore deposits. Ore in Iron Mountain at Lake Oswego (then Sucker Lake) near Portland had led to the erection of a small furnace there in the 1860s. Encouraged by Henry Villard, the building of western railroads which needed iron, and the advantages of pioneering an industry in an undeveloped economy, Simeon G. Reed undertook to expand this beginning into a plant which he believed would supply the whole Pacific Coast and as far east as Salt Lake. The Oregon Iron and Steel Company was doomed from the outset. Costs of development far exceeded estimates; local iron ore and coal were of low grade; importing supplies made costs skyrocket; the finished iron goods found little if any market. Railroad iron shipped in was cheaper than the local product. The plant costing initially more than $500,000 closed in 1894; reactivated briefly during World War I, it was soon afterward dismantled.

At Port Townsend, California capitalists built the Irondale furnaces, thinking to use bog ores of Chimacum mixed with richer ores from Texada Island. Twice rebuilt and remodeled during the 1880s, Irondale produced 10,000 tons of iron in 1889 but suspended production soon afterward. From 1900 to 1918 the firm went through repeated reorganizations, each with pretentious designs that somehow went awry. A short interval of activity during World War I lasted only so long as prices remained high.

At one time or another, Tacoma, Spokane, Sedro-Woolley, and Bellingham had notions of becoming steel producers. Seattle promoters were as ambitious for their city as Reed was for Portland. Peter Kirk, an experienced ironmaster from England who had supplied British iron for the Seattle, Lake Shore and Eastern Railroad, should have known better than most men whether he could manufacture iron profitably on Puget Sound. The Great Western Iron and Steel Company was organized with a paid-up capital of $1,000,000, and as the plant went up in the spring of 1891 the town of Kirkland was born on the eastern shore of Lake Washington. People blamed the panic of 1893 for shattering the dream, and perhaps it did. The plant never got into production and Kirkland became a ghost town even before the mill brought it fully to life. When general prosperity returned, the mill failed to revive and Kirkland remained a country town for half a century afterward.

438

The question seems not to be what made the westerners fail, but what made them think they could succeed. The fundamental obstacles were wholly inadequate deposits of ore and the national character of Pittsburgh's industry. The eastern industry was capitalized, not in millions, but in billions of dollars and it turned out products in the millions of tons. The needs of the entire country could be met by the mines and mills of half a dozen states. In this kind of game the Northwest could not compete.

THE NORTHWEST'S BASIC INDUSTRY

The manufacturing industries that did develop in the Pacific Northwest were lumber mills, meat-packing houses, flour mills, food processing plants, foundries, printing plants, bakeries, and breweries (see Graphs XIV, XV, XVI, pp. 627, 628). Unquestionably lumber manufacturing was primary. However, while it contributed a large percentage of the total of value added by manufacture, it did not follow that these lumbering states enjoyed the economic growth that would have accompanied full industrial development. For example, when locally produced lumber was made into furniture that could compete with Grand Rapids, then the region's economy could be said to be in a different stage of industrial growth.

Nor did the lumber industry directly contribute to the growth of cities. Portland turned out only a third of Oregon's total product, while Seattle, Tacoma, and Spokane produced together less than 20 percent of the Washington total. Mills had to operate near their log supplies; thus communities of fewer than 10,000 people, which comprised about half the populations of Washington and Oregon, accounted for 45 to 48 percent of the value added through manufacturing in their respective states.

In other kinds of manufacturing the role of the cities was much more important. More than 40 percent of the states' totals of value added could be traced to urban centers where manufacturing was often a matter of corporate enterprise and large plants. At least 85 percent of the activity in the principal cities was handled by corporations and 75 percent of the output was from plants producing $100,000 worth of goods or more annually. Forty percent of Seattle's manufactures came from mills doing a million dollars worth of business each year. Portland foundries and printing plants supplied three-fourths of the state's demand. Washington cities turned out two-thirds of the locally manufactured leather goods

439

and 73 percent of the bakery goods; Seattle and Tacoma produced 46 percent of the milled flour. Seattle alone did half of the state's meat packing and brewed 40 percent of its beer.

These figures, however, do not tell the whole story. The diversity and balance of urban industrial activity stands out in the development of a considerable number of lesser lines of manufactures which, though individually small, added a significant portion to the whole. In Seattle 209 food-processing establishments in 1914 employed as many workers and supported as large a total payroll as did 55 lumber mills, and the value of the food products was four times that of products derived from lumber. In no large city did any one line of manufacturing account for more than 17 percent of the total value of production; seven different lines in Seattle made up 60 percent of the total. Miscellaneous unspecified small lines represented another 28 percent, while the remaining 12 percent came from a number of industries which reported production between $140,000 and $1,500,000 annually.

It would appear that the worker in the city was not nearly so dependent on a single industry as was his counterpart in Kansas City, Kansas, or Youngstown, Ohio. If, however, one reconsiders the fact that lumber manufacture was the principal supporting industry of the region, second only to that of farming, he can rightly conclude that these secondary industries depended largely on the prosperity of agriculture and the lumber industry.

THE PACE SLACKENS

By 1910 the pace of progress showed evidences of slowing up, a decline reflected in manufacturing. Seattle plants increased their payrolls by only $2,000,000 in five years (1909–1914); the number of jobs rose by only 1000. In a number of lines which might be classified as durable consumer goods—furniture and mattresses, stoves and furnaces—demands were less on the eve of World War I than they had been earlier. As early as 1906–1909 lumber production began to drop.

When a principal economic support weakens, secondary manufactures and service industries are immediately affected. It is easy to suggest that the lumber industry, plagued by price fluctuations, shipping difficulties, and overproduction, was the source of trouble. But if, as was the case, a large part of lumber production went into local markets, the question focusses on local consumption. Probably the overbuilding of the cities themselves contributed something to the decline of prosperity. Speculation had created unreal values. Over a period of twenty years many millions of dollars had been poured into construction, and the major part of the task was approaching completion. Too, after 1910 net immigration was not increasing at the same rate as it had since 1890. And this led to a slackening of demand, hence of production. Oregon, which had not boomed to the same degree or as exuberantly as Washington, also felt the pinch. Incomes from investments in farm and city properties shrank 30 percent, and men who had been cautious in borrowing consoled themselves that they were now less encumbered with debts.

The region as a whole, and the nation too, were entering a new stage of economic development. Perhaps the period of easy expansion was completed and the economy stabilizing. If so, the future promised less than the past had performed. The slowdown in population growth and production that marked the years before World War I tempered and disciplined enthusiasms. No one could see then that war would bring another boom and another bust before the Pacific Northwest found its "take off" point in economic growth.

PART IV

The Pacific Northwest and the Nation

OVERVIEW

IN TRANSITION *to an urban society the Pacific Northwest manifested strong and sometimes unique reactions to social and economic changes occurring throughout the nation. In the following chapters we look at the Far West during fifty years of national crisis: world wars, depression, and fragile peace.*

"If any large generalization about Western History is possible in the face of the vast amount of it that historians have yet to explore," Earl Pomeroy wrote in 1965, "it is that the West itself as an area separate and different from the rest of the United States is disappearing."[1]

By mid-twentieth century, characteristics of westerners were not distinguishable statistically from those of the nation at large. The phenomenal influx of war workers in the 1940s gave the region a percentage increase in population almost as great as that of the first decade of the

[1] Earl Pomeroy, *The Pacific Slope: A History of California, Oregon, Washington, Idaho, Utah, and Nevada* (1965), 373.

443

century. Fifty percent of the inhabitants in 1960 were immigrants. Like earlier migrants, most were from the Midwest and North Central states, but the pattern of post-World War II migration indicated increased movement within the region and between it and California.

While the Northwest has continued to demonstrate some political idiosyncracies, these have not been as outstanding as in the first decade of the century. World War I distracted the voters from domestic discontents. Having achieved limited socioeconomic reforms, established political procedures which gave them greater participation in government, and weakened an already tenuous two-party system, the electorate was content to let well enough alone. World War I bred hysterical reactions to political attitudes which under conditions of peace, isolation, and optimism in the first decade of the century had not seemed either subversive or treasonable. After the war, a conservative reaction led the western states and the nation to accept Republican guidance "back to Normalcy." It was a futile journey. In 1932, the Pacific Northwest turned to the Democrats, Franklin Delano Roosevelt, and a New Deal.

Prior to World War I, the region suffered from a depression that seemed particularly acute in comparison with the booming first decade of the century. The twenties proved that neither the region nor any of its component states was a little island unto itself. Each was, rather, very much a part of the whole. Thus the Pacific Northwest, despite traditional antagonism toward centralized government, accepted the benefits of national planning and the recovery programs of the depressed thirties. The local labor movement which had displayed a firm devotion to independence—and idiosyncracy—was disciplined and strengthened as national organizations increased their powers with federal recognition of collective bargaining. Furthermore, as Pomeroy points out, the states of the Pacific slope had, without full awareness, skipped that phase of economic development in which they "could get along without much government," so that the "high percentage of officials sent out, in effect, to preside over the liquidation of the federal government's colonial responsibilities merged into the high percentage necessary to provide the kind of services (including higher education and the production of energy) that private initiative had provided to a greater extent in the older states."[2] The federal government, through various agencies, played a large role not only in the conservation and development of Pacific Northwest natural resources, but also in subsidizing the development of a more diversified economy.

The production of hydroelectric power has been the outstanding factor of economic change in the Far West since 1937. Possessed of over two-fifths of the nation's known potential waterpower, the region had less than one-tenth developed by 1936. The need to generate employment during the Depression and then to meet war demands led to the struc-

[2] Ibid., 395.

ture of a federally owned power system, and eventually to the establishment of industries not immediately related to other natural resources.

A conception of physiographic regionalism which had been embodied in the HBC's administration of the Columbia Department was not natural in the thinking of Americans. During the Great Depression when the federal government was pouring great sums of money into the Far West to stimulate its recovery, the idea that the states of the Northwest had more in common than boundary lines encouraged some to hope that regional planning and cooperation might quicken the economic growth of the three states. When the postwar conservative reaction set in, the first phase of regional planning which had brought worldwide attention to the Pacific Northwest's experiment was abandoned. Nevertheless, new uses and the fuller utilization of Northwest waters and their products have tended to force the individual states to concern themselves with this common treasury; and national administrations, however reluctantly, have had to recognize that regional resources are also national resources. Much of Northwest history in the past fifty years has, therefore, been a struggle to achieve cooperation between private and public interests, among the states, between the states and the federal government, and even between the United States and Canada. With this underlying theme, then, this history of the Pacific Northwest concludes.

CHAPTER
TWENTY-EIGHT

Politics and Pressures in the Progressive Era

BOOMING PROSPERITY relieved particular economic discontents; it did not allay political unrest. The Populists failed to accomplish the reforms for which they had crusaded, but the spirit of reform was still abroad.

At the turn of the century, Americans witnessed a rapid decline of nineteenth-century liberalism and laissez-faire and experienced a traumatic awakening to a new era for which old values seemed to have no meaning, but to which people now clung with desperate tenacity. Modern America posed questions of fundamental political significance about the structure of power and the functions of the state; about individual freedom and social good. In their quest for social justice men who emphasized the collective nature of society sought to eliminate the paradoxes of individual freedom by substituting the idea of social freedom. Others, clinging to a federalistic theory of society—of orders or groups held in balance by the interplay of interests—conceded that the balance was drastically upset and should be adjusted. Many who were unconcerned with political philosophy but found the traditional functions of government inadequate to the times, argued for a reformed state and dreamed of a disciplined society agreeably conforming to their optative designs for a good life.

447

From one point of view three postures can be distinguished. Rigid conservatives and equally rigid radicals, accepting deterministic forces of nature or economics, put their faith accordingly in either status quo or revolution; middle-of-the-roaders, abhorring the idea of revolution but accepting the idea of change, tried to give new meaning to old political framework and thereby to direct change to socially useful ends. From this group emerged the Progressive Movement, the Progressive Era, and a Progressive Party.

John Dewey, expositor of systematic progressivism but at the turn of the century hardly known outside a small academic circle, identified "progressive" with an attitude toward change. The "hard and fast conservative" thought of the "existing constitution, institutions, and social arrangements" as ends in themselves; the "progressive" thought of them as "mechanisms for achieving social results" at a given moment in an infinite extension of change or progress.

> Progress depends not on the existence of social change but on the direction which human beings deliberately give that change. . . . it depends upon human intent and aim and upon acceptance of responsibility for its production . . . the positive means of progress lie in the application of intelligence to the construction of proper social devices.[1]

Dewey's dicta might help to explain the value framework of progressivism and point up the progressive's optimistic assumptions that men were rational and could solve their problems; and that individualism, not dependent upon social organization or natural endowment, was a consequence of an "inner logic of an awakened cultural life," made possible by a new kind of education and a new type of leadership. But it does not explain the movement as politics.

William Allen White contended that progressives "caught the Populists in swimming and stole all their clothing except the frayed underdrawers of free silver." Some recent historians have denied this continuity. Analyzing the membership of the Progressive Party, they find that the "typical progressive" was

> . . . a member of the urban middle class, a professional man or independent business man, comfortable financially, well educated, a native-born Protestant, probably of New England stock. These men felt themselves overshadowed and threatened by the wealth and power of the masters of capital, and their progressivism was a reaction to this "status revolution." . . . Professor George E. Mowry finds the progressives hoped to "recapture the older individualistic values in all the strata of political, economic, and social life." "The central fear,"

[1] John Dewey, *Character and Events*, Joseph Ratner, ed., 2 vols. (1929), II, 820.

448

declares Professor Richard Hofstadter, "was fear of power," and the progressive movement "at its heart, was an effort to realize familiar and traditional ideas" that had taken form under the conditions of a predominantly rural society with a broad diffusion of property and power.[2]

Benjamin DeWitt, writing in 1915 near the close of the Progressive Era, explained the movement by what it accomplished. He found three marked tendencies in its "incoherent and chaotic" agitations. The best men in all parties insisted on the eradication of corruption in government; on the modification of government so that it would be easier for the many to control; and on the extension of governmental functions to relieve social and economic distress. These tendencies, he said, were seen "in the platform and program of every political party; they are manifested in the political changes that are made in the nation, the states, and the cities, and because of their universality and definiteness, they may be said to constitute the real progressive movement."[3]

To ascribe ideological consistency to progressives is to ignore differences among participants in the movement and their motives at both national and local levels. Farmer, businessman, Prohibitionist, suffragette, single taxer, silver, gold, and conscience Republicans, Democrats of different complexions, old-style bosses reformed and new-style emergent, all could be blanketed under the rubric "progressive" by one or more indices that one might set up. But one factor appears common to all who called themselves progressive: they seemed to believe or profess that superior to private interests was a public interest which could best be served by extended public participation in lawmaking processes. Mechanisms to achieve popular government had been advocated by the Populists at Omaha in 1892; similar ones were adopted by Californians who organized a Progressive Party in 1910. The National Progressive League, founded early in 1911 by senators Robert LaFollette (Wisconsin) and Jonathan Bourne (Oregon) advocated constitutional amendments to provide for the initiative, referendum, recall, and corrupt practice acts as well as for the direct election of senators, direct primaries, and presidential preferential primaries. Theodore Roosevelt's Progressives built on the same foundation, adding goals such as equal suffrage, restriction on the powers of the Supreme Court, government control of currency, conservation of natural resources, and matters of social and industrial justice, health and safety standards, child labor, and minimum wages

[2] John Braeman, "Seven Progressives," *Business History Review*, Winter 1961, 581.

[3] Benjamin Park DeWitt, *The Progressive Movement* (1915), 4.

and hours. Direct government was also a mechanism useful to groups who demanded social conformities—to Prohibitionists and racists—and to those who wanted to achieve some one specific goal, a single tax or woman suffrage.

Using simply advocacy of political reform as an index of "progressive," we find that the Pacific Coast states were progressive; indeed they pioneered the movement.[4] California and Washington, fastest growing of the coast states, under the impact of urbanization and industrialization first organized parties they called "progressive" and moved farther and faster along the broader path of progressivism, including social and economic reforms, than did Oregon. But Oregon, oldest in years of settlement, least affected by contemporary changes, and most conservative politically, pointed the way.

An account of Oregon's engagement in the Progressive Era, of how its citizens created and used the tools of reform, and of its leadership, may help us to understand the complexities of the Progressive Movement and the difficulties which face historians who attempt to generalize about it.

The mastermind of Oregon's successful political revolution was self-educated William S. U'Ren (1859–1949), born in Wisconsin, the son of English immigrants.[5] In search of health and a means of livelihood, U'Ren arrived in 1889 in Milwaukie, on the outskirts of Portland, where he set up in the practice of law, spiritualism, and the fine art of politicking. He had early become an ardent disciple of Henry George, whose passages of prose poetry exercised a hypnotic effect on thousands of readers, but whose single-tax remedy for poverty in the midst of progress made no headway in legislative halls. In James W. Sullivan's *Direct Legislation by the Citizenry Through the Initiative and Referendum* (1892), U'Ren believed he had found the key which would not only achieve the single tax but also give direction to other urges toward political change.

Sullivan's message was simple: Reformers had failed to recognize that to accomplish social reconstruction it was necessary to abolish the "law-making monopoly." Direct legislation through the initiative and referendum would destroy this monopoly and with it "class rule, ring rule, extravagance, jobbery, nepotism, the spoils systems, every

[4] Thomas A. Bailey, "The West and Radical Legislation," *American Journal of Sociology*, January 1933; William T. Ogburn, "Social Legislation on the Pacific Coast," *Popular Science Monthly*, March 1915; Earl Pomeroy, *The Pacific Slope: A History of California, Oregon, Washington, Idaho, Utah, and Nevada* (1965), chap. 8.

[5] Robert C. Woodward, "William S. U'Ren, a Progressive Era Personality," *Idaho Yesterdays*, Summer 1960. This issue contains three papers on Northwest "progressive personalities."

jot of the professional trading politician's influence." If farmers, wage earners, and other citizens would unite to effect direct legislation, it seemed "improbable that certain political and economic measures now supported by farmer and wage-worker alike could long fail to become law."

"I forgot, for the time, all about Henry George and the single tax," U'Ren later recalled. "The important thing was to restore the law-making power where it belonged—into the hands of the people.... Once given that we could get anything we wanted—single tax, anything." In 1893, he fathered a Joint Committee on Direct Legislation, composed of members of the state executive committees of the Knights of Labor, Portland Federated Trades, Grange, and Farmers Alliances. The same year he abandoned the Republican Party for the Populists, whose votes elected him to the legislature in 1897.

This was a session in which a United States senator was to be chosen. Customarily, legislators balloted until the price of a vote was high enough to win a majority; professionals handled the election, wheeling and dealing openly and without regard for public opinion. In 1897 the legislators demonstrated once again the processes of representative democracy.

U'Ren capitalized on a serious factional split in Republican ranks which, in effect, gave the few Populists the balance of power. Jonathan Bourne (1855–1940), cynical, politically ambitious scion of a wealthy old Massachusetts family, was a power in Republican councils. He was the Southern Pacific's legal counselor and paymaster for legislators who had a price. He owned silver mines near Baker, Oregon, and at Republic, Washington. As a Silver Republican he was outraged when the machine's Senator John H. Mitchell, candidate for reelection, came out for gold. U'Ren, quick to see a silver-plated opportunity, offered to help defeat Mitchell if in return Bourne would support a voter registration bill, an election procedure bill, and an initiative and referendum constitutional amendment. The bargain having been struck, U'Ren arranged a boycott of the Republican caucus while Bourne provided lavish hospitality for truant legislators. Without a quorum the House could not organize; as a result, no senator was elected. After this public demonstration of how to control a legislature, Bourne and U'Ren, working hand in hand, carried the next two legislatures along the path of reform.

For the first time since adoption of the Australian ballot (1891), the sessions of 1899 and 1901, by no means graciously, set about tidying up Oregon politics. A registration bill (1899) made voter qualifications and residence a matter of record; the Holt Bill (1901) allowed parties filing candidates to be represented on election boards and

THE PACIFIC NORTHWEST

113   109   105

CALGARY

Qu'Appelle
MOOSE JAW   REGINA

SWIFT CURRENT

A L B E R T A   S A S K A T C H E W A N

Oldman   MEDICINE HAT

LETHBRIDGE

AL FLATS

49

Milk   Poplar

EUREKA   Waterton
Glacier
International
Peace Park   CUT BANK

HAVRE

FORT PECK

NBROOK

WHITEFISH   Marias

BBY   JENNINGS   KALISPELL

Teton   FORT
BENTON   Missouri

GLENDIVE

ACE   Flathead
Lake   Swan

THOMPSON FALLS   GREAT FALLS

MISSOULA   M O N T A N A

PPE   HELENA

Musselshell   MILES CITY

Lochsa   Selway   HAMILTON   BUTTE

Rosebud Cr.   Tongue   Powder

ELK CITY   ANACONDA   Hole   THREE FORKS   Yellowstone   BILLINGS

Jefferson

Salmon   BOZEMAN   LIVINGSTON

45

Middle Fk.   SALMON   Big Hole   ALDER GULCH   GARDINER   SHERIDAN

LEMHI   DILLON   VIRGINIA CITY   Yellowstone
Nat'l   Yellowstone
Lake   Shoshone   CODY

Beaverhead   Red Rock   Park

Bighorn

I D A H O

Lemhi

KETCHUM   Henrys Fk.   Jackson Lake   105

Grand Teton
Nat'l Park   W Y O M I N G

Snake   IDAHO FALLS   Wind   RIVERTON

RUNEAU   Blackfoot   North Platte
CASPER

GOODING   POCATELLO   LANDER

AMERICAN FALLS

TWIN FALLS   BURLEY   MONTPELIER   RAWLINS

Bear   Green   LARAMIE

Hams Fork   GRANGER   ROCK SPRINGS

41

LOGAN   BRIGHAM

Great
Salt
Lake   OGDEN   EVANSTON   Blacks Fork   COLORADO

A   WELLS   STEAMBOAT SPRINGS

U T A H   SALT LAKE CITY   CRAIG

ELKO   113   109

SHERMAN

stipulated procedures to improve administration of elections. These measures materially lessened opportunities for fraud and made unlikely a repetition of the 1896 scandals.

After a long-drawn-out, harrowing session to choose between Henry W. Corbett and John H. Mitchell for the United States Senate, the 1901 legislature passed the Mays Law which permitted voters in a general election to express their preference among party candidates for the office. The same legislature considered and passed two primary nominating laws, one of which applied only to Portland. The other, statewide in scope, permitted cross-filing, and for this reason was declared unconstitutional.

But the major step in reform was initiated in the 1899 session when U'Ren presented an initiative and referendum amendment backed by strong public opinion generated by his Non-Partisan Direct Legislation League. The constitution required that two successive legislatures act upon an amendment and that it then be ratified by the people. Adopted by the legislatures of 1899 and 1901, the amendment was ratified by 62,024 to 5668 popular votes in 1902. This was the first amendment to Oregon's constitution since its adoption in 1859.

Seven years of tireless campaigning, education and propaganda; distribution of thousands of leaflets and wide circulation of Sullivan's book on direct legislation; drum-beat repetition of the words "initiative and referendum," "direct legislation," "people's government," "popular government," and "direct democracy," had finally paid off. The tremendous currency of those words was important not only to adoption of the amendment but also to the test of the initiative and referendum in the next few years.

THE OREGON SYSTEM AND HOW IT WORKED

The initiative and referendum amendment of 1902 (a second amendment applied the initiative and referendum to all local, special, and municipal laws in 1906) was the keystone of the Oregon System of direct legislation. The other elements of the system were added by initiative petitions: the Direct Primary Law (1904), the Corrupt Practices Act (1908), and the recall amendment (1908).[6] The recall,

[6] Allen H. Eaton, *The Oregon System, the Story of Direct Legislation in Oregon* (1912); James D. Barnett, *Operation of the Initiative, Referendum and Recall in Oregon* (1915); Waldo Schumacher, "Thirty Years of the People's Rule in Oregon: an Analysis," *Political Science Quarterly*, June 1932; Joseph G. LaPalombara, *The Initiative and Referendum in Oregon: 1938–1948* (1950).

giving the people power to call special elections for public offices, has seldom been used in Oregon. One important feature of the Corrupt Practices Act, regulation of campaign expenditures, has been largely ignored. But second only to the initiative and referendum amendment, the Direct Primary Law produced the most significant change in Oregon politics.

The hope that the legislature would follow voter advice under the Mays Law was dispelled when, in 1903, Governor T. T. Geer won the popular vote, but Mitchell finagled the election of his friend Charles W. Fulton. The next year, under U'Ren and his associates' persuasion, the Direct Primary Law was adopted by a comfortable majority, 47,678 to 16,735. It broke the back of political machines and weakened party politics by taking nominations of candidates from party conventions and putting them into the voters' hands. Any individual could run for office in primary or nominating elections, provided that 10 percent of the number of voters who voted for supreme court judge in the previous election, signed a petition to put his name on the ballot. This applied also to candidates for the United States Senate, but here it was a useless gesture, as the Mays Law had demonstrated, so long as legislators felt free to ignore the people's preference.

However, in the 1904 law, U'Ren inserted an ingenious method of circumvention—a permissive clause stipulating that a candidate for the state legislature might publicly declare which of two courses he would follow in electing a senator. By subscribing to "Statement Number One," he committed himself to vote for the people's choice as indicated in the primary election; in subscribing to "Statement Number Two" he declared for party regularity.[7] No legislative candidate had to "take" either statement, but when U'Ren's People's Power League educated the voters to ask whether a candidate did or did not, the provision became mandatory in effect.

During the 1906 campaign Jonathan Bourne's propaganda mill turned out letters to the electorate, explaining how voting for a Statement Number One candidate would give the people control over the election of the senators; provided, of course, that the voters also expressed their choice of a senatorial candidate in the primary election. Bourne incidentally enclosed literature promoting himself as the "Popular Government" candidate. He won the primary but his election by the 1907 legislature was no proper test of the efficacy of Statement Number One.

While the constitutionality of the direct primary was being challenged in the courts, the People's Power League initiated a bill *in-*

[7] Burton J. Hendrick, "Statement Number One," *McClure's Magazine*, September 1911.

structing the legislature to vote for the people's choice for United States senator, and the voters approved it, 69,668 to 21,162 (1908). The next legislature, strongly Republican and with a bare majority of members having "taken Statement Number One," elected—reluctantly indeed—the people's choice, Governor George E. Chamberlain, the first Democrat senator elected since 1879.[8]

Twenty-one other states had adopted the Oregon plan or a similar one before ratification of the Seventeenth Amendment (1913) made it unnecessary. "Statement Number One" was, according to a contemporary student, "a genuine invention, the rarest of phenomena in politics." In 1913, by a 2000 majority vote, Oregon adopted the presidential preference primary law rounding out the framework of the people's government.

U'Ren won national recognition for his role in shifting power from parties and bosses to the people—from old machines and bosses to new ones, such as the Grange, Federation of Labor, and People's Power League, according to one critic of direct legislation in Oregon. U'Ren was undeniably the prime mover of legislative reforms; he and his close associates drew up most of the early initiative bills. "My sole purpose in this life is to secure for the people the direct control of the government and every officer in it," he had said when under vituperative attack from anti-Statement Number One groups in the 1908 campaign.

But although U'Ren succeeded in these respects, he was not a charismatic leader. He worked behind a desk as secretary of organizations. He failed in the purpose for which he first advocated popular government; the single tax, pure or impure, was rejected time after time. By 1916, his influence was gone and the People's Power League had become suspect of having too much in common with North Dakota's Farmers' Non-Partisan Political League.

THE LABORATORY OF POLITICAL DEMOCRACY

Following adoption of the initiative and referendum, and while parts of the system were being fitted into place, Oregon became a glass-walled laboratory of political experimentation. Fears that direct legislation would mean the end of responsible government in legislative and executive branches, and that in their zeal to destroy bos-

[8] Russell G. Hendricks, "Election of Senator Chamberlain, the People's Choice," *OHQ*, June 1952.

sism "ballot-box legislators" would unwittingly open the door to dema-
gogues and encourage a dangerous trend toward class legislation, were
not realized.

Just as the urban-rural cleavage was not of paramount importance,
neither was class consciousness an important factor in the legislation
of the reform era. In Oregon the strongest support for direct legislation came from Portland and from wealthy wards as well as from
those in which working men predominated. In the state at large, it
came from the prosperous agricultural counties as well as from those
whose economies were dominated by timber and mining interests,
hard-fisted cannery operators, or baronial ranches. The Willamette
Valley, an area of small towns and small farms, and Union County,
where the "Missouri element" was strong, gave less support to direct
legislation. On the other hand, these areas ranked highest in support
of social conformity legislation such as prohibition, and were lukewarm
on economic measures like the eight-hour day. Multnomah County
stood sixth among Oregon's thirty-three counties in support of political
reformation, first in support of economic legislation, and twenty-ninth
in support of social conformity laws.[9]

Put to the test, the people performed well despite handicaps. The
intent of a bill was not always clearly defined. Ballot titles limited to
twenty-five words, and descriptions limited to 100 could scarcely con-
vey all features of bills that were sometimes deliberately complicated.
The use of double negatives in titles confused even informed and
literate voters.

Any measure that could induce eight percent of the total number of
legal voters to sign an initiative petition, any measure referred by the
legislature, or any legislative measure ordered referred by petition of
five percent of the voters, was placed on the ballot. In 1912 the people voted a "bedquilt," a ballot 18¼ by 34½ inches, containing thirty-
seven measures (thirty statutory and six constitutional amendments);
six candidates for the United States Senate and more than 130 candidates for state, county, and local offices. In seven general elections
between 1902 and 1914 the voters considered sixty constitutional
amendments.[10] Of these, twenty-nine were adopted, including the
initiative and referendum that opened the floodgates. In general and
special elections, Oregonians voted on sixty-seven statutory measures
that had been initiated by petition, four referred by the legislature,

[9] Richard Lehne, "An Analysis of Popular Support for Initiative and Referendum Measures in Oregon, 1902–1916," unpublished thesis, Reed College, 1965,
43.

[10] Burton J. Hendrick, "Lawmaking by the Voters in Oregon," *McClure's
Magazine*, August 1911.

and fourteen by popular order. Of eighty-five measures submitted between 1902 and 1914, 32 were enacted; between 1902 and 1950, 164 out of 397 became law.

The people's major accomplishment was the Oregon System itself. Woman suffrage (1912) and prohibition (1914) were, in total votes cast, (118,369 and 237,204) the people's greatest initiative victories. Initiative bills gave home rule to cities (1906), required indictment by grand jury (1906) and a three-fourths verdict in civil cases (1910), and abolished capital punishment by a bare 157 votes in 1914 (restoring it in 1920 and abolishing it again in 1964). Thumping majorities voted for taxes on earnings of railroad car, telephone, and telegraph companies (1906), and doubled liability of bank stockholders (1912). Employers bitterly but unsuccessfully fought an employer's liability act (1910); labor achieved a law forbidding private employment of convicts (1912).

The people adopted an eight-hour day on public works (1912) but rejected a universal eight-hour day (1914) and an "eight-hour day and room ventilation" law for women (1914). A measure to permit organized districts to vote bonds for railroad construction, which U'Ren believed might open the way to public ownership of utilities was buried, but a mild legislative measure to regulate public utilities was approved. On referendum, the voters approved a workmen's compensation act (1913) and disapproved Dr. Bethinia Owens-Adair's bill for sterilization of the criminally insane.

Consistently the voters were opposed to spending money. By majorities of 50,000 (1908) and 100,000 (1914) they refused to increase the $120 compensation for legislators. Their parsimony struck down good legislation while saving them from bad. They would not increase the number of judges or reorganize the courts (1908); they limited state and county indebtedness for roads and refused *both* authority to issue road bonds (1912); refused a millage tax base for the University and agricultural college, and ordered referenda on University appropriations they thereafter rejected. They refused money for irrigation and power projects in 1914, but two years later approved a rural credits amendment which provided relief for farmers.

Tax bills were suspect because Oregonians were devoted to a general property tax levied at an "equal and uniform rate" on all tangibles—personalty, credit instruments, and improvements—a system unjust, antiquated, and primitive, according to its critics. The single tax was repeatedly offered as an alternative. To support the Georgists' campaigns, Philadelphia soap king Joseph Fels poured funds into the state where it was believed conditions were especially favorable for adoption. These conditions were the existence of a group of deter-

458

mined advocates of the idea in its most radical form, direct legislation which lent itself to manipulation, exclusive reliance on the general property tax, and idle lands for speculation. The voters were not trapped by single-tax manipulators.

In 1909 and again in 1913, they rejected not only amendments to repeal the "equal and uniform" provisions of the tax law but also to create a State Tax Commission which might "open the way for all sorts of 'isms.'" However, they adopted an amendment prohibiting poll and head taxes (1910) which contained two clauses: one wiped out all existing constitutional limitations and restrictions on the taxing powers of the state, and the other reserved to the people the right to vote on all measures pertaining to taxation. Not until 1923 was a state income tax amendment adopted, and then by only a 516-vote margin.

In a real sense, the Oregon System was a nonpartisan accomplishment. However, with Republicans outnumbering Democrats four to one, it is obvious that Republicans made reform possible (see Graph X, p. 625). With the perennial machine senator, John Mitchell, convicted of fraudulent conspiracy in 1905 and Joseph Simon dead shortly thereafter, the party lost its entrenched leaders. Yet Oregon lacked what Washington and California both had—an organized group of Republicans, influenced by national reform trends, ready to take on the progressive mantle. Oregon's reputation for progressive legislation in social and economic areas should in fact be credited to recalcitrant Republican legislators under two strong and energetic Democratic governors.

Despite years of strong Republican domination in the legislature and in congressional representation, Democrats were elevated to the governorship. Between 1859 and 1902, five Republicans and five Democrats, none a tower of political strength, held this relatively unimportant office. In 1902, under the compulsion of reform, the voters chose George Chamberlain whose political reputation was above reproach, who was favorable to reform and committed to economy.

The son of a Mississippi doctor, Chamberlain (1854–1928) arrived in Oregon in 1876. Having earned a reputation for scrupulous honesty as attorney general, he was elected governor with a plurality of 246 votes over the Republican candidate, W. J. Furnish, and was reelected in 1906 with a 3000 plurality. As governor, Chamberlain defended the Oregon System from subtle attacks, such as one that would have weakened the referendum by tacking emergency clauses to nonemergency bills. He effected much needed prison reforms: the water cure, flogging, and the infamous "Oregon boot" were abolished;

[11] Virginia Lee Jardine, "George E. Chamberlain, Governor of Oregon, 1903–1909," unpublished thesis, Reed College, 1963.

courts were empowered to fix minimum sentences and to provide for paroles. A Railroad Commission Act that had some teeth in it was set up.[12] A state labor bureau was established, a child labor law passed, and a state library commission with a modest budget was authorized to support traveling libraries.

Chamberlain did not have smooth sailing with legislators. His predecessors seldom used the veto; Chamberlain vetoed twenty-nine bills in 1905, at least thirty in 1907, another fifty-seven before resigning in 1909. Most of the measures he so disposed of (few were passed over his veto) were, by his definition, extravagant or so poorly drawn that they would lead to costly failures. Some were outright raids on the treasury; others were foolish or vicious tests of legislative integrity. He could have left these decisions to public referenda; instead, he activated the office of governor by taking the burden on himself.

Chamberlain's career as governor and his election as United States Senator (1909), which proved the effectiveness of Oregon's primary law and Statement Number One, did not sit well with Republicans or the vested interests of the state. To get nominations back into party hands, Harvey Scott called for a Republican "assembly," since a "convention" was illegal under the Oregon System. "There will be a reform of reformers in Oregon by means of an assembly convention," he proclaimed. "Partyism will reassert itself and shut out political adventurers and self-called candidates. . . . Against all pretended Republicans, who take Statement Number One, 'the knife' will be used with the utmost vigor and the knife to the hilt." To this Judge Henry McGinn, a progressive Republican, replied in words that suggested another dimension of the political struggle:

> You say you are going to have an assembly. I ask you who will be there, who will compose it? I will tell you. The agents of the electric light company will be there. The agents of the street railways and the gas companies and the predatory trusts and combinations and of the big railroad companies will all have seats. . . .[13]

No senator was to be elected in 1910, but a governor was. Chamberlain had given that office a distinction it seldom enjoyed. He had, in fact, made Democrats—not just reformers—a threat to the Establishment. The Republican assembly, then, was a device to put a regu-

---

[12] The 1907 Railroad Commission Act spelled out greater powers for the Commission and included other utilities under its jurisdiction. The commissioners were appointed by the governor, secretary of state, and treasurer, who formed a Board of Control on budgetary matters and to whom other powers were sometimes delegated, as in this case, to curb the governor's powers.

[13] *Oregon Journal*, July 15, 1910.

lar Republican, Jay Bowerman, in the capital. It was a most inept device; the voters in the Republican primary dealt a blow to assembly candidates: only Bowerman and two legislative candidates were nominated.

The Democratic primary nominated Oswald West whose declaration of principles left no doubt that he followed the Chamberlain model:

> If I am nominated and elected I will . . . keep in mind those principles of the social compact found in our constitution, which declares this to be a government . . . by the people, and I will fight . . . any attempt of a legislature to repeal or nullify the initiative and referendum, the direct primary law, the corrupt practices act or the recall. The people must rule the corporations or the corporations will rule the state.

Ralph Watson, political editor of the *Oregon Journal* which supported West, predicted he would win by the votes of farmers, small merchants and working men. West received 54,853 votes to Bowerman's 48,751.

Oswald West (1873–1960), a native of Canada, was brought to Oregon when still a baby. Poverty haunted the family. He had little formal education, but read assiduously while driving a butcher's wagon or herding sheep and cattle. Starting as an errand boy, he became a teller in Ladd and Bush Bank, Salem. He worked for Chamberlain's election in 1902 and was appointed state land agent to dig into the activities of the school-land ring. His report to the Marion County grand jury in 1905 brought Francis J. Heney, special prosecutor for the United States Attorney General's Office, to Oregon and members of the ring to trial. West's next job was on the Railroad Commission. Even the *Oregonian* admitted admiration for his work there. "He does not worry himself over whether the commission has power . . . if it is something that ought to be done, he believes in doing it. . . ."

West needed an aggressive spirit to face the 1911 legislature composed of fifty-seven Republicans, two Democrats, one Independent in the House; twenty-six Republicans, three Democrats, and one Independent in the Senate under the presidency of Jay Bowerman. The *Oregonian*'s news columns reported that lobbyists were "oozing through the state house in crowds. . . ." Telephone, telegraph, railroad, power and light companies' agents were on the ground and "the moment an anti-corporation bill appears they hit the telephone for Portland. The next train brings a block of corporation lawyers and avid lobbyists to see what can be done."

West's method of dealing with the legislature was simple: he announced that if the legislators persisted in killing off all his measures, he would "veto any bill that they fathered . . . whether it had merit or not." In the 1911 session he vetoed sixty-three bills.

The next session was as strongly Republican as the former, but in ten minutes it elected Democrat Harry Lane to the United States Senate and in thirty-one days considered 939 bills and passed thirty-one. West drove through the measures he wanted; if the legislature did not act, he saw to it that initiative measures appeared on the voters' ballots. Surprisingly, however, some measures that the voters rejected were passed by the legislature and not subsequently referred. Thus Oregon got a Blue Sky Law, new banking laws and laws regulating loan sharks, and nearly all public service corporations were placed under the jurisdiction of the Railroad Commission, which later became the Public Utility Commission. A budget system for state departments and institutions was set up. Entered on the statutes were a widow's pension act, a minimum wage law, an industrial welfare law regulating wages and working hours of women, and a child welfare commission. A workmen's compensation act (with an Industrial Accident Commission set up to administer it) was referred to the people, bitterly fought by insurance companies, and passed. "We have from time immemorial been giving more thought to property than to personal rights," West declared in defense of reform.

West stood firmly for good roads and with inspired foresight saw that ocean beaches (under the guise of a public highway) were reserved to public use. Several conservation laws were passed, one providing for a state forester and fire protection, with promise of some slight progress toward West's goal of "the development and utilization of the natural resources . . . under regulation." However, his recommendations for a study of taxation of forested and deforested lands were not implemented. Prison reforms were carried far beyond Chamberlain's beginnings.

West's retirement from office (1915) coincided with a general weakening of the progressive pulse, but the Oregon System remained intact. In time it became enveloped in such an aura of sanctity that efforts to remedy its more obvious weaknesses were interpreted as assaults on the people's rule.

One further note should be added to this account of Oregon's reform era. Dr. Harry Lane is one of the forgotten men in Oregon history, perhaps because in 1917 he was one of the six United States senators who voted against American entrance into World War I. The grandson of Oregon's first territorial governor, Harry Lane (1855–1917) was closely affiliated with the reform movement in Portland where he practiced medicine.

From 1902 until 1908, the city and county had been controlled by Walter F. ("Jack") Matthews, a boss of classic type who held no office but managed those who did. Matthew's front was Mayor George H. Williams (1820–1910), the city's "Grand Old Man" of Republicanism. As United States senator from 1865 to 1871, Williams had figured prominently in the Republican Party. He served as United States Attorney General in Grant's cabinet and the President nominated him in 1874 for the office of Chief Justice of the Supreme Court. Charges of conflicts of interest in his administration as Attorney General led him to request withdrawal of his nomination, and he returned to Portland where he engaged in private law practice until Matthews pulled him out of political retirement.

Williams was unable or disinclined to combat the various rings of corruption in the city. When in 1908 he stood for a third term, Harry Lane was offered as a reform candidate and was elected. "Fearless and free, as courageous as he was honest," Lane "threw the searchlight of pitiless publicity on abuses and practices of whose existence the people had not dreamed." In 1912, he was the popular candidate for the United States Senate on the Democratic ticket and was elected by the legislature. Never strongly partisan, Lane was strongly progressive in his opposition to "privilege and power based on privilege." He supported most of Wilson's program and his reelection in 1916; but he broke with Wilson on the Armed Ships Bill and declaration of war.

THE PROGRESSIVES IN IDAHO AND WASHINGTON

While Oregon was swept by the spirit of reform, progressivism was also taking hold in Idaho and Washington. In both states, early reforms were the work of legislatures, parties, and party leaders rather than of the people. In both states the initiative and referendum came fairly late (1912). The leaders were party men, sometimes ambidextrous, whose progressivism was often more a matter of national politics than of interest in local reforms, as it was with Oregon's leaders.

The "Idaho plan" for administration of higher education and public schools in an integrated system (1913) was a unique accomplishment, setting a precedent for other states beset by institutional rivalries.

Otherwise Idaho's reforms were similar to those adopted elsewhere on the wave of progressive politics. It was among the first states to adopt woman suffrage (1905), four years earlier than Washington and seven before Oregon. It had a Sunday closing law in 1907, local option in 1909, and a bone-dry law in 1915. Provision for a state bank commissioner (1905) and a public utilities commission (1913) suggested that the legislature felt the state had an obligation to scrutinize bank activities and monitor rates for public services. In 1907 the legislature restricted and regulated lobbying, something Oregonians did not face up to for several decades. On the other hand, while labor troubles led to violence in the Coeur d'Alene mines and Governor Frank Steunenberg was assassinated in 1905, farmer and merchant legislators seemed more interested in land reclamation and economy than in authorizing the state to do more than police the disturbed area. Not until 1917 when labor troubles again threatened did the state adopt a workmen's compensation law.

But Idaho had a direct primary law in 1907 and in 1912 the initiative, referendum, and recall were adopted. Idaho was thus in the progressive ranks, and such was its reputation in Congress. Republican United States Senator Fred T. Dubois (1851–1930) had helped secure passage of the Reclamation Act in 1902. Returned to the Senate in 1900 as a Democrat, he had championed Teddy Roosevelt's conservation policies at the risk of losing all Idaho voters, who were strongly opposed to the creation of national forest reserves in their state. Dubois might have done well with Republican patronage from a grateful Roosevelt if he had returned to the Republican fold. This he could not do, partly because he was more strongly anti-Mormon than he was Progressive Republican. Returned to Idaho in 1906, he split the Democratic Party wide open on the Mormon issue.

Leadership passed into the hands of William E. Borah (1865–1940). As United States Senator from 1907 until his death Borah led a double life politically: he was progressive in Congress, conservative at home. In Congress he sponsored two major pieces of progressive legislation, the income tax and the direct election of senators; also the establishment of a children's bureau and the Department of Labor. He moved with the progressive wing of the Republican Party but never joined the Progressive Party. At home, he built up a reputation for service to his state, "without mortally offending any really vital interest group . . ." The progressive reputation was useful in Idaho, since neither conservative Republicans nor conservative Democrats had done well in local politics since 1890. Local politics were chaotic, and parties riddled by factions within factions. Idahoans tended to vote in protest rather than toward constructive party ends.

A student of the Washington Progressive movement finds that its leadership resembled Mowry's California "urban gentry," but that it included a "rural gentry" as well. Leaders in the movement who did not become members of the Progressive Party were scarcely distinguishable from those who did. Furthermore, support for progressive legislation came from strongly Populist counties of eastern Washington as well as from urban-industrial areas where Populism had been weak. According to William T. Kerr,

> Progressivism did not evoke the overwhelming allegiance of the various underprivileged elements that supported Bryan in 1896; it drew most heavily upon the native born, the moderately prosperous, and the better educated elements of the state. In this regard, it would appear that the progressives not only maintained the reform enthusiasm of the relatively prosperous one-crop wheat areas which had supported Bryan in less prosperous days, but that they also expanded this enthusiasm to include the middle-class elements of both town and country.[14]

Republicans carried out progressive legislation in Washington, but they went further than did either Oregonians or Idahoans and tested the issues more thoroughly. Both the Railway Commission Law (1905) and the direct primary (1907) were the result of mounting protest against intervention of the railroad lobby in politics. For years the railroads had defeated all attempts to establish a regulatory agency, although the Washington constitution authorized one. Nominating conventions were made a hollow mockery as in 1904 when James J. Hill's troubleshooter, J. D. Farrell in his curtained private car ordered party leaders to drop the railroad commission and scotch the renomination of Senator Henry G. McBride who supported it. This was one of many episodes that made the Republican convention of 1904 "the lowest point in the degradation" of the party.

Widespread reaction against such practices affected the next legislature. The railroad commission bill passed with only eleven negative votes in the House, four in the Senate; the direct primary passed in the Senate by a vote of thirty-nine to one. Here was a revolt of the party itself against its bosses. Even Senator John L. Wilson, party boss of the old school, friend of the railroad and timber interests and despoiler of the Colville Indian reservation, reformed in order to keep his hand in affairs. National progressivism was also reflected locally. Miles Poindexter (1868–1946) a Tennessee-born lawyer who had been successively attorney for Walla Walla and Spokane counties (1892–

[14] William T. Kerr, Jr., "The Progressives of Washington, 1910–1912," *PNQ*, January 1961, 26.

LEFT. *Kwakiutl canoes under sail. The length of one is decorated with a serpent having a well-defined eye, teeth, and tongue. The Kwakiutl built fine houses as well and made beautiful household boxes, dishes, masks and totem poles.*

RIGHT. *The river Indians transported themselves and their goods in dugout canoes and on that faithful old device, the back.* Old Fort Walla Walla *was painted by William Cary during a western journey.*

Transportation

RIGHT. *Mining operations in remote areas had to be supplied by pack train. In* Bell Mare *(detail), Charles M. Russell painted the custom of a belled mare leading a train of donkeys and mules.*

At the turn of the century, a pack is ready to depart from Grangeville to Buffalo Hump. Spring rains have done their worst for Main Street . . . but six inches of mud will all too soon be "Dust—Everywhere Dust."

But coaching could be fun for city folk. Two clubs, the Berkeley Glee and the Standford Mandolin, performing at the Marquam Grand Opera House, leave the elegant Portland Hotel in the Tallyho "Jupiter," 1895.

ABOVE. *A Gold Rush ship leaves Seattle for Alaska or the Yukon with a full passenger list, to judge from the thronged deck. The building extreme left announces that tickets are available for California, Mexico, South America, Antwerp, Havre, Southampton, and Cork.*

LEFT. *Pack trains can transport supplies but not heavy freight. Oxen haul freight in covered wagons into Last Chance Gulch, Montana, 1887.*

In the 1870s, rails, a steam engine and cars connected the Upper and Lower Cascades, over the Bradford Portage, on the Washington side of the Columbia.

The trim Columbia River steamers Spokane and Lewiston take on cargo and passengers.

Samuel Lancaster, the bold designer and construction engineer, and his party en route to celebrate the opening of the newly-completed Columbia River Highway, July, 1915.

Modern highway building, RIGHT, accomplishes what Lancaster could only dream of. BELOW. Modern highways, major railroads and frequently ocean vessels, serve cities throughout the Northwest.

LEFT. *The diesel train* City of Portland, *with its special scenic cars, sweeps up the banks of the Columbia.*

BELOW. *Air traffic fans out from Sea-Tac International Airport (Seattle-Tacoma) to every part of the world.*

1904) and a judge of the superior court (1904–1908), was strongly anti-railroad.[15] Elected to Congress in 1908, he joined the House insurgents. In 1910 he ran for the Senate as a Progressive Republican and carried the state to a landslide victory with 57 percent of the votes cast.

The next session of the Washington legislature responded to further progressive demands. With affirmative votes of three to one, it passed such measures as an eight-hour day for women, the initiative and referendum amendment, and a workmen's compensation act. A small group of diehards opposed these measures. But if there was any pattern in their alignment it was insignificant, merely that three of the five were from rural western Washington where one student has found "a consistent hostility to the progressive reformers."

Easy victories did not mean that support for progressive legislation was spontaneous. On the contrary, it was the result of skillful agitation, lobbying, and careful organization. The adoption of woman suffrage (passed by the legislature 1909, ratified by the people 1910), was a case in point. Washington had displayed a peculiar ambivalence on this issue. Women were permitted to vote in the Territory from 1883 to 1887; but in ratifying the constitution the people had revoked the privilege. Usually, the equal suffrage movement was tied in with prohibition. Oregon's Abigail Scott Duniway, an advocate of temperance rather than prohibition, had pointed out that this mingling of issues hindered the accomplishment of both; and it was been suggested that brewery interests in Oregon helped finance prohibition suffragettes in order to wreck the suffrage movement. Taking their cue from Mrs. Duniway, Emma Smith DeVoe and May Arkwright Hutton, Washington's suffrage leaders, carefully kept the two issues separated. In 1910 "this was possible," says Norman H. Clark, historian of Washington's Dries, "because each movement was vigorous enough to do without the other."

The initiative and referendum was likewise deftly handled. Having engineered the drive for the amendment in Oregon, U'Ren helped in Washington as well. The Direct Legislation League, counterpart of the People's Power League in Oregon, marshaled popular support, steered desired measures through the legislature, and got out votes for ratification of constitutional amendments. Little was left to chance.

Legislation designed to ameliorate the worker's lot was moderate by present standards, yet in the progressive spirit. Child labor laws of 1903 and 1907 protected minors against more flagrant forms of exploitation. A 1911 law gave women workers an eight-hour day. Two

[15] Howard W. Allen, "Miles Poindexter and the Progressive Movement," *PNQ*, July 1962.

years later the legislature enacted a minimum wage law that benefited both women and children. A wage commission was set up and
minimum wage levels established for several occupational groups
though enforcement left something to be desired. Substantial gains
were made through a Workmen's Compensation Law (1911), which
recognized the principle of collective liability and set up an industrial insurance department and accident fund administered by the
state. The most drastic of its kind enacted in the United States up to
that time, the law was tested in the State Supreme Court and upheld in a decision reflecting a progressive philosophy: "The state's
power to regulate industry is found in the effect the pursuant of the
calling has upon the public weal rather than in the nature of the calling itself."[16] Decried as state socialism, the law nevertheless dis-
armed critics and astonished even its proponents with its success.

PROGRESSIVES FORM THEIR OWN PARTY

This, then, was the record of progressive legislation in the Pacific
Northwest. Outwardly it might seem to have been accomplished without intraparty struggle. Republican control of the legislatures was
never in question. In Washington and Idaho most legislators rode the
groundswell of progressive sentiment and supported social and economic measures without feeling that their loyalty to party or faction
was open to question. Perhaps. Republicanism was gradually changing its spots and the GOP was coming to accept a new political
philosophy.

But the Old Guard gave ground grudgingly. Progressivism was not
always a political philosophy; often it was a convenient posture to
win votes when a candidate lacked regular party organization endorsement. Insurgency was at first a personal and individual matter.
Later it indicated an alignment within the Republican Party and, even
before 1912, led to serious defections and ultimately to a third-party
explosion.[17]

[16] John Bauer, "Documents and Reports," *American Economic Review*, March
1912, 187; Hamilton Higday, "Washington's Unique Compensation Law," *Independent*, October 1912.

[17] Keith Murray, "Republican Party Politics in Washington during the Progressive Era," unpublished thesis, University of Washington, 1946; "Issues and Personalities of Pacific Northwest Politics, 1889–1950," *PNQ*, July 1950; "Aberdeen
Convention of 1912," *PNQ*, April 1947.

Jonathan Bourne exploited the possibilities of the progressive movement in Oregon, especially the direct primary, to win a seat in the
United States Senate; Miles Poindexter did the same in Washington.
Both men achieved national prominence through speeches and writings on progressive themes, though the depth of their convictions
might be questioned. Borah's success was based on direct popular appeal and the claim that he was independent, owing little or nothing
to any political machine or to the favor of Big Business.

The emergence of Democratic leadership such as had occurred in
Oregon had no parallel in Washington or Idaho. Washington's Republican governors, Mead, Cosgrove, and Hay, took the initiative in
recommending legislation, and the voters found in Senator Wesley
Jones of Yakima a party regular who, without taint of insurgency,
proved to be a hard-working, conscientious public servant. Since the
Washington Republican Party was taken out of the hands of old-
school politicians and made increasingly responsible, Washington voters, unlike those of Oregon, did not need to cross party lines.

However, progressivism and reform encouraged independence in
candidates and voters. In the Pacific Northwest, Democratic votes
were heavier in 1908 than in 1900 and 1934 (see Graphs III, IV,
V, VI 5 pp. 622, 623). The most important expression of independence came in 1912 when Roosevelt and Taft contested for leadership of the Republican Party. In Washington the split went to the
grass roots. Early in 1912 a dozen county conventions wrangled in-
terminably as Taft and Roosevelt men fought for control, and finally
sent rival delegations to the state nominating convention at Aberdeen. Here too, the issue of control was fought bitterly and incon-
clusively, with the result that two state delegations went to Chicago.
Since the national committee on credentials was controlled by Taft
forces, the Roosevelt delegation was refused admission. Washington
Progressives then joined with other Roosevelt contingents to organize
the Progressive, or Bull Moose, Party.

In the national elections that fall, Roosevelt carried Washington by
a plurality of 26,000. The Bull Moose captured two of Washington's
four seats in the lower house of Congress and thirty-eight seats in the
state legislature. It was a signal show of strength, yet it demonstrated
more the size of the independent vote than a significant change of
party affiliation between Republicans and Democrats. A comparison
of the 1908 election with that of 1912 shows that only one county
(Douglas) shifted from Republican to Democrat.

In Oregon and Idaho the third-party movement had different effects. At first glance, the swing to Wilson appeared greater since he
carried both states and won a plurality in twenty-three of thirty-four

counties in Oregon and in fourteen of twenty-three in Idaho. However, though defections from the regular Republican organization were serious enough to lose the election for Taft, they were not enough to win for Roosevelt who came in second. In all three states the Democratic vote in 1912 constituted a smaller fraction of the total than in 1908, and the Progressive vote in Idaho and Oregon ran lower than in Washington. In Oregon and Idaho together Taft won a plurality in fifteen counties and led Roosevelt in thirty-six. On the other hand, the Socialists received a larger proportion than formerly (in Idaho, 30 percent) of the non-Democratic protest vote. Since the total protest vote was smaller than in 1908 and was divided between Socialists and Progressives, it gave the Democrats control by default.

Socialism, whether Marxian ("scientific") or non-Marxian ("utopian"), had not previously offered a serious third-party threat. In the 1890s Eugene V. Debs captivated Utopian Socialists with visions of a cooperative commonwealth—an idea widely popularized in Edward Bellamy's *Looking Backward* (1888)—and the party seriously considered colonization to promote reconstruction experiments. Washington and Idaho were believed to be ideal for the purpose because they were rich in natural resources, sparsely populated, and because Washington already ranked highest in the nation in Socialist membership and second in Socialist vote.[18] Despite a hard core of Marxists whose basic aim was a labor movement oriented toward revolutionary goals, Washington Socialists were conservative supporters of political and economic reforms rather than of revolution. The Party's 1908 platform showed the rightists in ascendancy. It called for legislation to abolish labor injunctions, child labor, and residence requirements for voting; and for establishment of the eight-hour day and 44-hour week, freedom of speech and press, the initiative and referendum, and equal suffrage. The next year the left wing, led by Herman Titus, walked out leaving A. H. Barth in charge of the conservative victors. In Oregon the Socialist Party pledged itself to use city and state governments to support labor. (Table III demonstrates the strength of the protest vote in presidential elections.)

The temporary nature of the 1912 alignment of parties became

[18] Ira Kipnis, *The American Socialist Movement, 1897–1912* (1952), 55, 61, 373. Kipnis says that "two small colonies with a total membership of 110 were eventually established in the state of Washington." Washington had several colonies; the Puget Sound Cooperative Colony, Port Angeles, antedated the Social Democrat project; Equality at Edison, according to Mary W. Avery, *History and Government of the State of Washington* (1961), 244, had 100 colonists from Maine. It is possible that this was the Social Democrats' colony. The Mutual Home Colony Association, founded in 1897 near Tacoma, had a brief but famous history.

TABLE III

Socialist Votes in Presidential Elections in Washington, Oregon, Idaho, 1900–1960[a]

Year	WASHINGTON Socialist	Per-cent	Social-Labor	Per-cent	OREGON Socialist	Per-cent	Social-Labor	Per-cent	IDAHO[b] Socialist	Per-cent
1900	2,006	1.9	866	.8	1,494	1.8				
1904	10,023	6.9	1,592	1.1	7,619	8.4			4,949	6.8
1908	14,177	7.7			7,339	6.6			6,400	6.6
1912	40,134	12.4	1,872	.6	13,343	9.7			11,960	11.3
1916	22,800	6.0	730	.2	9,711	3.7			8,066	6.0
1920	8,913	2.2	1,321	.3	9,801	4.1	1,515	.6	38	.0
1924			1,004	.2			917	.3		
1928	2,615	.5	4,068	.8	2,720	.8	1,564	.5	1,308	.8
1932	17,080	2.8	1,009	.2	15,450	4.2	1,730	.5	526	.3
1936	3,496	.5	362	.1	2,143	.5	500	.1		
1940	4,586	.6	667	.1	398	.1	2,487	.5	497	.2
1944	3,824	.4	1,645	.2	3,785	.8			282	.1
1948	3,534	.4	1,133	.1	5,051	1.0			332	.2
1952	254	.0	633	.1						
1956			7,457	.6						
1960			10,895	.9						

[a] Percentages are of the total vote cast by all parties.

[b] No votes reported for Socialist Labor.

Source: Compiled from Sverd Petersen, "A Statistical History of the American Presidential Elections" (1963).

plain during the next few years. Republicans bent every effort to heal their party schism, and largely succeeded. In all three states, third-party protest votes, Progressive and Socialist, declined to less than 8 percent of the total, and the region, like the nation, returned to the two-party system. The healing of Republican wounds did not bring immediate restoration of GOP power. C. C. Dill, Spokane Democrat, served two terms in Congress, and in the 1916 presidential election Wilson carried Washington and Idaho with a margin of some 15,000 votes in each state. Nineteen counties in Washington and nine in Idaho which had been Republican in 1908 and Progressive in 1912, voted Democratic in 1916, indicating the extent to which the independent vote of 1912 merged with the Democratic vote of 1916. Domestic issues were, however, so intertwined with questions of foreign policy that the final eclipse of insurgency cannot be clearly traced or defined. It is significant, by way of comparison, that only nine Oregon counties followed the transition to the Democrats while fourteen of the Progressive counties of 1912 reverted to the Republican column. Hughes carried the state in 1916 by a slender plurality, and the Republicans recaptured more independent votes in Oregon than in either of her sister states.

The Progressive Party had died. Progressivism itself was in sad decline. If it had been, as some have held, a resurgence of liberalism in the tradition of Jefferson, Jackson, and Lincoln, it was not strong enough to survive World War I. It should be kept in mind, however, that progressivism was a product of prosperity and optimism. For those who believed that human will could direct change to socially beneficial ends, the Progressive Era was one of great hope and good will.

CHAPTER
TWENTY-NINE

War and Peace:
Problems of Economic
Adjustment

As we have indicated, the full flush of prosperity that marked the first decade of the twentieth century had begun to fade by the opening of the second. Immigration slowed to a trickle and urban growth and construction fell off. Real estate dealers complained that sales were few and far between. Wheat that brought 93 cents a bushel in 1909 was selling at 72 cents in 1913. Douglas fir dropped three dollars a thousand and mill workers were laid off. It was apparent that the region faced another period of depressed prices and sluggish growth.

The outbreak of war delayed fulfillment of gloomy prophecies. Europe's demands sent the price of Northwest wheat up to $1.97 a bushel and pushed lumber up six dollars a thousand in 1917. Two years later, wheat farmers were receiving an average of $2.04 a bushel and Douglas fir was selling at three times its 1915 price.

476

LUMBER AND LABOR

During the war years, Seattle's employment totals leaped from 11,000 to 40,000, and the amount of manufacturing capital doubled. As a result, Seattle's rank among the nation's industrial cities rose from 62nd to 28th place, and Portland's from 58th to 40th. In value of products, the three Northwest states increased their output from $383,000,000 to $1,125,000,000—a figure which, however, also represented the general rise in prices throughout the economy.

In the war boom three components were prominent: development of food industries, expansion of the lumber trade, and shipbuilding on a large scale. Farmers turned their plows on almost a million and a half acres of new wheat land and increased their harvests by six and a half million bushels. In 1919, Washington stood seventh among flour milling states, eighth in canning and preserving (it produced 70 percent of the national output of processed salmon), and eleventh in dairy products.

Lumber remained the predominant Northwest industry in war as it had been in peace. Building army cantonments created an unusual demand on the national supply; but measured in board feet rather than in inflated dollars, local production rose only 28 percent over the slack year of 1914. Nevertheless, the industry was markedly affected by the war. Spruce became an important export item, and the federal government, through a military agency, controlled logging, milling, and labor relations.

At the outbreak of hostilities in 1914, England and France turned to the United States for lumber suitable for airplane construction. Wing beams, for instance, required a tough but not brittle, lightweight, straight-grained wood, free from flaws, in minimum lengths of forty feet. The Sitka spruce in the Coast range of Oregon and Washington was such a wood. Between 1914 and 1917, Oregon increased its production of spruce from 65,000,000 to 120,000,000 board feet. However, the purchasers found that only about 10 percent of the lumber met specifications. When the United States entered the war, the need for a larger supply of properly prepared wood became critical.

The Council of National Defense set up the Aircraft Production Board and made it responsible for producing planes as rapidly as possible. At first the Board believed that if it contracted for the full output of Northwest spruce, providing inspection to insure quality, the need could be filled. By October, 1917, it became evident that

477

this did not suffice. Mill operators seemed incapable of meeting specifications, and the Northwest's industry was involved in a disastrous strike over wages and hours. The Board then set up a military division to take over spruce production. Five thousand enlisted men, under Brigadier General Brice P. Disque, were sent to Vancouver Barracks in 1917 as the first contingent of the Spruce Division. By the following spring, 27,000 soldiers were at work in camps and mills in western Oregon and Washington. To eliminate military red tape, the Board authorized organization of the United States Spruce Production Corporation, with General Disque as president, and empowered it to make contracts, purchase properties, build mills, roads, and railroads, and otherwise act as a civil corporate body.[1] Within the year, the Spruce Division demonstrated what could be done with military authority, adequate capital, a disciplined labor force, and technical innovation.

Expert timber cruisers selected perfect tree specimens; engineers built thirteen short-line railroads and miles of planked truck roads to haul out the trees. Unable to handle the forest giants as whole logs, army-employed technicians devised a method of riving or splitting the straight-grained outer layers of a log into four sections, or cants. The cants could easily be moved to the mills to be sawed into flitches —slabs 3 to 4½ inches thick, one to five feet wide, and forty or more feet long. Since no Northwest mill was equipped to cut and kiln-dry flitches to specifications, the Corporation built, in forty-five days, a huge "cut up" plant at Vancouver. In operation by early February, 1918, within a year the plant turned out 14,000,000 feet of wing beam stock, 85 to 90 percent of which met specifications.

In a little more than a year the Corporation purchased and produced as a side product to the manufacture of wing beams, 143,-000,000 board feet of lumber—54,000,000 from Oregon's forests and 88,000,000 from Washington's. Of this total the Allies received 91,000,000 feet and the United States consumed the rest. At the end of the war, Corporation assets in plants (including a completed mill at Port Gamble that had not been put into operation, and an incompleted mill at Toledo, Oregon), trucks, railroads, land and other inventory amounting to $24,000,000, were liquidated over a period of years on generous terms to private concerns.

In the area of labor relations the Corporation asserted federal war powers over both employers and workers and won an unhappy reputation among labor organizations. At the war's outbreak, labor was or-

[1] United States Spruce Production Corporation, *History of the Spruce Division, United States Army* (n.d.).

478

ganized in practically all Northwest industries.[2] Unions had tested their strength and demonstrated their weaknesses at Roslyn and New-castle mines in the 1890s. By 1912 the United Mine Workers had entered Washington, and after Renton miners held out for two years for a closed shop, most operators signed contracts with the union. In the lumber industry, shingle weavers were the first to organize (1890). Although comprising only a small part of all mill employees, they were a strongly motivated and cohesive group because of the nature of their work. A piecework system of payment set a premium on skill and speed and at the same time put the workers under great pressure to earn a living wage. The dependence of an entire crew upon the pace set by the shingle sawyer bound the weavers together.

By 1903 the West Coast Shingle Weavers' Union, through a series of strikes, had bettered their wages and had a membership of 1300 organized in twenty-four locals, chartered individually by the American Federation of Labor (AFL) and loosely associated in a "grand council," the International Shingle Weavers' Union of America. However, in 1906 and 1913 efforts to win statewide and local recognition for the union failed.

The AFL had made several attempts to organize sawmill workers and loggers. In 1905 a charter was issued to the International Brotherhood of Woodsmen and Sawmill Workers, and, within a year or so, the organization had about 1250 members. However, the union lacked vitality, membership fell off, and in 1911 it was suspended by the Federation for failure to pay the per capita tax. The next year, the Shingle Weavers virtually took over the old Brotherhood under a new charter as the International Union of Shingle Weavers, Sawmill Workers, and Woodsmen. The new organization was wrecked within two years by an unsuccessful struggle for an eight-hour day. Operators at Everett and Raymond, anticipating the strike, countered with a lock-out, and when the men went back to work, it was to an open shop and the ten-hour day. Having failed in economic action, the Union tried political action, putting an eight-hour day to the voters on an initiative petition. This, too, failed. Within a year the number of affiliated locals dropped from twenty to five; membership fell from 1768 to 118. The Union once more reorganized with the shingle weav-

[2] Samuel Gompers visited Portland in 1883 and helped to found the Portland Federated Trades Assembly, which joined the AFL when it was organized in 1886. On Gompers' second visit (1887) representatives of 400 trades union men formed the Portland Federated Trades Assembly and within a year the Oregon Assembly was second strongest on the Coast. In 1902 the Oregon State Federation of Labor was organized with a membership of 10,000.

ers retaining jurisdiction only over their own group, and several timber workers' locals received a charter as the International Union of
Timber Workers. The early attempts of the AFL to organize the lumber industry as a whole were failures.

Northwest labor was self-consciously and often militantly union-
minded; but it was also parochial and headstrong. AFL locals asserted independence of action beyond the tolerance of Federation
principles. Local unions were strongly attracted to industrial organization, in part because of its practicality in the lumber industry, but
also because industrial unionism appeared less autocratic than craft
unionism. For these reasons and others, in the logging camps the Industrial Workers of the World (IWW) seemed to have the advantage over the AFL.[3]

A small faction broken off from the revolutionary wing of the Socialist Party, the IWW rejected political action and craft organization.
It maintained that economic action was the only effective weapon in
the class struggle and industrial unionism—"One Big Union" or syndicate—the only effective organization with which to form "the structure
of the new society within the shell of the old." Bound together by a
theory but lacking any centralized authority or plan of action, the
IWW organizers converged on localities where conditions bred discontent. They were present in Idaho mines when the Western Federation
of Miners, an industrial union under the leadership of IWW William
"Big Bill" Haywood, lost the 1899 Coeur d'Alene strike. They were
present in 1905 when Governor Frank Steunenberg was assassinated
by Harry Orchard and his pals who implicated Haywood and his
lieutenant, Charles Moyer. While labor charged that Orchard was
agent provocateur for the Mine Owners' Association, Idaho officials
kidnapped Haywood and Moyer and brought them to the state for
trial. Prosecuted by William E. Borah and defended by Clarence Dar-
row, both of whom made national reputations in this widely publicized trial, Haywood and Moyer were acquitted. But the IWWs had
won infamous reputations as revolutionaries, syndicalists, and an-
archists.

In the nomadic western logger, fearful of nothing, cheerfully cynical, with "frank and outspoken contempt for most of the conventions
of bourgeois society," and thwarted in his efforts to improve his lot, the
IWW saw the natural advance guard for a labor army, the guerrilla of
the revolution. Among loggers, the IWW was popular. In its membership, the logger saw an aggressiveness he could admire; if the "One
Big Union" was theoretical, the idea of an industrial union seemed

[3] Robert L. Tyler, "IWW in the Pacific Northwest: Rebels of the Woods,"
OHQ, March 1954.

appropriate to the industry and eminently practical in winning labor's goals. When the chips were down, few loggers or mill workers thought of revolution; but since the IWW supported the causes on which lumber workers felt strongly, they found Wobbly agitators useful guerrillas in their own particular war.

In 1905, the IWW reported that their Seattle group numbered 800. Two years later, they had locals at Portland, Vancouver, Astoria, Aberdeen, Hoquiam, Tacoma, Ballard, and North Bend. It was not unusual for IWW and AFL locals to work together. In 1907, for example, with full approval of the Central Labor Council, the IWW intervened in a Portland mill strike for a nine-hour day and a daily minimum wage of $2.50. For a time the Shingle Weavers considered affiliating with the IWW, but in the final vote the proposal lost. But IWW membership was not stable; it increased or decreased as circumstances were tense or relaxed. During the Portland strike, the local claimed 1847 members. At Hoquiam mills when strikes were called over wages (1912), 250 men joined in a single day. Yet in 1913 national headquarters reported only 640 members among lumber workers.

The Wobblies made up in mobility and vigor whatever they might lack in numbers. Organizers took the initiative and often assumed leadership in a local dispute, regardless of whether it was originally their own fight. When a demonstration was called for or civil rights threatened, the "foot-loose working stiffs" converged by the hundreds to fill the jails and embarrass the police. The Everett "massacre" (1916) was precipitated when the Seattle IWW chartered the *Verona* and took some 250 members to the neighboring city to demonstrate for striking shingle weavers. The sheriff and a company of armed citizens met them at the wharf. In the ten-minute shooting battle that followed seven men were killed and fifty wounded.

IWW tactics varied. They encouraged strikes and sought converts by haranguing listerners on street corners. In 1914 they shifted from organizing locals in towns to recruiting in the camps. The job-delegate worked until he was identified and fired; another soon replaced him. The wooden shoe and the black snarling cat became well-known symbols of IWW sabotage. Often, having precipitated trouble, the Wobbly disappeared, leaving the consequences of his acts to AFL and local unions.

In the summer of 1917 troubles in the camps reached a climax. Both AFL and IWW had built up their memberships, the first to 2500 men, the second to about 3000, representing both the pine sections of the Inland Empire and the fir timber camps and mills along the coast. The Shingle Weavers and Timber Workers drew up demands for an eight-hour, or at most a nine-hour day, and for higher wages and improved living conditions in logging camps. They also promoted the idea of union recognition, though this was not the principal issue. The employers refused to negotiate and organized the Lumbermen's Protective Association to resist union demands, using common antistrike funds and assessing penalties against mills that ran less than ten-hour shifts.

The AFL then set July 16 (1917) as a strike date. The strike took place as planned; 40,000 to 50,000 men were idle, and by August 1 not more than 15 percent of the West Coast mills were running. A boycott element entered the situation when ship carpenters at Grays Harbor refused to handle lumber from ten-hour mills. However, public pressure mounted against the strikers and the few mills that had conceded the eight-hour day soon retracted it. The IWW then transferred their fight to a strike-on-the-job, slowing down work by deliberate inefficiency and making what trouble they could through sabotage.

Such was the labor situation when the Spruce Division was sent into the Pacific Northwest. From labor's point of view, the army was employed as strikebreakers; from the employers', it appeared that the army was bullying them into accepting labor's demands. General Disque forced on employers what they had earlier refused to concede: the eight-hour working day and improved living conditions in logging camps. Private operators were forced to observe these precedents when the industry reverted to their control after the war.

For the Spruce Division wage problems were more complicated. In using enlisted men as workers in camps and mills, the military had to avoid the appearance of conscripting labor or affording special privileges to private operators. As it was worked out, the soldier-worker was paid civilian wages, minus his army pay, and was charged civilian mess rates. The Corporation set maximum wage rates to halt competition for civilian labor in a market of short supply but also as *quid pro quo* for employers' concessions on hours and camp improvements. With the hearty approval of the operators, the Corporation then set up under Disque a "fifty-fifty" employer-employee organization, the Loyal Legion of Loggers and Lumbermen (4–L), which was in effect a tremendous industry-wide company union. It outlawed strikes and boycotts and prohibited coercion of nonunion workers and employers. Under the demands of patriotism and as a necessary qualification for employment, 100,000 civilians, pledged not to strike for the duration, were enrolled in the Legion before the war ended.

A recent study concludes that Disque, to his credit, kept the Spruce Production Division "tightly controlled and set its major goals in harmony with those of civilian directors of the war administration. The SPD did not threaten civil government." Under army administration the Legion did not represent a conspiracy against labor, but the "SPD-Legion combination during the war did threaten and violate civil liberties."[4] The 4-L continued in existence after the war. Despite the best intentions of some members of the civilian board that inherited army leadership, the postwar Loyal Legion exerted its strength indiscriminately against AFL and radical labor movements, contributed to the fomentation of the "Red Scare" which made all labor suspect, and thereby weakened the development of labor organizations and encouraged disaffection in labor ranks.

SHIPBUILDING AND LABOR

A new and important factor in the Northwest's war industry was the mushroom growth of both wood and steel shipbuilding.[5] This enterprise was introduced into the Northwest on so large a scale that it dwarfed every other industry except lumber. It brought millions in capital investment to the region, gave employment to more than 50,000 men, and stimulated expansion of many secondary bread-and-butter industries that served the population working in the yards.

Although Coos Bay had launched some remarkably fast sailing clippers in the 1870s, shipbuilding was a minor industry in the Northwest. Some of the schooners and barkentines that made up Puget Sound's prewar lumber fleet were foreign "tramp" vessels; nearly all those of American registry were built on the East Coast. When in 1915 these ships were diverted to Atlantic routes, Westerners began to build for themselves. Late in 1915 Martin Erismann of Seattle designed a five-masted lumber schooner; J. A. McEachern of Astoria, Andrew Peterson and George Mathew of Grays Harbor, and John McAteer of Seattle built schooners with characteristic "bald-headed" (no topmast) rigs and auxiliary engines, which attracted considerable attention to Pacific Coast yards. Hastily constructed and poorly equipped, the locally built fleet was nevertheless a significant development of the early war years.

Norwegian companies and the French government placed orders for Northwest sailing ships and the Foundation Yards at Tacoma and Portland built twenty five-masted schooners, all named for French

[4] Harold M. Hyman, *Soldiers and Spruce: Origins of the Loyal Legion of Loggers and Lumbermen* (1963), 339, 341.

[5] John Lyman, "Pacific Coast-built Sailers of World War I," *Marine Digest*, May 30, 1942; Portus Baxter, "Growth of Shipbuilding," *Argus*, December 15, 1917.

battlefields, which carried lumber, flour, and nitrates to Europe. In 1918 the Swan Island Shipyard Corporation took over the Olympia Shipbuilding Company and built a number of wooden motorships for the Australian government. When the United States entered the war, the Emergency Fleet Corporation (EFC), a federal agency designated to build and manage American war shipping, also turned to the Northwest for ships. By the end of the war, twenty-eight separate yards in Seattle, Portland, Astoria, Aberdeen, Anacortes, Tillamook, Vancouver, and Columbia City were turning out wooden vessels. In Seattle, wooden ship building gave employment to several thousand men, supported a $3,000,000 payroll in 1919, and turned out $11,000,000 worth of ships.

In December, 1915, the Seattle firm of Skinner and Eddy had begun to build standardized steel construction steam vessels, and their *Niels Nielson* won the Norwegians' highest rating. The EFC placed orders for similar vessels and within a year the Pacific Northwest had nine steel yards in production, among them Skinner and Eddy, Ames, and J. F. Duthie in Seattle, Todd in Tacoma, G. M. Standifer, Northwest Steel, and the Columbia Shipbuilding Company at Portland and Vancouver. Skinner and Eddy, the giant of the group, put $4,600,000 into a 27-acre plant on the Seattle waterfront. Later it leased a second yard and doubled its capacity. Plant number 1 was the teacher and pacemaker of the world, launching ships in fifty-five days and having them ready to commission in another twenty.

These and the other steel shipyards boasted the finest plants money could buy, complete with bending slabs and furnaces, heavy cranes and air hoists, sectional floating dry docks, and well-equipped foundries and machine shops. Apart from the private capital invested, the United States government spent $2,000,000 on the Todd yard in Tacoma and almost as much on housing for workers there and in Vancouver, and on essential transportation facilities in Seattle, Tacoma, and Portland. The United States Shipping Board reported in June, 1919, that in the Northwest, forty-one yards (wood and steel) with a total of 193 launching ways, had delivered at a cost of $458,000,000 297 vessels (1,792,000 ship tons); 141 wooden sailers, and 156 steel freighters of 3500 to 8800 tons capacity. This was a dramatic demonstration of the region's industrial potential when conditions favored full development.

Shipyard workers not only set proud records of accomplishment but they also engaged with the EFC in disputes over wages. From the start, Northwest war industries were plagued by labor shortages, despite a drift of people from rural areas to cities and a heavy influx of workers from Idaho and Montana. Faced with a difficult task of

484

recruitment, shipyards offered higher wages than the national scale allowed, and individual plants raided the ranks of local competitors. Some small establishments had to pay premiums in order to get any men. Skinner and Eddy paid at rates so much higher than others offered that Portland builders lost men to Seattle yards.

The Macy Board, a wage adjustment agency created by the EFC, had established a uniform national scale, arrived at by averaging going rates in various cities across the nation. When applied in the Far West, where living costs were high, the scale led to severe wage cuts. Shipyard unions, particularly the Metal Trades Council of Seattle, requested exceptions for Northwest workers and, in the course of negotiations, got the impression that Charles Piez, vice-president of the EFC, was sympathetic to their cause and would make some kind of adjustment. However, in January, 1919, the war having ended but not wartime wage controls, and no adjustment having been made, the Council asked for a minimum $6 a day (as against the current Macy award of $4.16), and threatened to strike if refused. Piez was not now sympathetic. "The government is not so badly in need of ships that it will compromise on a question of principle," he declared. "If they [the workers] were successful in securing their demands by this means, the future of the entire shipbuilding industry in your district would be jeopardized." The Council appealed to the Seattle Central Labor Council for support in the form of a general strike.

One after another, AFL unions voted to go out in sympathy for the shipyard workers, and a 300-man General Strike Committee set February 6 as the day for the walkout.[6] "We are undertaking the most tremendous move ever made by *Labor* in this country," wrote Anna Louise Strong in the *Union Record* on February 4, "a move which will lead *no one knows where!*" But the same paper maintained that organized labor would conduct a peaceful sympathy strike, carrying it out in orderly fashion.

On Thursday morning, February 6, 1919, the city suddenly became strangely quiet. Streetcars stopped rolling and taxicabs disappeared from the streets. Restaurants closed their doors, stevedores trooped off the docks, and commercial traffic ceased, save for a few vehicles that carried placards of exemption. The mails continued to move and water and power stations were kept manned. Otherwise, business came to a standstill. The day passed without disorder. Police blotters showed no unusual activity and citizen deputies found little

[6] Robert L. Friedheim, *The Seattle General Strike* (1964); Wilfred H. Crook, *General Strike* (1931); General Strike Committee, *Seattle General Strike* (1919); Robert B. Gibson, unpublished manuscript, "The Radical Experiment," University of Washington, 1951.

to do. That night troops from Fort Lawton were quartered at the Armory, but no untoward incidents occurred. Twelve kitchens distributed food at low cost to the workers; milk stations provided milk for babies and invalids; hospitals were supplied without interruption. Workers were urged to remain peaceful and unions policed their members to avoid disturbances with public authorities and private citizens. Friday passed without violence and the atmosphere of tense apprehension relaxed somewhat.

But among the members of the General Strike Committee and the Executive Committee conflicting opinions arose as to what they were striking for and how long they should stay out. If the strike was an expression of sympathy with shipyard unions, that expression had been made, and the shipyard workers were no better off for the show of labor solidarity. The leaders urged that a terminal day be set lest labor lose the general public tolerance it thus far had enjoyed.

On Friday, Mayor Ole Hanson, a practiced opportunist, sensing labor's dilemma, issued several proclamations. Describing the strike as a revolution, he called on the citizenry to "clean up" the United States, and threatened to impose martial law if the strike was not ended by 8:00 A.M. Saturday. Mark A. Matthews, pastor of the First Presbyterian Church and a power in the community, led a Citizen's Committee in echoing the cry of "revolution." Newspapers, locally and abroad, carried banner headlines describing Seattle as in the throes of revolution. Anna Louise Strong's words were echoed abroad.

There is no evidence that either AFL leadership or labor rank and file contemplated seizing power and starting down a road that might lead "*no one knows where*." James Duncan, president of Seattle's Labor Council and an influential figure in the General Strike Committee's deliberations, was conservative by nature and, while tolerant of radical ideas, was opposed to radical action. The Committee had taken no steps toward a take-over of either the city or its industries. The strike, though inconvenient, was peaceable; its leaders were cautious, the rank and file restrained, and the Executive Committee solicitous that no one suffer damage or deprivation. By Saturday afternoon some of the striking unions were returning to their jobs. On Monday the General Strike had ended, though the Executive Committee had set the following day as its official termination.

Seattle's four-day "revolution" was over, but its reverberations appeared in the national and local reaction to the "Red Scare." The IWW had contributed to this hysteria in the Northwest. In western Washington, townspeople would have no truck with socialism or radicalism, and their reaction to the "Red Scare" was violent, as was demonstrated in Centralia on Armistic Day, November 11, 1919. Eleven years after the event, the "Centralia Massacre" was the subject of investigation and a joint report of the Committee of the Federal Council of Churches, National Catholic Welfare Conference, and the Central Conference of American Rabbis. (*The Centralia Case, A Joint Report on the Armistice Day Tragedy at Centralia, Washington, November 11, 1919*, October, 1930). Their findings revealed the following: The American Legion planned an Armistice Day parade down Centralia's main street. The local IWW, believing that the paraders intended to attack their hall, prepared to resist. The Legionnaires passed the IWW hall and returned, then stopped in front of the hall, allegedly for a rest. Shots were fired—whether first by Legionnaires or Wobblies was not determined—and four paraders and two IWW were killed. Vigilantes then rounded up men believed to be Wobblies. One, Wesley Everest, an ex-serviceman and known IWW, shot a Legionnaire while defending himself against the mob. Everest was arrested, but later a band of men dragged him from the jail, emasculated him, and hanged him from a railroad bridge. Ten Wobblies stood trial and were convicted of first-degree murder; later the sentences of eight were reduced to murder in the second degree. In 1933, Governor Roland Hartley pardoned five of these and in 1939 commuted the sentences of the last of the eight.[7] Everest's lynchers were never identified.

Thereafter the IWW was not an influential factor in Northwest labor conflicts. In the 1920s the practicalities of getting a job and earning a living were more important than theories and sporadic action. Old Wobblies, unregenerate to the last, could be found in skid road and waterfront pool halls; but for their reminiscences and their dreams of a classless society, they had no audiences but themselves. However, the idea of industrial unionism, without revolutionary undertones, remained very much alive and was revived in the 1930s to threaten AFL jurisdiction over Northwest labor.

Although in postwar days labor was suspect in some quarters, it was nevertheless a force to be reckoned with. The National Labor Board's wartime emphasis on the principle of a living wage and its recognition of labor's right to organize, like the Spruce Division's enforcement of the eight-hour day, had set precedents hard to break. The Oregon legislature encouraged unionism by passing the Horne Bill (1919) which prohibited court injunctions against pickets so long as their activity did not damage property or person. On the other hand, the sudden collapse of the regional economy in 1920 weakened union membership just when unions had real cause for concern, not only over wages but also with regard to a drastic decline in employment.

---

[7] Robert L. Tyler, "Violence at Centralia, 1919," *PNQ*, October 1954.

The shipyard industry, which had done so much to boom the economy, was first to collapse. Born of the war and nourished with war contracts, with the Armistice it lost its reason for being. For a brief time the United States Shipping Board had thought otherwise: "A new industry has been created and bids fair to remain an important feature of our commercial structure" was the bold prophecy of 1919. Even as these words were written, the Board's action belied them. In the nation as a whole, employment in the industry had peaked at 385,000; by June, 1920, it had dropped to 75,000. The Emergency Fleet Corporation cancelled Pacific Northwest orders for 146 vessels; Skinner and Eddy terminated their lease for Yard No. 2 in November, 1919. The Columbia River Shipbuilding Corporation put its facilities up for sale but found no buyers. In 1921, fewer than 1000 men were employed in shipbuilding; the total tonnage launched did not exceed 50,000. For the next twenty years shipbuilding had comparatively little importance in the economy of the region.

The severe decline that hit shipbuilding was experienced to a lesser extent by other industries. Industrial payrolls in Washington dropped by $100,000,000; output was half what it had been during the war. Employment in Oregon dropped 31 percent. Preference in employment was given to war veterans, but there were more applicants than jobs except in seasonal farm work. In mid-1920, the price of Douglas fir dropped abruptly from $34 to $17 a thousand; spruce from $37 to $21. The cause of this has been ascribed to operators who, without thought of the effect of overproduction on the market, turned out the largest cut of lumber in the history of the industry up to that time. Washington mills and camps laid off 15,000 men; Oregon, 7000. While the average wage remained slightly higher in these two states than in the rest of the country, the spread between real and dollar wages was growing critical. The cost of living had increased by 70 percent over 1913 figures, wages by only 50 percent. Wheat which had brought $2.04 in 1918 was selling at 84 cents in 1921. In short, Northwest production of goods and labor was back at prewar selling prices, but Northwest consumers were still buying at inflated prices.

Labor did not want to lose what it had gained during the war, fearing that in the recession old working conditions would be reestablished and wages so reduced that it would take years of struggle to restore them to a semblance of cost-of-living parity. For example, in 1919, Pacific Coast seamen had received a long-delayed wage rise; two years later, but before the shipping industry had shown significant signs of declining revenues, the seamen were asked to take a 25 percent cut. During the 81-day strike that followed, the operators' strikebreaking policies were supported by the United States Shipping Board, the ultimate authority in the dispute. Portland police interference with picket lines led to rioting and violence that seriously injured the union cause. When the strike folded, the open shop prevailed, and the whole coastal shipping industry had suffered by the deflection of trade to other channels.

Between 1919 and 1923, few industries and services were free from controversy, nationally as well as locally. Labor in most instances was the loser; yet one student of this era of Oregon's history concludes:

> In this period of extreme price and wage adjustments, nothing was definitely settled as to which principle should prevail in the settlement of industrial disputes: the principle of living wage, or the principle of reasonable and equitable profits. The difficulties of management under the trying conditions that existed were given adequate recognition, however, and the justness of the demands of the laborers for comfort and security was also accepted by fair-minded citizens. Whichever way the decision went, the justice of the case for the loser was in some way recognized. Yet no formula was found under which mutually constructive adjustments might be effected. The years between 1919 and 1923 formed a period in which Oregon, by trial and error, was coping with her wage problems in a more judicial spirit than might have been expected.[8]

Despite the setback that accompanied the return to "normalcy," by 1923 employment and production became stabilized at figures above those of prewar years. Graph XIII (see p. 627) shows a remarkable rise in employment indicating that the Pacific Northwest was sharing to some extent in the national prosperity of the mid-twenties. However, one should bear in mind that the increase in the number of production workers in the Pacific Northwest was also a consequence of almost uniform adoption of the eight-hour day. In 1914, 85 percent of wage earners in the region, (that is, of all persons gainfully employed) worked sixty or more hours a week. In 1920, 90 percent worked forty-eight hours or less.

By 1929 the lumber industry was cutting 11.7 billion board feet of lumber at a price level that supported 1,000,000 jobs. Particularly encouraging was the development of pulp and paper manufactures. Construction was resumed in a new building boom that employed several thousand workers. To hopeful contemporaries, it appeared that good times were in store for the Pacific Northwest.

However, the figures show that, although the Washington and Oregon net increase in population between 1920 and 1930 was larger than

[8] Harvey E. Tobie, "Oregon Labor, 1919–23, Part III," *OHQ*, December 1947, 321.

TABLE IV

Net Intercensal Migration, 1900–1950
(Persons over the age of ten)

	1900–1910	1910–1920	1920–1930	1930–1940	1940–1950
Washington	464,700	97,500	81,600	109,200	351,300
Oregon	189,900	56,000	96,500	94,100	244,000
Idaho	104,100	37,300	−50,600	20,500	−29,600

Source: Everetts, Lee, and others, "Population Redistribution and Economic Growth: United States, 1870–1950" (1957).

for the preceding decade, the total was far below that of the 1900–1910 boom years. Furthermore, after the war 50,000 native Oregonians left home for greener pastures elsewhere, and Idaho's small population suffered a devastating net loss. It is also significant that the birthrate notably declined; in 1930 Oregon's was lowest in the nation. While statistics might demonstrate advances in freight car loadings, postal receipts, and department store sales, these indices suggest a much lower growth rate than the region had previously enjoyed. The regional share in the national economy was actually becoming smaller. The situation was like that of Alice in Wonderland; one had to run as fast as one could to stay in the same place. Such, however, appeared to be the case for any region whose economy was underdeveloped, dependent upon agriculture and primary extractive industries, and lacking secondary industries that multiplied job opportunities and payrolls.

CHAPTER
THIRTY

The Futile Journey and
a New Horizon,
1920–1940

IN THE NORTHWEST, as in the nation, World War I marked the end of the Progressive Era and a decline of popular interest in legislating economic and social reforms. Issues of neutrality and then war distracted attention from domestic questions to world affairs. Both major parties supported America's entry into the war and political dissent was discouraged. The sense of moral urgency that accompanied the Quest for Social Justice was diverted to the Great Crusade to save the world for democracy.

POSTWAR POLITICS

In the decade following the Peace of Versailles, the Great Crusade was discredited. Reaction against involvement in European affairs was intensified by fear of revolutionary ideologies. The American people

491

wanted to return to "normalcy" and unalloyed enjoyment of what appeared to be prosperity of unparalleled magnitude. This attitude left the Democrats without a cause, and restored the Republicans to power.

In the Pacific Northwest, the presidential elections of 1920, 1924, and 1928 resulted in Republican majorities, and congressional delegations were Republican almost to a man (see Tables XIII–XVIII, pp. 614–620; and Graphs IV–VI, pp. 622–623). The only significant upsets were the elections of Spokane Democrat Clarence Dill, who replaced Miles Poindexter in the Senate, and of Sam B. Hill, who held a seat in the House for the next six terms. Republican habits of voting were so confirmed that incumbents in Congress were returned with monotonous regularity. Burton French (Moscow) served Idaho for thirty years (1903–1933); Addison Smith (Twin Falls), twenty years (1912–1932); and Borah was a fixture in the Senate from 1907 until his death in 1940. Oregonians treated their Congressmen in much the same way, keeping Willis Hawley (Salem) in the House from 1907 to 1933, and Nicholas J. Sinnott (The Dalles) from 1912 to 1928. Republicans succeeded Democrats George Chamberlain and Harry Lane in the Senate; Charles McNary (Salem) held office from 1918 to 1944 and Fred Steiwer, from 1927 to 1938. From 1918 to 19-32, Washington voters changed only three names in their entire congressional delegation. In the House, Republicans Mills and Summers, Johnson and Hadley worked as a team for twelve years without a substitution, Hadley serving nine consecutive terms and Johnson ten. Wesley Jones was a member of the Senate for twenty-two years. The citizenry of Washington, as of Idaho and Oregon, showed unusual confidence in their spokesmen in national affairs.

On the state level, Republican governors maintained succession in the capitals of Washington and Idaho, and only a handful of Democrats challenged them in the legislatures (see Tables XIII–XV, pp. 614–616). The wheels of party machinery turned with remarkably little squeaking. Legislation was confined mainly to necessary measures of finance and taxation, road-building, irrigation projects, and veterans' benefits. In all three states, consolidation and reorganization of governmental agencies occupied considerable attention.[1] In 1919 Idaho adopted a cabinet system consolidating forty or more departments into nine departments under commissioners responsible to the governor. In 1940 a further consolidation was effected. In

[1] Walter S. Davis, "New Civil Administration Code in Washington," *American Political Science Review*, November 1921; Charles McKinley, "Oregon Voters Defeat State Administrative Reorganization, But—," *National Municipal Review*, November 1931.

492

Washington, Governor Louis F. Hart took the initiative in a major governmental reorganization which abolished seventy-five regulatory commissions and boards and in the 1921 Code established ten administrative departments. While the executive authority remained divided among nine elective officials, the governor's patronage was strengthened by the creation of the new, well-paid positions. As lines of authority were gathered in the governor's hands, he gained importance in the party organization, but not without a struggle. (In 1965 Governor Dan Evans proposed to make seven of the remaining elective offices appointive.)

Oregon rejected consolidation. The legislature ignored the Mathews Report (1919) recommending comprehensive consolidation similar to that adopted in Washington and Idaho. In 1931 the voters defeated, 135,000 to 51,000, a referendum measure which would have created a cabinet form of state government. (Thirty years later Governor Mark Hatfield recommended the same change, but to no avail.) In the 1920s, Oregon's Republican legislators did not want to increase the governor's powers, and influential elements in the state, particularly bankers and utility companies, were averse to any reorganization which would put public utility and banking commissions under the governor's control. Since Chamberlain and West had given the office a new prestige, the office did not fall automatically into Republican hands, though the party seemed strong in other respects. In 1914, six candidates for governor appeared on the ballot. The 32,421 votes given the Progressive, Non-Partisan, Socialist, and Independent candidates, added to the 94,594 votes cast for the Democratic candidate, Charles H. Smith, totaled almost 6000 more than were given James Withycombe, the successful Republican. In a light vote in 1918, Ben Olcott had a margin of 15,627 votes over Democrat Walter M. Pierce, but a plurality of only 9147 over Pierce and the Socialist candidate together. Pierce, an eastern Oregon dirt-farmer and a persuasive politician, was too much in the tradition of Pennoyer, Chamberlain, and West, for Republican peace of mind.

Despite superficial appearances, Pacific Northwest politics were far from serene. In both major parties, organized blocs of protest votes seriously disturbed party regulars and party harmony. The Republican Party was not wholly free of residuals of Progressive ideology; at the same time, it entertained a highly reactionary faction which saw a "Red" tinge in all dissent. The Democratic Party was susceptible to unorthodoxy, but before it adjusted to being a coalition of the discontented it was split by third-party movements.

In each state, party solidarity was threatened, but under different circumstances and for different reasons. In Idaho and Washington, the Non-Partisan League was a storm center; in Oregon it hardly caused a ripple.

In the spring of 1916, representatives of the Farmer's Non-Partisan Political League of North Dakota appeared in the Northwest states to organize and to agitate for farm-labor unity and the North Dakota program. In Idaho the League called for "state-owned flour mills, terminal elevators, packing plants, sugar factories, warehouses and storage plants; state ownership and distribution of water power, rural credit banks. . . ." League members supported Borah and John F. Nugent for the United States Senate, and for a brief time held control of the Democratic Party. "Idaho, having scored the first complete victory outside North Dakota, was . . . henceforth entitled to be known as 'the second League State,' " according to the League's official organ.[2]

Wherever League organizers appeared, they met strong opposition, sometimes violence. In western Washington, law enforcement officers at Winlock, Toledo, and Sultan refused to protect the organizers when irate citizens tarred and feathered them. On the other hand, the League had considerable success in eastern Washington, despite anti-League demonstrations in Walla Walla County. By 1919, the Non-Partisan League was absorbed by the national Farmer-Labor Party, and in Washington a bloc of fifteen Republicans was identified with the new party. The next year Farmer-Labor cast 77,246 votes in the presidential election and 121,371 votes for the party's gubernatorial candidate, giving Republican candidate Louis Hart victory by a small plurality. The new party showed its strength in forcing referendums on legislative measures that would have inhibited independent voting, and throwing its support in 1922 to Democrat Clarence Dill for the United States Senate. But neither Non-Partisan League nor Farmer-Labor Party was successful in promoting state ownership of utilities or other radical economic measures. In Oregon, Non-Partisan League candidates made no showing and the Farmer-Labor Party did not even appear on the ballot. However, the threat of infection contributed to the distress of conservatives in both major parties.

Oregon's politics were vastly complicated by the emergence and rapid growth of organizations claiming to be special guardians of American virtues and institutions: the American Protective Association (APA), the Federation of Patriotic Societies (FOPS), and the Ku Klux Klan. Reportedly, the societies together could muster 40,000 to 50,000 voters in support of their measures. The KKK claimed 14,000 members, 9000 in Multnomah County, the remainder pri-

[2] Robert L. Morlan, *Political Prairie Fire; the Non-Partisan League, 1915–1916* (1955), 204–205.

marily in Jackson and Clatsop counties. Undoubtedly the "Red Scare" contributed to their proliferation, the KKK claiming that they were not anti-Catholic, anti-Semitic, or anti-Alien, but rather, "pro-American"; but they all appealed to racial and religious prejudices well rooted in the region's past.

The Catholics, comprising about 8 percent of the population, were attacked in the Compulsory School Bill, an initiative measure requiring all children to attend public schools. It was sponsored by Scottish Rite Masons, supported by the Klan and FOPS, and passed in the 1922 general election by a vote of 115,506 to 103,685. In 1924 the State Supreme Court declared the law unconstitutional and was upheld by the United States Supreme Court a year later. Since 1900 the Chinese population had notably declined, from 12,898 to 7000. Hence anti-Alien legislation was directed against the Japanese, whose number had increased from 2000 to 4000, largely concentrated in the Hood River Valley and in Portland. The Alien Property Act of 1923 which in effect prohibited Japanese from owning and leasing land, was in line with California and Washington legislation for the same purpose and was upheld in federal courts. The attack upon the Jews, about one percent of the population and largely resident in Portland, was directed against individuals rather than the group and was therefore less easily identifiable. In one instance, in 1922 the Klan tried overtly and unsuccessfully to prevent the appointment of Julius Meier to a city commission considering the possibility of holding a municipal exposition.

While one must conclude that many Oregonians were susceptible to racial and religious prejudices, their responses did not fall into any consistent pattern. In 1930 Julius Meier was elected governor. In 1926, the voters approved a legislative bill to repeal the constitutional provision prohibiting admission of Negroes to the state, which had long been a dead-letter law.

The Klan under Grand Dragon Fred T. Gifford tried to assume leadership among the patriotic societies, and failed in a spectacular bid in 1922–1923 to gain control of the state government through the Republican Party. As a consequence the party was badly split. Republican Ben Olcott, candidate to succeed himself as governor, having courageously sent state officers into Jackson County to prosecute Klan "necktie parties" which local officials ignored, publicly denounced the organization on the eve of the primary election. Olcott's margin of victory in the primary was so narrow that the Klan candidate, Charles Hall, demanded a recount but Klan endorsement proved to be the kiss of death for Republicans seeking nomination; only C. P. Hoff survived both primary and general election to become state treasurer. However, in Multnomah County the Klan succeeded in putting its nominees in the state legislature.

During the campaign, nearly all political hopefuls of both parties either courted Klan favor or remained discreetly silent about its activities. Walter M. Pierce, Democratic nominee for governor, did not publicly oppose or reject Klan support. He had long been opposed to Catholics holding office, and he favored the Compulsory School Bill; he was against admission of Orientals to the United States and their ownership of land. But he refused to campaign on these issues. His friends advised him to ignore religious and racial issues and to profit from the Republican split over them. "No matter how rotten or weak the Democrat may be," wrote one not altogether friendly advisor, "he will be elected on account of the greatest religious split which the Republican Party has seen in the history of the state." Sidestepping the Klan issue, Pierce campaigned on proposals that were politically more hazardous in a period of conservative reaction: consolidation of state offices, a severance tax on timber holdings, a gross earnings tax on certain utilities, and a state income tax. On the other hand, George Putnam, forthright editor of the Salem *Capital Journal*, warned the party that invisible government, not taxation, was the vital issue; and he chided Pierce, who by his silence, appeared to be trying to run with the hare and the hounds.[3]

Pierce's Republican opposition had little to say about his failure to take a position on the Klan, but they loudly made the most of his radicalism. They recalled that as state senator in 1919, he alone had voted against the criminal syndicalism act which made advocacy of revolutionary class struggle a felony.[4] They charged that he was secretly a member of the Non-Partisan League and was trying to "Sovietize" the state. "The real issue is radicalism against Americanism," declared Walter L. Tooze, Republican state chairman, juxtaposing on the one side the Klan candidate and on the other "Pierce, the Non-Partisan League candidate . . . now masquerading as a Democrat and backed by every radical in the State. . . ."

Despite vociferous opposition, Pierce was elected by the largest vote (133,392) given a gubernatorial candidate up to that time and with

[3] For Putnam's career as a fighting editor, see George S. Turnbull, *An Oregon Crusader* (1955). For data on Pierce and the Klan issue, I am indebted to Arthur H. Bone of Salem, who is working on a biography of the governor. *The Oregon Voter*, W. W. Chapman editor, has much material on the Klan during 1922–1923.

[4] After the United States Supreme Court found in favor of a defendant charged under the Oregon Syndicalism Act (*DeJonge* v. *State of Oregon*, 1937), the legislature repealed the act and substituted a conspiracy law.

a plurality of 32,228. The Klan immediately asserted that its votes had given Pierce the victory—a claim difficult to prove. Undoubtedly, Klansmen voted for Pierce. They had no alternative; their own candidate, Charles Hall, had not survived the Republican primary and they could not support Olcott who had excoriated them. But the question of whether Pierce had made a deal for Klan votes plagued him the rest of his life. He flatly denied it, insisting that when the Klan asked him for patronage—as they did Senator McNary—he refused, declaring that he was his own master and owed the Klan nothing.

According to contemporary observers, Klan and Klansmen were tools in the hands of Pierce's real opposition. A month before the election, Ralph Watson of the *Oregon Journal* identified Pierce's enemies as "holders of hidden wealth, now exempt from taxation, the utility corporations, affronted by his suggestion of a gross earnings charge against them; by the timber cruisers and operators who see in his severance tax proposal a hostile move against them." Within a few months after Pierce took office, petitions for his recall were circulated by groups Pierce identified as the "interests" he was attacking:

> The Public Service Corporations were being notified that their assessments are all being raised a total of fifty million dollars a year and they are alarmed. . . . The Corporations desiring water power sites are alarmed because I have appointed a new state engineer that cannot be fooled or bamboozled. . . . The big timber interests are alarmed because I have stated . . . that we ought to have a tax on natural resources. . . .

An article in *World's Work*, August 1923, reported that Klan leadership in Oregon was "closely allied with certain electric light and power corporations, and it is common gossip among politicians that it was organized, or encouraged, as a counter-irritant against reform movements which might impair the corporate interests." George Putnam editorialized to the same effect:

> The Klan in Oregon represents the capitalization of religious prejudices and racial animosity by public service corporations as the means of sidetracking the public mind from economic issues. With the people foolishly fighting over religion and fanning the fires of fanaticism, they have forgotten all about agitation against 8 cent street car fares, high telephone and other service rates and reduced wage scales. . . . The Grand Dragon . . . who now aims to be the political boss of Oregon [Gifford], was formerly the labor "fixer" for one of the big power companies . . . he evidently made good for he has been promoted from "fixing" labor to "fixing" the general public. . . .

The recall movement failed. It was rumored that thousands of signatures had been obtained for the recall petitions, but for reasons best known to the backers, the issue did not come to election. According to Pierce's unpublished memoirs, the recall was part of a large plan to force him to come to terms with "the interests" and when he refused to do so, threatening in retaliation to go to the people with charges of bribery and other disclosures, he was permitted to fill out his term of office.

The 1923 legislature with which Pierce worked was dominated by the Klan and FOPS. The Senate was composed of twenty-six Republicans, four Democrats; the House had fifty-nine Republicans and nine Democrats. KKK members organized the Senate under Jay Upton, and K. K. Kubli, said to be "leader of the 'Kublic Klan,'" was elected speaker of the House. The legislature passed and Pierce signed a bill prohibiting sectarian garb in school rooms and the anti-Japanese Alien Property Bill; it petitioned Congress to halt Oriental immigration. Otherwise, Klan-sponsored bills did not occupy the legislature as much as Pierce's legislative program.

A bitter debate on the governor's bill to abolish sixty-four boards and commissions and reorganize other functions of government into four departments resulted in a compromise bill which Pierce vetoed because it so thoroughly eliminated all the benefits that might have ensued from consolidation. The governor's income tax bill was passed, referred to the people, and approved by a margin of slightly more than 100 votes out of 117,707 cast; it was repealed a year later in a special election by a vote of 123,799 to 111,055. Pierce's effort to set up a hydroelectric power commission died in committee; his severance tax bill introduced in the Senate was withdrawn.

The strength of Republican opposition to his program made Pierce early realize that he had little chance of reelection. He might have capitalized on the independent vote for LaFollette in the 1924 presidential election, but despite his sympathy with LaFollette Progressives, Pierce was a straight party man, and Democrats made a poor showing against LaFollette in Oregon. In 1926, Oregonians gave Republican Isaac L. Patterson a plurality of 14,201 and retired Pierce. Six years later in the Roosevelt landslide, he went to Congress as representative from Oregon's Second District. During his ten years in the House he was a strong champion of Roosevelt policies, consistently working for public power and farm relief measures.

The 1924 presidential election seriously jolted both major parties in the Northwest. In 1923 the Farm-Labor Party had given way to the Conference for Progressive Political Action which invited Robert La-

Follette to run for president on his own ticket. Protest that had been evident in flurries of support for the Non-Partisan League and the Farm-Labor Party rolled up impressive backing for their successor, LaFollette's Progressive Party. LaFollette proposed a program which included farm relief measures, public ownership of railroads and water-power, and recognition by law of collective bargaining.

Northwest Republicans who stood staunchly for Coolidge and party regularity barely survived the election. Democrats who reluctantly accepted compromise candidate John W. Davis made a worse showing than the Republicans. In Idaho, LaFollette trailed Coolidge by only 15,000 votes out of 148,295. In nineteen counties out of forty-four the Progressives were a real threat to the Republicans; in all but five they surpassed the Democrats. The greatest challenge to Republicanism in Washington emerged in rural counties: Douglas, Grant, Benton, Kittitas in the central part of the state; Skagit, Island, Kitsap, and Snohomish on the Sound. Yet all three urban counties were invaded too. In King and Spokane, Republicans eked out a four to three victory over the Progressives, while in Pierce they won by 2000 votes in 44,818. Oregonians went for Coolidge, but LaFollette received 10,000 more votes than Davis, and Republicans won only a plurality in eleven counties including Portland and the northeast corner of the state.

Republican congressional delegations from the northwestern states interpreted the election returns as another agrarian protest. Senator Charles L. McNary (R-Oregon) sponsored the McNary-Haugen Bill which proposed price support through government purchase of surplus farm products. A bipartisan bloc of supporters failed to override Coolidge's veto (1927), but every northwestern senator except Borah, and every congressman except Albert Johnson (R-Grays Harbor) and Franklin F. Korell (R-Portland), voted for the bill.

In 1928 the magic of Hoover's name, for many people synonymous with business efficiency, not only kept Northwest voters in the Republican fold but seemed to entrench the party more firmly than ever. In 1928 and 1930 third-party voting dropped to the lowest level in nearly thirty years. The percentage of votes cast for Hoover was considerably larger than for Harding in 1920. But faith in Republican prosperity was shattered in the months following the market crash of October 1929. Farmers were desperate, yet no relief was offered them. On the contrary, Oregon's Willis P. Hawley, from the First Congressional District, co-sponsored the Smoot-Hawley high tariff (1930) which was a direct blow for wheat exporters.

In Oregon, Republicans experienced a trauma when a member of their own party attacked the sacred principle of free enterprise and carried the voters along with him. Throughout the twenties, George Joseph, a Portland attorney, was the apostle of public power. During his several terms in the legislature he fought private power at every turn and repeatedly sponsored constitutional amendments that would have allowed the development of public ownership. In 1930 he ran against Henry Corbett and Walter Norblad in the Republican primary for governor on this one issue. The campaign was hard-fought and bitter, and Joseph's victory was bought at a high price. Only a few weeks after his nomination he died of a heart attack. However, the movement he had started was by then so strong that Julius Meier, one of his closest friends, agreed to run as an Independent in the general election. He pressed the cause of public power vigorously and, in the same election which put him in the governor's office, the voters approved legislation which permitted formation of public utility districts.

The utility issue was important in Washington, where support of public power became identified with liberal elements in both parties. In the Republican Party, Homer T. Bone all but succeeded in winning conservative Albert Johnson's seat in Congress. Legal councillor for Tacoma, which had a municipally owned electric power system, Bone had been prominently identified with the power issue. He moved from party to party, running with the Socialists in 1912, the Progressives in 1924, and thereafter with the Republicans until 1932; but he remained constant in his advocacy of public power.

Roland Hartley in 1930 saved the governorship for the Republicans by 67,000 votes, but his challenger, Scott Bullitt, representing the liberal wing of the Democratic Party, had had no trouble in edging out conservative Stephen Chadwick. Democrats also won another term in the Senate for Clarence Dill. "Unless things take a decided change for the better within six months," a worried Republican wrote Senator Wesley L. Jones in December 1930, "you are going to see a party spring up in the country that will make the old Populist party of 1896 look conservative. . . ."[5] Although Clarence Dill was returned to the Senate, there was little to suggest a Democratic resurgence. The party had profited by the disappearance of Farm-Labor and Progressive minorities, but not so much as had the Republicans. In 1928, Al Smith had won a heavier percentage of votes than had Wilson in 1920 and had proved himself stronger than John W. Davis in 1924. Yet in 1930 Democrats had captured only one vote in three and gave no promise of winning a majority anywhere. The party lacked a program for economic recovery and it offered nothing to dissidents. And of these there was an increasing number as 1932 approached.

[5] Quoted in Keith Murray, "Issues and Personalities of Pacific Northwest Politics, 1889–1950," *PNQ*, July 1950, 230.

THE GREAT DEPRESSION AND THE NEW DEAL

No number of cheerful platitudes could disguise the fact that the nation was in the throes of economic disaster. The Pacific Northwest reeled as its economy, which had not fully recovered from the postwar depression, plummeted to a new low and breadlines formed. Lumber exports dropped to less than half of what they had been in 1929. Twenty-cent wheat did not pay freight charges in southern Idaho; thirty-seven cent wheat cast a pall over eastern Oregon and Washington. To escape maintenance costs, apple and prune growers pulled up their trees and burned them for fuel. The 1932 salmon pack was 120,000,000 pounds under that of 1929. Mining output in Idaho declined from $32,000,000 to $9,000,000 between 1929 and 1932. General conditions reflected these reverses in the major resource industries. Wholesale trade fell off 47 percent.

In 1933 the number of production workers in Washington was 59.1 percent of the number in 1929; in Oregon the figure was 62.8 percent, and in Idaho, 49.1 percent. Individual incomes fell to about 55 percent of the 1929 level. Tax delinquencies in Oregon amounted to $40,000,000 and private lands, largely in timber and totaling an area as large as Delaware, reverted to counties. Although Northwest banks had serious difficulties, they weathered the storm better than those in the Mountain States and the Midwest border. On the other hand, the rate of business failures for Oregon and Washington was generally

TABLE V

Number of Production Workers Employed, 1927–1939, as Percents of Number Employed in 1929, for Selected States

	1927	1929	1931	1933	1935	1937	1939
United States	94.6	100	73.8	68.6	83.6	97.1	89.4
New York	97.1	100	76.7	66.4	81.1	90.2	86.8
Illinois	89.3	100	57.5	39.5	52.5	65.3	58.2
Iowa	89.2	100	66.8	44.2	57.9	66.4	63.9
California	91.0	100	72.3	68.1	87.5	107.4	97.9
Washington	21.2	100	61.8	59.1	71.4	88.4	78.8
Oregon	87.4	100	64.5	62.8	79.9	100.9	97.3
Idaho	86.4	100	60.0	49.1	67.3	81.8	69.8

Source: Calculated from the Bureau of the Census, Department of Commerce data.

higher than in other states. (Oregon, which had the highest rate in the nation between 1927 and 1929, had a lower rate in 1932 when other states were experiencing their highest.)

Where formerly the Northwest states had encouraged immigration, they now discouraged it. Newcomers intensified competition for scarce jobs, and put added pressure on relief agencies. Years of drought in the Dust Bowl sent thousands of refugees into the green haven of the Northwest but, unfortunately, to cheap, unproductive, cutover lands or to cities already burdened with the unemployed. Two persons left Oregon for every three who arrived.[6]

DEPRESSION POLITICS

When voters went to the polls in 1932 they demonstrated that the party of prosperity no longer had their confidence. In all three states, third-party votes increased, but the victory of the Democrats was unqualified. Never had there been such a complete reversal, so unanimous a disposition for the Democrats. In 1928, Fremont County (Idaho) had enjoyed the distinction of being the only county in the three states to give a plurality to Al Smith; in 1932, Bear Lake County (Idaho) and Benton County (Oregon) were the only ones that remained loyal to Hoover. Some counties in which protest voting was habitual and every third-party candidate usually had some support, now voted Democratic. Counties which had not declared for a Democrat in two generations did so in 1932. The voters put Democrats in the governor's offices and in the state legislatures. Oregon sent two Democrats to Congress and in 1934 elected a Democratic governor.

One could not say that the Democratic Party in the Pacific Northwest states was prepared to make the most of the Roosevelt landslide. While the New Deal program was welcomed in the Inland Empire and on the Sound where in earlier days the Democracy had prevailed, in neither area had the party developed anything resembling a disciplined machine. The Republicans had much the better organization, but neither party, as we have shown earlier, could control the independent vote in crises. As one commentator explained, the Washington voter had never been roped or branded by any political party. In 1932 he was under no restraints and felt no compulsion to follow the dictates of existing party organizations.

Instances of eccentricity and opportunism attracted national atten-

[6] Davis McEntire and Marion Clawson, "Migration and Settlement in the Pacific Northwest, 1930–1940," *Social Science*, April 1941.

tion to Washington's "circus politics." The man elected attorney general was a lawyer who, it was said, had not practiced in fifteen years; one of the newly chosen members of the legislature did not have the price of a ticket to Olympia; another was in jail. Vic Meyers, the new lieutenant governor, was a popular band leader who had once campaigned for the office of Seattle mayor promising to install a hostess in every streetcar. The thoughtless exuberance in these elections in time of severe crisis left observers amazed and breathless. Andrew Jackson had once expressed the view that there was nothing mysterious about government that ordinary people could not understand and manage. Now it looked as if Washington were testing Old Hickory's thesis.

Radicalism, discredited since the days of the Wobblies and the 1919 General Strike, in 1933 found vent in the Washington Commonwealth Federation (WCF). Composed of dissident left-wingers, rival labor unions—AFL, CIO, and WPA Workers' Alliance—the Unemployed Citizens League, Townsendites (old age pensioners), Technocrats, and liberals of varying degrees and causes, the Federation echoed Upton Sinclair's EPIC (End Poverty in California) movement, proposing to End Poverty in Washington (EPIW). John C. Stevenson, popularly known as the Voice of Painless Parker on radio networks and the "most colorful public character who ever blossomed in the state," in 1933 ran for governor on the EPIW slogan, promising monthly pensions of $100 for the aged, tax-free homes, and electricity for farms. Stevenson was defeated by Clarence Martin, a well-to-do middle-of-the-road Democrat. On the other hand, erratic and ailing Marion Zioncheck, idol of labor, was sent to Congress, and Homer T. Bone, having become a Democrat for the cause of public utilities, went to Congress with WCF help. But Senator Clarence Dill, backed by the Federation, was defeated by a more conservative member of his own party, Lewis Schwellenbach.

If the elections of 1932 and 1934 had had strange results, that of 1936 was chaotic. One of the first orders of business of the new regime had been the adoption of the blanket primary (1935) which in effect made all nominations for office nonpartisan and abandoned party distinctions. "Only in the State of Washington," wrote one critic, was it possible for an individual "to vote at the same primary for a Republican as the nominee for governor, for a Socialist as the nominee for attorney general, for a Democrat as the nominee for state treasurer, for a Communist as the nominee for sheriff."[7]

[7] Clarence A. Berdahl, "Party Membership in the United States," *American Political Science Review*, February 1942, 23; Claudius O. Johnson, "Washington Blanket Primary," *PNQ*, January 1942, and "Washington's Blanket Primary Review," *PNQ*, October 1957.

Under the leadership of thirty-two year old Howard Costigan, the WCF in 1936 captured the Democratic state convention which adopted the Federation program in toto. Considerably to the left of Sinclair's California program, it called for public ownership of natural resources, munition plants, and utilities, and for federal ownership and operation of national banks. The heart of its program was embodied in the slogan "production for use," and the WCF introduced and supported unsuccessfully Initiative 119, a vaguely worded measure which would permit the state to organize "unused productive forces" in the interests of the entire population.

Mary McCarthy found her native state in ferment; "wild, comic, theatrical, dishonest, disorganized, hopeful; but it is not revolutionary."[8] The voters rejected all WCF measures on the ballot and the WCF did not capture the state. A combination of moderate and conservative elements in both parties proved strong enough to keep the radicals in check. Several thousand Republicans took advantage of the blanket primary to vote for Clarence Martin who, while accepting the essentials of the New Deal program, nevertheless resisted the extreme demands of the WCF. Four years later (1940) Clarence Dill defeated Martin in the primaries, but conservative Democrats voted with Republicans to elect Arthur Langlie. Confronted with Democratic majorities in both houses of the legislature and in the other elective offices, Langlie's administration was hardly a happy Republican victory, but it indicated that the political pendulum was swinging to the right. The New Deal lost favor in the rural counties and Republicans captured several seats in Congress (see Graph IX, p. 625). Ten counties in the central and eastern part of the state voted Republican in the presidential elections of 1940 and 1944. By 1948, four congressional districts were safely Republican once again. In senatorial elections the Democrats were still in control. Harry Cain of Tacoma upset for one term a succession of Democratic victories unbroken since 1932. Though Bone left the Senate to become a federal judge, and Schwellenbach to become Secretary of Labor, the roll of Washington senators—Monrad Wallgren, Warren Magnuson, and Henry Jackson—continued to be weighted in favor of Democrats. In the First Congressional District, (King and Kitsap counties) which had been WCF strongholds, the strength of the Federation diminished. Hugh Delacy was defeated after a single term in Congress and thenceforth the Democrats presented candidates more discreet in their liberalism.

Idaho Democrats also showed unprecedented strength during the early years of the New Deal (see Graph VIII, p. 624). The northern

---

[8] Mary McCarthy, "Circus Politics in Washington State," *The Nation*, October 17, 1936; "Progressives in Seattle," *New Republic*, October 20, 1937.

congressional district, which for thirty years had been Republican, entered upon twenty years of Democratic control. Compton White was returned to the House of Representatives as faithfully as had been Burton French before him. D. Worth Clark (Pocatello) served two terms in the lower house, while another Democrat, James P. Pope (Boise), joined Borah in the Senate. In 1938 Clark succeeded Pope and was followed in turn by Glen Taylor.

The Democratic Party promised much to Idaho. Roosevelt's monetary policies put miners back to work and silver output, which had dropped from $32,000,000 to $1,500,000, increased to $15,000,000 by 1937. New Deal conservation policies encouraged hope that the federal government would install Civilian Conservation Corps (CCC) to work in forests ridden with blister rust and put the unemployed to work on needed irrigation projects. The appointment of Idaho's Theodore A. Walters as First Assistant Secretary in the Department of the Interior seemed reassuring.[9] The state did get seventy CCC camps and, under the Public Works Administration, appropriations for reclamation projects. However, federal largesse was nothing like that expended in Washington and Oregon and Idaho Democrats suffered internal dissensions that boded no good.

Popular "Cowboy" C. Ben Ross won election as governor three times in succession, though custom had decreed a limit of two terms. Ross was an able administrator and a veteran politician possessed of some of the arts of demagoguery as well as consuming political ambition. In the early thirties his machine could deliver votes where and when they were needed. But Ross was not invincible. In 1936 he failed to unseat Borah and thereafter his influence diminished; his organization split and Democrats of differing persuasions came forward, each with his own constituency and speaking out for his own political views. D. Worth Clark, isolationist and conservative, spoke for a wing of the Democratic Party which became increasingly critical of the New Deal. Francis Ristline and Glen Taylor emerged as the leaders of the liberal wing.

When Borah died in 1940, a Republican, John Thomas, took his seat in the Senate. For several years thereafter no one could say that Idaho was either Democratic or Republican. Democrats were strong in Lewiston, Kellogg, and the Coeur d'Alene country, while Republicans controlled Canyon and Payette counties. In the Snake River Basin Boise went Republican while Pocatello continued Democratic. Rooseveltian policies could not satisfy all Idahoans, divided as they were by geography and economic interests. Farmers and livestock

9 Elmo R. Richardson, "Western Politics and New Deal Policies; a Study of T. A. Walters of Idaho," *PNQ*, January 1963.

men were worried over the consequences of reciprocal trade agreements; cattlemen opposed the Taylor Grazing Act (1934) regulating grazing on the public domain. The Idaho Power Company threw its weight against New Deal public power policies. Idaho had no urban centers and no strong labor vote; in this respect it differed from both Washington and Oregon.

Oregon Democrats demonstrated their idiosyncrasies with vigorous in-party fighting, but they lacked the carnival spirit that marked Washington's Depression politics. The Third Congressional District sent General Charles Martin to Congress in 1930. Four years later he became governor by a narrow margin over the combined votes for Republican Joe E. Dunne and left-wing Democrat Pete Zimmerman running as an Independent. Walter Pierce went to Congress for five terms; Nancy Honeyman, daughter of Charles E. S. Wood, served one term in Congress, so that two of Oregon's three seats in the House were held by Democrats. In the 1935–1937 legislature, Democrats had a comfortable majority in the lower house and only four fewer senators than the Republicans. Multnomah County Democrats captured eleven out of twelve Republican seats between 1930 and 1934.

Oregon also had a Commonwealth Federation. Under the leadership of Monroe Sweetland and Stephenson Smith, the OCF evaded the blandishments of the Popular Front while supporting wholeheartedly the more radical aspects of the New Deal and particularly the cause of organized labor during a period of violent disputes. When Governor Martin revealed himself as less sympathetic to labor than to employers, the OCF led the fight against his renomination in 1938.

LABOR WARFARE

Labor was a factor in New Deal politics in the Pacific Northwest, and during the years of economic recovery the Western Coast became a proving ground for labor organizations and labor policies. In 1930 unionism was at the nadir of its fortunes. Along the waterfront, gains that had been made in "decasualizing" longshoremen during World War I were lost and membership in the Seamen's Union and International Longshoremen's Association had dwindled.[10] In the lumber industry labor unions had almost disappeared. The AFL had

[10] Longshoremen had first organized on Puget Sound in 1913 and from this area the movement spread along the coast. "Decasualization of Dock Labor in Seattle," *Monthly Labor Review*, October 1924; John Blanchard and Dorothy Terrill, *Strikes in the Pacific Northwest 1927–1940; a Statistical Analysis* (1943).

some strength in the building trades but practically none in the woods where a logger, if he had a job, was getting 25 cents an hour in 1933.

Section 7A of the National Recovery Act (1933) declared it to be government policy that "employees shall have the right to organize and bargain collectively through representatives of their own choosing," and further stipulated that employers should comply with maximum hours of labor, minimum rates of pay and other conditions of employment approved or prescribed by the President. In 1934 the International Longshoremen's Association, charging that employers had not complied with the code, went out on strike for recognition of their AFL union as a bargaining agent and for higher wages and shorter hours. They successfully challenged the "blue book" (company) unions and with the aid of federal arbitrators won a six-hour day, 30-hour week, a basic wage rate of 95 cents an hour, and joint control of hiring halls. In 1935, the ILA united with seamens' unions to form the Maritime Federation of the Pacific; management immediately responded by organizing the Waterfront Employers Association, and asking for a modification of the 1934 agreements, particularly with regard to hiring halls. In the summer of 1935 the Maritime Federation went out on another strike which tied up Portland's slowly reviving commerce for a discouraging three months.

The NRA had a short life but the principle it set forth with regard to labor was embodied in the National Labor Relations Act (1935), usually referred to as the Wagner Act, which also set up the National Labor Relations Board to adjudicate labor disputes. Before the Board was functioning, the AFL led half the men in the Douglas fir belt off their jobs in a successful drive for union recognition. For two years the AFL Carpenters Union functioned as the timber workers' bargaining agency. However, the old issue of industrial versus trade unionism was revived and given new meaning under the NLRA stipulation that workers could elect the agency to represent them in collective bargaining. When in 1937 the Committee for Industrial Organization withdrew from the AFL to form the Congress of Industrial Organizations (CIO), West Coast longshoremen also withdrew from the AFL International Longshoremen's Association and formed the International Longshoremen's and Warehousemen's Union affiliated with the CIO. From 1937 on, the waterfront was a CIO stronghold defended by longshoremen, fishermen, salmon cannery workers, and inland boatmen. Harry Bridges, their leader, was repeatedly charged with having Communist associations and his enemies demanded that he be deported to his native Australia. The charges were never proved, but some members of the union followed the party line and gave the organization a distinctly reddish appearance. Despite favorable contracts, strife and controversy haunted west coast harbors. Picket lines gave trouble repeatedly, and loading operations were interrupted when CIO men refused to handle nonunion cargo. Organized slowdowns and disputes over lift-boards and labor-saving machinery doubled costs on the docks. Not until December 1940 was there material improvement in efficiency and a more satisfactory adjustment of conflicting interests of labor and management.

In the spring of 1935 loggers and sawmill men walked out and by late summer had won a five-cent-an-hour wage increase and recognition of the AFL in camps and sawmills. The AFL Carpenters were the leaders but they immediately met with opposition from timber workers, who, as we have shown earlier, found the AFL too conservative and too narrowly specialized. No single leader succeeded in dominating timber workers as Bridges did longshoremen or Dave Beck, AFL teamsters. Insurgents formed the International Woodworkers Association (IWA) under the CIO, and almost at once workers were involved in jurisdictional struggles. Beginning in late summer of 1937 and continuing for a year and a half, Portland was the scene of bitter "goon" fights between CIO Woodworkers and AFL Carpenters and Teamsters. When workers at the Inman-Poulson Mills voted to join the CIO, the AFL refused to recognize the election, continued the strike, and boycotted lumber from CIO mills. At Grays Harbor, Everett, and Tacoma, mills were repeatedly shut down while locals wrangled. Elections were held, the results challenged. Conferences were summoned to meet in Washington, D.C., only to adjourn without decision. Wage agreements, hours, and specific contract provisions were worked out on short-term bases with any union that seemed to be the top dog at the moment. Eventually, a rough division of control was worked out which left the AFL stronger in the mills, the CIO in the forest. But the National Labor Relations Board was hard put to settle the problems the struggle perpetuated.

Employers generally favored the AFL over the CIO. They preferred, for example, to deal with Dave Beck.[11] Beck and his teamsters union made their first conquests in Seattle, where truck drivers used wrenches and jack handles when necessary to "perfect their organizations." Having thus established themselves, they extended their power by bringing within their control subsidiary groups—warehousemen, milkmen, brewery workers, even department store clerks. They failed to establish control over loghaulers and Boeing machinists. Nevertheless, Beck made himself one of the strongest labor

[11] "After the Battle; Present Relations Between Labor and Management," *Fortune*, February 1945; "Dave Beck," *Ibid.*, December 1948.

leaders in the country, which carried him to the presidency of the International Brotherhood of Teamsters in 1952. Ingenious and resourceful, he was quick to adapt to circumstances. Strong-arm methods gave way to negotiations which emphasized the common interests of unions and employers. Laundrymen and dry cleaners, bakers and garage owners came to see the advantages of paying higher wages to employees when costs could be offset by charging higher prices, and when they had some assurance that unprofitable competition would be discouraged. Beck fell into step with the Chamber of Commerce and Seattle became a peaceful closed-shop town. Portland's labor difficulties also quieted down with the AFL in control.

From this digressive episode of labor history we can perhaps better understand the temper of the public when, in 1938, the AFL-CIO conflict was still violent. The jails were full of goon-squads awaiting trial; employers wanted peace but not at the price of strong unions, and federal mediators were thwarted by labor and management suspicions of the NLRB. In defeating the renomination of Governor Martin on the labor issue, the Oregon Commonwealth Federation split the Democratic Party and in effect gave the state back to the Republicans.

By 1938 Oregonians had had second thoughts about the local Democracy and were less enthusiastic about Roosevelt's New Deal. Republican Charles Sprague, editor of the Salem *Oregon Statesman*, succeeded Martin and the GOP held the governor's office thereafter until 1956. Homer D. Angell replaced Nan Honeyman in Congress; Rufus C. Holman defeated Willis Mahoney in the Senate race; and the Republicans regained control of the legislature and two years later, Multnomah County. Roosevelt's 1936 plurality of 144,027 slipped to 38,860 in 1940. Thus the Republicans gained in strength and the Democrats progressively weakened; until 1956, Oregon was once again almost a one-party state.

But among Oregon Republicans, Governor Sprague was identified as an independent-minded liberal; Senator McNary seldom opposed Roosevelt policies. Those who directed party councils (from Portland's Arlington Club, it has been said) tended toward the "essence of Whiggery"—compromise and accommodation to the times. New Deal benefits were not to be associated exclusively with the Democratic Party.

Contemporary historians have tried to put the New Deal in perspective with antecedent reform movements of the Populist and Progressive Eras. It has been argued on the one hand that the New Deal was not revolutionary, that it failed to come to grips with basic issues because it chose to work in a traditional framework of reform; on the other, that the Roosevelt Era was a definite break with the past. To some observers, the New Deal was an American step toward Caesarism and totalitarianism; to others, it was a commitment to a broader based democracy.[12]

What the New Deal meant to the Pacific Northwest was what it offered in specifics rather than in theories. The New Deal spoke in familiar terms to those who for fifty years had agitated for federal irrigation projects, development and planned use of natural resources, regulation of corporations, protection of labor and consumer interests, farm relief, and fiscal policy more responsive to the market. Pump-priming as a means of bolstering a sagging economy had been advocated by Coxey's followers in the 1890s. Forty years later the Pacific Northwest showed no reluctance to test the Keynesian thesis that public spending encouraged private investment. The New Deal proposed little that was novel to an area which had experienced protest and reform movements in depression and in prosperity, in both agricultural and urban settings. Keith Murray has concisely summarized reasons for Roosevelt's popularity in the Far West:

> During the 1930s, Franklin Roosevelt became the symbol of what the Northwest wanted. He stood for hydro-electric development and irrigation projects. He urged currency inflation and directed that the gold standard be abandoned, to the delight of those to whom Populism was "not a political party but rather an attitude." His sponsorship of laws to regulate the securities and commodities exchanges along with the act to guarantee bank deposits was the type of legislation that had been urged by numerous Westerners since 1896. Farmers were soothed by crop-control checks, and labor benefited from the Wagner Act. The way of any Republican candidate who opposed these measures was hard indeed.[13]

Those who witnessed the shift from the Democratic upswing back to Republicanism disagreed as to how to interpret it (see Graph VII, p. 624). Some said that Oregon voters accepted the main purposes and features of the New Deal, but were only half-hearted in support of the Democratic Party. Palmer Hoyt, editor of the *Oregonian*, admitted the almost magical personal influence of Roosevelt, but insisted Oregon was basically opposed to New Deal paternalism, citing as proof voter rejection of tax proposals and free-spending measures. A case could be made for both opinions. In one amazing instance, Oregonians demonstrated the conflict between their habitual economy-

[12] *The New Deal: What was It?* Morton Keller, ed., American Problem Studies (1963).

[13] Murray, *op. cit.*, 231.

510

mindedness and their new concern with economic security. Like Washington and California, Oregon had a population older than that of the nation at large. Old age assistance was, therefore, an issue of prime importance. The Social Security Act of 1933 pressed the states to set up unemployment insurance legislation, but old age assistance was still a matter of local provision. The legislature passed a modest bill that nowise met the demands of Townsendites, who in 1938 prevailed upon the voters, 183,781 to 149,711, to adopt a Townsend Plan. However, in the same election the voters rejected (219,557 to 112,172) a transactions tax to implement the measure.

On the other hand, Oregonians took advantage of federal matching funds for old age assistance, social security, and grazing loans. They welcomed federal funds for the development of hydroelectric power, though, as we shall see, they were not of one mind with regard to public ownership of power facilities. Farmers in the grain belt accepted crop controls reluctantly but endorsed their wheat checks without pain. Management had no objection to provisions of the National Industrial Recovery Act which limited competition, but objected to the recognition of collective bargaining and minimum wages and hours. In short, different segments of the community accepted and approved those features of the New Deal which served their own interests and howled with anguish over those that did not. So long as no large group of interests was consistently hurt and so long as New Deal measures, though "radical," were expedient to economic recovery, no cohesive opposition took shape. But with the second phase of the New Deal (1935–1938) was posed the question whether the "whole American cause and tradition must stand or fall with one economic dogma."[14] Accepting the particulars of New Dealism, Oregon voters evaded disruptive debate on political theory and abandoned the party of the new Democratic Dogma.

In these terms one can interpret the ambiguous statement of an Oregon political scientist commenting on the 1938 elections which returned the state to Republican control:

> To a surprising extent the political situation in Oregon reflects that of the nation. In a state which for many years has been so predominantly Republican in its political preference, the recent upheaval should be interpreted not so much as a revolution as a return to a normal condition after four abnormal years [1934–1938] induced by a nation-wide economic situation.[15]

[14] C. Vann Woodward, *The Burden of Southern History* (1961), 184.
[15] Philip A. Parsons, *The* [Oregon] *Commonwealth Review*, January 1939, 719.

The New Deal left its mark upon the Pacific Northwest. In the following chapter we shall look at two important areas in which the consequences of government policies were most apparent; in the development of hydroelectric power, in the confrontation of regional, national and state interests in the future of the region's economy, and in the building of World War II industries.

CHAPTER
THIRTY-ONE

The Columbia River in a New Role: Hydroelectric Power and Economic Development, 1933–1967

ALTHOUGH HARD TIMES gripped the Northwest—Washington with particular severity—by 1933 Roosevelt's program had brought assistance to the region, conferring more permanent benefits here than in many other sections of the country. Federal emergency relief (FERA) and public works (PWA) funds put thousands of jobless men to work and generated secondary activities that created more jobs. Between 1935 and 1937, Washington manufacture payrolls increased by about $45,000,000, output by $200,000,000. Income figures rose fairly close to those of 1929, and an estimated two-fifths of this increase can be attributed, directly or indirectly, to recovery programs. Grand Cou-

513

lee and Bonneville dams were started as such projects but their greater significance lay in the long-run effects they had upon the regional economy.

GRAND COULEE DAM

The Grand Coulee project had its genesis in schemes to build up underpopulated eastern Washington with attractive offers of irrigated lands at prices users could afford. Since 1914, irrigation had become an increasingly expensive undertaking. High costs placed a tremendous burden on water users. Financing projects was more than ever difficult during the decade following World War I when agricultural prices slumped from their former levels. In many places where small water systems had been built during the first flush of reclamation enthusiasm, the 1920s brought failure for many, retrenchment and readjustment for others. In Idaho, commercial irrigation companies went out of business almost entirely, and in Oregon and Washington their operations dropped to less than half of what they had been. Many districts were unable to finance improvements or to pay interest on outstanding bonds.[1] Consequently the Corps of Engineers of the United States Army and the Reclamation Bureau had to carry more and more of the burden.

Despite years of depressed agricultural prices, Pacific Northwest promoters continued to think in terms of increasing farm production and supporting a larger farm population. For Washington expansion must, of necessity, lie in the Columbia Basin. The Reclamation Bureau hesitated to go into this section, mainly because the cost of bringing water to the parched soil appeared prohibitive. However, in 1918 two plans that staggered the imagination were put forward. One called for a gravity system bringing water to the Columbia Basin from Lake Pend Oreille (Idaho) a hundred miles to the northeast. The entire cost for canals, tunnels, and siphons necessary to carry the water at the proper grade through intervening ridges and across or under the Spokane River, was estimated at $300,000,000. Although this was thought of as exclusively an irrigation project, it was proposed that water not required for agricultural purposes at certain times of the year could be turned into the Spokane River for the benefit of hydroelectric power plants. This plan, originating with E. F. Blaine, horticulturist for the Sunnyside Division of the Yakima Project, received

[1] For a more detailed account of these developments, see Dorothy O. Johansen and Charles M. Gates, *Empire of the Columbia*, 1st ed. (1957), chap. 32.

514

its principal support from Spokane. Private power interests thought well of it, since it would benefit them without threatening competition from public power installations.

Almost at the same time that Blaine was promoting his gravity-flow plan, James O'Sullivan and William Clapp of Ephrata and Rufus Woods, editor and publisher of the *Wenatchee World*, proposed an alternative even more spectacular—a dam on the Columbia and a storage basin in the Grand Coulee. Glacial ice had once blocked the course of the Columbia River, forcing it to carve out a new channel and valley bed extending south toward Soap Lake. When the glaciers withdrew, the ice dam melted and the river resumed its old channel, eroding it slowly but relentlessly until the waters flowed some 600 feet below the basalt rim of the plateau. O'Sullivan proposed to dam the river, raise the water level, and pump the water over the rim into the upper end of the Coulee for storage and distribution to more than a million acres of fertile but arid soil. It was a bold and imaginative scheme. The dam would have to be a colossal structure, at least 400 feet high and more than 4000 feet long—"the biggest thing in one piece that man had ever made"—but O'Sullivan was convinced that the only difficulty was one of magnitude. No problems of engineering were involved that had not been solved on a smaller scale in construction of dams elsewhere.

For a decade, a storm of local controversy raged over the relative merits of the Pend Oreille and Grand Coulee plans. In the end, the latter prevailed. One could not say that Ephrata and Wenatchee argued more persuasively or lobbied more effectively than Spokane. The Blaine plan involved complex legal and political factors. For example, Idaho agricultural interests, fearful of competition from Columbia Basin irrigated lands, were opposed to the diversion of Lake Pend Oreille waters. Furthermore, though estimates were lower than those for Grand Coulee, the costs of the gravity-flow system charged against the land would raise prices to an estimated $400 per acre. On the other hand, if revenues from electric power generated at the Grand Coulee were allocated to irrigation, costs to farmers would run as low as $85 per acre.

The government's changing attitude with regard to development of the nation's rivers also entered into the decision favoring Grand Coulee. Recurring disastrous floods, depletion of domestic water supplies, and growing awareness of the importance of hydroelectric power in the national economy moved Congress to consider its policy—or lack of policy. Historically, Congress had justified federal appropriations for river improvements as benefits to commerce and navigation. Traditionally, the Corps of Engineers was responsible for surveys and construction of such improvements. Western demands for aid to irrigation had enlarged the area of federal activities and such projects were assigned to the Bureau of Reclamation in the Department of the Interior. Normally, there was no conflict between the two agencies because there were no overlapping functions; on the other hand, there was also no overall planning for the full utilization of the waters and the most efficient use of moneys spent on river improvements.

REGIONAL PLANNING

In 1907, Theodore Roosevelt had appointed an Inland Waterways Commission to study the whole question of river development. The Commission's report emphasized the need for a federal policy to encourage multiple use instead of haphazard, unrelated, single-purpose projects. In submitting the report to Congress (1908) Roosevelt stated that:

> It is poor business to develop a river for navigation in such a way as to prevent its use for power. . . . We cannot afford needlessly to sacrifice power to navigation or navigation to domestic water supply, when by taking thought we could have all three. Every stream should be used to its utmost. . . . Each river system from its headwaters in the forest to its mouth on the Coast is a single unit and should be treated as such.

He recommended a "definite and progressive policy" and a "concrete general plan" of comprehensive river development with a responsible authority to administer policy. Not until the twenties, however, was Congress moved toward policy-making and long-range planning, and then only by fits and starts. Between 1923 and 1928, a series of acts authorized the Corps of Engineers to proceed with river surveys covering such matters as flood control, power development, irrigation, navigation, and domestic water supplies. In 1927, Congress and President Hoover approved Boulder Dam, planned as a self-supporting multipurpose project under the Bureau of Reclamation. By 1931 it was apparent that the Corps of Engineers would approve the Grand Coulee project.

Their recommendations were embodied in a report on the Columbia River (1932) usually referred to as the "308 Report" because the survey was authorized in House Document Number 308 (1925). The engineers found that the Columbia River and its tributaries, through integrated development, could provide flood control, irrigation for potentially valuable lands, a major waterway from the sea to the interior, and "could be developed into the greatest system of low-cost hydro-electric power in the United States." For these multiple purposes, the Corps proposed ten dams on the Columbia between the Canadian border and tidewater, to be erected at Grand Coulee, Foster Creek, Chelan, Rocky Reach, Rock Island, Priest Rapids, Umatilla Rapids, John Day Rapids, The Dalles, and Bonneville at the Cascades.

Under strong pressure from O'Sullivan and Woods, the Washington state legislature set up a Columbia Basin Commission to promote the Grand Coulee project and state relief funds were used to do some preliminary work on the site, employing 250 men in 1933 and 2500 in 1934. When, in March 1933, Roosevelt created the Public Works Administration (PWA) to channel moneys into the states to generate employment, $60,000,000 was allocated to the Bureau of Reclamation to build a low dam at Grand Coulee.

In the meantime, the President had created by executive order a cabinet-level National Resources Committee which, through its Advisory Committee and staff, undertook to make a general study of regional factors in planning and development through state and regional bodies. To the Pacific Northwest Regional Planning Commission was assigned the immediate task of determining:

1. What should be the policy for future planning in the great area drained by the Columbia River?
2. How can the enormous resources of water, forests, and minerals in the area be best utilized and conserved for the benefit of present and future generations?
3. How can these resources be organized for the benefit of the whole region?

With the help of a staff directed by Roy F. Bessey and including economists, political scientists, and engineers, notably Charles McKinley, Blair Stewart, Charles E. Carey, P. Hetherton, and James C. Rettie, the Regional Commission drew up in 1936 the first general regional planning report. It found that the states of Oregon, Washington, and Idaho, and western Montana comprised a "coherent subnational region" with the Columbia Basin at its core for purposes of "planning, conservation, and development." The resources of this region were of such a nature as to warrant a national interest in public works already under way, Grand Coulee and Bonneville, and in a "competent and comprehensive basic plan for public works for the entire region with a continuing program adjusted to regional and national needs and controlled by advance planning." The Commission therefore recommended the following.

Planning should be continued along organizational lines which are now established, with provision for more permanent legal basis and for effective coordination of Federal agencies and State and local government.

Construction of public works should be integrated into a harmonious scheme of regional development.

Federal power plants now under construction, or to be constructed, should be considered as units of a single integrated power system.

A new operating body in the form of a Federal corporation should be created and assigned all Federal power operations.[2]

According to staff members who wrote this unique report the most important idea in it was

related to the concept of a federally-built and operated regional grid system with the highest voltage and technical factors of reliability possible at that time. This was the work of Charles E. Carey, consulting electrical engineer, who before the depression had been one of Westinghouse's engineers. Carey also originated the idea that the grid, in addition to handling the power generated by Federal dams, should be available to carry the energy of other systems in the region. Thus the basis for the later "Northwest pool" idea and practice was laid.

Carey also advocated adoption of the postage stamp rate system—the same wholesale charge for power regardless of regional location—which had been used by the Tennessee Valley Authority. This allowed choice of an industry location to be made on factors of transportation, labor supply, social amenities for work, and other advantages. Carl E. Magnussen of the University of Washington and Carey also pioneered the idea of using a kilowatt year as a basic unit of rate measurement in order to encourage continuous utilization of power and thus to stabilize employment.

By 1935, state and federal agencies not only advocated comprehensive, integrated development of the Columbia River, but had gone far beyond the idea of a low dam at Grand Coulee and the idea of electric power as simply a by-product of irrigation and flood control facilities. This was a turn of events which private power companies could not accept with equanimity. When it became evident that they would fight a high dam and the development of a single integrated power system, the Columbia Basin Commission and other advocates of public power asked Congress for formal authorization of a high dam and appropriations for its completion. In hearings held on the pro-

[2] National Resources Committee, *Regional Planning, Part I: Pacific Northwest,* May 1936, vii; Roy F. Bessey, *Pacific Northwest Regional Planning—A Review,* State of Washington, Bulletin No. 6, Division of Power Resources (1963).

posals, Homer T. Bone and Lewis Schwellenbach of Washington and Charles McNary of Oregon urged the high dam, emphasizing the generation of power as a factor important to the region's total economy and arguing that cheap power would compensate the area for its lack of other energy bases—natural gas, inexpensive coal, and petroleum.

In the Rivers and Harbors Act of 1935, Congress formally approved the work on the dam which, thus far, had been carried on with FERA and WPA funds by presidential order.[3] Construction of Grand Coulee Dam then proceeded apace, and with spectacular engineering ingenuity. Completed, it was the largest concrete structure built up to that time; as high as a 46-story building; twelve city blocks in length at the spillway, and 500 feet at the base. World War II delayed construction of storage basin and canals; however, plans and regulations for the irrigation project were ready to be applied.

When Grand Coulee was ready to produce power in 1941, Congress had already arrived at a decision with regard to administration of federal power facilities on the Columbia. Completion of Bonneville Dam in 1937 forced a decision as to its administration. The Engineers had recommended the project in their 1932 report, and they had the support of Oregonians. Campaigning in Portland in 1932, Roosevelt had advocated local power projects as a means of improving the region's economy, but he had not specifically come out for federal projects. The first New Deal Congress adjourned without any promise of government aid, when Congressman Charles Martin and Senator Charles McNary made strong personal appeals to the President for approval of the project as a public work. He allotted $26,000,000 in PWA funds (later increased to $36,000,000) and the Corps of Engineers was assigned the task of construction. Two years later Bonneville Dam was ready to deliver power. The double-barrelled question, then, demanded an answer: What agency was to administer the operation, and for whose benefit—private or public interests?

THE STRUGGLE FOR PUBLIC POWER

In Chapter Twenty-Nine we suggested that private utilities occupied a sensitive spot in Oregon and Washington politics. In Washington, the issue of public versus private power had been aired since the turn of the century and the positions of the antagonists had been

[3] George Sundborg, *Hail Columbia: the Thirty-Year Struggle for Grand Coulee Dam* (1954).

loudly articulated. The state constitution permitted municipalities to incur debt for municipally owned utilities: water, artificial light, and sewers. Seattle and Tacoma pioneered municipal electric systems in the face of the "fiercest competition . . . ever staged in the country," according to J. D. Ross, Superintendent of Seattle's highly successful City Light.[4] The principal opposition came from Puget Sound Power and Light, owned by Stone and Webster of Boston, which served most of western Washington. Its practices, and those of other companies, did not win friends for private utilities.

State utility commissions sanctioned rates that would give utility investors a fair return. The methods of bookkeeping kept those rates high. For example, a company might secure waterpower rights with only a small outlay but capitalize the acquisition at high value. Against this capitalization it could charge proportionately higher rates. Rate experts showed that one Portland distributor charged its customers on the basis of 8 percent return on an operation with a book value of $8,000,000 and a real value of less than $1,500,000. Another company capitalized at $10,000,000 a development which cost only $1,230,000.

Within a few years after its establishment, Seattle City Light rates provided a yardstick which private utilities had to meet; as a consequence, units of power which had formerly cost 20 cents could be had for six cents or less. Private operators did not welcome this kind of competition. They argued that public utilities were socialistic and did not help to carry costs of local government and services because they were tax-free. Municipal operators replied, in effect, that reductions in rates more than repaid the community for what it lost in taxes; they ignored the charge of socialism. Throughout the Northwest, private companies joined forces to block legislation extending or establishing public power installations, and, reportedly, spent large sums in anti-public power campaigns.

Nevertheless, to an increasing number of persons it seemed strange that in a land of abundant potential, hydroelectric power was a scarce and expensive commodity. Washington Grangers demanded legislation to permit municipal systems to serve surrounding rural districts. Initiative No. 52 was approved in 1924, placing the issue before the legislature. Neither house acted favorably, and subsequent efforts were

[4] Elliott Marple, "Movement for Public Ownership of Power in Washington," *Journal of Land and Public Utility Economics*, February 1931; James K. Hall, "Washington's Public Ownership District Power Law," *National Municipal Review*, June 1931; William A. Smith, "Development of Public Utility Districts in Washington," unpublished thesis, University of Washington, 1950; Carl Dreher, "J. D. Ross, Public Power Magnate," *Harper's Magazine*, June 1940.

no more rewarding. Only as the Grange was joined by other pressure groups did public power win at the polls and in the legislature. In 1930 Homer T. Bone's Public Utility District Law was passed. Under this law, an otherwise unincorporated area could organize as a utility district (PUD) to build dams and to generate, purchase, and distribute power. The door was now open to statewide public power in Washington. In Oregon, a similar first step had been taken in 1930 as a result of George Joseph's battle for public power.

Some contemporary political observers believed that the popular vote enabling establishment of PUDs was more a protest against private corporations than an affirmation of the principle of public ownership. True, little progress was made in putting PUDs into operation (see Graph XIX, p. 630). Spokane County organized a district (1932) but it remained inoperative. Of the three counties that took action in 1934, only Mason was able to provide service. By 1939, four districts were producing and/or distributing electricity. In Oregon, private utilities persistently and successfully fought public power through legislative lobbies and appeals to Oregonians' fears of indebtedness, and the voters rejected bills that would put the state in the power business. By the end of 1940, voters had rejected organization of twelve PUDs and approved twelve. Two of the latter reorganized as cooperatives with REA funds. Four authorized issuance of bonds, but none was operational.

The financing of dams, installations, and transmission lines was a formidable problem for a PUD. To purchase power from private operators promised no reduction in rates; to condemn private operations was expensive and suits might drag through the courts for decades. As in building transcontinental railroads and major irrigation systems, the pioneer phases of public power (other than municipal systems) required resources that only the federal government could provide. However, government had been extremely reluctant to extend its powers in this direction.

Since World War I, Congress had engaged in occasional debate on regulations of private utilities. In 1920, the Federal Water Power Act created the Federal Power Commission (FPC) to license companies constructing facilities on navigable waters which, by definition, came under federal jurisdiction. The Commission also had power to regulate rates for power distributed in interstate commerce. But private companies evaded federal supervision by building on non-navigable streams and escaped rate regulations through the same devices by which they successfully evaded state regulations. Senator James Couzens of Michigan led a fight to extend federal regulatory powers, but received no support from either Coolidge or Hoover.

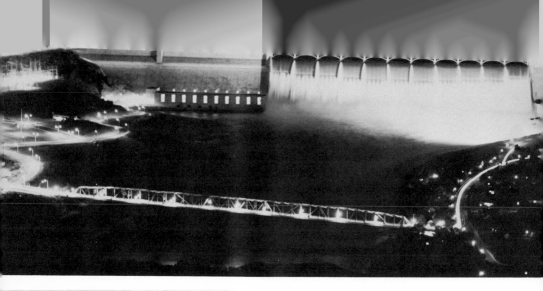

Industry At Mid-Century

ABOVE. *Grand Coulee Dam at night, power-house left and right of the spillway. Water—its storage, distribution and use for power—has increased not only the productivity of land but kinds and numbers of industries, economic opportunities and payrolls.*

LEFT. *A Bonneville Power Administration maintenance crew makes a routine run by helicopter to inspect power lines. The name Bonneville honors Benjamin Bonneville of fur trading days.*

RIGHT. *A fish hatchery at Underwood, Washington. Expanding conservation programs protect the fishing industry.*

BELOW. *A deep well of sweet water, pumped by water-generated electric power, irrigates desert land.*

Two ornithologists check conditions on the Malheur National Wildlife Refuge, Blitzen Valley, Oregon. The preservation of natural resources is itself an industry of importance to the region.

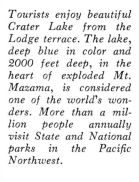

Tourists enjoy beautiful Crater Lake from the Lodge terrace. The lake, deep blue in color and 2000 feet deep, in the heart of exploded Mt. Mazama, is considered one of the world's wonders. More than a million people annually visit State and National parks in the Pacific Northwest.

BELOW. The Aluminum Company of America's Vancouver, Washington, plant. In 1940, the first primary aluminum west of the Mississippi was produced here. Today there are six primary-producing companies. The Vancouver plant alone employs more than 1500 persons and has an annual payroll of $10½ million.

RIGHT. Molten aluminum pours from the crucible into a 700-pound ingot mold.

The front "face" of a giant plutonium reactor as uranium fuel elements are loaded into the fuel tubes which pierce the reactor. The Atomic Energy Commission built six reactors at Hanford, Washington during World War II. General Electric now operates the plant where one of the reactors is a dual purpose unit producing plutonium and electric power.

The Boeing Company, Seattle. manufactures planes for much of the United States airlines industry and for national air lines in countries all over the world.

Boeing contributes to the Space Age. This giant chamber is used in the space environment laboratory. It can furnish an atmospheric vacuum equal to that at 400-miles altitude and a temperature of minus 320° Fahrenheit. LEFT. Imaginative new methods increase the engineering and uses of wood: these huge laminated, arched trusses bear heavy roof loads without a single support.

Tektronix, Inc. manufactures oscilloscopes in a complex of sleek modern buildings scattered through a landscaped rural acreage near Portland. The highly-skilled employees, many of them women, enjoy a profit-sharing system and many other liberal benefits.

More efficient ship-to-shore loading methods eliminate heavy manual labor and in turn call for better machine skills.

BELOW. *The Columbia River port of Vancouver, Washington, sparkles with the lively traffic of bridge, highway and river which moves the goods of the waterfront industries: grain, malt, wood products, chemicals, carborundum, cement.*

Neither were these administrations friendly to Senator George W. Norris' efforts to put the federal government in the power business for the purpose of establishing a national yardstick for power rates, and demonstrating the advantages of public ownership of power. Norris made Muscle Shoals a test case of public policy. There the government owned a World War I nitrate plant and power-producing facilities whose product was sold to a private company which distributed it at monopoly rates. The Norris-Morin Resolution (1928) called for the creation of a government corporation to use the Muscle Shoals plants for production of cheap fertilizer and for the production and distribution of electric power. The resolution passed both houses of Congress but was killed by Coolidge's pocket veto. Hoover vetoed a similar resolution in 1931.

Roosevelt however supported Norris, and in May 1933 the Norris-Morin Resolution was enacted into law. It created the Tennessee Valley Authority (TVA), a regional public body endowed with the legal characteristics of a corporation and with some administrative freedoms not usually found in governmental agencies but common to private enterprise. The Authority was responsible for the development of navigation, flood control, land management, and reclamation in the seven states of the Tennessee Valley, and as a corporate body it could construct, own, and operate power plants and sell electricity.

The TVA and the Rural Electrification Administration (1935), which was also empowered to produce and distribute power to rural areas, together involved the government in long-range operations directed toward economic growth as well as recovery. TVA demonstrated what an authority could do, not only in establishing a yardstick for power rates but also in rehabilitating a severely depressed area. However, the United States Supreme Court warned that it would not look with favor on government in the power business unless electricity was merely a by-product of projects sanctioned by traditional interpretations of the general welfare clause of the Constitution—navigation, flood control, and defense of the nation.

BONNEVILLE POWER ADMINISTRATION

Against this background, Congress in the spring of 1937 had to make a fundamental decision with regard to the Northwest projects. As has been pointed out, the question was how, and by what agency,

Bonneville was to be administered, and for whose benefit. A decision with regard to Bonneville on these matters would affect Grand Coulee, Boulder, and other projects being considered; it would affect the future of private power and the economic development of other western areas. Hence, when the House Committee on Rivers and Harbors considered Resolution 7642, a bill to "authorize completion, maintenance and operation of Bonneville project for navigation and other purposes," more than local interest was attached to the hearings.

The hearings revealed that sentiment in the Pacific Northwest was divided not only on the fundamental issue of the administrative agency but upon corollary issues as well.[5] Farmers and Grangers wanted administration by the Bureau of Reclamation which already administered power plants in connection with irrigation projects and was traditionally responsive to farmers' wishes. Some proponents of long-range planning wanted an authority similar to the TVA so that reclamation, soil and timber conservation, recreational and industrial uses of water could be integrated in a rational plan for economic growth. Washington PUDs wanted power widely transmitted over government-built lines. Other public power advocates wanted an intertie of installations and postage-stamp rates to spread the benefits. Private power wanted government responsibility to rest at the bus-bar, (roughly, the generating plant) leaving transmission to purchasers. Portland and the Corps of Engineers were opposed to an intertie, wanting bus-bar rates that would favor communities nearest the dam. The Portland Chamber of Commerce and private utilities, maintaining that the region had little demand for power that could not be met by existing facilities, argued against any kind of administration that would put Bonneville in competition with private companies, and asked for pooling operations and distribution under the Corps of Engineers with supervision by a local board of utility management familiar with the local situation.

The 1937 Bonneville Administration Act that emerged from the long-drawn-out hearings stipulated that Bonneville facilities should be maintained and operated by the Corps of Engineers, while Coulee Dam would be managed by the Bureau of Reclamation. A civilian administration, appointed by the Secretary of the Interior, was to have charge of marketing the energy produced at both dams. "To encourage the widest possible use of all electric energy that could be generated and marketed," the administration was authorized to construct facilities for transmission of power "within economic transmis-

[5] U.S. House of Representatives, Committee on Rivers and Harbors *Hearings*, March–June 1937.

sion distance" to "existing and potential markets, and for the purpose of interchange . . . to interconnect the Bonneville project with other Federal projects." To insure that the facilities would benefit the general public, and "particularly domestic and rural consumers," the administrator, in contracting for sales of power, was to give "preference and priority to public bodies and cooperatives," reserving for them 50 percent of capacity. As Grand Coulee and other Columbia River power projects came into operation, they also came under BPA marketing jurisdiction and their revenues were to pay for the dams and Coulee irrigation projects.

The Bonneville Administration was a far cry from a corporation or authority like the Tennessee Valley project. Bonneville's administrator was responsible to the Secretary of the Interior; he could recommend rates subject to review by the Federal Power Commission; he had to seek congressional appropriations for funds to extend and operate plant and transmission lines. Under administrators J. D. Ross and Paul Raver, BPA undertook to serve as a clearinghouse and research center for economic planning not unlike TVA. Charles E. Carey, the first chief engineer, planned the interties by which power from federal projects was distributed in a grid system over most of the region.[6] In Washington, PUDs sprang up like magic to take advantage of the preference clause. (As of 1965, Oregon had four operative PUDs, Washington, 24; Oregon had 11 municipally owned systems, Washington, 21; Oregon had 16 cooperatives, and Washington, 20.) By 1952, nearly 70 percent of regional hydroelectric power was produced by locally or federally owned public power installations.

On December 7, 1941, the Pacific Northwest Power System was organized to deliver energy to war production industries. Between 1939 and 1944, energy sold increased from 120,000,000 to 9,000,000,000 kilowatt hours (see Graphs XVII, XVIII, p. 629). So great was the demand that the War Production Board ordered the pooling of public and private electric output and interconnections with Bonneville extended as far east as Fort Peck Dam (Montana), south to Salt Lake City, and north to Vancouver, B.C. Shipyards, aircraft industries, and food processing plants made their demands on output. A whole new development in electro-process industries was made possible by the power supply. Twelve large plants were built at a cost of $160,000,000 for processing alumina and making calcium carbide and ferroalloys. In 1943 the United States Atomic Energy Commission chose Richland (Washington) as the site for the Hanford Atomic Works.

[6] Charles McKinley, *Uncle Sam in the Northwest; Federal Management of Natural Resources in the Columbia River Valley* (1952).

WORLD WAR II INDUSTRIES

In the Pacific Northwest, all factors of growth were stimulated by World War II, but the "battle of production" affected business even before Pearl Harbor. With the entry of the United States into the war, government contracts for ships and aircraft produced a tremendous expansion in manufacturing. Seattle ranked among the top three cities in per capita war orders, and Washington near the top among the states. In four years' time, 1941–1944, government contracts amounted to $5.59 billion in Washington alone.

Shipbuilding was once again the principal war industry. The Bremerton Naval repair yards sent most of the Pearl Harbor fleet back to sea and to the crucial battles of the Pacific. About 210,000 persons (including women) were employed on Puget Sound and on the Columbia River, where Henry J. Kaiser opened his first yard in 1941. In a few months, his mammoth operations had turned out fifty flattops and hundreds of Liberty and Victory ships built by amazingly fast methods of welding and assembly from steel produced by Kaiser Mills at Fontana (California) and Provo (Utah).

The aircraft industry was relatively new in the Pacific Northwest, but one of the nation's largest operations had its roots in Seattle, where early in the century William Boeing, a flying enthusiast, built a few planes. During World War I Boeing produced fifty Model C planes for the Navy and, in 1920, 200 pursuit planes. Despite some lean postwar years, he succeeded in building a staff of engineers and technicians who by 1934 had developed the design of Project 299, grandfather of the Flying Fortresses. Two years later the Army Air Corps placed an initial order for thirteen heavy bombers, which were delivered in August, 1937. War orders began to pour in, and by 1943 more than 40,000 persons were employed at the main plants in Seattle and Renton and in shops at Bellingham, Chehalis, Everett, and Aberdeen.

Modern aviation was made possible by the development of cheap aluminum, which depended on cheap power. Through the Northwest power pool and intertie more power was available in the region than elsewhere. Consequently, bauxite was imported from Arkansas, Alabama, and Louisiana to reduction plants at Vancouver, Tacoma, Spokane, operated by Alcoa, Reynolds, and Ollin. Until the Spokane rolling mills were built, the ingots were sent east and then returned to the Boeing plants as rolled sheets or extruded products.

Other new industries emerged to meet war demands. Manufacturing plants, large and small, were caught up in the web of war production, no matter where they were located or what their previous experience. Agricultural Walla Walla made castings for Portland shipyards; implement factories in Yakima turned to the production of destroyer parts. Liberty and Victory ships took their propellers from brass foundries in Seattle, their galley stoves, windlasses, and steering engines from iron works in Everett. Pacific Car and Foundry Company produced General Sherman tanks and tank retrievers, while in nearby Kent a small garbage can factory became an important supplier of rifle clips.

The war also made great demands on the Northwest's staple industries and boomed the economy. The regional index of business activity climbed sixty-three points. In 1946, the farmers' cash receipts were 244 percent above 1935–1939 figures. Miners, lumber workers, and fishermen worked at peak production figures. Food plants increased production of processed goods, Yakima Valley alone processing close to 5,000,000 cases of fruits and vegetables and 39,000,000 pounds of beet sugar. Workers were recruited from all over the country; a new immigration, concentrated in the three major metropolitan areas, swelled the population figures.

The Northwest was in a period of industrial growth; yet pride of achievement was tempered by doubts as to the permanence of the changes. With the return of peace shipyards might disappear as they had in 1920; aircraft contracts would be cancelled. What would be the prospects of employment and industrial reconversion then? Research analysts figured what measures of postwar adjustment were possible and likely, but generally a lugubrious pessimism settled over the region as the war drew to a close.

The worst fears were not realized. Although many war workers left the region, newcomers took their places with the result that the gain in population was maintained and even increased. Business activity hardly faltered with the end of the war; thereafter, the general index continued its strong steady rise until, in 1952, it stood at 261. After watching it for several years, statisticians shifted their base year from the 1935–1939 average to 1947. Henceforth, the new postwar level would be taken as the normal state of affairs with which subsequent changes would be compared.

The situation in 1947 was, in some ways, so different from 1939 that it did seem the region was entering upon a new stage of economic development. Even though factory employment had dropped nearly 100 points on the index at the end of the war, it stabilized at a level 50 points above the prewar figure. Aircraft plants employed twice as many men as in 1939, and shipyards three times as many. In nine of sixteen major industrial groups, Northwest manufacturers registered important gains and conserved them. The total value added by manufacturing for the region as a whole increased 265 percent (see Graphs XII, XIV, pp. 626, 627). Building and private construction, long neglected during the years of depression and war, rose to a level five times that of the middle 1930s. Business activity in banks and department stores was two and three times greater.

Several factors accounted for the industrial growth. Large government expenditures continued because of the disturbed state of world affairs. Manufacturing plants constructed during the war were available to private industry at bargain prices. The pent-up demand for consumers' goods expanded the market, now proportionally larger because of the increase in population.

Yet, those who made careful appraisals of the postwar economy were not persuaded that the new conditions were basically different from the old. The development of the region was still dependent upon raw material resources, and was directly related to the extractive industries; 80 percent of its manufacturing continued to be concentrated in five major groups: lumber, food processing, paper, transportation, and primary metals (see Graphs XIV, XV, XVI, pp. 627, 628). Industrial diversification increased somewhat within these groups, but the general balance as between groups (save for the aluminum and aircraft industries) was not greatly changed from what it had been earlier.

THE POST-WORLD WAR II ECONOMY

Despite its gains, manufacturing occupied a comparatively small proportion of the population. The region accounted for only two percent of the national increase in number of production workers. With a few exceptions, important ones to be sure, the Northwest was still a place of small shops and branch plants. It was still an area set apart by great spaces and long distances from the more populous sections of the country. The pattern of freight rates still presented serious obstacles to the establishment of industries which were at all sensitive to transportation costs. Hydroelectric power promised to give the region an advantage in attracting new industries. Yet, the first major industries attracted by this cheap facility, such as alumina reduction plants and electro-process industries, consumed tremendous amounts of power and employed only small working forces. This was demonstrated in the mid-fifties when the economic growth rate dropped but the consumption of power increased. By 1956 the region had a power shortage and "brown-outs" became a familiar experience at peak-load periods.

The Eisenhower Administration was committed to the policy of partnership of public and private interests in hydroelectric development. It encouraged private companies to build dams and generating plants on tributary streams, and to continue to pool their output with that of publicly owned facilities. Although The Dalles and McNary dams were completed and John Day Dam, the largest on the lower river, was scheduled for the late 1960s, the federal government retired from further development of hydroelectric development in the Columbia Basin. On the other hand, in the face of strong opposition from public power advocates and individuals committed to integrated river development, private operators, whose capacity to build had been greatly enhanced by the availability of cheap capital of one kind or another, expanded their facilities in Idaho and Oregon.

The conception of a regional integrated power system was also seriously challenged as Washington PUDs and municipal systems vied not only with each other but with Oregon and Idaho private companies and promoters of federal developments for power sites and facilities.[7] Furthermore, the Pacific Northwest's cheap power rates created antagonism in eastern industrial areas dependent upon private operations and thermal energy bases, coal, and oil. Congress looked with skepticism at Bonneville reports of revenues and estimated expansion costs, often failing to consider that Bonneville Administration revenues bore the costs of Columbia Basin irrigation. From time to time, efforts were made to create a Columbia Valley Authority or an independent corporation to free Columbia Basin hydroelectric development from political pressures. In 1958, Senator Richard Neuberger (D-Oregon) sponsored a bill to create a Columbia Valley Corporation similar to TVA which would free Bonneville Administration from these handicaps. As proposed, the bill would also encourage industrial growth with assurances of firm power supply as well as cheap rates by removing the preferential clause which restricted 50 percent of the output to the use of cooperatives and PUDs. Since the proposal affected almost every organized interest in the region, it, like other proposed reforms of the BPA, was defeated.[8]

[7] Roy F. Bessey, *The Public Issues of Middle Snake River Development; the Controversy Over Hell's Canyon and Nez Perce Reaches*, State of Washington, Division of Power Resources, Bulletin No. 9 (1964).

[8] U.S. Senate, Committee on Public Works, *Hearings on the Bonneville Project Act Amendments, May–June*, December, 1958.

On the other hand, power generated by federally owned installations wheeled through private as well as public transmission lines. The intertie system originally fought by private utilities has in many cases become essential to their existence. A Bonneville transmission line to Klamath Falls, a step toward an intertie with federal projects in California, was halted by Eisenhower's Secretary of the Interior, Douglas McKay (R-Oregon). However, in 1965 an intertie of Bonneville with private California companies neared completion. The same year the "nation's biggest public-versus-private power fight" seemed to be approaching a solution, since "Idaho Power Company knows Bonneville is here to stay and Bonneville knows that Idaho Power Company is here to stay," according to Idaho's John A. Carver, Undersecretary of the Department of the Interior.[9] Idaho Power, with the support of Utah Power and Light and other private utilities, has defeated efforts to bring public power to serve the phosphate processing plants of southern Idaho, and Bonneville power will move over private lines to serve only its preference customers, cooperatives, and publicly owned systems, when a wheeling agreement between BPA and Idaho Power can be reached.

THE COLUMBIA RIVER AS AN INTERNATIONAL RESOURCE

However, in twenty years the river has come to have a wholly new significance in the life of the region and the nation, and as a consequence many agencies and many interests are concerned with its utilization and management. Private and public interests, and federal, state, and even international relations have become involved. An instance of international concern illustrates the complexity of the situation.

The Columbia and two of its tributaries—the Kootenai and the Pend Oreille—are boundary rivers. Problems incident to such waters led to the Boundary Waters Treaty of 1909 and an International Joint Commission (IJC) to deal with them. With the completion of Grand Coulee Canada and the United States agreed upon the terms of reference by which the IJC would be authorized to investigate the "practicability and desirability of a further development of the water resources of the Columbia River basin for a number of purposes, including the efficient development of water power" in the public in-

[9] *Oregonian*, November 8, 1965.

533

THE PACIFIC NORTHWEST
RECLAMATION AREAS
AND DAM SITES

118

49

MONTANA

Milk

Libby

Hungry Horse

Marias

KALISPELL

Teton

Missouri

Noxon Rapids

Flathead
Lake

Thompson Falls   Kerr

Swan

Clark

Fk.

Musselshell

shak

Canyon
Ferry

HELENA

Lochsa

Selway

Bitterroot

Jefferson

Yellowstone

rwater

Ilole

Salmon

Madison

MONTANA   45
WYOMING

Middle Fk.

Ruby

Red Rock

Big

Lemhi

Hebgen

Yellowstone
Lake

Shoshone   CODY

yelte
ke

Lima

Buffalo Bill

ascade

Island
Park

Bighorn

Deadwood

Jackson Lake

McKay

Henrys Fk.

Jackson Lake

Wind   Boysen

wrock

Boise

Anderson Ranch

Palisades

Magic

Snake

Blackfoot

Falls

k

Bliss

American Falls

Blackfoot Marsh

Lower Salmon

Minidoka

AMERICAN FALLS

Hams Fork

Green

Upper Salmon

Bruneau

Milner

Bear

Salmon Falls

Oakley

IDAHO
UTAH

Horse

Blacks

Fork

ROCK SPRINGS

Great
Salt
Lake

OGDEN

Flaming Gorge   41

118

109

SHERMAN

terest as the two governments interpreted it.[10] The International Columbia River Engineering Board, composed of a United States and a Canadian committee, was set up for this purpose and worked amicably together until relations between the United States and Canada became strained over the latter's assertion of economic nationalism. This was manifest when, in 1955, General A. G. L. McNaughton, chairman of the Canadian section of the IJC, took the position that Canada's interests in water resources took precedence over international considerations. He cited a proposal by which Canada would divert the Kootenai to the Columbia at Canal Flats (not far from David Thompson's winter camp of 1807) and thence by tunnel carry a great part of the Columbia flow to the Fraser River and to the potential industrial development of British Columbia. The implications of this proposal were not diminished by McNaughton's statement that Canada would consider the "exploitation and use of certain portions of those waters which we may find it advantageous to permit to continue to flow from Canada across the boundary."[11]

If the Canadians chose to divert the Columbia, imitating United States nationalistic policy on the Rio Grande above the Mexican border, it was claimed that the effect upon the water supply of the Pacific Northwest would be disastrous and would render practically useless the billion-dollar dams and power installations already built. Representatives of the United States, notably Idaho's Governor Len Jordan, chairman of the American section of the IJC, argued for—but Canada rejected—the conception of the river as a continental resource. Yet that it was one in fact handicapped the Canadian stand for unilateral action.

The Eisenhower Administration attempted to smooth matters over with the "partnership" idea. Douglas McKay, replacing Len Jordan on the Commission, had both as governor of Oregon and as Secretary of the Interior, presided at the abdication of governmental planning on both state and federal levels. The proposals he made to the IJC called for a *quid pro quo* arrangement by which Canada would realize "downstream" benefits in exchange for "upstream" storage. This proposal led to further studies by the International Columbia River Engineering Board and a highly significant report (1959) which made planning the keystone of Canadian-American relationship with regard to the Columbia. The report, which laid the foundations for a master plan for the development of Columbia River water resources in Canada, was based essentially on engineering and economic con-

[10] Richard Dougall, "Economic Cooperation with Canada, 1941–1947," U.S. Department of State *Bulletin*, June 22, 1947, 1190.

[11] U.S. Department of State *Bulletin*, December 12, 1955, 980–988.

siderations, without regard to the fact or effect of the international boundary.[12] The report provided the framework for direct negotiations between the two nations in 1960. Noteworthy on this occasion was the strong leadership of Pacific Northwest congressional delegations, who assumed rather unusual roles in what was ordinarily a strictly executive function. Senator Richard Neuberger (Oregon), chairman of the subcommittee of the Senate Committee on Interior and Insular Affairs, showed qualities of statesmanship; Senators Mike Mansfield (Montana), Frank Church (Idaho), and Wayne Morse (Oregon), members of the Senate Foreign Relations Committee, gave outstanding support through the yearlong negotiations. The result was the Columbia River Treaty of January 17, 1961, attesting to the belief that "many more advantages at much less cost would flow from joint development and control than from two competing and often conflicting operations, founded on the unilateral pursuit of rights based on claims of absolute sovereignty and exclusive jurisdiction." Under the terms of the treaty Canada will build three storage dams above the boundary at an estimated cost of $345,000,000 and operate the storage facility to provide maximum benefits in flood control and hydroelectric power production. The United States will operate existing power facilities and new ones as constructed. Canada will receive one-half of the downstream power benefits, defined as "the difference in the hydroelectric power capable of being generated in the United States and without the use of Canadian storage, determined in advance." The United States pays Canada over a nine-year period $64,400,000 for flood control benefits to be realized from Canadian storage. The treaty also grants the United States an option to construct Libby Dam in Montana; and provides for procedures to govern diversion of waters in case need arises.

The Senate ratified the treaty March 16, 1961 with only Senator Wallace F. Benton of Utah dissenting. In January 1963, President Kennedy and Prime Minister Pearson signed important agreements clarifying and adjusting certain aspects of it which were possible sources of controversy. But the treaty remains inoperative, lacking Canadian ratification. This depends upon the settlement of jurisdictional issues between the Canadian federal government and the Province of British Columbia.

The Canadian problem is not unlike that of the United States where federal, state, and private interests are involved in every considera-

---

[12] Charles E. Martin, "International Water Problems of the West; the Columbia Basin Treaty between Canada and the United States," in *Canada-United States Treaty Relations*, David R. Deener, ed. (1963), 58. Full text of the treaty can be found in U.S. Department of State *Bulletin*, February 13, 1961.

tion of water resources. In 1946 attempts to reconcile interests of this nature led to the creation of the Columbia Basin Inter-Agency Committee which, it was hoped, would coordinate federal and state "planning and execution of works for the control and use of the waters of the Columbia River system and the streams of the Coastal drainage areas." By the mid-forties, however, state and regional planning boards had disappeared and no local agencies existed to represent the states. The Northwest governors' Columbia Interstate Compact Commission (1952) proposed intergovernmental cooperation by negotiating a compact between the states, to avoid if possible an authority like TVA or the strong hand of federal control. The Commission served a purpose in providing a forum for public discussions, but no compact emerged satisfactory to the several states. Idaho and Montana did not want a commission with powers to act; Oregon and Washington rejected drafts submitted to the legislatures in 1963–1964 because they were "toothless," and their delegates withdrew from the organization. According to the *Oregonian*, August 28, 1965:

> The obvious need, if upper basin states and politics in Oregon and Washington are chiefly motivated by fear of federal invasion, is to set up a compact, ratified by Congress, with revenue bond and other financing and capability of doing the numerous jobs itself. These purposes could include power generation, distribution of water including diversion to the Southwest, controlling pollution and regulating all land uses in the greater interest of the Northwest public. The concept obviously is too big for our junior statesmen to grasp. So, while they fulminate, the federal government perforce must step in to do what needs to be done.

All this suggests that planning—statewide, interregional, and international—is inherent in the Columbia River's role in the twentieth century economy.

These issues have cut across party lines locally as well as in national affairs. The benefits of the New Deal and hydroelectric power issues were not identified simply with Democratic votes; Republican McNary supported river development, and Guy Cordon, who took McNary's place in the Senate, labored energetically to secure federal appropriations for transmission lines that would round out the Bonneville power system and feed into private systems. It was characteristic of the Oregon Republican Party to accommodate moderately to changing needs.

Thus the Republicans had gained in strength while the Democrats progressively weakened until during the 1940s Oregon was, as we pointed out earlier, almost a one-party state. By 1952 Richard L. Neuberger, one of the few Democrats in the legislature, referred to himself and his legislator wife as the "poor relations" of Oregon politics, pointed out as curiosities to visitors in the galleries. It was noteworthy that in four years (1938–1942) the number of Democrats in the state Senate dropped from twelve to three; in the House of Representatives, from thirty-eight to nine. Oregonians had tried the Democracy under exceptional conditions and felt that Democratic control savored of labor unions, pensioners, and the heavy hand of federal bureaucracy. The Republican tradition was strong and Oregon found it easy to return to it.

Still, it was hardly accurate to call Oregon a one-party state; its politics were marked by too much independence exercised both by the voters and by their representatives. Wayne Morse, elected to the Senate as a Republican in 1944, was a law unto himself and finally bolted the party eight years later. Although its organization left much to be desired, the Democratic Party had the strength of votes. In 1950 the number of registered Democrats exceeded the Republicans by some 6000. Two years later, despite the Eisenhower victory, Democratic registrations dropped below the Republican by only a few thousands (see Graph X, p. 625). Neuberger was hardly to be called a poor relation when his Democratic supporters were strong enough to send him to the United States Senate, and Edith Green to the House in 1954. Thus the balance of political forces was more even than might at first appear. Oregon's tradition was Republican, but its Republicanism was not reactionary.

THE ECONOMIC GROWTH

Future historians writing of the Pacific Northwest will probably use the war decade of the forties as the turning point—or, to use Walter Rostow's figure of speech, the "take-off"—in the development of the region's economy.[13] How they will explain it will depend upon definitions of "underdeveloped" and "mature" economies and the significance attached to certain factors of growth: increase in population; the number of production workers; the relation of imports and exports to local purchasing power and standards of living to local and interregional markets; and the development of secondary and other levels of manufacture.

[13] Walter Rostow, "The Take-Off into Self-Sustained Growth," *Economic Journal*, March 1956; *The Stages of Economic Growth* (1960); and for criticisms of the theory, *The Economics of Take-Off into Sustained Growth*, W. Rostow, ed. (1963).

539

In the late sixties, the Pacific Northwest demonstrates some peculiar features. The region as a whole is still, theoretically, "underdeveloped." Yet, since the war the development in Oregon and Washington metallurgical and chemical industries and manufacture of electronic appliances and aircraft—which tend to balance exports against imports—suggests an approach to a "mature" economy. So, too, do value added by manufacture, the relatively high income level, and the growth rate of manufacturing employment.

TABLE VI

*Percent of Increase in Manufacturing Employment
for Selected Years*

	1955–1956	1958–1965
United States	6	12.9
California	24	14.5
Oregon	5	12.1
Washington	10	4.0

Source : From "Table of Employment in Manufacturing Employment," compiled by Oregon State Division of Planning and Development.

Between 1958 and 1965 the rate of growth for California and Washington temporarily declined as the production of war industries tapered off. Washington's prosperity has largely depended upon government contracts for aircraft, missiles, and spacecraft produced chiefly in the Puget Sound area, upon supplying military establishments in Alaska, and upon military bases and operations. The state has tended toward specialized industrial development which is affected, for better or worse, by government policies in war preparations and by outer-space ventures. The federal payroll for civilian and military employees alone was $601,000,000 in 1964. Oregon incomes deriving from federal payrolls totalled $190,000,000 (see Table X, p. 610).

Oregon's rate of growth, measured in terms of manufacturing employment, more than doubled between 1958 and 1965. The state's industrial growth has come about in diversified production, not only in the development of secondary manufactures from forest products, but also in rapidly growing new industries unrelated to basic raw resources. Locally founded industries such as Tektronix, which manufactures such electronic instruments as cathode ray oscilloscopes and auxiliary accessories, had sales of $75,000,000 in 1964; Sawyer's Incorporated, a photo industry, and Omark Industries' saw-chains, fasteners, and cutters, are multi-million dollar industries selling in worldwide markets. These are relatively small operations compared with Boeing's $2 billion contract for commercial jets; but the expansion of diversified small and middle-size enterprises in Oregon has been described as "regionally and nationally exceptional."

Oregon's situation may demonstrate the thesis that the area's

> . . . growth depends not so much upon whether exports are concentrated in broad groups such as "primary products" or "industrial products," but upon the particular types of products from either or both groups, and upon the region's competitive position vis-a-vis other regions in supplying the particular products.[14]

In 1945, opinions differed as to the economic future of the Pacific Northwest, but there was general agreement that resource development was still an imperative. Emphasis upon management that included state and federal, private and public bodies gave a new importance to endeavors that had been going on, not too successfully, for several decades. In the sixties, the necessity for action becomes more evident if consideration is given to the characteristics of regional "product-mix." The resources of water and waterpower, forest and soil, remain important factors of the region's economy and of its future prosperity. In the following chapter we examine further efforts to preserve and to utilize some of these resources.

[14] Richard L. Pfister, "External Trade and Regional Growth; a Case Study of the Pacific Northwest," in *Regional Development and Planning: A Reader*, John Friedmann and William Alonzo, eds. (1964), 294.

CHAPTER
THIRTY-TWO

Timber and Fisheries in a Regional Economy

THE INHABITANTS of the Pacific Northwest had exploited the resources of the land and sea with little thought for the future. It was hardly noted, for example, that in 1908 to keep the mills of Portland alone in operation eighty acres of forest had to be cut every twenty-four hours. But in those early years of the century an articulate few, led by Gifford Pinchot, a professional forester, raised their voices to point out the probable effects of depletion on the national economy.

THE EARLY CONSERVATION MOVEMENT

Standing timber remaining in the nation was estimated at 2500 billion board feet of which 100 billion were annually cut or destroyed by fire or disease. Since the yearly growth rate of new forest was at best only 40 billion feet, simple arithmetic indicated that the supply would be exhausted within a single generation. Assuming the problem was a relatively simple one of "saving" the forests, conservationists proposed a simple solution—the creation of national forest reserves in the public domain. When Theodore Roosevelt, by executive order, swept

542

150,000,000 acres into national reserves and placed Pinchot in charge of them as chief of the Forest Service, a great howl went up from the Far West. By Roosevelt's dictum, five-sevenths of Idaho's standing timber, one-fourth of Oregon's and slightly over one-fifth of Washington's was believed to be "locked up" forever.

Westerners did not accept the conservationists' gloomy predictions. Using different figures and a different rationale, they estimated forest stands at 1500 billion feet and the annual cut at little more than five billion. The regional economy demanded expansion of the industry. To "lock up" this essential resource was to constrict the region in an economic straitjacket, and furthermore it was an abuse of federal power and an assault on the states' rights. Erastus Brainerd of the Seattle *Post Intelligencer* protested

> . . . the recent abuses of power have grown to the point that there will be bitter revolt against the entire policy of forest reserves and an appeal to Congress to repeal all of the laws on the subject. The growth of such a great state as Washington can no longer be hampered, . . . to please a few dilettante experimentalists, however well intentioned and patriotic in purpose they may be.

The Washington legislature let its anguish be known, and Oregon's Senator Charles Fulton, long a friend of lumber interests, tacked on to the Forest Service appropriation bill (1907) a rider stipulating that in the future no forest reserves should be created in western states except by act of Congress.

While the populace generally appeared to approve the idea of conservation in theory, problems of practice rested with state and federal administration. For example, state land commissioners were usually more concerned with the administration and sale of public lands than with the forests on them. Legislation commonly had to do with taxation of private timber holdings and requirements and immunities extended to lumber companies. None of the Northwest states had a state forester or a code of laws spelling out a long-range forest policy. Only through institutions of higher learning did the states encourage systematic studies of lumbering and forestry. Washington launched its School of Forestry (1907) at the University, and Oregon set up a school at the State College; but while these bodies carried on studies of the industry and increased understanding of the complexities of conservation and the industry's administrative and economic problems, they had little direct influence on state practices.

In one area, the states early assumed a measure of responsibility for timberlands. Fire, roaring with frightening speed through pine and fir country, had scorched and ravished the land even before settlement.

Charles E. Laughton, Washington's first lieutenant governor (1889–1893), termed fire "the most insidious enemy we have to contend with." During the dry summer months the forest jungle became, in Stewart Holbrook's phrase, "the biggest box of tinder on earth." Whatever the source of the spark—lightning, a careless logger's match, or a locomotive smokestack—the result was a holocaust that brought desolation and often death.

1902 was the year of the Yacolt Burn in Lewis County—a raging fire that devastated 700,000 acres of timber, killed thirty-five people, wiped out a score of villages, left farmers and stump ranchers destitute and saw and shingle mills in ashes, and whose blaze formed a mighty torch visible from Bellingham to Eugene. That year, fire losses in Oregon and Washington were estimated at $12,767,000.

Within a few years thereafter the Northwest states established a system of fire wardens, and private lumber companies organized their own fire-fighting crews. In 1908 a group of larger timber owners formed the Washington Forest Fire Association, assessed themselves a penny an acre, and kept some eighty men in the field throughout the dry season. A cautious partnership between state and industry was not unnatural in this case, for common action was clearly advantageous and a fire-fighting program involved no controversy over public and private rights. Furthermore, the pattern of land ownership, resembling a great checkerboard with state and federal lands interlaced in alternate sections with private holdings, made it obvious that only a cooperative effort could be efficient. Working relationships were further improved when federal funds for fire protection were allocated to the states under the Weeks Act (1911). The amounts were small—$10,000 each to Washington and Oregon, and $10,500 to Idaho and Montana—and were available on a matching basis on the assumption that for every federal dollar allocated, a conservative estimate of three to five dollars would be spent from state or private funds. (In 1917 the United States Forest Service experts estimated that costs of fire protection ranged from 1/10 of a cent to 1/3 of a cent per thousand board feet.) The Oregon legislature, impelled by Governor West and public opinion, in 1913 passed a compulsory fire patrol law, "the capstone of a triple alliance" of state, federal, and private timber owners. At the same time a beginning, though a small one, was made in reforestation of state-owned lands by sowing seed and planting cutover areas. Idaho made the best showing, with more than 10,000 acres reforested in 1913; Oregon rehabilitated over 8000 and Washington nearly 3000 acres. The record was modest, but it gave at least token recognition to the task to be done.

State forests were but a small fraction of the regional total (15.6

billion of a total of 1131.5 billion feet) and state forestry agencies were never more than frail reeds to lean upon. In the contest to determine what timberlands should be set aside, and to establish standards of good forest practice and sustained yield, Uncle Sam took the initiative. National forests and national park reserves were of such a scale as to constitute an important element in both protecting the timber supply and perpetuating the forest industries.

Because Uncle Sam was a powerful absentee landlord whose benevolence was by no means proved and might fairly be doubted, federal forest policies were viewed with alarm. However, the Forest Service record did not substantiate fears. In policies and regulations, high purpose was tempered with frank recognition of the Service's limited powers and the realities of the national as well as local demands. The national forests were not "locked up." Whenever there was a real demand for lumber, reserve stumpage was offered for sale at fair minimum prices, the quantity and variety depending on the market and offering from private forests. In 1910, 574,000,000 feet of stumpage was sold from the national forests of the Northwest, of which two-thirds was cut, representing about 7 percent of the total cut for the year. In 1913 several large contracts allowed private purchasers to cut over a period of twenty-two years at prices adjusted every five years to meet market conditions.

THE FOREST SERVICE PROGRAMS

In setting up conditions for cutting on reserves, the Forest Service demonstrated its concern for reforestation and devised a practical and flexible approach to the problem, which was recommended for private operators as well. For example, Douglas fir forests grow in stands of uniform size, and in the natural state destroy themselves because the mature trees shut out the light which would permit the seedlings to grow. Hence the Service first required clean cutting in which nursery-grown stock could be planted. Stocks of seedlings were raised in nurseries at Pocatello, Helena, and at Snoqualmie, their annual capacity reaching 10,000,000 plants in 1910. However, the Service also discovered that if clean or strip cutting were used only in small tracts and seed trees left on each tract, then natural reproduction would take place. Thus a combination of planned cutting and replanting could make the forests a permanent resource to be farmed over the centuries.

The Forest Service program was widely publicized. Foresters and rangers became a corps of educators who did much to influence public opinion in the areas to which they were assigned. These men identified themselves with the region, and the Forest Service policy of decentralizing the administration of the reserves served to relieve local resentment against the "absentee landlord."[1]

By 1917 problems of the lumber industry and of forest policy had been well explored, but a full meeting of minds between foresters and lumbermen had by no means been reached. Only a few private operators paid more than lip service to principles of forest management. Most approved it insofar as government policies encouraged fire protection and curtailment of logging, which sometimes helped to support prices. Some were reassured when they realized that national forests relieved them of the burden of maintaining a future timber supply, while providing them with stumpage for current needs. Some of the largest companies made only token gestures toward conforming to good management practices; others condemned them and, inveighing against government interference, went on to strip the lands and leave them unplanted to erosion and economic waste.

Demand for timber after World War I superseded any demand for forest management or approved cutting practices. Federal reports documented depletion with impressive statistics. The nation as a whole, it appeared, was using up its trees four times as fast as they were growing. In the Pacific Northwest privately owned forests were being cut at an alarming rate. Yet the lumber industry had little incentive to curtail production or to cut on a scientific basis when the margin of profit was narrow and uncertain. Fred Ames of the Forest Service admitted that sound forest policy would appeal to the lumbermen only when it would pay.

While progress in private forestry was extremely slow during the 1920s, the decade was nevertheless important, for a program of cooperation between government agencies and the lumber industry was now being outlined in federal and state legislation. The idea of mutual interest and common responsibility was acknowledged more readily when the alternative was regulation by law. Cooperation as against governmental control was argued at length in Congress. Conservationists of the Pinchot school urged strict regulations under federal law to limit the cut of timber on private lands as well as in national forests. There was likewise a disposition to have the government purchase cutover lands, rehabilitate them, and set them up as reserves.

---

[1] Charles McKinley, *Uncle Sam in the Pacific Northwest*, chap. VII; Thornton T. Munger "Recollections of My Thirty-Eight Years in the Forest Service, 1908–1946," *Timberlines*, U.S. Forest Service, December 1942.

Such proposals came from strong critics of the industry for its disregard of its role in the economy and who, from general conviction, felt that the answer to the problem lay in the direct exercise of federal authority. However, these views did not prevail. The mood of the postwar years was similar to that after the Civil War: speculative, devoted to laissez-faire, and politically attached to the status quo.

COOPERATION IN FOREST PRACTICES

On the other hand, prominent western leaders, William B. Greeley and Fred Ames of the Forest Service, professors Fred R. Fairchild and Burt Kirkland, and lumbermen like George Long, encouraged new attitudes toward federal and private cooperation in the management of forests and in solving some of the problems of the industry such as taxation and marketing. Greeley, for example, maintained that national forests should serve "as a governor of the industrial machine which manufactures and distributes forest products by maintaining not only competitive but stable conditions in the lumber trade." Public interest demanded that both monopoly and wasteful overproduction be avoided. Conservation and long-range logging practices would not stifle enterprise but sustain it. Oregon Senator Charles McNary was notably influenced by these views as he was by his background in Oregon where conservation and cooperation among state and federal agencies and private and public interests had long been urged if not explicitly adopted.

According to a recent study, Oregon occupied a unique role in providing leadership for this movement toward cooperation in its pioneer days. Of twenty-five leaders in the movement, seventeen were residents of the Willamette Valley from which came the earliest plans for cooperation:

> [John] Waldo's plan of 1889 for federal-state partnership in the management of the timber lands of the Cascade Range: [John] Minto's numerous and original ideas on resource management, based on private self-interest aided by state and national supervision, and foreshadowing closely the tree-farm idea of the present time; Chamberlain's "spirit of compromise and patriotism" which enabled the Democratic governor to get through the Republican legislature a state fire law drafted by a Forest Service employee; the defense by Joseph Teal for the lumber industry and by Oswald West for the state governments and federal policies against states' rights groups. This

547

tradition of moderation and accommodation was typical of the conservation movement in the Pacific Northwest.[2]

In the Clarke-McNary Act (1924) Congress wrote the principle of cooperation into every paragraph. The Secretary of Agriculture was authorized to cooperate with state officials or other suitable agencies to recommend systems of fire protection for "the continuous production of timber" on suitable lands. He was also to cooperate with the states to provide tree seeds and plantings and to give aid in managing woodlots. Other provisions looked toward the purchase of cutover lands and the acquisition of other forest lands by mutual agreement with the owner "to insure future timber supplies." The Knutson-Vandenberg Act (1930) expanded the tree-planting program in national forests and provided that purchasers of timber from these reserves could be required to pay part of the cost of clearing and planting. Washington and Oregon also passed state forest codes which, unfortunately lacking provisions for rigorous enforcement, required operators to burn slashing and to leave cutover lands in condition for re-seeding.

The next few years saw noteworthy improvement in fire protection and taxation, and in forestry experimentation. Federal appropriations for fire fighting were considerably increased, as were state appropriations and industry contributions. These were not always sufficient, however. For example, assuming that weather conditions in the Coast Range would provide some protection against holocaust, private operators were not prepared to fight the fire that broke out in Tillamook County on August 14, 1933. Out of control, flames swept over 311,000 acres (270,000 acres in twenty-four hours) containing a stand of 12.5 billion feet of mature Douglas fir, and devastated the already depressed economy of Tillamook County.

The industry's degree of participation in reform programs was affected by good times and bad. During prosperous years, eagerness for maximum profits often led to disregard of both laws and cooperative agreements; during hard times, expenses were cost across the board, and inevitably, state tax laws were attacked.

The question of tax revision was brought before the state legislatures, in Washington by Governor Roland Hartley and in Oregon by Governor Oswald West, and new tax laws were adopted. By their provisions a low annual assessment on forest lands was combined

---

[2] Lawrence Rakestraw, "Before McNary; The Northwest Conservationists, 1889–1913," *PNQ*, April 1960, 56; "Uncle Sam's Forest Reserves," *PNQ*, October 1953; "The West, States' Rights and Conservation," *PNQ*, July 1957; Elmo R. Richardson, "Conservation as a Political Issue; The Western Progressives' Dilemma, 1909–1912," *PNQ*, April 1959.

with a yield tax amounting to 12.5 percent of the value of the timber. By levying the yield tax only as the lands brought returns, the state encouraged landowners to undertake long-term plans for conservation and reforestation. However, the low annual assessment worked to the disadvantage of the industry, especially in depression periods. The timber tax, in 1936, averaged about two cents per thousand board feet on standing timber. In heavily forested Douglas fir country, this amounted to about 70 cents an acre, and was a basic revenue source for state and counties. To keep revenues from diminishing, the tax was increased as stands of timber were depleted; thus on depleted forest lands, owners paid three to four dollars per acre. Under these conditions, operators were understandably antagonistic to laws which placed further burdens on them.

The measures with which we have been concerned thus far had mainly to do with protection and replacement of forests, and avoided the more controversial problem of establishing a long-range balance between timber cut and rate of forest growth. The McSweeney-McNary Act (1928) was an approach to this problem, authorizing forest experiment stations and research programs to determine ways and means of balancing a timber budget of growth and cut in a sustained yield program. The principle underlying the Act was cooperation between public agencies and private owners.

Cooperation was a two-way street. Greeley later recalled that when a lumberman applied to cut trees from national forests the long-term contract was approved on condition that the applicant adopt for his own timberlands the practices enforced in the national forests. During the dark days of the Depression the national lumber code, drawn up in 1934 for the National Recovery Administration, embodied much the same kind of bargain. The industry wanted price increases and was willing to accept wage and hour standards along with them; its representatives also agreed to the inclusion of Article X which pledged operating companies to put into effect "practicable measures" of good forestry to protect against fire, prevent damage to young trees, and provide for restocking cutover areas. Cooperation was to be reciprocal and carried obligations for governmental agencies as well. When the NRA was declared unconstitutional and the code lost legal authority, the industry volunteered to continue its main provisions as an undertaking in industrial self-government. Skeptics were doubtful that good intentions would survive any strain.

When it came to fixing limits on the amount of lumber to be put on the market, the industry took the initiative in seeking cooperation. Now it was distrustful of the Forest Service, not because it locked up timber, but because it made too much available. When the industry was beset by overproduction and falling prices even before the Great Depression had set in, David T. Mason and Carl M. Stevens, consulting foresters in Portland, in 1927, proposed to use the idea of "sustained yield" to take from the market federal timber which, if sold at auction according to prevailing practice, threatened to depress prices further.

Farming the Forests: Sustained Yield

The conception of sustained yield had been advanced earlier. Burt P. Kirkland, in an article entitled "Continuous Forest Production of Privately Owned Timberlands in the Solution of the Economic Difficulties of the Lumber Industry," (*Journal of Forestry*, XV, 1917), had outlined its principal features. In essence, this was a matter of farming the forests. To be properly preserved, they should not only be protected but also harvested as a crop in such a manner that the cut did not exceed growth, with new stock continuously planted and protected for future harvesting.

The Mason plan called for the establishment of sustained yield units, each a large tract of timber, part of which was privately owned and part in reserves. For each unit, a cutting schedule was calculated for a period of forty years or more, the time that existing timber would last at the going rate of cutting. Such a plan would not require curtailment of cutting below the current level, but would hold back reserves until some time safely in the future when they could be drawn upon without upsetting prices. Thus the supply would be stabilized. The plan assumed, however, commitments on the part of the Forest Service to make timber available as needed and self-interest on the part of the stronger companies that would lead them to endorse the plan.[3]

The program was tested in an application to the Oregon and California Railroad revested lands, 3,000,000 acres including some of the best timberlands in Oregon. When the federal government finally recaptured this grant from the Southern Pacific in 1917, Congress had provided for its administration under the Bureau of Land Management and under stipulated conditions. The law required that this timber be sold as applied for at current market prices. Mason, recognizing that this was a threat to prices, actively promoted legislation (1937) which modified the terms of administration and applied to the

---

[3] David T. Mason, "Sustained Yield as a Remedy for Overproduction," *West Coast Lumberman*, October 1, 1927; *Forests for the Future: the story of Sustained Yield as Told in the Diaries and Papers of David T. Mason, 1907–1950*, Rodney C. Loehr, ed. (1952).

lands the principles of sustained yield "for the purpose of providing a permanent source of timber supply, protecting watersheds, regulating stream flow, and contributing to the economic stability of local communities and industries, and providing recreational facilities." Thus some social benefits were written into an economic document. In setting up units, the Department of the Interior was directed to recognize the need for a permanent source of raw materials to support dependent communities, and to give "due consideration" to established lumbering operations. This assumed, in effect, that a strong company, assured of a source of supply from public forests through long-term contracts, could stabilize its operations, add to its investments in mill facilities, and adopt a reforestation program that might support a town indefinitely.

The annual cut was limited to 500,000,000 board feet or as much of that total as could be sold at reasonable prices on a normal market. But timber sales from a forest unit were to be limited to its reproductive capacity and the same principle was to be applied to the whole grant as soon as the annual growth rate was determined. Cooperative agreements could be negotiated with federal or state agencies and with private forest owners and operating companies to put the program into effect on lands not administered directly by the Department of the Interior. Thus the main features of the Mason plan were written comprehensively into law for the Oregon area.

In 1944 Congress extended the sustained yield plan from Oregon to other states by further general legislation. Under individual agreements, sustained yield units could be set up on public and private lands, with coordinated management and a single schedule for havesting and reforesting. In situations where a particular community depended upon wood-processing industries, sustained yield units could be established wholly from federal timberlands harvested, without competitive bidding, for the community benefit. Here the cut was not necessarily pledged to a single company, though operators who supplied local industries were preferred. Through special agreement timber properties administered by state or local agencies could be included in either type of unit.

Despite the broad terms of the 1944 law, few new units were actually set up. Forest Service policy stipulated that at least 20 percent of salable timber assigned to a unit should be owned by private cooperators. So long as prices remained high, landowners were reluctant to accept restrictions entailed by long-range commitment. Consequently, few applications were submitted. In 1946 the Forest Service and the Simpson Logging Company of Shelton, Washington, agreed

551

to a 100-year plan covering approximately 270,000 acres on the Olympic peninsula. Its terms obligated the company to practice fire and insect control and approved silviculture. In return, the Forest Service pledged for company use timber from the national forest up to 80 percent of the total stand in the unit. This agreement was designed as a model for future plans, but since its restraints applied at once while the benefits were deferred, the arrangement had limited appeal. In setting up federal units for dependent communities, the Forest Service again moved slowly. After prolonged negotiation, a plan was effected for the benefit of the Grays Harbor communities, but difficulties of administration and of determining the proper requirements of dependency were so great that the federal unit approach found little if any usefulness elsewhere.

The sustained yield unit law was born of a period of depression and was hardly suited to the problems of World War II and subsequent markets. The "s.y." agreements no longer served either the lumber industry's purpose or the conservationists'. The latter felt little enthusiasm for a partnership that pledged four trees in the national forest to one on private lands, and there was opposition to committing large tracts of national forest to any single timber company. Furthermore, the industry under boom conditions wanted more timber from the national forests and had no reason not to engage in competitive bargaining for it.

But conditions of prosperity actually did promote wider acceptance of an idea fundamental to the concept of sustained yield—the growing and harvesting of timber as a crop. Foresters had long realized that a distinctive feature of the Pacific Northwest's forests was their profuse and rapid reproduction. A clear cut slope, divested of its trees but relatively safe from fire and disease, would produce thick and flourishing "junior" forests in little more than twenty years. So with prosperity, the industry and the Service placed less emphasis upon limitations of cutting and greater emphasis upon efficient forest reproduction and use. Large companies hired foresters and gradually made logging more systematic and responsive to local conditions.

Lumbermen took pride in their accomplishments and advertised them widely. In 1941 the Clemons Tree Farm, near Elmo and Montesano, initiated a movement that spread to thirty-six states. By 1954, Washington had more than 200 tree farms; 129 in the Douglas fir country, 80 in the pine section, for a total of 3,000,000 acres. Weyerhaeuser found the farms to be good business as well as good public relations and set the pace for the industry.[4]

[4] Richard Lillard, "Timber King," *The Pacific Spectator*, Winter 1947.

By mid-century, the industry had come to accept public ownership and administration of timberlands as practiced by the Forest Service and on some of the municipal watersheds. However, the point was vigorously urged that timberlands should, so far as possible, be in private hands. It was argued that public ownership took land off tax rolls, and though the government made payments in lieu of taxes to counties in which national forests were located, this objection was never stilled. It was voiced most loudly and persistently when large tracts of timber were set aside in national parks where logging policies were more restrictive than in national forests. Congressman Mon Wallgren's 1938 bill establishing Olympic National Park of nearly 1,000,-000 acres was strenuously opposed not only by the industry but by the Washington State Planning Council as well.

On the other hand, the public was not assured that the industry had proved its good intentions so far as forest management was concerned. Exploitation still threatened the forests, and the nation at large looked to federal agencies as a sure safeguard of the region's vital resources. However, changes in demand for forest products and within the industry itself were doing what legislation could only attempt. Technological changes made possible the full utilization of every log, and new processes created products in which not only mill waste but also forest-burn debris and lodge pole pine, formerly considered worthless, could be used.

CHANGES IN THE FOREST INDUSTRIES

At one time the forest industry meant the manufacture of lumber, rough or planed. Its by-products were waste: mountains of sawdust and slab that were clouds of smoke by day and pillars of fire by night. In 1925, the Northwest began to manufacture paper and pulp, which has followed historically in the wake of a large and well-established lumber industry. By 1960, pulp and paper production stood second to lumber in terms of value added and third in numbers of persons employed. Production of veneer, third most important by-product of the industry; of fibre-boards and pressed wood products, even chemical by-products, have diversified the lumber industry and each has reinforced the argument for efficient forest farming. An interesting consequence of these changes has been the recovery of millions of board feet of wood, once thought to be irrecoverable waste, from the great Tillamook Burn. Salvage has permitted reforestation and replanting. In 1966, in accessible parts of the Burn, one sees only a few denuded spars, standing out above the thick new forest growth like ghosts to remind the traveler of the holocaust.

Another evidence of change in the industry is the gradual disappearance of the small "gyppo" outfit and the concentration of the forest product industry in the hands of large producers. Weyerhaeuser and Georgia Pacific capital resources enable them to develop, through technology and research, new uses for wood products and, through coordination of production, to survive price fluctuations. The large producers tend to spread out their lumber operations in small mills, which feed chips and sawdust to their pulp and paper mills, so that concentration of the industry has in some measure led to decentralization, with the result that more villages have become mill towns and derive support from the forests.

Any consideration of the lumber industry today must include the effects that population growth has had on the demands for construction and building materials. According to some estimates, the "Westward Tilt" that pulls population to the Pacific Coast promises to expand the industry in the next forty years by more than 80 percent of its present production. Thus lumbering has developed from a primary extractive process to a complex of primary manufactures to which secondary wood product industries are attached; thus forest resources have become an integral part of the industrialization of the Pacific Northwest.

NORTH PACIFIC FISHERIES

The development of logging and lumbering into a complex industry producing a wide range of manufactured products provides a sharp contrast to fishing, which remains largely a primary extractive industry, its by-products limited to fertilizers and fish extracts. However, the industry is important and the threat of depletion has led to interesting instances of ingenious rehabilitation and interstate and international cooperation.

Before World War I, William F. Thompson showed that while the total catch of halibut had increased between 1907 and 1913, the returns per skate were so much less that fishermen were forced to fish more intensively and to range farther north into Alaska waters. Thompson's views were sustained in testimony given at the American-Canadian Fisheries Conference (1918) where it was generally agreed that both a closed season and a thorough study of the life history and habits of the halibut species were necessary. But since fishing was done outside the limits of territorial jurisdiction, any effective controls had to be exercised jointly by the United States and Canada.

A halibut fisheries treaty negotiated in 1922 set a closed season from November to February and authorized a special international commission to study the halibut population on the various banks and to recommend means for preservation and development of the industry. The commission's study showed that depletion was caused by increasingly intensive fishing. It therefore recommended that fishing boats be licensed and that the total annual catch be reduced to a point where yield could be stabilized, the use of certain kinds of gear prohibited, the existing closed season extended, and areas populated by immature fish closed altogether. These recommendations were incorporated in a new treaty (1930) and the International Fisheries Commission was transformed from a research body into a full-fledged regulatory agency.

The program adopted was successful. In a short time the catch per skate increased 89 percent west of Cape Spencer and 77 percent south of the cape. The initial quota of 46,000,000 pounds was raised by 2,000,000 in 1938 and by 6,000,000 pounds more in 1940.

Although regulations were set and administered by the International Fisheries Commission, the fishing industry was consulted at each step. With commission approval boat owners and fishermen's unions set up the Halibut Product Board (1932) to govern individual boat operations over the whole fishing area and to stabilize prices throughout the year by means of "orderly marketing." Under auspices of the Board, representatives of Canadian and American halibut fishers annually negotiate a "Halibut Curtailment Program."

The rehabilitation of salmon runs in the Columbia and Fraser rivers presented problems no less pressing than those of the halibut fisheries. Programs of research and experimentation were equally demanding, particularly the tracing of the long migrations which carried salmon from the streams where they were spawned to the open sea and back again. Most perplexing of all, practical solutions were difficult to plan and execute because of the conflicts of interests not only between Canadian and American fishermen but also between fishermen who would keep the rivers open and engineers who would dam them for purposes of irrigation, flood control, or power development.

Experts repeatedly urged Canadian-American action in restocking the Fraser River system, potentially the best sockeye river in the world. An international convention (1930) set up a joint commission to control border fisheries, setting quota catches to be divided equally between the nationals. At the time Americans were taking more fish than the specified limit for both Americans and Canadians, and the Senate did not act upon the convention. During the next few years, however, Americans lost their competitive advantage and were more amenable to controls. Supplementary articles protecting the rights of Washington fishermen were drawn and thereafter the Fraser River Sockeye Salmon Treaty of 1930 was ratified, opening the way at last to rehabilitation of the Fraser salmon streams. Under the direction of a joint commission, biologists and engineers determined the kind of regulations needed to protect the salmon runs and to improve their access to spawning streams.

The most urgent problem was removal of a mass of rock blasted into Hell's Gate Gorge during railroad construction in 1913. This had been a formidable barrier to the migrating sockeye, and until the fish channels were reopened other measures of rehabilitation were of little value. A three-year (1945–1948), $1,500,000 project removed some rock from the main stream to allow the fish a normal run, and at other places ladders and tunnels provided means for them to bypass or go through the obstacles. Within three years, the increased catch repaid ten times the cost of improving the river. In 1953 the Fraser yielded 4,000,000 sockeye worth $10,000,000, the largest catch since 1917. On the strength of this record the State of Washington embarked upon an elaborate program of fishways and stream improvement designed to rehabilitate its salmon streams in the same manner.

The Columbia River, like the Fraser, was one of the great salmon streams of North America. Yet its productivity was seriously threatened by intensive fishing, by construction of hydroelectric and irrigation dams, and by neglect of the smaller tributaries which in many instances were so clogged with brush and other obstructions that salmon could no longer spawn in them.

Measures designed to insure adequate escapement of fish were more than ordinarily complicated, since the lower Columbia was a boundary between Oregon and Washington and the two states did not agree on laws and regulations. In 1910, the legislatures established a joint committee on fisheries to work for uniformity in policies. A few years later, 'with congressional approval they formed an interstate compact (1918) which established concurrent jurisdiction over the lower river. Unfortunately the compact failed in its purpose. In test cases the courts ruled that despite common jurisdiction each state could still act independently in regulating its own citizens. Thus Oregon outlawed fish wheels in 1927; in Washington they were legal until 1935. That same year Washington prohibited fish pounds and fixed gear on its side of the river; but Oregon permitted their use on its river banks below the Cascade rapids.

The building of dams on the Columbia River created another problem. At Bonneville, McNary, and Rock Island dams, fish ladders and elevators enabled salmon to proceed upstream. Grand Coulee Dam, however, could be neither scaled nor skirted, and more than a thousand miles above it had to be abandoned. The situation called for artificial propagation to shift runs to tributaries of the lower river. Adult fish were intercepted at Rock Island, their eggs stripped and fertilized, and the fry reared in pools at a large hatchery at Leavenworth on the Wenatchee River. Tank trucks then took the fingerlings to planting areas in tributaries that entered the Columbia below Grand Coulee. These fish returned to spawn in the streams in which they had been placed, and the stock of fish in the lesser streams was greatly multiplied to offset losses on the upper river.

Artificial propagation has required continuing and extensive research. The Oregon Fish Commission, for example, supported an Oregon State University program to develop from cannery scrap an inexpensive and efficient hatchery food that did not transmit fish diseases. The result was so encouraging in economy and in the quality and number of mature salmon returning to spawn that all sixteen of Oregon's hatcheries now use the wet pellet feed. At the University of Washington, an experiment in selective breeding and hybridization has produced larger Chinook that appear somewhat resistant to water pollution and that return to spawn in two or three years instead of the customary four.[5]

The growing importance of the lower tributaries led to still other measures of conservation, some undertaken by the individual states, others cooperatively. But here too were legal snags. The Washington legislature in 1949 declared the lower Columbia watershed a sanctuary for the special purpose of building up native stocks. Tacoma, having a rapidly expanding municipally owned power system, contested the provisions of this law since it had applied to the Federal Power Commission for permission to build a hydroelectric power dam on the Cowlitz River. Federal, state, and municipal authorities came into conflict on the issue of fish versus kilowatts. The FPC gave Tacoma permission to build, and construction started on Mayfield Dam in 1955; the state instituted court action on behalf of the state fisheries program, and in 1958 the supreme court ruled against it. A second dam, Mossy Rock, was under construction in 1965; but a strenuous program of planting fish in waters below the dams promises some measure of compensation for the loss of the last large spawning stream in the watershed.

[5] Murray Morgan, "College Bred Fish for Man's Delight," *Harper's Magazine*, July 1965.

The working relations of the state fishery departments of Washington and Oregon with the United States Fish and Wildlife Survey were far happier. In 1948 the three agencies entered into a cooperative, 20-year research and development plan. New hatcheries were built in the lower Columbia watershed, fishways were erected at obstruction points, and a comprehensive plan of stream clearance was undertaken. Experts estimated that with a sustained program of river improvement the Columbia River system could be made to yield annually nearly double the 28,000,000 pounds of fish currently produced.

With urban growth and industrial development, cooperation among state and local agencies, between states and federal government and among the states themselves, become increasingly necessary. Air pollution is a problem that transcends local solutions. Water pollution not only affects fish life but human life as well. Rapidly growing communities postpone building expensive sewage disposal plants. The inhabitants of Oregon's most heavily populated area have been slow to recognize and take steps to remedy pollution of the Willamette River. Industries vital to the region's economy, such as pulp and paper mills, use tremendous quantities of water. The $90,000,000 Crown-Zellerbach plant at Wauna (Oregon) when in full production will daily draw 44,000,000 gallons from the Columbia, and the effluent must be treated to remove primary waste. But as the number of such plants multiplies on both sides of the river, industries and states are faced with the necessity of full cooperation in safeguarding the quality of waters they mutually share. Pollution limits recreational as well as industrial uses of the waters. Only as the public becomes aware of its stake in the physical environment do political bodies tend to consider interagency and regional cooperation. Thus full and efficient utilization of the Pacific Northwest's natural resources appear to reinforce arguments for planning earlier demonstrated in the development of the region's hydroelectric power complex.

CHAPTER
THIRTY-THREE

Metropolitan Centers and People

IN THE PRECEDING several chapters we have been concerned with the economic resources of the region. Here we will briefly consider the human resource, the people, and the environment in which they live in the 1960s.

During the 1950s immigration slowed down and natural increase accounted in considerable measure for Washington's 19.9 percent increase, Oregon's 16.3, and Idaho's 13.3 percent. By way of comparison, in the same interval the national increase was 18.8 percent and California's a noteworthy 100 percent. Slightly more than 50 percent of Washington's inhabitants had been born in the state; 54.2 percent of Idaho's population and 47.9 percent of Oregon's were native born. Historically the population of the Pacific Northwest had its roots in the Midwest and North Central states. The old pattern of migration was still evident, but increasing interchange within the region and between California and the more northerly states indicated that the movement now followed the dominant national pattern in which people tended to move to contiguous areas. About the same number of California-born were resident in Oregon and Washington in 1960; but for every Californian who moved to Oregon, two Oregonians moved to California. Among the top twenty states contributing to the latter's

559

growth, Oregon ranked sixteenth. Few Washingtonians moved to California, but for every nine who moved from Oregon to Washington, ten from the Evergreen state moved to Oregon. Utah continued to contribute more than any other state to Idaho's population.

The general composition of the regional population was native American, Protestant, and white. The foreign born in each state were less than one percent of its total population, and the largest number came from Canada. War industries attracted Negroes from the South in the forties and their number continued to grow in the next decade. In 1959 more than 40,000 were settled in Washington and 16,000 in Oregon. Their concentration in urban areas, (Oregon, 95.5 percent; in Washington, 85.4 percent) led to problems with which the inhabitants were not immediately prepared to cope, but by 1953 both states had antidiscrimination laws. In 1964 when de facto school segregation and minority discontent disturbed Portland, a citizens' biracial committee under chairman Judge Herbert Schwab recommended a plan of school improvements and "free attendance" options which appeared to relieve the situation insofar as schools were concerned. None of the Pacific Northwest states has experienced violent racial incidents.

Compared to southern Negroes whose median income was less than $2000, those employed in the Northwest enjoyed a measure of the high income which distinguished the region. (In studying Table VII one should bear in mind that the median income of all families in the United States was $5620.)

In 1946 a significant part of all personal incomes came from proprietorships, farm and business ownership, and from property holdings.[1] However, by 1960 five-sevenths of the incomes in Washington, half in Oregon, and eight-thirteenths in Idaho derived from wages. Of Idaho's employed, 20.8 percent earned less than $3000 a year and 10.5 percent more than $10,000; 15.3 percent of the employed in Washington and 17 percent in Oregon were in the low-income group and 16.6 and 13.9 respectively in the higher range. On the national level, 22 percent received $3000 or less, 10 percent $10,000 to $15,000, and four percent $15,000 and above.

The ratio of nonworker to worker in Idaho was 1.66; in Washington, 1.58; and in Oregon 1.54. Fifty to 55 percent of the labor force was employed 50 to 52 weeks a year, a larger percentage than before World War II when heavy dependence on lumbering and agriculture created high seasonal unemployment.

[1] M. Lee, "Appraisal of the Pacific Northwest," *Harvard Business Review*, May 1948.

TABLE VII

Median Family Incomes, White and Nonwhite, 1960

	Washington	Oregon	Idaho
White			
urban	6622	6322	5818
rural-urban	5642	5441	5046
rural-farm	5046	4817	4292
Nonwhite			
urban	5063	4540	3456
rural-urban	3686	4344	3162
rural-farm	3748	5864	4419

Source: Department of Commerce, Bureau of the Census, "Population Characteristics by States," 1960, vols. I, II, III.

The West in 1960 had about 50 percent fewer single men than in 1900, and the ratio between men and women narrowed to a closer approximation of the national ratio. The median age, while higher than in 1900, was lower than it had been in 1940 when the Pacific and Rocky Mountain states had the highest fertility (and lowest mortality) rate in the nation. Between 1950 and 1960 the number of five-to-nine year olds increased 70 percent in Washington and 79 percent in Oregon—statistics which sent school districts into flurries of school building and consequently to unwelcome tax rises to pay for all levels of education. Since 1900, the Far West (and the western North Central states) have had the lowest illiteracy rate in the nation. Idaho had the highest rate among the Pacific states (1.9) and Oregon shared with Nebraska the lowest rate (1.2) nationally. Urban illiteracy was less than one percent in all three states. Ninety-three percent of the fourteen-to-seventeen age group were in school, and for the population twenty-five years or older the median number of years of schooling was 11.8 in Oregon and 12.1 in Washington.

Graph II (p. 621) illustrates the national and regional trend toward urbanization since 1900. Until 1950, the Bureau of the Census automatically classified population concentrations of less than 2500 inhabitants as "rural places"; cities and unincorporated places with more than 2500 inhabitants were "urban places." By this definition (which for comparative purposes was used in Graph II) Washington in 1960 was 58.4 urban; Oregon, 53.9, and Idaho, 42.9 percent. In 1950 the Bureau changed the definition so that cities and unincorporated places of over 2500, densely settled urban fringes, and counties having no incorporated municipalities but with a density of 1500 persons or more to a square mile, were classified as urban. By this revised definition, Washington was 68.1 percent urban; Oregon, 62.2, and Idaho, 47.5.

Not density of population, but rather the degree of urbanization is the interesting phenomenon of contemporary America and of the Northwest. The United States is 69.9 percent urban, yet only 29 percent of its inhabitants live in cities of 100,000 or more; 42 percent live in aggregations of 20,000 or more. However, the modern city functions far beyond its corporate borders. Hence the Bureau of the Census defines as an "urbanized area" one in which there is a central city (or cities) of 50,000 inhabitants and a built-up urban fringe.

In addition to urbanized areas, the Bureau has a category for areas having major cities, satellite clusters, and contiguous related counties that are metropolitan in character. Such a unit—an "integrated functional unit of interdependent constituent cities, towns, villages, and even rural places"—is a Standard Metropolitan Statistical Area (SMSA).[2] There were 212 SMSAs in the United States in 1960; ten were in California and five in Oregon and Washington combined. Of Washington's 2,853,000 inhabitants, 1,800,945 live in SMSAs, as do 890,978 of Oregon's total of 1,768,687. Between 1950 and 1960 the population of Washington living in these areas increased 10.6 percent; Oregon's increase was 13.1.

Spokane is the center city of an SMSA confined to Spokane County, and Tacoma the center city for Pierce County. Others are the Seattle-Everett SMSA (King and Snohomish counties); the Portland, Oregon-Washington SMSA (Multnomah, Washington, and Clackamas counties in Oregon and Clark County, Washington); and Eugene, which is the center city for Lane County. Thus the metropolitan and urbanized areas of the Pacific Northwest, with the exception of Spokane (and Yakima which is an urbanized area but not yet an SMSA), are primarily concentrated on Puget Sound and in the Willamette Valley. The imagination is tempted to picture a future Northwest Megalopolis, a linear city stretching from north to south with hardly a break of rural character.

[2] United States Census, 1960, *Characteristics of the Population*, Vol. I; Summary, Part I, 31. The two criteria for metropolitan areas are: (1) at least 75 percent of the labor force of the county is engaged in nonagricultural work, or (2) 50 percent of the population is living in contiguous areas of at least 150 persons per square mile in an unbroken chain of minor civil divisions with such density radiating from the central city.

Metropolitan Centers and People

The components of the SMSA are integrated economically. But each metropolitan area is beset by problems of nonintegration which are universally called "problems of the fringe areas." For example, the Portland Tri-County complex (Multnomah, Clackamas, and Washington not including Clark County, Washington), in 1956 had three county governments, 23 municipal administrations, and 13 zoning districts; 49 water districts and 40 fire districts, 10 sanitary, 10 drainage, and 26 highway lighting districts; 133 school districts, one port district, one park and recreation and one water control district—a total of 310 independent units of local government with taxing powers. Indicative of both the growth of the urban fringe and the costs of providing facilities for them was the increase in tax levies between 1940 and 1956; those of county governments were up 127 percent; school districts, 452 percent; and other kinds, 270 percent.[3]

One solution for most of these problems is annexation with the center city or cities. In the Pacific Northwest cities have tended to look upon the fringes as burdens on their tax structure and the fringes wish to keep Suburbia independent of Metropolis. Portland had customarily remained neutral when suburban areas moved toward annexation, and only three percent of the city's population lives in annexed territory. However, the complexity of transportation, highway construction, refuse disposal, and water supply as well as the duplication of police and other governmental functions on county and city levels inexorably forces the residents of the Tri-Counties to some kind of cooperative action. Pressure from the state sanitary authority and public concern over water pollution has led to a Tri-County major sewage disposal system, an important step forward in meeting a common problem.

The municipality of Metropolitan Seattle, where 15 percent of the population lives in annexed territory, has managed to avoid legal controversy or the open warfare that so often harasses city and fringe governmental units. The metropolitan area has been enabled by law to provide and distribute water, develop rapid transit and refuse disposal systems, parks and recreation areas, and to set up an advisory planning board. But the voters approved only one metropolitan area service, the Seattle Metro sewage system encompassing 230 square miles, the city of Seattle, ten incorporated towns, and unincorporated King County. This undertaking suggests that Seattle has a modest degree of urban sophistication that some other cities of the region do not share.

[3] State of Oregon, Legislative Interim Committee on Local Government, *The Problems of the Urban Fringe: Portland Area* (July 1956), 10, 14.

THE PERSONALITIES OF THE CITIES

One could expand indefinitely on the statistical characteristics of population and environment. But people in their infinite variety, and cities in their individuality (which some critics claim is lacking) are more than numbers. According to a contemporary writer, "The modern city is not a social community. At best it is an association of different classes on an economic basis, at worst an agglomeration of human atoms."[4] No Northwestern city would admit to such a charge. Seattle has demonstrated in more than one instance a strong community spirit. It points with pride to its 1963 Exposition for which the community spent generously and was rewarded with financial success. The site chosen permitted utilization of the existing Armory, High School Memorial Stadium, and the Civic Auditorium which was remodeled to become the Opera House. The monumental verticality of the Space Needle dramatized the Fair theme—"Century 21"—and dominated the site, which is under continued development as a cultural center. The United States Science Pavilion, a serene and beautiful building designed by Seattle architect Minoru Yamasaki, has been leased to the city and continues as a science museum supported initially by the National Science Foundation and subsequently by funds from local government and private donors.

Unlike Seattle, which is in its own promotional vocabulary a "go-ahead" city, Portland moved in 1965 as slowly and deliberately as it did in 1865, and there remains considerable sentiment, even on the part of newcomers to "keep things as they are." The idea has been advanced that Portland is a community only in the sense that it is continuously involved in trying to arrive at consensus, which is the essence of community. In 1958, just about the time Seattle began to plan its Fair, Portland took the initiative in urging an Oregon Centennial Exposition for 1959–1960. Small appropriations from the state legislature dominated by upstate sentiments and alienated from the city, and much indecision as to whether the affair was to be predominantly "cultural" or "commercial" doomed the enterprise to the dimension of an overgrown county fair. The city gained no benefits in the way of permanent improvement.

Within the city itself, rival interests of the east and west sides of the Willamette River frustrate city planning and generate feuds. Two elections were necessary before a bare majority voted to build a Coliseum Sports and Recreation Center on the East Side, rather than at

[4] E. A. Gutkin, *Twilight of Cities* (1962), 28.

Delta Park or in an urban renewal area on the West Side. Whether the city should build a new stadium and where, or purchase and re-model an old and privately owned one, was still an unresolved to-do in 1965. In the 1940s the inhabitants voted for an urban renewal project in the northwest part of the city, but rejected a measure to put up the small funds for a federal grant. During a business recession in 1957 the voters approved a Portland Development Commission in hope that it would start projects to generate employment. Out of this came a major urban renewal project in the southwest part of the city. At the beginning of 1966, a bridge on the Willamette was suspended for months in mid-river while city, state, and county authorities and residential and business communities argued where the highway with which the bridge was to connect should be located. Seattle, on the other hand, without noticeable public protest, tunneled hills and cut a wide swath through a densely populated area for an express high-way, built double-deck ramps that march on columns of steel and concrete above the waterfront, and put a floating bridge of concrete on Lake Washington.

ARCHITECTURE AND THE ARTS

In both cities, the demands of urban life have changed the sky-lines. High-rise apartments, office buildings, and hotels have come late to Portland. So too have the sweeping parabolas and cloverleafs of concrete that speed traffic on and off bridges and freeways. But as with Spokane, Tacoma, Eugene, and Salem, an immense pride moves Portland residents to look upon their own as fairest of them all.

As the cities have expanded in a prosperous mood, public and pri-vate structures reflect the spirit of innovation and modernity. During the 1920s tradition dominated architectural design; stately churches lifted their spires high above the city streets. Residential architecture exhibited a variety of styles and designs; two-story cottages and "ramblers" were popular on Puget Sound. The one-story, eyebrowed frame box prevailed in Portland's new low-income developments; Tudor brick mansions, discreetly hidden behind high hedges and approached by winding roads through natural groves, appeared on Palatine Road and the high view points of the western hills. So far as there were trends, the twenties were not distinguished by originality. For the most part they witnessed a conformity to accepted designs and national tastes. But in some instances local works demonstrated talent. Morris Whitehouse and his associate, Herman Brookman, exe-

cuted the design for Temple Beth Israel. (1927), as handsome in monumental design as in minute detail, and William G. Purcell's First
Church of Christ Scientist (1926) brought the ideas of the Chicago
School to Portland. The firms of A. E. Doyle and Associates, Lawrence
and Holford, Whitehouse and Brookman, Sulton and Whitny, and
Fritsch and Aandahl created noble structures within the bounds of
tradition.

Beginning in the 1930s the region began to know modern architecture as the liveliest of the Seven Arts. Architects everywhere were
breaking away from the traditional, and in the Northwest, where old
ties were not so strong and the setting was provocative, they were
able to design with a maximum of freedom. An intermingling of influences from East and West took place. Pietro Belluschi, trained in
Rome and at Cornell, developed in Oregon a fresh interpretation of
architectural design and became one of the region's most prominent
spokesmen. Students of Walter Gropius went out from his classes
at Harvard to practice their profession in the Far West. Van Evera
Bailey and Richard Neutra influenced western schools which produced a generation of designers capable of holding their own in any
community, and some, like Welton Beckett and Minoru Yamasaki,
achieved distinction outside the Northwest. Others contributed richly
to the architecture of the region itself, and freed it to a considerable
extent from its dependence upon eastern firms.

The region gained greatly in stature and competence during and
after the thirties. Regional firms made a very real impact on the architecture of home and church, hotel and office building. Carl Gould's
plan for the Seattle Art Museum (1933), dignified and beautiful in its
external simplicity, admirably suited its specialized purposes. Belluschi's plan for the Portland Art Museum (1936) was marked by the
same qualities, and he won national recognition for churches that contributed significantly to the new trend in religious architecture. John
Yeon, in the A. R. Watzek house (1937), set an influential pattern for
construction that adapted local materials to the special opportunities offered by climate and landscape; so too have Walter Gordon's
W. W. Wessinger house (1950) and John Storr's Forest Products Building on the Centennial site. Belluschi's design for the Equitable Savings
and Loan Building (1948) seemed at the time to be the last word in
its application of modern principles, a reenforced concrete frame encased almost completely in glass. In 1951 Belluschi returned to the
East, to become dean of the School of Architecture and Planning
at Massachusetts Institute of Technology while associates continued
his practice in Portland. In 1965 he was appointed head of the School
of Architecture at the University of Oregon, to which the former head,

Walter Gordon, and Professors Marion Dean Ross and Lewis Crutcher had lent distinction.[5]

In Seattle, Naramore, Bain, Brady, and Johanson designed such major structures as the Public Safety Building, the Veterans' Administration Hospital, and the University of Washington Health Sciences Building. Young, Richardson, Carleton, and Detlie did the Children's Orthopedic Hospital. Paul Thiry and John Durham were known for their churches and George Wellington Stoddard for his dramatic football stadiums.

In the late 1950s and early 1960s, urban renewal replaced slum areas with stark high-rise apartment complexes, office buildings, and industrial plants whose mundane functions are hidden by novel and sometimes exciting exteriors accentuated by landscaping and tree-lined avenues. In every city shopping centers have multiplied and spreading urban fringes have stimulated architectual ingenuity. John Grant planned the Northgate Shopping Center (Seattle), a model grouping of retail stores that attracted wide attention. The Seattle firm of John Graham and Associates prepared the plans for Portland's multi-million dollar Lloyd Center, covering fifty-six acres, housing more than 100 stores and numerous offices, with an ice arena in the Mall and 8000 parking spaces of which 3500 were under roof. Seattle and Portland artists contributed architectural sculptures and embellishments. Jean Johanson's mosaic pool reflects George Tsuakawa's sculptured figures; Ray Jensen's delightful animal figures grace the Mall fountain, and Tom Hardy executed the delicate metal sculpture, "Flight of the Birds," which catches and reflects sunset lights in a water pool.

In Portland Ernest B. MacNaughton used his influence to encourage builders in the new mode and artists working with new techniques. A trained architect, MacNaughton had come to Portland from Harvard and Massachusetts Institute of Technology in 1905 and had become a key figure in property management, banking, and education. Never timid about asserting himself, he spoke firmly for innovation and sculptural design. Thus Frederic Littman's sculptures enhanced the clean features of the First National Bank at Salem and his low relief bust of Franklin D. Roosevelt memorialized the president at Lake Roosevelt, created by the impounded waters of Grand Coulee Dam. Tom Hardy's metal sculptures of Northwest flora and fauna form handsome screens for the first-floor windows of Portland State College's College Center Building and Manuel Izquierdo's sculptures are found in public and private buildings.

[5] Victor Steinbruck, *Seattle Cityscape* (1962); Marion D. Ross, *A Century of Architecture in Oregon, 1859–1959* (1959).

ABOVE. Game of Al-kol-lock (played by the Chualpay Indians of Fort Colville) *painted by Paul Kane, whose notes state that it was a popular game among the Indians all along the Columbia.*

ABOVE. *A sack race "event," Thunder Mountain, Idaho. New buildings in this new town were waiting to be finished, but why not take out a little time for fun?*

RIGHT. *The main street in an 1881 Montana frontier town boasts a music hall, an opera house and a billiard parlor.*

BELOW. *Indian canoe races, probably in the early 1900s.*

Recreations

The 1891 photographer titled this "A Bountiful Day in the Wallowas."

BELOW. *The Lewis and Clark Exposition, held in Portland, 1905, was conceived primarily to promote the city and the west. The same was true of Seattle's Alaska-Yukon-Pacific Exposition held in 1909.*

A latter-day Indian potlatch, Tatoosh, Washington. Originally an occasion for wealthy chieftains and nobles to build their prestige by giving away or destroying quantities of valuable property, including slaves, it has by this year of 1912 become a social affair, frowned upon by whites.

ABOVE. The Huckleberry Pickers *painted by C. S. Price, a fore-most contemproary artist of the northwest and of the country. The painting is owned by the Portland Museum of Art, one of the fine small museums of the United States and having a large collection of northwest painters.*

LEFT. Seattle Art Museum is *noteworthy for its beautiful archi-tecture and setting and its world-famous Oriental Collection.*

Fishermen can have almost any kind of dream come true: LEFT. *The cheerful turmoil of setting out for a day's salmon fishing off shore. Or* ABOVE. *The peace and privacy of trout-stream angling in Oregon's Collier State Park.*

ABOVE. *Nationally known Sun Valley, Idaho, in surprise summer dress. Six months from now it will be draped in its familiar snow, with its ski buff population.*

A favorite mountain sport everywhere in the Northwest.

The Space Needle is the proud landmark of the Century 21 Exposition, *1962, Seattle's very successful World's Fair.*

The decade of the 1920s did not encourage artists. Mark Tobey, who came west in 1920 and joined the faculty of the Cornish School in Seattle, later remarked that the mood of the day would turn any creative heart into a bloodless organ. Tobey did not find intellectual nourishment and stimulation in the Northwest, and left after a short while to spend several years in Europe and the Near East. For much the same reason, Portland lost Clayton S. Price for fourteen years. Born in Iowa, Price (1874–1950) spent his early years in Wyoming, Canada, and California with one year (1905–1906) at the St. Louis School of Fine Arts. There he met a fellow cowboy-turned-artist, Montana's Charles M. Russell, who strongly influenced his early style. For a time Price was an illustrator for Portland's *Pacific Monthly*; but having seen his first examples of modern European painters at the San Francisco Panama and Pacific International Exposition, he turned seriously to painting in the Bay City.

Yet others came and remained in the Northwest. Ambrose Patterson came to Seattle (1919) with the full equipment of a professional, having been trained in Paris and Australia. Walter Isaacs, who also had his instruction from French masters, had learned from Othon Friez simplification of form and color, and from Charles Guerion rigorous exactitude. These men and Raymond Hill, the watercolorist, gave the University of Washington new importance as a center of artistic work.

The depression decade of the thirties saw years of trial and testing, but they were fruitful years, thanks to substantial encouragement given to artists by government agencies and individual patrons. Price, Kenneth Callahan, Guy Anderson, and Morris Graves, all significant names among Northwest painters, were among those who grew in maturity and kept their creative talents alive through commissions from the WPA Federal Art Project.

Painters in the Northwest have been torn between tradition, the dominating land and seascapes, and the trend of modern art to abstract forms. Walter Isaacs did portraits of University of Washington faculty—Savery, Cory, and Lee Paul Sieg—though he was known also for his scenic studies and still life. Raymond Hill established a small "Art Vacation" program at Chelan, a choice spot for landscapes. Ambrose Patterson journeyed to LaPush and, after careful observation and delineation, painted his interpretation of an Indian Shaker Meeting. Kenneth Callahan found inspiration both in logging camps and in the Seattle skyline. Even the abstractionists were not wholly indifferent to their environment; witness Morris Graves' "Joyous Young Pines." Despite Graves' sense of cultural starvation, Puget Sound pulled him back from his wanderings repeatedly. When he went to paint in Ireland, he remarked that he had memorized the Northwest and took it with him to use as he might need it. Mark Tobey, who enjoyed his studio in the University district until a supermarket came in across the street and drove him from his familiar haunts, also took nourishment from the regional environment and put down on canvas his impressions of crowded wartime Seattle. Always prolific, Tobey ranged from violent caricature to the most involved abstraction, from scenes of brilliant color to designs of tortured fantasy. Outward appearance was to him but superficiality. The products of no particular region or locality, his paintings spoke of the turmoil and excitement of the cities and of man's hopeless entanglement in a world of confused and changing values.

Morris Graves' subject matter, intricately symbolic, was elaborated in sequences and series, in birds and fish and pine trees, each of which represented something elemental in life. His art was not intellectual but intuitive, as if he could fathom the deepest meanings in men's existence by "stilling the surface of the mind and letting the inner surface bloom." Some critics spoke of his compelling honesty, his abiding taste, his attempt to combine, not altogether successfully, the decorative qualities of Asiatic art with Western abstraction. Others confessed that his paintings left them with a sense of riddles that had no answers, of symbols with lost meanings, like artifacts from a vanished age. Drawn from some remote spiritual level, they seemed to dissolve beneath one's gaze yet continued somehow to haunt and captivate the imagination.

C. S. Price returned to Portland in 1928 and until his death in 1950 worked quietly on the canvases that have since won him wide recognition. His painting was of the West, but his interpretation of it transcended the landscape and the myths of frontier life. He gave monumental dignity to the pathos of the Indians' and homesteaders' lines. His "Feller on a Horse Going the Other Way" is a vignette of lonely parting. In his later style, "Form and subject are joined to a mysticism," latent in his earlier works. "The Far Northwest," says critic Harris K. Pryor, "has a way of stimulating this . . ."

> [Price] begins to rework old themes and to introduce a few new subjects. The animals and birds become dematerialized and ghostlike. . . . Color becomes muted; forms vague. . . . he slashes through all surface appearances, until form and feeling fuse to his satisfaction"[6]

[6] Harris K. Pryor, "C. S. Price and the Real West," *C. S. Price, 1874–1950, A Memorial Exhibition* (Portland Art Museum, 1950); "Mystic Painters of the Northwest," *Life*, September 28, 1953.

573

The power of his style is demonstrated in "The Huckleberry Pickers," with its vague figures of Indian women and horses, and mountain slopes all in muted earth tones.

That the Pacific Northwest could produce, or at least give asylum to such a group as this entitled it to more than casual notice. However one might interpret the artists and their work and whatever one might think of their style, these men developed a new language in painting that challenged both critics and fellow artists. Tobey and Graves were spoken of in Paris as leading "une école du Pacifique." Their canvases and those of other Northwest moderns were acquired and exhibited by the great metropolitan museums.

The fine arts were also encouraged by improved museum facilities and the enrichment of art collections both in Oregon and Washington. The University of Oregon acquired an outstanding collection of Oriental art assembled by Murray Warner. In 1933 Seattle built its Art Museum through the generosity and civic spirit of Mrs. Eugene Fuller and her son, Richard E. Fuller. The Fullers also gave the city a valuable collection of Oriental jades, Chinese snuff bottles, and Japanese art treasures; and through the years they broadened the scope of the collection to cover the entire field of Asiatic art, and encouraged the building up of a representative group of traditional and modern works. Other patrons joined in the effort, especially Mrs. Donald E. Frederick and Mrs. Thomas D. Stimson, both of whom contributed outstanding items. The Museum gave tangible support to the efforts of Northwestern artists, and acquired a considerable number of their paintings.

The Portland Art Museum not only continued its lively art school but built up a discriminating collection through gifts and purchases, making a practice of acquiring contemporary pieces and the works of promising local artists. In shunning pedestrian works, the Art Museum roused the ire of those who looked upon modern art as subversive.

It has been said that young musicians in the Northwest show promise but that it remains unfulfilled for those who remain in the region. Perhaps here again provincialism and tradition inhibit the expression of a highly individualistic art. In Portland the symphony has been maintained through the efforts of a few dedicated individuals. Conductors Willem Van Hoogstraten (1925–1928), James Sample (1949–1953), Theodore Bloomfield, (1954–1959), and recently Jacques Singer (1962–   ) have maintained a high level of performance with professional musicians. Tacoma has been host to Eugene Ormandy; Seattle experienced Sir Thomas Beecham. Composer Ernest Bloch (1880–1959) spent his last years on the Oregon Coast where he completed several of his more complex works, among them the

"Second Concerto Grosso"and "Concertino for Viola, Flute and Strings," but so far as one can discover, the presence of this master had no noticeable effect upon regional musicians or musical life. On the other hand, Jacob Avshalomov has been an outstanding influence on young artists. Avshalomov made Portland his home as a young man; he taught at Columbia University for eight years, and won the Alice Ditson and New York Music Critics Circle Award for his compositions. He returned to Portland as director of the Junior Symphony and successor to his friend and patron, Jacques Gerskovitch.

Surprisingly, considering the early popularity of theater in the Pacific Northwest, its cities are not "good theater" towns. Road shows are few and far between. However, Seattle has long had a Civic Repertory Theater and the University has had a successful record of production. Like other civic theaters, Portland's alternates box office attractions with avant-garde productions; and "off-Broadway" theaters bring the offbeat show to small audiences. But Ashland (Oregon), where Angus L. Bowmer built his replica of the London Globe, has its summer Shakespeare festival sold out months in advance. Young actors mingle with famous professionals, and for several months each summer the town becomes a school for the concentrated study of seventeenth-century music and drama.

LITERATURE AND LEARNING

In the twenties and thirties, literary emphasis was still upon cultural autonomy. Undoubtedly there was too much provincialism in this, too much straining to point out to the world the unique possessions of the Northwest without establishing rigorous standards either for significance of subject matter or excellence in style. In 1939 Russell Blankenship commented wryly on the preoccupation with frontier hardship and scenic grandeur which gave much of the regional writing a distressing sameness and marked it for mediocrity. Ten years later a conference of writers and critics, assembled at Reed College to consider the strengths and weaknesses of regionalism in literature, heard Joseph Harrison enter a plea for the elements of universality rather than local uniqueness as the key to greatness in literary expression.[7]

One of the most significant achievements of the 1920s stemmed

[7] Russell Blankenship, "Half Century of Cultural Progress: Literature," in *Building a State: Washington 1889–1939* (1940); Joseph B. Harrison, "Regionalism is Not Enough," in *Northwest Harvest, a Regional Stocktaking,* V. L. C. Chittick, ed. (1948).

from a critic rather than a poet or novelist. Tracing the progress of American writers in producing an indigenous literature, Vernon Louis Parrington explored the theme in the larger area of colonial and national experience and found a new importance in it. His *Main Currents of American Thought* (1928), which won recognition throughout the nation as a pivotal study, had a particular relevance for the writers of his own region, for he interpreted literature as the expression of social and economic values and the crystallization of experience which linked the American scene with the broader background of English and European thought. Parrington's views were novel for the day. He was a hero to the rebellious young; a threat to the smug belles-lettres of the elders.

Although the Pacific Northwest produced no literary giants, in the early thirties it was the home of a number of gifted writers who, in retrospect, have been considered the region's finest craftsmen. James Stevens wrote his *Paul Bunyan Stories* that did much to endear to America this folk hero of western logging camps. Harold Lenoir Davis completed his Pulitzer prize-winning book, *Honey in the Horn* (1935), a picaresque novel of herders and horse traders, sawmill workers, hop pickers, and home-hungry wanderers projected against an early twentieth-century Oregon background. It was a man's book, pungent, unconventional, a "literary long drink and a heady one" which sent Oregonians into a dither of protest. This was not the Oregon of their image.

Davis began writing for the *American Mercury* in 1929. Almost all the short stories and sketches appearing in its pages related to his major work-in-progress—"Crop Campers," "Back to the Land, Oregon 1907" (1929), "A Town in Eastern Oregon," "Water on the Wheat" (1930), "Team Bells that Woke Me," and "A Pioneer Captain" (1931). Like his short stories and first novel, his later novels used regional materials, but Davis was never inhibited by them. *Beulah Land* (1940); *Harp of a Thousand Strings* (1947), *Distant Music* (1957), and *Kettle of Fire* (1959), written after he left Oregon, won no wide reading public, for Davis was a writer's writer.

Stevens and Davis did not believe that regionalism or regional themes explained the failure of Northwest writers to achieve stature. Rather they indicted the region's provincialism, Oregon's Puritanism, and the public's lack of discrimination. In 1935 the two privately published a statement, now a rare piece of Americana, under the title *Status Rerum; a Manifesto upon the Present Condition of Northwestern Literature, Containing Several Near-Libelous Utterances upon Persons in the Public Eye*, in which they complained that

> . . . The Northwest . . . has produced a vast quantity of bilge, so vast, indeed, that the few books which are entitled to respect are totally lost in the general and seemingly interminable avalanche of type. . . . Is there something about the climate, or the soil, which inspires people to write tripe? Is there some occult influence, which catches them young, and shapes them to be instruments out of which tripe, and nothing but tripe, may issue?

These Angry Young Men of 1935 pointed the finger at Colonel Ernest Hofer's Oregon poetry monthly, *The Lariat* and Seattle's *Mirror and Muse*, at local clubs of versifiers, and at the universities' commercialized "creative" writing courses—as corrupters of literary standards. Stevens, in an *American Mercury* article, especially attacked small-town Puritanism and the seduction of potentially good writers by local boosterism.

The effect of all this, of course, was to silence the few yearning boosters and the meek majority of artists. All conformed to Webfoot Puritanism, at least in lip service. Some of them finally fled the region, as Edwin Markham, Joaquin Miller, and Charles Erskine Scott Wood had done before them. H. L. Davis did not stop until he was in the deep of Old Mexico. The last I heard of Albert Richard Wetjen he was in the South Seas, and still going. Such free-spirited novelists as Vardis Fisher and Nard Jones kept great open spaces between themselves and the Portland literary pillories. Only one heretic of consequences lingers on in the Willamette, and he has lately appeased the bishops by giving up strong drink.[8]

Vardis Fisher's moving trilogy, *In Tragic Life* (1932), *Passions Spin the Plot* (1934), and *We are Betrayed* (1935), was also strong medicine for the provinces, though the intensity of his style, like his brooding, tragic sense of life, seemed indigenous to the Snake River country he used as setting:

> All the elemental passions of life were dramatized here. From sky to earth, in one hour, was a mute brooding quiet, deep as despair; but in the next hour, the west opened, the sky was a wilderness of lightning-paths, and storm howled from ledge to ledge.
> It was a beautiful place but a haunted place. It got hold of you, wormed into your blood, became part of your bone . . .

[8] James Stevens, "Portland: Athens of the West," *American Mercury*, March 1936, 348. Markham was only a child when he left Oregon. It is seldom remembered, however, that Mary McCarthy, "the lady with the switch blade," whose *Groves of Academe* (1952) and *The Group* (1963) irritated the academic world and titillated the reader of less conservative tastes, was a Washington expatriate.

Nard Jones' *Wheat Women* (1933), a novel of life in the Walla Walla country, was of uneven merit but had a power Jones lost in subsequent novels built from historical documents, such as *Swift Flows the River* (1940), that deals with incidents of steamboat days. Archie Binns's *Lightship* (1934) and *The Laurels are Cut Down* won plaudits from reviewers for faultlessly simple prose and sympathetic understanding of the Puget Sound country. Robert Cantwell's *Land of Plenty* (1934) was a proletarian novel of a mill town which contrasted with Binns almost savagely stressing the rough and brutal side of life when industrialism made its impact on the Northwest.

During the next twenty years a considerable number of regional novels and nonfiction volumes found their way into print. Allis McKay's story of settling the Wenatchee country, *They Came to a River* (1941), was more than competent. Nard Jones not only wrote several novels but added a work of general regional characterization in *Evergreen Land*. By mid-century Murray Morgan was known for his *Skid Road*, an informal history of Seattle, *The Dam*, a popular account of Grand Coulee, and *Last Wilderness*, a delineation of past and present on the Olympic Peninsula. Stewart Holbrook with engaging spirit wrote on many topics in the development of the American West, his best works about the woods, *Holy Old Mackinaw* and *Burning an Empire*. In *Far Corner* he offered thumbnail sketches of a number of lesser characters and places in the Northwest, done with deft touch and sure sense of human interest. In 1948 Holbrook surveyed the regional field in *Promised Land*, a book of representative selections from Northwest novels and essays, which proved to be something of a landmark in the literary history of the area. In the variety of their interests, in their professional competence and in their appreciation of literary values, these authors were entitled to be considered able spokesmen for their generation.

The latter years, dominated by free-lancers and journalists, have been distinguished by technical skill and by an amazing productivity rather than by the more lasting qualities of thoughtfulness and philosophic penetration. Holbrook went on tirelessly from one book to the next. Richard Neuberger wrote numerous articles for the popular magazines. His biography of George W. Norris, *Integrity* (1937), written in collaboration with Stephen S. Kahn, was a tribute to his political hero; *Politics: We go the the Legislature* (1954), was the story of his and his wife's experiences as the only Democrats in Oregon's Republican legislature. But it was Washington's Betty McDonald who established a sales record for a Northwest author when *The Egg and I* sold more than a million copies. Each year saw a yield of novels which, while they cast interesting sidelights on the region and witnessed its great desire to be heard and understood, also testified to modest talents and an unsophisticated literary environment.

In the sixties young Don Berry (1932–   ) has given the Northwest its best novel. In *Trask* (1960), successfully, and in its sequel *Moontrap* (1962), less expertly, he has demonstrated that a historical setting does not inhibit the artist; in *A Majority of Scoundrels* (1964), that the talented writer can compose a history with dramatic effect.

Scholarship and research have been pursued assiduously in every branch of higher learning. Anthropologists distilled the results of field work into closely packed monographs, while economists and sociologists studied the communities of their day and incorporated their findings in descriptive and technical studies. Works of formal history and biography appeared, some treating of regional subjects while others evidenced the writer's interest in broad areas of knowledge which had no advantage in local perspective. J. Allen Smith finished a second book, *The Growth and Decadence of Constitutional Government* (1930), in which he raised searching questions as to the impact of political and administrative centralization on American democracy. Scientists gauged the resources and products of the region and offered their proposals for their further development.

Such activities were centered for the most part in colleges and universities. These schools experienced rapid expansion during the two periods of postwar development when population increases and high enrollments greatly spurred their growth. New laboratories and dormitories went up on the college campuses, faculties were enlarged, and a number of new programs of research and publication were undertaken which contributed significantly to the advance of knowledge.

The University of Washington had grown from a school of 4000 to one of 10,000 students between 1914 and 1926. The campus quadrangle took shape with the construction of several classroom buildings and the first wing of the Suzzallo Library, a college-gothic cathedral type structure designed to be the architectural focus of the entire development. These years witnessed also a number of administrative reorganizations which gave new importance to law and journalism, marine biology and business administration. The State College of Washington doubled its enrollment and strengthened its program not only in agricultural fields, but in the arts and sciences, engineering, mining, and home economics as well. A legislative survey (1915) attempted to define the areas of special interest of each school, but for a number of subjects it was not felt to be necessary to assign responsibility exclusively to either institution.

Jurisdictional problems plagued Oregon much more than Washing-

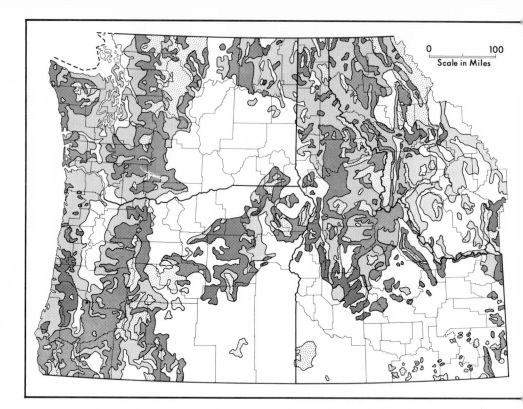

ton. The rivalry of Eugene and Corvallis became increasingly intense and finally produced a full-scale inquiry (1931) and reorganization, accompanied by screams of anguish and political hay-making. The two schools were put under a single governing board and policies were formulated that envisaged a considerably sharper division of functions than was attempted in Washington. Specialization was logical enough, but institutional loyalties were strong; the concept of a university was never wholly fulfilled so long as programs of studies were split between two institutions forty miles apart. The later trend was less severe in its separation of sciences and arts and allowed the development of programs at both schools though still preserving special emphases for each.

Private colleges continued to occupy a prominent place in higher education. Church-sponsored schools felt the same general impulse that produced the growth of the public insitutions, and joined in the movement to improve and enlarge their facilities. The College of Puget Sound moved to a spacious new campus in Tacoma (1924) while Willamette University (Salem) carried out a "forward movement" that brought money for several new buildings, higher faculty salaries, and a larger endowment. Lutherans reorganized and combined their schools at Parkland, Washington, and the Seventh-day Adventists im-

THE PACIFIC NORTHWEST GENERALIZED FOREST CONDITIONS

Old-Growth Sawtimber

Young-Growth Sawtimber, Unstocked Forest Land, Pole-Size Mature Timber in High Mountains

Non-Commercial Forests

Non-Forested

Compiled from U. S. Forest Service maps by Jon Leverenz for ATLAS OF THE PACIFIC NORTHWEST, *edited by R. M. Highsmith, Jr., Oregon State University Press. Reprinted by permission.*

proved their college at Walla Walla. Catholic institutions of higher education were strengthened, especially Gonzaga (Spokane) and Seattle. Though funds came slowly and the problems of finance were constant worries, private colleges nourished the traditions of scholarship and claimed many devoted supporters who continued to think of most of them as less godless than public institutions.

Depression years were lean years on the campus. Salaries were cut sharply and minimum budgets discouraged all but essential activities. However, following World War II a further transformation took place, the importance of which would be hard to exaggerate. Millions of dollars went into the expansion of physical plants, so that returning alumni would hardly recognize the old familiar places. With grants and aid from public and private sources, the schools of the Far West were able to attract able scholars and executives. A medical school was established at the University of Washington; the University of Oregon School of Medicine at Portland was immensely strengthened. Research funds became available in substantial amounts; contract research became such an important factor that only good judgment and firm policies kept the guidelines directed toward university learning rather than to applied mechanics. In mid-century, the colleges and universities race to keep up with mounting enrollments. The rapid development of junior colleges and community colleges has taken some pressure from older institutions; but the multiplication of campuses increases costs and so endangers the quality of instruction at all levels.

The educational programs of public schools was as vital to public welfare as the growth of the colleges, and offered fully as great a challenge. In terms of finance and administration, curriculum development, and teacher training, the problems in expanding the elementary and secondary school systems throughout the region were formidable indeed. From World War I until World War II there was a relative relaxation; but as the war babies entered the schools pressures mounted.

Methods of financing varied from state to state but in all cases were marked by increasing reliance upon state funds since revenues from local real estate taxes were uneven and often inadequate. Washington shifted the sources of school support more completely than Oregon and Idaho to state appropriations. By 1948 more than 70 percent of the money Washington spent for common schools came from state taxes. While both Oregon and Idaho have recognized the necessity of state support and have raised increasing sums from general taxes, neither state has reached a constantly receding goal. School taxes have become the largest single item in the expenditure of the tax dollar in Oregon, the burden lying heaviest on local property holders. State equalization funds are a bone of contention in legislative sessions and almost every biennium there is a lobby for a state sales tax to reduce the burden on property, but labor remains adamantly opposed.

The general trends in school administration lay in the direction of more comprehensive coordination and supervision at the state level. For a time the superintendent of public instruction and the state boards of education maintained only small offices and occupied themselves mainly with fact-finding and advisory functions. After 1930, however, they became increasingly concerned with specific questions of statewide administration. During the depression years there was an urgent need to effect economies by consolidation and uniformity in business matters so that every dollar spent on education would bring the greatest possible return.

Later, when huge sums were being spent on construction of new buildings, on buses and equipment, the states exercised even greater vigilance in supervision wherever state dollars were used. Through their control of teaching credentials, their vigorous sponsorship of education programs before the legislatures, and through the lobbying of professional educational associations, state educational agencies came to exercise a powerful influence over local administrators and classroom teachers as well. School boards still played an important role in individual districts, but the management of schools lost much of the grass-roots democracy of the earlier years. Furthermore, the small sized unit of school administration was found not only inefficient but deficient in providing greatest opportunities for the children. The creation of consolidated school districts has taken place, but not without anguish in districts where the little red school house was presumed to be quite satisfactory for local needs.

As for the classroom itself, the region followed the national trend in its concern for the nonacademic student. For some years college preparatory work went out of fashion while the curriculum was shaped and adjusted to the needs of those whose education would go no further than high school. Not until mid-century, when entrance into college once more became competitive, did the schools turn again to the more intensive training of those who must meet the rigors of examinations and high scholarship.

RECREATION AND SOCIAL AGENCIES

The Northwest found it necessary to plan and develop recreation facilities more systematically as the population grew larger. In earlier times hunting and fishing and mountain climbing were enjoyed by a comparatively small number of people who asked no conveniences as part of their pleasure. As the years passed, however, spokesmen for recreation urged that more of the region's beauty spots be made generally accessible. During the 1930s the National Forest Service encouraged extensive and varied recreational programs, supported and served by concessions at places where small commercial establishments were practicable. Mount Baker and Stevens Pass attracted skiing enthusiasts on weekends, and Snoqualmie and Naches Pass were favored by city dwellers who could reach them in little more than an hour's drive. In the years following World War II skiing became not only sport but good business, and equipment shops found a ready market for the finest skis, boots, and bindings. Hunting and fishing became businesses as well, the latter involving outlays of millions of dollars on boats and gear.

The sheltered waters of Puget Sound and inland lakes and rivers give the Northwesterner many opportunities for pleasure boating. Yachtsmen cruise off shore or spend vacation periods in the San Juan Islands and the Strait of Georgia. Small sailboats of half a dozen racing classes dot Lake Washington on a breezy day. Chris-Crafts, Century Runabouts, and speedy outboards skip lightly over the waves, their water skiers swinging in wide arcs across the foaming wake. With Stan Sayres' racing hydroplanes, Slo-mo IV and Slo-mo V, Seattle has made its August Sea Fair the principal festival of the year for civic promotion. Water sports likewise have became a favorite recreation on the slack waters above many dams on the Columbia and its tributaries, as well as on impounded waters of irrigation such as Ochoco and Owyhee.

States have acquired recreation areas at well-chosen sites throughout the region. This program developed comparatively late, for natural beauty was so common that it hardly seemed necessary to buy acreage to preserve it. After World War II, however, park and recreation commissions became more active, and more funds were made available. State parks were crowded with tourists and campers. Historical museums offered entertainment and instruction to those who were curious to learn what personages had been there before them, and what events had taken place. Washington took the lead in this movement; it was more important there, since federal and local agencies largely met the need in Oregon and Idaho.

The last areas to be served with recreational facilities were the suburbs, which circle the cities in ever-widening rings. Speculative builders and promoters were quite capable of putting up homes for several thousand new inhabitants within the space of a few months, creating settlements that were virtually towns, yet with scant if any provision for civic and social needs. School boards had to buy land at a speculator's price, and developers felt no responsibility to include playgrounds in their plots. At the same time county park agencies rarely had the money—or the vision—to purchase and develop sites on a comprehensive plan. Even where planning commissions pointed the way, the establishment of civic and recreational facilities came slowly.

As recreation came to require more and more planning and conscious civic effort, so too did various other programs of social concern. The establishment of churches to serve growing populations did not take place spontaneously. Sometimes individual city churches sponsored new churches in rapidly growing areas nearby. More often interdenominational councils of churches made comity assignments to one denomination or another, and the machinery of denominational planning and guidance supported the efforts of local communities. In these activities the Northwest took its place in a national movement, receiving new strength in the churches founded there. At the same time the region contributed leadership to national organizations. The election of Dr. Paul Wright, pastor of Portland's First Presbyterian Church, as national moderator of the United Presbyterian Church and of E. B. MacNaughton as moderator of the Unitarian Universalist Association are but two illustrations of the growing participation of the region in the religious affairs of the nation at large.

In most fields of social welfare and community effort, the Far Northwest followed the general trend in organization and program. The cities had their Good Neighbor funds, their councils of social agencies. State institutions and juvenile programs reflected the influence of improved professional leadership, though politics and costs were obstacles to rapid improvement in administration. Hospitals in far western communities received their share of grants from the national foundations for the enlargement of their facilities and services.

In some few instances one could say the region was in the vanguard. The Group Health Cooperative of Puget Sound was one of the country's pioneer ventures in the field of prepaid medical coverage, and met with a strong popular response. The program of orientation and guidance for foreign students, set up at the University of Washington under the direction of James Davis, was commended throughout the nation. John Richards won election as national president of the American Library Association for his record of energetic and resourceful leadership in library administration, not only for his own institution, the Seattle Public Library, but in the wider field as well. These evidences of progressivism and imaginative leadership in humanitarian endeavor, no less than the Pulitzer awards won by Northwest poets and scientists and the Rhodes scholarships captured almost regularly by the students of Reed College and the University of Washington, indicated that the region was coming of age socially and intellectually.

In some ways the Pacific Northwest was still, at mid-century, the "far corner" of the United States. In general viewpoint, as in economic enterprise, it made a difference that the broad belt of mountains and plains separated this section of the country from the more populous eastern states. Professional and business people lived and worked in an atmosphere far removed from the hustle of Chicago and New York. Their thinking was likely to be that of the provinces, not of the brain centers where the major decisions of the nation were formulated and determined. Many who grew up by Pacific shores had never seen New England or the deep South, had never visited the national capital or enjoyed an eastern concert stage or theater.

However, notwithstanding the great open spaces, distance was not the dimension of living that it had been earlier. By ordinary air transport New York and Washington were a few hours away. Scholars and salesmen, clerics and politicians attended the national meetings of their guilds. Corporations and colleges recruited from the entire nation, and did much to bring about an intermingling of people from every section. Foundation grants and fellowships opened new opportunities for travel and study, and numbers of westerners began to visit Europe and Asia. Radio and television largely destroyed cultural provincialism, bringing to Northwest homes a varied fare of entertainment and instruction, ranging from prizefighting to grand opera.

In 1833 a lonely trader in a Hudson's Bay Company post wrote of his exile on the Columbia; by mid-twentieth century isolation was more a local and individual matter than regional. The country as a whole was knit together and the Pacific Northwest was one with the nation.

.   .   .

History portrays only the shapes of events, pictures only the silhouettes of men in time and place, discovers only what has been already revealed by accident or design. The limitations of history are implicit in Kenneth Hanson's thoughts on "Graves at Mukilteo":

> Between what was the town
> and what is still the sea
> they placed their dead. Remorse
> born hatred, passing love
> transform themselves to these
> impassionate doves in stone,
> a name, two dates, a sentiment.
> "Kind father, loving son."
> "The beautiful flower has faded."
>
> Now crabgrass hides the skewed
> endurances of grief. What
> once they bore, who lie beneath,
> their private good or ill,
> despair, envy, the range of pain,
> no carved inscriptions tell.
> Knock of the sea, thin sun,
> the changing weather, they share
> neighborhood and stone, together.[9]

But to historians who read the records of the past it is apparent that men marched to the sound of distant music, to the promise of the future. For those who came to the Far Northwest, this was a land of promise, though not of the riches of Quivira or the fabulous cities of Cibola. A new land only yesterday, it was within a matter of a short time, an old land to which a native might return. Vancouver-

[9] *New Orleans Poetry Journal*, vol. IV, no. 3.

born Mary Barnard in "The Rapids" has written the epilogue for twentieth-century Columbians.

> No country is so gracious to us
> As that which kept its contours while we forgot them,
> And whose valleys, closed under receding hills,
> Open to our return.
>
> The water we saw broken upon the rapids
> Has dragged silt through marshland
> And mingled with the embittered streams of the sea.
> One might have kept sweet pailsful and kept nothing.
>
> But the ungatherable blossoms floating by the same rock,
> The chisel marks on a surface in full flight
> Have flung light in my face, have made promises
> In unceasing undertone.[10]

[10] In *Five Young American Poets* (1940).

APPENDIXES

Supplementary Readings, Tables, and Graphs

Supplementary Readings

THIS BIBLIOGRAPHY has been compiled by Priscilla Knuth, research assistant at the Oregon Historical Society, and associate editor of the *Oregon Historical Quarterly*, and by Keith A. Murray, Professor of History at Western Washington State College. It provides readings in editions usually accessible to the general reader either in college libraries or in good public libraries.

For complete coverage, a scholar should be familiar with the following publications:

Belknap, George N., *McMurtie's Oregon Imprints*, appearing originally in the *Oregon Historical Quarterly*, "1st Supplement," (December 1950), "2nd Supplement," (June 1954), and "3rd Supplement," (September 1958), 4th Supplement, LXIV:2, June, 1963.

McMurtrie, Douglas C., *Oregon Imprints, 1847–1870*. (Eugene: University of Oregon Press, 1950.)

For general bibliography:

Appleton, John B., *The Pacific Northwest, A Selected Bibliography . . . 1930–1939*. (Portland: Northwest Regional Council, 1939).

Judson, Katharine B., *Subject Index to the History of the Pacific Northwest, Alaska, as Found in U.S. Government Documents . . . , 1789–1881*. (Olympia: Washington State Library, 1913).

Pollard, Lancaster, "A Checklist of Washington Authors." *Pacific Northwest Quarterly*, 31:1, January 1940.

Pollard, Lancaster, "A Pacific Northwest Bibliography, 1947." *Pacific Northwest Quarterly*, 39:2, April 1948.

Smith, Charles W., *Pacific Northwest Americana*. (Portland: Binfords & Mort, Publishers, 1950).

Winther, Oscar O., *A Classified Bibliography of the Periodical Literature of the Trans-Mississippi West, 1811–1957*. (Bloomington: Indiana University Press, 1961).

For students interested particularly in political history of the region:

Jonas, Frank H., ed., *Bibliography on Western Politics, Supplement to the Western Political Quarterly*. (December 1958).

A listing of unpublished theses and dissertations, divided by general subject follows.

Bromberg, Erik, "A Bibliography of Theses and Dissertations Concerning the Pacific Northwest and Alaska." *Pacific Northwest Quarterly*, 40:3, July 1949. Manuscripts found in colleges and Universities of the Pacific Northwest.

Bromberg, Erik, "A Further Bibliography of Theses and Dissertations Concerning the Pacific Northwest and Alaska." *Pacific Northwest Quarterly*, 42:2 April 1951. Manuscripts found in colleges and Universities outside of the Pacific Northwest.

Bromberg, Erik, "A Bibliography of Theses and Dissertations Concerning the Pacific Northwest and Alaska Supplement, 1949–57." *Oregon Historical Quarterly*, LIX:1, March 1958.

Bromberg, Erik, "A Bibliography of Theses and Dissertations Concerning the Pacific Northwest and Alaska Supplement, 1958–1963." *Oregon Historical Quarterly*, LXV:4, December 1964.

For paperbacks on Northwest topics see:

Deutsch, Herman J., "The West in Paperbacks." *Pacific Northwest Quarterly*, 54:3, July 1963.

GENERAL REFERENCES FOR COMPREHENSIVE COVERAGE

Avery, Mary W., *History and Government of the State of Washington* (Seattle: University of Washington Press, 2nd ed., 1965) Probably the best of the studies on Washington state government.

Bancroft, Hubert Howe, *The Works of Hubert Howe Bancroft* (San Francisco: The History Company, Publishers) Tedious to read, but still probably the single most valuable aid for primary source material.
History of the Northwest Coast, 1543–1800. Vol. XXVII, 1884.
History of the Northwest Coast, 1800–1846. Vol. XXVIII, 1884.
History of Oregon, 1834–1848. Vol. XXIX, 1886.
History of Oregon, 1848–1888. Vol. XXX, 1888.
History of Washington, Idaho and Montana, 1845–1889. Vol. XXXI, 1890.
History of British Columbia, 1792–1887. Vol. XXXII, 1887.

Corning, Howard M., ed., *Dictionary of Oregon History* (Portland: Binfords & Mort, 1956).

Federal Writer's Project, *Oregon, End of the Trail*. American Guide Series (Portland: Binfords & Mort, 1951).

Fisher, Vardis, ed., *Idaho, A Guide in Word and Picture*. American Guide Series, (Caldwell, Idaho: Caxton Printers, 1938). Historical tours of the state.

Fuller, George, *A History of the Pacific Northwest* (New York: Alfred A. Knopf, 1947). Out of date, nothing significant after 1890. Good treatment of Indian Wars and Northwest geology.

Gates, Charles M., ed., *Readings in Pacific Northwest History, 1790–1895* (Seattle: University of Washington Press, 1941). Limited to 19th century materials.

Idaho Yesterdays, See composite and annual Indexes of articles published.

McArthur, Lewis A., *Oregon Geographic Names*, reprint of 1952 ed. Out of print, but parts are to be found in Oregon Historical Quarterly.

Meany, Edmond S., *History of the State of Washington* (New York: The Macmillan Company, 1924). Highly detailed. Includes many pioneer names and the roles of individuals in the story of the Northwest.

Supplementary Readings

Meany, Edmond S., *Origin of Washington Geographic Names* (Seattle: University of Washington Press, 1923). Long out of print, but may be obtained in most libraries. The only book of its kind for Washington.

The New Washington, A Guide to The Evergreen State, American Guide Series, (rev. ed. 1950.)

Oregon Historical Quarterly, see composite and annual indexes in addition to articles listed below, under notation O.H.Q.

Pacific Northwest Quarterly, see composite and annual indexes in addition to articles listed below, under notations: P. N. Q. Earlier issues called *Washington Historical Quarterly* (Noted as W.H.Q.).

Smith, Henry Nash, *Virgin Land: The American West as Symbol and Myth* (Cambridge: Howard University Press, 1950). In paperback.

Winther, Oscar O., *The Great Northwest: A History* (New York: Alfred A. Knopf, 1950). A standard textbook. Better for Oregon history than Washington or Idaho.

PHYSICAL ENVIRONMENT

Baldwin, Ewart N., *Geology of Oregon* (Oregon State System of Higher Education, 1964).

Campbell, C. W., *Introduction to Washington Geology and Resources* (Pullman: Research Studies of the State College of Washington, Vol. 21:2, 1953).

Dicken, Samuel N., *Oregon Geography* (Ann Arbor, Michigan: University of Oregon Bookstore, 1959).

Douglas, William O., *My Wilderness: The Pacific West* (New York: Doubleday & Company, Inc., 1960). Except for chapters on the Alaskan Brooks Range, and California's High Sierra, a colorful description of the best parts of the Pacific Northwest.

Ekman, Leonard C., *Scenic Geology of The Pacific Northwest* (Portland: Binfords & Mort, 1962).

Freeman, Otis, and Martin, Howard, *The Pacific Northwest: A Regional Appraisal* (New York: John Wiley & Sons, 1954). The tables and charts are badly out of date, but the coverage is among the best.

Gilkey, Helen M., and Powell, G. M., *Handbook of Northwest Flowering Plants* (Portland: Binfords & Mort, 1961).

Haig-Brown, Roderick L., *Return to the River: A Story of The Chinook Run* (New York: Morrow and Company, 1941). Life cycle of the salmon.

Highsmith, Richard W. Jr., ed., *Atlas of the Pacific Northwest: Resources* and *Development* (Corvallis: Oregon State University Press, 1962).

Holbrook, Stewart H., *The Columbia*, Rivers of America Series (New York: Rinehart & Co., Inc., 1956) A highly readable account of some of the history and folklore of the river from its headwaters to its mouth. In paperback.

Hutchinson, Bruce, *The Fraser*. Rivers of America Series (New York: Rinehart & Co., Inc., 1950). Particularly good for the explorations of Simon Fraser in British Columbia.

McKenny, Margaret, *Wildlife of the Pacific Northwest* (Portland: Binfords & Mort, 1954).

Randall, Warren R., *Manual of Oregon Trees and Shrubs* (Corvallis: Oregon State University Press, 1961).

Rue, Leonard Lee III, *The World of the Beaver* (Philadelphia: J. B. Lippincott Company, 1964).

Van Wormer, Joe, *The World of the Bobcat* (Philadelphia: J. B. Lippincott Company, 1964).

Van Wormer, Joe, *The World of the Coyote* (Philadelphia: J. B. Lippincott Company, 1964).

REGIONALISM

Binns, John H., "Northwest Region—Fact or Fiction?" *Pacific Northwest Quarterly* 48:3, July 1957. Before World War I, the Pacific Northwest had a distinct character.

Chittick, Victor L. O., ed., *Northwest Harvest, A Regional Stocktaking* (New York: Macmillan Co., 1948). An anthology of opinion by leading Northwest writers on the regional character of the Northwest.

Deutsch, Herman J., "A Prospectus for the Study of the Governments of the Pacific Northwest States in Their Regional Setting." *Pacific Northwest Quarterly*, 42:4, October 1951.

Frykman, George A., "Regionalism, Nationalism, Localism: The Pacific Northwest in American History," *Pacific Northwest Quarterly*, 43:4, October 1952.

Holbrook, Stewart H., *Far Corner: A Personal View of The Pacific Northwest* (New York: The Macmillan Company, 1952). Partly reminiscence.

Jensen, Merrill, ed., *Regionalism in America* (Madison: University of Wisconsin Press, 1952). The sections on the Pacific Northwest.

Morgan, Murray, *The Northwest Corner: The Pacific Northwest, Its Past and Present* (New York: Viking Press, 1962).

Pollard, Lancaster, "The Pacific Northwest: A Regional Study," *Oregon Historical Quarterly*, LII:4, December 1951.

Stratton, David H., "The Dilemma of American Elbowroom," *Pacific Northwest Quarterly* 56:1, January 1965. Psychological problems of Oregon settlers caused by the hugeness of the land.

Warren, Sidney, *Farthest Frontier: The Pacific Northwest* (New York: The Macmillan Company, 1949) Good material on utopian experiments.

INDIAN CULTURES

Boas, Franz, "The Art of the Northwest Coast of North America," in his *Primitive Art* (New York: Dover Publications, Inc., 1955) paper.

Clark, Ella E., *Indian Legends of the Pacific Northwest* (Berkeley: University of California Press, 1953).

Collins, J. M., "Growth of Class Distinctions and Political Authority among the Skagit Indians during the Contact Period," *American Anthropologist*, 52:3 (July, 1950).

Cressman, Luther S., Williams, Howel, and Krieger, Alex D., *Early Man in Oregon: Archeological Studies in The Northern Great Basin* (Eugene: University of Oregon Press, 1940).

Cressman, Luther S., *The Sandal and the Cave* (Portland: Champoeg Press, 1964).

David, R. T., *Native Arts of The Pacific Northwest* (Palo Alto: Stanford University Press, 1949).

Supplementary Readings

Drucker, Philip, *Cultures of The North Pacific Coast* (San Francisco: Chandler Publishing Company, 1965).

Drucker, Philip, *Indians of The Northwest Coast* (New York: McGraw-Hill, 1955).

DuBois, Cora Alice, *The Feather Cult of The Middle Columbia* (Menasha, Wisc.: George Banta Publishing Company, 1938) The religion of Smohalla.

Gunther, Erna, "The Indian Background of Washington History," *Pacific Northwest Quarterly* 41:3, July 1950.

Hagan, William T., *American Indians* (Chicago: University of Chicago Press, 1961) Mainly governmental policies relating to Indians.

Haines, Francis, "Horses for Western Indians," *The American West*, III:2, Spring 1966.

Josephy, Alvin M. Jr., ed., *The American Heritage Book of The Indians* (New York: Simon & Schuster, Inc., 1961) Particularly the chapters "Kayakers and Cannibal Dancers," and "Beulah Land."

Ray, Verne, "Native Villages and Groupings of the Columbia Basin," *Pacific Northwest Quarterly* 27:2, April 1936.

Seaman, Norma G., *Indian Relics of The Pacific Northwest* (Portland: Binfords & Mort, 1946).

Schaeffer, Claude, *Map of Indian Tribes and Tribal Languages of The Oregon Country* (Portland: Oregon Historical Society, 1958).

Smith, Marian W., "The Cultural Development of the Northwest Coast," *Southwestern Journal of Anthropology*, 12:3, 1956.

Smith, Marian W., *Indians of The Urban Northwest* (New York: Columbia University Press, 1949) Mainly Salishan cultures.

Spier, Leslie, *Tribal Distribution in Washington* (Menasha, Wisc.: George Banta Publishing Company, 1936).

Strong, Emory M., *Stone Age on The Columbia River* (Portland: Binfords & Mort, 1959).

Taylor, Herbert C., Jr., "Aboriginal Populations of the Lower Northwest Coast," *Pacific Northwest Quarterly* 54:4, October 1963. Population estimates.

Underhill Ruth M., *Indians of The Pacific Northwest*, U.S. Department of Interior, Bureau of Indian Affairs, Education Division. (Riverside, California: Sherman Institute Press, 1945).

EXPLORATION AND DISCOVERY

Bakeless, John E., *Lewis and Clark, Partners in Discovery* (New York: W. Morrow, 1947).

Cline, Gloria G., *Exploring the Great Basin* (Norman: University of Oklahoma Press, 1963) Particularly Peter Skene Ogden.

Coues, Elliott, ed., *History of The Expedition Under The Command of Lewis and Clark* (3 vols, Dover Publications, Inc. 1964) In paperback.

Coues, Elliott, ed., *New Light on The History of The Greater Northwest: The Manuscript Journals of . . . David Thompson 1799–1814* (New York: F. P. Harper, 1897).

DeVoto, Bernard, ed., *The Journals of Lewis and Clark* (Boston: Houghton Mifflin Company, 1963 sentry edition) In paperback, selections from *Journals*.

Ghent, William J. *The Early Far West: A Narrative Outline, 1540–1850* (New York: Longmans, Green and Co., 1931).

Golder, Frank A., *Russian Expansion in The Pacific, 1641–1850* (Cleveland:

The Arthur H. Clark Company, 1914). Discovery and occupation of Eastern Siberia and Alaska.

Jackson, Donald D., ed., *Letters of The Lewis and Clark Expedition, with Related Documents, 1783–1843* (Urbana: University of Illinois Press, 1962).

Johansen, Dorothy O., ed., *Voyage of The Columbia: Around the World With John Boit, 1790–1793* (Portland: Champoeg Press, 1960) Paperback.

Munford, James Kenneth, ed., *Journal of Captain Cook's Last Voyage* (Corvallis: Oregon State University Press, 1964) Good material on John Ledyard.

Meany, Edmond S., *Vancouver's Discovery of Puget Sound* (Portland: Binfords & Mort, 1942) A standard work, which would have been improved by better footnoting giving exact modern counterparts for the place names Vancouver used.

Nevins, Allan, *Fremont: Pathmarker of The West* (New York: Longmans, 1955) A sympathetic study of Fremont.

Sheppe, Walter, ed., *First Man West: Alexander Mackenzie's Journal of His Voyage to The Pacific Coast of Canada in 1793* (Berkeley: University of California Press, 1962).

Wagner, Henry R., *Sir Francis Drake's Voyage Around the World: Its Aim and Achievements* (San Francisco: J. Howell, 1926).

THE MARITIME AND CONTINENTAL FUR TRADE

Barry, J. Nielson, "Columbia River Exploration, 1792," *Oregon Historical Quarterly*, XXXIII: 1, March 1932.

Beidelman, Richard G., "Nathaniel Wyeth's Fort Hall," *Oregon Historical Quarterly*, LVIII: 3, September 1957.

Chittenden, Hiram M., *The American Fur Trade of The Far West* (Stanford, Calif.: Academic Reprints, 1954) The earliest definitive work in this area.

Galbraith, John S., *The Hudson's Bay Company as an Imperial Factor, 1821–1869* (Berkeley, University of California Press, 1957).

Goebel, Dorothy Bourne, "British Trade to the Spanish Colonies," *American Historical Review*, XLIII: 2, January 1938.

Graebner, Norman A., *Empire of The Pacific* (New York: Ronald Press Co., 1955).

Howay, F. A., "Early Navigation of the Straits of Fuca," *Oregon Historical Quarterly*, XII: 1, March 1911.

Howay, F. A., ed., *The Dixon-Meares Controversy* (Toronto: The Ryerson Press, 1929).

Hussey, John A., *A History of Fort Vancouver and Its Physical Structure* (Tacoma: Washington State Historical Society, 1957).

Irving, Washington, *Astoria* (any recent edition).

Irving, Washington, *The Adventures of Captain Bonneville, U.S.A. in The Rocky Mountains and the Far West*, edited with introduction by Edgeley W. Todd, (Norman: University of Oklahoma Press, 1961).

Kenyon, Karl, *The Seals, Sea Lion, and Sea Otter of the Pacific Coast*, (U.S. Department of the Interior, 1955).

Lewis, William S., and Phillips, Paul C., eds., *The Journal of John Work* (Cleveland: The Arthur H. Clark Company, 1923).

Manning, William R., *The Nootka Sound Controversy*, American Historical Association *Annual Report*, 1904, 279–485.

Supplementary Readings

Merk, Frederick, *Fur Trade and Empire* (London: Oxford University Press, 1931).

Norris, John, "The Policy of the British Cabinet in the Nootka Crisis," *English Historical Review*, CCLXXVII, October, 1955.

Porter, Kenneth W., *John Jacob Astor, Businessman*, 2 Vols. (Cambridge: Harvard University Press, 1931).

Rich, E. E., *History of The Hudsons Bay Company, 1670–1870* (New York: The Macmillan Co., 1960–61).

Schaeffer, Victor B., "The Sea Otter on the Washington Coast," *Pacific Northwest Quarterly*, 31:4, October 1940.

Sheppe, Walter, ed., *First Man West: Alexander Mackenzie's Journal of His Voyage to the Pacific Coast of Canada in 1793* (Berkeley: University of California Press, 1962).

Sparks, Jared, *Life of John Ledyard, The American Traveller* (Cambridge: Hilliard and Brown, 1828).

Spaulding, Kenneth A., ed., *Alexander Ross: The Fur Hunters of the Far West* (Norman: University of Oklahoma Press, 1956). Fort Okanogan.

Stewart, Edgar I., and Jane R., eds., *Ross Cox: The Columbia River* (Norman: University of Oklahoma Press, 1957) Activities around Spokane House and Astoria.

Tobie, Harvey E., *No Man Like Joe: The Life and Times of Joseph L. Meek* (Portland: Oregon Historical Society, 1949).

Vestal, Stanley, *Joe Meek: The Merry Mountain Man, A Biography* (Caldwell: Caxton Printers, 1952).

Wallace, W. Stewart, ed., *Documents Relating to the Northwest Company* (Toronto: The Champlain Society, 1934).

Wallace, W. Stewart, ed., *Pedlars from Quebec, and Other Papers on the Nor'Westers* (Toronto: The Ryerson Press, 1954).

MISSIONARIES AND THE OREGON TRAIL

Applegate, Jesse, "A Day With the Cow Column," *O.H.Q.*, I:4 December 1900.

Bischoff, William N., S.J., *The Jesuits in Old Oregon* (Caldwell: The Caxton Printers, Ltd., 1945).

Bright, Verne, "Folklore and History of the 'Oregon Fever'," *Oregon Historical Quarterly*, LII:4, December 1951.

Davis, William L., S.J., "Peter John DeSmet: The Journey of 1840," *Pacific Northwest Quarterly*, XXXII:1, 2; XXXIII:2; XXXV:1, 2; January, April 1941, April 1942, January, April 1944.

DeVoto, Bernard, *The Year of Decision: 1846* (Boston: Little, Brown and Company, 1943) Particularly the Oregon Trail material. In paperback.

Drury, Clifford M., *First White Women Over the Rockies*, 4 Vols. (Glendale, Calif.: Arthur H. Clark Company, 1963–1966) Diaries of Narcissa Whitman, Eliza Spalding, Mrs. Wm. H. Gray, Mrs. Asa B. Smith, Mary Richardson Walker, and Mrs. Cushing Eells.

Drury, Clifford M., ed., *Diaries & Letters of Henry H. Spalding and Asa B. Smith Relating to the Nez Perce Mission, 1838–1842* (Glendale: Arthur H. Clark Company, 1958).

Drury, Clifford M., *Elkanah and Mary Walker: Pioneers Among the Spokanes* (Caldwell: The Caxton Printers, Ltd., 1940).

Drury, Clifford M., *Henry Harmon Spalding* (Caldwell: The Caxton Printers, Ltd., 1936).

Drury, Clifford M., *Marcus Whitman, M.D., Pioneer and Martyr* (Caldwell: The Caxton Printers, Ltd., 1937).

Drury, Clifford M., *A Tepee in His Front Yard, A Biography of H. T. Cowley* (Portland: Binfords & Mort, 1949).

Ghent, W. H., *The Road to Oregon, A Chronicle of the Great Emigrant Trail* (New York: Longmaus, Green and Co., 1929) To 1859.

Hafen, LeRoy R., and Ann W., Eds., *To the Rockies and Oregon, 1839–1842* (Glendale: Arthur H. Clark Company, 1955) Diaries of travelers.

Jacobs, Melville C., *Winning Oregon: A Study of an Expansionist Movement* (Caldwell: The Caxton Printers, Ltd., 1938) International diplomacy of Oregon settlement.

Jessett, Thomas E., ed., *Reports and Letters, 1836–1838, of Herbert Beaver* (Portland: Champoeg Press, 1959).

Lamb, W. Kaye, ed., "The James Douglas Report on the 'Beaver Affair'," *Oregon Historical Quarterly*, XLVII:1, March 1946.

Landerholm, Carl, trans., *Notices and Voyages of The Famed Quebec Mission to the Pacific Northwest* (Portland: Oregon Historical Society, 1956) Blanchet, Demers, and others.

Lavender, David, *Land of Giants* (New York: Doubleday & Company, Inc., 1958).

Lyons, Sister Letitia Mary, *Francis Norbert Blanchet and the Founding of the Oregon Missions, 1838–1848* (Washington, D.C.: The Catholic University of America Press, 1940).

McNamee, Mary D., *Willamette Interlude* (Palo Alto: Pacific Books, 1959) Activities of Sisters of Notre Dame de Namur.

Monaghan, Jay, *The Overland Trail* (Indianapolis: Bobbs-Merrill Co., 1947).

Place, Marian T., *Westward on the Oregon Trail* (New York: American Heritage Publishing Company, 1962).

The *Oregon Historical Quarterly*, *The Pacific Northwest Quarterly*, and the *Oregon Pioneer Association Transactions* (issued yearly, 1876–1928) include many overland journey diaries. See indexes for each and Oregon Historical Society sale book catalog for list of OPAT diaries.

NINETEENTH-CENTURY POLITICS AND GOVERNMENT

Barth, Gunther, ed., *All Quiet on the Yamhill: The Civil War in Oregon* (Eugene: University of Oregon Books, 1959).

Ellison, Joseph, "Design For a Pacific Republic, 1843–62," *Oregon Historical Quarterly*, XXXI:4 December 1930.

Hicks, John D., *The Constitutions of The Northwest States* (Lincoln: University of Nebraska Press, 1923).

Jackson, W. Turrentine, "Indian Affairs and Politics in Idaho Territory, 1863–1870," *Pacific Historical Review*, XIV:3 September 1945.

Johannsen, Robert W., *Frontier Politics and The Sectional Conflict: The Pacific Northwest on the Eve of the Civil War* (Seattle: University of Washington Press, 1955).

Johannsen, Robert W., "National Issues and Local Politics in Washington Territory, 1857–1861," *Pacific Northwest Quarterly*, 42:1, January 1951.

Supplementary Readings

Johannsen, Robert W., "The Oregon Legislature of 1868 and the Fourteenth Amendment," *Oregon Historical Quarterly*, LI:1, March 1950.

Kaplan, Mirth Tuft, "Courts, Counsellors and Cases: The Judiciary Department of Oregon's Provisional Government," *Oregon Historical Quarterly*, LXII:2, June 1961.

Kingston, C. S., "Walla Walla Separation Movement," *Washington Historical Quarterly*, 24:2, April 1933.

Knuth, Priscilla, "Nativism in Oregon," Reed College *Bulletin*, Armitage Essays, January 1946.

Murray, Keith A., "The Movement for Statehood in Washington," *Pacific Northwest Quarterly*, XXXII:4, October 1941.

Nelson, Herbert B., and Onstad, Preston E., eds., *A Webfoot Volunteer: The Diary of William M. Hilleary, 1864–1866* (Corvallis: Oregon State University Press, 1966). The Civil War in Oregon, east and west of the Cascades.

Pomeroy, Earl S., *The Territories and The United States, 1861–1890: Studies in Colonial Administration* (Philadelphia: University of Pennsylvania Press, 1947).

Seagraves, Helen Leonard, "The Oregon Constitutional Convention of 1857," Reed College *Bulletin*, Armitage Essays, June 1952.

Wells, Merle W., "The Creation of the Territory of Idaho," *Pacific Northwest Quarterly*, 40:2, April 1949.

Wells, Merle W., "Clinton DeWitt Smith, Secretary, Idaho Territory, 1864–1865," *Oregon Historical Quarterly*, LII:1, March 1951.

Wells, Merle W., "David W. Ballard, Governor of Idaho, 1866–1870," *Oregon Historical Quarterly*, LIV:1, March 1953.

Wells, Merle W., "Territorial Government in the Inland Empire: The Movement to Create Columbia Territory, 1864–1869," *Pacific Northwest Quarterly*, 44:2, April 1953.

Wells, Merle W., "Politics in the Panhandle," *Pacific Northwest Quarterly*, 46:2, March 1955.

Wells, Merle W., "The Idaho Admission Movement, 1880–1890," *Oregon Historical Quarterly*, LVI:1, March 1955.

Wells, Merle W., "Idaho Anti-Mormon Test Oath, 1884–1892," *Pacific Historical Review*, XXIV:3, September 1955.

Woodward, Walter C., *The Rise and Early History of Political Parties in Oregon, 1843–1868* (Portland: J. K. Gill Company, 1913) Out of print but available in *Oregon Historical Quarterly*, Vols. 11, 12, 13.

NINETEENTH-CENTURY INDIAN RELATIONS

Beal, Merrill D., *"I Will Fight No More Forever": Chief Joseph and the Nez Perce War* (Seattle, University of Washington Press, 1963).

Bischoff, William N., "The Yakima Campaign of 1856," *Mid-America*, 31: New Series, 23:3, 1949.

Burns, Robert Ignatius, S.J., *The Jesuits and the Indian Wars of the Northwest* (New Haven: Yale University Press, 1966).

Culverwell, Albert, "Stronghold in the Yakima Country: Fort Simcoe and The Indian War, 1856–1859," *Pacific Northwest Quarterly*, 46:2, April 1955.

Drake, John M., "Cavalry in the Indian Country, 1864," *Oregon Historical Quarterly*, LXV:1, March 1964.

Glassley, Ray H., *Pacific Northwest Indian Wars* (Portland: Binfords & Mort, 1953).

Guie, H. Dean, *Bugles in the Valley, Garnett's Fort Simcoe* (Yakima, Wash: Republic Press, 1956).

Haines, Francis, *The Nez Perces: Tribesmen of the Columbia Plateau* (Norman: University of Oklahoma Press, 1955).

Hart, Herbert M., *Old Forts of the Far West* (Seattle: The Superior Publishing Co., 1965).

Jessett, Thomas E., *Chief Spokan Garry, 1811–1892: Christian, Statesman, Friend of The White Man* (Minneapolis: T. S. Denison & Co., 1960).

Josephy, Alvin M., *The Nez Perce Indians and the Opening of the Northwest* (New Haven: Yale University Press, 1965).

Murray, Keith A., *The Modocs and Their War* (Norman: University of Oklahoma Press, 1959).

O'Callaghan, Jerry A., "Extinguishing Indian Titles on the Oregon Coast," *Oregon Historical Quarterly*, LII:3, September 1951. With particular reference to the Tillamooks.

Shane, Ralph, "Early Explorers Through Warm Springs Reservation Area," *Oregon Historical Quarterly*, LI:4, December 1950.

Spaid, Stanley S., "The Later Life and Activities of General Joel Palmer," *Oregon Historical Quarterly*, LV:4, December 1954.

Stern, Theodore, "The Klamath Indians and the Treaty of 1864," *Oregon Historical Quarterly*, LVII:3, September 1956.

Victor, Francis Fuller, *The Early Indians Wars of Oregon* (Salem, Oregon: F. C. Baker, 1894).

Voegelin, Erminie Wheeler, "The Northern Paiute of Central Oregon: A Chapter in Treaty-Making," Parts 1, 2, 3, in *Ethnohistory*, 2:2, 3, and 3:1, Spring, Summer 1955, and Winter 1956. Useful on the Snake Indians in Oregon.

NINETEENTH-CENTURY INTERNATIONAL DIPLOMACY

Clark, Robert C., ed., "Aberdeen and Peel on Oregon," *Oregon Historical Quarterly*, XXXIV:3, September 1933.

Deutsch, Herman J., "The Evolution of Territorial and State Boundaries in the Inland Empire of the Pacific Northwest," *Pacific Northwest Quarterly*, 51:3, July 1960. Mostly Oregon, Idaho, and Washington.

McCabe, James O., *The San Juan Water Boundary Question*, Canadian Studies in History and Government #5 (Printed in The Netherlands: University of Toronto Press, 1964).

Merk, Frederick, "Genesis of the Oregon Question," *Mississippi Valley Historical Review*, XXXVI:4, March 1950.

Merk, Frederick, "Oregon Pioneers and the Boundary," *American Historical Review*, XXIX:4, July 1924.

Miller, Hunter, *San Juan Archipelago: Study of the Joint Occupation of San Juan Island* (Bellows Falls, Vt.: The Wyndham Press, 1943).

Savelle, Max, "Forty-Ninth Degree of North Latitude as an International Boundary, 1719: The Origin of an Idea," *Canadian Historical Review*, XXXVIII:3, September 1957.

Van Alstyne, R. W., "International Rivalries in the Pacific Northwest," *Oregon Historical Quarterly*, XLVI:3, September 1945.

Supplementary Readings

TRANSPORTATION AND ECONOMIC GROWTH

Abdill, George B., *Pacific Slope Railroads from 1854 to 1900* (Seattle: Superior Press, 1959) Photographs.

Adams, Kramer A., *Logging Railroads of the West* (Seattle: Superior Press, 1961).

Albright, George L., *Official Explorations for Pacific Railroads* (Berkeley: University of California Press, 1921).

Baker, W. W., "The Walla Walla and Columbia River Railroad," *Washington Historical Quarterly*, XIV:1 January 1923. The "Strap Iron" road from Walla Walla to Wallula.

Clarke, S. A., "The Oregon Central Railroad," *Oregon Historical Quarterly*, VII:2 June 1906.

Eggenhofer, Nick, *Wagons, Mules, and Men: How the Frontier Moved West* (New York: Hastings House, 1961).

Ellis, David M., "The Oregon and California Railroad Land Grant, 1866–1945," *Pacific Northwest Quarterly*, 39:4, October 1948.

Frederick, J. V., *Ben Holladay: The Stagecoach King* (Glendale: The Arthur H. Clark Co., 1940).

Ganoe, John T., "The History of the Oregon and California Railroad," *Oregon Historical Quarterly*, XXV:3, September 1924.

Gaston, Joseph, "The Genesis of the Oregon Railway System," *Oregon Historical Quarterly*, VII:2, June 1906.

Glasscock, C. B., *The War of the Copper Kings* (New York: The Bobbs-Merrill Company, 1935).

Gill, Frank B., "Oregon's First Railway," *Oregon Historical Quarterly*, XXV:3, September 1924.

Hedges, James B., *Henry Villard and the Railways of the Northwest* (New Haven: Yale University Press, 1930).

Holbrook, Stewart, *James J. Hill: A Great Life in Brief* (New York: Knopf, 1955).

Howard, Addison, "Captain John Mullan," *Washington Historical Quarterly*, XXV:3, July 1934.

Jackson, Turrentine, *Wagon Roads West* (Berkeley: University of California Press, 1952).

Johansen, Dorothy, "The Oregon Steam Navigation Company," *Pacific Historical Review*, X:2, 1941.

Kenny, Judith K., "Early Sheep Ranching in Eastern Oregon," *Oregon Historical Quarterly*, LXIV: 2, June 1963.

Libbey, F. W., "An Outline of Oregon's Mineral Industry," *Oregon Business Review*, (Eugene: University of Oregon Press) May 1945.

Livingston-Little, Dallas E., *An Economic History of North Idaho, 1800–1900* (Los Angeles: *Journal of the West*, 1965).

Livingston-Little, Dallas E., "Discovery and Development of the Coeur d'Alene Mines," *Journal of the West*, III:3 July 1964.

Lomax, Alfred L., *Pioneer Woolen Mills in Oregon . . . 1811–1875* (Portland: Binfords & Mort, 1941).

Lucia, Ellis, *The Saga of Ben Holladay: Giant of the Old West* (New York: Hastings House, 1959).

Mills, Randall V., "A History of Transportation in the Pacific Northwest," *Oregon Historical Quarterly*, LXVII:3, September 1946.

Mills, Randall V., *Sternwheelers up the Columbia, A Century of Steamboating in the Oregon Country* (Palo Alto: Pacific Books, 1947).

Mills, Randall V., *Railroads Down the Valleys: Some Short Lines of the Oregon Country* (Palo Alto, Pacific Books, 1950).

Newell, Gordon, *Ships of the Inland Sea, The Story of the Puget Sound Steamboats* (Portland: Binfords & Mort, 1951).

Nunis, Doyce B. Jr., ed., *The Golden Frontier: The Recollections of Herman Francis Reinhart, 1851–1869*, (Austin: The University of Texas Press, 1962).

Oliphant, J. Orin, "History of the Livestock Industry in the Pacific Northwest," *Oregon Historical Quarterly*, LI:1, March 1950.

Oliphant, J. Orin, "The Cattle Herds and Ranches of the Oregon Country, 1860–1890," *Agricultural History*, 21:4, October 1947.

Paul, Rodman W., *Mining Frontiers of the Far West, 1848–1880* (New York: Holt, Rinehart and Winston, 1963).

Pollard, Lancaster, "The Salmon Fishery of Oregon, Washington and Alaska," *Americana*, XXXVI:4, October 1942.

Quiett, Glenn, *They Built the West: An Epic of Rails and Cities* (New York: D. Appleton-Century Company, Inc., 1934).

Riegel, Robert E., *The Story of the Western Railroads* (Bison Book: University of Nebraska Press, 1964).

Spence, Clark C., *British Investments and the American Mining Frontier, 1860–1901* (Ithaca, N.Y.: for American History Association, by Cornell University Press, 1958).

Stewart, Earle K., "Transporting Livestock by Boat up the Columbia, 1861–1868," *Oregon Historical Quarterly*, L:4, December 1949.

Stewart, Earle K., "Steamboats on the Columbia: The Pioneer Period," *Oregon Historical Quarterly*, LI:1, March 1950.

Throckmorton, Arthur L., *Oregon Argonauts: Merchant Adventurers on the Western Frontier* (Portland: Oregon Historical Society, 1961).

Throckmorton, Arthur L., "The Role of the Merchant on the Oregon Frontier: The Early Business Career of Henry W. Corbett, 1851–1869," *Journal of Economic History*, XVI:4, December, 1956.

Vinnedge, R. W., "The Genesis of the Pacific Northwest Lumber Industry and its Development," *The Timberman*, CCV:2, December 1933.

Winther, Oscar O., *Old Oregon Country: A History of Frontier Trade, Transportation, and Travel* (Palo Alto: Stanford University Press, 1950).

Winther, Oscar O., *The Transportation Frontier: Trans-Mississippi West, 1865–1890* (New York: Holt, Rinehart and Winston, 1964).

LATE NINETEENTH- AND TWENTIETH-CENTURY POLITICS

Barnett, James D., *Operation of the Initiative, Referendum, and Recall in Oregon* (New York: Macmillan, 1915).

Brooke, Leonie N., "Voting Behavior in Oregon: An Analysis," *Oregon Historical Quarterly*, LIII:1, March 1952.

Clark, Malcolm H. Jr., "The War On the Webfoot Saloon," *Oregon Historical Quarterly*, LVIII:1, March 1957.

Clark, Norman D., *The Dry Years: Prohibition and Social Change in Washington* (Seattle: University of Washington Press, 1965).

Supplementary Readings

Eaton, Allen H., *The Oregon System, The Story of Direct Legislation in Oregon* (Chicago: A. C. McClurg & Co., 1912).

Johnson, Claudius O., "Washington Blanket Primary," *Pacific Northwest Quarterly*, 33:1, January 1942.

Kerr, William T., Jr., "The Progressives of Washington, 1910–1912," *Pacific Northwest Quarterly*, 55:1, January 1964. An analysis of the socio-economic background of the leaders of the Progressive Party in Washington.

LaPalombara, Joseph G., *The Initiative and Referendum in Oregon: 1938–1948* (Corvallis: Oregon State College Press, 1950).

Murray, Keith A., "The Aberdeen Convention of 1912," *Pacific Northwest Quarterly*, 38:2, April 1947.

Murray, Keith A., "Issues and Personalities of Pacific Northwest Politics, 1889–1950," *Pacific Northwest Quarterly*, 41:3, July 1950.

Rakestraw, Lawrence, "Before McNary; The Northwest Conservationists, 1889–1913," *Pacific Northwest Quarterly*, 51:2, April 1960.

Rakestraw, Lawrence, "The West, States Rights, and Conservation," *Pacific Northwest Quarterly*, 48:3, July 1957.

Richardson, Elmo R., "Conservation as a Political Issue; The Western Progressive's Dilemma, 1909–1912," *Pacific Northwest Quarterly*, 49:2, April 1958.

Richardson, Elmo R., *The Politics of Conservatism: Crusades and Controversies, 1897–1913*, University of California Publications in History, Vol. 70 (Berkeley: University of California Press, 1962). Mainly the Bellinger-Pinchot Affair.

Richardson, Elmo R., "Western Politics and New Deal Policies; A Study of T. A. Walters of Idaho," *Pacific Northwest Quarterly*, 54:1, January 1963.

Schumaker, Waldo, "Thirty Years of the People's Rule in Oregon: An Analysis," *Political Science Quarterly*, June 1932.

Woodward, Robert C., "W. S. U'Ren and the Single Tax in Oregon," *Oregon Historical Quarterly*, LXI:1, March 1960.

Woodward, Robert C., "William S. U'Ren, A Progressive Era Personality," *Idaho Yesterdays*, 4:2, Summer 1960.

TWENTIETH-CENTURY ECONOMIC DEVELOPMENT

Bessey, R. F., "Resource Conservation and Development Problems and Solutions in the Columbia Basin," *Journal of Politics*, 13:3, August 1951.

Blanchard, John, and Terrill, Dorothy, *Strikes in the Pacific Northwest, 1927–1940: A Statistical Analysis* (Portland: Northwest Regional Council, 1942).

Cohn, Edwin J., *Industry in the Pacific Northwest and the Location Theory* (New York: King's Crown Press, 1954).

Coulter, C. Brewster, "Victory of National Irrigation in the Yakima Valley, 1902–1906," *Pacific Northwest Quarterly*, 42:2, April 1951.

Gates, Charles M., "A Historical Sketch of the Economic Development of Washington Since Statehood," *Pacific Northwest Quarterly*, 39:3, July 1948.

Hidy, Ralph W., Hill, Frank Ernest, and Nevins, Allan, *Timber and Men: The Weyerhaeuser Story* (New York: The Macmillan Company, 1963). Chapters 12 through 30 deal with the Pacific Northwest.

Mitchell, Bruce, *The Story of Rufus Woods and the Development of Central Washington* (Wenatchee, Wash.: *The Wenatchee Daily World*, 1965).

Seymour, W., "Partnership Policy in Regional Power Planning," *American Economic Review, Papers and Proceedings*, 46, May, 1956.

Stanberg, V. B., *Growth and Trends of Manufacturing in the Pacific Northwest, 1939–1947* (U.S. Dept. of Commerce, Office of Field Service, 1950).

Strong, Dexter K., "Beef Cattle Industry in Oregon, 1890–1938," *Oregon Historical Quarterly*, XLI:3, September 1940.

Sundberg, George, *Hail Columbia: The Thirty Year Struggle for Grand Coulee Dam* (New York: The Macmillan Company, 1954) Stressing mainly the career of James O'Sullivan.

Voeltz, Herman C., "Genesis and Development of a Regional Power Agency in the Pacific Northwest, 1933–43," *Pacific Northwest Quarterly*, 53:2, April 1962.

NINETEENTH-CENTURY CULTURAL, SOCIAL, AND LABOR MOVEMENTS

Caswell, John E., "The Prohibition Movement in Oregon, 1836–1904," *Oregon Historical Quarterly*, XXXIX:3, September 1938.

Down, Robert H., "Oregon's Century of Education," *Oregon Historical Quarterly*, XXXIV:4, December 1933.

Elliott, Eugene C., *History of Variety-Vaudeville in Seattle from the Beginning to 1914* (Seattle: University of Washington Press, 1944).

Jessett, Thomas E., "Origins of the Episcopal Church in the Pacific Northwest," *Oregon Historical Quarterly*, XLVIII:3–4, Sept.-Dec. 1947.

McDonald, Norbert, "The Business Leaders of Seattle, 1880–1910," *Pacific Northwest Quarterly*, 50:1, January 1959.

Powers, Alfred, *History of Oregon Literature* (Portland: The Metropolitan Press, 1935).

Relander, Click, *Strangers on the Land: . . . The Yakima Indian Nation's Efforts to Survive Against Great Odds* (Yakima; Franklin Press, 1962). Nineteenth and twentieth century.

Ross, Marion D., "Architecture in Oregon, 1845–1895," *Oregon Historical Quarterly*, LVII:1, March 1956.

Stern, Theodore, *The Klamath Tribe: A People and Their Reservation*, Monograph 41, The American Ethnological Society (Seattle: University Press, 1965).

Stone, Harry W., "The Beginning of the Labor Movement in the Pacific Northwest," *Oregon Historical Quarterly*, XLVII:2, June 1946.

Turnbull, George S., *History of Oregon Newspapers* (Portland: Binfords & Mort, 1939).

TWENTIETH-CENTURY CULTURAL, SOCIAL, AND LABOR MOVEMENTS.

American Academy of Political and Social Science, *American Indians and American Life, The Annals*, Philadelphia, May 1957.

Bolton, Frederick E, and Bibb, Thomas W., *History of Education in Washington* (Washington: U.S. Govt. Printing Office, 1935).

Botting, David C. Jr., "Bloody Sunday," *Pacific Northwest Quarterly*, 49:4, October 1958. The 1916 Everett Riot.

Caswell, John E., "The Prohibition Movement in Oregon, 1836–1904," *Oregon Historical Quarterly*, XXXIX:3, September 1938.

Supplementary Readings

Caswell, John E., "The Prohibition Movement In Oregon, 1904–1915," *Oregon Historical Quarterly*, XL:1, March 1939.

Clark, Malcolm H. Jr., "The War On the Webfoot Saloon," *Oregon Historical Quarterly*, LVIII:1, March 1957.

Clark, Norman D., "Everett, 1916, and After," *Pacific Northwest Quarterly*, 57:2, April 1916.

Down, Robert H., "Oregon's Century of Education," *Oregon Historical Quarterly*, XXXIV:4, December 1933.

Elliott, Eugene C., *History of Variety-Vaudeville in Seattle from the Beginning to 1914* (Seattle: University of Washington Press, 1944).

Friedham, Robert L., *The Seattle General Strike* (Seattle: University of Washington Press, 1964). The first General Strike in the United States, 1919.

Hyman, Harold M., *Soldiers and Spruce: Origins of the Loyal Legion of Loggers and Lumbermen* (Los Angeles: University of California at Los Angeles Press, Institute of Industrial Relations, 1963). World War I Labor Relations.

Jessett, Thomas E., "Origins of the Episcopal Church in the Pacific Northwest," *Oregon Historical Quarterly*, XLVIII:3–4, Sept.-Dec. 1947.

Kornbluh, Joyce L., ed., *Rebel Voices: An I.W.W. Anthology*, (Ann Arbor: University of Michigan Press, 1964).

McClelland, John M. Jr., "Terror on Tower Avenue," *Pacific Northwest Quarterly*, 57:2, April 1966. The Centralia riot of 1919.

McDonald, Norbert, "The Business Leaders of Seattle, 1880–1910," *Pacific Northwest Quarterly*, 50:1, January 1959.

Martin, W. T., "Continuing Urbanization on the Pacific Coast," *American Journal of Sociology*, 62, November, 1956.

O'Conner, Harvey, *Revolution in Seattle: A Memoir* (New York: Monthly Review Press, 1964). The Seattle General Strike from the viewpoint of one of the participants.

O'Hara, Edwin Vincent, *Catholic History of Oregon* (Portland: Catholic Book Company, 1925).

Sheppard, Edward, and Johnson, Emily, "Forty Years of Symphony in Seattle, 1903–43," *Pacific Northwest Quarterly 35–1*, January 1944.

Stone, Harry W., "The Beginning of the Labor Movement in the Pacific Northwest," *Oregon Historical Quarterly*, XLVII:2, June 1946.

Tobie, H. E., "Oregon Labor Disputes, 1919–23," *Oregon Historical Quarterly*, XLVIII:1,3,4, March, September, and December 1947.

Tyler, Robert L., "I.W.W. in the Pacific Northwest: Rebels of the Woods," *Oregon Historical Quarterly*, LV:1, March 1954.

Tyler, Robert L., "Violence at Centralia, 1919," *Pacific Northwest Quarterly*, 45:4, October 1954.

Tyler, Robert L., "The I.W.W. and the Brain Workers," *American Quarterly*, XV:1, Spring 1963.

TWENTIETH-CENTURY BIOGRAPHY AND LOCAL HISTORY

Allen, Howard W., "Miles Poindexter and the Progressive Movement," *Pacific Northwest Quarterly*, 53:3, July 1962.

Bingham, Edwin, "Oregon's Romantic Rebels: John Reed and Charles Erskine Scott Wood," *Pacific Northwest Quarterly*, 50:3, July 1959.

Brimlow, George F., *Harney County, Oregon, and Its Range Land* (Portland: Binfords & Mort, 1951).

Brogan, Phil F., *East of the Cascades* (Portland: Binfords & Mort, 1964).

Cooper, John Milton Jr., "William E. Borah, Political Thespian," *Pacific Northwest Quarterly*, 56:4, October 1965. An unflattering treatment.

Edson, Lelah Jackson, *The Fourth Corner: Highlights from the Early Northwest* (Bellingham, Washington: Cox Brothers, Inc., 1951). A local history of the counties of Northern Puget Sound.

Fargo, Lucille, *Spokane Story* (New York: Columbia University Press, 1950).

French, Giles, *The Golden Land; A History of Sherman County, Oregon* (Portland: Oregon Historical Society, 1958).

French, Giles, *Cattle Country of Peter French* (Portland: Binfords & Mort, 1964).

Jackman, E. R., and Long, R. A., *The Oregon Desert* (Caldwell: Caxton Printers, 1965).

Johnson, Claudius O., *Borah of Idaho* (New York: Longmans, Green and Co., 1936) A favorable account.

McClintock, Thomas C., "J. Allan Smith, A Pacific Northwest Progressive," *Pacific Northwest Quarterly*, 53:2, April 1962.

Morgan, Murray, *Skid Road: An Informal Portrait of Seattle* (New York: Viking Press, 1951).

Morgan, Murray, *The Last Wilderness* (New York: Viking Press, 1955) The Olympic Peninsula.

Nesbit, Robert C., *"He Built Seattle:"* A Biography of Judge Thomas Burke (Seattle: University of Washington Press, 1961).

Neuberger, Richard L., *Adventures in Politics: We Go to the Legislature* (New York: Oxford University Press, 1954).

Oliver, Herman, *Gold and Cattle Country* (Portland: Binfords & Mort, 1961).

Redford, Grant H., ed., *That Man Thomson* (Seattle: University of Washington Press, 1950).

Shaw, James G., *Edwin Vincent O'Hara, American Prelate* (New York: Farrar, Straus & Cudahy, 1957).

Smith, Arthur Robert, *The Tiger in the Senate: The Biography of Wayne Morse* (Garden City, N.Y.: Doubleday, 1962).

Turnbull, George S., *An Oregon Crusader* (Portland: Binfords & Mort, 1955). A biography of George Putnam and his battle for freedom of the press.

Tables

TABLE VIII

Population of Pacific Northwest States, 1850–1965

Year	Washington	Oregon	Idaho
1850		13,294	
1860	11,594	52,465	
1870	23,955	90,923	14,909
1880	75,116	174,768	32,610
1890	349,390	313,767	84,385
1900	518,103	413,536	161,772
1910	1,141,990	672,765	325,594
1920	1,356,621	783,389	431,866
1930	1,563,396	953,786	445,032
1940	1,736,191	1,089,684	524,873
1950	2,378,963	1,521,341	588,637
1960	2,853,214	1,768,687	667,191
1965	3,078,120	1,938,220	(not computed for whole state)

Source: Department of Commerce, Bureau of the Census. Figures for 1965 are from Pacific Northwest Bell Telephone Company, Business Research Division, "Population and Household Trends, 1960–1980" (April, 1965).

TABLE IX

White and Nonwhite Population, 1900–1960

	1900	1910	1920	1930	1940	1950	1960
WASHINGTON							
Total	518,103	1,141,990	1,356,621	1,563,396	1,736,191	2,378,963	2,853,214
White	496,304	1,109,111	1,319,777	1,521,661	1,698,147	2,316,496	2,751,675
Percent	95.8	97.1	97.3	97.3	97.8	97.4	96.4
Negro	2,514	6,058	6,883	6,840	7,424	30,691	48,738
Percent	0.5	0.5	0.5	0.4	0.4	1.3	1.3
Indian	10,039	10,997	9,061	11,253	11,394	13,816	21,076
Percent	1.9	1.0	0.7	0.7	0.7	0.6	0.7
Chinese	3,629	2,709	2,363	2,195	2,345	3,408	5,491
Percent	0.7	0.2	0.2	0.1	0.1	0.1	0.2
Japanese	5,617	12,929	17,387	17,837	14,565	9,694	16,652
Percent	1.1	1.1	1.3	1.1	0.8	0.4	0.6
Filipino	—	17	958	3,480	2,222	4,274	7,110
Other	—	186	1,150	3,610	2,316	4,858	9,582
OREGON							
Total	413,536	672,765	783,389	953,786	1,089,684	1,521,341	1,768,687
White	394,582	655,090	769,146	938,597	1,075,731	1,497,128	1,732,037
Percent	95.4	97.4	98.2	98.4	98.7	98.4	97.9
Negro	1,105	1,492	2,144	2,234	2,565	11,529	18,133
Percent	0.3	0.2	0.3	0.2	0.2	0.8	1.0

Indian	4,951	5,090	4,590	4,776	4,594	5,820	8,026
Percent	1.2	0.8	0.6	0.5	0.4	0.4	0.5
Chinese	10,397	7,363	3,090	2,075	2,086	2,102	2,995
Percent	2.5	1.1	0.4	0.2	0.2	0.1	0.2
Japanese	2,501	3,418	4,151	4,958	4,071	3,660	5,016
Percent	0.6	0.5	0.5	0.5	0.4	0.2	0.3
Other (incl. Filipino)	—	312	268	1,146	637	1,102	2,480
IDAHO							
Total	161,772	325,594	431,866	445,032	524,873	588,637	667,191
White	154,495	319,221	425,668	438,840	519,292	581,395	657,383
Percent	95.5	98.0	98.6	98.6	98.9	98.8	98.5
Negro	293	651	920	668	595	1,050	1,502
Percent	0.2	0.2	0.2	0.2	0.1	0.2	0.2
Indian	4,226	3,488	3,098	3,638	3,537	3,800	5,231
Percent	2.6	1.1	0.7	0.8	0.7	0.6	0.8
Chinese	1,467	859	585	335	208	244	311
Percent	0.9	0.3	0.1	0.1	—	—	—
Japanese	1,291	1,363	1,569	1,421	1,191	1,980	2,254
Percent	0.8	0.4	0.4	0.3	0.2	0.3	0.3
Other	—	12	26	130	50	168	510

Source: Compiled from Department of Commerce, Bureau of the Census population statistics, 1900–1960.

T A B L E   X

Some Major Sources of Personal Income, 1964
(in millions of dollars)

	Washington			Oregon			Idaho		
	1962	1963	1964	1962	1963	1964	1962	1963	1964
Total personal income	7,426	7,575	7,861	4,324	4,568	4,876	1,351	1,366	1,398
Wages and salaries	5,070	5,160	5,365	2,758	2,948	3,195	824	831	868
Contract construction	309	307	307	166	197	210	82	54	60
Manufacturing	1,479	1,486	1,514	783	826	907	158	106	161
Wholesale and retail trade	935	963	1,009	561	600	654	158	163	172
Services	449	451	485	266	283	310	79	83	92
Government									
Federal									
Civilian	307	321	335	130	144	152	44	50	52
Military	273	245	266	34	35	38	28	30	32
State and local	599	637	681	360	386	414	104	109	116
Proprietors' income									
Farm	213	186	173	118	106	103	126	128	108
Nonfarm	655	650	656	529	551	570	142	133	137
Property income	890	957	1,012	566	609	643	152	164	173
Transfer payments	593	626	656	360	375	388	109	114	115

Source: From Department of Commerce, Office of Business Economics, "Survey of Current Business," July 1965, 16.

TABLE XI

Concentrations of Population: Washington, Oregon, Idaho, 1900–1960

	1900	1910	1920	1930	1940	1950ᵃ	1960ᵃ
WASHINGTON							
Number of places with population:							
Under 2500	74	150	177	183	182	183 (189)	191 (196)
Over 2500	15	27	33	38	40	55 (72)	74 (96)
2500–10,000	11	19	23	23	26	35	47
OREGON							
Number of places with population:							
Under 2500	103	153	175	176	173	172 (178)	168 (172)
Over 2500	11	18	23	28	34	47 (50)	63 (63)
2500–10,000	10	16	19	22	27	36	41
IDAHO							
Number of places with population:							
Under 2500	32	89	124	129	125	159 (161)	172 (174)
Over 2500	2	12	20	21	26	29 (33)	29 (34)
2500–10,000	2	11	18	19	19	20	19

ᵃ Figures in parentheses use 1950–1960 definition of urban. Up to the 1950 census, "urban" applied to "cities and other unincorporated places" having 2500 or more inhabitants. In 1950 and 1960, "urban" was defined as:
(a) places of 2500 inhabitants or more incorporated as cities, boroughs, villages, and towns;
(b) the densely settled urban fringe, whether incorporated or unincorporated;
(c) unincorporated places of 2500 inhabitants or more;
(d) counties in states other than the Northeastern States that have no incorporated municipalities within their boundaries and have a density of 1500 persons or more per square mile.
Source: Compiled from Census Reports.

TABLE XII

Marital Status of the Population 14 Years and Older

	1900	1910	1920	1930	1940	1950	1960
WASHINGTON							
Male Total	228,748	515,201	557,211	642,595	732,846	914,430	1,003,704
Percent:							
Single	51.4	49.5	40.1	37.2	35.1	26.1	24.7
Married	42.1	44.9	53.7	55.7	58.0	66.3	68.5
Widowed	3.9	3.5	4.3	4.5	4.4	3.9	3.3
Divorced	0.7	0.9	1.5	2.3	2.5	3.6	3.5
Female Total	140,766	344,467	449,459	559,240	663,421	860,455	1,001,924
Percent:							
Single	28.0	28.4	24.8	24.3	22.8	15.4	16.3
Married	63.3	62.3	64.1	63.0	63.2	70.1	68.6
Widowed	7.6	7.7	9.3	10.0	11.2	11.1	11.4
Divorced	0.9	1.1	1.7	2.5	2.8	3.4	3.7
OREGON							
Male Total	173,098	302,275	314,861	389,855	453,644	572,035	616,766
Percent:							
Single	49.1	48.5	37.8	35.7	32.8	22.7	22.6
Married	45.0	45.6	55.7	56.9	60.1	69.7	70.5
Widowed	4.7	4.2	4.6	4.7	4.3	3.7	3.3
Divorced	0.8	1.1	1.8	2.6	2.8	3.9	3.6

Female Total	122,542	209,323	268,249	347,407	421,909	560,800	634,518
Percent:							
Single	31.3	29.2	24.8	23.9	22.4	15.1	16.2
Married	59.4	61.2	63.4	63.0	63.8	70.9	68.7
Widowed	8.3	8.4	10.1	10.5	11.2	10.5	11.3
Divorced	0.9	1.1	1.9	2.5	2.8	3.4	3.8
IDAHO							
Male Total	64,991	133,528	160,554	168,295	205,381	211,235	226,097
Percent:							
Single	50.5	47.2	40.0	38.3	35.5	25.3	24.3
Married	44.6	48.0	54.8	55.5	58.5	68.3	69.8
Widowed	3.9	.3.3	4.0	4.2	3.7	3.7	3.0
Divorced	0.7	0.7	1.0	1.8	1.9	2.7	2.9
Female Total	41,053	89,919	127,602	140,880	179,509	199,130	221,295
Percent:							
Single	26.6	27.3	25.4	25.6	23.2	16.1	16.4
Married	65.5	65.5	66.3	65.1	66.4	72.6	71.4
Widowed	7.1	6.2	7.4	7.8	8.7	9.1	9.7
Divorced	0.7	0.6	0.9	1.4	1.7	2.2	2.5

Source : Compiled from Department of Commerce, Bureau of the Census statistics, 1900–1960.

TABLE XIII

Washington: Vote for Governors, 1900–1964

Year		Elected	Vote	Opposition Vote
1900	D	McBride	51,944	R 49,860
1904	R	Mead	75,278	59,119
1908	R	Hay	*a*	
1912	D	Lister	97,125	R 96,629; Prog. 77,792
1916	D	Lister	181,642	R 167,802; Soc. 21,117
1920	R	Hart	210,622	D 66,079; Farm–Lab. 121,371
1924	R	Hartley	220,162	D 126,477; Farm–Lab. 40,073
1928	R	Hartley	281,991	D 214,334
1932	D	Martin	352,215	R 207,497; Liberty 41,710
1936	D	Martin	466,500	R 189,141
1940	R	Langlie	392,522	D 386,706
1944	D	Wallgren	428,834	R 400,604 (Langlie)
1948	R	Langlie	445,958	D 417,035 (Wallgren)
1952	R	Langlie	567,822	D 510,675
1956	D	Rossellini	588,748	R 471,560
1960	D	Rossellini	590,390	R 574,857
1964	R	Evans	(Plurality of 245,000 in 1,250,000 votes cast)	

a Figures unavailable.

TABLE XIV

Oregon: Vote for Governors, 1902–1962

Year		Elected	Vote	Opposition Vote	
1902	D	Chamberlain	41,857	R	41,611
1906	D	Chamberlain	46,022	R	43,508
1910	D	West	54,853	R	48,751
1914	R	Withycombe	121,037	D	94,594
1918	R	Olcott	81,067	D	65,400
1922	D	Pierce	133,392	R	99,155
1926	R	Patterson	113,118	D	87,569
1930	Ind	Meier	135,642	D	63,044; R 48,233
1934	D	Martin	116,677	R	86,923
1938	R	Sprague	214,062	D	158,744
1942	R	Snell	220,188	D	62,561
1946	R	Snell	237,681	D	106,474
1948	R	McKay	271,295	D	226,958
1950	R	McKay	334,160	D	171,750
1954	R	Patterson	332,522	D	244,179
1956	D	Holmes	362,288	R	356,323
1958	R	Hatfield	331,900	D	267,934
1962	R	Hatfield	345,947	D	265,359

Idaho: Vote for Governors, 1900–1962

Year		Elected	Vote	Opposition Vote		
1900	D	Hunt	28,628	R 26,468		
1902	R	Morrison	31,874	D 26,021		
1904	R	Gooding	41,877	D 24,192		
1906	R	Gooding	38,386	D 29,496		
1908	R	Brady	*a*			
1910	D	Hawley	40,856	R 39,961;	Prog. 5,342	
1912	R	Haines	35,056	D 33,922;	Roosevelt Prog. 24,325	
1914	D	Alexander	47,618	R 40,349;	Prog. 10,583	
1916	D	Alexander	63,877	R 63,305;	Soc. 7,321	
1918	R	Davis	57,626	D 38,499		
1920	R	Davis	75,748	D 38,309		
1922	R	Moore	50,538	D 36,810;	Prog. 40,516	
1924	R	Moore	65,508	D 25,081;	LaFollette-Prog. 58,167	
1926	R	Baldridge	59,460	D 24,837		
1928	R	Baldridge	87,681	D 63,046		
1930	D	Ross	65,235	R 51,484		
1932	D	Ross	116,663	R 68,863		
1934	D	Ross	93,313	R 75,659		
1936	D	Clark	115,098	R 83,430		
1938	R	Bottolfsen	106,268	D 77,697	(Clark)	
1940	D	Clark	120,420	R118,117	(Bottolfsen)	
1942	R	Bottolfsen	72,260	D 71,260	(Clark)	
1944	D	Gossett	109,527	R 98,532		
1946	R	Robins	102,233	D 79,131		
1950	R	Jordan	107,642	D 97,150		
1954	R	Smylie	124,058	D104,981		
1958	R	Smylie	(Plurality of 4,574 votes in 239,046 cast)			
1962	R	Smylie	(Plurality of 23,702 votes in 255,454 cast)			

a Figures unavailable.

616

TABLE XVI

Oregon: Vote in Federal Elections, 1920–1964

Year		President		Senate	House (Congressional Districts by Party) Republican	Democrat
1920	R	Harding Pl. 48,662	R	R. N. Stanfield	2, 3[a]	
1922					1, 2	3
1924	R	Coolidge Pl. 5,502	R	C. L. McNary	1, 2, 3	
1926			R	F. Steiwer	1, 2, 3	
1928	R	Hoover Pl. 90,740			1, 2, 3	
1930			R	C. L. McNary	1, 2	3
1932	D	Roosevelt Pl. 58,934	R	F. Steiwer	1	2, 3
1934					1, 3	2
1936	D	Roosevelt Pl. 119,445	R	C. L. McNary	1	2, 3
1938			R	R. C. Holman	1, 3	2
1940	D	Roosevelt Pl. 219,555	R	A. G. Berry	1, 3	2
1942			R	C. L. McNary	1, 2, 3, 4[b]	
1944	D	Roosevelt Pl. 17,123	R	W. Morse	1, 2, 3, 4	
1946			R	G. Cordon	1, 2, 3, 4	
1948	R	Dewey Pl. (R/D) 17,757	R	G. Cordon	1, 2, 3, 4	
1950			R	W. Morse	1, 2, 3, 4	
1952	R	Eisenhower Pl. 146,571			1, 2, 3, 4	
1954			D	R. L. Neuberger	1, 2, 4	3
1956	R	Eisenhower Pl. 77,189	D	W. Morse	1, 4	2, 3
1958					1	2, 3, 4
1960	R	Nixon Pl. 39,699	D	M. Neuberger	1, 4	2, 3
1962			D	M. Neuberger	1	2, 3, 4
1964	D	Johnson Pl. 315,729	D	W. Morse	1	2, 3, 4

[a] W. C. Hawley elected in CD 1 by a coalition of Democratic, Republican, and Prohibition parties.
[b] New Congressional District created.

TABLE XVII

Washington: Vote in Federal Elections, 1920–1964

Year	President	Senate	House (Congressional Districts by Party)	
			Republican	Democrat
1920 R	Harding Pl. 48,880	R W. L. Jones	1, 2, 3, 4, 5	
1922		D C. C. Dill	1, 2, 3, 4	5
1924 R	Coolidge Pl. 18,899		1, 2, 3, 4	5
1926		R W. L. Jones	1, 2, 3, 4, 5	
1928 R	Hoover Pl. 164,996	D C. C. Dill	1, 2, 3, 4	5
1930			1, 2, 3, 4	5
1932 D	Roosevelt Pl. 91,706	D H. T. Bone		1, 2, 3, 4, 5, 6[a]
1934		D L. B. Schwellenbach		1, 2, 3, 4, 5, 6
1936 D	Roosevelt Pl. 226,820		(219,024)[a]	(425,985)[b]
1938		D L. B. Schwellenbach	(227,958)	(357,686)
1940 D	Roosevelt Pl. 130,467	D L. B. Schwellenbach	(313,614)	(430,442)
1942			3, 4, 5	1, 2, 6
1944 D	Roosevelt Pl. 117,220	D W. G. Magnuson	1, 2, 3	4, 5, 6

1946		R	H. P. Cain	(157,886)	(100,512)
1948	D	Truman Pl. 47,271		(187,718)	(164,485)
1950		D	W. G. Magnuson	(176,873)	(132,564)
1952	R	Eisenhower Pl. 95,506	D H. M. Jackson	1, 2, 3, 4, 5, 6[c]	CL
1954				1, 2, 3, 4, 5, 6	
1956	R	Eisenhower Pl. 89,971	D W. G. Magnuson	(240,519)	(209,052)
1958		D	H. M. Jackson	1, 2, 3, 4, 5[d]	
1960	R	Nixon Pl. 16,974		1, 2, 4, 5, 6	3, 7[a]
1962		D	W. G. Magnuson	1, 2, 4, 5, 6, 7	3
1964	D	Johnson Pl. 302,000	D H.M. Jackson	(584,000)	(613,000)

[a] New district created.
[b] Figures not available by district.
[c] In this year a congressman-at-large (CL) was elected but vote not available.
[d] Figures for District 6 and CL not available.

Idaho: Vote in Federal Elections, 1920–1964

			House (Congressional Districts by Party)	
Year	President	Senate	Republican	Democrat
1920	R Harding Pl. 44,343	R F. R. Gooding	1, 2	
1922			1, 2	
1924	R Coolidge Pl. (R/D) 45,623	R W. E. Borah	1, 2	
		R F. R. Gooding	1, 2	
1926				
1928	R Hoover Pl. 35,466	R J. Thomas	1, 2	
1930		R W. E. Borah	1, 2	
1932	D Roosevelt Pl. 36,101	D J. P. Pope		1, 2
1934			(63,169)[a]	(99,870)[a]
1936	D Roosevelt Pl. 51,743	D J. P. Pope	(68,793)[a]	(126,179)[a]
1938		D J. P. Pope	(83,167)[a]	(95,517)[a]
1940	D Roosevelt Pl. 20,526		(107,803)[a]	(123,833)[a]
1942		D J. P. Pope	2	1
1944	D Roosevelt Pl. 6,477	D G. H. Taylor	2	1
1946		R H. C. Dworshak	2	1
1948	D Truman Pl. (D/R) 5,856	D B. H. Miller	2	1
1950		R H. Welker	1, 2	
1952	R Eisenhower Pl. 85,160	R H. C. Dworshak	2	1
1954		R H. C. Dworshak	2	1
1956	R Eisenhower Pl. 60,969	D F. Church	2	1
1958			1, 2	
1960	R Nixon Pl. 22,744	R H. C. Dworshak		1, 2
1962		D F. Church		1, 2
1964	D Johnson Pl. 89,100	R L. B. Jordan	(144,000)[a]	(140,000)[a]

[a] Figures not available for districts.

Graphs

I

POPULATION GROWTH

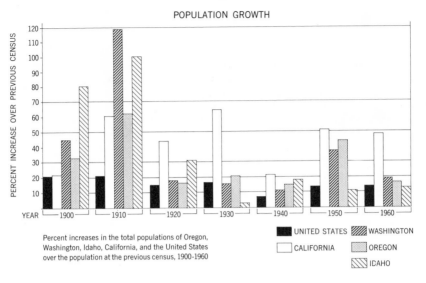

Percent increases in the total populations of Oregon,
Washington, Idaho, California, and the United States
over the population at the previous census, 1900-1960

II

URBAN-RURAL POPULATION PERCENTAGES

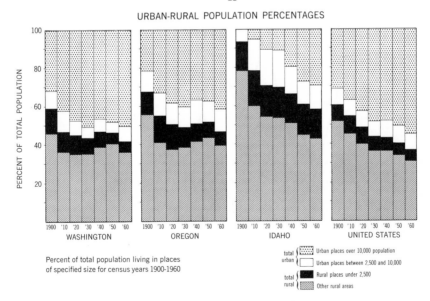

Percent of total population living in places
of specified size for census years 1900-1960

III

PRESIDENTIAL VOTES: WASHINGTON, OREGON, IDAHO

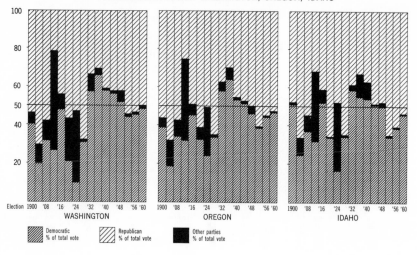

| Democratic % of total vote | Republican % of total vote | Other parties % of total vote |

IV

IDAHO: MAJOR PARTY VOTE FOR PRESIDENT, 1900-1960, IN PERCENTAGES OF TOTAL VOTES CAST

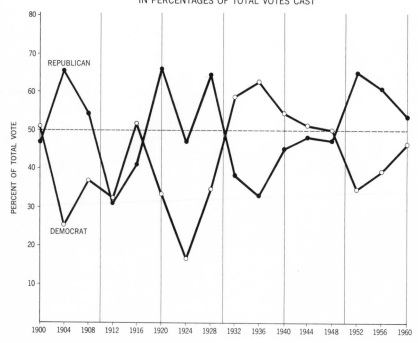

Source: A Statistical History of the American Presidential
Elections, by Sverd Petersen

V

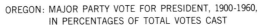

OREGON: MAJOR PARTY VOTE FOR PRESIDENT, 1900-1960,
IN PERCENTAGES OF TOTAL VOTES CAST

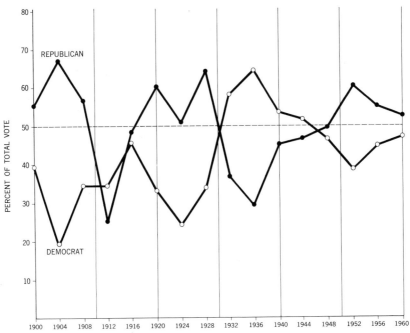

Source: A Statistical History of the American Presidential
Elections, by Sverd Petersen

VI

WASHINGTON: MAJOR PARTY VOTE FOR PRESIDENT, 1900-1960,
IN PERCENTAGES OF TOTAL VOTES CAST

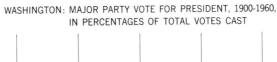

Source: A Statistical History of the American Presidential
Elections, by Sverd Petersen

 OREGON: MAJOR PARTY VOTE FOR REPRESENTATIVES IN CONGRESS, 1926-1960
IN PERCENTAGES OF TOTAL VOTES CAST

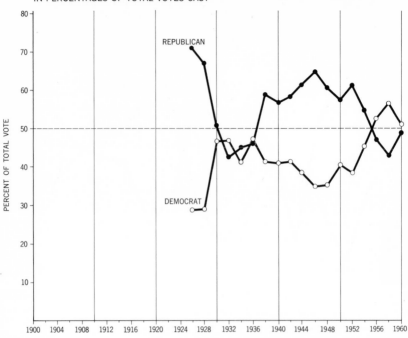

Source: State of Oregon, Secretary of State, Voting Trends in Oregon, 1858-1960

VIII

IDAHO: MAJOR PARTY VOTE FOR REPRESENTATIVES IN CONGRESS, 1928-1960
IN PERCENTAGES OF TOTAL VOTES CAST

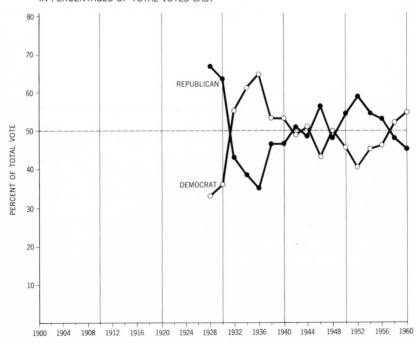

Sources: 1952-1960, Congressional District Data Book, Bureau of Census
1946-1950, Statistical Abstract of the United States
1928-1944, Vote Cast in Presidential and Congressional Elections, 1928-1944,
Bureau of Census

IX

WASHINGTON: MAJOR PARTY VOTE FOR REPRESENTATIVES IN CONGRESS, 1928-1960 IN PERCENTAGES OF TOTAL VOTES CAST

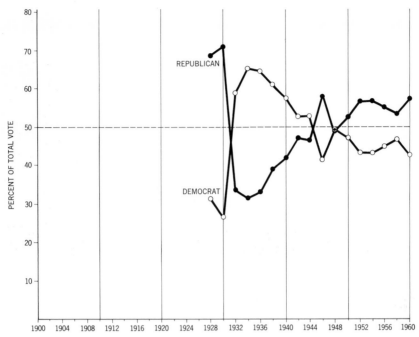

Sources: 1952-1960, Congressional District Data Book, Bureau of Census
1946-1950, Statistical Abstract of the United States
1928-1944, Vote Cast in Presidential and Congressional Elections, 1928-1944,
Bureau of Census

X

PARTY REGISTRATIONS FOR GENERAL ELECTIONS IN OREGON, 1908-1960

Source: Drawn from data in Compilation of Election Statistics,
Secretary of State, Oregon. 1962

XI
WHEAT PRODUCTION AND EXPORTS IN PACIFIC NORTHWEST

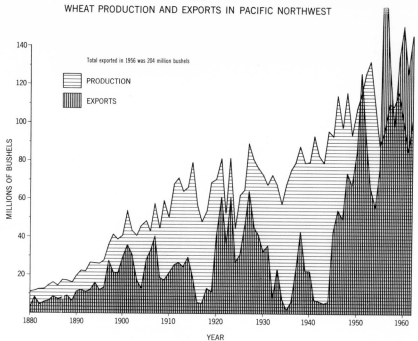

Total exported in 1956 was 204 million bushels

PRODUCTION

EXPORTS

MILLIONS OF BUSHELS

YEAR

Source: Western Wheat Associates, U.S.A., Inc., in cooperation with U.S. Department of Agriculture, Wheat: Supply, Distribution and Value in the Pacific Northwest, 1963. pp. 12-13, 60-61, 61-65.

XII
REAL VALUE ADDED BY MANUFACTURING, 1909-1962

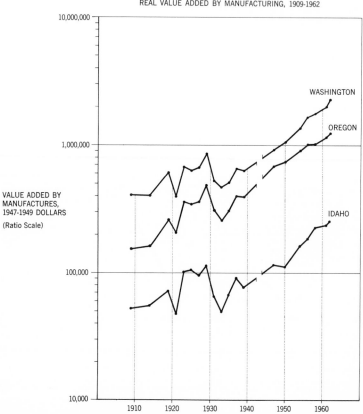

WASHINGTON

OREGON

IDAHO

VALUE ADDED BY
MANUFACTURES,
1947-1949 DOLLARS

(Ratio Scale)

1947-1962 not strictly comparable to earlier
series where price data was unavailable.

XIII

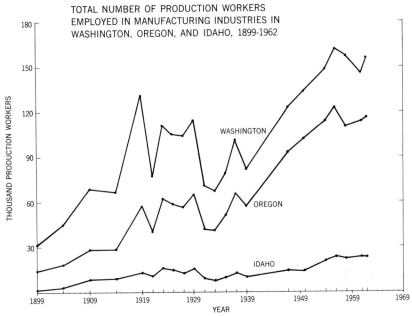

TOTAL NUMBER OF PRODUCTION WORKERS
EMPLOYED IN MANUFACTURING INDUSTRIES IN
WASHINGTON, OREGON, AND IDAHO, 1899-1962

Sources: Department of Commerce, Bureau of Census
Census of Manufactures, 1899-1958
Survey of Manufactures for 1950, 1956, 1961, 1962

XIV

OREGON: COMPOSITION OF VALUE ADDED BY MANUFACTURE

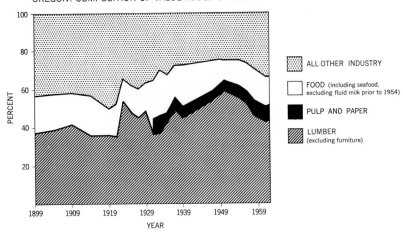

Sources: Department of Commerce, Bureau of Census
Census of Manufactures, 1899-1958
Survey of Manufactures for 1950, 1956, 1961, 1962

XV

WASHINGTON: COMPOSITION OF VALUE ADDED BY MANUFACTURE

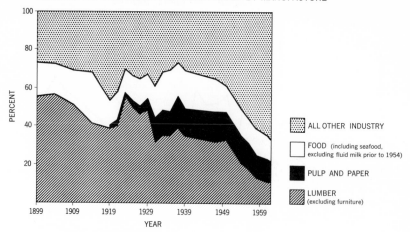

Sources: Department of Commerce, Bureau of Census
Census of Manufactures, 1899-1958
Survey of Manufactures for 1950, 1956, 1961, 1962

XVI

IDAHO: COMPOSITION OF VALUE ADDED BY MANUFACTURE

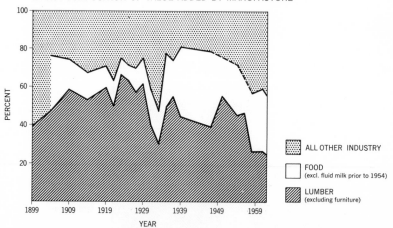

Sources: Department of Commerce, Bureau of Census
Census of Manufactures, 1899-1958
Survey of Manufactures for 1950, 1956, 1961, 1962

XVII

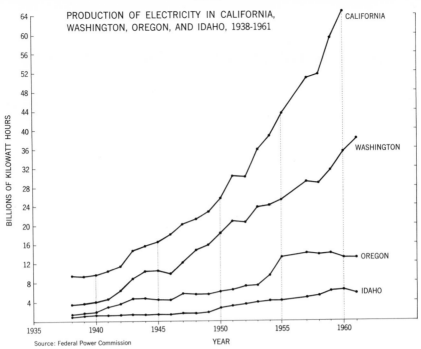

PRODUCTION OF ELECTRICITY IN CALIFORNIA, WASHINGTON, OREGON, AND IDAHO, 1938-1961

BILLINGS OF KILOWATT HOURS

CALIFORNIA

WASHINGTON

OREGON

IDAHO

YEAR

Source: Federal Power Commission

XVIII

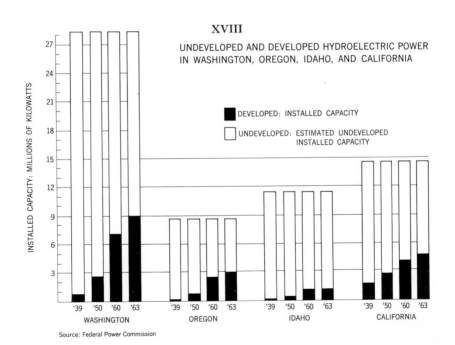

UNDEVELOPED AND DEVELOPED HYDROELECTRIC POWER IN WASHINGTON, OREGON, IDAHO, AND CALIFORNIA

INSTALLED CAPACITY: MILLIONS OF KILOWATTS

■ DEVELOPED: INSTALLED CAPACITY

□ UNDEVELOPED: ESTIMATED UNDEVELOPED INSTALLED CAPACITY

WASHINGTON   OREGON   IDAHO   CALIFORNIA

Source: Federal Power Commission

ELECTRICAL POWER GENERATED BY PRIVATELY AND PUBLICLY OWNED UTILITIES
AS PERCENT OF ELECTRICITY GENERATED BY ALL UTILITIES

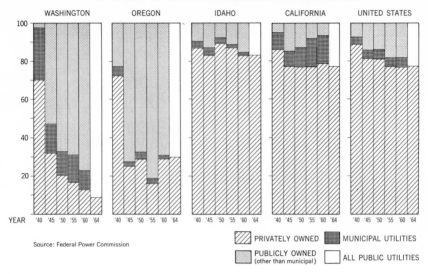

Source: Federal Power Commission

PRIVATELY OWNED   MUNICIPAL UTILITIES

PUBLICLY OWNED
(other than municipal)   ALL PUBLIC UTILITIES

Illustration Credits

Pictures are identified by page number and position.

Aluminum Company of America, Vancouver, Washington 523 bottom left

The American Museum of Natural History, New York 16 all pictures

The Anaconda Company, New York 327 bottom

The Boeing Company, Seattle, Washington 524 middle, 524 bottom right

Bonneville Power Administration, USDI, Portland, Oregon 239 middle, 240 top, 240 middle, 241 top, 354 bottom, 522–523 top, 522 middle left, 523 bottom right

Bureau of Indian Affairs, USDI, Portland, Oregon 19 five small bottom pictures

Bureau of Sports Fisheries and Wildlife, USDI, Portland, Oregon 522 middle right, 523 top

Canned Salmon Institute, Seattle, Washington 290 middle, 290 bottom, 291 all pictures

Cyrile van Duser, Missoula, Montana 425 top

Eastern Washington State Historical Society, Spokane 101 middle, 169 bottom left, 422 top, 468 top

Greater Vancouver Chamber of Commerce, Washington 525 bottom

History of Idaho Territory, 1884 by Wallace Elliott 326 top

Hudson's Bay Company, Winnipeg, Manitoba 99 middle, 101 bottom

Idaho Department of Commerce and Industry, Boise xiv bottom, 424 bottom

Idaho Historical Society, Boise xv top, 19 second from top, 166 bottom left, 169 top, 238 top, 238 third from top, 324 top right, 324 bottom, 325 all pictures, 236 middle, 326 bottom, 327 top, 423 top, 466 bottom left, 568 middle left

International Pacific Salmon Fisheries Commission, New Westminster, British Columbia 290 top

Montana Historical Society, Helena 568 middle right

National Park Service, Scotts Bluff National Monument, Nebraska 167 top

The New-York Historical Society, New York 17 top left

Oregon Historical Society, Portland 101 top, 166 bottom right, 168 bottom, 169 bottom right, 238 second from top, 238 bottom, 239 top, 288 top, 288 third from top, 288 bottom, 289 top, 289 middle, 352 top, 352 bottom left, 352 bottom right, 353 bottom, 422 middle left, 422 middle right, 467 top, 468 middle, 468 bottom, 569 top, 569 middle

Oregon State Highway Department, Salem xii top, xii bottom, xiii top, xv top right, xv bottom, 167 bottom, 241 bottom, 355 top, 423 middle, 469 top, 523 middle, 570 bottom right

Portland Art Museum, Oregon 570 top

Portland Chamber of Commerce, Oregon 422 bottom

Provincial Museum, Victoria, British Columbia 288 second from top, 466 top

Royal Ontario Museum, Toronto, Canada 17 middle, 17 bottom, 18 all pictures, 568 top

Seattle Chamber of Commerce, Washington 469 bottom right, 570 middle, 570 bottom

Seattle School District, Washington 425 bottom

631

Index

633

647